Lorenzo Dow, Peggy Dow

The Life, Travels, Labors, And Writings Of Lorenzo Dow

Lorenzo Dow, Peggy Dow

The Life, Travels, Labors, And Writings Of Lorenzo Dow

ISBN/EAN: 9783741118265

Manufactured in Europe, USA, Canada, Australia, Japa

Cover: Foto ©Andreas Hilbeck / pixelio.de

Manufactured and distributed by brebook publishing software (www.brebook.com)

Lorenzo Dow, Peggy Dow

The Life, Travels, Labors, And Writings Of Lorenzo Dow

THE LIFE,

TRAVELS, LABORS, AND WRITINGS

OF

LORENZO DOW;

INCLUDING HIS

Singular and Erratic Wanderings in Europe and America.

TO WHICH IS ADDED

HIS CHAIN JOURNEY FROM BABYLON TO JERUSALEM; DIALOGUE BETWEEN CURIOUS AND SINGULAR; HINTS ON THE FULFILLMENT OF PROPHECY, ETC., ETC.

AND THE

VICISSITUDES, OR JOURNEY OF LIFE,

AND

SUPPLEMENTARY REFLECTIONS BY PEGGY DOW.

COMPLETE IN ONE VOLUME.

NEW YORK:
R. WORTHINGTON, 770 BROADWAY.
1881.

PREFACE.

SINCE the days of George Whitefield, it has not fallen to the lot of another minister of the gospel to enjoy so great and wide-spread a celebrity as that of the late LORENZO DOW. In England and Ireland, in the United States and the Canadas, there are probably few persons now living who have reached adult age to whom his name is not familiar. There is not a State in our Union that he has not visited, and there is scarcely a town in the older States in which he has not been listened to by hundreds, if not thousands, of the present generation.

It is hardly possible that one who attracted so much of the public attention during his life should soon cease to be an object of interest. Many among those who have listened to his public teachings, as well as those who know him only by reputation, would doubtless be gratified to possess the means of forming a true estimate of the character of the man—the causes of his singularities, the secret of his influence, and the peculiar bent and power of his mind. It is to gratify this desire that the present edition of his collected works is given to the public. His Journal, which comprises the history of his life to his fortieth year, will suggest to an attentive reader a clew to the enigma which his apparently mysterious conduct often presented.

It may be said of Lorenzo Dow with more truth than of most men, that he knew himself. He had carefully studied his own disposition and endowments, both physical and intellectual, and his great object was to obtain a field which would give free exercise to all his powers. At an age when such reflections are seldom made, he had the sagacity to foresee that the beaten track of the many would consign him to utter uselessness, if not to insignificance and contempt. Those who are familiar with his history will credit him when he says, as he often does, that he had no desire to be singular for the *sake* of singularity. Awkward and ungainly to the last degree by nature, with a harsh voice, and no imposing presence; tortured with a restless desire of locomotion, which seemed as necessary to his health as to the gratification of his impulses, he yet felt the wish, and believed he had the ability, to better the moral and spiritual condition of his fellow-men. But to do this, he knew he must be allowed to do it in his own way. Nature had hedged up the usual avenues to usefulness, and he must travel in the way left open to him, or not travel at all. It is clear that no amount of labor or study would have raised him even to mediocrity as a preacher of the ordinary stamp.

The deep and touching sorrow he often evinces at the rebuffs of his Methodist brethren, who could not countenance his eccentricities, clearly proves that an obstinate will was not the motive that impelled him; while his unfeigned love of the doctrines of the Methodist church, and his invariable refusal to be instrumental in any manner in creating a schism in that body, or in forming a sect or party of his own, are evidence that he was wholly free from ambitious or worldly designs. There is no rational or charitable solution of the apparent mystery which his character and conduct often presented, but that which admits him to have been mainly actuated by a strong desire to benefit mankind.

PREFACE.

The fastidious and educated will probably suggest, that whatever may have been his motives, he was wholly mistaken as to his ability to improve the moral condition of men; they themselves have listened to his harangues with indifference, if not with contempt, and they cannot conceive how a different effect could be produced on the minds of others by the same humble means. This is hasty, if not shallow reasoning. The calm appeal, and the eloquent, but subdued fervor, that sometimes stir the inmost hearts of an orderly and refined assembly, would be utterly powerless to arrest the attention of a lawless and vicious mob. Men of every degree of intelligence, and in every stage of civilization, are to be reached by the efforts of a Christian ministry; and the problem to be solved is, what are the means best adapted to attain the proposed end. Whoever carefully studies the character of the people to whom Dow principally confined his labors, and the effects of his ministrations among them, will see that he was not mistaken. We cannot deny the fact, theorize as we will, that, aside from much of what will be termed mere fanaticism and transient excitement, many were induced by his preaching to reform their lives, and to shun evils as sins against God. That they did not immediately become models of Christian liberality and refined sentiment may be granted; but their rampant, sallying vices were subdued, and thus an opportunity for further advancement, and the ministration of a more intellectual priesthood, was gained at least for their posterity if not for themselves.

The following anecdote, by an eye-witness, of the powerful effect of Lorenzo's preaching upon his most inveterate enemies, is but one of many similar instances that might be enumerated:—

"In 1807, at a camp-meeting held at Niskeuna, between Troy and Schenectady, I first became acquainted with the eccentric Lorenzo Dow, who was at that time, I think, in possession of a truly Christian spirit, though extremely odd and exceptionable in his manners. He seemed to possess the ability or art to transform himself into almost any, and every human character. He could become ludicrous in the extreme—could satirize, or speak ironically to admiration, and yet I have heard him deliver some of the most solemn discourses to which I ever listened. At this camp-meeting, he had given offence to some of the multitude, by his cutting remarks, and a number had associated together without the camp, and formed a company of from fifty to one hundred, and chosen a leader or captain, and having armed themselves with clubs, were preparing to march into the camp-ground, and take Dow by force, and carry him off and punish him at their leisure, for the insult which he had offered them.

"Dow got information of their movements before they were ready to enter the camp, and determined to go out and meet them. Several friends strove to dissuade him from this, but he had made up his mind; and taking Peggy, his wife, by the arm, he immediately started for the road, which was some fifty rods distant. I immediately followed, to see what would be the result. On coming to the highway, where were hundreds, perhaps thousands of people, he asked leave of the owner of a huckster's establishment, to stand in the door of his shantee, and address the people. But the occupant objected, saying that should he do it, his building would be torn down at once, and his goods destroyed. He then made application to one or two others who had similar establishments, but being refused by all, he went to a stump where a large oak tree had lately been felled, and there taking his stand, commenced addressing the multitude, who immediately gathered around him. Presently, the hostile band were seen approaching and pressing through the crowd, preceded by their leader, a large and lion-like looking man, whose mouth, like that of many who followed him, was full of cursing and bitterness. They pressed on until the leader stood directly facing Dow, at the foot of the stump.

"He there paused for a moment or two, while the speaker looked him full in the face and continued his discourse. Some one of the band from the rear called out with an oath, 'Why don't you knock him down!' and many voices were soon raised, crying, 'Pull him down, knock him down!' But the speaker continued, and the leader stood silent and almost motionless, when some who were in the rear attempted to press through to the stump, being impatient at the delay of their leader. But on their coming up, and making an attempt to pull Dow from the stump, the leader called out, 'Let him alone until he has finished his speech.' But many voices replied with awful oaths, that they would have him down at once. Their captain then raising his club, cried out in a threatening voice, 'Let him alone until he has finished his discourse,' and added, 'I will knock down the first man that attempts to disturb him until he has finished his speech.' This brought them to a full stand; for I suppose they knew the man whom they had chosen as their leader, and did not think it safe to provoke his wrath against themselves.

"Dow went on with a solemn address for the space of thirty minutes or more, and when he had closed, this captain or leader offered him his hand to assist him down from the stump, and asked him in a very civil manner, where he wished to go. Dow informed him that his design was to return to the camp-ground. The other replied, 'Here are men that will injure you if they can, but if you will accept my services I will not leave you until I see you safe among your friends.' Dow thanked him, and he then called out, 'Who of you will unite with me to see this man safe among his friends on the camp-ground?' Some twenty voices responded, 'I will.' Dow then took his wife by the arm, and these volunteers formed around them, and in that order they marched to the ground, the leader having notified all, that if any one offered any violence, it would be at his peril.

"At this meeting, Dow gave something like a prophetic view of the future state of the world and of the church, which made a deep impression on my mind, and led me to watch more closely the progress of events as they have since transpired. I will not here detail the national events to which he alluded, but will give two particulars concerning the church, which he told us we might look for within the next fifty years. The first was the revival of the power and influence of the church of Rome, and that it would be especially realized in these United States: and that if not ourselves, yet some of our children might through that power and influence be called to seal their testimony for Christ with their blood. Now all this seemed very improbable, as the papal power was at that time prostrated by the French revolution, and the subsequent reign of Napoleon Bonaparte: and comparatively little was known of that church in this country, except what was found in the history of former ages. The second item in this seemingly prophetic declaration was, that the church of England would, either secretly or openly, become a co-worker with the agents of the church of Rome, in re-establishing its power and influence. Also, that as the Protestant Episcopal Church in this country sympathized with, or was influenced by, the Church of England, we might expect to find men among ourselves, who would lend their aid to bring about these results. I shall make no comment on the above. I simply give the statement as I received it."

There are many points in the moral character of Lorenzo Dow well worthy of study. It is not often that we meet with a tenderer heart, or one more open to all the sympathies of life. His friendships were deep and lasting. His affection for his parents, for his beloved Peggy, and for his little infant, will find a hearty response in every honest breast. There are few more genuine traits of simple-heartedness and love of country to be found in any biography than in the Journal of Lorenzo Dow; and these are the more valuable, as he relates his tale with perfect artlessness, and without the least attempt or desire to produce effect. Though evidently possessed of the finest sympathies, and desiring the good-will of his fellow-men, he yet, at length, became somewhat inured to their contemptuous and scornful treatment. Bu nature would at times assert her rights, and get the better of all his philosophy. It is singular to see a man who had been steeped in misery, and was thoroughly accustomed to every species of cold-hearted selfishness, bursting into tears, —as he did on one occasion in Ireland, when attempting to sell his watch to supply his wants,—simply on being asked what countryman he was. It is easy to imagine the crowd of tender recollections that came thronging upon the heart of the poor wanderer at such a question.*

Another highly commendable trait in the character of Lorenzo Dow was his manly independence. Though never too proud to receive help from the humblest source, when honestly intended, he yet preferred to suffer the extremest misery rather than accept the smallest favor at the hands of those who would consider him obligated by their bounty to pursue a course contrary to his own convictions of duty. If he relates the truth, and there is no reason to doubt it, more than one attempt of this kind was made upon his destitution, and that by persons high in honor in the church; but Lorenzo valued such proffers at their true worth, and declined them with a firmness which ought to have gained him the esteem of all good men.

The intellectual endowments of Lorenzo Dow were far from contemptible. He had great natural shrewdness, great firmness, and invincible energy and perseverance. His advantages of early education were small, and he seems never to have attained the power of treating a subject methodically, or of pursuing a course of consecutive reasoning. Still there are many valuable observations for the conduct of life in his writings, and a vein of homely good sense and sound morality pervades them all. He considered the press next to the pulpit for usefulness, and therefore, as he says, he " collected the quintessence" of his writings for the benefit of posterity.

These writings are here given to the public, together with the " Journey of Life," by his wife, Peggy Dow. That they may be useful in exciting a desire to imitate the virtues of their authors, is the earnest wish of the writer of this Preface.

* At length I went into another watchmaker's, who looked at me and said, "Tell me your cheapest price." I said, "A guinea," it being not half the value. He asked me what countryman I was *I burst out a crying;* he then gave me a breakfast, a guinea, and a shilling.—*Dow's Journal* p. 80

CONTENTS.

PREFACE.................................. PAGE 1
CERTIFICATE OF HON. CADWALLADER D. COLDEN, NOTARY PUBLIC 9
CERTIFICATE OF JAMES MADISON, SECRETARY OF STATE.............................. 10
CERTIFICATE OF HIS EXCELLENCY JOHN PAGE, GOVERNOR OF VIRGINIA 10
CERTIFICATE OF HIS EXCELLENCY JONATHAN TRUMBULL, GOVERNOR OF CONNECTICUT .. 11
CERTIFICATE OF HIS EXCELLENCY JOHN MILLEDGE, GOVERNOR OF GEORGIA 11
CERTIFICATE OF TWENTY-NINE MEMBERS OF THE LEGISLATURE OF GEORGIA 12

JOURNAL OF LORENZO DOW.

PART I.

CHAPTER I.

Lorenzo's Birth and Parentage—Early Childhood—Dread of death—Draws a prize in a lottery, in answer to prayer—Severe illness—Dream of the prophet Nathan—Another dream—Deep religious impressions—The Bible a sealed book—Election and Reprobation—Feelings of despair—Meditates suicide, and goes to the woods with a loaded gun to accomplish it—The Methodists—Reports and opinions concerning them—Preaching of Hope Hull—Powerful effect of his sermon upon Lorenzo, who again meditates suicide—A dream of hell and the devils—Lorenzo's conversion—Happy frame of mind—Doubts and fears .... PAGE 13

CHAPTER II.

Lorenzo's call to preach—Temporary blindness—Weak state of health—Despaired of by friends—Convalescence—Exhorts in public—Opposition of parents—A dream of Adam and Eve—Another dream, in which mankind are seen in the air, suspended by a brittle thread over hell................................ 20

CHAPTER III.

Lorenzo begins to travel—Receives discouraging advice—Is lost in a wilderness—Dreams of John Wesley—A horse is offered him—Sets out for Rhode Island—Reflections on the journey—Gives out a text for the first time—Harsh judgment of T. C.—Receives a dismission from the Presiding Elder, with orders to go home—Deep affliction on account of it—Attends Conference, is examined by the Bishop, rejected, and sent home—Continues to travel and preach—Visits New York, Massachusetts, New Hampshire, and Vermont—Is publicly accused by a Baptist preacher of laying down false doctrine—Crosses the mountains in a snow-storm—The Ruling Elder disapproves of his travelling—Lorenzo's reply—He is again sent home—Approved by the Quarterly Meeting, and sent on a Circuit—Temptations to commit suicide—Opposition from preachers and people—Is encouraged by a dream—Is permitted to travel by the Conference, but is not admitted on trial, and his name refused a place in the minutes—Publicly gives up the name of Methodist—Friends supply his necessities—Goes to Vermont—Attends Quarterly Meeting—Is encouraged—Resolves to get up a revival—Success of his efforts—Offence taken at the plainness of his dress and expressions—Is known by the name of Crazy Dow—Hires a woman for a dollar to spend a day in prayer—A serious dialogue—Effects of thunder and lightning—Solomon Moon's declaration—Conversation with a Calvinist Baptist preacher—Joyful meetings in the new countries—Terrible declaration of a sick woman—A stranger attempts to wring Lorenzo's nose—Lorenzo preaches in Swanton—Publicly opposed by three Baptist preachers—Is seized with a fever at Danby—Relieved by drinking plentifully of cold water—Carried to a rich man's house—Cold reception—Reports of his death—An act of Faith—Restoration to health........................... PAGE 25

CHAPTER IV.

Lorenzo is admitted on trial—Sets off for the north—Rides twenty-three miles in a snow-storm—The wild geese driven from their course—Lorenzo calls the sun, moon, and stars, the fowls of the air, and beasts of the field, to witness against the people—Attends Quarterly Meeting in Ashgrove—Is complained of and whipped by brother Hutchinson—Six hundred join the Methodists—Lorenzo starts for the south—Bread thrown upon the waters—Fall of a reprobation preacher—Lorenzo preaches at Green River—Enters the meeting-house in a borrowed great-coat and two hats—Alarm and excitement of the people—Visits New Concord—Prays God in public that something awful may happen in the neighborhood—Awful fate of a blasphemous young man—The gingerbread lottery—The fiddler thrown out of employ—In Alford Lorenzo preaches Methodism, inside and outside—A lady imagines her elegant dress is aimed at—Lorenzo shames her—He visits Stockbridge, Lenox, Pittsfield, and Bethlehem—Writes to conference for permission to visit Ireland—Visits his parents—Preaches a funeral sermon with great effect—Leaves home again—Crosses the Canada line—Preaches to the offscouring of the earth—Strong desire to visit Ireland—Discouraged by the brethren—Sells his horse—Goes to St. Johns—Is examined by the officers—Bargains with a sea-captain for a passage to Dublin—Sails for Quebec—Is tarred and tallowed by the sailors—Suspected of being a spy—Offers are made him to enlist—Finds friends at Quebec—Sails for Dublin—A terrible gale—Reflections on the voyage—Narrow escape from shipwreck—Arrives at Larne, in the north of Ireland—Goes ashore—Inquires for Methodists—Finds a few—Is scolded by a woman for not praying for the king—Preaches frequently—Great improvement in his health... Page 45

CHAPTER V.

Lorenzo goes to Dublin—Finds Methodists and attends meetings—Calls on the preachers—Is advised to return to America—Is publicly reproved by Mr. Tobins—Great discouragements—Is comforted by a dream—Is invited by a Scotch soldier to preach in the barracks—A mysterious dream explained—Lorenzo parts with half his money to a starving woman—Visits Belfast, Carrickfergus, Ballycary, Strode, Cogray, and Carley—Dialogue with a magistrate—Is threatened with the guard-house—Preaches in the streets near Belfast, and is sent to prison—Preaches to the prisoners, and is discharged—Goes to the Isle of Man—The sailors steal his provisions—Returns to Dublin—Goes to Hull—Speaks in a Quaker meeting, for which he is reproved—Ideas on Grammar, the Bible, and Christianity—On Baptism and the Lord's Supper—Goes to Kilkenny—Returns to Dublin and meets Dr. Coke, who proposes to him a missionary station at Halifax or Quebec, which he declines—Is threatened with the vengeance of Lord Castlereagh—Is discountenanced by the conference, and his way completely hedged up—Prints a sketch of his experience... 61

CHAPTER VI

Lorenzo sickens of the small-pox—Is kindly treated and recovers—Is solicited to play at cards—Consents to play one game—Goes to Hacketstown, and inquires for swaddlers—Is solicited to accept a razor, which he refuses—Is blamed for not drinking wine and dressing ministerially—Visits the famous Vinegar Hill—Has eleven shillings forced on him, but refuses two shirts—Is closely questioned by a magistrate—Sells his watch for a guinea, and gives half of it to a poor man—Returns to Dublin—Prints three thousand handbills to warn the people of Dublin—Directs one to the Lord Lieutenant of Ireland—Visits Tullemore, Tuam, Hollymount, Foxford, &c. 72

CHAPTER VII.

Lorenzo takes leave of his friends and sails for America—Arrives at New York—Is stationed on the Dutchess and Columbia circuit, Freeborn Garrettson presiding elder—Visits his parents—Multitudes flock to hear him............... 86

CHAPTER VIII.

Lorenzo resolves to travel the continent at large—Sails from New York for Savannah, Georgia—Arrival—Spends some hours in a churchyard—Andrew the black preacher—Jealousy of a brother preacher—Reflections on the hooping crane—Visits Augusta—Inquires for Methodists, and is directed to a Frenchman, who treats him with great contempt—Stops with a black family—A young clergyman gives him a broadside in a flowery prayer—Hope Hull leaves him to paddle his own canoe—Is near being knocked over by the falling of a black woman—Meets Stith Mead—Visits Charleston—Finds the preachers friendly, but shy—Holds picked meetings—Sails for New York........ Page 90

CHAPTER IX.

Is sick at New York—The preachers are shy of him—Preaches at the State Prison and Almshouse—Goes to New Haven—Stones are thrown at him through the windows while preaching there—Visits Middletown and Eastbury—Selling the Gospel not in good demand—Obtains the blessing of sanctification by an act of faith—Visits Coventry, Lebanon, Scotland, Canterbury, Preston, Stonington, Groton, New London, &c.—In Hartford his horse throws him and runs away—Returns to New York—The preaching-houses shut against him—Visits Turkey, in New Jersey................ 102

CHAPTER X.

Lorenzo visits Massachusetts—Fails to obtain a hearing in Boston—Sets off for Georgia—Gets into the wrong pulpit by mistake, and is driven out by the sexton—Reaches Philadelphia—Is severely hatchelled by Mr. Cooper and Elder Ware—Visits Wilmington and Baltimore—Stops in North Carolina—A woman warns the people against him as a horse thief—Reaches Georgia and attends a camp meeting—Visits Augusta—The governor offers him money—A narrow escape from a raving heifer—Sets off for the west—Travels through the Choctaw nation—Reaches Natchez—A ride through Cumberland woods—Is seized by a party of Indians—Escapes by flight—Hears the cries of the catamounts—Reaches Nashville—Preaches in a grog-house—Travels to Kentucky—Preaches at Frankfort in the playhouse—Arrives in Virginia, ragged and dirty—Preaches in Bedford county—Takes his text from *The Age of Reason*—Finds Jesse Lee—A constable in Raleigh attempts to arrest him as a *horse thief*—Returns to Georgia—Rules for Holy Living. 114

PART II.

CHAPTER I.

Lorenzo visits the upper counties of Georgia—Preaches on A-double-L-partism—Preaches at Louisville in the Statehouse—A Baptist preacher attempts to upset him from a chair—Receives a recommendation signed by the governor of Georgia, the secretary of state, and twenty-eight members of the legislature—Visits Savannah—Returns to Augusta—Meets Dr. Coke—Goes to South Carolina—Preaches at Charleston—Goes to Raleigh, N. C., and preaches in the Statehouse—Preaches in Buncombe—Starts for Tennessee—Singular phenomena of the *jerks*, and their extensive prevalence..... 126

CHAPTER II.

Lorenzo starts for Virginia—Preaches in Culpepper, before one of the President's daughters—Preaches at Prince Edward before the lawyers—Prepares an Address to the people of Virginia—The Snake and the Hedgehog—Preaches at Yorktown—Scarcely a white Christian in the place—Hears of the death of his mother.. 135

CHAPTER III.

Lorenzo returns to New England—Preaches in Boston—Visits New York and Albany—Sees his future wife Peggy—Story of a bird's nest.. 148

CONTENTS.

CHAPTER IV.
Lorenzo's Courtship and Marriage..... PAGE 151

CHAPTER V.
Lorenzo starts for the Mississippi—Visits Ohio, Tennessee, and Louisiana................ 153

CHAPTER VI.
Lorenzo returns to the North—Various adventures on his journey...................... 157

CHAPTER VII.
Lorenzo's tour through New England—Incidents and anecdotes............................ 166

CHAPTER VIII.
Lorenzo's journey to North Carolina—Anecdote of Old Sam—Calls the people who had threatened his life "a pack of d—d cowards"—Returns to New York...................... 171

CHAPTER IX.
Lorenzo, accompanied by his wife Peggy, sails for Liverpool—Arrival—Reflections on the ancient castles—Preaches in Liverpool—Visits Manchester—Calls on Jabez Buntin, who refuses to see him—Goes to London—Gets the king's license to stay in the kingdom—The "wooden walls" of the British—Returns to Manchester—Preaches in a salt pan—Kind reception by Adam Clarke—Cool contempt of Dr. Coke—Goes to Dublin—Finds a hearty welcome—Visits and preaches in several places—Returns to Liverpool—Visits Leeds and Yorkshire—Conversation with Adam Clarke—Returns to Dublin—Meeting with a coxcomb—Defends himself in a public meeting—Is injured by a stone thrown at him by a boy—The mob assemble at his meetings—Reflections on his thirtieth year—Returns to Liverpool—A dumb boy attends Lorenzo's preaching, and is enabled to speak—A Deist converted—Great effects of his labors at Macclesfield and Congleton—Illness of Peggy—Returns to Ireland for a general visit—Death of his only child—Remarkable experience of Mr. Averill—A Roman priest, with a whip and club, drives away the people who are listening to Lorenzo—He returns to Liverpool—Six kinds of Methodists in England—Comparative state of religion in England and America—Returns to America............ 180

CHAPTER X.
A short account of "Eccentric Cosmopolite." 215

CHAPTER XI.
Lorenzo's labors and travels in Virginia—Is collared by lawyer Baker, who threatens to break his neck—The ladies take his part—Has to apologize for wearing a single-breasted coat—Sees the wife of the "Wild Man of the Woods"—Meets Jesse Lee—Retributions of Providence 222

CHAPTER XII.
Conclusion—Lorenzo's temporal affairs—Moral and religious reflections—Visits New York and Philadelphia—Reflections on historical incidents—Visits Ohio and Kentucky—A great earthquake in Missouri—Goes to New Orleans—Visits the battle ground of General Jackson's victory—Returns to New York—Completes a tour through Vermont, New Hampshire, and Connecticut, 1816................... PAGE 228

THE CHAIN OF LORENZO 247

REFLECTIONS ON THE IMPORTANT SUBJECT OF MATRIMONY 284

ANALECTS UPON NATURAL, SOCIAL, AND MORAL PHILOSOPHY.

Introduction 298
Of the Law of Nature..................... 299
Of Personal Rights 299
Of Social Rights 300
Of Moral Rights........................... 302
Of Governments 305
Of Divine Delegation 305
Of the Pope's Power...................... 308
The Dawn of Liberty..................... 311
Of Forms of Government 314
Right of Property held under Monarchs.... 315
Of Representation......................... 316
Nature and Design, and Enaction of Law.... 316
Of the Law of Nations 317
Recapitulation 318
A Contrast................................. 318
Of Punishments........................... 318
Of Political Existence 321
Of the Spread of the Gospel............. 322
Summary Review......................... 331
Conclusion 336

A JOURNEY FROM BABYLON TO JERUSALEM; OR, THE ROAD TO PEACE.

Introduction 340
Reflections on Nature 341
Miscellaneous Reflections 342
Moral Inquiries 344
Of Hieroglyphic Babylon 344
Of Jerusalem 346
Of Moral Evil............................. 347
Of Man's Fall............................. 349
Of the New Birth 350
Of Repentance............................ 351
Of Faith................................... 352
Of Hope 355
Of Charity................................ 355
Of Fasting 356
Of Prayer 357
Of Watching 358
Of the Night of Death................... 360
Of Hell and Paradise 361
Of the Day of Judgment................. 361
Of Providence in Nature................ 363
Of Spirits Good and Evil................ 364
Of the Resurrection 366
Of the Lake of Fire 367
Of the Heavenly Jerusalem.............. 367
Conclusion 369

A DIALOGUE BETWEEN THE CURIOUS AND SINGULAR 372
HINTS ON THE FULFILMENT OF PROPHECY .. 382
ON THE MINISTRY 396
DOW'S LAWSUIT 397

Appendix.................................. 416

VICISSITUDES OF THE JOURNEY OF LIFE. By PEGGY DOW....................... 425
SUPPLEMENTARY REFLECTIONS............ 470

UNITED STATES OF AMERICA.

STATE OF NEW YORK, ss.

[SEAL.] By this public instrument, be it known to all whom the same may or doth concern, that I, CADWALLADER D. COLDEN, a Public Notary, in and for the State of New York, by Letters Patent under the Great Seal of the said State, duly commissioned and sworn, and in and by the said Letters Patent invested "with full powers and authority to attest deeds, wills, testaments, codicils, agreements, and other instruments in writing, and to administer any oath or oaths to any person or persons," do hereby certify, that on the day of the date hereof, personally appeared before me the said Notary, the Reverend Lorenzo Dow, whose person being by me particularly examined, appears to me to be of the age of twenty-eight years, or thereabouts ; of the height of five feet ten inches : rather light complexioned, and much marked with the small-pox ; having small light eyes, dark brown hair and eyebrows, small features, and a short visage, a scrofulous mark on his neck under his chin, on the right side : and the said Lorenzo Dow being by me duly sworn on the Holy Evangelists of Almighty God, deposeth and saith, that he was born in the town of Coventry, in the State of Connecticut, in the United States of America, of Humphrey B. Dow, and Tabitha his wife, who was Tabitha Parker; that his said parents were also born in the said town ; that his mother is dead, but his father is yet living, and resides in the same place. And the said deponent further saith, that he is the person named, intended and described as Lorenzo Dow, in all and each of the several documents hereunto annexed, which are respectively lettered A, B, C, D, and which are now produced to me, the said Notary, and lettered as aforesaid by me, the said Notary, and my notarial firm thereon written.

And I, the said Notary, do further certify, that on the same day and year last aforesaid, also appeared before me, the Reverend Nicholas Snethen, of New York, and James Quackenbush, of the State of New York, gentleman, who being by me also sworn on the Holy Evangelists of Almighty God, depose and say : and first the said Nicholas Snethen saith, that he is well acquainted with the said Lorenzo Dow, and has known him from his youth to this time ; and this deponent has been also well acquainted with the parents of the said Lorenzo Dow : that the said Lorenzo Dow is a native of the United States of America, and a Minister of the Holy Gospel, and the said deponent doth verily believe that all the facts herein stated and set forth by the said Lorenzo Dow, are true. And the said James Quackenbush saith, that he hath known the said Lorenzo Dow, for four years last past, and upwards—that he hath always understood, and doth believe him to be a native citizen of the United States of America, and doth believe that all the facts to which the said Lorenzo Dow hath above deposed, are true. And the said Lorenzo Dow being such native citizen as aforesaid, of the United States of America, is entitled to all the advantages and privileges thereof, and to the friendly aid and protection of all persons, Potentates and States, with whom the said United States are in peace and friendship.

Whereof an attestation being required, I have granted this under my notarial firm and seal.

    Done at the city of New York, in the United States of America, the said deponents having first countersigned the same, this fifth day November, in the year of our Lord one thousand eight hundred and five.

                                                CADWALLADER D. COLDEN,
                                                              Not. Pub.

LORENZO DOW,
NICHOLAS SNETHEN,
JAMES QUACKENBUSH.

A

Cadwallader D. Colden, Not. Public.

To all to whom these presents shall concern, *Greeting:*

THE BEARER HEREOF, LORENZO DOW,

A citizen of the United States of America, having occasion to pass into foreign countries, about his lawful affairs, these are to pray all whom it may concern, to permit the same Lorenzo Dow, (he demeaning himself well and peaceably,) to pass wheresoever his lawful pursuits may call him, freely without let or molestation in going, staying, or returning, and to give him all friendly aid and protection, as these United States would do in the like case.

IN FAITH WHEREOF

SECRETARY OF STATE'S SEAL. OFFICE.
(GRATIS.)

I have caused the seal of the Department of State for the said United States, to be hereunto affixed. Done at Washington, this 23d day of October, in the year of our Lord one thousand eight hundred and five, and of the independence of these States the thirtieth.

JAMES MADISON,
Secretary of State.

B

Cadwallader D. Colden, Not. Pub.

VIRGINIA, to wit.

Be it known to all whom it may concern, that the Reverend Lorenzo Dow, who declares himself a native of Connecticut, one of the United States of America, has for two or three years past occasionally travelled through this commonwealth, as an itinerant preacher of the Gospel; that his appointments to preach have, according to report, been attended by considerable numbers of the inhabitants of this state; that on all occasions his conduct has been inoffensive, and his manners impressive. It is believed that his views are confined to the promotion of human happiness, by diffusing, to the utmost of his abilities, a knowledge of the Christian religion, and by a conviction, on his part, of its tendency to that desirable object. This certificate is granted to the said Reverend Lorenzo Dow, at the request of his friends, in consequence of a meditated voyage to Europe for the restoration of his impaired health.

[SEAL.]   Given under my hand as Governor, with the Seal of the Commonwealth annexed, at Richmond, this 19th day of October, 1805.

JOHN PAGE

C

Cadwallader D. Colden, Not. Public.

Humphrey B. Dow and Tabitha Parker were joined in marriage, Oct. 8th, A. D. 1767.

Lorenzo Dow, son of Humphrey B. Dow and Tabitha his wife, was born in Coventry, October 16th, A. D. 1777.

(A true copy of record, examined by)

NATHAN HOWARD, *Town Clerk.*

STATE OF CONNECTICUT, ss.

COVENTRY.

October 11th, A. D. 1805.

I, the subscriber, do hereby certify that by the law of the State aforesaid, al.
rriages, births and deaths are to be recorded in the records of their respect-
towns, and Nathan Howard, Esq. who hath attested the aforesaid from the
vn records, is the clerk of said town, duly appointed and sworn, and that the
ove signature is in his own proper handwriting, and that faith and credit is
be given to his attestation in court and country.

In testimony hereof I have subscribed my hand and seal.

[SEAL.]   JESSE ROOT,
                   Chief Justice of the Superior Court

STATE OF CONNECTICUT, ss.

TOLLAND COUNTY, COVENTRY.

October 15th, 1805.

This certifies that the above Lorenzo Dow was born in Coventry, as above
ted, of a *reputable family*, and he the said Lorenzo is by profession a *Metho
t preacher;* he is a man of *decent morals* and of *peaceable behavior*, so far as
r knowledge of him extends. And that the above said Jesse Root is the
ief Justice of the Superior Court in the State of Connecticut, and that full
dit is to be given to his certificate in court and country.

           JEREMIAH RIPLEY, one of the Judges of the Court of
              Common Pleas, County of Tolland.
           ELEAZER POMEROY, Justice of Peace.

[SEAL.]   HIS EXCELLENCY JONATHAN TRUMBULL, GOVERNOR IN
           AND OVER THE STATE OF CONNECTICUT.

To all who may see these presents—*maketh known*,
That *Jesse Root*, Esq. the person whose signature is set to the within *Certi-
ite* is *Chief Judge* of the *Superior Court* within said *State*.—That *Jeremiah
pley*, Esq., signer of the within Certificate, is one of the *Judges* of the Court
Common Pleas, for the County of Tolland in said State.—That *Eleazer Po-
roy*, Esq., also one of the within *signers*, is a *Justice of Peace*, within and for
mentioned *County*.
That each of the above named gentlemen have been legally qualified and
ly appointed to do and perform all and singular the duties appertaining to
ir several offices. And that full faith and credit is to be given to their several
ts and signatures in their respective capacities. In faith and testimony where-
I have hereunto set my hand and affixed my seal of office, at the *City* of
w *Haven*, in said *State*, the 15th day of October, in the year of our Lord 1805.
                    JONATHAN TRUMBULL.

               D

          Cadwallader D. Colden, Not. Pub.

GEORGIA.

his excellency JOHN MILLEDGE, *Governor* and *Commander-in-Chief* of
the *Army* and *Navy* of this *State*, and of the *Militia* thereof.—To all whom
these presents shall come, *Greeting:*

KNOW YE, that Abraham Jackson, Risden Moore, Bolling Anthony, Za-
ariah Lamar, James Terrell, John Clark, David Dickson, Solomon Slatter,
alter Drane, Jared Irwin, Thompson Bird, Robert Hughes, Drury Jones,

George Moore, Wormly Rose, Joel Barnet, William H. Crawford, Samuel Alexander, George Philips, John Hampton, Elijah Clark, William W. Bibb, David Bates, Buckner Harris, Allen Daniel, William Fitzpatrick, James H. Little, John Davis, and James Jones, Esqrs., who have severally subscribed their names to the annexed recommendation, in favor of the Reverend Lorenzo Dow, are Members of the Legislature of this State, and now in Session.

THEREFORE all due Faith, Credit and Authority, are and ought to be had and given to their signatures as such.

JOHN *MILLEDGE

IN TESTIMONY whereof, I have hereunto set my Hand, and caused the Great Seal of the said State to be put and affixed, at the State House in Louisville, this third day of December, in the year of our Lord, eighteen hundred and three, and in the twenty-eighth year of American Independence.

By the Governor,

Hor. MARBURY,
Secretary of the State.

STATE OF GEORGIA.

To all whom these presents shall come or concern.

BE it known, that the Reverend Lorenzo Dow, an Itinerant Preacher of tne Gospel, hath travelled through this state several times, in the course of two years, and has maintained the character of a useful and acceptable Gospel Preacher; and now being about to leave the State, We, in testimony of our high regard for him, recommend him to all Christians and lovers of virtue, as a man whose sole aim appears to be the propagating useful Principles through the Christian religion.

Given under our hands at Louisville, this 3d December, 1803.

ABRAHAM JACKSON,	JOEL BARNET,
RISDEN MOORE,	W. H. CRAWFORD,
BOLLING ANTHONY,	SAMUEL ALEXANDER,
Z. LAMAR,	GEORGE PHILIPS,
JAMES TERRELL,	JOHN HAMPTON,
JOHN CLARK,	ELIJAH CLARK,
DAVID DICKSON,	WILLIAM W. BIBB,
SOLOMON SLATTER,	DAVID BATES,
W. DRANE,	BUCKNER HARRIS,
JARED IRWIN,	ALLEN DANIEL,
THOMPSON BIRD,	WILLIAM FITZPATRICK,
ROBERT HUGHES,	JAMES H. LITTLE,
DRURY JONES,	JOHN DAVIS,
GEORGE MOORE,	JAMES JONES,
WY. ROSE.	

---

* This publication is for the benefit of society when I am dead and gone.† The press is next to the pulpit, for usefulness, and many having desired the "quintessence of my writings," with difficulty they have been collected and concentrated accordingly.—L. D.

† *Note by the Editor.*—After a course of thirty years' preaching, having travelled over England and Ireland, and visited almost every part of the United States, Mr. Dow died at Georgetown, in the District of Columbia, on the 2d of February, 1834.

THE JOURNAL

OF

LORENZO DOW

CHAPTER I.

MY CHILDHOOD.

I was born, October 16, 1777, in Coventry, Tolland County, State of Connecticut. My parents were born in the same town and descended from English ancestors. They had a son, and then three daughters, older than myself, and one daughter younger. They were very tender towards their children, and endeavored to educate them well, both in religion and common learning.

When I was two years old, I was taken sick; and my parents having been a long journey and returning homeward, heard of my dangerous illness, and that I was dead, and they expected to meet the people returning from my funeral. But to their joy, I was living; and beyond the expectation of all, I recovered.

When I was between three and four years old, one day, while I was at play with my companion, I suddenly fell into a muse about God and those places called heaven and hell, which I heard people converse about, so that I forgot my play, which my companion observing, desired to know the cause. I asked him if ever he said his prayers, morning or night; to which he replied, "No." Then said I, "You are wicked, and I will not play with you." So I quit his company and went into the house.

My mind, frequently on observing the works of creation, desired to know the cause of things; and I asked my parents many questions which they scarcely knew how to answer.

Being for a few weeks in another neighborhood, I associated with one who would both swear and lie, which proved some harm to me. But these serious impressions did not leave me until in my eighth year, when my parents removed to another vicinity, the youth of which were very corrupt; and on joining their company, I too soon learned their ways, grieved the tender feelings of my mind, and began to promise myself felicity when I should arrive to manhood.

One day I was the means of killing a bird, and upon seeing it gasp, I was struck with horror. And upon seeing any beast struggle in death it made my heart beat hard, as it would cause the thoughts of my death to come into my mind. Death appeared such a terror to me, I sometimes wished that I might be translated as Enoch and Elijah were; and at other times I wished I had never been born.

About this time a query arose in my mind, whether God would answer prayer now as in primitive times; and there being a small lottery in the neighborhood, and I wishing for the greatest prize, promised within myself, that if it was my luck to obtain the prize, I would take it as an answer to prayer, and afterwards would serve God. No sooner had I gotten the prize, which was nine shillings, than I broke my promise. My conscience condemned me, and I was very uneasy for some weeks.

After I had arrived to the age of twelve years, my hopes of worldly pleasure were greatly blasted by a sudden illness, occasioned by overheating myself with hard labor, and drinking a quantity of cold milk and water. I than murmured and complained, thinking my lot to be harder than that of my companions; for they enjoyed health, while I was troubled with an asthmatical disorder or stoppage of breath. Oh! the pain I endured!

Sometimes I could lie several nights together and sleep sound; and at other times would be necessitated to sit up part or all night. And some times I could not lie down at all for six or seven days together. But as yet I did not consider that the hand of God was in all this. About this time, I dreamed that I saw the prophet Nathan, in a large assembly of people, prophesying many things. I got an opportunity to ask him how long I should live. Said he, "UNTIL YOU ARE TWO-AND-TWENTY." This dream was so imprinted in my mind, that it caused me many serious and painful hours at intervals.

When past the age of thirteen years, and about the time that JOHN WESLEY died, (1791,) it pleased God to awaken my mind by a dream of the night, which was, that an old man came to me at mid-day, having a staff in his hand, and said to me, "Do you ever pray?" I told him, "No." Said he, "You must;" and then went away. He had not been long gone before he returned; and said again, "Do you pray?" I again said, "No." And after his departure I went out of doors, and was taken up by a whirlwind and carried above the skies. At length I discovered, across a gulf, as it were through a mist of darkness, a glorious place, in which was a throne of ivory overlaid with gold, and God sitting upon it, and Jesus Christ at his right hand, and angels and glorified spirits celebrating praise.—Oh! the joyful music! I thought the angel Gabriel came to the edge of heaven, holding a golden trumpet in his right hand, and cried to me with a mighty voice to know if I desired to come there. I told him I did. Said he, "You must go back to yonder world, and if you will be faithful to God, you shall come here in the end."

With reluctance I left the beautiful sight and came back to the earth again. And then I thought the old man came to me the third time and asked me if I had prayed. I told him I had. "Then," said he, "BE FAITHFUL, AND I WILL COME AND LET YOU KNOW AGAIN." I thought that was to be when I should be blest. And when I awaked, behold it was a dream. But it was strongly impressed on my mind, that this singular dream must be from God: and the way that I should know it, I should let my father know of it at such a time and in such a place, viz. as he would be feeding the cattle in the morning, which I accordingly did. No sooner had I done it than keen conviction seized my heart. I knew I was unprepared to die. Tears began to run down plentifully, and I again resolved to seek the salvation of my soul. I began that day to pray in secret; but how to pray or what to pray for, I scarcely knew.

I at once broke off from my old companions and evil practices, which some call innocent mirth, which I had never been told was wrong; and betook to the Bible, *kneeling* in private, which example I had never seen. Soon I became like a speckled bird among the birds of the forest, in the eyes of my friends. I frequently felt, for a few seconds, *cords of sweet love* to draw me on; but from whence it flowed, I could not tell. I since believe this was for an encouragement to hope in the mercy of God.

If now I had had any one to instruct me in the way and plan of salvation, I doubt not but I should have found salvation. But, alas, I felt like one wandering and benighted in an unknown wilderness, who wants both light and a guide. The Bible was like a sealed book; so mysterious I could not understand it. And in order to hear it explained, I applied to this person and that book; but got no satisfactory instruction. I frequently wished I had lived in the days of the prophets or apostles, that I could have had sure guides; for by the misconduct of professors, I thought there were no Bible saints in the land. Thus with sorrow many months heavily rolled away.

But at length, not finding what my soul desired, I began to examine the cause more closely, if possible to find it out: and immediately the doctrine of unconditional *reprobation* and particular *election* was exhibited to my view—that the state of all was unalterably fixed by God's "eternal decrees." Here discouragements arose, and I began to slacken my hand by degrees, until I entirely left off secret prayer, and could not bear to read or hear the scriptures, saying, "If God has foreordained whatever comes to pass, then all our labors are vain."

Feeling still condemnation in my breast, I concluded myself reprobated. Despair of mercy arose, hope was fled, and I was resolved to end my wretched life; concluding the longer I live, the more sin I shall commit, and the greater my punishment will be; but the shorter my life, the less sin, and of course the less punishment, and the sooner I shall know the worst of my case. Accordingly I loaded a gun, and withdrew to a wilderness.

As I was about to put my intention into execution, a sudden solemn thought darted into my mind, "Stop and consider what you are about: if you end your life, you are undone for ever; but if you omit it a few days longer, it may be that something will turn up in your favor." This was attended with a small degree of hope, that if I waited a little while, it should not be altogether in vain. And I thought I felt thankful that God prevented me from sending my soul to everlasting misery.

About this time there was much talk about the people called Methodists, who were lately come into the western part of New England. There were various reports and opinions concerning them. Some said they were the deceivers that were to come in the last times; that such a delusive spirit attended them, that it was dangerous to hear them preach, lest they should lead people out of the good old way which they had been brought up in; and that they would deceive if possible the very elect. Some, on the other hand, said they were a good sort of people.

A certain man invited Hope Hull to come to his own town, who appointed a time when he would endeavor, if possible, to comply with his request. The day arrived, and the people flocked out from every quarter to hear, as they supposed, a new gospel. I went to the door and looked in to see a Methodist; but to my surprise he appeared like other men. I heard him preach from—"This is a faithful saying and worthy of all acceptation, that Christ Jesus came into the world to save sinners." And I thought he told me all that ever I did.

The next day he preached from these words: "Is there no balm in Gilead? Is there no Physician there? Why then is not the health of the daughter of my people recovered?" Jer. viii. 22.

As he drew the analogy between a person sick of a consumption and a sin-sick soul, he endeavored also to show how the real balm of Gilead would heal the consumption; and to spiritualize it, in the blood of Christ healing the soul; in which he described the way to heaven, and pointed out the way-marks, which I had never heard described so clearly before. I was convinced that this man enjoyed something that I was destitute of, and consequently that he was a servant of God.

He then got upon the application, and pointing his finger towards me, made this expression: "Sinner, there is a frowning Providence above your head, and a burning hell beneath your feet; and nothing but the brittle thread of life prevents your soul from falling into endless perdition. But, says the sinner, What must I do? You must pray. But I can't pray. If you don't pray, then you'll be damned." And as he brought out the last expression he either stamped with his foot on the box on which he stood, or smote with his hand upon the Bible, which both together came home like a dagger to my heart. I had like to have fallen backwards from my seat, but saved myself by catching hold of my cousin who sat by my side, and I durst not stir for some time for fear lest I should tumble into hell. My sins, and the damnable nature of them, were in a moment exhibited to my view; and I was convinced that I was unprepared to die.

After the assembly was dismissed, I went out of doors. All nature seemed to wear a gloomy aspect; and every thing I cast my eyes upon seemed to bend itself against me, and wish me off the face of the earth.

I went to a funeral of one of my acquaintance the same day. but durst not look upon the corpse, for fear of becoming one myself. I durst not go near the grave, fearing lest I should fall in, and the earth come in upon me; for if I then died, I knew I must be undone. So I went home with a heavy heart.

I durst not close my eyes in sleep, until I first attempted to supplicate the throne of grace for preservation through the night. The next morning, as I went out of doors, a woman passing by told me that my cousin the evening before had found the pardoning love of God. This surprised me, that one of my companions was taken and I was left. I instantly came to a resolution to forsake my sins and seek the salvation of my soul. I made it my practice to pray thrice in a day for about the space of a week; when another of my cousins, brother to the former. was brought to cry for mercy in secret retirement in a garden, and his cries were so loud that he was heard upwards of a mile. The same evening he found comfort.

Shortly after, several persons in the neighborhood professed to have found the pardoning love of God, among whom was my brother-in-law Fish, and his brother.

Sorrows arose in my mind, to think that they were heavenward, whilst I, a guilty one, was in the downward road. I endeavored to double and treble my diligence in prayer, but found no comfort to my soul. Here the doctrine of unconditional reprobation was again presented to my view, with strong temptations to end this mortal life. But the thought again arose in my mind; if I comply, I am undone for ever, and if I continue crying to God, I can but be damned at last.

One evening there being, by my desire, a prayer-meeting appointed by the young converts, I set out to go; and on my way, by the side of a wood, I kneeled down and made a solemn promise to God, if he would pardon my sins and give me an evidence of my acceptance, that I would forsake all those things wherein I had formerly thought to have taken my happiness, and lead a religious life devoted to him; and with this promise I went to meeting.

I believe that many present felt the power of God. Saints were happy and sinners were weeping on every side: but I could not shed a tear. Then I thought within myself, if I could weep I would begin to take hope; but, oh! how hard is my heart! I went from one to another to know if there was any mercy for me. The young converts answered, "God is all love; he is all mercy." I replied, "God is just too, and justice will cut me down." I saw no way how God could be *just* and yet show me mercy.

A certain woman bound upon a journey, tarried at this house that night; and discovering the distress of mind I was in, broke through the crowd with the hymn-book in her hand, and after reading a part of a hymn, said to me, "My friend, I feel for you; my heart aches for you; but this I can tell you, that before I leave town in the morning, you will come down here praising God." I told her, "No; I believed I should be in hell before morning."

After the meeting had concluded, which was about nine o'clock, and previous to the foregoing circumstance, I had, by the advice of my parents, set out for home thrice; but by a strong impression, as it were a voice whispering to my heart, "You must not go yet; but go back and pray to God;" I turned about and went into a wheat field, and kneeled down; and striving to pray, I felt as if the heavens were brass and the earth iron; it seemed as though my prayers did not go higher than my head.

At length I durst not go home alone, fearing I should be carried away by the devil, for I saw destruction before me.

Several of the young converts accompanied me on my way; one of whom was Roger Searle. They since have told me that I fell down several times by the way, which I do not remember, as my distress was so great that I scarcely knew what position I was in. When I got home, I went into my bedroom; and, kneeling down, I strove to look to God for mercy again; but found no comfort. I then lay down to rest, but durst not close my eyes in sleep, for fear I should never awake, until I awaked in endless misery.

I strove to plead with God for mercy, for several hours, as a man would plead for his life; until at length being weary in body, as the night was far spent, I fell into a slumber. In it I dreamed that two devils entered the room, each with a chain in his hand; they laid hold on me, one at my head, the other at my feet, and bound me fast, and breaking out the window, carried me a distance from the house, and laid me on a spot of ice; and whilst the weaker devil flew off in flames of fire, the stronger one set out to drag me down to hell. And when I got within sight of hell, to see the blue blazes ascending, and to hear the screeches and groans of devils and damned spirits, the shock it gave me I cannot describe. I thought that within a few moments this must be my unhappy lot. I cannot bear the thought, I will struggle and strive to break these chains; and if I can, and get away, it will be gain; but if I cannot, there will be nothing lost. In my struggle I waked up; and, oh! how glad was I that it was only a dream! Still I thought that within a few hours it would surely be my case. I again strove to lift my heart to God for mercy—and these words struck my mind; "In that day there shall a fountain be opened to the house of David, and to the inhabitants of Jerusalem, for sin and for uncleanness." A thought darted into my mind that the fountain was Christ; and if it were so deep and wide for the wicked inhabitants of Jerusalem to wash in and be clean, why not for the *whole world?* why not for me? Here hope sprang up that there was a Saviour offered to *all*, instead of a certain few; and if so, possibly there might be mercy yet for me. But these words followed; "Wo to them that are at ease in Zion." Here discouragements arose; I concluded that if there had been a time when I might have obtained mercy, yet as I had omitted it so long, the day of grace is now passed, and the wo denounced against me. I thought myself to be the unprofitable servant, who had wrapped his talent in the napkin, and buried it in the earth. I had not on the wedding garment, and was unprepared to meet God.

I thought I heard the voice of God's justice saying, "Take the unprofitable servant, and cast him into utter darkness." I put my hands together, and cried in my heart, " The time has been, that I might have had religion, but now it is too late; mercy's gate is shut against me, and my condemnation for ever sealed:—Lord, I give up; I submit; I yield; if there be mercy in heaven for me, let me know it; and if not, let me go down to hell and know the worst of my case." As these words flowed from my heart, I saw the Mediator step in, as it were, between the Father's justice and my soul, and these words were applied to my mind with great power; " Son! thy sins which are many are forgiven thee; thy faith hath saved thee; go in peace."

The burden of sin and guilt and the fear of hell vanished from my mind, as perceptibly as a hundred pounds weight falling from a man's shoulder; my soul flowed out in love to God, to his ways and to his people; yea, and to *all* mankind.

As soon as I obtained deliverance, I said in my heart, I have now found Jesus and his religion, but I will keep it to myself. But instantly my soul was so filled with peace, and love, and joy, that I could no more keep it to myself, seemingly, than a city set on a hill could be hid. At this time daylight dawned into the window. I arose, and went out of doors; and, behold, every thing I cast my eye upon, seemed to be speaking forth the praise and wonders of the Almighty. It appeared more like a new world than any thing else I can compare it to. This happiness is easier felt than described.

I set out to go down to the house where the meeting was held the preceding evening; but the family not being up, and I being young, I thought it not proper to go in and disturb them. Seeing a wicked swearer coming down the road, I wished to shun him, and accordingly I went down to the barn. As he drew near me, I went round it, and looked up towards the house, and saw the *woman who was bound on the journey* coming out at the back door. I made to her with all the speed I could. It seemed to me that I scarcely touched the ground, for I felt so happy, that I scarcely knew whether I was in the body or out of it.

When I got to her, she said, "Good-morning." "Yes," said I, "it is the blessedest morning that ever I saw;" and, walking into the house, the first words that I said were, "I am happy, happy, happy enough." My voice penetrated almost every part of the house; and a preacher coming down stairs, opened his hymn-book on these words:

"O! for a thousand tongues to sing
My dear Redeemer's praise."

Indeed, I did want a thousand tongues, and ten thousand to the end of it, to praise God for what he had done for my soul.

About nine o'clock I set out for home; when to behold the beautiful sun rising in the east above the hills, although it was on the twelfth of November, and the ground partly frozen, was to me as pleasant as May.

When I got home to my parents, they began to reprove me for going out so early, as they were concerned about me. But when I told them where I had been, and what I had been upon, they seemed to be struck; it being such language as they had never heard from me before, and almost unbelieving to what I said. However, my soul was so happy that I could scarcely settle to work; and I spent the greatest part of the day in going from house to house, through the neighborhood, to tell the people what God had done for me.

I wanted to publish it to the ends of the earth, and then take wings and fly away to rest. In this happy situation I went on my way rejoicing for some weeks, concluding that I should never learn war any more. Some said that young converts were happier than those who were many years in the way. Thought I, Lord, let me die whilst young, if I may not feel so happy when I am old.

One day relating my past experience and trials, in a prayer meeting, my mother, upon hearing thereof, said to me, "How do you know that you are converted? How do you know but what you are deceived, if you have passed through such trials as I understand you have?" I said, "God has given me the evidence of what ground I stand upon, and he cannot lie." Afterward, walking out of doors, it was suggested to my mind, "Here are many in town that have professed religion thirty or forty years, and say they do not know their sins forgiven; and can it be that a young upstart stripling could have more knowledge and experience in these things than they? Nay; you have only lost your conviction: you think you are converted, but your peace is a false one."

I then began to reason with the tempter, instead of going to God in prayer to show me my state, "Can all these things I have met with be a deception?" Unbelief began to arise; and my Beloved hid his face from me. I ran to the fields and woods, sometimes kneeling and walking, and bemoaning my loss; for I felt as if something of more value than silver or gold was departed from me; but I found no comfort to my restless mind. I then set out to go to a house where some converts lived, hoping God would enable them to speak something for my comfort; but before I got to the house, I met my BELOVED in the way; he was the chiefest among ten thousand, and altogether lovely. And I went home happy in the Redeemer's love, and with twelve others, among whom was my cousin Roger Searle, I joined the Methodist Society.

CHAPTER II.

CALL TO PREACH, ETC.

ONE day being alone in a solitary place, whilst kneeling before God, these words were suddenly impressed on my mind: "Go ye into all the world, and preach the gospel to every creature." I instantly spoke out, "Lord, I am a child, I cannot go; I cannot preach." These words followed in my mind: "Arise, and go, for I have sent you." I said, "Send by whom thou wilt send, only not by me, for I am an ignorant, illiterate youth, not qualified for the important task." The reply was, "What God hath cleansed, call not thou common." I resisted the impression as a temptation of the devil; and then my Saviour withdrew from me the light of his countenance. I dared not believe that God had called me to preach, for fear of being deceived; and durst not disbelieve it, for fear of grieving the Spirit of God: thus I halted between two opinions.

When I nourished and cherished the impression, the worth of souls was exhibited to my view, and cords of sweet love drew me on; and when I resisted it, a burden of depression and distress seized my mind.

Shortly after this, my trials being very great, I took an opportunity to open my mind to my friend, R. Searle, who said his mind had been impressed the same way for about four months.

One day, as I went to meeting, being in August, 1793, a certain person said to me, "My friend, it appears to me as though you never had any trials." My reply to her was, "Although my soul had been happy the greatest part of the time these nine months past, yet the remainder of my life will be a life of grief, and trouble, and sorrow." Said she, "I hope not." Said I, "You may wish so in vain; for what is revealed will surely come to pass." Very shortly after this, as I was riding along one day, I was seized with an unusual weakness, and my eyesight entirely failed me, whilst my horse carried me forward about the space of half a mile, when my sight returned, and strength, in some degree. Soon after this, whilst retired in a wood, I was taken in a similar manner, and for some time I thought I was dying; but my mind was calmly stayed by God. My bodily strength continued gradually to decline, till at length it was concluded I had the quick consumption; and by physicians and friends I was given over to die. In the beginning of this illness, the sacrament was administered to the society, at which I attended.

It was suggested to my mind, "What good does it do to kneel down there and eat a little bread and drink a little wine; why is it not as good to eat bread and milk at home?" I replied, "It is a command of God;" and threw it out of my mind. I partook, and felt measurably happy. But the same suggestion returned in the evening, and so harassed my mind for a space of time, that I, instead of resisting it by watching unto prayer, began to give way, by querying with the enemy, until my happiness of mind was fled: and shortly after this, being brought apparently near the borders of eternity, and not enjoying that consolation as heretofore, the language of my heart was,

> "I have fall'n from my heaven of grace,
> I am brought into thrall,
> I am stript of my all,
> And banished from Jesus's face."

Oh! how I felt cannot be described by tongue, at this critical period of life, not to see my way so clearly as formerly! But it was not long before God blessed these words to the comforting of my soul, though all but my confidence was given up before:

> "Peace! troubled soul, thou need'st not fear—
> Thy great Provider still is near:"

so that now I could look beyond the grave, and see my way to joys on high.

One thing I desired to live for, viz., to attain to higher degrees of holiness here, that I might be happier hereafter; and what I desired to depart for was, to get out of this trying world, and be at rest with saints above. Yet I was resigned to go or stay. But it pleased kind Providence to rebuke the disorder beyond the expectation of all, and in a measure to restore me to health, so that, after about five months' confinement, I was enabled once more to attend meeting; and falling into conversation with R. Searle about the dealings of God towards us, the impression came upon my mind stronger than ever, that I should have to call sinners to repentance. After returning home, I began to consider the matter on every side more attentively than I had done before, and to make it a matter of earnest prayer to God, that if the impression was from him, it might increase; but if not, that it might decrease. My mind soon became so powerfully exercised as to cause some sleep to depart from me; till at length my trials were so great, that I was resolved to fast and pray more fervently, that if the will of God was to be known I might find it out; and on the twenty-third day of my so doing, according to what my bodily strength would admit of, it being one Sunday afternoon whilst engaged in prayer in the wilderness, in an uncommon manner the light of God's countenance shined forth into my soul, so that I was as fully convinced that I was called to preach as ever I was that God had pardoned my sins.

This continued for about the space of forty-eight hours, when I again began to doubt; but after eleven days it pleased the Lord to banish all my doubts and fears, and to fill me with his love.

1794. One day a prayer meeting being appointed in the town, and I feeling it my indispensable duty to go, I sought for my parents' consent in vain. Still, something was crying in my ears, "Go, go;" but fearing that my parents would call me a disobedient child, I resisted what I believe was required of me, and felt conscience to accuse me, and darkness to cover my mind. But at length, finding a spirit of prayer, I had faith to believe that God would bless me, though from the fourteenth of May to the ninth of June, I felt the sharp, keen, fiery darts of the enemy.

June 12th. This scripture afforded me some strength: "Fear not, the night is far spent, the day is at hand."

I heard G. Roberts (the one who had taken me into society) preach from these words: "Our soul is escaped as a bird out of the snare of the fowlers; the snare is broken, and we are escaped."

June 14th. These words afforded my soul great comfort: "I will not leave you comfortless, but we will come unto you, and take up our abode with you." And whilst retired in devotion, my soul did taste of the powers of the world to come.

24th. I was still satisfied that it would be my duty to preach the gospel, though several reasons occurred to my mind against it, viz.: 1st, According to human appearance, my bodily strength would not endure the fatigues and the inclemencies of the weather which must attend such a life. 2dly. My parents and relations would be against my travelling, from whom I must meet with much opposition. 3dly. My weakness and want of learning, and my abilities, did not seem adequate to the task. But upon hearing my father read this expression in Whitfield's sermons, "*Where reason fails, there faith begins,*" my mind was strengthened to meditate on the work.

Sunday, October fifth, was the first time that I (with a trembling mind) attempted to open my mouth in public vocal prayer in the society.

A little previous to this time, upon considering what I must undergo if I entered upon the public ministry, I began to feel discouraged, and had thoughts of altering the situation of my life to excuse me from the work; but I could get no peace of mind until I gave them entirely up, though my trials in this respect were exceedingly great.

November 14th. About this period, I attempted to speak a few words of exhortation in public, which my parents hearing of gave me a tender reproof, which was like a sword to my heart, fearing lest I should run too fast.

One day I felt impressed to exhort again, but fearing the reproof of my relations, (as the old enemy was now raised,) I neglected my duty, in order to shun the cross: but horror and condemnation seized upon my mind; and I began to reflect if, in the beginning of my pilgrimage, I have such trials to encounter with, what will it be if I attempt to go into the vineyard to face a frowning world? Nay, let the consequence be what it may, saved or damned, I am resolved I will not preach the gospel. And if ever one felt the pains of the damned in this world, it appeared to me that I did.

I was willing to be a private member of society, but not a public teacher. I had rather retire to some remote part of the earth and spend my days; but I could not feel myself excused from preaching the gospel.

Filled with horror and darkness whilst awake, and with fearfulness and frightful dreams by night, for near the space of four weeks, one night I was awaked by surprise; and, in idea, there were represented to my view, two persons, the one by the name of *Mercy*, with a smiling countenance, who said to me, "If you will submit, and be willing to go and preach, there is mercy for you," he having a book in his hand; the other by the name of *Justice*, with a solemn countenance, holding a drawn, glittering sword over my head, added, "If you will not submit, you shall be cut down: now, or never." It appeared to me that I had but one half hour for consideration; and if I still persisted in obstinacy, that it would be a gone case forever.

I put my hands together, and said, "Lord, I submit to go and preach thy gospel: only grant my peaceful hours to return; and open the door."

At the dawn of day, I arose and withdrew to the wilderness to weep and mourn before God. At length the light of his countenance shined into my soul, and I felt humble under his mighty hand, willing to become any thing as God should see fit.

About this time, I made known to my parents the exercise of my mind, which previously I had kept from them. They immediately began to oppose me in this thing; and advised me to reject it by all means, concluding it to be a temptation, as it appeared to them an impossibility that I should be called to such a work as this, which apparently I could not fulfil.

1795, July 16th. Last night the hand of the Lord was heavy upon me. I was much afflicted in body and mind; in body, by the want of breath, so that I was scarcely able to exist, by reason of my asthmatical disorder—in mind, by much heaviness; whilst the enemy suggested, "You will never go forward in public, because of the weakness of your body and the violence of your disorder; and you are deluded by that impression which you think is from God: besides, none will equip you out, and you will one day perish by the hand of Saul." Here my faith was greatly tried, for I saw no way for my equipment, unless the hand of the Almighty should interpose; for my parents had hinted already that they would neither give their consent nor assistance. My discouragements therefore became exceedingly great.

August 4th. I feel tried and tempted by the world, the flesh, and the devil; and if I think of pursuing any other course of life but that of preaching, I sink into horror and find no peace in any other way.

22d. About this time, my mind was much exercised concerning the doctrines of unconditional election and final perseverance. I dreamed that I saw Adam and Eve in the garden of Eden; and God, after talking to them as written in Genesis, said, "I shall be faithful on my part, and it depends upon your being faithful to the end, to receive a crown of glory: but if you are not faithful you will be exposed to the damnation of hell." He then said to me, "Write these things, for they are true and faithful."

October 28th. Being greatly pressed in spirit for a number of days to know my *father's* will, whether, provided a door was opened, *he* would give his consent for me to go out to travel, or whether he would withhold me by his authority, when I think the time is come that I should go, he said, "I shall not hinder you; only give you my *old* advice, not to harbor the thought; and I shall not give you any help." I told him I did not desire any help, only liberty of conscience. I concluded that my father thought that some persons, and not God, had raised such thoughts in my mind, which occasioned him to restrain me; so I told him if this was the case, that he judged the matter wrong.

November 9th. Being again tried in my mind with regard to preaching, fearing lest I should run too fast or too slow, and querying from what quarter my impression came, I dreamed that I was walking in the solitary woods beside a brook, and saw a beautiful stalk about eight feet high: from the middle and upwards, it was covered with beautiful seeds. I heard a voice over my head, saying to me, "Shake the stalk that the seeds may fall off, and cover them up: the seed will be of great value to some, though not to thyself; but thou shalt receive thy reward hereafter."

I shook the stalk, and beautiful speckled red seeds fell off, and I covered them up with earth and rotten leaves, and went on my way to serve the Lord.

Some time after, I thought I was there again, and saw a large number of partridges or pheasants that had been scratching up a great part of the seed. I discovered them and was very sorry, and went and drove them away; and watched it to keep them away, that the remainder, with my nourishing, might bring forth fruit to perfection.

Then I thought I began to preach, and immediately awaked, when the parable of the sower came strongly into my mind.

19th. My mind has been buffeted and greatly agitated, not tempted in the common sense of the word, so that my sleep departed from me, and caused me to walk and wring my hands for sorrow. Oh, *the corruption of wicked* nature! I feel the plague of a hard heart, and a mind prone to wander from God; something within which has need to be done away, and causes a burden, but no guilt, and from which discouragements frequently arise tending to slacken my hands.

I dreamed that I saw a man in a convulsion fit, and his countenance was expressive of hell. I asked a bystander what made his countenance look so horrible. Said he, "The man was sick and relating his past experience, his calls from time to time, and his promises to serve God; and how he had broke them; and now, said he, I am sealed over to eternal damnation, and instantly the convulsion seized him." This shocked me so much that I instantly awaked, and seemingly the man was before my eyes.

I dropped asleep again, and thought I saw all mankind in the air suspended by a brittle thread over hell, yet in a state of carnal security. I thought it to be my duty to tell them of it, and again awaked; and these words were applied to my mind with power: "There is a dispensation of the gospel committed unto you, and wo unto you if you preach not the gospel." I strove to turn my mind on something else; but it so strongly followed me, that I took it as a warning from God. And in the morning, to behold the beautiful sun to arise and shine into the window, whilst these words followed—"Unto you that fear my name, shall the Sun of Righteousness arise, with healing in his wings"—Oh! how happy I felt! The help of kings and priests is vain without the help of God.

December 31st. The year is now at a close. I see what I have passed through. What is to come the ensuing year, God only knows. But may the God of peace be with me, and grant me strength in proportion to my day, that I may endure to the end, and receive the crown of life. I felt my heart drawn to travel the world at large; but to trust God by faith, like the birds, for my daily bread was difficult, as my strength was small; and I shrunk from it.

CHAPTER III.

MY BEGINNING TO TRAVEL.

1796. January 7th. I received a message, with orders from C. Spry, the circuit preacher, to go to Tolland to the brethren there, for a few days, that he might get some knowledge of my gifts. This visit caused some opposition. Afterwards, I was directed to go and meet L. Macombs, a preacher on New London circuit, who after two days constrained me to part from him; so I turned and went to East Hartford, having my brother-in-law's horse with me. In this place I attended several meetings. From thence to Ellington, where I met C. Spry—who directed me to fulfil three of his appointments, Warehouse Point, East Windsor, and Wapping, at one of which, whilst speaking, I was taken suddenly ill, even to the losing of my sight and strength: so I was constrained to give over.

15th. I rode near forty miles to Munson and met N. Snethen, with whom I travelled through his appointments a few days, when he likewise constrained me to part from him, after giving me the following hints:—"You are but eighteen years of age; you are too important, and you must be more humble, and hear and not be heard so much. Keep your own station, for by the time that you arrive at the age of twenty-one years, you will see wherein you have missed it. You had better, as my advice, to learn some easy trade, and be still for two or three years yet; for your bodily health will not admit of your becoming a travelling preacher at present; although, considering your advantages, your gifts are better than mine were when I first set out to preach. But it is my opinion that you will not be received at the next conference."

19th. I feel gloomy and dejected; but the worth of souls lies near my heart. O Lord! increase my faith, and prepare my way.

After travelling several days and holding a few meetings, I attended the quarterly meeting at Wilbraham. C. Spry hinted that there were many scruples in his mind with regard to my travelling; as many thought my health and behavior were not adequate to it.

February 5th. I set out for home, and in the town of Somers I missed my road, and got lost in a great wilderness, the snow being about two feet deep, on which was a sharp, icy crust. After some time, as the path divided into branches, so that I could not distinguish one plainer than another, and those extending over the woods in all directions for the purpose of getting ship timber, I went round about till I was chilled with cold, and saw nothing but death before me. At a distance I could see a village, but could discern no way to get to it; neither could I find the passage out by which I entered; and night drawing on, no person can tell my feelings, except one who has been in a similar situation. I at last heard a sound, and by following it, perhaps about half a mile or more, I found a man driving a team, who gave me a direction so that I could find a foot-path made by some school-boys, by which I might happen to get through. Towards this I proceeded, and by means of leaping my horse over logs, frequently stamping a path for the horse through the snow banks, with much difficulty made my way, and late at night got to my brother-in-law's, in Tolland, and the next day went home, and my soul was happy in God. I am glad that I went, although there was great opposition against me on every side. I am everywhere spoken evil of, &c. I feel the worth of souls to lie near my heart, and my duty still to be to preach the gospel, with a determination to do so, God being my helper.

20th. I dreamed that, in a strange house as I sat by the fire, a messenger came in and said, "There are three ministers come from England, who in a few minutes will pass by this way." I followed him out, and he disappeared. I ran over a wood-pile, and jumped upon a log, to have a fair view of them. Presently three men came over a hill from the west towards me: the foremost dismounted; the other two, one of whom was on a white horse, and the other on a reddish one, both, with the three horses, disappeared. I said to the first, "Who are you?" He replied, "John Wesley," and walked towards the *east*. He turned round, and looking me in the face, said, "God has called you to preach the gospel; you have been a long time between hope and fear, but there is a dispensation of the gospel committed to you. Wo unto you, if you preach not the gospel."

I was struck with horror and amazement to think how he should know the exercise of my mind, when I knew he had never heard of me before. I still followed him to the eastward, and expressed an observation, for which he with his countenance reproved me, for the better improvement of my time. At length we came to a log house, where negroes lived. The door being open, he attempted twice to go in, but the smoke prevented him. He said, "You may go in, if you have a mind, and if not, follow me." I followed him a few rods, where was an old house, two stories high, in one corner of which my parents looked out at a window, and said to him, "Who are you?" He replied, "John Wesley." "Well," said they, "what becomes of doubting Christians?" He replied, "There are many serious Christians who are afraid of death. They dare not believe they are converted, for fear of being deceived; and they are afraid to disbelieve it, lest they should grieve the Spirit of God: so they live and die, and go into the other world, and their souls to heaven with a guard of angels." I then said, "Will the day of judgment come as we read, and the sun and moon fall from heaven, and the earth and works be burnt?" To which he answered: "It is not for you to know the times and seasons which God hath put in his own power, but read the word of God with attention, and let that be your guide."

I said, "Are you more than fifty-five?" He replied, "Do you not remember reading an account of my death in the history of my life?" I turned partly round, in order to consider, and after I had recollected it, I was about to answer him, "Yes;" when I looked, and behold, he was gone, and I saw him no more. It set me shaking and quaking to such a degree, that it waked me up.

N. B. The appearance of his person was the very same as he who appeared to me three times in the dream when I was about thirteen years of age, and who said that he would come to me again, &c.

March 14th. About this time my uncle made me the offer of a horse, and to wait a year for the payment, provided I would get bondsmen. Four of the society willingly offered. O! from what an unexpected quarter was this door opened! My parents seeing my way thus beginning to open, and my resolution to go forward, with loving entreaties and strong arguments strove to prevail against it. But as they promised some time before not to restrain me by their authority, in case a door should open from another quarter, (they not expecting it would,) and seeing they could not prevail upon me to tarry, they gave up the point, and gave me some articles of clothing and some money for my journey.

Not having as yet attempted to preach from a text, but only to exercise my gifts in the way of exhortation, I obtained a letter of recommendation concerning my moral conduct: this was all the credentials I had.

About the tenth of last month, I dreamed that C. Spry received a letter from Jesse Lee, that he wanted help in the province of Maine, and that the said C. S. and L. Macombs concluded to send me. N. B. These were the two preachers who afterwards signed the above-mentioned letter of recommendation.

1796. March 30th. This morning early I set out for Rhode Island in quest of J. Lee, who was to attend a quarterly meeting there. As I was coming away, we joined in prayer, taking leave of each other; and as I got on my road, I looked about, and espied my mother looking after me until I got out of sight; this caused me some tender feelings afterwards.

Until this time I have enjoyed the comforts of a kind father's house; and oh! must I now become a wanderer and stranger upon earth until I get to my long-home!

During this day's journey, these words of our Lord came into my mind: "The foxes have holes, and the birds of the air have nests, but the Son of man hath not where to lay his head."

The language of my heart is, "What is past, I know; what is to come, I know not. Lord, bless me in the business I am set out upon." I feel more than ever that God has called me to this work.

April 1st. Upon my arrival at Cranston, in Rhode Island, I found that J. Lee had gone to Boston. I accordingly set out after him, and found the preachers' boarding-house at Boston, and they told me that Lee had gone to the east, and that I could not overtake him short of two or three hundred miles; and their advice was, to go to Warren, in Rhode Island, with Thomas Coope, a native of Manchester, who was going to set out that afternoon. Accordingly I joined him in company thirty-six miles to Easttown.

Sunday, 3d. This day, for the first time, I gave out a text before a Methodist preacher; and I being young, both in years and the ministry, the expectations of many were raised, who did not bear with my weakness and strong doctrine, but judged me very hard, and would not consent that I should preach there any more for some time.

Having travelled a few days with T. C., we came to Reynham, where attempting to preach, I was seized with sudden illness, such as affected me at Warehouse Point, with the loss of sight and strength, so that I was constrained to give over, and T. C. finished the meeting. After this, lots were cast to see whether I should pass the sabbath here, or go to Easttown. It turned up for me to tarry here, which I accordingly did, and held three meetings, which were solemn.

I met T. C., who said, if I was so minded, I might return home; which I declining, he said, "I do not believe God has called you to preach." I asked him why? He replied, "First, your health; second, your gifts; third, your grace; fourth, your learning; fifth, sobriety: in these you are not equivalent to the task." I replied, "Enough! Lord, what am I but a poor worm of the dust, struggling for life and happiness."*

The time now drawing near when I expected to leave these parts, the society where I first attempted to give out a text desired to hear me again; and, contrary to my entreaties, T. C. appointed a meeting, and constrained me to go, threatening me if I refused. Accordingly I went, and gave out these words: "Am I therefore become your enemy, because I tell you the truth?" Gal., iv. 16.

June 30th. I rode twenty-four miles, and preached once, and saw J. Lee, the presiding elder, who had just returned from the east. I gave him my recommendation.

July 3d. This evening, our quarterly meeting being over, from the representation that was given of me by T. C., I received a dismission from the circuit, with orders to go home, which was as follows:

"We have had brother Lorenzo Dow, the bearer hereof, travelling on Warren circuit these three months last past. In several places, he was liked by a great many people; at other places, he was not liked so well, and at a few places, they were not willing he should preach at all. We have therefore thought it necessary to advise him to return home for a season, until a further recommendation can be obtained from the society and preachers of that circuit.

"JOHN VANIMAN,   JESSE LEE, Elder.
"THOMAS COOPE.
"*Rhode Island, July* 3, 1796.
"To C. Spry, and the Methodists in Coventry."

The time has been when I could easier have met death than this discharge. Two or three handkerchiefs were soon wet through with tears. My heart was broke. I expostulated, and besought him for further employment, but apparently in vain. The next morning, as we were about parting, he said, "If you are minded, you may come to Greenwich quarterly meeting next Sunday, on your way home."

This evening I preached in Greenwich courthouse, as I once dreamed, and the assembly and place looked natural to me.

After travelling through Sepatchet, Smithfield, (in which I formed a class, for the first time,) Providence, and Wickford, where attending a prayer meeting among the Baptists, I asked liberty to speak, which seemed to give them a surprise; and, after some time, they said, "If I had a message from God, they had no right to hinder me." I spoke a few minutes, had their attention, and their leader seemed satisfied, and bid me God-speed.

From thence to South Kingston I set out for my native town, at which I arrived, and met my friends, who were glad to see me.

My parents asked me whether I was not convinced that I did wrong

---

* He is since expelled the Connexion!

in going? I told them, "No; but was glad." Others began to mock, and cry out, "This man began to build, and was not able to finish."

After a few days I set out for Granville, to meet C. Spry, who gave me a written license, and orders to come to the ensuing quarterly meeting at Enfield, where he would give me a credential for the conference; and, if I was so minded, and brother Cankey willing, I might travel Tolland circuit until that time.

But, as the circuit extended through my native town, I thought proper to forbear, and set off for Hanover, in the state of New Hampshire, to see my sister, whom I had not seen for about five years. But J. Lee coming to town next day, lodged at a house where I had inquired the road, and they informed him of me. He sent for me, and querying me whether I still preached, and by what authority, and what I came there for, showed his disapprobation at my coming hither, and then we parted.

I tarried a few days, and held several meetings, and for the time met with no small trials of mind and opposition from without, and then returned to Connecticut, fulfilling several appointments by the way.

I went twenty-eight miles to Enfield quarterly meeting, for my credential, and C. Spry sent me to Z. Cankey, who could not give it to me, according to discipline. He sent me back to S., and he again to Z. C., several times; but at length Z. C. said, "Have you not a written license?" I told him, "Yes, to preach." Said he, "That is as good as a recommendation to the conference," which I believed; though C. Spry knew that, according to the *letter* of the discipline, I could not be received with this, yet he told me to attend the conference.

September 20th. Conference came on in the town of Thompson, and I passed the examination by the bishop before them; and after some conversation in the conference, T. Coope, J. Lee, and N. Snethen bore hard upon me after I had been sent out of the room, and those who were friendly to me durst say but little in my favor; so I was rejected and sent home, they assigning as the reason, the want of a written credential, though the greatest part of them were personally acquainted with me. This so affected me, that I could take no food for thirty-six hours.

After my return home, still feeling it my duty to travel, I accordingly resolved to set off the next Monday; but Philip Wagar, who was appointed for Orange circuit, being in Tolland, sent for me, and I went twelve miles to see him.

After he had criticised and examined my credentials, he concluded to take me on his circuit. I accordingly got prepared, and bidding my friends farewell for a season, met him in West Windsor.

Some weeks ago, whilst I was in Rhode Island, being troubled with the asthmatical disorder, I was necessitated to sit up some nights for the want of breath; but at length laying down on the carpet, I found that I could sleep and breathe easy.

Accordingly, I was resolved to try the experiment until the fall of the year, which I did without much trouble. But September twenty-seventh, being on my way with P. Wagar, he said the people would despise me for my lodging, and it would hurt my usefulness; and accordingly he insisted upon my lying in bed with him, he thinking it was a boyish notion that made me lie on the floor.

To convince him to the reverse I went to bed, but was soon much distressed for want of breath, and constrained to arise and sit up all night; after which, I would be persuaded to try the bed no more. After travelling with him a few days into the state of New York, he gave me a direction when and where to take the circuit. I travelled to New Lebanon, where I saw one who experienced religion about the time that I did, and our meeting in this strange land was refreshing to our souls.

Monday, October 10th. I rode twenty miles to Adams, and thence to Stanford: at these places we had refreshing seasons.

Wednesday, 12th. I rode thirty miles across the Green Mountain, in fifteen of which there was not a sign of a house; and the road being new, it frequently was almost impassable. However, I reached my appointment, and though weary in body, my soul was happy in God.

From Halifax I went to Guilford; and on entering a chamber where the people were assembled, it appeared natural to me, as though I had seen it before, and brought a dream to my remembrance, which so overcome me that I trembled and was obliged to retire for some minutes. In this meeting, three persons were stirred up to seek God.

Leaving the state of Vermont, I crossed Connecticut river, through Northfield to Warwick, Massachusetts, where we had a refreshing season.

Thence I went to Orange, and preached in the Presbyterian meeting house, the clergyman having left the town. Being this day nineteen years old, I addressed myself to the youth. I spent a few days here; and, though meeting with some opposition, we had refreshing seasons. Oh! how fast is the doctrine of unconditional reprobation falling, and *infidelity* and the denial of *future punishment* prevailing! Men thus going from one extreme to the other, as they wish to lull conscience to sleep, that they may go on in the enjoyment of the world without disturbance. But, oh! would they wish to be deceived in a dying hour?

I never felt the plague of a hard heart as I do of late, nor so much *faith* as I now have that *inbred corruption* will be done away, and I filled with perfect peace, and enabled to rejoice evermore.

I never felt the worth of souls so near my heart as I do of late, and it seems as if I could not give vent enough to it. Lord! prosper my way, and keep me as under the hollow of thy hand, for my trust is in thee.

October 20th. Satan pursues me from place to place. Oh! how can people dispute there being a devil! If they underwent as much as I do with his buffetings, they would dispute it no more. He throwing in his fiery darts, my mind is harassed like punching the body with forks and clubs. Oh that my Saviour would appear and sanctify my soul, and deliver me from all within that is contrary to purity!

23d. I spoke in Hardwick to about four hundred people, thence went to Petersham and Wenchendon, to Fitchburgh, and likewise to Notown, where God gave me one spiritual child. Thence to Ashburnham, where we had some powerful times.

November 1st. I preached in Ringe, and a powerful work of God broke out shortly after, though some opposition attended it; but it was very solemn.

Some here, I trust, will bless God in the day of eternity that ever they saw my face in this vale of tears.

In my happiest moments I feel something that wants to be done away

Oh! the buffeting of Satan! if I never had any other hell, it would be enough.

Thence proceeded to Marlborough, where our meetings were not in vain.

Whilst I am preaching I feel happy. But as soon as I have done, I feel such horror, without guilt, by the buffetings of Satan, that I am ready to sink like a drowning man, sometimes to that degree that I have to hold my tongue between my teeth to keep from uttering blasphemous expressions; and I can get rid of these horrible feelings only by retirement in earnest prayer and exertion of faith in God.

From Marlborough I went to Packersfield, and thence to Chesterfield, where I had one seal of my ministry. Leaving New Hampshire, I crossed into Vermont, and came to Marlborough.

Thus I continued round my circuit until I came to Belcher. A few evenings previous, I dreamed that a minister came and reproved me harshly, whilst I was preaching. In this place it was fulfilled; for a Baptist preacher accused me in the congregation of laying down false doctrine. Presently a Presbyterian affirmed the same likewise; because that I said a Christian would not get angry.

Here also appeared some little fruit of my labor, among which were some of my distant relations.

About this time I visited Mary Spalding, who had been suddenly and miraculously restored, as was said, from an illness which had confined her to her bed about the space of nine years. Her conversation was so profitable, that I did not grudge the journey of several miles to obtain it. I found it to strengthen my confidence in God. The account was published by a Presbyterian minister, with her approbation.

On the 29th, I met P. Wagar, which seemed to refresh my mind. I had to take up a cross and preach before him. But, oh! the fear of man! The next day I parted with him and went on my way.

My discouragements were so great, that I was ready to leave the circuit. I would think within myself, I will go to my appointment to-day and then go off; but being refreshed during the meeting, my drooping spirits would be revived, and I would be encouraged to go to the next. Thus it would be, day after day; sometimes I was so happy, and the times so powerful, I would hope "the winter was past and gone:" but soon it would return again. Thus I went on, during the three first months on the circuit; at length, my discouragements being so great, and inward trials so heavy, I concluded to go further into the country and spend my time in the best manner I could, about the neighborhood where my sister lived.

December 15th. I rode fifteen miles to Brattleborough. About this time, on my way, I took a severe cold on my lungs, and almost lost my voice. The next day my friends advised me not to go to any other appointments, as they thought it presumption; but I feeling impressed in my mind, could not feel content to disappoint the people. Accordingly, in the name of God, I set out in a hard snow-storm, over the mountains, about ten miles, and a solemn time we had. The storm still continuing to increase, the snow had now fallen about knee high, so that the mountains were almost impassable by reason of snow, steepness, mud, and logs; the people here thought my life would be endangered by the fall.

ing of trees, or the extreme cold in the woods, as there was no house for several miles, and the wind blew exceedingly hard. However, out I set, relying upon the Strong for strength. The snow being driven in banks more than belly deep, I frequently was obliged to alight and stamp a path for my horse; and though I was much wearied and chilled, yet by the goodness of God, I arrived at my appointment, fourteen miles. We had a good time, and I did not begrudge my labor. I believe these *trials* will be for my good, to qualify me for *future usefulness* to others: and a secret conviction I feel, that if I prove faithful, God will carry me through, and support me to see the *cause* that should *ensue*.

After my arrival at my sister's, I had thoughts of spending my time principally in study; but feeling it my duty to call sinners to repentance, I could not enjoy my mind contented without travelling in the neighboring towns, there being no Methodists in this part of the world.

I went to Enfield several times during my stay, (being first invited by a Universalian,) by which there seemed to be some good done. Here I received an invitation to fix my residence among them, as their stated preacher. This was somewhat pleasing to nature, as by it I could have ease and acquire wealth; an elegant new meeting house being also ready; but something within would not suffer me to comply.—Still feeling it my duty to travel, I went into Canaan, Lyme, Dorchester, Orford, Hebron, New Lebanon, Strafford, Tunbridge, Chelsea, Hartford, with many other adjacent towns; and the feather edge of prejudice was removed, and some few were awakened and hopefully converted to God.

1797, June 4th. At Vershire in Vermont, I met with N. Snethen, who informed me that he had seen J. Lee, and that I must come down to the quarterly meeting; and, said he, "J. Lee disapproves of your travelling into so many new places, and what will you do provided that he forbids your preaching?" I told him it did not belong to J. L. or any other man to say whether I should preach or not, for that was to be determined between God and my own soul; only it belonged to the Methodists to say whether I should preach in their connection; but as long as I feel so impressed, I shall travel and preach, God being my helper; and as soon as I feel my mind released, I intend to stop, let people say what they will. But, said he, "What will you call yourself? The Methodists will not own you; and if you take that name, you'll be advertised in the public papers as an impostor." Said I, "I shall call myself a friend to mankind." "Oh!" said he, "for the Lord's sake don't; for you are not capable of it—and not one of a thousand is; and if you do you'll repent it." I sunk into a degree of gloominess and dejection—and told him I was in the hand of God, and felt submissive; so I bade him farewell and rode ten miles on my way. The next day I rode fifty miles to Charlestown, where I overtook J. Lee, to my sorrow and joy * * * * * He mentioned some things, particularly that if ever I travelled I must get a new recommendation from my native circuit, or else not offer myself to conference again.

We then rode to Orange quarterly meeting. But J. Lee forbade P. W. to employ me any more, and then set off.* I ran after him and said, "If you can get no text to preach upon between now and conference, I

---

* This was the fourth time I had been sent home.

give you Genesis xl. 14," and then turned and ran, and saw him no more for some years, when we met at Petersburg in Virginia.

I then returned home to my parents, after an absence of eight months; having travelled more than four thousand miles, through heat in the valleys, the scorching sun beating down, and through cold upon the mountains, frequently sleeping with a blanket on the floor, where I could look up and see the stars through the bark roofs, the frost nipping me so that I lost the skin from my nose, hands, and feet; and from my ears it peeled three times—travelling through storms of rain and snow; this frequently drifted into banks, so that I had no path for miles together, and was obliged at times to alight and stamp a way for my horse for some rods: at other times, being engaged for the welfare of souls, after preaching in the dark evening, I would travel the chief part or the whole of the night, from twenty to forty miles, to get on to my next day's appointment; preaching from ten to fifteen times a week, and oftentimes no stranger to hunger and thirst in these new countries; and though my trials were great, the Lord was still precious to my soul, and supported me through.

The preacher of Tolland circuit, (Evan Rogers, who since hath turned churchman,) after some close and solemn conversation, advised me to preach in my native town, and provided that I could obtain a letter of recommendation concerning my preaching gifts as well as my conduct, he saw no hindrance why I should not be received at conference. The thought was trying. The cross was great, to think of preaching before my old acquaintance and relations; besides, my parents were opposed to it, fearing how I should make out. However, there being no other way, and necessitated thereto, the people flocked out from every quarter, and after my feeble manner, I attempted to perform; and I obtained a credential by the voice of the *whole* society; which was approved of by the preachers at the quarterly meeting; after which it was thought proper to send me to Granville circuit.

During my stay at and about home, though I went into several other places, not in vain to some souls, yet my trials were very great, so that many almost whole nights' sleep departed from me. I walked the floor and woods, weeping until I could weep no more, and wringing my hands until they felt sore. When I was in the north country, being under strong temptations to end my life, I went down to a river to do it, but a thought of futurity darted into my mind; the value of my soul! oh! Eternity. I promised and resolved if God would grant me strength to resist the temptation, and see my native land in peace, that I would discharge my duty to my friends. This he had done, and now my promise began to stare me in the face.

I felt it my duty to visit from house to house; but the cross was so heavy, I strove to run round it. But the thorns beside the way scratched me: and to take up one end of the cross, it dragged hard. Here the old temptation returned so powerful, that I durst not go from one appointment to another alone, nor without one to go with me, and sometimes one to sleep in the same room, lest I should end myself at night; and for the ease and enjoyment of my mind, I was necessitated and did visit about sixty different families, and then set off to Granville circuit, under the care of Sylvester Hutchinson, with Smith Weeks and Joseph Mitchell. Weeks was at first unwilling I should come on the circuit, fearing how I would make out; but seeing I was under trials, consented. Accordingly I went round until I came to Suffield. Upon my entering the neighborhood, I fell into conversation with an old man, and he invited me to hold a meeting at his house. Accordingly I appointed to preach to the youth in the evening; and went to my other appointment not far off. The man of this house shut his door and would entertain no more meetings. This was a trial to me, not knowing what the society would do for a place to meet in.

When I began to meditate what I should say to the youth, I could think of no subject, felt distressed, and was sorry I had made the appointment.

I withdrew to a field to seek help from the Lord; but I felt as if all the powers of darkness were combined and compassed me about.

When I saw the people began to collect, I thought I would have given the whole world, if I possessed it, that the meeting had not been appointed; but as it was now given out, and circumstances being as they were, I durst do no other than go to the house. I went with this burden to the house, and by an impression, spoke *ironically* from the words of Solomon, which mightily pleased the youth at first. My burden was soon gone; the power of God seemed to overshadow the people, as I turned the discourse upon the judgment which the youth must be brought into: and one of the ringleaders was cut to the heart, and brought to seek God. Here a good work broke out; and where about thirty or forty used to attend, now the congregation was increased to hundreds, and this wilderness seemed to bud and blossom as the rose.

In Northampton, a society was collected likewise, though Methodists had not preached there before.

August 6th. After preaching in Conway, I went to Buckland; and when the people saw my youth, and were disappointed of the preacher they expected, they despised me in their hearts. However, God made bare his arm, and I have reason to believe that about thirty persons were stirred up to seek God from this day.

The year past was remarkable for very many persons complaining of uncommon trials of mind from the enemy of souls, and scarcely any revival to be heard of either in Connecticut, Massachusetts, or the upper part of New York.

The flame kindled and ran into several neighboring towns, and some hundreds of souls professed to experience the forgiveness of their sins.

A great deal of opposition, both from preachers and people, Baptists and Presbyterians, was in this quarter; professing to be friends to God and truth, whilst to us they were secret enemies, seeking to get people converted to their way of thinking, and proselyted to their denomination.

I dreamed one night that I saw a field without end, and a man and boy striving to gather in the corn, whilst thousands of birds were destroying of it. I thought there was such a necessity for the corn to be gathered, that let the laborers work ever so hard, the labor would not wear out their strength until the harvest was past.

This dream encouraged me to go on in this work; and in the space of twenty-two days, I travelled three hundred and fifty miles, and preached seventy-six times, besides visiting some from house to house, and speaking to hundreds in class-meetings. In several other places, there was a good revival likewise. At the quarterly meeting, I obtained a *certificate*, concerning my *usefulness* and *conduct* here; and as S. Hutchinson thought not proper to take all the preachers to conference, he concluded to leave me to help the revivals, and that he would there transact my business for me. So I gave him my *dismission* from Rhode Island, and my *two* last *recommendations* to carry into conference.

September 19th. Conference began in Wilbraham. My case was brought forward, to determine whether I should be admitted on trial to preach, or sent home, or expelled.

J. Lee and several others, of whom some were strangers to my person, took up hard against me, from say and hear-say; and only one at first espoused my cause. This was Joseph Mitchell, with whom I had travelled these last few weeks. After some time a second joined him. The debate was sharp and lasted for about three hours, when Mitchell and Bostwick could say no more, but sat down and wept; which seemed to touch the hearts of some. At length, it being put to the vote whether I should travel or not, about two thirds of the conference were in my favor. All that saved me, in this conference, from an expulsion, was the blessing which had attended my labors. But still those who were against me would not suffer me to be admitted on trial, nor my name printed in the minutes. One said, if they acknowledged me fit to travel, why not my name to be put on the minutes? If he be fit for one, why not for the other, &c. So I was *given* into the *hands* of S. Hutchinson, to *employ* me or *send* me *home*, as *he should think fit*. He sent me a message to meet him on Long Island, which I did not receive in time to go; and the first preacher, Daniel Bromley, who came to me after conference, I asked, "What hath the conference done with me?" He replied, "They have done by you, as they have done by me." "What's that?" said I. He replied, "They have stationed me on this circuit." And that was all that I could get out of him concerning the matter; only he ordered me to take his appointments round the circuit, whilst he should go to see his friends, until he should meet me again. Accordingly I set out to go round the circuit. I had been on my way but a day or two, before I came to places where the preachers, on their way from conference, had been, and told the *accusations* against me, and my *rejection*. Thus it was, day after day; people telling me the same story.

From this circumstance, as the conference had given me no station, and Hutchinson's message had not reached me, I concluded I should be sent home again, as I had no license according to discipline, which one must have, if his name is not printed in the minutes.

My trials were so great, I was afraid I should become insane; and seeing no chance for my life, I publicly gave up the name of Methodist, and assigned the reasons why, viz.: because the preachers would not receive me as a brother to travel with them, &c. I was resolved to set out for some distant part of America, out of sight and hearing of the Methodists, and to get societies formed, and the next year to come and offer myself and them to the connection, and by this method to get my character established; for J. Lee had said, if I attempted to travel in the *name* of a Methodist without their consent, he would advertise me in every paper on the continent, &c., for an impostor.

But now arose a difficulty from another quarter. I had lost my great coat on the road whilst travelling, and my coat was so worn out that I was forced to borrow one; my shoes were unfit for further service, and I had not a farthing of money to help myself with, and no particular friends to look to for assistance. Thus one day, whilst riding along, facing a hard, cold, northeast storm, very much chilled, I came to a wood; and alighting from my horse, and falling upon my knees on the wet grass, I lifted up my voice and wept, and besought God, either to release me from travelling and preaching, or else to raise me up friends. My soul was refreshed, and my confidence was strengthened, and I did believe that God would do one or the other. And thus it was: people a few days after this, of their own accord, supplied all my necessities, and gave me a few shillings to bear my expenses.

Jeremiah Ballard, whom I had esteemed as a pious man, was expelled at the Wilbraham conference, and, as he represented it to me, it was unjustly. He went with me to the north, and in a number of places he saw, with me, the outpouring of God's Spirit. He was minded to form societies, and call ourselves by the name of Separate Methodists. I told him no, for God did own the Methodists; and of course I durst not do any thing to their injury. This caused a separation between him and me. He formed societies on his own plan, and afterwards I saw him no more; but by what I could learn, he and his people differed, and then he and some of them removed off to the western country. It appears that the conference were under the necessity of excluding him for a foolish thing, as he would show no humility, but was stubborn and impenitent. O! how blessed is the spirit of meekness!

I accordingly left the circuit, and set off for the north. I had not gone far till I came to Deerfield river. In riding through it, the cakes of ice going down the stream had like to cost me my life. But this did not discourage me; I still went on my way, upwards of a hundred miles, till I came to the town of Windsor, in Vermont, where God poured out his Spirit, and several were turned to him. I thought it not my duty to leave the young converts to the devouring wolves, but to tarry and strengthen them for a season; and whilst here, I wrote back to some of my old friends, who told the preachers where I was, and what I was about. They wrote, requesting me to come back to a quarterly meeting. At first I concluded not to go, thinking what should they want but to scold me. But feeling it impressed upon my mind in a powerful manner, one evening, after holding two meetings, I called for my horse, and set out for Claremont, and continued travelling twenty-five hours, excepting the times of baiting my horse; during which space I rode about a hundred and seventeen miles, and got back to Conway on my old circuit. From hence, I proceeded to Buckland, where was held the quarterly meeting, and met the preachers, wishing to know what they wanted with me.

Hutchinson began to be very crabbed and cross, seemingly, at first, in his questioning me why I went away. I assigned him as the reason, because I had no chance for my life. "Why," said he, "did you not receive the message I sent you, to come to me?" I replied, "No; not until it was too late," &c., which I could hardly persuade him to believe at the first.

L. Macombs asked what I came back for? I told him, "I was sen for, and I came to see what they wanted of me." Said he, "What do you intend to do?" I replied, "I expected to go back to the north." Then he and Hutchinson went and talked together. I was sorry I had gone away, after I had found out the mistake and Hutchinson's friendship for me. Accordingly, in answer to a query which was proposed, viz., What satisfaction can you make? I replied, "That I was willing to acknowledge that I was sorry, but not guilty, as I did it in sincerity, not hearing soon enough of his message." Which acknowledgment I made, first, in quarterly conference, before about thirty preachers, leaders, and stewards, with exhorters, and then he required it in a public assembly of about eight hundred people.

After this, I travelled several days in company with S. Hutchinson, who was going to take me to Cambridge circuit; and on the way, said he, "The conference have had a great deal of talk and trouble concerning you, and now you are under my care, and you shall *live* or *die* at the end of three months: if you are faithful, and your labors blest, so that you can obtain a recommendation from the circuit, all shall be well; but if not, you shall die."

Accordingly, after reaching the circuit, a saying I remembered, viz., you had as good be hanged for stealing an old sheep as a lamb, and finding the people in a very low state of religion, I was convinced that nothing but a revival could save my life; I was therefore resolved to do my endeavors to get up a revival, or else to get the circuit broke up. So I went visiting the people from house to house, of all denominations, that were in the neighborhood; and where there was freedom, to exhort them, collectively or individually, as I felt in my mind, after joining in prayer.

Pittstown, New York, was the first place I thus tried on this circuit, and preached at night. Thus I did here, for several days successively, and it caused a great deal of talk. Some said I was crazy; others, that I was possessed of the devil. Some said one thing, and some thought another. Many it brought out, to hear the strange man, who would go away cursing and swearing, saying that I was saucy, and deserved knocking down; and the uproar was so great among the people, that the half-hearted and lukewarm Methodists were tried to the quick, and became my warm opposers, complaining of me to my travelling companion, Timothy Dewey, whose mind at first was prejudiced. However, it was not long before I had the satisfaction to see some small fruit of my labor here, which gave me encouragement to strive to raise the inquiry of the people to consideration, though the devil should be raised round the circuit.

In this place I visited about a hundred families, some of them twice or thrice over. In Ashgrove I walked about four miles, and visited every family in the way, and generally met with a good reception, though the cross of visiting thus was the hardest and happiest that ever I took up. From thence I set out to go to an appointment in Wilson's Hollow, which was surrounded by mountains, except one small entrance, and coming to a house, I felt impressed to go in and pay them a visit; but the cross being heavy I strove to excuse myself and go by, saying, the other preachers, who are older in years, and in experience and learning, do not visit thus, and yet enjoy the comforts of religion, and I will take them for my pattern—thinking it impossible that God should call me to such a peculiarity, who was so weak and ignorant. Instantly I felt distress in my mind. When I came to a second house, I felt impressed as above; but still supported my mind against it with the same arguments, when I cast a look to the sky, and I felt as if God was about to revive religion there, and, if I did not visit them, their souls would be required at my hand. It seemed as though the sun frowned upon me: accordingly I resolved, if the impression continued, that I would go into the next house, and if I met good reception, I would thus go through all the families in the Hollow, which amounted to about thirty in number. I called, and finding a good reception, I went to a second and third, but was turned away. To all the village, however, I went. Some thought one thing, and some said another. However, they came out, to hear a crazy man, as they thought, and were struck with a great solemnity, whilst I spoke from these words: "Thus saith the Lord, set thine house in order, for thou shalt die and not live." The second and the third day I held meetings likewise, and said, at such a time, I hope to be here again, God willing. Accordingly I came, and proposed a covenant to the people, if they would attempt to pray three times a day, four weeks, on their knees, I would remember them thrice in the twenty-four hours during that space, God being our helper to perform; and requested those who would endeavor to do it, to signify it by standing on their feet, and those who would not, to keep their seats, for God is about to revive religion here; and those who put in for a share may freely obtain, but those who neglect will find it to their sorrow.

About twenty rose up, to which I called God to witness; and whilst we were at prayer, one who had not agreed caught hold of a loom to avoid falling down, whilst his knees smote together. The evening after I was gone, the youth assembled to take counsel about their souls, and were so concerned that the cries became general, and were heard afar off, and eight persons found comfort before they disbanded.

To this place Hutchinson came, just after he reached the circuit, though I had not heard of this effect of my labors.

Thus round the circuit I went, visiting from house to house, getting into as many new neighborhoods as I could, and sparing no character in my public declarations. Many were offended at my plainness, both of dress, expressions, and address in conversation about heart-religion, so that the country seemed to be in an uproar. Scarcely one was found to take up my cause, and I was mostly known by the name of Crazy Dow. At length quarterly meeting came on in Welsh Hollow, and I expected an expulsion, the uproar being so great. T. Dewey had come thirty miles to give me a scolding for my conduct, to whom I said, "I make a conscience of what I do, and for it I expect to give an account to God; if you should ever turn against me, I cannot hearken to you in this matter." After this, God gave me favor in his sight; so that he took my part, and defended my cause (round the circuit, like a champion) to the lukewarm, unknown to me at first.

Of him I was the more afraid, as I knew that he had promoted the expulsion of Ballard.

So I went to Hutchinson, and besought him to exclude me, that I might go my way, and be of no more trouble to them, which he refused, and gave me some snarp words, and said he would not, but that I should tarry on that circuit another quarter; adding, "But before the quarter is up, I expect you'll leave the circuit and run away." So we parted. But I was resolved he should be disappointed in me for once, at least, if no more.

At Claridon and Castleton the society were watching over me for evil, and not for good. These two places I visited, likewise, from house to house. Next I went to Fair Haven, where I met with hard speeches. Then to Poultney, where was no regular preaching. Here lived a young woman, whom I began to question about her soul, but met with cool answers. "Well," said I, "I'll pray to God to send a fit of sickness upon you, if nothing else will do, to bring you to good; and if you won't repent then, to take you out of the way, so that you shall not hinder others." Said she, "If you'll pray for such things, you can't be the friend you pretend to be to my soul, and I'll venture all your prayers;" and she was much displeased, and so was her mother likewise. She soon, however, began to grow uneasy and restless, and went into one room and into another, back and forth; and at last sat down, but could get no relief. The whole family, except the father and one son, began to grow outrageous towards me, which occasioned me to go seven miles late at night, for the sake of family quietness.

Shortly afterwards the young woman began to seek God, and, with two of her sisters, was soon found walking in the ways of wisdom; and a society was shortly formed in the place, although I saw them no more.

In Hampton and Skeinsborough, on the south end of Lake Champlain, was some revival, likewise.

Here was a woman who found fault with me for exhorting the wicked to pray, saying, "The prayers of the wicked were an abomination to the Lord." But I told her that was homemade scripture, for there was no such expression in the Bible; and after bringing undeniable passages to prove it was their duty, I besought her to pray. She replied, "I cannot get time." I then offered to buy the time; and for a dollar she promised to spend one day as I should direct, if it were in a lawful way, provided she could get the day, she not thinking I was in earnest. I then turned to her mistress, who promised to give her a day. Then throwing a dollar into her lap, I called God, and about thirty persons present, to witness the agreement. She besought me to take the dollar again, which I refused, saying, "If you go to hell, it may follow and enhance your damnation." About ten days elapsed, when her conscience roaring loud, she took the day, and read two chapters in the Bible, and retired thrice to pray to God to show her what she was, and what he would have her to be, according to my directions.

Afterwards, I had the satisfaction to hear that before night she felt distressed on account of her soul, and before long found the comforts of religion. From thence I visited Kingsborough and Queensborough, where many were brought to a sense of themselves, among whom was Solomon Moon.

One evening, just as I had dismissed the assembly, I saw a man to whom my mind was impressed to go; and before I was aware of it, I was breaking through the crowd; and when I had got to him, I said,

"Are you willing I should ask you a few serious questions?" He replied, "Yes." "Do you believe," said I, "there is a God?" Said he, "Yes."

Q. "Do you believe there is a reality in religion?"
A. "I am uncertain; but think we ought to do as we would be done by."
Q. "Are you willing for some good advice?"
A. "Yes."
Q. "Supposing I shall give you some that you can find no fault with the *tendency of it*; are you willing, and will you try to follow it for four weeks?"
A. "Yes, if it is no unreasonable request."

I then desired him not to believe what authors, ministers, or people said, because they said so; but to search the scriptures to seek for light and instruction there; to read but a little at a time, and read it often, striving to take the sense of it.

2dly, Not to stumble over the unexemplary walk of professors of religion, nor the contradiction in ministers' sermons; and to forsake not what other people thought was wrong, but what he himself thought to be wrong: and then to take his leisure time, and go where none would see him but God, twice or thrice a day, and upon his knees beseech the Almighty to give him an evidence within, that there was a heaven and a hell, and a reality in religion, and the necessity of enjoying it in order to die happy. "And then," said I, "I do not believe the time will expire before you will find an alteration in your mind, and that for the better."

Q. "Is the advice good or bad?"
A. "I have no fault to find; the natural tendency of it is to good, if followed."

I then said, "You promised, if the advice was good, and you had no fault to find with it, that you would follow it four weeks: and now I call God to witness to your promise." So left him.

He went away, and began to meditate how he was taken in the promise before he was aware of it, and for forty-eight hours neglected it—when his conscience condemned him, and for the ease of his mind he was necessitated to go and pray.

From hence I went to Thermon's Patent, and held several meetings, not in vain; and riding across the branches of Hudson's river, I called the inhabitants together, and we had a refreshing season from the presence of the Lord. In eternity, I believe, some will be thankful for that day.

After preaching at Fort Edward, (where one took fire mysteriously, and was burnt to death,) I went to Easttown. Here the youth, under plain dealing, would frequently leave the house. Accordingly, after procuring a school-house, I invited all the youth to come and I would preach to them; and the house was filled from end to end: and then placing my back against the door, to prevent their running away, gave out the text, and did not spare, and was soon confirmed that God was about to visit the place.

Solemnity rested on every countenance; and in the morning the congregation was treble its usual number, and there was a shaking among the dry bones. This neighborhood I visited from house to house likewise, conversed personally with the youth, and found that about two thirds of them were under serious impressions, but durst not expose it to each other for fear of being laughed at, though some fled from me for fear of being talked to. In this private conversation, they promised to pray for a season, one of which broke her promise and strove to escape my sight; but following her to a neighboring house, I sat in the door and would not let her out till she promised to serve God or the devil for a fortnight. The latter she chose, saying, "I can't keep the other." I called God to witness, and said, "I'll pray that you may be taken sick before the fortnight's up;" and left her. Before night she began to grow uneasy and was sorry she made the promise. She soon broke it, and began to seek the salvation of her soul; and in about a week was hopefully converted to God.

After I had gone through the visiting, in public meeting I set forth plainly the state of the youth, as above-mentioned, and besought them not to be afraid of each other, but to continue seeking the Lord. And one evening, whilst T. Dewey was exhorting, a flash of forked lightning pierced the air, and rolling thunder seemed to shake the house. Some screeched out for mercy; and some jumped out at the windows, and others ran out at the door.

From this night the stir became visible, and thirteen of the youth that night resolved together to pursue religion, let their companions do as they would. A young man by the name of Gideon Draper, said, "If I can stand the crazy man, I will venture all the Methodist preachers to convert me." And when I heard of his expression, faith sprang up in my soul, and I felt a desire to talk to him. He objected, "I am too young;" but here God brought him down, and he is now an itinerant preacher.

As our quarterly meeting was drawing near, every society round the circuit promised, such a day, as much as their labor and bodily strength would admit, to observe as a day of prayer and fasting to God, that he would meet with us at the quarterly meeting, which came on June 20th at Pittstown.

Here, after S. Hutchinson had finished his sermon, J. Mitchell began to exhort, when there commenced a trembling among the wicked; one, and a second, and a third fell from their seat; and the cry for mercy became general. Many of the backsliden professors were cut to the quick; and I think for eleven hours there was no cessation of the loud cries. No business of a temporal nature could be done at this quarterly meeting conference.

The next day, Solomon Moon, who had come more than forty miles, stood up in the love-feast and declared how he was caught in a promise, and to ease his mind, was necessitated to fulfil, and within three days, found the reality of what he had doubted; and he besought others not to be afraid of promising to serve God. "For," said he, "I bless the day that ever I saw the face of brother Dow." It was curiosity, as he testified, which first induced him to come out to hear him that was called the crazy man. In this love-feast, the cry began again, and continued till within two hours of sun-setting, when I went off to an appointment, leaving about twenty who were resolved not to go away until they found pardon.

This day's meeting was a season not soon to be forgotten. I have reason to believe, from observation round the circuit, that not less than a hundred souls were blessed and quickened here.—N. B. It had continued from nine in the morning.

During these last three months, I had six hundred miles to travel in four weeks, besides meeting in class upwards of six hundred members and spectators, and preaching seventy or seventy-five times, and some visiting.

As we were enlarging this circuit, there being a vacant place of upwards of sixty miles, I, with some trouble, got a few places for preaching. As I was travelling, at a distance I saw one dressed in black, whom I overtook; and I asked, in our conversation, if he knew any thing of the Methodists and their doctrine lately in these parts. He was a Calvinist Baptist preacher, and from my dress and questions he supposed that I was no preacher, but a stranger to the Methodists; so he talked just like a prejudiced Calvinist about them; and when he had found me out, he colored, and invited me to dine with an acquaintance of his. I requested permission to pray with them, which caused some surprise. "Prayers," thought they, "in the middle of the day!" Through this medium, the door was opened at Brandon, where I made a covenant with the people. Here curiosity brought out one of the chief men, a merchant, with his proud niece, to hear, as he expected, a great man; but being disappointed in the looks of the person, he was almost ready to go home. But considering in his mind, "I have come a mile and a half distance, through a difficult road; now I am here, I'll stay to the end." He rose up in the covenant, with his niece, not thinking what they were about, but seeing others rise. I called God to witness to the covenant, and went on my way. The consciences of these two persons began to condemn them for breach of promise; and to ease their minds, they were constrained to fulfil, and soon found comfort: and they, with his wife, at the end of four weeks, came out to join society; and twenty-two others followed their example the same day. In nine days after, twenty-five others joined likewise.

The commonalty said, "The Methodists have done some good, by turning the mind of the blasphemer, from collecting in his debts, to religion, and so we are kept out of jail."

In New Huntingdon. I made a covenant with the people, which proved not altogether in vain. Shortly after, about forty were joined in class. This place I visited from house to house, with Hindsburg. Monkton, and Starksborough; where the wilderness seemed to bud and blossom as the rose. O! the joyful meetings we had in these new countries, will not soon be forgotten.

When in Williston, an uncle of mine with his family came out to hear, but behaved very rudely, and strove to persuade me to leave the town, and have no more meetings there; "for," said he, "you will break up our good order."

From hence I proceeded to Richmond, where was a woman, who, being told by her physician that death was now upon her, cried out, "Why, Doctor Marsh, you have been deceiving me, promising me life and health, not letting me know my danger, that I might prepare for death. Twice I have been brought to the gates of death, and promised God, if I might be restored, that I would serve him, and after recovering broke my promise, and went on in the ways of sin; and now I am brought to the gates of death, and have not time to repent: and turning to a man in the company, said, "Whilst the minister is preaching my funeral sermon, know ye that my soul is in hell," and then expired.

Here whilst I preached, some liked, others mocked, and were unwilling to converse with me, lest I should ensnare them into a promise. From hence I crossed Onion river (through some danger by reason of its depth) to Underhill, where God gave me one child in the gospel, as I found next year. From thence to Cambridge, where I met with some opposition; and then crossed the river Demiles to Fairfield and Fairfax, where the people were serious, but some afterwards spoke evil of this way.

Thence to St. Alban's, where one made disturbance in meeting, which I reproved. After meeting, he said if I did not make him satisfaction, by a public acknowledgment that I had abused him, he would prosecute me at law. I defied him to do his worst, knowing that the law was in my favor. "Then," said he, "lay out for the worst." In another meeting, although he thought himself a gentleman, he came in and publicly attempted to wring my nose; but I dodging my head, his hand slipped by; and although I was a stranger, a man attempted to take my part. So I was forgotten by the first. The wrangle in words was so sharp between them, that the woman of the house turned him out of doors.

The next day he waylaid me until he was tired and chilled, and went in to warm himself; and just then I rode by the house where he was.

I preached in Swanton, likewise; and though I had many critics, and was publicly opposed by three Baptist preachers, yet three persons dated their conviction and conversion from this meeting. At the close of it, I appealed to the people that I had proved every disputed point from the scriptures; whereas my opponents had not brought one whole passage of scripture in support of their assertions. So having first recommended them neither implicitly to believe me or my opponents, but to search the scriptures for their own information, we parted. But the Baptists held a council among themselves, and came to a conclusion, that it was best to come no more to hear such false doctrine, as they deemed mine to be. From Canada, I visited all the towns on the Lake shore, to Orwell, to my uncle Daniel Rust's, and God was with me on the way.

The circuit was now divided, and I was to take the part which lay towards Albany.

September 10th, having travelled on foot the preceding week about ninety miles, and preached nearly twice a day, I thought that something broke or gave way in my breast. I borrowed a horse, and proceeded from Wells to Danby. Whilst speaking in the chapel, my strength failed and I gave over, and brother Lobdel concluded the meeting.

To his house I went, but was soon confined to the floor with a strong fever, being destitute of money, bound in body. They had but one room in the house, and several children in the family; and the walking across the floor (the sleepers being long) caused a springing, which gave me much pain, as I had but one blanket under me. A wicked physician was employed, without my consent, whose prescriptions I did not feel freedom to follow; but being over-persuaded by some who wished me well, I at length complied, and found a very bad effect attended. Being in this situation, I began to meditate what course to take, knowing that unless I could get help soon I must die; when I recollected an account I had heard of a man in a fever, who was given over to die: by persuading his watcher to give him plentifully of cold water, which was contrary to orders, he recovered in a few hours. I endeavored to follow the example, by asking it in teacupfuls, from both of my watchers alternately, (so that they should not mistrust my intention, lest they should withhold it from me,) as they waked up in the night, until I had taken twenty-four cups, which promoted a copious perspiration, and the fever left me. But I was so weak that I could not bear the noise and shaking, and the extremes from heat to cold, occasioned by the fire being sometimes large and sometimes nearly out. The man of the house, with J. Mitchell, was now gone to the conference at Granville. I hearing of another family of Methodists who were rich, persuaded a young man without religion, to make a *bier* and sew a coverlet upon it; with which (the neighbors being called in) they carried me up and down hills, like a corpse, several miles to the rich man's house, where I expected the best of attendance. But, alas! I was much disappointed, for they seemed unwilling to assist me with nursing or necessaries; neither could I send to where I had friends, by reason of the distance. Here I despaired of life, and some who were no friends to my manner of conduct, reported that I was dead, from which it appeared they wished it were the case. This report gained much ground, and circulated for some hundreds of miles; so that my parents heard of it, and believing it, gave me up for dead, and my sisters dressed in mourning; and the preachers on hearing it so credibly, ventured to preach my funeral sermon in several places where I had travelled.

The first relief that I got during this illness, was from a Quaker (a namesake of mine, though no relation) who had accidentally heard me preach.

He came ten miles to see me, on hearing I was sick, and I hinted to him my situation. He went away, and the next day came again, and brought a quart of wine, a pint of brandy, a pound of raisins, and half a pound of loaf sugar. These articles seemed to give me new strength, but were soon out. My nurse, who was a spiritual child of mine, offered to get me what I had need of at her own cost; but she having herself and two children to maintain by her labor, being forsaken by her husband, my heart was so tender that I could not accept of her kind offer. Then she prevailed upon the man of the house, with much difficulty, to get me a bottle of wine. The reason, I suppose, they were so unwilling to supply me with what I stood in need of, was because they expected no recompense.

The floor overhead was of loose boards, on which they poured, day after day, baskets of apples and Indian corn in the ear; which with the working of a loom, and spinning-wheels in an adjoining room, besides the cider-mill near hand, all together, caused such noises as in my very weak state distressed me much. In addition to the above, the youth of the neighborhood made noisy visits, without restraint of the family.

A man who had heard of, but never seen me, came fifteen miles to know my state, and gave me a dollar. Soon after, two men who had heard that I was dead, and then alive, and again dead, came about thirty miles to find out the truth concerning me. I was glad to see them, and would take no denial, until they promised to come with a wagon and take me away, which they were unwilling to do, thinking that I should die by the fatigue. But they at length consented.

The wagon came, and a message from a young woman, that if I would come to her father's house, the best of care should be taken of me. Her name was Mary Switzer.

I waited thirty-six hours for the rain to abate; but seeing it did not, persuaded them to wrap me in a coverlet, and with straw under and over me we set out—and over rugged hills and mountains, they carried me twenty-seven miles in eight hours, to the house where I was invited; and beyond their expectation, I received no harm. At this time I was so weak, that I was obliged to be carried, not being able even to stand alone.

The young woman made good her promise, and the young friends who had joined society when I was in this part before, spared no pains for my comfort—she being up with me four and five times every night, whilst I was still despairing of life. One evening, as the young people were holding a prayer meeting in the adjoining room, a thought came into my mind, "Why is not God as able now to raise me to health as those in primitive days?" Something answered, "He is." "Why is he not as willing?" Something replied, "He is." Another thought arose, "Why don't he do it?" The answer was, "Because you lack faith." It struck my mind, "Is faith the gift of God? or is it the creature's act?" The reply was, "The power to believe is the gift of God; but the act of faith is the creature's." I instantly strove to see if I could act faith; and I did believe, if the young people which were in the room, would intercede with God faithfully during that week, that God would, in answer to many prayers, restore me to health.

I made this request of them, (to pray for my recovery,) if consistent with God's will. About two hours afterwards I fell asleep, and had a singular dream, by which I was convinced I should see my native town in peace once more; and within fifteen hours after I perceptibly began to amend, and by the goodness of God, after about ten weeks' confinement, from the beginning of my illness, I was able to ride alone.

During this illness, I was frequently asked if I did not repent having exposed myself to such toils and hardships through the year past? I replied, "No; if it was to do, I would do it again; it brought me such peace and consolation, that now my very soul was lifted up above the fear of death, so that the grave appeared lovely."

What I wished to live for, was principally these: First, to attain to higher degrees of holiness here, that I might be happier hereafter; and, secondly, I felt the worth of souls to lie near my heart, and I desired to be useful to them. What I desired to die for was, to get out of this troublesome world, and to be at rest with saints above.

CHAPTER IV.

MY ADMITTANCE ON TRIAL.

I OBTAINED a letter of recommendation, signed by above thirty local preachers, stewards, and class leaders, &c., concerning my usefulness and moral conduct, which T. Dewey carried to the conference, and gave his opinion concerning me, when nine others and I were admitted on trial. My name was now printed in the minutes, and I received a written license from Francis Asbury. Then said S. Hutchinson to J. Lee, "This is the crazy man you have been striving to kill so much."

November 20. I set off with brother Dewey for the north, though still so weak that I could neither get on nor off my horse alone.

In Argyle we had a solemn season. Then we parted, and I revisited Thermon's Patent and Queensborough; after which, I rode twenty-three miles, facing a cold, northeast snow-storm—I think the hardest that I ever was exposed to; even wild geese could not keep their course, but flew round and round. The next day but one I rode through Rutland thirty-six miles to Brandon, where I stayed a week, met the societies, and preached fifteen times. Bidding them farewell, I returned southward, visiting some places until the quarterly meeting came on.

I took my leave of the classes and people in the different places, taking them to record that I had spared no pains, either by night or day, in public or in private, to bring them to good; and if they did not repent, I should appear against them at a future day, calling the sun, moon, and stars, with the fowls of the air and the beasts of the field, to witness against them, that my skirts were pure from all their blood.*

December 27th. I puked almost to death before it could be stopped; but, far beyond expectation, God enabled me to speak at night. On the twenty-ninth I held three meetings, which appeared not in vain. On the twenty-ninth our quarterly meeting began in Ashgrove, where I was complained of, and was whipped (in words) by brother Hutchinson for jealousy.

The next day we had a refreshing season, and about two hundred communicants; and after giving them my farewell, I felt as pure from the blood of the people as if I had never been called to preach.

During my stay upon these two circuits, in ten months, about six hundred were taken into society, and as many more went off and joined the Baptists and Presbyterians.

From thence I started with brother Sabin for the south. I rode through Bennington in a cold storm, and through tedious drifts of snow to Williamstown.

January 1st, 1799. I again renewed my covenant to be more faithful to God and man than I had been. I proceeded to Stockbridge, and met friend Hubbard, who was to go where I came from, and I to supply his place on Pittsfield circuit, while brother Sabin was to go to Litchfield. This circuit was in a very low situation, and the most despised of any in New England; and as they had frequently sent complaints to conference against their preachers, I at first refused to go to it, lest I should be injured by false brethren, knowing that J. Sawyer, with whom I was to travel, had been prejudiced against me. But upon conditions that Dewey and Sawyer would stand by me, as far as consistent with truth and discipline, I consented to go.

On the third I began to pursue the circuit regularly, after my irregular manner, and preach especially to sinners and lukewarm professors, with backsliders.

---

* I have not seen them since.

From Lenox, going across the mountain to New Canaan, I met with a loss, and had like to have perished with the cold and snow-drifts.

6th. I preached in Pittsfield. The members were high in profession, but low in heart. Their prejudice being great, they did not invite me to their houses, but were sorry I came on the circuit.

7th. Windsor. In the lukewarm class, the power of God was felt. From hence to Adams and Stanford, where revivals soon broke out. But the Baptists did us much harm, pretending to be friends, but with the reprobation doctrine opposing as enemies behind our backs.

Thence through Clarsburgh to Pownal, where the people were once engaged in religion, but now were hardened; so we gave up the place.

Thence to Hoosac, where several were cut to the heart, and shortly after a beautiful society was formed. This town being large, I went into several other parts to break up fresh ground.

One day a man said to me, "Fourteen months ago I met you coming out of Troy; and you, after inquiring the road, asked, 'Was my peace made with God?' I replied, 'I hope so,' knowing it was not, for which my conscience condemned me. But the pride of my heart would not suffer me to acknowledge that I lied; and you, after giving me good advice, went on your way, which advice has not left me yet; and now I am resolved to serve God the remainder of my life." This was an encouragement to me not to be discouraged, as bread thrown on the waters is found after many days. Hence I went to Troy, where was some revival in the class. Thence to Greenbush, where a glorious work of God began.

The second time I went to that place, the people flocked out by hundreds to hear the strange man preach up his principles. I told the people that God had promised me two souls to be converted from that day, and if my labors were not acknowledged, they might brand me in the forehead with the mark of liar, and on the back with the mark of hypocrite.

They watched my words. However, two who were in the assembly thought, Oh! that I might be one of these two; and shortly after both found pardon. A reprobation preacher sought to do us much harm, when I publicly besought God, if he was a true minister, to bless his labors, and make it manifest; but if he had jumped presumptuously into the work, that God would remove him, so that he should not hurt the people. Shortly after he fell into a scandalous sin, and so his influence was lost.

At Canaan Gore a number of backsliders and sinners were brought to a sense of themselves, and joined in a class; one of whom invited me to preach in Green River meeting-house, as we had a right to it two days in the year.

The time arrived; the people came out, and I went: but having a hard day's journey of twenty-five miles, and to preach five times, and to speak to three classes, I had to be in earnest.

As I entered the meeting-house, having an old, borrowed great-coat on, and two hats, the people were alarmed, and thought it singular that I did not bow to every pew as I went towards the pulpit, which was the custom there. Some laughed, and some blushed, and the attention of all was excited. I spoke for about two hours, giving the inside and outside of Methodism. Many, I believe, for that day will be thankful, though I was strongly opposed by a reprobationist in the afternoon. My hat was taken from me without my consent, and two others forced upon me: I was carrying one to give a young man.

In New Concord, religion being low, I visited the people three miles, taking every house, and (being persuaded) I told the people that God would soon surely revive his work; which words they marked, and sought to do me harm, as instantly the work did not appear.

I besought God in public, that something awful might happen in the neighborhood, if nothing else would do to alarm the people. For this prayer many said I ought to be punished.

A company of young people going to a tavern, one of them said, "I will ride there as Christ rode into Jerusalem." Instantly his horse started, ran a distance, and threw him against a log. He spoke no more until he died, which was next morning.*

In this neighborhood the young people assembled again to a gingerbread lottery; and I preached from—"If they hear not Moses and the prophets, neither will they be persuaded though one rose from the dead." They were so struck, that the fiddler whom they employed had nothing to do.

At length the revival appeared visible, and the mouths of gainsayers were shut: numbers were added to class.

On my way to Spencertown, at a distance, I discovered a place in a hilly country, where I thought God would immediately revive his work. Coming to a house, I inquired my road, but found I had gone out of my way; but upon being righted, I came to the place which just before I had seen from the top of a mountain, where I thought God would revive his work.

I began immediately to visit the neighborhood from house to house. The people thought it strange, I being a stranger, and came out to see where it would end.

Here too it was soon reported I was crazy, which brought many out to the different meetings: among whom was an old man, who came to hear for himself, and told the congregation that I was crazy, and advised them to hear me no more. I replied, people do not blame crazy ones for their behavior; and last night I preached from the word of the Lord; but when I come again I will preach from the word of the devil. This tried our weak brethren: however, the people came out by hundreds to hear the new doctrine. I spoke from Luke iv. 6, 7, and an overshadowing season we had of the Divine presence. I besought the family to promise to serve God; but upon receiving a refusal, my soul was so pained with concern on their account, that I could not eat my breakfast, and set out to go away in the rain. Conviction seized the minds of the family; they followed me at a distance with tears, and made me the promise, and not altogether in vain. Here the society was greatly enlarged · those that were in darkness were brought into marvellous light.

In Alford, I preached Methodism, inside and outside. Many came to hear; one woman thought I aimed at her dress. The next meeting she ornamented far more, in order that I might speak to her. But I in my discourse took no notice of dress, and she went away disgraced and ashamed.

---

* His name was Valentine.

The brethren here treated me very coldly at first, so I was necessitated to pay for my horse-keeping for five weeks: and being confined a few days with the ague and fever, the man of the house not being a Methodist, I paid him for my accommodation.

I had said in public that God would bless my labors there; which made the people watch me for evil and not for good. I visited the whole neighborhood from house to house, which made a great uproar among the people. However, the fire kindled; the society got enlivened, and several others who were stumbling at the unexemplary walk of professors, were convinced and brought to find the realities of religion for themselves. When leaving this place, I was offered pay for my expenses, but I refused it, saying, "If you wish to do me good, treat the coming preacher better than you have done me."

Stockbridge. Here the minister of the place had done his endeavors to influence the people to shut the preachers out of the town; but by an impression I went into one part, and by an invitation to another; and though the opposition was great from the magistrates and quality, yet they found no way to expel us out of the place; but the revival began, and several were stirred up to seek God. Now reprobation lost ground: the eyes of many were enlightened to see a free salvation offered to all mankind.

In Lenox the society and people were much prejudiced at first, but the former were quickened afresh. Here lived a young woman, who, by the unexemplary walk of professors, was prejudiced against the advice to religion, saying, "I see no difference between their walk and others." Her parents besought me to say nothing to her about her soul, lest she should be prejudiced and hardened more. I began to consider what to do; and after seeking to God for wisdom and success, said, "Sophy, if you'll read a chapter every day till my return four weeks hence, I'll give you this Bible." She thinking I was in jest, said she would. I instantly gave it to her, at which she blushed. At my return, as she said she had fulfilled, I requested a second promise; which was that she would pray twice a day in secret another four weeks. She said, "You'll go and tell it round if I do:" which I assured her I would not, if she would only grant my request. Said she, "I'll retire, but not promise to kneel," so we parted. At the expiration of the time I came round the circuit here again, and requested one promise more, viz. to pray once a day kneeling, which I would not take a denial of: and to get rid of my importunity she promised; and before the time expired she was convinced of the necessity of being made holy, and was willing that all the world should know of her resolution to serve God during life.*

I visited Pittsfield extensively, and had the satisfaction to see the Methodists and others stirred up to serve God. Now they offered me presents, which I refused, saying, "The next preachers invite home and treat well, for my sake."

In Bethlehem, whilst preaching, I was suddenly seized with puking, and expected to expire. Here also God revived his work.

Conference drawing near, and finding that my food did not nourish and strengthen me as heretofore, I was convinced that unless I could get

---

* A few years after she died happy.

help, I must be carried off the stage. I accordingly wrote to conference concerning my state, and requested permission to take a voyage to sea as I had no hope of escaping any other way; and IRELAND lay particularly on my mind. Feeling a particular desire to visit Lansingburgh and Albany, which the preachers had restrained me from going to, I embraced the opportunity whilst they were gone to conference.

June 17th, I preached five times and rode thirty-five miles. On the 18th, I rode fifty-five miles; preached five times, and spoke to two classes. On the 19th, I preached six times, and rode twenty-five miles. On the 20th, I preached twice and went to Albany, and preached eight nights successively, one excepted, which I improved in Lansingburgh.

In the daytime, I went to Coeyman's Patent and Niskeuna. These visits were not altogether in vain; wherefore I did not grudge the above mentioned hard days' works to gain this time.

29th. I rode thirty miles, preaching twice on the road, to Handcock; which place I had visited extensively, it being newly taken into the circuit, and about forty members joined in the class. Our quarterly meeting coming on, the congregation was so large, we were constrained to withdraw to the woods; for no building we had would contain them. It was a powerful time indeed, and many were refreshed from the presence of the Lord.

My state of health being so low, I bade them farewell until we should meet in a future world, as I expected to see them no more on earth.

I took them all to record, that my skirts were pure from all their blood, as I had spared no pains to bring them to good.

When I at first came on this circuit, I felt like one forsaken, as they all appeared to be sorry to see me, and almost unwilling to feed me or my horse. For all my toil here, I received ten dollars, when my extra expenses were upwards of six pounds; so that when leaving it, I was fifteen pounds worse in circumstances than when coming: yet it afforded me comfort that I could leave them in peace, and have a joyful hope of enjoying some of them as stars in my crown of glory, which I expected soon to obtain.

As the preachers who had just come from conference told me that my request was rejected, and my station was on the bounds of Canada; this information grieved me at first: however, I consented to go according to orders, after I had visited my native town.

Leaving this circuit, to which there were added one hundred and eighty, and about five hundred more under conviction for sin, I set off for Coventry, and riding through Granville circuit, it caused me to weep and mourn when I saw some who were awakened when I was there, now in a backslidden state. Oh! the harm done by the laziness and unfaithfulness of preachers! But some who were alive then are alive still, and I trust to meet them in a better world.

July 3d. I reached my native town, and found my parents and friends well in body, but low in religion. Next evening I preached; many flocked out to hear the preacher who had risen from the dead, as was the common say.

I told the people, once I was opposed by them about preaching: I have come home before now to see you and bid you farewell for a season; but now I have come home, not a-cozening, as some children do to see their parents, but to discharge my duty and bid you farewell once for all; and if God does not give me seals of my labor, you may still say he has not called me to preach.

I went to New London, to see if the salt water would do me any good, and c ming through Norwich I met with a cool reception from the society: but in New London all seemed friendly. We had several powerful meetings; two were awakened, and one found pardon during my stay.

I besought God to let me preach one funeral sermon in my native town; where, having visited many, I preached in about twenty different houses. Having spent about four weeks, the time drew near when I must set off.

The class-leader, S. Parker, having received a wound, bled to that degree, that he died in consequence of it, happy in the love of God.

I took leave of the dear families of my acquaintance, and August 4th, preached the funeral sermon to many hundreds of people. Both gentry and commonalty were drawn out by curiosity to hear one of their native town, whom they had heard so much about; thinking it would do to go to a funeral, when it would not to go to another of my meetings; taking the funeral for a cloak.

After discharging my duty as God gave me strength, to old and to young, to professor and non-professor, I said, "Ye all see the decline I am in, and take you to record my walk and conversation since I first professed religion, and my faithfulness to you now; and if God permit, I intend to see you again at the end of eleven months; but it is impressed on my mind as though I shall never see you in time, unless it should be in answer to many prayers; I therefore bid you farewell till the judgment day;" and then taking my youngest sister by the hand—(from whom I had obtained a promise to pray twice a-day till I should be twenty-two years old, reminding her of my dream; she then being in the height of fashion, pleaded she should have none to go with her; I said, I myself had to go alone and was enabled to endure—and you, after I am two-and-twenty, if tired of the service of God, can turn back and the devil will be willing to receive you again; then tears began to roll)—I bade her farewell, and to strive to meet me in heaven, and rather than have her turn back to sin, would come and preach her funeral sermon. Another sister, and my mother, and brother-in-law, I shook hands with likewise. My father's trials were so great, he withdrew, (I suppose to weep;) and then mounting my horse, all this being in the sight of the assembly, and the sun shining from the western sky, I called it to witness against that assembly if they would not repent, that my skirts were pure from their blood; and then putting the whip to my horse, I rode off forty miles that evening before I dismounted. On the 5th, I rode seventy miles to Chesterfield. A family with whom I was acquainted, being, as I thought, unwilling to receive me, I went to the next house, and so pleaded that they took me in.

The next day I rode sixty-four miles, to Hanover, and the day after saw my brother-in-law and two sisters; to whom I discharged my duty, and left them and went to Vershire.

A swelling appearing on my horse's leg, I left him and borrowed another to reach my circuit. On my way across the mountain, I preached in Berry, and the power of God was present. The next morning crossing Onion river, reached my circuit at Essex, being two hundred and fifty miles from my parents. Cold winter now approaching, my clothes considerably worn and few; and no way apparently to get any more, having but one penny in my pocket, and a stranger in a strange land; and unless God gives me favor in the sight of the people, shall have to walk on foot. My trust is still in God; my mind is solemnly stayed upon him, and I do believe he will bless me here by numbers.

I met brother Sabin, a local preacher, who came to my assistance in Jericho. After meeting, we set off, whilst one rode the other went on foot, to Fletcher: here a powerful work of God immediately broke out.

The next day, we swam the horse across the river Demile, ourselves crossing in a canoe; proceeded through a wood without any path, for some miles, and late at night came to Fairfield, about thirty miles in all. My body was weary but my soul was happy.

It was not long until I was sorely tempted to desist from travelling, and wait till my change come; but then considering the value of souls, I am constrained to exert the little strength I have.

On hearing brother Sabin preach in Sheldon, I was comforted. The next day we crossed the Canada line into Dunn's Patent: here God began a good work. From thence to the Dutch manor, brother Miller's, where I had been before.

I held meeting, and a proud young woman was stirred up to seek the Lord, and found comfort. Borrowing a horse, I went to break up fallow ground, and proceeded to Dunham towards Mumphrey Magog Lake, and held meetings in different parts of the town. Some were angry and spake evil of the way; and some were serious and tender, and desired to hear again. The people in this part of the world were the offscouring of the earth, some having ran hither for debt, others to avoid prosecution for crimes, and a third character had come to accumulate money. These were like sheep without a shepherd, having only two ministers, one of whom believed one principle and preached another. Hence I went to Sutton, and got into three parts of the town; in two of which there was a prospect of much good; but in the other, reprobationism shut up the hearts of the people, and I must speak there no more.

Returning through these places to Mussisque bay, the prospect of good increased. From thence I proceeded round the north end of the bay to the west side, as far as I could find inhabitants. The roads were so sloughy and miry that they were almost impassable. However, I got places to accommodate the inhabitants for meetings, all along. Here for thirty miles there was no preaching until I came: but the Lord made bare his arm.

Returning, I held meetings at the same places, and found the prospect to increase. Then going up the lake shore, held meetings where I had the year past, until I came round to Fletcher: here the work increased. Hence I proceeded through Johnston, up the river Demile to Morristown. Here the people had not heard a sermon for two years: we entered into a covenant to serve the Lord; and many were keenly convicted, and their hearts were like wax before the sun.

Hence to Stowe, where for three miles I could get no house at first. Night drawing on, I scarcely knew what to do, as the families would not take me in; but at length I met a company of men, who had been marking out land in the woods; to these I made known my errand, and they invited me to go back about two miles; and the house was soon filled with people, and solemn times we had that evening and the next morning.

Ten years ago, this was a howling wilderness, inhabited only by wild beasts, and now contained near one hundred families. Oh! what an alteration there is in the earth!

From hence I went to Waterbury, on Onion river, where a reprobationist gave me these words to preach from: "No man can come to me except the Father who hath sent me draw him." The Lord loosed my tongue, and good I believe was done.

From thence I returned to Mussisque bay, under trials and discouragements of mind, but was revived on meeting brother Sabin. As I could not readily find a horse to borrow, I set out on foot towards Magog: but my body being weak, I disappointed one congregation, to my sorrow, but reached the next day's appointments in Sutton and Dunham, and God gave me favor in the sight of some, who with horses conveyed me to the several places.

During my walk, I found one fourth of a dollar, and reasoned, why have I found this? I have not had any for some time past.

I had to walk from Dunn's Patent to the bay, which was about ten miles, the nighest way, on which lived but few inhabitants. I set out, hoping to get through that night, but falling short by reason of weakness, came to a house and requested they would guide me through the woods, but in vain. I then entreated liberty to tarry under their roof all night, as it had now become dark, and impossible for a stranger to keep the road, it being narrow and miry, and closed overhead by the branches of thick-topped trees: besides, it was exceedingly dangerous, by the flocks of bears, which were uncommonly numerous this fall; but at first my entreaties were in vain: then remembering the piece of money which I had found, I offered it to them for the privilege, which, on this condition, I obtained. The next morning, with much difficulty I got through to a friend's house.

After breakfast I obtained a horse, and set out to fulfil my appointments round the bay, which were five. Far beyond my expectation, I was enabled to go through these, riding twenty-five miles that day, and visiting the isle of Noah and Hog Island, (in the latter of which I held the first religious meeting that was ever in it; and a solemn time it was.) I returned to the Dutch manor and sold my watch, saddle, and portmanteau.

For some months past, I had no hope of recovering from my declining state, unless it were by a long voyage to sea, but the impossibility of it, as I thought, was so great that I rejected the idea. I had been strongly impressed these few weeks past, that if I tarried I should die according to the dream; but that if I were to cross the ocean to Ireland, it would be the means which God did choose to bless to the restoration of my health, and preservation of my life for future usefulness, for some particular end unknown to me. But when I considered the dangers by sea, by reason of storms and tempests, at that season of the year, and of being taken by pirates or privateers, into whose hands I might fall in this declining state, and what care would be shown me I did not know: and supposing I were even to get well to Europe, what might follow I did not clearly foresee: the country being in scarcity, with great disturbances, and who would receive me I could not tell—and if rejected by all, having no trade to pursue, I saw nothing but that death would follow. These things weighed so heavy in the balance of reason, that I rejected the impression, and threw it out of my mind as a temptation: it returned with more force, and pursued me from day to day. By nourishing it, I had peace; and by rejecting it, depression, which caused great distress; so that many hours of my sleep departed from me. This I made known to the preachers and some others, who had importuned me to tell them what was the matter.

After being informed, all with one voice entreated me not to entertain such a thought as coming from God, seeing that my labors were here acknowledged, and that there was a prospect of a universal revival. "Wherefore it is inconsistent," said they, "that he could require you to g away three thousand miles, into a strange country, without friends, leaving the circuit in this situation, forfeiting the confidence which the conference have placed in you, by giving you the care of the circuit, and none to supply your place."

These arguments were powerful, and so confounded me that I could not answer them. Still there was something in my mind that said, Go; and by putting it away I could get no peace.

September 26th. I preached in Highgate, Swanton, and St. Alban's, for the last time; in Georgia and in Milton likewise. In the latter I once made a covenant, which they broke, and afterwards they hated me so, that they could not bear to see me.

28th. Our quarterly meeting began in Essex. I made my exercise known, and the declining state I was in, to S. Hutchinson and J. Mitchell, who would hearken nothing to it, but brought up the above-mentioned arguments. I besought for a certificate concerning my moral conduct, but was refused, with a strict injunction not to go. S. Hutchinson said, "I shall appear like a fool in the eyes of the conference for supporting your cause in the manner I have done, as some said that you would never prove true to the connection, which, by going away, will appear to be the case. But, if you'll tarry, as I ever have been, so I still will be your friend; and the next conference your probation will be ended, and you will be ordained." I bid him farewell, giving him Hezekiah's lamentation—Isaiah, xxxviii. 9, &c. He gave me Paul's charge to Timothy, and so we parted, after that I had given my farewell to the people.

I now proceeded to fulfil what appointments I had made for myself, riding with J. M. to Fletcher. He again entreated me for his, and my, and the work of God's sake, to tarry, saying, "If you go away and leave us thus, I believe the curse of God will follow you;" and kneeling down, besought God, if he had called me to go, to make it manifest, and if not, to hedge up my way; and so parted for a while. I went to Cambridge, Johnston, Morristown, Stowe, Waterbury, and Duxbury, and the quickening power of God was sensibly felt in every place.

About this time I met with Dr. Whipple, of New Boston, in New Hampshire, who gave me some things for my voyage, saying he felt for me in this great undertaking.

My trials of heart were great to think of leaving my people and country, and particularly my parents, probably to see them no more, so contrary to the minds and advice of all those who wished me well; but I have endeavored to weigh the matter candidly before God, as for eternity, and after making it a matter of earnest prayer to know my duty, that, if the impression be from God, it may increase, and if from the enemy, it may decrease; and, according to the best judgment I can form, I do believe it to be the will of God that I should go, as I can enjoy peace of mind in no pursuit but this, and accordingly I am resolved to proceed as the door opens.

My horse being brought from Vershire, which cost eighty-four dollars, I now sold for a small part of that sum; and all which I could collect, including the price of my saddle, &c., amounted to six guineas and some provision.

October 12th. I met brother Mitchell again; he would not bid me farewell, saying, "I can't give my consent you should go." I bid him farewell, saying, "I know you have ever been my friend, and are such to the present day; it is hard to go contrary to your advice, and if you think I am wilful in this matter, you judge me wrong and hard: it is in tender conscience before God that I leave you this day, for the sake of peace of mind, which if I could otherwise enjoy, I would take up with your advice, 'to stick and die by the stuff:'" and kneeling down, whilst at prayer our hearts were melted with a feeling sense of the goodness of God; and, as Jonathan and David's, our parting was hard. From thence I proceeded (in a canoe which had come for me and started back, I being about twenty minutes behind the time, but hailed him, so he stopped and took me in. This was a stranger, as the first man who was to have come for me was dead) down the Mussisque river, across the bay, to what is called the Ridge, where God has begun a good work. Here some of my friends from the Manor met me with entreaties not to go, which to prevent did not bring my chest, as apparently I must die with sufferings among hard-hearted sailors; but if I would tarry with them, I could have friends and a decent burial. But my mind was to go; so they went back and brought my chest to South River. We kneeled down on the bank, and besought God, if it was his will I should go, to prosper my way, but if not, to shut it up. Said they, "We expect to see you again." But I replied, "It is in my mind as though I should never see you again." Some were minded not to have brought my chest, that I might thereby be detained until it was too late for going, as the fleet was to sail in a short space. Being disappointed of a canoe which was promised, we took another, which sprang a-leak before we had gone far; but we got a second down the river, and soon got into the lake.

The waves ran high, and the people had advised us not to go, as they thought there was great danger of upsetting.

The man who had promised to take me to St. John's breaking his word, I had to look out for another, who said, "Such a day, I went out of curiosity to hear a strange man who had come to the neighborhood, whose words reached my heart. And now I believe God has pardoned my sins, and I bless God that ever I saw your face."

Cutting down a bush, and hoisting it for a sail, we reached St. John's about three in the afternoon; and after wandering up and down the town for about two hours, I found a man who, for two dollars, engaged to carry me in a cart to Lapareri, the mail stage having gone off just before I arrived there.

After being examined strictly by the military officers, and my name recorded, I parted with the canoe-man, and went on my way; being now entirely among strangers, and probably I shall be so, I know not but for life. The cart broke down on the road, and he had to borrow another About three o'clock after midnight I arrived at Lapareri, being very much chilled.

The market boats at break of day started for Montreal, and on my way I discovered several vessels lying at the wharf, one of which particularly attracted my mind; and after landing, I walked on board, inquiring where she belonged and was bound to.

The captain answered, "Belongs to Quebec, and bound for Dublin." (The very place where I wanted to go.)

Q. "Will you give me a passage?"
A. "Have you plenty of money?"
Q. "What shall you charge?"
A. "Sometimes people give fifteen guineas, but I will carry one for eight."
Q. "I'll give you five guineas and find myself; will you carry me for that? If not, I must return to the states."
A. "I will; but you are a devilish fool for going from a plentiful country, with peace, to that disturbed island."

I then gave him his money, and bought some more provisions, and had a few shillings left.

After attempting to preach in a congregation of the hardest of the hard, I went on board the vessel, and put down the river a few leagues.

October 16th. I this day was twenty-two years old. The dream of the prophet now lay with weight upon my mind, which said that I should live until I was two-and-twenty, and the hours passed solemnly away. A woman passenger said, "I judge this man's a Methodist." I, turning away as with an air of disdain, said, "What do you lump me with that despised people for?" She replied, "Because you don't drink, and be jovial and cheerily as what the rest of us are, but are gloomy and cast down—like that people, always melancholy." "Well," said the sailors, "we'll try him over the ground, and see what he is made of." Then they began to put tar on my face, and tallow on my clothes, until I told the captain he ought to make them behave more civil, being commander of the ship. However, I was the object of all their sport for seven days on our way to Quebec, during which time I suffered much with cold, having no blankets, and lying either on the cable, or across some barrels filled with potash, and my garments being thin, and nothing but a side of leather to cover myself with. But the last night I found a small sail, and begging it of the captain, I wrapped myself in it, and thought myself comfortable. There was no fire below decks at this time.

One morning a lieutenant came on board before I was up, and describing my dress, inquired of the captain if such a person was on board. I came up, and the captain told me what had passed.

The officer then said, "You were seen at Lapareri, &c., and was thought to be one of M'Clen's party, as a spy, and I have come a hundred miles to apprehend you, and now you must clear yourself, or go before the chief commander." I showed him my license and some private letters, and told him my business. He then replied, "I believe you are an honest man, and if you will enlist, I'll give you so much bounty and a sergeantcy, and if not, you shall be pressed." I replied, "Fight I cannot in conscience for any man; because it would be inconsistent for a man one hour to be praying for his enemies, and the next hour learning to handle a gun to shoot them; but if you take me on board I shall preach." At length I found a strange piece of money in my pocket; and he attempted to take my hat to put a cockade on it; I snatched it out of his hand and pushed him away; to which he said, "Remember you are not in the States now; here it is treason to resist an officer." I making as if I would throw them overboard, he besought me not, as the cockade was costly: on condition of his letting me have peace till I got to Quebec, I gave them up. At our arrival, it being evening, I would not stay on board in the captain's absence, knowing the sailors would abuse me. The lieutenant, as I carried his little chest or trunk to his lodgings, said he would send his servant to pilot me to the house of a piece of a Methodist; but it being now late, altered his mind, and gave me entertainment all night, with blankets and fire, which was refreshing to me. He and his captain exerted themselves to lead me into sin; but before we parted I obtained liberty to pray with them.

The next morning I inquired for Methodists, and through the medium of an English lad, the people being mostly French, found a few backslidden ones, some of whom came from Europe. The week preceding, a society of about twenty-six, belonging to the army, had gone to Halifax, but two or three of their wives were left. I found the place where they used to hold their meeting, and collected about a dozen English to a meeting in the evening.

The next evening the congregation increased to about thirty; thus on to about a hundred and fifty the five days I was there. A woman, the first day, on finding out who and what I was, invited me to dinner; then her husband invited me to eat and drink as I needed, as often and as long as I stayed. This I looked upon as providential. This woman was very inquisitive to know all the particulars of the materials I had procured for the voyage; and the day but one before I was to set sail, gave me all the small materials that were lacking; and the last evening, after I had done preaching, one, and a second, and a third, &c., of their own accord, without any hint from me, came forward and laid down pieces of money, amounting in the whole to several dollars, which I stood in need of at this critical time: and a buffalo skin dressed with the hair on (which I had to lodge on while here in the city) and a blanket, were given me by one person for my bed on the voyage. Now I began to meditate, when I entered this city, according to human appearance, I must fall short of the voyage for want of necessaries, and no place to lodge in whilst here; but that God who I believed had called me to go, to him I looked (when in retirement under a fort wall) and found my wants supplied; and if he thus far had opened the way step by step, what reason had I to doubt but that all my journeys might be made as prosperous as this through trials, and I preserved for future usefulness, and yet see my native land in peace; and my soul was strengthened to put my trust in God and go forward. I think about twenty were stirred up to seek God during this short stay, who earnestly entreated me to give over my voyage and tarry with them; but not prevailing, sought a promise for my return in the spring, which I gave them not, but said, "If God will, perhaps I may see you again."

October 28th. I went on board, and the fleet fell down the river. I thought of my parents, but said, "To tarry is death—to go, I do but die."

October 31st. I informed my parents of my departure, and got into the Gulf of St. Lawrence. I felt some little sea-sick, but did not puke much; but my bodily sickness increases fast, and 'tis more than probable, according to human appearance, that I shall not see Dublin.

November 2d. I saw Newfoundland covered with snow, and left it to the left. My sickness still increases, and I am scarcely able to sit up ten minutes in twenty-four hours. The captain, though deistical and profane, is as kind as I could expect from a religious man. Though the agreement was to come in the steerage, my birth is in the cabin, and the boy has orders to wait upon me as I have need.

I feel the want of some religious person to converse with. Oh! how do people misimprove their privileges, and some don't prize them until deprived of them. But religion is that which the world can neither give nor take away. I still feel the Lord to be precious to my soul in my critical place. Surely in the deep waters are the wonders of the Almighty to be seen.

The whole fleet consisted of about twelve sail. We had pleasant sailing for about a week, the ships frequently calling to each other; but at length the sea began to rise, first like hills, then like mountains, then it seemed to run to the skies: the whole fleet was scattered, but the next day collected again, and within two hours after so scattered that we saw each other no more. This gale lasted five days. The captain said, that for fifteen years he had not seen the like. The mate replied, " I have followed the sea these twenty-five years and have never seen the like." But through the goodness of God, we were not driven any out of our course, and sustained no damage except the breaking of the main yard. Though the crew appeared terrified once or twice, I don't know that my mind was ever more calm in my life. I frequently said to myself, "My body may sink to the bottom; but my soul will fly to the paradise of God." At length the wind abated, and the sea fell, and I spent a little time on deck: I could see no land. Farewell to America. Oh! shall I ever see my native country again? I am now going to a strange land, to be a stranger among strangers, and what is before me I know not.

I gave the name of my father, and the place of his residence, to the captain, that if he gave me to the sharks, my parents should have information, which he promised to send. If I live to do good, I will bless God: and if I die, O God! thy will be done.

What am I going to Europe for? For the sake of riches? From whence will they come? For honor? Who will give me this? For ease? Lord, thou knowest my heart, that I have no other end in view, but thy glory and the salvation of immortal souls. And though I pass through trials I will fear no evil, whilst God is on my side. I know the time has been when I was a guilty sinner, and I have a witness within myself that all my guilt is done away through the mediation of Christ, and my soul is in a state of acceptance with God. I frequently, whilst enjoying this evidence, am greatly distressed and compassed about, as with all the powers of hell, so that a horror seems to run over my mind, when I feel not the least degree of guilt, but love to God and all mankind, and none of the slavish fear of hell; neither would I commit a known sin for my right hand. If any one should ask, how that a sanctified saint could have such feelings or trials; I ask again, cannot spirit pray or operate upon spirit, as well as matter upon matter? If any one should deny, let him prove it. Experience is the greatest evidence; a person may be powerfully depressed by the infernal powers of darkness, and still retain the right and sure evidence of his acceptance with God, so as to read his title clear to heaven. Tempting to actual evil is one thing, and buffeting of the mind is another. At particular times, to feel either the one or the other, is no sin, whilst the whole soul cleaves to God.

After being under some weighty exercises, I fell asleep, and God comforted me in dreams of the night; for first, I thought I saw myself in some place, and the people seemed to be struck with wonder what I came for. Shortly after I heard some young converts tell their experience; then I saw the work go prosperously on; after which I saw myself surrounded by a wicked company of people; but their words were like empty sounds, though their tongues were sharp; yet their weapons were like feathers, for my forehead was like brass. But God raised me up friends in time of need. From this, I infer that some trouble is at hand, yet I am more than ever convinced that this voyage will turn for my good, and for the glory of God. Trouble I expect is near, but my trust is in God: all is well now; to-morrow may take thought for itself.

I remember once when I was in trouble with my asthmatical disorder, I besought God to heal my body and let my heaviest trials be in mind; but now I find it is not good to be our own choosers, but submit to the will of God; remembering that all things shall work together for good to them that love him.

25th. The sun in the sky was not seen for several days, which made it dangerous sailing; but fearing privateers, did not lay to. One evening, the captain grew uneasy and could not sleep, and got up and lay down several times in a short space, and as the mate came below to warm himself, the captain said, "Mr. Tom, is there land near?" The mate said, "I can see three leagues ahead, and there is no land in sight." The captain's trouble continuing, the reason he could never assign, immediately lay down, and then rose up and went on deck, and being strong-sighted, beheld land within a mile! All hands were called; they tacked the vessel about. Oh! what a providence was this!—Less than twenty minutes no doubt would have wrecked the ship. This was in latitude fifty-seven, off the Highlands of Scotland.

26th. The sun broke out pleasant; this evening we came to anchor at Larne, in the north of Ireland; having no contrary wind all the way until we got off this port; when the wind turning suddenly round, drove us in here, where we were bound nineteen days. O! what a mercy of God! I have seen his wonders in the deep, and through his goodness have escaped the roaring waves. I yet cannot say I am sorry that I have come ; although I know not what awaits me on the shore : my trust is still in God, who has the hearts of all men in his hand.

27th. This morning I went on shore, having no proper recommendations with me. The captain said, "I wonder what the devil you are going to do here." I told him perhaps he might see before he left town.

As I entered the village, I inquired for Methodists, and a lad directed me to inquire for John Weares, a schoolmaster, and came to a house and met the man in the door. Said I, "Are there any that love God here or in town?" Said he, "My wife makes more ado about religion, than all the people in town ; come, walk in." I went in, but found him an enemy to truth.

In this place, for more than forty years no regular society could be established till a few days since, when nine women were joined in a class, one of whom kept a school, and sent me word that I might occupy her room for meeting. With much difficulty, through the goodness of God I got a few collected in the evening, to whom I spoke. A loyal woman after meeting scolded me because I did not pray for the king. I replied, that I came from a country where we had no king, and it was not natural for me ; so she excused me and invited me to breakfast. Noise began to be in town, "There is an American come." Accordingly the next day I gave a crown for a large ball-chamber, and put up a public notice, requesting all hands to turn out. Many came to see the babbler ; to whom I spoke, and then caught near the whole of them in a covenant : which the greater part, I suppose, broke that night.

God gave me favor in the sight of the people ; and I received invitations to breakfast, dinner, and supper, more than I needed during all my stay. The next evening, after preaching, said I to the people, " As many of you as will pray for yourselves twice in the twenty-four hours for two weeks, I will endeavor to remember you thrice, God being our helper: and you that will, come forward, that I may take your names in writing, lest that I forget."

A few came forward that night ; some more next day, and so on ; now and then serious countenances appeared in the streets : at length, one and another was telling what God had done for their souls. The congregations were very large. I had a desire to visit the adjacent country ; but no door opening, as no one might travel without a pass, the country being under martial law.

When I arrived at Larne, the captain said, " When I sailed from Quebec, you was so weak and low, that I never expected to bring you to land again : I thought I should give your body to the sharks ;"—" But now," said the mate, " you look ten pounds better." The inhabitants said, " We evidently perceive that since your coming here you have altered for the better every day : you are become quite another man than when we first saw you."

The first night after I came on shore, I went into my room, and was going to pull off the coverlet of the bed and spread it on the floor, according to my usual custom in America ; and behold the floor was earthen or ground, which I had never seen before. I felt amazed, to think what I should do : to sleep in a bed, thought I, I cannot ; to sleep on the ground, I shall be chilled and take a fever. At length I came to this resolution ; I'll go into bed with my clothes on, and if it comes to the worst, I'll get up: so I lay down, thinking it was more than probable I should have to rise within half an hour, on account of my asthma. I soon fell asleep, and slept sound until morning.

CHAPTER V.

MY DUBLIN RECEPTION.

DECEMBER 15th, after two days sail, I landed in Dublin. Having a letter, I sought to find him to whom it was directed; and a customhouse officer, for two-and-sixpence English, piloted me there—but in vain, he not being at home; and night coming on, I scarcely knew what to do, as the family would not suffer me to stay within, fearing who or what I might be. I inquired for Methodists; and a chaise-man said, "I know where there is one lives;" and for a shilling I got him to pilot me to the house.

After rapping, the door was opened by a boy, who informed the mistress that a stranger wanted her husband. She said, "Let him come in till he comes home:" so I went in, and sat down in the shop. By and by in came her husband, William Thomas, who stopped and looked, and then with a smile shook hands with me; which gave me some hope. After I told him my case, he invited me to tarry all night; which I accordingly did, and in the evening attended meeting at Gravel-walk, where I was called upon to pray.

The next day I called to see the preachers, and when I saw Mr. Tobias, made my case known to him. He heard me, and then with plain dealing advised me to go on board again and return to America, though he did not attempt to scruple the account I gave of myself. He offered me half a crown, which I refused, and with tears left him, though I had only *two* shillings left.

In the evening, at Whitefriar-street meeting-house, I was again invited to pray and sing; but Mr. Tobias, the preacher, on whom I had called, checked me in the meeting, and took the hymn out of my mouth, commanding the persons who prayed to stand on their feet; and after meeting gave me a sharp reprimand: and then called the local preachers and leaders into a room, and, I suppose, charged them, and reprimanded him who had invited me, as he ever after was shy to me.

Now my door seemed to be completely hedged up, and I saw nothing but death before me, having no money to pay my passage back, and did not know how to do ship-work, and no trade to follow for my bread, and I could not expect *this family* to entertain me long; no acquaintance round about, and three thousand miles from my friends. No one can tell my feelings but those who have been in the like circumstances. It was a trial of my faith, yet I could not say I was sorry that I had come; though it seemed to me I should sink. But these words strengthened my confidence, "The very hairs of your head are all numbered;" immediately I lay down and fell asleep, and dreamed that I saw a person put leaven in a bowl of meal; it leavened and leavened till it swelled clear over on the ground, then leavened under ground till it got a distance of some score rods, imperceptible by the inhabitants: at length it broke out in the furthermost place; and then appeared in several other spots. This dream strengthened my confidence in God, that my way was preparing, though imperceptible to me. When I awaked, my trials of mind we-e greatly lessened. I besought God if he had any thing for me to do n this country, to open a door and prepare my way; but if not, to take me to himself; for now I was only a burden to myself and others: and I did believe that one or the other he would grant.

20th. Whilst we were at family prayer, a Scotch soldier overheard us, and came in and invited me to preach in the barracks at Chapel-izod; which I did several times. Several other doors opening in different barracks, I improved the opportunities; one of which was at Island-bridge, where God began a revival, and a small society was formed. Having a desire to visit the country, at first the door appeared shut; but one, (who for a scruple of conscience had been expelled society,) upon hearing thereof, sent word to me that he was going to the Queen's County, and if I was minded to go, would bear my expenses.

26th. Taking the canal boat, we proceeded to Monastereven, whence we walked to Mount Mellick.

Here I found a man out of society, who had been abused, which occasioned the separation of about thirty, who held meetings by themselves. I held several meetings in different parts of the neighborhood, and refreshing seasons we had from the presence of the Lord. A quarterly meeting was held here. I petitioned for liberty to go into the love-feast, but was denied, saying, you belong to no particular people.

My congregations were so large that no private house could contain them, for which reason some got open the preaching-house doors, contrary to my advice, lest it should look as though I wanted to cause divisions, as the preacher had left strict orders not to let me in, &c.

Here I heard two women from my own country preach, called Quakers, for the first time of my hearing any of their society.

A question arose in my mind whether I had done wrong in coming away from my own country: Is it not possible that I lay under a mistake after all? Thus I fell asleep, and dreamed that I died, and was buried under a hearth; the lid which composed a part of the hearth was marble. My father coming into the room, said, "What is there?" One replied, 'Your son lies there." He then pulled off the lid, and, behold, it was truth. And I stood and looked at my body, and, behold, it began to putrefy and moulder. I was then a mystery to myself, to see my body in one place, and I standing in another. I began to feel, to see if I was flesh, when a voice seemed to answer, "I will explain the mystery to you. If you had tarried in America, you would have died as the prophet predicted, and your body would have been mouldering as you now see it: but you are now preserved for future usefulness." I waked up with the queries gone.

From hence (Mount Mellick) I returned to Dublin. I received two letters from the north, requesting me to return with all speed to Larne. I had received money enough from the withdrawn members to return.

After holding some more meetings in the barracks, and paying my passage, and procuring some provisions, (having two shillings left,) 1 set sail, but was put back by a contrary and tempestuous wind, after being out thirty hours.

I believe there was the peculiar hand of God in this, for a powerful time we had at Island-bridge the same evening.

January 20th, 1800. After walking some miles, I embarked again, and just as I was going on board, heard the shrieks of a woman, and turning round, saw a door shut t , and one weeping as if her heart would break. I asked the cause. She said she had three children at home, who had eaten nothing since yesterday, and that she had not a sixpence to buy bread for them, and this family would not lend a shilling, and that her husband would not receive his wages until Saturday night. There was a dialogue in my mind whether duty required me to relieve her want, as I reflected how much better my present circumstances were than hers. However, I did not leave her till I had given her one of the shillings I had left; and, oh, how grateful she appeared! The wind was not entirely fair; however, we put to sea. The storm increased, and the sea seemed to run mountains high, and washed several valuable things overboard; but what surprised me was, I never once heard the captain swear or take an oath during all the time.

On the twenty-second we gained Belfast harbor, and came to anchor within two miles of the town, where I jumped into the pilot's boat, and gave my remaining shilling to be taken ashore, and, through cold wind and rough sea, reached the town about six o'clock in the evening. I wandered up and down for some time, the way I felt my heart inclined,[*] till recollecting a letter I had in my pocket; but how to find the person to whom it was directed I did not know, but feeling my heart drawn up an alley, I went to the door and rapped. The people desired to know what I wanted. I told them, and they invited me to take tea, which favor I received as from the hand of God; then a lad piloted me to the house where I wished to go, where I found the mother of Sergeant Tipping, in whose room I preached at Island-bridge, he having sent by me a letter to her.

Here I had lodging, and continued a few days. I went to see the preacher, Andrew Hamilton, jr., to whom I related all my situation; and, after a little conversation, he gave me the right hand of fellowship, with liberty to improve round his circuit, so long as my conduct should be such as it had been at Larne. He could not be blamed for this precaution, for if I behaved bad he would be blamed. I told him I hoped he would not by me have cause to repent giving the liberty. He likewise gave me money to pay the passage of a letter to New York, to get justice to my character.

From thence to White Abbey, where I was questioned very close, and it was judged I did wrong in leaving America; but J. Morrison, whom I had seen at Larne, (the local preacher who formed the class, and questioned me very close, to know where I came from and was going to,) persuaded them to call an assembly, to whom I spoke.

Thence to Carrickfergus, (where a jailer apparently died and remained

---

[*] By the light of lamps, famine and death now stared me in the face in this large town, yet I could not say I was sorry I had left America.

for some hours, then revived again for some hours, and appeared to be in great horror.) and held several meetings; to these two places I had notes of introduction from a preacher.

Thence to Ballycarey, and held three meetings, which were very serious. From thence to Larne, which I gained about twelve o'clock. I took breakfast, and visited two or three families, and though my dress was somewhat altered, the people knew me, and were staring from their doors and windows.

I spent some more time about here, not altogether in vain. The society when I left it amounted to about sixty in number. Such a village as this I never met with before, for universal friendship to me, considering I was such a stranger.

One man, by the name of Martin, showed every possible kindness whilst I was confined by a breaking out, which was generally thought to be the small-pox.

One morning the shop door under the same roof was found wide open, though late in the evening the mistress had examined particularly, as was her constant custom, to see that it was locked and barred just before she retired to rest, and nothing was missing, though money and valuable articles were in it.

The man who said his wife made so much ado about religion, at first was unwilling to hear me preach, or even to pray in his family, being much given to jesting, &c.; but when sickness came upon him, he made vows to serve God, and sent for me to visit him, and a few hours before his departure found acceptance.

Isle of Magee. Here was no society. Many were the opposers to a free salvation, contending for reprobation, and blinding the people tnereoy. However, many tender minds of the youth appeared to be stirred to consideration during the few meetings I held among them.

In Strade and Cogray were a tender people. At Doe, the officer of the guard, taking the letter of the law, would suffer no meeting in the evening, so scores were disappointed. However, I held meeting in the morning, and several times afterwards, and the disappointment brought more out to hear, by which means I hope good was done.

One morning I went to the barracks, and found many of the soldiers round the card table, which seemed to dash them. I threw a pamphlet on the table, and walked off. These things so attracted their attention, that on a sabbath day the parade was omitted, that the men might come and hear me. The greatest part of the assembly were caught in a covenant to pray to God, but some were angry, and said I *swore* the people to be religious.

In Carley, the family had not notified the people according to expectation, fearing the martial law. However, they thought and said it was a pity I should lose my visit, and calling in the neighbors, we had a refreshing season. Some more meetings I held in this vicinity, and some good I hope was done. In Ballinure and at Bryantang we had comfortable seasons. At Kilwater the Lord has begun a good work. In Belleast:n church I spoke to the young people from, "Is it well with thee?" having walked fourteen miles and spoke four times.

Sunday, February 23d. I went fourteen miles, and preached four times. Many felt the word, and it was a happy day for me.

March 6th. A magistrate hailed me on the road, and said, "Where are you going?"
A. "To Larne."
Q. "Where did you come from?"
A. "Ballycarey."
Q. "What's your occupation?"
A. "I have got none."
Q. "Where do you belong?"
A. "Nowhere."
Q. "What, are you strolling about the country?"
A. "Yes, I have no particular place of residence."
Q. "Where's your pass?"
A. "I have got none."
Q. "Where was you born?"
A. "North America."
Q. "Well, to America you shall go again.—Come, go along with me to the guard-house."
Q. "What do you follow, and what did you come after?"
A. "I follow preaching, and come on account of my health; and Methodist preachers don't apply to magistrates for passes."
"Well," said he, (upon observing I could not walk fast, my feet being sore,) "if ever I see you this way again, I'll send you to prison." I replied, "You are at your option, and can do as you think proper." Then he put the whip to his horse and went on.

My mind has been much exercised of late, as though it would be my duty to travel the vineyard in other lands, and the time of my departure from about here, I believe, is nigh.

I feel the worth of souls near my heart, and as willing to spend and be spent in the ministerial work as ever. My trust is still in God; but oh! the hindrances of Zion!—stumbling-block professors, I fear, are the ruin of many souls.

When I feel an uncommon impression to do such and such things, if, when I resist them, it brings a burden, and if when I cherish them it brings love, I generally prosper in following it.

My soul is pained on Zion's account. The sores upon my feet grow worse, and I have no one who can sympathize with me in my singular state. Sunday, 16th. I preached in Larne, for the last time, from "Finally, brethren, farewell," &c., to many hundreds of people, and a melting season it was: hard to part with the young beginners; but the will of God be done.

On the 17th, contrary to the advice of my friends, I walked to Caron Castle. There I held some meetings, and there seemed a prospect of good. From thence to Glenarm and Canayla; here we had solemn seasons. Returning to Carrickfergus, I held several meetings; as when I left this place before, I put up a public notice, requesting the people to turn out when I should come again, and hear me, not as critics, but as sincere inquirers after truth. Word flew over the town, "The American's come, the American's come;" so I told them I would speak to the youth, which brought out a multitude. Then I said, "Invite out the deists, and I will preach to them." So the deists in town were invited personally, and came out. After several meetings, I felt myself clear from the place and went away. The power of God was sensibly felt here, and one soul, I trust, found religion, whom some months after I met in Dublin. From this, I infer that I ought not to be discouraged if the fruit of the word does not immediately appear.

April 1st. Quarterly meeting was held in Belfast, where I met several preachers who treated me with love and friendship, as much as I could expect in my situation. One's name was Wood. A woman at Newry, who had got her mind prejudiced, had said, "God has forsaken the Methodists, and will bless them no more, and the Evangelical society have got the crown." Wood said, "God has not forsaken them, but will bless them again, and twenty souls will be converted before Saturday night." And how he came to speak these words, he could not tell. It was the beginning of the week, and no visible appearance of a revival, until the next evening, when some were awakened powerfully, and just twenty before sunset on Saturday professed to receive remission of sins; and some hundreds were shortly taken into society.

I walked to Antrim, and held a few meetings that were solemn and tender, and returned to Belfast. Round this place I had some meetings in the streets, for which I was sent to prison. But A. Hamilton said to the officer, "Preaching in the streets is a privilege allowed us by government, and they will give you no thanks for your loyalty in sending this young man to prison; for he seeks to do no harm, if he can do no good." I got a good opportunity to speak to the prisoners by this means, and shortly was let out. I bless God for this singular event, for it brought more people out to meeting.

Feeling my spirit inclined to the south, I bought a passage. These words were running through my mind, "and the waters assuaged." I told the people I believed we should have a rough passage. Some advised me not to go; but feeling my work done here, I set forward on Friday, 11th. On Saturday night the wind began to blow, and the waves to toss the vessel, which drove the captain and hands to their Romish duties, as they got affrighted.

The wind drove us into Ramsay bay, in the Isle of Man; and we anchored about a mile from land. The waves being high, I did not venture on shore for several days.

The sailors ate up my provisions whilst I slept, and their provisions my weak stomach could not endure; so for more than eighty hours I did not break my fast, except with cold water, and I despaired of life.

The wind and storm increased. A schooner near us slipped her cable and drove off towards Scotland. Our captain, the night following, got terrified, as did all the hands and passengers; but my mind was calmly composed and stayed on God.

The captain had thoughts of running the vessel on shore to the mercy of God. But at length the day broke. A signal of distress was hoisted, and a boat came from shore and towed the vessel to the quay, and I went on shore to get something to eat, having but one sixpence with me. And after much difficulty I found a Methodist boardinghouse, and made known my situation to them, who gave me some food: and eating rather hearty in my weak state, it seemed to give me much pain. Here also I obtained a lodging for the night. My soul was melted to tenderness under a sense of the Divine goodness, in turning my present captivity. The next day a preacher came to town, to whom I made known my situation; and God gave me favor in his sight.

The preaching-house doors were opened to me, where some hundreds of people came to hear me the first night; and conditionally if the vessel id not sail, I intended to speak the next.

The vessel attempted to sail out unknown to me, but broke her anchor against the quay, which detained her another tide; so I fulfilled the meeting and did not lose my passage. The captain said I was either a witch, or a wizard, or a devil, or something, and if it had not been for me, he would have had a good passage, and before he would take me again, I should pay five pounds. He and the crew came to hear me preach.

I visited about twenty families, which times were tender indeed. The disposition of the inhabitants seemed exceedingly hospitable. They were minded I should tarry for some weeks; but not prevailing, gave me the necessaries for my passage; so we set sail for Dublin.

I did not regret all my sufferings, considering the good times we had in this place.

The night before I got on shore, (whilst the waves were running over the deck, every now and then the water coming into the forecastle where I was, which made me wet and chilled,) I dreamed that I got on shore, and held two meetings. This I related to the people before I held the first meeting.

After a passage of forty-eight hours, I landed in Dublin, and was glad to escape the sailors, who twice threw me across the cabin.

I went to my old lodgings at W. Thomas's, where I continued twelve days, to let my feet grow a little better; but the same shyness still appeared among the Methodists.

During this stay was held the Quaker yearly meeting. Several meetings I attended, and found it not altogether unprofitable.

Here I saw one, who when hearing I was sick in the north, sent something for my relief, and here gave me more to bear my expenses.

May 6th. I took the canal boat for Monastereven, where I tarried a few days, and the edge of prejudice seemed to be removed in general; and some refreshing meetings we had, though the preaching-house was shut against me by strict orders from the preachers. The class-leader said, "I believe you mean well, but did wrong in coming away without liberty; for which reason these *afflictions* in body, &c. pursue you; but if you are faithful, will at last work for your good."

A door being opened, I rode three miles and held four agreeable meetings.

A man carried me to Knightstown, near Mount Mellick, as my feet were so sore I could not walk; my hands likewise so swelled, that I could neither dress nor undress myself: so I tarried with T. Gill for several days, holding meetings in the evenings, the fruit of which I expect to see in the day of eternity. Thence I rode to Maryborough, where I found kind friends, and held four meetings. Thence to Mount Mellick, where we had some refreshing times. Then I hobbled along about two miles to T. Gill's, and spent a little time more. My trials concerning my singular state, and the exercise of faith God calls me to, and to see so little fruit of my labor, and the cause of God so wounded by ministers and professors of all denominations, made me wish to retire to some lonely part of the earth, and weep and mourn out my days. But I cannot feel myself released from the important duty of sounding the gospel trumpet; from which, if I had the riches of the Indies, I would have given them for a release: but in vain were my thoughts. I sometimes thought I knew the feelings of Moses, in some small degree, with Jeremiah and Jonah; but not long after I found the Lord to breathe into my soul the spirit of my station: I felt resigned; my discouragement subsided, and I was filled with holy resolutions to go forward in the name of, and relying on God alone. O God! keep me as in the hollow of thy hand, meek and patient, strong in faith, and clean from the stain of sin.

Taking my farewell leave of the people, I set out for Hall, near Moat, as a Quaker had invited me at the yearly meeting. Here I tarried several days, and experienced much kindness, and I improved the time in reading their books, with the journal of George Fox,* which I long had a desire to see, but never had an opportunity until now. Oh! how are this dear people degenerated from the state of their forefathers! I spoke a few words in one of their meetings, for which I got a gentle reproof. I rode to Athlone, and sent a man through the town to notify the people.

I soon had a considerable congregation collected in the session-house, where many were melted to tenderness. I believe much good might be done here, if the gospel was faithfully preached; but I must go to another place: here the Methodists looked upon me shy. In Moat I held two meetings, and had out, as I was told, some scores of Quakers.

Thence I rode on a car to Tullamore, where I found prejudice had been imbibed by the people. Hence I walked with much pain to Mount Mellick, and rested two days. Thence to Mountrath, where we had several comfortable meetings.

As I lay on the bed, a preacher came in and looked, and went out and inquired, and came in again, and calling me brother, shook me by the hand. I questioned him as to his mind about my leaving America, and having a meeting appointed in his preaching-house; said he, "It is hard to judge in a case where it comes down on a man's conscience." So he parted with me in love, saying, "I cannot encourage you according to discipline; and so I will let you alone, &c. But brother Averill told me if saw you, to bid you call on him."†

About this time the following ideas came into my mind. 1st. About the plain language, so called: first, grammar—second, Bible—third, Christianity teaches us plainness and not superfluity. 2d. That no man has a right to preach except God call him to it by his Spirit; and though words be ever so good in and of themselves, yet unless attended by the power of God to the heart, will not profit; therefore it must be delivered in the power and demonstration of the Spirit to be useful; and likeness will beget likeness, and a stream cannot rise higher than the fountain; therefore what is not done in the Spirit cannot please God; consequently we must be subject to the Spirit, passive and active: passive, having no

---

* In meetings with the world's people he generally spoke · though silent at times in silent meetings.

† He travelled at large by the consent of the conference.

will of our own, but what is conformed and swallowed up in the will of God: active to do what God requireth of us, &c.

As past experience is like past food, the present enjoyment of the love of God, is what makes the soul happy. Therefore there is a necessity of momentary watching and constant prayer; to have our minds uplifted, drawn out after and solely stayed on God; and to have one fixed resolution in all things, to please, and know, and enjoy God: and accordingly begin, spend, and close every day with him. And in order to do this, we must have the agency of the Spirit; its strivings and assistance; but can we have this at all times at our disposal? To command the Spirit we cannot: this is the free unmerited gift of God. Yet as he gives it freely, and as the Spirit is never found wanting to convince considerate minds and make them serious and solemn; and as the scriptures command a steady acting, walking, and striving; and saith "eth" the present tense, (and yet requires no impossibilities,) I therefore conclude we may sensibly feel the Spirit continually; and the fault must be on the creature's side, if we do not, &c.

But can a man have the Spirit to preach and pray, when and where he will? It appears the apostles could not work miracles when and where they pleased: and in order that souls may be quickened, the word must be attended by the same power and Spirit, though in a different calling; consequently we must be under its influence, direction, and impression. But how shall we know the light and Spirit of God from that of the devil?

1st. There is no true, solid, lasting peace but in the knowing and enjoyment of God: and the calls of the Spirit of God bring tenderness and solemnity; and in following them there is great peace and content in the mind, which affords a joy or happiness that is very sweet and full of love: it draws them more after God, and they have greater affection for the future happiness of God's creatures; and to resist the Spirit of God's calls, brings, 1st, depression and burden, and, if persisted in, darkness and condemnation will come and overshadow the mind, and the tender place will become hard; and great bitterness and unhappiness will fill the mind: and as it is God's will and delight to make us happy, it is our duty to follow the leadings which give true content and solid joy to the inquiring mind: and they that do not, sin against God, and wrong themselves. As for a person's having the discerning power positively to know the state of the people, I know not; but God knoweth the state and hearts of all; and his Spirit may influence and impress a person's mind to such and such discourses, or to speak to such and such states or cases of men, though we may not know the particular object; and as there is no particular form of church worship or government pointed out in the scripture, I therefore have no right to stick down a stake, and tie all preachers to that particular form, mode, or rule in public meetings: for what is one's meat is another's poison. In some cases among men, there is no general rule without an exception to it; what will be suitable at one time, will not always do at another: therefore we are daily to inquire the will of God, and to follow the leading of God's Spirit.

When God is about to make use of an instrument to some work, a little previous he frequently permits them to pass through great buffetings of Satan, and deep trials of mind. Trials denote good days; and good days denote trials at hand; but the darkest hour is just before the break of day.

With regard to asking a blessing, either vocal or in silence, or rather giving of thanks, previous to eating, it is scriptural: but after, appears to be the addition of men; except it be inferred from the writings of Moses.

Water baptism I have seen God acknowledge, by displaying his power, whilst the ceremony was administered in sprinkling, plunging, and pouring: but as Paul said God had not sent him to baptize, but to preach, so say I.

With regard to bread and wine, God has blessed my soul in the use of them, when I looked through the means to the end. But ceremonies others contend enough about; and all I have to do is to save souls. If I could feel my mind released, oh! how soon would I retire to my father's house, or to some retired place, and spend my days; but I feel wo is me, if I preach not the gospel. Some can go or stop, just as man directs; and preach, and have no seals of their ministry from year to year, and yet feel contented and think all is well; but how they get along with it is unknown to me. But some I believe God accepts as Christians, but not as preachers.

My mind is pained to see so many resting in means short of the power; and others so closely attached to particular forms. Oh! my bowels yearn over the different denominations; my soul mourns before God on Zion's account. I am willing to spend and be spent in the vineyard of the Lord; but I know in vain I labor except God's Spirit attend the word and work.

I believe God intends and will lead me by the still waters, in a way I have not fully known; and trials at hand I believe await me, and afterwards I trust God will bless my labors.

From Mountrath I called upon Mr. Averill, on my way to Donoughmore. With him I had an agreeable conversation. Said he, "I believe you are sincere, but lie under a powerful temptation in coming away from America." He gave me the liberty of his pulpit; from which I spoke to the people, and a refreshing time we had. In Donoughmore likewise, at two meetings. From hence to Durrow, where we had two meetings, and I received a kind reception, though a stranger. Thence I walked to Kilkenny; my feet being bad, I was detained here for several days, during which time I had a number of meetings; the latter of which were very refreshing, and one soul I since hear has been brought to good. Here a stranger sent a horse with me twelve miles to Innisteague. Thence I walked to Ross. Here a Quaker lived who had invited me from the yearly meetings; I spent near a week at his house, perusing some books which I found profitable.

I once went into a prayer-meeting in the Methodist chapel, and they gave me the hymn-book, which I took as providential; for I was impressed to speak concerning the dealings of God with me, though I sang not. Thus God opens my door step by step. The next morning I set out on my way some distance; the further I went, the more depressed I felt, and the more impressed to return; and for peace of mind through necessity I went back, and requested permission in the preaching-house to call the people.

After they had considerable talk among themselves, and some with me, they opened the door; at first, the discipline seemed to hinder, and then they durst not deny.

The commanding officer of the town, with many of the quality and commonalty, filled the meeting-house, to whom I spoke an hour or more; this was a refreshing time, and not soon to be forgotten.

Very early the next morning feeling my mind free of this place, I set out for Enniscorthy, and found an opportunity to ride on a car, which greatly eased my feet.

I spoke a few words in the Methodist meeting, and at night put up with a Quaker, in whose house I spoke to a number of his servants. Thence I walked to Carnew. I here was received as a friend by a Methodist supernumerary preacher, who gave me the right hand of fellowship; and in his house I had some meetings. Attempting to ride on a car from thence, I had not gone far before I was overtaken with an express from the widow Leonard, who wished to see me. Here I called another meeting, which was tender. Thence I walked to Gorey, where I spoke to a few hundreds, and a solemn time it was.

From thence to Eicon, holding one meeting on the way, and two here, which were times not soon to be forgotten.

Thence to Rathdrum: here I spoke to a few, among whom was the preacher who had shut me out of the love-feast at Mount Mellick. Here he pretended some friendship, with color in his face.

Thence to Wicklow, where Cooper preached, and then a Methodist: after which I was permitted. But some gentry being here, they could not bear the truth.

From thence I came to Dublin about the fifteenth of July. Here I met Doctor Coke, who had just returned from America. By him I received a letter from my dear friend J. Mitchell, who was so unwilling that I should come away; and also another from R. Searle. These gave me some refreshment. About this time I received a letter from my parents and sister; which gave me comfort to hear my parents were well, and my sister still endured.

Dr. Coke requested me to go a missionary to Halifax or Quebec: and upon conditions that I would promise obedience to what he should direct, for six years, he would bear my expenses; and I should want nothing of books, clothing, &c. Having twenty-four hours' consideration, I weighed the matter, and returned my answer in the negative; as in tender conscience I durst not leave the kingdom yet, believing it the will of God I should stay. At which time tears flowed plentifully, and it seemed as if my head was a fountain of waters. The doctor grasped me in his arms, gave me a hug, and went his way.

At the time he made me the proposal, (whilst we sat at breakfast,) one preacher came and sat down by my side, and said, "What do you desire or request of the conference that they should do for you?" I replied, (supposing him to be my friend,) nothing; only that the preachers should not speak against me, to blacken my character; whereby to prejudice people against me, to hedge up my way, and hurt my usefulness. He then removed to the opposite side of the table, and said, "If he attempts to travel in the name of a Methodist and preach in the streets, the mob will be upon him; and if they once begin, they will attack every preacher that comes along, and fall on our Irish missionaries next: and if they begin, it will be hard to stop them; and government will immediately conclude we are at the head of these disturbances, or the occasion of them ; by which means they will deem us enemies, and take away some of our privileges. Whereas," said the doctor, "there was never such a thing known, when in the midst of external and internal wars and commotions, that preachers were permitted to travel and hold meetings as often as they pleased." He then added, " I don't know but your travelling about may do more harm than the conversion of five hundred souls may do good ; take it upon all accounts, I can't say but I shall be under the necessity of writing to Lord Castlereagh, to inform him who and what you are ; that we disown you, &c. : then you'll be arrested and committed to prison, and if you once get in jail, it will be hard to get out."

These things were mentioned for my consideration, during the above-mentioned twenty-four hours.

But the impression upon my mind was so strong to tarry, that if government had threatened to send me to prison in irons, as yet I durst not consent to go.

After this, it was talked over in conference, and agreed that the connection should show me no countenance, but disapprobation, which they requested the doctor to tell me, though he never did his errand ; but Tobias, upon finding out his mission, took upon himself to do it, without being appointed ; and forbid me coming to Waterford (where he was stationed) among the Methodists, or to the meeting-house, and if I did, he would preach against me in public and in private. Upon this, several of the preachers who were friendly in their hearts, durst not show it outwardly, &c.

Now, according to appearance, my way was hedged up all around. My trials were keen ; but God was my support, in whom I put my trust, believing he would pave my way step by step.

About this time I had a short sketch of the general run of my experience committed to the press, in order to give away for the benefit of mankind—it contained about twenty small pages, the edition was near three thousand—none of which I sold ; but sent some of them to different parts of the country.

CHAPTER VI.

SMALL-POX CONFINEMENT.

I TOOK a walk out of town, in order to preach to a garrison ; but could not get them together ; so I gave them some pamphlets, and set out to return ; and on my way from the pigeon-house I was suddenly taken unwell, and thought I should have died on the spot ; and staggering along I got into Ringsend ; when after some little refreshment in a grocer's shop, I gained some strength, and visited a couple of prisons, and got to my lodgings. This was the first Lord's day in August. I took tea with the family, and retired to my chamber, where I was confined about thirty-two days, without the sight of the sun.

In the beginning of this confinement, it was thought I had the measles, but an apothecary being called in, on examining closely, he said the eruption was too prominent for this, and therefore it must be something else, perhaps the small-pox. So my friends halted between two opinions, scarcely knowing what to do—I being unwilling to have any physician who had not the fear of God before his eyes; knowing I had suffered so much from them, with very little good.

But a Quaker woman, who heard of me, came to see me, and said, "I wish he was in the care of Doctor Johnson, and I should feel my mind easy." I, upon hearing the words, made some inquiry concerning the man, and consented he should come; and being sent for, he came without delay, as he had heard of me just before, and was considering in his mind whether he should come of his own accord and offer me his assistance.

My eyes at this time were entirely closed, and continued so about a fortnight; and for about ten days nothing passed through my bowels.

Here I despaired of life, and expected to die: but the Lord was precious to my soul as ever. Three things I desired to live for, which were :—

1st. I wanted to attain higher degrees of holiness, that I might be happier hereafter.

2d. I felt the worth of souls, and an anxious desire to be useful to them.

3d. My parents I wished to see once more in this world, lest when they heard of my death, it would bring them to the grave with sorrow. But at length I was enabled to give them up, and leave them in the hand of God to protect and support.

What I wished to die for was, to get out of this troublesome world and to be at rest with saints above. Yet I felt resigned to go or stay, as God should see fit; sensibly feeling the presence of God and reading my title clear to the mansions of glory. The very sting of death was gone; so that it appeared no more to me to die, than to fall asleep and take a nap.

During this time, there was something whispering in my mind, as though this sickness, by the will and wisdom of God, came, and would turn to his glory in this world, and yet I must travel other countries to preach the gospel; but the possibility of it seemed so contrary to human appearance, that I did not give much heed to the whispering voice; but my soul was happy all the time.

Some thought it strange that I did not speak more than I did about religion; but I feeling my mind weak, and my thoughts sometimes to wander, was fearful lest I should speak amiss, and thereby perhaps hurt tender minds, as some had already said that I was better in my heart than in my head. After twenty-two days thus passing away, hope began to spring up in my mind that I should recover, and yet labor in the vineyard of the Lord.

The physician, Dr. Johnson, had attended me faithfully from the time he first came; sitting up with me about ten whole nights, and visiting me repeatedly through the day; and as soon as he thought I was able, had me carried in a sedan chair to his own house, though he was neither in membership with the Quakers nor Methodists.

Here I continued seven weeks. I think for about twelve days after I came, the blood would gush out of my sores upon attempting to rest the weight of my body upon my limbs; but upon the forty-fourth day of my sickness, I attempted to venture out with help. During this space of time God gave me favor in the sight of the people, though a stranger in this land, and having but one guinea when I was first taken ill, yet I wanted for nothing during the whole time.

Oh! how different are the dealings of man to me now from those in America, when confined with the bilious fever! Surely there must be the hand of God in this. He let me know what it is to want and to abound, that I might feel my weakness and dependence, and prize my privilege by feeling for my fellow-mortals, and improve my time for eternity.

I think of all the people I have met with for four years and seven months' travel, this doctor has showed me the greatest kindness and friendship, for which may God reward him in the day of eternity!

After some little recovery, feeling a desire to do good, I asked for Whitefriar-street preaching-house, but was denied. Then for Lady Huntingdon's society meeting-house in Plunket-street, but could not get it. Then I applied to the Quaker society, but they could not, consistent with their religious principles; yet they behaved very kind and friendly to me. Then I sought for a play-house in vain. Thus my way seemed to be hedged up.

The first place that presented to view was the Weavers' Hall, on the Coombe, in the Liberty, which was occupied by the Separate Methodists, by some called Kilhamites, but by themselves, the New Connection. Here I held several meetings. Some laughed, others stared, but in general were solemn and quiet, and some were melted to tenderness. I formed a covenant in one of these meetings, which appeared not altogether fruitless. In their meetings, also, I had liberty to speak what I felt.

About this time I received a letter from S. Hutchinson, dated New York, July twenty-first, in which I found he was now reconciled to my coming, and sent my character to this country, to A. Hamilton, doing me justice; which letter I showed to one of the stationed preachers, and had my character read in a public assembly, to let people know what I was, as many had been scrupulous concerning me.

At length, recovering my health to such a degree, I had thoughts of leaving Dublin and going to the country, but could not feel my mind free, until I first had visited several prisons, and held a meeting at the doctor's house.

October 16. I was twenty-three years old; the prophet's prediction was fresh in my mind, not only the year past, but now. What is past and gone, I know; but what is to come, I leave the event to God, believing he who hath preserved me and brought me through the mountains or waves of affliction and trials, will still be with me, and grant me strength in proportion to my day, if I cleave to him with all my heart, and have but the one thing in view, viz., the glory of God and the salvation of immortal souls.

18th. I have held a few meetings of late in Chapel-izod, which seem not to be altogether in vain.

On the 19th I held my last there, and at the Coombe.

On the 20th I visited several prisons, holding meetings with the prisoners, and gave them some bread and books; and called some of the most serious and decent of the neighborhood into the doctor's house at even, to whom I spoke about an hour, and all was solemn and quiet; so for the present I feel my mind released to go and visit the country. What is before me, I know not; I expect trials and hardships in the way; but as soon as I can find my mind released and free, and the door open, I intend to return to my own country.

22d. In company with my doctor I went to Rathcool, but the woman of the house who had invited me being absent, I met with a cool reception; however, I spoke to a few, and with grief went to Leixlip, where I had been invited, but the family holding some different sentiment, my situation here was trying too.

At Lucan I was disappointed, and then began to grow discouraged, querying in my own mind whether the preachers were not right, and I under a mistake. Whilst spending some time solitarily and walking the floor, I besought God, if he would make my journey prosperous, and give me favor in the sight of the people, to give me a token for good; and upon this I lay down to rest, and soon fell asleep, and dreamed I was walking up a river's side through a smooth plain, and began to feel faint and weary, and meditated what I should do for refreshment; and suddenly coming to the door of a cottage which was open, I saw the table spread, and as I rapped, the mistress came, and grasping me by the hand, gave me a hearty welcome, to my astonishment. Said I, "How do you know me?" Said she, "Our little Jemmey (as I thought a boy about twelve years old) dreamed last night that God sent two angels to us, clothed in white, with a message to entertain a traveller, with such and such a dress and features, who should come in the afternoon, and you answer the very description; therefore you are welcome." I then looked, and, behold, my robe was white, fine, unspotted linen; and oh, how joyful I felt, to think that angels were sent to prepare my way! I then awaked, with my mind solemnly stayed on God, and my spirits refreshed to pursue the journey.

Taking the canal boat at Hazelhatch, I went to Athy, and on the way the passengers solicited me hard to play cards. I replied, "I will play one game when you have done, but must have the captain's consent." They then looked and laughed, and played on, now and then turning a joke on me.

I gave one of my pamphlets to the captain, and in the evening, as soon as the gaming was over, after they had done playing, I offered to buy the cards. The captain replied, "I don't sell cards, but will give them to you." I thanked him, and played my game by throwing them out at the window into the canal. The company seemed to be thunderstruck and conscience-convicted, and their merriment was soon over. Solemnity seemed to rest on every countenance; they now and then forced out a word, as though they took my conduct as an imposition; but in a manner they seemed dumb or confounded. But I felt justified in my conduct.

In Athy I met with a kind reception, and had the liberty of a chapel which was not the Methodists'. I held two meetings, but the curate thought I was for party, as I preached up free salvation, he knowing it was a controverted point, and at first would not consent for a third meeting, till reviewing the matter, he would take no denial but I should hold a third. These meetings were quickening.

Thence to Carlow, where I held three meetings. Here I was troubled with the asthma, for the first time to prevent my rest since I came into this country. Thus I perceive the seeds of death are in my body, which if I am not faithful, I expect will carry me suddenly hence.

I walked to Hacketstown through the rain, thirteen long Irish miles. I inquired for swaddlers, (for if I asked for Methodists, the Romans there would immediately direct me to the worst enemy they had, through an evil spirit,) and was directed to a house, (not a member, but a hearer,) and asked for liberty to tarry all night, as I could not hear of a man who had invited me to come previously. The woman said, "If you will accept of some straw, you may stay;" which I thanked her for, as I felt so weary I scarcely knew how to walk any further. But the man, perceiving my thoughts of tarrying, objected. I then rummaged my papers, and found a few lines to a man out of town, who was not in a capacity to entertain travellers; so I walked to his father's, (being piloted by a lad, who returned immediately,) about half a mile, and came to the door and rapped. The family were unwilling to let me in, as several persons the night before had been robbed, and house robberies were frequent in that quarter. I now was called to an exercise of my faith, as there were several dogs to guard the house without, and apparently I should not be let in, as they questioned me back and forth through the door, with entreaties to go to a tavern; yet they recollected none near, but what was filled with soldiers. At length the old man, who was the only Methodist in the house, whilst sitting in the corner, felt these words run through his mind (as I was about to go and take up my lodgings on the bank of a ditch) repeatedly with power: "Be not forgetful to entertain strangers, for thereby some have entertained angels unawares." He began to grow restless and uneasy, and finally prevailed on the family to open the door and see who and what I was. As I came in, I saw fear in their countenances, and began to sing an American hymn, and talk with them about their souls, and soon it was gone. The old man says, "I think I have heard of you before from Mount Mellick." They entertained me all night. As I was going away in the morning, the old man said, "Will you not hold a meeting?" I said, "If you will get the people convened." During the day two daughters were following the new fashions; observing the superfluities they were fixing on some new clothes, I said, "Every time you wear them, remember another suit you'll have—the muffler and the winding-sheet,"- which seemed to sink in their minds; and since, I have had the satisfaction to hear (several ways) these young women were found walking in the ways of wisdom.

In all I had four meetings here. In Tinnehely I had two in a house and one in the street. In Killiveany we had several refreshing seasons. At Rednah we had two powerful meetings. At Roundwood we had two likewise. At Castle Cavan the people were hard, but I hope some good was done. At Echon I fell in with Mr. Matthew Lanktree, who I expected would treat me with coldness, considering what had passed at conference, but was agreeably disappointed.

He gave me liberty to travel on his circuit as long as I pleased. He, I think, is one of the holiest men I have met with in Ireland. He strove to persuade me to accept from him a razor, which something within had in times past prevented me from using, and forbid it still, as it was a guard, sentry, or watch to remind me of my duty, and that if ever I fell away to become a backslider, properly speaking, I should never be re-claimed.

Arklow had lain with some weight on my mind for several weeks: I accordingly paid it a visit. No Methodist being in the town, I knew not where to go; but God put it into the heart of a man to open his ball-chamber, in which I held several meetings, which were very tender. A man who had opened a malt-house to other missionaries, denied it to me.

On my way to Carnew, a preacher who had treated me with coolness at Ross, and had some trying reflections for it, took me upon his horse, and he himself walked six miles. He now gave me the right hand of fellowship, and I spoke for him at night.

Here lives a widow who was strangely preserved in the rebellion; she is liberal, 1st, in sentiment—2d, in alms—3d, in plain dealing. She has built a large preaching-room, which is open to all; is prudent in temporal and external matters, and in religious things, sees men as trees walking.

Here some blamed me for not being more cheerful, and take a glass of wine, and dress more ministerial, &c. But there is a certain something within, which is tender, and to grieve or go contrary to it, pains me, and I know not but condemnation might follow if I persisted in going contrary to its dictates. Here I had several refreshing seasons. A few days since, as I was credibly informed, there was heavenly melodious music heard, from whence could not be ascertained: and at the same time a young woman died happy.

At Castletown, Arklow-rock, Ballymurtah, Minerrock, and Sally-mount, we had melting times. In Wicklow, two solemn meetings. In Gorey, I held three in a house, and one in the street. The chief commanding officer, as the sergeant said, was coming to stop me; and when within a few yards turned and went off muttering.

At Clough, I had one meeting. In Ballycanew, two. Clinganny, one. Ballymore, one. Ferns, two. Newtonbarry, four, and one in its vicinity, which was quickening.

At Enniscorty, after holding two meetings, I went out of town on my way, but going burdened and distressed, returned back and held two more for the ease and enjoyment of my mind.

I went on Vinegar Hill, and took a view of the place where much blood was shed on account of religion. Oh! when will the time come, when the earth shall be of one heart and of one mind, and the nations learn to war no more. Many who say they are enlightened, being still in darkness, rest contented, and fight for the form of religion, but know not the power nor the purity of it.

At Wexford, I met M. Lanktree again; I told him he must prepare for a scolding at the next conference, provided he gave me such liberties. He replied, "I dare not oppose you. 'Tis evident God is with you; and I look upon your coming here as providential, and so does my wife, as she has found it a blessing to her soul; and I entreat you to tarry longer on the circuit;" and as we were about to part, to see each other no more, as we supposed, he could hardly refrain from weeping.

I held three meetings here, and one at the barony of Forth, which was the most refreshing I had seen for some time.

On my way to Ross, I saw one sitting by the way-side, reading the Bible, to whom I gave a pamphlet.

As I called at a tavern to refresh, I found a young man under some convincement. I conversed plainly with him, though a stranger, and gave him a pamphlet.

At Ross, I held three meetings, and some said I was Quakerized; others said I was too much of a Methodist, and some that I was a mystic.

From thence I set off for Waterford, where M. Tobias was stationed, as this place lay upon my mind for several weeks. I was now called to a trial of my faith, as I did not expect one Methodist in the place would receive me. But this afforded me some comfort, that I could appeal to the Searcher of hearts. I had no other end in view than to do his will, believing it my duty to go.

Having a letter to a class-leader which was not particularly directed as to his residence, I inquired for the man. One said, he lived in one street; another said, in another. Thus I wandered up and down the town for some time, and suddenly I discovered a man: a thought arose, that man won't lie; I ran to him and showed the letter. Said he, "Do you think I know the man?" I told him I wanted information. He asked me several questions, and piloted me to the door. The man of the house read the letter, and after tea, took me to the preacher's house to hear what he would say; and behold it was the man I had seen in the street, Zechariah Worrel.

He gave me the right hand of fellowship. I told him to look out what he did, lest others should blame him. I spoke at night, and on sabbath morning too; but at night he durst not give me the liberty, as then was the great congregation. On Monday evening, through the intercession of the leaders, I held a third meeting, and appointed for the fourth. The house was well filled, and in the congregation were several Quakers. There was a considerable movement among the people.

The next morning, I held my last meeting; the class-leaders, of their own accord, gave me a recommendation; first, that they believed I preached the gospel as held by the Methodists; and second, that my labors were blessed to the people.

Here I had several valuable articles of clothing and money offered to me, which I refused; however, about eleven shillings were forced on me. I visited several backsliders and quitted the place.

In Pilltown we had a shaking time; here I pasted up some printed rules for holy living, in the streets; as I had done some written ones in several other places.

To Carrick-on-Suir, I had several letters, which paved my way to getting the preaching-house; in which I had five meetings that were tender. The chief person of the society, when I first came here, was absent: but on coming home, offered me two shirts and some money, which I refused. Said he, " It argues a sound heart, but a weak head; and if I had been at home when you first came, I would not have given you the preaching-house, as that would have been an encouragement to impostors; but you might have preached in my private house as often as you pleased." I had several other things offered by other persons also, which I refused and went to Clonmel; having about five hundred papers printed—*rules for holy living*. Here I got the preaching-house, likewise; which some previously said, I would not get: however, the congregations were larger than had been known for many months; and the power of God was sensibly present.

Earnest entreaties were made for my tarrying longer; but feeling my mind free, after holding three meetings, and after pasting up some rules, I quitted the town.

I had accepted a small note and two shillings, but feeling burdened in my mind, gave up the former to the person.

At night, I put up with a Roman Catholic, at Capperquin, which took all the money I had, amounting to 2s. 6d. English.

On my way to Tallow, a magistrate overtook me.

Q. "What have you got in your bundle?"
A. "Papers."
Q. "What papers?"
A. "Rules for Holy Living."
Q. "Where did you sleep last night?"
A. "Capperquin."
Q. "You made good speed this morning. Where was you born?"
A. "North America."
Q. "What did you come here after?"
A. "Partly on account of my health, and partly by an impression on my mind, believing it to be the will of God."
Q. "What do you do here?"
A. "I strive to persuade people to serve God."
"Well," said he, "that is a good practice; but d you meet with much success?" I replied, "I am striving to do what I can; but it is the Spirit of God that must accomplish the work." He then proposed several of the questions again and again, with some others, I suppose, to see if I would contradict myself. I then gave him a paper and a pamphlet, and told him if he wanted further information, to search me.

He said, "There are many who go about to stir up the minds of the lower class," (alluding to politics, riot, and rebellion,) "but my mind is satisfied concerning you," and so he rode on.

In Tallow I held two meetings, the house being opened to me; but now I had another trial, my feet being so sore, apparently I could walk no further. But a man who was going my road, took me up before him on a horse, and carried me six miles: and another man afterwards let me get upon his car now and then; and now and then I would hobble along a spell. So I got to Cork late in the evening, and having a letter to a man, I was provided with food and lodging.

Next day I went to see the assistant preacher, who was also chairman of the district. Said I, "What privilege will you grant me?" Said he, "Go away and come at such an hour and I will tell you;" which I did. Said he, "I have talked with some of our most respectable friends, who think it not proper to give you any encouragement, as it would be too great encouragement to impostors; and we think you to be out of your sphere. "But," said I, "suppose I hold meetings in town, not to intrude upon your meeting hours, nor yet say any thing against you, neither lay down contrary doctrines?" Said he, "It will be taken as opposition, if you hold any meetings anywhere at any time here." So I parted with him, this being Saturday evening.

Sabbath morning I heard one preach, and then took breakfast with a Quaker, who treated me cool enough. I attended their meeting, and then by an impression upon my mind took upwards of a hundred of my hand-bills, or printed rules, and went through the town distributing them to the gentry, and heard a preacher at night. The next morning, feeling the want of some money, I attempted to sell my watch, but could find none that would buy it. At length I went into another watchmaker's, who looked at me and said, "Tell me your cheapest price." I said, "A guinea," it being not half the value. He asked me what countryman I was. burst out a crying; he then gave me a breakfast, a guinea, and a shilling. He asked then my religion; and I gave him a pamphlet and paper; and then requested a guide out of town, to whom I gave half the guinea, with orders to carry it to the man who had provided my bed and board, as he had a wife and three others of his family sick at that time.

In the night, I arrived at Bandon, and inquired for Methodists. The woman said, "What do you want with them?" A. "To tarry all night." Q. "Are there any near?" A. "There is one near you." Q. "Did you ever hear of an American in this country?" A. "What is he doing?" A. "Wandering up and down striving to do good, and he has had the small-pox of late." Q. "Are you he?" A. "Yes. Come, walk in." I felt thankful to God that he had provided me lodging for the night, &c.

Next day I went to see the preachers, one of whom treated me rather cool. The other said, "I can give you no encouragement, and I will give you no opposition; I am willing you should go round the circuit and do all the good you can." From this, I perceived that he felt more love in his heart than he durst show out. But in a dream of the night, my mind was so impressed, that I quitted the town early in the morning, leaving my staff behind, and bidding none farewell. It took me more than seven hours to walk nine miles, to Kinsale. On the way, I was near being stopped by a magistrate. I sat down by the road-side and reflected thus:—"Here I am, a stranger in a strange land, but little money, and few that show me friendship; I am going now to a place, and I have no ground to expect reception; I cannot walk much further; I cannot buy a passage to a distant part, and what shall I do, seeing I have no way to get bread? Once I had a father's house and tender parents, and how would they feel if they knew my present case? Unless God works wonders for me soon, I shall surely sink." Then I lifted up my voice and wept.

The first Methodists I met in town treated me coolly; but recollecting to have seen a young woman in Dublin who lives here, I inquired and found her. She at first was sorry to see me; she being in a low uncomfortable state of mind, and her parents not Methodists. However they invited me to tarry; and so it happened by the overruling hand of Providence, that I got the preaching-house: first, by talking with the members individually, and provoking them to say, "I have no objection if the rest have none;" and then by making bold to stand up on Christmas night, after a local preacher had dismissed the people, and spoke a few words, and formed a covenant with the assembly to pray three times a day for a week, and the greater part of which agreed, and I called

God to witness to the engagement. And when the society met to speak on the privilege of the meeting-house, there was none to object.

Early the next morning many came out to meeting, and at evening likewise; thus for several days together; and God's power was felt by several who were quickened to start afresh for the kingdom of glory.

I held one meeting to preach to the children. The preacher who had treated me with slightness in Bandon, came to the stairs and listened. At a love-feast there was never such a refreshing time known there before.

I wished for a passage to Dublin, a vessel being ready for sea; but the owner would not consent that the master should take me on board; saying, "Where they have got priest, minister, or preacher on board, there is no prosperity or good luck;" and the vessel was wind-bound for several days.

During my stay here, I frequently thought every meeting would be the last, and would appoint no more, hoping by some means to get away; but no door opened. I received invitations to breakfast, dine, and sup, more than I supplied. At length, some people (not in society) procured me a passage, unknown to the owner, by persuading the captain to take me on board, and provided sea-stores, and then gave me information that the wind was coming fair, and if I would, I could now sail for Dublin. The people at a venture would come out to meeting, and seemed as though they could not keep away. I requested my departure might be notified that night; and within two hours after hearing that the captain would take me, went on board and was under sail; and, after fifty-two hours' passage from Oyster-haven, I landed in Dublin, and went to my old home, Doctor Johnson's, where I was cordially received, having been absent eleven weeks and two days, and travelled by land and water about seven hundred English miles.

It lying weightily upon my mind, what the Cork preacher said, I wrote to him the following purport:

"I don't see how you could in justice take it as wicked opposition, if I did nor said nothing against the Methodists, provided I held meetings, without judging me hard. I acknowledge you treated me with less severity in harsh words than I expected; but lest you should write letters before me and hedge up my way, I left Cork as I did; and now remember, if souls be lost in consequence of it, that will lie at your door; for God knows, if I could have kept my peace of mind, I would not have left America, but in tender conscience I was constrained to come."

The person who carried the above, delivered it as follows:—

Bearer. "Sir, here is a letter from Lorenzo."

Preacher. "Oh! is he in Kinsale? (reads the letter without changing countenance) He is displeased I did not let him preach. Did he preach in Kinsale?"

Bearer. "Yes, sir, to large congregations, and a prospect of good."

Preacher. "I'm glad there is a good prospect; he has been a zealous preacher in America, and came away against rule or order of his assistant: he follows his own feelings too much; he is Quakerized."

Bearer. "I believe, sir, he is led by the dictates of the Spirit, for his labors are owned of God."

Preacher. "Poor man, he fatigues himself; I told him he ought not to walk so much. I bid him call on me in the morning, in order to give him some assistance, but was too ill to see him."

Bearer. "I don't think Lorenzo would accept of it, sir. He is not a burden to any of our societies."

Preacher. "I hear he is abstemious, and will not take sufficient nourishment. He won't take clothes, and such a poor figure as he cuts! Why, when he went to Bandon and stood at the people's door, they could not tell what to make of him;" and so he concluded with saying something concerning my heart and head.

January, 1801. The greater part of this month I spent in this city. I went to see John Dinnen, who treated me with more friendship than ever before; yet there seemed to be something out of order between us.

Here I found Alice Cambridge, (who lives with Mrs. Stafford, from whom I received manifested kindness,) who had been very hardly treated in the south, and turned and kept out of society for no other cause than because, in conscience, she could not desist from holding public meetings. She was kind to me during my illness, and was the occasion of the preachers first coming to see me. Oh! prejudice and austerity, when will ye be done away! By the means of Alice I procured a large room for meeting, in Stephen-street, where thrice I spoke to some scores. In Capel-street, twice; some seemed to feel the word, others were angry. In Thomas-street I met a few. In New-street I had four meetings; some people were solemn, others noisy. I spoke twice at the Coombe, three times in Spitalfields, twice in Ransford-street, once in Cathedral lane, besides family visits, at which came in a few in different parts of the city. At Elephant lane I had two solemn and attentive meetings.

For some months I had a desire to preach at Black Rock, but saw no way till now. The young curate, by the name of Mitchell, whom I had seen at Athy, gave me the privilege of Mr. Kelly's chapel, in which I spoke to an attentive, serious people.

Having it impressed on my mind for several months to give the inhabitants of Dublin a general warning, I never saw my way clear to proceed until now; and believing the judgments of God hanging over the place, I got about three thousand handbills printed, such as lay upon my mind, and the greatest part I distributed among the quality and decent kind of people, leaving them in their shops or houses; and one I enclosed in a letter, and gave it to a sentinel in the castle yard for the Lord-lieutenant; but fearing he would not get it, I got a second framed and directed in gilt letters, *for the Lord-lieutenant,* sealed in black wax and paper, and tied tape round it; this I left in the porter's lodge.

I got two others framed in black, and directed in gold letters; one *for the merchants,* the other *for the lawyers.* The first I hung up in the Royal Exchange, the other I left on the floor, in the sight of the lawyers, in the hall of the four courts, and walked out, it being court time.

A local preacher said he was willing I should have a meeting in his house, if it would not grieve his brethren. At the leaders' meeting it was objected to.

At John Jones's, my printer, in Bride-street, I held my last meeting, which was solemn and refreshing, having had near thirty since this time of my coming to town.

Feeling my mind at present free from the city and college, (as I had left a pamphlet on every floor in the letter-box,) and bound to the west of Ireland, I took leave of a number of my Dublin friends, saying, "I know not that I shall ever see you again in time." But several said it was impressed on their minds I should return to the city before I went to America.

February 1st. I took leave of my dear Paul and Letitia, who had showed every particular kindness and attention to me during this visit, which parting was painful to me, and taking the canal boat, I arrived in Tullamore after night-fall. This day one passenger called for a pack of cards, and another reproved him, saying, "It is sabbath day." This opened a door for me to distribute some of my handbills and pamphlets, some of which passed into the first cabin, which influenced the passengers to send for me in there. Some of these cross-questioned me concerning my leaving America and travelling through the kingdom, with other parts of my conduct which they had heard of. I endeavored to return my answers to the purpose, and yet in such a manner as should be profitable to the whole. God was my helper, and his power seemed to come over them. These people spread over town what a strange man they had in company. The Methodists who heard of it came to the house where I was confined with sickness to my bed near all day, and asked if I would hold a meeting at night. I said, "Yes, provided you will give me the preaching-house, and get the people notified." Here prejudice had formerly shut the door and the hearts of the people against me.

In the evening the seats were filled; the next night the house was filled; the third night all the people could not get in. The next morning early the seats were filled, and I gave my last. The day but one preceding, I put up one of the *rules for holy living* in the market-place, which occasioned a Protestant and a Roman or two to come first to words and then to blows; and then one of the Romans, who held the Protestant whilst the other beat him, was obliged to run into his house and not show his head in the market all day, lest the Orangemen should give him a beating: he was one of the richest merchants of his profession in town. I spoke that day in the street to near fifteen hundred people, generally well behaved. Here I was offered half a guinea, and the offer of a return carriage, to carry me sixteen miles, which I refused, knowing that example goes before precept, and that the eyes of many are upon me. I walked nineteen miles to Birr, but here met with a cool reception. Likewise at Cree, to which I had a letter from their friend; nevertheless, I was coolly enough received. "Well," said I, "I have come about twenty-two miles out of my way to see you, and, if it is convenient, should be glad to hold a meeting; but if you call not the people together, I shall be pure." And leaving them immediately, after giving them two pamphlets, I reached Eyrecourt that night.

The next day I walked twenty-two miles, and got benighted; I called at a farm-house, and got liberty, for money, to tarry all night, but found no freedom to eat in the house, except two or three roasted potatoes.

Next morning walked on, and a car overtook me; I hired a driver to carry me into Tuam, at which town, upon my arrival, I felt a sudden halt in my mind. Inquired for Methodists, and after getting some refreshment found one, who treated me kindly, and got me the preaching-house and ten score of hearers that night.

For several days past, feeling the necessity of a preacher's being assisted by the supernatural grace of God, or else h s labors to be but of little use, and feeling my own weakness, trials began to arise and discouragements to desist; but here God revived my spirits, by granting the quickening influence of his grace, to assist me to go through the meetings both at night and morning.

At Hollymount we had two solemn meetings, though the class-leader had treated me with some neglect.

At Castlebar, where Mr. Russel and his wife were kind and friendly more than I expected, I held a number of meetings, which were refreshing and powerful. Here one woman said she had seen me in a dream two weeks before.

At Newport good was done. Here I was met by Sir Neal, who observing me to have a bundle of papers under my arm, which I had got printed a few days before as a warning to the people of the country, being more and more convinced there is an awful cloud gathering over the land, he questioned me very harsh and sharply what those were, and who and what I was; and after taking me to his house and examining different papers, said he believed I was an honest man, and gave me a pass.

At Nappogh the people were cold and hard. At Westport, in the day of eternity, I expect the fruit of two meetings will appear.

At Tullagh, a country place, about two hundred came out at night, and as many the next morning, though the ground was white with frost.

At Cappavico the Lord's power was to be felt, and at Menalo we had memorable times. About this time I fell in with the Rev. Mr. Averill, who entreated me to tarry longer on the circuit, saying, "The cries of the people are after you, which I look upon to be the voice of God in their hearts; for it is evident God is acknowledging you among them, and if you will tarry another year, I'll give you a guinea a month to bear your expenses, and provided the next conference set their faces against you, as they did the last, I'll pay your passage home to America." I told him I believed the time was near that it was the will of God I should return home; therefore durst not engage to tarry.

At Foxford we had good times. At Ballina we had three powerful meetings. About this time I had some articles of clothing and money offered to me; but a small part I felt free to accept, though I would have to live by faith about my passage.

I walked about thirty Irish miles in a day, and coming to Sligo, I met Mr. Averill again. He preached and administered the sacrament, the latter of which was refreshing.

In the evening, I spoke at the courthouse to about a thousand people, and entreated them to prepare for trials, which I expected were coming on the land. The next morning, after speaking to about two hundred, went to Manor-hamilton, where was a great ado about religion, and some good doing.

I attempted to speak at night, and about two thirds through my discourse, I was suddenly stopped, like one confounded, and other preachers carried on the meeting, and concluded it.

The next morning, feeling greatly depressed in mind, I wrote a letter for Mr. Averill, leaving it on the table, and quit the house before the family was up, and walked twenty-one miles to Enniskillen, where I spoke to a few at night, not in vain. The next morning, speaking to a number more, I went to Tempo, and at a tavern where I took some refreshment, I missed my pocket-book, in which were a number of letters to people's friends in America. At night, I called in a market-town, and after distributing a number of handbills, called at a house, and for the sum of thirteen shillings English, could have supper, and lodging, and breakfast, and liberty of holding two meetings. The man was a Methodist, the woman a Presbyterian.

The Methodists then besought me to tarry a day or two, in vain.

Partly in the rain, I walked twenty-one miles to Dungannon, and whilst distributing handbills through the town, a soldier I met, who knew me, though it was night, and took me to a sergeant's house, who said, "When we lay at Chapel-izod last year, when you came there and formed the covenant, a corporal who agreed thereto, afterwards became serious and died in peace."

Here I had an ulcer broke in my lungs whilst I was asleep, which had like to have strangled me at first. I felt cold chills, after this, running through my body, and feverish, and my bodily strength greatly reduced. The sergeant, who a few days previous was wishing that he knew where I was, that he might send for me to come to that place, asked the circuit preacher if I might have the meeting-house, who said, "By no means." However, the sergeant knowing my desire to hold a meeting, after the preacher had dismissed the people, spoke out, and said: "Take notice, there is an American in town, who will hold a meeting to-morrow evening, but the place is not determined on;" then walking and whispering to the preacher, said, "Will you forbid its being here?" Who replied, "I will neither approve nor oppose it." The sergeant turned to the people and said, "It will be here."

I had four meetings in the house, and two in the street, which were solemn and attentive.

I held several in the neighborhood of this place, which seemed to be attended with some degree of power; at one of which, a seceder's schoolhouse would not contain the people, and church service just being over, I got the liberty of its pulpit, which I looked upon as singular and providential. I spoke to near seven hundred people, and mentioned, I believed trials were near. Thence I proceeded to Lisburn, and put up with one who had been a Quaker, but had withdrawn. He appeared to be a conscientious man, but the scriptures bear but little weight with him, and the divinity of Christ he seems to stumble at. Thence to Belfast. On my way I called at Lambeg to inquire concerning a singular circumstance, respecting one's losing his hair, which was thought to be supernatural; it has produced a great effect upon the man of the house.

CHAPTER VII.

RETURN TO AMERICA.

ALL the vessels in Belfast were full of passengers, except two; one of which being dear, and her provisions not such as I required, I declined. But a Quaker said, "Lorenzo! I would not wish to transport thee; but if thy mind is clear to go home, we will make thee out a passage; thee speak to thy friends, and I to mine;" which I did, but no notice was taken of it. Then the Quaker, with a friend, gave me two guineas to engage my passage on board the other; but the captain, who was bending towards Quakerism, observing I had the small-pox some months before, refused to take me; saying, "I know not but the infection may still be in your clothes, and five of my hands have not had it, and if they should be taken unwell, I shall be knocked up on my voyage."

About this time, I received three letters from Dr. Johnson, giving some account of my last visit in Dublin, and with an anxious desire for my return; but if I did not see my way clear to come, might draw on him for as much as should be needful for my voyage, and receive it either as a gift or loan, whichever might be most agreeable to me: but I in a letter replied, "I cannot see my way clear to ask the Methodists for much help, lest they should lay claim to me and seek to tie my hands: nor to ask too much of the Quakers. I must look all around; and for you to pay it out of your own pocket, I cannot consent, no not in my mind: but if people are willing to do the same, I shall look upon it as providential."

In one of his letters, he expressed a desire, if consistent with the Divine will, he, with his dear Letitia, might see me once more, to take leave of me, and see me properly equipped under their own inspection. Accordingly, as my way now seemed hedged up in the north, and feeling my mission to be nearly ended, unless it were a desire to visit two or three neighborhoods, and feeling that I could go without condemnation, I took the mail-coach to Lisburn, where I held a meeting in what is called the new connection, which was solemn and tender.

Thence, being an outside passenger, I came to Dublin the next day, chilled and tired, and if it had not been for the kindness of the guard accommodating me with his seat, I must have given out on my way.

About six o'clock in the morning, I arrived at my friend Dr. Johnson's, to their agreeable surprise. Here follows one thing of the doctor's singular conduct, in sending some notices to persons of different persuasions, that, "If any person of ability had a desire, and would consider it a privilege to assist in sending Lorenzo Dow comfortably home to his own country, such assistance would be accepted by Letitia Johnson, 102 New-street." In consequence of this, they received somewhat more than the voyage required.

I held two meetings in Bride-street, the latter of which was solemn and tender, and the two Dublin preachers were present.

March 28th. It was now rising of sixteen months since I first came on to the Irish shore, and whilst others have been robbed and murdered, I have been preserved by land and sea. Though a few days ago, I was informed, the crew with whom I sailed, when drove into the Isle of Man, were plotting to throw me overboard, if an Englishman had not interposed. I have known of less hunger in this country of scarcity, than ever for the space of time in my own, since travelling.

To-morrow, God willing, I expect to embark for America. What is past I know; what is to come, I know not. I have endured trials in my own country, and have not been without them in this, even from those whom I love and wish well, both outward and inward, temporal and spiritual: but my trust is still in God, who I believe will support me, and give me a blessing upon my feeble labors in my native land, though I expect to wade through deep waters there.

I know not but I may come to Europe again, though there is but one thing which will bring me, viz. to save my soul.

April 2d. I took my farewell leave of Paul and Letitia Johnson, and William and Nancy Thomas, with whom it was hard parting, and embarked for America on board the ship Venus, S. Taber, master, 250 tons burden, seventy-three passengers, mostly Roman Catholics.

3d. At one o'clock, A. M., took in our anchors, hoisted sail, and in about fifteen days after losing sight of land, we were half across the ocean, when the wind came against us, so that we were driven to north, and south, about two weeks, making but very little headway.

26th. I held meeting on board; good attention appeared among those who could attend. After forty-seven days' passage, we hove in sight of land, and shortly after came to the quarantine ground, Staten Island, where I was detained thirteen days; during which time I got relief from some persons in New York, whereby I escaped those *vermin* that are troublesome on long voyages with a number of people, &c. On our passage, my life was despaired of, through costiveness, (as in thirty-three days no means of medicine answered but thrice,) by some gentlemen on board, who with the captain showed me kindness. After holding two meetings, and my clothes cleansed, I got permission from the doctor to come into the city: where I was cordially received by S. Hutchinson, and some other kind friends; but they durst not open the preaching-house doors to me for fear of the censure of the conference now at hand.

Dr. Johnson had given me a paper signifying that if I were brought to want in any part of Ireland, I could draw on him for any sum I chose, by any gentleman who traded in Dublin, which paper I never made use of. He sent a library of books by me, with orders to sell them, and make use of the money to buy me a horse to travel with, &c. and if I were minded might remit it to him in a future day. These books were of singular service to aid me in my travels, which I thought to be my duty, viz. instead of being confined on a circuit, to travel the country at large, to speak on certain points which I considered injurious to the kingdom of Christ in this world, &c. Not knowing the value of these second-hand books, one took the advantage of my ignorance to get them under price; but my friends insisted he should give up the bargain; to which he with a hard demand of ten dollars consented, with the proviso that Kirk (who sold them for a hundred and fifteen dollars) should have no profit. Oh! the cursed love of money!*

---

* I paid the Doctor afterwards.

June 16th. Conference came on, and some of my old friends were minded I should take a circuit; but did not blame me for going to Europe, considering the advantage I had got to my health, &c. I could not feel my mind free to comply, feeling it my duty to travel more extensively. Their entreaties and arguments were hard to resist; and on the other hand the discouragements if I rejected, or discomplied, would be great. It would not only by them be deemed wilful, and must expect their disapprobation, but still be like the fowls of the air, to trust Providence for my daily bread. Here I was brought to halt between two opinions, thinking it was easier for one to be mistaken than twenty: yet I felt it my duty to travel the continent at large. Here my trials were keen.

A pamphlet of my experience coming to America, Kirk was minded to reprint it; but Bishop Whatcoat said I belonged to them, and they ought to have the first privilege of printing my experience: and being under great trials of mind, concluded to give up my judgment to theirs, and take a circuit; which I had no sooner consented to *try for a year, the Lord being my helper*, than an awful distress came over my mind; but I could not recall my words. My mind being somewhat agitated, gave the bishop some encouragement relative to my journals, of which on reconsideration I repented, as the time was not yet.

I was restored by the conference where I was on going away, viz. remaining on trial. The conference was more friendly than I expected when on my voyage home; but I did not make my acknowledgment that I did wrong in going away. Some thought I had broke discipline; but on re-examination it was found I had not, as one on trial has a right to desist as well as they to reject.

My station was on the Dutchess and Columbia circuit, with David Brown and William Thatcher; Freeborn Garretson, presiding elder. Thus distressed, I sailed to Rhinebeck; on which way, one attempting to go on board the vessel was knocked out of the boat, and carried down the stream more than a mile before he could be picked up. Oh! what dangers are we in! How uncertain is life! When I arrived at the flats, I called at a Methodist's and got a meeting appointed for the night. One of the principal Methodists came to inquire, "Who is stationed on our circuit?" I replied, "Brown, Thatcher, and Dow." Said he, "Dow, I thought he had gone to Ireland!" I replied, "He has been there, but has lately come back." Said he, "Dow! Dow! why he is a crazy man; he will break up the circuit." So we parted. After meeting, I appointed another at the new meeting-house then building, which tried them at my boldness, they not knowing who I was (but supposed a local preacher) and intended Mr. G. should preach the first sermon there, for the dedication. Next day some desired to know my name, which I desired to be excused from telling. I held a number of meetings in this place, mostly cold and lifeless, though we had some good and pious friends; yet I could not speak with life and power as formerly; but felt as if was delivering my message to the *wrong* people. For it had been in my mind to return to my native town, and there begin and travel extensively; first, in the adjacent places, and so abroad, as I might find Providence to open the door.

When I got to this place I had two shillings left, and hearing of a place called Kingston-sopus, I was minded to visit it, (contrary to the advice of my friends,) and having got a few together with difficulty, and leaving two other appointments, returned, having paid away all my money for ferriages, and when the time commenced in which I must go and fulfil the appointments, saw no way to get across the ferry; and whilst walking along in meditation on past providences, and raising my heart that a way might be opened for my getting across the ferry, I cast my eye upon the sand and espied something bright, and on picking it up found it to be a York shilling, the very sum I wanted in order to cross over. And when I had fulfilled my first appointment, and was going to the second, a stranger shook hands with me, and left near half a dollar in my hand, so I was enabled to get back. Thus I see Providence provides for them that put their trust in him. Having some scripture pictures framed sent by me from Europe to dispose of, some I gave away, and the remainder I let go to a printer for some religious handbills, &c. in Poughkeepsie, some of which I distributed through the town, and hearing the sound of a fiddle, I followed it, and came to a porch where was a master teaching his pupils to dance. I gave some handbills, which he called after me to take away, but I spoke not a word but went off. Here the people are hardened. At Fishkill and the Highlands the people were hard, and apparently sorry to see me. At Clove and Snarlingtown likewise, I visited some neighboring places, and had some tender meetings. At Amenia and Dover the Methodists seemed shy; I put up at a tavern several times. Swago, I visited from house to house, but have not the art nor the spirit of visiting as when in the north country. Sharon: I found two classes here, the first hard and sorry to see me; the other tender with Christian love. In Salisbury and Canaan, Connecticut, I had sundry meetings, but still felt as if not in my right sphere. A report that crazy Dow had got back from Ireland, brought many out to hear. Mount Washington, Sheffield, and Egremont, Massachusetts, I visited: thence to Hudson, and so to Rhinebeck.

After quarterly meeting I went home to see my friends, and found my parents well, and one sister, who had become more serious within the course of a few months, which was a matter of consolation to me.

The expectation of the Methodists was raised, expecting such times as we had before, not looking enough beyond the watchman. Once some were prejudiced against me, but now too much for me; so I was clogged with their expectations and shut up. Walking to Norwich, gave away my pocket handkerchief to get a breakfast, and took shipping to New London, where we had three meetings that were large and tender. One who was near and dear to me did not come to see me, neither durst I go to see him, which caused me some pain of heart.

September 3d. I went forty miles to Middletown, and had four meetings, which were good and tender. At New Hartford I hired a ball-room, which cost me a dollar and a half. The man thought I was going to have a play at first; many came to hear, to whom I spoke from, "After I have spoken, mock on." Some were tender, and some disputed, saying, "All things are decreed; and they hoped they were Christians, and no man can be a Christian unless he is reconciled to God's decrees." I replied, "If all things are foreordained, it was foreordained that I should talk as I do, and you are not reconciled to it, and of course are not

Christians; but deceiving yourselves according to your own doctrine." The young people smiled, and so we parted.

Oh, when shall the time commence when the watchmen shall see eye to eye, and the earth be filled with God's glory? Thence I went to my circuit, and continued round with my mind burdened, as when sailing up from New York; and have been burdened and depressed whilst on this circuit ever since. I do not have such meetings as formerly, though the cause of God and the worth of souls lies as near my heart as ever. What can be the cause, unless out of my sphere? I felt a pain in my right side, and on the seventh day an ulcer, as I suppose, broke in my lungs, and I raised a putrefied matter, and was forced to cut my labor short the next day through weakness of body. After this, I had hardly strength to keep up with my appointments; but frequently was obliged to lie upon the bed whilst addressing the people. At length I got a little more free from my pain, and was in hopes that the raising would cease, and the place heal.

October 24th—25th. After quarterly meeting, I left this circuit, by G.'s direction, and proceeded for Litchfield circuit, but did not ask for location, as I wished to go through the year if possible, considering my engagement, and the nature of my standing.

26th. The Methodists being low and lazy here, I walked through the town and gave notice for meeting, and invited the people; and some ministers and lawyers, with the people, accepted. The second meeting scores could not get in. At Milton, God has begun a good work. In Kent, the people are hard. New Milford, Washington, Woodbury, Goshen, Winchester, Bristol, I visited. Some were hard; some were prejudiced; and with some I had comfort; among whom were some Seventh day Baptists near the last place. In Farmington and Northington religion seemed low; in the latter, harm was done by the minister opposing the work under brother M. In Granby and Barkhemsted it is low. Hartland Hollow, once a flaming place for piety, seems to be diminished greatly; yet of late some small quickening. Colebrook and Winstead I visited; in the latter is a large society, but not so much engaged as they used to be. Thus I have got round the circuit—scarce any blessing on my labors, and my mind depressed from day to day

---

CHAPTER VIII.

GEORGIA TOUR.

Of late it hath lain upon my mind that I should not recover whilst I continued in this sphere of action, and that my ill health came in consequence of not doing what I had felt to be my duty, viz., to travel the continent more at large; and the only remedy to escape and recover from this decline, would be by a change of air and climate, &c., and as though Providence chose to make use of this means for my recovery, for some end unknown to me. And the more I made it a matter of prayer—

that if it were a temptation, it might decrease, but if it were from Him, it might increase—and the more I think upon it, and weigh it as for eternity, the more it increases, and cords of sweet love draw me on.

The thoughts of leaving the circuit without liberty is somewhat trying, as I had done it once before; and some perhaps may conclude there is no confidence to be put in me. The island of Bermuda, or Georgia, is what I had in contemplation.

November 21, 22. Quarterly meeting was in Cornwall. I told brother Batchelor that my mind was under the above trials; he said he was willing I should go. But Garretson, my spiritual grandfather, would not consent, but offered me a location on the circuit, if I would say I could travel no longer; but would not consent that I should leave it on any condition at first. I could not say but that I could travel a space longer, and yet apparently but a very little while. At length I strove to get him to say, if it was the opinion of brother Moriarty, that my health was declining, he would not charge me with disobedience at the next conference. He said I must then labor not in my usual way, but like the other preachers, viz., the regular appointments only. And thus indirectly it was left; so I continued on.

27th. My strength, I think, declines.

December 1. I reached my parents again, tarried four days, had two meetings, and told my parents of my intention of visiting the southern climes. They did not seem to oppose it, as I expected, but said, "Once it would have been your delight to have been received and regularly travelling on a circuit, and now they are willing to receive you, you cannot feel contented to tarry on a circuit, which, if we were to have our choice, it would be to have you continue; then you will have friends, and can come and see us. But you must be your own judge in this matter; weigh it well, and act accordingly."

I left my horse, saddle, bridle, and watch, in the hands of Nathaniel Phelps, and had some money of a neighbor, viz., my horse, with the man who came fifteen miles to see me, and gave me a dollar, when I was sick in the north country. Peter Moriarty, the assistant preacher of the circuit, having gone home to wait till God should send snow that he might move his family, it was uncertain when I could get his judgment respecting my decline, and there being no probability of my obtaining Garretson's consent, I was now brought into a straight. Being unable to fulfil the appointments with propriety any longer, I got brother Fox to take them in my stead.

My license being written in such form by Mr. G., it would only serve for the Dutchess and Columbia circuits, so that when he removed me to Litchfield it was good for nothing; so I destroyed it, and, of course, now had no credentials to aid me in a strange land. The thought of going away under the above difficult circumstances was trying, both to my natural desire and to my faith; yet it appeared to me I was brought into this situation by my disobedience, and the only way would be to obey in future.

December 9. A friend, N. P., carried me to Hartford, and, being disappointed of shipping, I set off on foot for New Haven, and though weak in body I went twelve miles, and stopped at a tavern; but it being the freemason lodge night, they made such a noise I could not sleep, so I went to a farm-house.

I set off at the dawn of day, and a man in Meriden saw and knew me, gave me a breakfast, and sent a horse with me several miles; so I reached New Haven that night, and spoke to a few. The next evening I spoke again, and God gave me favor in the sight of some. At length I set sail for New York, and making a mistake, as the passengers divided when going on board, I carried away two bottles which belonged to the other packet where my things were; and on our arrival I paid the damage of the porter, which the people drank up without my consent. However, they were so kind as to rummage my things, and write in my journal some scurrilous language belonging to seafaring people. After my landing, I went to my old home at the house of brother Jeffrey. I took the advice of several physicians, whose advice it was to go; and finding a vessel bound to Bermuda, was denied a passage on account of my religion. But Captain Peleg Latham, going to sail for Savannah, offered to take me and throw in a fifth part of my passage, considering the cause of my going.

Through Dr. Johnson's books I had procured my horse, got some religious handbills printed, containing *rules for holy living*, &c., paid my passage, and had about one dollar and a half left me, eighteen dollars still being in G.'s hands. My friends made out my provisions. My cough and weakness increase. I am more than ever sea-sick. I said, "To tarry is death, to go I do but die."

January 3d, 1802. I am in latitude 34 deg. 38 min., longitude 76 deg. 2 min. My cough has almost left me, but my raising continues. The people are as kind and civil as I could expect from the circumstances. Natural and human prospects appear dark. What is before me I know not; my trust is in God. I have but one to look to or rely upon in this undertaking. My trials are keen; indeed, it is a trial of my faith to go; but Jesus is precious to my soul on this roaring sea. The winds these four days past have been contrary.

There is but one in all Georgia that I know. I have seen before Hope Hull, my spiritual father, and to him I never spoke. My mind was tried by the enemy of souls; something within said, "You will see such good days no more; the openings and favors you have had are now gone, and, as it were, death awaits you." But one evening, when thus tried, when lying down, a thought arose, "Why have I not as great a right to expect favors from God now, as in days that are past and gone?" Immediately hope and faith began to revive, and my heart to be drawn out in prayer. Soon after, the wind came fair, and we run from five to nine miles an hour, till we had run our latitude. On our way, a whale played round our vessel for an hour or two.

January 6. Saw land. It being foggy, did not venture into port. The night following, found we had but about two fathoms of water, as we sounded to cast anchor upon a hollow shoal; it being then high water the captain began to prepare the boats to flee. The noise waked me up I saw the people terrified, and preparing to escape. I began to examine whether I was sorry I had come, or was prepared to die; felt great inward peace, and no remorse, and fell asleep again. But their ado soon awaked me; I dressed myself, sung a hymn, and lay down. I observed some praying, and one man reproving another, saying, "It is no time to swear now." Soon the vessel struck; the cable they cut off in five blows, and hoisted a sail, leaving the anchor, and the tide carried us through a narrow place into deep water, striking twice on the way. Just before, was a smart breeze, but now a calm. Through this medium, by the providence of God, we escaped. Gladness appeared on every countenance, and soon drinking, cursing, swearing, and taking God's name in vain, appeared on the carpet. My heart was grieved to see this, and I could but reprove and counsel them. Oh, how frequently will people be frightened in danger, and deny it afterwards!

7th. Fog continued till afternoon, then got a pilot, and anchored in the river at night.

Friday 8th. I landed in Savannah, and walked through the town; I found a burying-ground, and the gate being down, I went in, and spent an hour or two in thanksgiving and prayer for my deliverance and a prosperous journey. Oh, the poor blacks! a boat of them, with some white people, came alongside of our vessel: my heart yearns when I view their sable faces and condition. I inquired for Methodists, and found no regular ones in town. But one of Hamet's party, Adam C. Cloud, a preacher, whom I did not know at first, gave me the liberty of his preaching-house that night, in which I spoke to about seventy whites and blacks; but to get them collected, I took upwards of a hundred handbills, and distributed them through the town, and threw one into a window where a man was dying. A Baptist preacher being present, read it to the family, as he afterwards told me, and that it was a solemn time. He (Mr. Halcomb) ever denied me his meeting-house. On Sunday and Monday evenings I spoke in the African meeting-house: it did my heart good to see the attentive blacks. Andrew, the black preacher, had been imprisoned and whipped until the blood ran down for preaching, as the people wanted to expel religion from the place, he being the only preacher in town. The whites at length sent a petition to the legislature for his permission to preach, which was granted. Said he to me, "My father lived to be a hundred and five years old, and I am seventy, and God of late has been doing great things for us. I have about seven hundred in church, and now I am willing to live or die, as God shall see fit." The whites offered me a collection, which I declined, lest wrong constructions should be put upon it, and I deemed an impostor, as I was a stranger. I gave my trunk, &c., to the family where I tarried. In pouring out some crackers, I found two dollars, which I suppose my friends flung in at New York: this I stood in need of. As I was leaving town, old Andrew met me, and, shaking hands with me, left eleven dollars and a half in my hand, which some had made out. So I perceived God provides for those who put their trust in him. I had not gone far before I fell in with a team; I gave the man a handbill, which he said he would not take half a dollar for, and bid me put my bundle in his cart. Thus, with help, I got on about twenty miles that day.

The captain with whom I sailed, said he discovered a visible alteration for the better in my health previous to our parting; as my cough left me, I raised less and less, and my strength returned more and more, far beyond expectation. It was thought when I sailed from New York, that I should not live to return.

The day after I left Savannah, a man overtook me who had heard of me, and said, "Are you the preacher who has lately come from the northward?" I replied in the affirmative. Said he, "I heard you in Savannah, and desiring to find you I saw one back in a wagon dressed in black, whom I asked if he was the man; he replied, "No, sir, I love rum too well."

He took me on his horse and carried me to old father Boston's, near Tukisaking. Here I was kindly received, and called in a few neighbors, to whom I spoke, and appointed a meeting for Sunday. In the interval they began to interrogate me where I came from, and for my license, or credentials; which, on the relation of my situation, caused them to think I was an impostor; but at length they found my name on the minutes, so their fears in a great measure subsided. A Methodist preacher on his way from conference fell in there on Saturday, and behaved as if he thought I was an impostor; however, my appointment was given out and could not be recalled. And while I was fulfilling it, the melting power of God was felt, and tears were rolling on every side. As I was leaving the assembly to go to my evening appointment, about ten miles off, several shook hands with me, and left pieces of money in my hand to the amount of some dollars, which I perceived increased the preacher's jealousy, as I refused the loan of a horse. I walked and fulfilled my evening meeting, where a collection was offered, which I refused; however, about four dollars were forced upon me.

18th. Continuing my course, I saw the sand-hill or hooping-crane, the largest kind of bird or fowl I ever saw; also, a flock of geese flying over. Sure—instinct! what is it? or who can tell? the power of attraction. Men are wise, yet the more they find out, the greater mysteries are presented to view, and the more puzzled they are relative to the book of nature. Oh, the wisdom of God! The birds of flight know their appointed time; and oh that the children of men would consider theirs. I dined gratis at an inn.

20th. I reached Augusta, (the place seemed familiar, as if I had seen it before, when I came within sight of it, as I had four times dreamed of preaching in a similar place, and seen some similar people,) and inquired for Methodists, and the first direction was to go to the house of a Frenchman, where the family treated me with great ridicule and contempt. From thence I was directed to the house of a Calvinist, where I was treated with equal coolness. Thence to a house where the fashionable preachers put up, but got no encouragement to tarry; but was directed to the common preachers' boarding-house, where I was thought to be an impostor, and so was sent to a private boarding-house: I went there, but could not get entertainment for love or money; and espying a grove of woods at a distance, concluded to go and take up my lodging there that night; and leaving a handbill, I set off and got about two-thirds of the way out of town, when a negro overtook me with an express that his mistress wanted I should come back. I went back and tarried all night, and for my supper, lodging and breakfast, they would take nothing, neither would they keep me any longer, though I offered them any sum they should ask for a week's board. Next night I offered a family pay for four nights' lodging; they said they would take me on trial; I did not eat or drink with them; they kept me three nights for nothing, but would not keep me the fourth. Next night I went down on the bank of the river to take up my lodgings there, and whilst walking back and forth meditating on my singular state and circumstances, a boat landed, from which came a negro, and called me by name. I asked him where he saw me? He replied, "I heard you preach in Savannah; did you not in such a place?" He asked me where I lodged; I told him I had no place. Said he, "Will you sleep where black people live?" I replied, "If they be decent ones." He went off, and after about half an hour came back, and piloted me to a black family who lived in as good fashion as two-thirds of the people in Augusta. I stayed all night, and though I offered them pay, yet they would not receive any, neither would they keep me any longer for love nor money. I procured my provisions and had them dressed at the house of Moses, a black man, who was a Baptist preacher. Whilst at his shop, I heard of a man who was friendly to the Methodists, to whom I sent a line, signifying that if he would make me an appointment, I would cross the river to Camelton, where he lived, and preach. He did as I desired, and I held three meetings. Here I had a singular dream, which seemed to be as singularly fulfilled in some degree shortly after. I spoke in the African Baptist meeting-house to some hundreds of blacks, and a few whites, the Methodist meeting-house being denied me by the society and the preacher, L. G., they supposing that I was an impostor.

30th. I tarried two nights at a plantation house, where the man was troubled with an uncommon disorder, which puzzled a council of physicians, who supposed it to be a polypus in the heart. In the night I was seized with an inward impulse to set off on the Washington road, (my things not having arrived up the river,) so that my sleep departed. In the morning when I arose, it was apparently gathering for a storm of rain, so I rejected the impulse as a temptation; but it returned with double force; and for the sake of peace of mind I set off; but what I was after I could not tell, and when turning it over in my mind, I appeared like a fool to myself. And after travelling about ten miles, an old man between seventy and eighty, who was riding very fast, stopped of a sudden as he met me and said, "Young man, are you travelling?" I answered in the affirmative, and gave him one of my handbills. He on finding the contents shook hands with me and said, "I am a Baptist, but my wife is a Methodist;" and invited me to his house, about seven miles off on the Uchee creek, and procured me a congregation the next day, among whom was a respectable family which attended, (Esquire Haynes and his wife,) who got their hearts touched under the word, and invited me to hold a meeting at their house, which I did the next day; and through this channel my door was open for visiting several neighborhoods, where the people seemed to be melted to tenderness; and so I was not examined for credentials. I begged two children of the above-mentioned family, (only they were to have the care of them,) which since have become serious. Appointments being sent on before me, I went from Haynes' to Pieman's; thence to Capt. Thornton's, on Upton creek.

February 10th. I got to Hope Hull's before sunrise, having walked nine miles that morning. I found him in a corn-house. I saluted him with, "How do you do, father?" His reply was somewhat cool. He agreed to make me an appointment in the courthouse, (he living above a mile from the town,) having influence among the people. After breakfast, before he had started for town, I took a quantity of handbills, and running through the woods got to the town first, and distributed them among the people, and cleared out before he got to town, having scarcely spoken to any one. This made a great hubbub among the people, who I was, and where I came from; but when he came in to make the appointment he unfolded the riddle: this brought many out to hear. Next night I spoke again. It was thought I could get no hearers; however, the latter congregation was larger than the first. A young clergyman from Connecticut, at the first meeting, said, I spoke many truths, but was incorrect, and was minded not to come again; however, he did; and after I had done, he voluntarily made a flowery prayer, in which he gave me a broadside.

I once had a sister who resided in this town; and her husband, who was a country lawyer, was ungenerously abused in a duel, and afterwards died at Charleston; his life and death, when I reflected on his future state, caused me some tender sensations of mind. One night, in a dream, I thought he appeared to me, and replied, "It is better off with me in the other world than what you think—it is well with me; when I was dying, and so far expired that I could not communicate to others, I was convinced of the truths of religion, and sought, and found acceptance." When I awoke, my mind was greatly relieved.

Hope Hull said to me, "The kindness you received in Ireland, might be accounted for on natural principles—the affection of the people taking pity on you; and if one was to come to this country, and behave well, he would have the same kindness shown him." He entreated me to give over this mode of travelling, and to return to New England, and agree to take a circuit and wander no more; "for," said he, "though it appears that Providence hath been kind to you, yet you will not always find Dr. Johnsons in your travels;" but said, he thought that trials and difficulties would devolve upon me, and involve me by and by. He mentioned that God suffered Balaam to go where he desired; likewise a young man that came to Charleston, who lay under a mistake on a certain occasion, and some other things similar to this; which, considering who he was, and my singular standing, and danger of running too fast or too slow, or going on one side or the other, discouraged me much, when I gave way to reasoning and doubting on the subject of my duty in so travelling; but when I put my confidence in God, and submitted the matter to him, I felt peace and happiness of mind, and an inward refreshment and courage to go forward. He said that he did not know, when travelling, that ever he felt it impressed on his mind to go to one place more than another; but said he, "If I heard of a place opened, or a meeting-house vacant of a minister, or a wicked neighborhood, why reason said I should go." In reading Alexander K—'s life, I could not but remark his dream, page 96, about the pit and spring of water, &c.

H. H. gave me a paper where to call on certain families. I cautioned him on what he did, lest he should be censured for opening my way. Said he, "I leave every man to paddle his own canoe." I left the house before the family was up, and walked nine miles. At Washington, where H. lived, a contribution was offered, as well as at Uchee creek, and some other places, which I refused, knowing that example goes before precept.

and that impostors are fond of money, and if I were not guarded should be esteemed as such. However, at the latter place eleven dollars were sent from the people by Mr. H. and forced upon me.

I found the great Baptist meeting would take off the people, so I continued on my walk until I got about twenty miles from H.'s, (giving away handbills on the road,) where I sat down in the forks of the path and meditated what I should do to preserve my journals from an approaching shower. Just then a man, whom I had given a handbill to, came along and invited me to his house: he dismounted from his horse, and I got on, and soon arrived there, which was about a mile, when as awful a shower of rain fell, I think as ever I beheld; so my journals were preserved. This man had no religion. In the night I felt uneasy, and my heart bound upon the road; the man perceiving that I was getting up, inquired the cause, and strove to discourage me; but not prevailing, arose and taking two horses from his stable, carried me across two or three streams of deep running water, and by a tavern where was a sharp, cross dog.—Soon as the day dawned he went back, and I continued my course a few miles, and found a family of Methodists, where I took breakfast; but thought that they supposed that I was an impostor; and being informed where a funeral sermon was to be preached I quit them, and went to hear Britain Caple, who spoke in the power and demonstration of the Spirit; after which, I asked and obtained permission and spoke a few words, as Caple thought I could do no harm, (I appeared so simple to him, as he afterwards said,) if I could do no good. Thence I went to Greensborough, and held meeting that night, and the night following, and then concluded to go, not among the Methodists, unless it came in my way: but principally around to the courthouses, &c. On my way to Oglethorp, I called at a house to rest, (having the night before travelled a considerable distance till two men overtook me, and on finding who I was, provided me lodging the remainder of the night,) and the man began to find fault about the Methodists, (he not knowing who I was,) by which means I found one in the neighborhood. I went there and left some handbills for the neighborhood; and as I was going off, the family found out who I was, and invited me to tarry and hold a meeting, after they had inquired and found that I was not one of O'Kelly's party. In the meeting, a black woman belonging to General Stewart, who was a brother to the man of the house, fell down and lay like a corpse for some time; and her hands seemed as cold as death. We were at prayer when she fell, and her falling had like to have knocked me over. After about an hour and a half she came to, and praised God. I gave her my pocket Bible, with orders to carry it home, and if she could not read herself, to get the whites to do it for her. I had a meeting next night, and morning following; and thence proceeded to three appointments, which the family had sent on; one was at Lexington, at Pope's Chapel. About this time I had a singular dream which induced me to cross the Oconee river, and tarried with a kind Baptist family that night. Next day I called on Tigner, a noted Methodist; and finding that the circuit preacher, T. C., would be there the next day, I left a parcel of handbills, and went on my way until evening, when I stopped for lodging; and hearing of a serious family, I called on them, but scarce knew how to introduce myself; however, the family, on asking me various questions, invited me to tarry all night; and in the evening, on finding out what I was,

7

invited me to hold a meeting next day, which I accordingly did; this being in Clark county; and at night in Jackson old courthouse, where a few dollars were forced upon me. I was solicited to tarry longer, but felt my heart drawn to travel with expedition over these interior countries and return to New England, as my health and strength had returned far, far beyond my expectation.

Monday, 22d. I walked thirty-five miles to Franklin, and had a meeting at night.

23. Yesterday espying some drunken people, apparently so, I left an appointment, which to-day I fulfilled, and such an attention is rare to be found.

24. An opportunity presenting, I rode a number of miles and had meeting at night in Elberton, and the night following. I got an opportunity of sending some handbills to the Tombigbee, where perhaps I may one day visit. What am I wandering up and down the earth for? like a speckled bird among the birds of the forest. What is before me I know not; trials I expect are at hand, my trust is still in God, my trials are keen: my mind seems to be led to return to the north by the way of Charleston.

26. I went to Petersburg, had a letter from Doctor Lester, of New York, to Solomon Roundtree there, who opened his house for meeting, and showed me the greatest kindness of any man, since I came to the south. I went through the town and dispersed some handbills, which brought many out to meeting. I visited Vienna and Lisbon, and continued my course towards Augusta, though strongly entreated to tarry longer, with the offer of a horse to ride about sixty miles, but could not find freedom to tarry, or accept, yet about ten dollars I was constrained to receive, lest in attempting to do good, I should do harm. Some good impressions appeared to be made. I called at a house on the road, where I saw a woman ask a blessing at a table, and I, to give her a sounding, talked somewhat like a deist; she was a Methodist, and was going to turn me out of doors, when a man said, "He is one of your own party;" which was the preventive. I tarried all night, which she would take nothing for, but gave me some advice; as she halted between two opinions who I was. Calling for some breakfast on the road, the old man insisted I should pay before I eat, which I did, and asked the cause of a collection of youths so early. The reply was, "To revive the yesterday's wedding." After some talk, I gave them some handbills; the old man took one and began reading like a hero, when feeling conviction, could hardly go through. I prayed with them, and went on my way, and some of the young people who came for the resurrection of the wedding, as they called it, followed me out of doors, with tears, and the old man forced back the quarter dollar which I had paid for my breakfast.

Tuesday, March 2d. As I was sitting down to rest, by the forks of some roads, four persons were passing by me, and I overheard the word meeting; which induced me to ask, if they were going to meeting: but the answer was cool. So I followed after them, and going along to see what they were after, about half a mile out of my road, I came to a large assembly of people at a Presbyterian meeting-house, waiting in vain for their minister. I gave them some handbills; the people read them, and then showed them through the assembly; and some persons present who had heard of me before, told it; so I was invited to speak, with this proviso that I must give over if the minister came. I spoke nearly an hour on free salvation, but the minister did not come. I received an invitation to a Methodist meeting-house, where I had two meetings, and some dated their awakenings and conversion from that time. From man we may receive favors, and ask again and be denied with resentment; but the more we expect from God, them ore we shall have in answer to faith and prayer, in sincere patience, in submission to the will of God. The longer I pursue the course of religion, the more I am convinced of the truth of these scripture passages, that all things shall work together for good to them that love God: if we don't bring the trials on ourselves needlessly; and no good thing will God withhold from them that walk uprightly. Lord, increase my faith. I expect trials are at hand; the devil can show light, but not love, and in going in the way of love's drawings I generally prosper; but in going contrary thereto, barrenness, distress, burdens, and unfruitfulness, and sorrow, like going through briers and thorns. As it is God's will to make us happy, it is our duty to go in the paths of peace, tender conscience, and melting joy: and in so doing, I don't remember the time I was sorry; though I perceive not the propriety of the thing immediately, yet I do afterwards; therefore, I act as a mortal being who possesses an immortal soul, and expect to give an account at the bar of God, as if my eternal happiness depended on the improvement of my time.—Improvement enlarges the experience, and experience enlarges the capacity; and consequently we know more and more of God; and God made us so that it might be the case with us: and if it were not so, we could neither be rewardable nor punishable, for there would be nothing to reward or punish, for one part of the punishment is bitter reflections, or accusations for misimproved time and talents, the natural consequence of which, hath brought them there, and this would make distress. As holiness constitutes the felicity of Paradise, what nonsense it is for unholy beings to talk of going there; for it would rather tend to enhance their pain to behold the brightness of that sweet world. Therefore I think they had rather be in hell; and the mercy, love, and goodness above, will in justice send them there; for it is the will and goodness of God, to send people or persons to the places suited to their nature, disposition, and choice. Oh, may God teach me the things I know not. A forced obedience is no obedience at all; voluntary obedience is the only obedience that can be praise or blame worthy. All good desires come not by nature, but by the influence of God's Holy Spirit, through the mediation of Christ, which are given to make us sensible of our weakness and wants, that we may seek and have the same supplied: and of course, it is our duty to adhere to the sacred influence by solemn considerations, and a resolution to put in practice the same, by breaking off from that which we are convinced is displeasing and offensive in God's sight, and looking to him for the blessings we feel we want, in earnest expectation that he will bestow it through the merits of the Son.

Crossing Little River in a canoe, I held a meeting at ten o'clock in the morning; and though the notice was short, sixty or seventy came out, and it was a tender time.

Sunday 7th. I arrived in the town of Augusta, and my things having arrived, I went through the town, distributing handbills from house to house; some I gave to black people, some I flung over into the door-yards and some I put in under the doors, or through the windows where the lights were out; and whilst doing this, a negro came after me three times to go to his master's house, saying that Mr. Waddle, a Presbyterian minister, wanted me. I went and obtained a breakfast. He being about to leave the town, and hearing of me before, and being a candid man, was the means of removing prejudice, in some degree, from that society. Then I went to the Methodist meeting-house, where the preacher beckoned me to come up into the pulpit, which I declined until the third time, and then went. Said he, "The elder, Stith Mead, will be in town this morning, and he wants to see you." He had got on my track, and some knowledge of my conduct, which had removed prejudice from his mind. At length, he came, and after preaching a funeral sermon, offered me, if I desired it, liberty of the pulpit, and the privilege of giving out my appointment for the afternoon, which I accordingly did, and then went off to the Presbyterian meeting, and told them of it as soon as the meeting was dismissed; and the African Baptist likewise, and then to my room: (the people said, I was a crazy man.) The bell was rung to give the people notice; this was for the convenience of the Presbyterians. I spoke in my feeble way, and appointed meeting for the next evening. The Methodists said, "You will have no hearers to-morrow evening, for Mr. Snethen was liked the best of any minister that was ever here, and he could not get but few hearers on a week-day night." However, the people flocked out more on Monday evening than Sabbath, and I appointed for Tuesday, and told the young people, if they would come out, that I would give them hymn-books, which accordingly they did, and the congregation was larger still; I proposed a covenant to the people, to meet me at the throne of grace daily in private devotion, which hundreds agreed to, by rising up, for a space of time, which I bound them by their honor to keep.

I expected to leave town next morning, but S. Mead prevailed on me to tarry till the following sabbath, considering the prospect of good. Solemn countenances were soon seen in the streets. On Wednesday evening we had meeting in Harrisburg; on Thursday evening the man who had just finished a job about the meeting-house kept the key, so that it was with much difficulty that we obtained it for meeting in the evening: he assigned as the reason, arrearage of pay; we told the people of it. I mentioned that I esteemed it a privilege to have such a house to hold meeting in, and for my share felt willing to give ten dollars towards the deficiency; and if they would come forward and subscribe liberally, perhaps they might not feel the loss of it, for God might bless them accordingly. We got upwards of seventy dollars that night. I told the youth, if they would come to a prayer-meeting the next evening, I would give them some more books; about six hundred persons came out, to whom I gave seventy hymn-books more, making a hundred in all. Saturday evening and next morning I held meeting in the vicinity, and the work evidently appeared, for mourners came forward to be prayed for. In the afternoon I gave my last discourse in Augusta, and then I requested those that were determined to set out and seek God, to let me take their names in writing, that I might remember them in my devotions when gone. About seventy, who had been careless, came forward.

Last evening we got about thirty dollars more for the meeting-house. It was expected that I should have a contribution last meeting, for my labors and well wishes to the town, &c., which I declined, and many thought it strange; yet five dollars I was constrained by my friends to take from a man out of society, lest my refusal should do harm. Next morning, Dr. Prentice, who had treated me as a friend, and was the first man that gave me an invitation to make his house my home in this place, sent his servant and chair with me nine miles; thence I continued on my way towards Charleston.

Wednesday, 17th. I set off before sunrise, but was taken unwell; so I walked about ten miles, and whilst lying down under a pine, I reflected thus: how do I know but this weakness of body came by the will and wisdom of God, and in a way to do good, as afflictions happen not by chance nor come from the dust, but are God's mercies in disguise. Presently there came along a Methodist backslider, who at times strove to reason himself into the belief of deism and Universalism; but still he could not forget the peaceful hours he once enjoyed, for the word preached would reach his heart, so that he but seldom went to places of meeting. I obtained a promise from him, however, that he would try to set out again; and as we parted, he was tender. I spoke at night and next morning to a few, and some wagons coming along, I got liberty to ride in some of them by turns. My shoes heating my feet, I gave them away for some bread, having a pair of moccasins with me, which preserved my feet from the sand.

Friday, 19th. I called at a number of houses to get entertainment, but could not for love or money, till about the middle of the night, when coming opposite a house or cottage, an old woman opened her door, and, as I saw the light, begged permission to tarry, which I obtained; she gave me some bread, and said, "I suppose the other families did not take you in, but supposed you to be some thief, as you did not appear to be in the character of a gentleman." I paid her for my lodging, but for the bread she did not require it. Next evening I travelled till late, likewise inquired at almost every house for entertainment, but could not obtain upon any conditions. At length I espied a light, but durst not venture near it for fear of the dogs, but found a convenient tree, where I could screen myself from the dogs, and then alarmed the family. After some time I was answered, and piloted to the house, where I found an old woman and her son, and she, to relieve my hunger, gave me such as her cottage afforded, viz., coffee and cakes, gratis. However, I paid her, and next morning I went to Dorchester, and called on a Mr. Carr, to whom I had a letter, and spoke in his house, where good seemed to be done, after I had heard a Mr. Adams, an Independent minister, in their meeting-house.

Monday, 22d. I came to Charleston, and found the preachers friendly, and yet shy, for fear of the censure of the conference; so the preaching-house was shut against me. I called on Mr. Matthews, then one of Hamet's preachers, for some handbills which were sent there by Adam C. Cloud for me, [here I took the measles,] and distributed about twelve hundred of them through the town, and then obtained the liberty of the poorhouse, in which I held several meetings. Matthews invited me to supply an appointment for him in the great meeting-house which was built for the Methodists, and about which Hamet made crooked work, &c. When M. was gone out of town I advertised the meeting, and about two thousand attended, to whom I spoke; it was thought to have been as still a meeting as had been known in that quarter, for such magnitude. A collection was offered me, which I refused. A gentleman opened a large room, in which I held several picked meetings. A collection was offered here, which I declined; however, a few dollars I received from some, partly through constraint and the medium of Mr. Monds, who appeared loving and kind. The family here, where Jones the preacher had piloted me, expected pay for my board. I found a little book here which I wanted, and when paying for it, left money in the man's hands, a sufficiency for my board, and quit the house, and took up my lodging with Esquire Terpin, who was inclined towards the Friends or Quaker society, where I held several picked meetings. The Hamet Methodists were low; the Asbury Methodists (so called) were shy. At length I took my departure for New York. The measles appeared on my voyage, and the captain and all hands were unkind, and one passenger fired a pistol off near my head, in the small, tight steerage, which seemed to injure me much in my low state.

CHAPTER IX.

RETURN TO NEW ENGLAND.

APRIL 8th. I landed in New York, (though on our way we had crossed the Gulf Stream,) and about two days after, my life was despaired of by Dr. Lester, as the inflammatory fever had set in. Whilst I was confined at the house of brother Quackenbush, the Lord was precious to my soul; the sting of death was fled, and sometimes I turned my thoughts on future joys, and realized that some of my spiritual children had gone before, and I absent from Jesus. Oh, how did my soul wish to be in those sweet realms above! But then, turning my thoughts on time, I considered the value of souls, and that poor sinners were in the dangerous, blind, dark road; the question arose, which I would choose, to depart to Paradise, or spend twenty or thirty years more in this vale of tears, in laboring in the spirit of a missionary for the sake of my fellow-mortals' salvation; and, after a short pause, I felt such a travail for souls, that if it might be consistent with the Divine will, I wished to recover for their sakes, and still be absent from my crown of glory; yet I felt resigned to go or stay, as God should see fit.

After about twelve days' confinement, I put on my clothes with help, though during that time I could sit up but a very few minutes at a time, and that not without assistance, to prevent fainting. The day that I got able to stagger abroad, the mistress of the house was taken ill. The Lord was good that we were not both sick together.

I went to the south without consent. Some of the preachers in the city appeared shy, who were dear to me, which hurt my feelings, not to be visited in my sickness, though one came at times for a morning walk, and at length another; but perhaps there was a cause.

May 2d. God opened the way for my getting into the state prison, which

I had long before felt a desire to visit, to hold religious meetings there. Brother Kerr, whom I had seen in Ireland, was one of the keepers, and obtained a verbal permit for a friend of his to hold meeting with the convicts, though in general written ones from two inspectors were required from those who are invested with powers to grant them. Two Calvinists preached there generally: but this Sunday one of them was called away to a sacramental meeting, and the other readily consented to give up his part of the day without examining who or what I was. (These three circumstances, of the *one inspector* and *two preachers*, I perhaps view in a different light from what some do.) I thought predestination was poor stuff to feed these prisoners with, considering their conduct and state; so I spoke upon particular election and reprobation, and a free salvation, not out of controversy, but to inform the mind. I had held but one short meeting since my sickness, and I was still so weak that I scarcely knew how to stand; yet I soon forgot myself, and stood an hour: and in the afternoon I stood about two, whilst speaking on deism, and the melting power of God seemed to be present, as we formed a covenant to meet each other at the throne of grace, &c. I believe there was between three and four hundred prisoners. I spoke at night in the poorhouse.

Monday, 3d. I received a letter from one of the prisoners, who was condemned to imprisonment for life for the crime of forgery. He was a deist when put in; but now he seems desirous of salvation: he, in the name of a number, requested me to visit them.

Tuesday, 4th. I visited the cells where some of the most impenitent were confined, and tears began to flow: through the iron grates I spoke to others in the different rooms of the mechanics, (nailers excepted)—I spoke with some and prayed also, and all was still and attention; so my heart seemed to melt towards them with love. Then I visited the bad women, and it was observed that some of the worst of them were brought to bow. I obtained the favor of visiting the prison through, and speaking to the prisoners on a week-day. This, I was informed, had not been granted to any one before. They were going to petition the governor for a permit for the visit, if I had not obtained it without, considering I could not tarry till the following sabbath. Afterwards I was informed that a number became serious; and one who aided in burning Albany, who was deistical and a bad prisoner, got convicted, and died happy soon after; which was a matter of consolation to me. The preachers visited the prison, and hearing of the impressions made on some minds, appeared more soft and friendly, and had thoughts of offering me the African meeting-house; but feeling my mind bound for Connecticut, I could not feel free to stay. I got some religious handbills printed, and procured some books to give away, so I had not money enough left to carry me home; and giving away about seventeen hundred handbills over the city, I found a vessel for Middletown, and went on board just as she was going off, though the captain was a stranger to me. The vessel put into New Haven, where I debarked, and the captain gave me my passage gratis, though he knew not but that I had plenty of money, which happened well for me. I held a few meetings in New Haven, which seemed not altogether in vain, though the devil was angry and a few stones flew from some of his children or agents, one of which came through the window in the pulpit and struck just by my side. A young man of no religion left a dollar in my hand, which enabled me to take the stage (though I still was feeble in consequence of my late illness) thirteen miles and procure me a breakfast. Then walking a few miles to Durham, I called at an inn to rest, and the landlord, who was a Methodist, knew me, and constrained me to tarry all night and hold two meetings. I then sent forward appointments into the neighboring towns and parishes, &c. in every direction, though I knew not how I should get on to fulfil them.

Thursday, 13th. I arrived in Middletown, expecting the society would treat me coolly, but was agreeably disappointed. When in the south, I found some minutes of a conference held between the Presbyterian, Baptist, and Methodist preachers, twenty-five in number, to form regulations, &c. how the different societies might be on more friendly terms together, as the contentions between the different sects had been a great injury to the cause of religion in the unbelieving world. These minutes met my approbation, so I got hundreds of them reprinted, and sent them to ministers and preachers through the north. And finding the congregation divided about an Independent meeting-house here in Middletown, and being informed that the parties were to meet, &c., I went in the dead of the night and had some of my union minutes pasted on three doors of the meeting-house. The next morning they were read by many. I suppose each party on the first sight concluded it was a threatening from the other, till they found its contents. When they met, I sent in a petition for the liberty of its pulpit, &c., and afterwards the Methodists had it more frequent.

Oh, the mercy of God! Oh, the rebellion of man! Discouragements are before me, but my trust is still in God.

Saturday, 22d. Having had seventeen meetings the week past, which were as hard as thirty common ones, on account of their length, &c., a friend aided me with a horse; so I came to Eastbury about ten at night, where was a quarterly meeting; the preachers treated me with more friendship seven times than I expected, particularly Broadhead the elder, who had written to me in Europe a friendly letter, that many preachers and people in my native land would wish to see my face again, though I had never seen him before. I had laid out for the worst, and if I were disappointed it should be on the right side.

Sunday, 23d. I was permitted to preach for the first time at a quarterly meeting, and the melting power of God seemed to be present, and a quickening was felt among the people. I sent forward about threescore appointments in different parts of the state from this meeting, though I saw no way how I could get on to fulfil them. However, Providence provided a way. Abner Wood, one of the preachers, having an extra horse, offered it to me very reasonable, so I gave him an order on Mr. Garretson, for the eighteen dollars in his hands, and let him take my watch, (which a woman had sent me just as I was embarking for America,) at what price it should be thought proper, &c. Brother Burrows gave me an old saddle, and one of the preachers, John Nicholes, gave me a whip.

Selling the gospel is not in so good a demand now as formerly, and bigotry through America is falling fast, and God is bringing it down, and Christian love prevailing more and more. This visit, which I am now upon, was what I felt to be my duty when on my passage home across the Atlantic.

When I was on the Orange circuit, I felt something within that needed to be done away. I spoke to one and another concerning the pain I felt in my happiest moments, which caused a burden but no guilt. Some said one thing and some another; but none spoke to my case, but seemed to be like physicians that did not understand the nature of my disorder. Thus the burden continued, and sometimes felt greater than the burden of guilt for justification, until I fell in with T. Dewey, on Cambridge circuit. He told me about Calvin Wooster in Upper Canada, that he enjoyed the blessing of sanctification, and had a miracle wrought on his body, in some sense; the course of nature turned in consequence; and he was much owned and blessed of God in his ministerial labors. I felt a great desire arise in my heart to see the man, if it might be consistent with the Divine will; and not long after I heard he was passing through the circuit and going home to die. I immediately rode five miles to the house, but found he was gone another five miles further. I went into the room where he was asleep; he appeared to me more like one from the eternal world than like one of my fellow mortals. I told him when he awoke who I was, and what I had come for. Said he, "God has convicted you for the blessing of sanctification, and that blessing is to be obtained by the single act of faith, the same as the blessing of justification." I persuaded him to tarry in the neighborhood a few days; and a couple of evenings after the above, after I had done speaking one evening, he spoke, or rather whispered out an exhortation, as his voice was so broken in consequence of praying in the stir in Upper Canada; as from twenty to thirty were frequently blessed at a meeting. He told them that if he could get a sinner under conviction crying for mercy, they would kneel down a dozen of them, and not rise till he found peace. "For," said he, "we did believe God would bless him, and it was according to our faith." At this time he was in a consumption, and a few weeks after expired; and his last words were, as I am informed, "Ye must be sanctified or be damned," and casting a look upward, went out like a snuff of a candle without terror. While whispering out the above exhortation, the power which attended the same, reached the hearts of the people: and some who were standing and sitting, fell like men shot in the field of battle; and I felt it like a tremor to run through my soul and every vein, so that it took away my limb power, so that I fell to the floor, and by faith saw a greater blessing than I had hitherto experienced, or in other words felt a Divine conviction of the need of a deeper work of grace in my soul; feeling some of the remains of the evil nature, the effect of Adam's fall still remaining, and it my privilege to have it eradicated or done away. My soul was in an agony; I could but groan out my desires to God: he came to me and said, "Believe the blessing is now." No sooner had the words dropped from his lips than I strove to believe the blessing mine now with all the powers of my soul; then the burden dropped or fell from my breast, and a solid joy, and a gentle running peace filled my soul.

From that time to this, I have not had that ecstasy of joy or that downcast of spirit as formerly; but more of an inward, simple, sweet running peace from day to day, so that prosperity or adversity doth not produce the ups and downs as formerly; but my soul is more like the ocean, whilst its surface is uneven by reason of the boisterous wind, the bottom is still calm; so that a man may be in the midst of outward difficulties, and yet the centre of the soul may be calmly stayed on God. The perfections of angels are such, that they cannot fall away; which some think is attainable by mortals here; but I think we cannot be perfect as God for absolute perfection belongs to him alone: neither as perfect as angels, nor even as Adam before he fell, because our bodies are now mortal, and tend to clog the mind, and weigh the spirit down. Nevertheless, I do believe, that a man may drink in the Spirit of God, so far as to live without committing wilful, or known, or malicious sins against God, but to have love the ruling principle within, and what we say or do to flow from that Divine principle of love from a sense of duty, though subject to trials, temptations, and mistakes at the same time. But it is no sin to be tempted, unless we comply with the temptation, for Christ was tempted in all respects like as we are, and yet without sin. James saith, count it all joy when ye fall (not give way) into divers temptations, which worketh patience, and experience, &c. Again, it is no sin to mistake in judgment, and even in practice, if it flows from the principle of Divine love; for Joshua wholly followed the Lord, as we read: for one sin must have shut him out of Canaan, as it did Moses; yet we find he mistook in his judgment and practice, in the matter of Eldad and Medad, prophesying in the camp, thinking they did wrong, &c., which was not imputed as sin; and many infirmities we are subject to whilst in this tabernacle of clay, which we shall never get rid of till mortality puts on immortality. But nevertheless, as before observed, I think a man may have love the ruling principle, which is the perfection in Christ I contend for, and why may we not have it? God gives us desires for it, commands us to pray for it in the Lord's prayer, and that in faith; and commands we to enjoy it, and love him with all our heart, and his promises are equal to his commandments, which are, that he will circumcise our hearts to love him, and redeem us from all our iniquities; and as death doth not change the disposition of the mind, what nonsense it is to expect a death or future purgatory—no, we should expect it now, as now is the time and day of salvation, saith the Lord. Enoch walked with God three hundred years; the ancient disciples were filled with joy and the Holy Ghost; and John, and those to whom he wrote, were made perfect in love. David, when a stripling, was a man after God's own heart, but not when a murderer, for no murderer hath eternal life abiding in him, saith John, but after his confession, God put away his sin; and Paul, in Romans vii, spoke to those who knew the law and rehearsed the language of one under it, when he said, "I am carnal, sold under sin;" but in the three first verses of the next chapter, he informs us, that himself was made free from the law of sin and death: if so, he could not be groaning under the bondage of it, unless you can reconcile liberty and bondage together, which I cannot do, because I cannot think that a man can be carnal, which is enmity against God, and yet be one of the best of men at the same time, because it is a contradiction, and a contradiction cannot be true. A garrison may have inward foes bound, and armies without, perhaps three, and yet have peace among themselves: destroy some of the inward foes, and there are some left; destroy the whole, and there are none left within, yet there are some without, viz. the world, the flesh, and the devil; and there is need for the garrison or person to keep up their watch afterward when the inward foes are destroyed, as well as before, or else the outward foes will come in, and then they will have inward foes again. Therefore, you see that the blessing of sanctification is not only obtained by a single act of faith, the same as justification, but kept likewise by a constant exercise of faith in God, as a man going towards heaven is like one rowing up a river, who when diligent, makes headway, but if he stops, the tide will take him back. Therefore, as a vessel, whilst a stream runs in it, will be kept full, if it be full; but stop the stream above, and it will grow empty by the outlet: so the Christian, whilst in constant exercise of faith, enjoys constant communion with his God; but if he does but neglect his watch, he will feel an aching void within. O Christian! can you not realize this, or witness to it from experience?

Tuesday, 25th. I found my friends well in Coventry—held some meetings, and then proceeded to fulfil the errand or work which I had felt to be my duty when coming home from Ireland, namely, to travel the continent at large, to speak on certain points, which I conceived to stand, or be in the way, to the no small injury of Christ's kingdom, which I had been persuaded to give over the year before, at the New York conference, and in consequence thereof, felt my mind distressed, and as if I was delivering my errand to the wrong people, until I arrived in Georgia, for a recovery from my decline, which I believed came in consequence of the distress of my mind, which originated from undertaking to do that which I thought not to be my duty; when giving up my judgment to the judgment of others, in a matter of magnitude and conscience. Though having to trust Providence for my daily bread in future, as when in Georgia and Ireland; yet the peace of mind that I have, and do enjoy in this critical line of life, more than compensates for all the discouragements as yet, and my trust and hope is still in God, who hath helped and supported me hitherto. Gilead and Hebron were the first of my visiting on this tour, and the power of God was to be felt. Lord, open my door and prepare my way through the state.

29th. I went to Lebanon, through the rain, and spoke; and at Windham courthouse at night; the people, except a few, were solemn and tender; then tarried at a house where I called the first day I set out to face a frowning world, who then were prejudiced against me, but now more friendly. Oh cursed, hard prejudice, what hast thou done to benight the understanding and prevent it from judging right! it is the devil's telescope, and will magnify and deceive according as you look through it.

Sunday, 30th. I spoke twice in Scotland, and twice in Canterbury.

31st. I rode to Preston, and had one meeting, and three in Stonington, and a quickening seemed to run through the people. I feel the want of more faith. Faith among the preachers and people causes good meetings from the presence of the Lord. I spoke at the head of Mistick river, and in Groton, and New London, to many hundreds of people.

My way was singularly opened in Georgia, and so it hath been since my return. Glory be to God—who would not serve so good a Being as this?

June 2d. I spoke at Quaker-hill, and in Colchester four times that day; I trust not in vain.

The conference is sitting, and I expect to be as a leper shut out of the camp—yet I have broken no discipline, for I was only a preacher on trial, and never in full connection, and of course cannot be expelled from the connection, seeing I was never in. And I never was a member of the quarterly conference, and of course am not accountable to any particular quarterly conference for my conduct. And the class that I once belonged to, is now broken up; and my standing happened to be such, that there was none in particular to call me to an account; yet I had plenty to watch over me either for good or evil. If my standing had been any other than what it now is, I must have had my heels tripped up at this critical time.

Sunday, 6th. I spoke in the congregational meeting-house, in my native town.

Monday, 7th. The dysentery took away my strength considerably. Wednesday, I visited one in despair of God's mercy, though a member of the congregational church; she had been the means of turning her son from pursuing religion, back into sin.

Friday, 11th. I preached in Andover, to about a hundred, generally well behaved; this parish had been, something like Jericho, shut against the Methodists.

Saturday, 12th. This day or two past, I have been somewhat distressed. I went to Thompson, and on my way the burden fell, and was encouraged to go forward, as God's Spirit seemed to run through the assembly. I spoke in Pomfret, Brooklyn, Canterbury, Franklin, Norwich, and at the landing, where the people appeared serious, and many tender; at the latter place, one came to me and said, "Last August I heard you preach, and it was the means of my conversion to God, and one more also."

Tuesday, 15th. I spoke in Sterling, where the Methodists had not spoken before, and in Plainfield; thence to Bozrah, and some adjacent places, and had meeting. About this time, I fell in with the bishops on their journey to the east. Mr. Asbury was more friendly than I expected—and said, he thought I missed it, that I did not tarry at the New York conference, adding, if I could have cleared up some things (which I suppose was about my deserting the circuit, &c.,) to the satisfaction of the preachers, perhaps I might have been ordained; and added further, that my name was taken off the minutes, as they kept none on but such as travelled regularly. Mr. Whatcoat said, "We should join as one man to go forth as an army to hold each other up; but if you attempt to travel at large, you will meet with continual opposition from your brethren, (though some approbate you,) and this will have a tendency to discourage you, and weaken your hands, and wean you from your brethren, so after a while you will fall away."

I visited New Salem, Chatham, Haddam, and Guilford, where one got religion;* thence to Wallingford and Cheshire, where bigotry is great in the hearts of the people.

Tuesday, 22d. I had four meetings, and having fulfilled the first appointment about sunrise, in Newington, I went to the second in Wethersfield, and when I had done, a woman, who was a stranger, shook hands with me, and left a dollar in my hand, which was the only money I had had for some time. On the way to the third meeting, my horse flung me in the city of Hartford, and ran, and I got him no more till November following; when I was falling, my horse started towards me as I was getting on, pitched me over him to the other side, which some people

---

* Who since has become a black preacher in the West Indies.

seeing, screeched out, supposing my brains would be dashed out against the pavement; however, it so happened that I did not get entangled in the harness, and received no material injury, except a severe shock. How far angelic interposition is present on such occasions, we shall more clearly see in a coming world. The before-mentioned dollar enabled me to take the stage, and go on my route to Windsor. At the time I fell, I had about a hundred appointments given out, and about seven hundred miles to travel—all to be performed in five weeks; but how to get on, I did not know, as my horse was taken up and advertised, and got away again, and then not heard of for some time; and the man in whose possession they were, would not deliver up my saddle and outward garment, unless I would pay him several dollars, after proving them mine; so I left him to his conscience to settle the matter. However, my trust was still in God, whom I did think would overrule it for good, which accordingly took place; for there were several neighborhoods which I had previously felt a great desire to visit, but prejudice and bigotry had entirely shut up the way until now, when the above incidents were overruled to the casting of my lot in those vicinities, where the door was opened, and I held meetings, the fruits of which I expect to see in the day of eternity. I got assistance to Suffield, Westfield, Springfield, Ludlow, Wilbraham, Stafford, Ellington, East Hartford, Wapping, Hartford-five-miles, Mansfield, Eastford, Thompson, Killingly, Abbington, Plainfield, Voluntown, Cranston, and Providence—where *Providence* opened my way, by raising me up friends to assist me to get from place to place, to speak to thousands of people.

A few appointments were not given out according to my expectation, so I disappointed them, as they clashed with my own; but those which were given out according to my direction I fulfilled all, except one, which I withdrew, so none were disappointed. I visited Lyme, and several neighboring places. About this time I lost my pocket-handkerchief, and borrowing another at tea, forgot to return it as I arose from the table, and immediately went to meeting: from this circumstance, an idea was conceived that I meant to steal it. Oh, how guarded should we be against a spirit of jealousy, which is as cruel as the grave! However, I sent the woman money, as I had lost hers likewise, while riding. In ten weeks and two days I rode about fifteen hundred miles, and held one hundred and eighty-four meetings, and feeling my mind drawn out to declare a free salvation, I frequently stood three hours, and generally near two. I received two letters from Dr. Johnson, which were a comfort to me.

Daniel Ostrander is appointed presiding elder of Connecticut. He gave me a recommendation for a local deacon's ordination, &c.; but I observed a clause in the discipline that was made whilst I was in Europe, that every local preacher should meet in class, and that if he did not, he should forfeit his license, which made me rather suspicious about being ordained, as it would be impracticable to meet in a class, and yet travel as extensively as what I expected; and if I travelled without meeting in a class, I should forfeit my license, (or rather credential,) and if I proceeded without it, must forfeit my membership and be excluded, &c., and to be so excluded without breaking discipline, as I only had been on trial, and never in full connection, and had a right of course to desist, as well as they to stop me if they chose, as a trial implies a trial on both sides; nor. yet guilty of false doctrine, contrary to Methodism, or immoral conduct, (I was unwilling to put a sword in the hand of another to slay myself,) and though I had appointed a day to fall in with the bishop for that purpose, yet could not see my way clear to proceed, and so gave up my recommendation, lest it should be said, I converted it to a different use from what it was intended—not but what I was willing to be accountable for my moral conduct, if I could in any way, that I might follow the dictates of my conscience. I was fearful of hurting brother Ostrander's feelings by this refusal. Some said that I construed that part of the discipline wrong; however, I explained it as I thought it read, and afterwards asked J. Lee, who observed that he would have made use of that very passage to prevent one of his local preachers from travelling in my way, because a *local travelling preacher* is a contradiction in terms, and would be a bad precedent. Another time I wanted to cross a ferry, and thought, what shall I do for money to get over? I had none, and could think of nothing I had with me to pawn, and as I was mounting my horse a half-dollar was put into my hand by two persons, so I was provided for. About this time, I wanted a horse shod, and had given the last farthing of my money to have a school-house lighted in Glastenbury, and knew not where to look: however, a way was provided in a strange congregation, who knew not my necessity.

In Milton, Woodbridge, Stratford, Meriden, and several other places, I found kind friends to aid me, and some appeared to believe more freely in a free salvation, and good I have reason to believe was done. At length feeling my mind free from Connecticut, I took water passage from Fairfield to New York, and having paid my passage and procured some provisions, I had no money left; and having a tedious passage, the last twenty-four hours I had no food. However, I arrived in the city, and found some kind friends, who knew not my wants; for previous to my sailing my small-clothes I had left to be washed, which were to have been brought to me, but was disappointed of their coming, so I had not a necessary change. However, God still provided for me. One day, as I was walking one of the streets, Solomon Roundtree, from Georgia, being here after goods, saw me, and knew me, and called me into the store to know if I wanted or needed any thing. He gave me a pocket-handkerchief, a change of linen, cassimere for vest and pantaloons, and four dollars in money, for which may he be rewarded in a future day. The preaching-houses were shut against me. I made application for, and obtained permission to hold meetings in, the poorhouse school-room; and then, with much difficulty, obtained liberty of the Universalists' meeting-house. They thought the Methodists had something against me of a bad nature, or why would they shut me out, and keep me so distant? I spoke in the Universalists' meeting-house to a large assembly, and one of their preachers attempted to answer my discourse afterwards, and gave notice of his intention that night.

Mr. Sergeant, one of the stationed preachers, who had been opposed, now (as he there told me) became friendly; but T. Morrell, the superintendent, was still opposed, so I must do as I could, if I could not do as I would. I perceived by wrong information he had formed wrong ideas of me, as many others through the same channel have done: therefore as they mean well, though they lie under a mistake, it is not worth while for me to give them bitter retaliations, as many do who are opposed to the Methodists, and thus become persecutors. I ought to do right, if other people do wrong, and the best way that ever I found to kill an enemy, was to love him to death; for where other weapons would fail, this hath the desired effect, and I hope with me it ever may. After holding meetings in different private houses, whilst hundreds were listening in the streets, I at length felt my mind free from the city; though during my stay, I had walked thirty miles one day into the country, and had meeting at night, and likewise had obtained permission from the mayor to hold meeting in the Park, who sent constables there to keep order, and some said the mayor himself was there in disguise. I visited Turkey, in New Jersey, and Elizabethtown, where the meeting-house was open to me, and Thomas M——'s father, who calls himself a Bible man, gave me a dollar.

I embarked and sailed for Newburgh, where I felt previously a desire to go. The captain gave me my passage, though a Calvinist, and admitted prayers with on the way. I procured with some difficulty the liberty of an academy, in which I held two meetings. The people complained to their minister that I had destroyed their doctrine, (as was said,) and he must build it up, or they would hear him no more. He replied, "That it would take him nine sabbaths to build up what I had pulled down." He spoke two Sundays and made bad worse; then calling in help, *they* disputed about construing scripture, got quarrelling, and it terminated in a lawsuit, as one charged the other with heresy, and so was prosecuted for slander, &c.

I called on Elder Fowler, who I expected would keep me distant, but was agreeably disappointed; he gave me a horse, for getting it shod, to ride several days. So I visited Lattentown, where I was expected the day before; however, the disappointment was overruled for good, and being notified, more came out. I visited Plattekill, Pleasant Valley, Shawangunk, and several other places. At the Paltz, I was taken with a violent puking for several hours; but at length I embarked and landed at Loonenburgh, and walked to Schoharie, and saw my brother-in-law Fish for the last time. I visited Halabrook, Schenectady, Clifton Park, Niskeuna, Troy, and Half Moon, where I saw my friend R. Searle,* whom I had not seen for about eight years, except about five minutes. It seemed natural to see him, and brought past times fresh into my mind when he and his sister were in our native land, who were the only young persons I had then to associate with on religious subjects. Our meeting gave me a tender sensation, but it appeared that he could not see the propriety of my travelling thus, so I thought it most advisable to retire that day, and went to another place and held a meeting. Albany friends met me at a distance, and invited me to town to hold a meeting, which I accepted; but the preacher, Cyrus S., would not consent for me to go into the meeting-house, so hundreds were disappointed, as the trustees did not like to hurt his feelings: as he said, "If they let me in, he should petition the next conference not to give them a preacher." The society in general appeared friendly, and John Taylor opened his house, in which

---

* I have not seen him since; he has withdrawn and joined the Church of England.

I held meeting. This, Cyrus did not like. The Lutherans, it appears, would have lent me a meeting-house, but supposed I was wicked, or why should Mr. Stebbins shut me out? So I went to him to get a paper that there was nothing against my moral conduct; which he refused to give, adding, "that I trampled on the bishop's power, by travelling so independent, which if he was to do, he would have been cut off long ago;" likewise, "that it would be inconsistent for him to pave the way for me to obtain another meeting-house when he denied me his own," and said, "that he would rather have given ten dollars than to have had such an uproar in the society and city as there was since I came; and ten to the end of that, if I could not have been kept away without." Just after I began to travel he appeared friendly, and his labors were owned and blessed of God, and then he was a noisy Methodist.*

In Cobuskill we had a good time, and at Skenevius creek, where I saw some who were stirred up to become serious about the time I was in my native land; likewise an old uncle of mine whom I supposed was dead. I remember once some of his words when I was young, which made great impression on my mind in one of his visits.

September 15th. A large meeting being appointed for all denominations in the country, to worship God together in the woods, my brother-in-law and sister had striven to prevail upon me not to go, and at first prevailed; but feeling distressed in my mind I went, (an awful hail-storm happened in the way.) Hundreds collected, to whom I spoke; when others were coming on the ground, orders were given for all the official characters of the different religious orders to retire to a council-room, to consult how to carry on the meeting; they went, but I did not *feel free* to go till their business was nearly over. They agreed not to meddle with their *peculiarities*, but to be as near alike as they possibly could; but I was not there when they took the vote, so my hands were not tied. There were about two thousand people, and upwards of thirty ministers or preachers of the Presbyterian, Baptist, and Methodist orders, and took turns in speaking, and I spoke in the night. Next day I had thoughts of leaving the ground but got detained, and Calvinism came upon the stage; but the preachers' hands were tied so that they could not correct it; but I felt in my heart to speak on certain points, which liberty I obtained, and began meeting without singing or prayer, and my text I did not tell until towards the close of the meeting. I stood near three hours, and after we were joining in prayer and rising up, when no one in particular was speaking, several persons observed that they saw something fall from the sky like a ball of fire, about the bigness of a man's hat-crown. I did not see it; however, just at that moment, a number fell like men shot in the field of action and cried for mercy. The meeting continued nearly all night, and many found peace. The next day as I was going off, the people were so kind as to give me a horse, saddle and bridle. So after visiting a number of places, and attending a quarterly meeting at Paris, I went to Western with brother Miller, who has no children, except an adopted daughter,† (Peggy * * * * * * *.) I visited several neighboring places, and spent a week not in vain. I had an oilcloth cloak

---

* But now he has withdrawn and joined the Church of England.
† Who has since become my companion in life.

given to me, and then took my departure for Upper Canada. I swam my horse across Black River, and arrived at Kingston, through a black, deep-soiled, flat country, and so muddy that my horse could but just walk, and for miles together seeing nothing but the wild beasts of the desert. I visited several neighborhoods within forty miles of Kingston westward. I had several dollars offered me, which I refused, lest the circuit preacher (who was supposed to be sick, as he had disappointed a number of congregations) should think I hurt his salary, and this be brought against me at a future day. I went down about a hundred and twenty miles, holding meetings as I went, and frequently only on mentioning Calvin Worster's name, and the blessing he was to me, people who had here felt the shock of his labors were stirred up afresh, and some would even cry out, &c. I saw the grave of a distant relation of mine who had been a great traveller, but ended his life on an island at the mouth of Lake Ontario. Thus I see we must all die. Oh, the solemn thought! but when I cast a look beyond the bounds of time and space, I see, methinks, a beautiful place where saints immortal dwell, and where I hope, by God's grace, one day safely to arrive.

I recrossed St. Lawrence River, from Cornwall to St. Regis, and passing through an Indian settlement, who live in the English fashion in some degree, I came into Shadigee woods, so through to Plattsburgh, missing the road by the way. However, I was not hurt by the wild beasts, and found good places to cross the rivers, and my road brought me nigher than the usual road. I called at a house where two of my spiritual children lived, who were awakened on Cambridge circuit; but could rally nobody: so I turned my horse in a pasture, and took up my lodging under a haystack for the night; but towards day I heard a child cry, so I gave another alarm, and was cordially received in. I held meetings about here, and saw my friend J. Mitchell. I went to the Grand Isle and had two meetings; then riding three-quarters of a mile through the water on a sand-bar I came to Milton; thence to Fletcher, and saw the man that took my horse when I was going to Europe; thence to Hardwick, (being now in Vermont,) where my brother Bridgman and two sisters lived. My youngest sister seemed to have lost her desires in a great measure, and I could not prevail on her to set out again. This grieved my heart; I told them I could not bid them farewell, unless they would endeavor to set out and seek God afresh, though I wished them well.

I visited several neighboring places, and souls were blessed by God. Thence leaving Vermont I came over Connecticut River, into New Hampshire, where I met Martin Rutter going to form a circuit. I had felt a desire he should go into that part where he had set out to go. I gave him the names of some families where to call.

I saw Elijah R. Sabin, who had been a zealous and useful preacher, but was now broke down and married, and about to locate. I had meetings in Haverhill; then rode to Plymouth, and Holdness, and Meredith, and Gilmington, and the melting power of God seemed to be present in many places.

CHAPTER X.

RETURN TO GEORGIA.

I MET one who wanted my horse, by the name of Sealy. I told him he might have him if two impartial men would appraise him, &c. The two men could not agree; so they called a third, who judged in such a manner that this bargain, which was in connection with two others, was about two hundred dollars damage to me. It was my intention to have sailed for the south, which was the cause of my putting myself in the way whereby I was cheated as above. I believe God suffered these trials to befall me, for not being more submissive to go to the south by land, &c. However, I proceeded on foot, being a stranger in this part, until I came to old Almborough in Massachusetts, where I saw Stephen Hull, with whom I once was acquainted: he went out from near my native place to travel, but at length cut the connection, assigning as the reason his family, &c., and that he could nor get a support among the Methodists. I observed his wife was a pious young woman when with her father, Colonel Lippet, in Cranston, but now appears to be in a cold, uncomfortable state. Here I observed Mr. Wilson, of Providence, and John Hill, who now are Congregational ministers, though once Methodists, and once could kneel at prayer, but now I observed they stood. They compared themselves to "fixed stars," and me to a comet, which is supposed to connect systems. I neither felt freedom to eat or stay long, having arrived there at night, and went off in the morning before they were up; though I expected to have had the privilege of a meeting-house if I had tarried. I thought of the words of Judas, "What will ye give me, and I will deliver him to you," &c.

I took the stage to Haverhill and came to Boston; and Thomas Lyell,* who had been chaplain to Congress, and was the stationed preacher, would not suffer me to hold meeting in the meeting-house, or anywhere else; but said, if I did he should publish me accordingly, saying, I was not a travelling preacher, nor a local one, and of course he could not suffer meeting consistently; and if I would leave the town in peace without meetings, he would let me depart in peace. He asked me if I was needy, and provided me with a breakfast, and offered me an old coat, &c. I hired my board and lodging, and no vessel going out soon, my money failed me; so I was obliged to leave the town on foot, and then took stage and came to Worcester that night; then walked eighteen miles by moonlight to Charlton.

November 7th. I had a meeting at Dudley. 8th, at Sturbridge, Woodstock, and Ashford. 9th, I saw my parents, and my mother for the last time. 10th, I left my parents and walked about twenty miles, and rode in a wagon eighteen miles more; and as we were crossing a toll-bridge one began to run the rig upon me, asking me how much money I had got, and wanted to swap purses with me, and he considering himself a gentleman, I reached him mine with a few shillings in it, though I had

---

* He hath withdrawn and joined the Church of England.

but six cents left. He gave me his purse, but was sure to take out the contents in season. I thought he felt some conviction; he offered to swap back; but I said, a bargain is a bargain. Then a friend went a distance to where I had about twenty-eight dollars due; so I took an old mare and my bridle, and an old saddle being given to me, and set off for Georgia, having one quarter of a dollar in my pocket.

About this time I heard that the horse which had flung me in the summer was found, and that the man of whom I had him had got him again; so I went and got the same mare which I had let him have for it, and then sold her for a watch and spending money; and collecting about five dollars, in the name of the Lord I set forth, not knowing what was before me.

I had an appointment to preach, and making a mistake in the meeting-house I went up into the pulpit, but was soon drove out by the sexton, it being another man's meeting. However, when he had done I got a peaceable hearing in another place.

In Reading the Lord blessed the people; and at North Castle, White Plains, New Rochelle, Tuckahoe, Tarrytown, Singsing, and several other places. Then crossing North River I preached at brother Smede's, in Haverstraw, where some dated their awakening and conversion.

Thence to Pequest and Asbury, and then to Philadelphia, where Mr. Cooper and Elder Ware hatchelled me in such a manner as I never was before, without bitterness. They reasoned and criticised on me as if they were determined to search me out from centre to circumference. I did not think proper to answer all their questions, neither to assign all the reasons I had for my conduct. Mr. Cooper said, "Your European brethren oppose you, and your American brethren oppose you; and you say our rules are good, and yet you go contrary to them, and two opposites cannot be right, and consequently one must be wrong. Do you think that you are wiser than all the rest of the world? Lorenzo Dow has set up his will in opposition to his brethren, and is wiser than they all." He then said, that wo is to him by whom offences come, and that I offended my brethren. He then gave me a pair of scales to weigh in, and put my arguments in one side, calling them a feather, and his arguments in the opposite side, calling them ten thousand pounds, and then see which will weigh the heavier, a feather or ten thousand pounds; and so left it ringing in my ears, a feather or ten thousand pounds. I told him, that in matters of opinion barely, we should give up our judgment to the majority; but in matters of tender conscience before God, we must be our own judges: for if by hearkening to the other in giving up my conscience I am brought into trouble, how can I expect to be acquitted at the bar of God? He asked me, if I did not think the preachers were as conscientious as myself? I replied, that I did not like to answer that question; but thought some went more by reason, and that was better known to themselves than me: I must answer for one, and of course act for myself.

I went on my way to Wilmington, and called on a preacher who treated me coolly; so I put up at an inn. However, what Ware and Cooper said, discouraged me much; but the Lord, after I had submitted the matter to him, comforted my soul. For he had previously warned me in a dream of the night, that trials awaited me in Philadelphia, which I had told to brother E. Wolsey. I went on into Delaware, and came to a vil lage which appeared familiar as though I had seen it before. A collection was offered me which I refused, and went to Cokesbury; saw a preacher, and then went to Baltimore. After I held a meeting and saw brother S. Coate, who was friendly, and suffered me to improve in a prayer-meeting, an old man gave me two dollars, which I needed, as I had but one dollar and a half left me. Wells, the assistant, was out of town that time. H—y, a preacher, refused to tell me where the Methodists lived that way to the southward; yet I set off and rode about thirty miles to a place where I found a family said to be Methodists, and held a meeting; and likewise in the neighborhood (being detained by a snowstorm) several others. Thence I proceeded on my way, and met Bishop Whatcoat just as I had crossed Georgetown ferry. He treated me with love and tenderness, and after he had inquired my journey, I inquired his welfare, and he told me where to call and put up in Alexandria and Dumfries. So I found brother Brien and the assistant preacher, brother Roen, to treat me kindly. Thence on to Culpepper, where I spent Christmas, and received a dollar and a half, which, with two dollars I received at Alexandria, were of great service to me; though they knew not my wants. Thence to Louisa county, where my mare was taken sick, so I left her and went on to Cumberland county on foot; and while at breakfast I turned in my mind, What an apparent enthusiast I am! Yet I felt peace, and said in my mind, that my late misfortune should turn to the glory of God, and I felt within myself that I should yet see good days in this weary land, where I am now a stranger. Thence to Prince Edward county. On the way I called to dine, and paid the man beforehand; but the family were so dilatory, that I went off without waiting for it to be got ready. So crossing Coal's ferry I came to Danville. I spoke in Halifax by the way, where I was thought to be an impostor. Here a man overtook me with a horse which he led, lame and bareback; he suffered me to ride it about sixty miles. So I came to Stetesville, Iredell county, in North Carolina. My money being nearly all gone, I wanted to sell my watch for spending money. I got the watch low, at eighteen dollars, and offered it for nine, if I could have supper, lodging, and breakfast with it. A watchmaker came in and said it was a good one; so the innkeeper offered me nine dollars, or eight dollars and a half with supper, &c. I took the latter, and while I was asleep the mistress of the house was so good or bad as to send all round the neighborhood, as I was informed, to notify the people that a horse-thief was at her house, and if they did not lock up their horses they must expect one to be gone before morning.

Next day, I had my feelings in this strange land, and retired in private and renewed my covenant with God, that if he would suffer the providences to open before me as in time past, I would give up to suffer his will; for I felt as if I was not quite so resigned to travel, and pass through trials as in time past. My soul was refreshed to put my hope in God and look forward. I got a few together, and spoke in the courthouse—likewise at a Methodist house, where I was thought an impostor. Having a letter, I went to where it was directed, and the man of the house happened not to be at home, which was well for me; so I got a meeting, and the people were so well satisfied, that I got liberty and an invitation to speak again. About the same time Philip Bruce, an old preacher and presiding elder, came home from Virginia, and arrived at his father' about six hours before his father died; he felt hurried in his mind to hasten on the road. It appears that his father expected to see his son Philip by a conviction in his mind.

Philip Bruce heard of me, and charged his friends to be aware of me; but on hearing of my having related some of my past experience, recollected to have heard of me before, and retracted his first charge, and wished them to receive me if I came to their house, which was a means of opening my way. A day or two after, I fell in with him; he treated me as I would wish to be received by the influential considerate servants of God, while my conduct is as becometh the gospel of Christ. Here lived some who were called Presbyterians, which I called Presbyterian-Methodists, or Methodist-Presbyterians. They had the life and power of religion. They gave thirty-three dollars of their own accord, and eleven more were subscribed. James Sharp took the money, and let me have a horse, and trusted me for the remainder, though he had no written obligation, and some said he would lose it.

An opportunity presenting by a traveller, I sent on a chain of appointments towards Georgia. After holding several other meetings in Iredell, I set off, and had meeting at Major M'Claray's, Spartanburgh, Enore, Abbeville courthouse, so to Petersburgh in Georgia, where I arrived on the 2d of February, 1803, having had some trials, and experienced some providences by the way. I felt the want of credentials, as the Methodists for hundreds of miles had treated me coolly. However, as soon as I entered Petersburgh, a lad knew me, and soon word flew over the town that the walking preacher had got back, and I spoke to an assembly of magnitude that night. A society of Methodists was raised here when I was walking this country last year, though religion was cold. Now it seemed to flourish, my way was opened, and I sent appointments, and visited the country extensively as Providence enabled me to succeed.

At Rolem's meeting-house, and at Thompson's, Cunningham's, Powelton, Sparta, Rehobeth, Washington, Sardis, Indian Creek, General Steward's, Burk's, General Dickson's, Baker's, Carroll, Redwine's, Paine's, M'Daniel's, Coldwater, Stenchcomb's, and Sest's neighborhood, &c., I held meetings.

A camp-meeting, the first I ever attended, was held on Shoulder-bone creek, where I arrived on the third day of its sitting, about the dawn of it. I spoke several times, and the Lord was with us; ten persons came forward, and testified that they had found the pardoning love of God, among whom was Judge Stith, who had been a noted deist. In this quarter God gave me favor in the sight of the people, and some were raised up to supply my wants, among whom was Doctor B. and S. Roundtree, Doctor Lee, &c., and another gentleman, who gave me a cloak; for these favors, may God remember those who administered to my necessities.

I visited Hancock, Clark, Jackson, Oglethorp, Franklin, and Elbert counties, quite extensively; the congregations were exceeding large, so that I mostly spoke under the trees, and the Lord overshadowed us with his divine presence: the fruit of this visit I expect to see in a future world. Though it was by a very sweet drawing that I undertook to wander here by land, yet it was trying to my flesh and blood to leave my friends and acquaintance in the north, and wander so many hundred miles among strangers, considering what I had passed through before among strangers;

yet something within would say, go and you shall see peace; and I went and saw it; so I do not grudge all my toil. However, I was not without my trials here, considering the cause of God, for many of the Baptists supposed me to be a Baptist preacher when I was on foot through this quarter at first, and now flocked out by crowds to hear me, as I had said but little about names or parties when here before, and was coolly received by those whose friendship I wished to retain. The Baptists (of whom many are pious) were sorely disappointed in me now, when they heard my doctrine, or ideas on election and reprobation; and instead of owning me now for a Baptist, reprobated me to the highest pitch, and several church meetings were held on the subject, the result of which was, that they should hear me no more. Some of their preachers spoke hard against me in public and in private, behind my back; and some things I was informed they said which they could not prove; and all this, because I endeavored to show the evil of that doctrine which had been such a curse to me, and for preaching up a free salvation; which caused brother Mead to say, (as they now preached up eternal decrees more than usual,) "It will be the means of drawing out the cloven foot to cut it off"—meaning, it would cause the people to know their sentiments more fully, which they frequently kept hid, and so deceived the people, by preaching an offer of mercy, when only a few, the elect, could possibly have it. And as some of them said that I preached or held to things that were false, brother Mead, and a number of others, advised me to prepare for publication my *Thoughts*, or *Chain*, on different religious subjects.

I visited Augusta, and found a good society formed there; also Wanesborough, Sandersville, and many other adjacent places, together with Louisville the capital, where the governor offered me money, which I did not feel free to accept, but was thankful for his good wishes.

March 25th, 1803. Camp-meeting came on at Jones's meeting-house, and lasted until the 29th. Some were convinced of error of sentiment, and some of sin, and a goodly number found peace in the blood of the Lamb, and the world's people were brought to acknowledge that something out of the common course of nature must have produced the effect in two instances. I found the people here kind, for as Hope Hull mentioned to them that I was about to go to the western country, and perhaps I might want some spending money, &c., upwards of a hundred dollars were given me; so I found the Lord to provide, who put it into the heart of General John Stewart to get me a pass on parchment from the governor, under the seal of the state, to pass through the Indian country.

My horse not being good for travelling, I sold him on credit, and a Methodist, so called, having one for sale, offered him to me for a hundred and fifty dollars. This man who was called a Methodist, did not show me the kindness to wait, as another man of no society and of no religion did; for the latter was bound for me, though he had not seen me before; and he also carried the money a distance for nothing; so I see that the hearts of all men are in the hand of God, and he can and doth work by whom he pleaseth.

Feeling my soul refreshed by my visit, and my work done here for the present, and my horse paid for, and I well equipped for travelling, and my heart drawn to the west, and a number of letters being given me to give to people, I was resolved to go to the westward. I accordingly told brother

Mead, who was going to Virginia, that if he was minded he might give out a chain of appointments for me, through that country, to which he agreed. (During this visit, I had a narrow escape from a raving heifer.) I felt a desire to hold meeting in a certain house of quality people; but knew not how to accomplish it. But a thought struck my mind; so I got one to go and deliver an errand in such a way as to provoke the man to say, "I'm willing if my wife is," and the woman to say, "I'm williug if my husband is;" which was effected by the errand being delivered to them separately. I then published the appointment, but it so happened, that the family were all from home, except the blacks, at the time of meeting; so I spoke before the gate in the road, and had a good time: but I received a few lines from one of the absentees, expressing grief on their side at the circumstance.

April 19th. Being provided with necessaries, I crossed the Oconee river, and there meeting some persons, set off for Tombigbee; but I had not proceeded a hundred yards, before I found that one on whom we depended as a guide, knew nothing about the road; of course, I must depend on my own judgment. I had procured a map of the road, a hundred and thirty miles to the Chatahochee river, and a pocket compass, &c. A young man from Connecticut, who was acquainted with some of my relations, was feeding mules in the woods, so we followed him a few miles, and then encamped in the wood for the night. Next day a woman and a child got flung from a horse, and thereby were ducked in the Ocmulgee river. So we proceeded on, frequently seeing Indians, (which a black woman of the company was much afraid of,) till we came to Flint river, where we hired an Indian to lead a horse through, and himself waded before it. Some of the land over which we passed, was miserable, and some was preferable to any I had ever seen in the south. We frequently saw wild game, among which were deer and turkeys. The Indians frequently came to our camp, and while we had our evening devotion, they would be solemn and mute: we could talk together only by signs, and I desired to know if they knew what we were about; they replied, that we were paying our addresses to the *Great Man* above, who is the author of breath, &c. Thus all intelligences have some idea of Divinity, futurity, and rewards and punishments. And what causes such universal acknowledgment, but an universal teacher? which must be God! I broke my umbrella, and likewise lost my whip, the latter while buying corn, and hiring a pilot.

One day a couple of us thought to get to the agent's house before the company to get provision, but had not gone far before an Indian alarmed us much, shooting a deer through, and the ball struck near us, which made us suppose some hostile intention was against us till we saw the mistake. We left a man and a woman in the woods, who were going to trade with the Indians, as they travelled slow.

Hawkins, the agent, treated us cool, so we quit him and went on. Next day we missed our road, or rather Indian path, which we were convinced of by some swamps and water-courses, and turning a little back, one of the company being a good woodsman took the lead, and striking across we came to a path, which divided the minds of the company at first; but at length we agreed to strike across it further through the woods, and that afternoon found a path which proved to be the right one. We at length found a man hunting horses, who piloted us to the first house in the settlement, which we made in thirteen days and a half from the time we set out, having travelled about four hundred miles.

The company supposed that they could save thirty or forty miles' travel by swimming across the Alabama River, and fording a swamp, which they attempted to do, and got detained by rain two days. But I left them and went down the river ten miles and stayed with a half-breed Indian, who charged me a dollar and a half for the night. I then left an appointment for Sunday in the Tensaw settlement, and went over the Alabama by the Cutoff, to the west side of Tombigbee, through a cane-brake or swamp, seven miles, and found a thick settlement, and then a scattered one seventy miles in length, through which I sent a chain of appointments, and afterwards fulfilled them, and the fruit I expect to see at a future day.

The river Tombigbee, like the Nile, overflows once a year, and is also a flood-tide river only once in twenty-four hours. It is navigable for vessels, and will one day become the glory of the south part of the United States, as the trade of Tennessee, &c., will pass through it. The inhabitants are mostly English, but are like sheep without a shepherd. Whilst under the Spanish government it was a place of refuge for bad men; but of late, since it fell to us, it seems to be in a hopeful way, and there is still room for great amendment. A collection was offered to me, which I did not feel free to accept; and I left the settlement, procured some corn, and had not a cent left. Three of my travelling companions fell in with me again, and accompanied me through the Choctaw nation to the Natchez settlement, which we reached in six days and a half, being about eight hundred miles from Georgia. On the way we met with a man going alone to Georgia; and in the sixth town I gave my saddle-cloth to the Indians for corn to feed my horse with.

Here I was called to another exercise of my faith, having no money, and a stranger in a strange land; but my hope was still in God, who hath helped me hitherto. The master of the house to which I first came was once a Methodist. He happened to hear of my coming the week preceding, by some travellers, and received me and the three men kindly, and the next day got me a meeting, and good I trust was done. The night after I held a meeting at the house of a Baptist; then rode on towards the town of Natchez, and parted with my three companions by the way, who were going to West Florida to see their father.

I called on a man who was said to be a Methodist, but found he was not; so I went to another house where they were called Methodists, but met with a cool reception at the first until I showed them the governor's passport, and likewise two papers, one from brother Mead and one from Hull, that I was an acceptable preacher, of moral conduct, &c.; then they were more kind, and kept my horse about two weeks. Brother Moses Floyd met me the same night, and having received letters by me from Georgia, was friendly; then the above family became more so. The governor, to whom I had an introductory letter, was also friendly.

I held two or three meetings in the assembly-room, with the permission of the mayor, though with difficulty obtained. The man on whom I called and found he was not a Methodist, reflected how far I had come to see them through the woods, and felt his heart inclined to lend me a horse to ride more than a hundred miles. So I went to Kingston, and procured a spot of ground (by selling my watch) for a meeting-house ; and then to the heights, and Pinckneyville, and held meetings. I stopped at a house in the edge of West Florida and sold my cloak. Thence I returned and visited several neighborhoods, and God's power was to be felt in some of them.

My horse was now taken lame, so that he was not fit to ride to Tennessee. I spoke at the Pineridge meeting-house, and at Washington, Sulsertown, and at Calender's meeting-house, where some were offended. Here quarterly meeting was held. Thence I went to Wormsville, Biopeer, and Bigblack, and preached the funeral sermon of a niece of the Rev. Tobias Gibson ; and the Lord was with us. I left my horse with brother Gibson, and took a Spanish race-horse, which he was to be responsible for, and I was to remit him the money by post when it should be due on my arrival in Georgia in November.

June 20th. Having got equipped for my journey through the woods of Cumberland, which was several hundred miles, and having been informed that a party of men was that morning to start into the wilderness, I intended to go with them, but on my arrival found they had started the day before ; so I must either wait for more, or go and overtake them. To wait I durst not, as my appointments had gone to Virginia. A Kentuckian had some time before, as I was informed, struck an Indian, who shortly after died ; and the other Indians supposed that his death was in consequence of the blow, and they complained to the governor, and the Kentuckian was tried and acquitted. Wherefore the Indians, according to their custom, were determined to kill somebody, as they must have life for life. And they had now become saucy, and had shot at and wounded several on that road, but had not killed any one yet ; and it was supposed that some one must shortly fall a victim. However, I set off alone and rode the best part of twenty miles, when I saw a party of Indians within a hundred feet of me. I was in hopes they would pass me, but in vain, for the first Indian seized my horse by the bridle, and the others surrounded me. At first I thought it was a gone case with me ; then I concluded to get off my horse and give up all in order to save my life. But it turned in my mind, that if I do, I must return to the settlement in order to get equipped for another start, and then it will be too late for my appointments. Again it turned in my mind, how, when I was in Ireland, somebody would frequently be robbed or murdered one day, and I would travel the same way the day before or the day after, and yet was preserved and brought back in peace, and the same God is as able to preserve me here and deliver me now as then. Immediately I felt the power of faith to put my confidence in God. At the same time I observed the Indians had ramrods in the muzzles of their guns, as well as in their stocks, so it would take some time to pull out the ramrods, and get their guns cocked and prepared up to their faces ready to shoot. At this moment my horse started and jumped sideways, which would have laid the Indian to the ground who held the bridle, had it not slipped out of his hands. At the same time the Indian on the other side jumped, seemingly like a streak, to keep from under the horse's feet, so that there was a vacancy in the circle, when I gave my horse the switch, and leaned down on the saddle so that if they shot I would give them as narrow a chance as I could to hit me, as I supposed they would wish to spare and get my horse. I did not look behind me until I had got out of sight and hearing of the Indians. I was not long in going a dozen or fifteen miles; so I overtook the company that day, and told them what I had passed through. They said that they had met the same Indians, and that a Chickasaw trader who was with them, told them, that two Chickasaw Indians with him said, that the Choctaws which I met informed them, that if the Chickasaw trader was not with these Kentuckians they should have taken their provisions from them. When I heard this, I reflected if such a small preventive was the only means of saving a party from being plundered, what danger was I exposed to? And I felt more solemn afterwards than when in the midst of dangers.

About forty-eight hours after, a party of twenty-five men were attacked by some ruffians, driven from their camp, and plundered of some thousands of dollars, and some of them came near starving before they got in.

I travelled on several days with the company, but they proceeded so slow that I resolved to quit them; and thinking I was within about forty miles of the Chickasaw nation, set off alone one morning in hopes of getting in the same night. So I travelled on all day as fast as I could conveniently, stopping only once to bait, until I came within about twenty miles of the settlements; and about ten at night came to a great swamp, where I missed the trail, and was necessitated to camp out without any company, (except my horse,) fire, or weapons of defence. As I dismounted to fix my bridle and chain together for my horse to graze, while fastened to a tree, I heard a noise like the shrieks of women, and listened to know what it might be; but it occurred to my mind that I had heard hunters say that the catamount or panther would imitate the cries of women. At first I felt some queries or fears in my mind; but I soon said, God can command the wild beast of the forest as well as he can command the Indians: so I knelt down and committed myself to the protection of a kind Providence, and then lay down and had a comfortable night's rest. The next morning I went on and joined the settlement about ten o'clock, and got some milk and coarse Indian bread for myself, and corn for my horse. I then went on about twenty miles further, and, through the good providence of God, did not miss my road, though there were many that went in different courses. At length I saw a man dressed like a gentleman: he came up and shook hands with me, and after some conversation invited me to his house, about a mile and a half off. I tarried with him a few days, and had two meetings with some reds, blacks, whites and half-breeds; and good I think was done in the name of the Lord. The post came along and I left Mr. Bullen, the missionary, with whom I spent my time, and set off with him. In three days and a half we travelled upwards of two hundred miles, and came to the settlements of Cumberland; and, having a letter, I called on Major Murray, who treated me kindly. I gave away the last of my money and my pen-knife, to get across an Indian ferry. I sold my chain halter for two dollars, and brother Murray lent me a horse to ride to Nashville, where I got two or three letters, which I consider as the hand of Providence, as it was the only means of opening my door. I inquired for Methodists, but found none—I strove to get a place for meeting that night, but all in vain: so I went about six miles and called upon a local preacher, who treated me with friendship, and I tarried all night. Next day early I returned to Nashville, and tried to get the courthouse, and several private houses; but all in vain. Then I went to a grog-house and began to talk ironically, as if I was one of their company: and soon the man offered me the liberty of his house for what I would choose to give him; he supposing I was not in earnest. But I let him know that I was, by giving him a dollar, and told him as a man of honor I should expect the room of him. I then went out and told the post-master, who advertised it for me, as he knew by the superscription of my letters that I was no impostor. I returned to Major Murray's, and delivered up my horse, where was a class-meeting. The circuit preacher was cool; but Mr. Cannon, a local preacher, being a man of consideration, prevailed. I met the class, and the Lord being with us we had a good time: so my way was opened through the country. The grog-house in Nashville would not contain the people, and somebody prepared the market-house for me. I spoke and described the character of a Christian, a gentleman, and the filth of the earth, which were the subjects of my discourse: and some, fearing of coming under the class of filth, behaved well. I appointed meeting again, in the courthouse, if it should be opened, if not, on the public square, or in an adjacent grove, as might serve best. The court sat in the mean time, and they ordered the courthouse to be opened, and I spoke to hundreds. Contributions were offered me, which I refused; however, several dollars were forced on me by some gentlemen. The cause of my refusing the above was this: I did not wish to put myself in the power of another, nor give Satan a sword to slay me, or power to hedge up my way, as the eyes of hundreds were upon me. A camp-meeting was held; but I believe good was prevented by their not following the openings of Providence.

I visited several other places, and then went to Kentucky, and visited Beardstown, Frankfort, and Lexington. Some Methodist local preachers treated me coolly, and strove to shut up my way; but God opened my way by the means of a Baptist, at Beardstown. At Frankfort I got the state-house: and at Lexington I first got the courthouse, then a playhouse, and afterwards, the Methodists opened to me their meeting-house—in several meetings God was with us. Thence I steered to Virginia. On the way I was informed of an old salt well being found and a large bed of ashes by it, and pieces of earthen kettles, denoting their size to be larger than potash kettles; and also vessels of stone like a salt-cellar, which must have belonged to the ancients.

At an inn I offered the man pay over night; but he refused, saying he would be up in season in the morning. However he was not, so I left what I supposed would be his demand, on the table, and went on: he afterwards reported that I had cheated him. At another place, all my money was gone to one dollar, and the landlord, attempting to accuse me of passing counterfeit money, would not exchange my dollar for my fare, but thought to injure me, until another man changed it for me. At length, I met two men, who told me that my appointments were made in Virginia, at Abington, where I arrived August 21st, about three hours before meeting time. I was now dirty and ragged, as my pantaloons were worn out, my coat and jacket worn through, as also my moccasins. I had only the smallest part of a dollar left: however, some gentlemen gave me seven dollars, and then a collection was made, which I refused, until they hurt my feelings and forced it upon me: some others held back their liberality. I had a convenient stage erected, and we had a solemn time. I left an appointment when I would be there again, and in the neighboring counties, and went on to Fincastle; then to Bedford county, where I spoke in the town of Liberty. I took my text from the *Age of Reason;* and some went off before I had cleared up the point, they supposing me to be a deist; but afterwards were sorry. I spoke in Lynchburgh, New-London, at Carmel Courthouse, and a number of adjacent places, and left hundreds of appointments for the spring. I saw Dr. S. K. Jennings, and found him to be a man of strong powers of mind, and great acquired information, and very pious. Oh, may he fill up that sphere of life, which he is qualified for.

In Cumberland county John Hobson, Jun., got awakened, and found peace, as he fell down while I was speaking. His dear companion was laboring under great trials of mind, for the loss of all her offspring, till God cast my lot in that quarter, when she got reconciled to the same, by the sanctifying influence of God's Holy Spirit. His mother, who was upwards of eighty years old, also found peace. I visited several other places, and the Lord was with us. Then I went to Richmond, and by the governor's consent, spoke in the capitol, (which somebody had advertised in the Argus,) and afterwards in the Methodist meeting-house several times: also in Manchester, and at New Kent quarterly meeting.

I rode twenty miles to Petersburgh in the rain, and seeing a man, inquired of him if he knew Jesse Lee. He replied, "he is my brother," and took me to his house. As soon as I passed the gate, I saw Jesse standing in the door, and I sat still on my horse, though I was wet through, (with a bundle of books under my arm.) I had no outer garment on; and there was not a word spoken for some time between us. At length, said he, "Come in." I desired to know whether it was war or peace. Said he "Come in." Said I, "Is it war or peace?" Said he, "Come in." I made the same reply. Said he, "*It is peace.*" So I dismounted and went in, and he, after some conversation, went and procured me a large assembly that night, in the Methodist meeting-house. I spoke there several times, and God was with us. Oh, how different was I now received from what I was formerly! Surely I was agreeably disappointed in my reception; and there must have been the hand of God in this. I visited several neighboring places not in vain. I got five hundred pamphlets printed, and as I was going to the office for them, a stranger called me out one side and put ten dollars into my hand, (though he knew not my necessity) which was just the sum I wanted for the printer.

I had much offered me in my travels through the state; but was unwilling to give Satan any ground to hedge up my way, and of course declined the most of it. One day I had an appointment to preach, and then started for South Carolina, through a part of some hundreds of miles, where I never was before, and had only a few cents at my command. However, my trust was still in God, who put it into the hearts of some, as we were parting and shaking hands, to leave about seven dollars in my hand: so I went on and saw more providences of God: I also saw some evils. Near Raleigh, North Carolina, a petty constable attempted to take me up as a *horse thief.* Col. Paul Rushian, of Chesterfield county, South Carolina, took me up also, examined my private writings, and gave me some of the most abusive, dirty language that I ever met with in my life. I found brother Dougherty, the presiding elder, had given me out a chain of appointments througn his district, of several hundred miles, which I fulfilled, and arrived back at Petersburgh, in Georgia, according to appointment when going away. Here my wants were relieved, mostly by Major John Oliver, who came and called me his spiritual father, and so did several others; and I saw a great alteration in the inhabitants.

RULES FOR HOLY LIVING.

SERIOUS *considerations* upon the value of thy SOUL; with the shortness and uncertainty of TIME, and the *duty* that you owe to GOD—with the awful consequence of *living* and *dying* in SIN!

REMEMBER that by *nature* you are a fallen, *degenerate* creature, therefore you must be *regenerated* and BORN of the SPIRIT—for without holiness no man shall see the LORD!

Consequently, be persuaded, and *resolve*, through grace, to *begin*, and *spend*, and *close* every day with GOD, forsaking all known sin, with unnecessary wicked company; having your heart drawn out after GOD, in a praying frame, with your mind solemnly staid upon HIM in quest of truth—that you may enjoy HIS favor here, and experience HIS benedictions for ever in CHRIST JESUS!

THE JOURNAL

OF

LORENZO DOW.

PART SECOND

CHAPTER I.

CAROLINAS AND TENNESSEE TOUR.

October 28th, 1803. After an absence of about seven months, I arrived back in Georgia, having travelled upwards of four thousand miles. When I left this state, I was handsomely equipped for travelling, by some friends whom God had raised me up in time of need, after my trials on my journey from New England. My equipment was as follows: My horse cost forty-five pounds, a decent saddle and cloth, portmanteau and bag, umbrella and lady's shove whip, a double suit of clothes, a blue broadcloth cloak, (given me by a gentleman,) shoes, stockings, cased hat, a valuable watch, with fifty-three dollars in my pocket for spending-money, &c., &c. But now on my return I had not the same valuable horse, and my watch I parted with for pecuniary aid to bear my expenses. My pantaloons were worn out, and my riding chevals were worn through in several places.

I had no stockings, shoes, nor moccasins,* for the last several hundred miles, nor outer garment, having sold my cloak in West Florida. My coat and vest were worn through to my shirt; my hat-case and umbrella were spoiled by prongs of trees, whilst riding in the woods. Thus with decency I was scarcely able to get back to my friends as I would. It is true, I had many pounds and handsome presents offered me in my journey, but I could not feel freedom to receive them, only just what would serve my present necessity, to get along to my appointments, as I was such a stranger in the country, and so many to watch me (as an impostor) for evil, and but few to lift up my hands for good.

As I considered that the success and opening of many years depended on these days, I was not willing to give any occasion for the gospel to be blamed, or any occasion to hedge up my way. For it was with seriousness and consideration that I undertook these journeys, from conviction of duty, that God required it at my hands. And, knowing that impostors are fond of money, I was convinced that Satan would not be found want-

---

* An Indian shoe.

ing to whisper in the minds of the people, that my motives were sinister or impure.

Major John Oliver came and took me by the hand, calling me father, saying, "When you preached in Petersburgh last, your text was constantly ringing in my ears, for days together, whether I would deal kindly and truly with the Master, &c.; so I had no peace until I set out to seek the Lord: and since, my wife and I have been brought to rejoice in the Almighty."

He gave me a vest, pantaloons, umbrella, stockings, handkerchief, and a watch, &c. Another gave me a pair of shoes and a coat, a third, a cloak, and a few shillings for spending-money from some others. Thus I find that Providence, whose tender care is over all his works, by his kind hand is still preserving me. Oh, may I never betray his great cause committed to my charge!

I visited the upper counties, and had refreshing seasons among my friends, from the presence of the Lord. General Stewart informed me of a remarkable circumstance, of a man who heard the doctrine of unconditional election and reprobation preached up. The devil told him that he was one of the reprobates, which drove him to despair; so he put an end to his life by blowing out his brains. An A-double-L-part minister, who held the doctrine of unconditional election and reprobation, preached up good works, saying, "it would do no good to preach his sentiments;" which caused my spiritual father (in the gospel) to observe to him, "that a doctrine which is not fit to be preached, is not fit to be believed."

I held a meeting in a republican meeting-house, that is, one free for all denominations. I spoke on A-double-L-partism. An A-double-L-part preacher present being asked how he liked the preaching; he replied, "that he held and preached no contrary sentiments himself." But afterwards, he did his utmost to cut my doctrine to pieces, and blacken my character. I preached in Georgetown, and set out at eight at night for Augusta; and travelling nearly all night, I came to a camp where some negroes were *toting** tobacco to market. I stopped with them until day, and one gave me some corn for my horse.

The next day, missing my road, I gave my pocket-handkerchief for a pilot.

November 20th. I arrived at camp-meeting at Rehoboth. I took, "Master, I am," for my text; with observing that he offered a great reward for runaways, whose marks I would describe. The auditory, amounting to about five thousand, sunk into a solemn silence, whilst I described the diabolical marks of sinners, and the reward for their return, &c.

About fifty souls were born to God. There were forty-four tents, eight wooden huts, forty-eight covered wagons, besides carriages, &c., of various sorts. Many I parted with here whom perhaps I shall never see more, and set off for St. Mary's, in company with several of the preachers. As we hove in sight of a town, I inquired its name, and felt an impulse to stop and hold meeting, which I did, intending to overtake my

---

* The mode of toting tobacco to market is by rolling it in casks, with a wooden axle through the middle, on the ends of which are fastened the shafts for the horse to draw it by. Fifteen or sixteen hundred weight may thus be pressed and carried to market.

company next day; but leaving Warrington late at night, I rode several miles, and stopped to inquire the road. The man within knew my voice, and persuaded me to alight and tarry until morning, when he accompanied me to meeting, in Bethel meeting-house, where I was drawn particularly to speak of murder and murderers; after which brother Mead observed, that two murderers were supposed to be present.

November 23. I spoke in Louisville to as many as could conveniently get into the statehouse. Brigadier-general John Stewart was then present. I attacked A-double-L-partism, and proposed a covenant to the auditory, to meet me at the throne of grace, for a limited period of time, when the gentlemen observing General Stewart to arise, followed his example, as a sign of their compliance with the proposal; which I observed, they were bound by the principles of honor and veracity to keep.

Whilst I was preaching, I pointed out the duty of rulers, as stewards of God and guardians to the people, that vice might be suppressed, and virtue encouraged. Whilst speaking, also, I perceived the chair on which I stood, on the writing-table, to move twice or thrice, the cause of which I could not then ascertain, but sat down to prevent my falling. After meeting, a young German, having observed a Baptist preacher to put his foot on my chair twice or thrice, apparently with a design to tilt me over and set the house in a laughter, (who was an A-double-L-part man,) went and shook his fist in his face, intimating that, if he had him out of doors, he would pay him for his insult to the stranger.

The A-double-L-part man, being a member of the legislature, complained of the young man to the house for having insulted him. The house ordered the young man to prison, and the next day to trial, as no member might be insulted whilst sitting in the house. The young man pleaded that the member was not sitting at the time, and so was acquitted. This cost him about thirty dollars, and the state about six hundred, as the trial lasted two days. It was a few days after this that I received a recommendation, as a preacher of the gospel to the world of mankind, signed by the governor, secretary, and twenty-eight members of the legislature, with the great seal of the state.

Bishop Asbury's appointments being given out, and it being uncertain whether he would attend, Stith Mead, who was presiding elder of the district, thought proper to send me on his own appointments to St. Mary's quarterly meeting, whilst he intended to take the bishop's plan.

25th. The high waters retarded; but to prevent disappointing the people in my circuitous route, I made the greatest speed; and a gentleman-traveller supposing, from my speed, that I was some murderer, clapped spurs to his horse and pursued me to a meeting, where God's power was manifested among us.

26th. I held a two days' meeting at Union meeting-house, where there was some quickening; but the A-double-L-part people were in this part also raking my character.

Hence to Kenootchy creek, and so to Tabor's creek; and Captain Mitchell, in whose house I held meeting, so interrupted, that we removed into the street. Then he ordered me down from the stage, and we retired to a neighboring plantation; but he took his horse and pistols, and interrupted us here also. Oh, the sin of drunkenness, which leads to murder!

My evening appointment was not given out near the Goose ponds, and I found it almost impossible to get a place to lodge.

December 3d. I crossed the Altamaha, and met brother Isaac Cooke, who came missionary from conference here, the most dismal, marshy part I ever was in. I found he had good success, though he was not without his enemies; but God, for his indefatigable labors, gave him upwards of a hundred members this year, and he had two meeting-houses erected for the connection.

A clear conscience is like a clear sky without a cloud. Oh, may I never live to be useless! I remember Doctor Johnson said, "Thou hast an ulcer or defect in thy liver, with which thou wast born into the world; and if thou livest high or intemperate, or bringest slight condemnation or burden on thy mind, or dost not labor hard, &c., &c., the nature of thy disorder is such, thou wilt be in danger of being suddenly cut off: but if thou art prudent, &c., thou mayest live as long as most others, unless some contagious disorder shall lay hold on thee." The propriety of these remarks I am convinced of from experience.

We took our departure from Savannah, where we parted, and I spent a few days. The curse of God seems to rest about here since the days in which they treated John Wesley ill, and confiscated the property of George Whitfield, which was appropriated to religious and charitable purposes.

Hence to Tukisaking, where old father Boston lived, who received me as I left Savannah the first time I came to Georgia. Last night, as brother Cooke was preaching, a black woman was struck under conviction, with the power of God. Her body was cold as a corpse, and laid aside sixteen hours as in a sweet sleep or state of insensibility, and no symptoms of life, except a regular pulse. Some thought that she would never come to; however, she revived, praising God. I spoke, and we had a refreshing time in the woods.

I sent an appointment to Lanear's ferry, on the Ogeechee river. On my arrival, I found a stage erected in the woods, and a vast concourse of people, few of whom had ever seen me before.

As I began meeting, I perceived a man uneasy. He got up, and sat down, and up and down again, and walked around, which denoted some unusual uneasiness in his mind.

After meeting, I set off for my evening's appointment. Several were going the same way. I abruptly spoke to one, "Are you not sorry you came to meeting?" (not recollecting him to be the above man.) He replied, "Yes; and I believe it would have been better for me to have stayed at home, and my horse eating grass. I understand," added he, "you can tell fortunes; and if you can tell what is to come, you can tell what is past. Tell me, did I ever kill anybody? If I did, I'll confess it before the people!"

Thus he twice or thrice strove to make me answer the question. It made a solemn impression on my mind, so that I did not speak; but looking him in the face as we rode a distance, viewing it necessary to be guarded in my conduct, as the company were strangers to me, I inquired his name as we parted at the forks of the road. However, it made such an impression on my mind, that I could not but relate it to the congregation in Springfield courthouse. After meeting, the gentleman where I lodged informed me that this Squire H. was supposed to be concerned in a murder with a man who was under sentence of death. It appears, from the best accounts I could collect, that this H. was an A-double-L-part man, and believed once in grace and always in grace, which brought me to reflection, (from the horrible circumstance,) what dangerous sentiments these are, not only in a religious point of view, to lull people to sleep, but also in a civil and political respect. For if one falls into public scandal, and retains an idea of being secured unchangeably in the favor of God, he cannot be under the influence of the principles of honor, nor yet the idea of future reward and punishment; and of course he is a dangerous person to society, seeing neither civil, nor honorable, nor moral obligation, will restrain him from his evil designs. This is the truth, and cannot be confuted.

I lost my horse and cloak, expecting they would be sent to me, and with difficulty reached Augusta, where the conference was beginning to sit.

Here I met Dr. Coke. He said, "How do you do, brother Dow? I am glad to see you. Your warning to the people of Dublin had liked to have proved too true."

Here Stith Mead brought me the parchment of recommendation from the governor, &c., and I gave him a testimonial of my sincerity and attachment to the Methodist body, and my approbation of the general tenor of their conduct, &c. Here I was talked over in conference; and after some conversation, the doctor observed that I had done the Methodist societies no injury that he knew of, but in sundry instances to the reverse.

Bishop Asbury directed the preachers to publish for me to preach in the meeting-house during the sitting of conference, which was done, and I gave my farewell to the people, and also my thoughts on different religious subjects, which were published under the title of, *The Chain of Lorenzo, by the request of his friends, as his farewell to Georgia,* as a present to the meeting-house, which was in debt.

The cause of this publication originated from the false reports and dust which the A-double-L-part people had raised against me; but my friends advised me to it, that the unprejudiced might judge for themselves where the truth lay, and so thus the cloven foot be drawn out, and cut clear off; that when God had killed the old stock, there should be none to carry the news, and thus A-double-L-partism be driven from the land, which concern had drawn me from Ireland, that precious "souls might escape as from the snare of the fowler."

I sold my watch for printing some religious handbills, (*rules for holy living*,) which I distributed around the town; and got some also printed on silk, for the higher class, lest paper would be too much neglected, one of which I had framed, and the doctor tied it up for me in paper, and superscribed it, "For his Excellency the Governor," which I left with an attorney to deliver, as I delivered one of my silk bills. Thus I left the conference, who had agreed not to hedge up my way, with weeping eyes and aching heart, and took my departure to South Carolina. With difficulty I crossed Savannah river, and a man who crossed with me, took me behind him on his horse, and carried me over several runs of water. I got assistance to where my horse was, having several good times, and the A-double-L-part people looked sour. A fresh had been in the river, so I could not get my cloak, neither had I a second shirt at this time. But my trust is in God, who hath helped hitherto.

On my way to Charleston I spoke in an old Methodist meeting-house, and at Cossahatchee; here was Mr. C., once an itinerant, sensible preacher, but now cold in religion. M. B. heard me also, but has quitted the Methodists, and preaches A-double-L-partism.

Monday, January 9th, 1804. I rode fifty-two miles, and arrived at Charleston late in the evening, and put up with W. Turpin, Esq., who received me when I first was in this place, and procured me picked meetings at his house. I find Mr. Hamet has gone to a world of spirits, to answer for the deeds done in the body. As it respects his division, it appears his motives were impure, arising from a desire of popularity; in consequence of which there was a breach of confidence by him as respected the incorporation of the house. Awful to relate, it appears he died drunk!

I spoke in his house called Trinity Church; also, in the Methodist meeting-house. Here I saw Dr. Coke; who informed me that he saw a recommendation for me at the house of brother John Harper, signed by some of the members of the legislature and the governor of the state, which has not yet fallen into my hands; the cause I know not, though I have sent for it repeatedly.

Friday, 13th. I left Charleston, crossing a ferry, and rode thirty-three miles, keeping up with the mail-stage.

14th. I crossed a bad ferry of several miles, in consequence of a fresh in the river, which took three hours with the stage. Hence we went on to Georgetown, where I held a few meetings, and then rode forty-three miles to Kingston; leaving brothers Mallard and Jones behind. The former was blessed in his labors here last year; and Hamet's conduct had done injury. Jones soon after was found drowned in a creek, supposed to have been seized with a fit of epilepsy, which he was subject to; but the verdict of the coroner's jury was that he had died drunk, though he was exemplary for temperance and piety.

I put up at a tavern, though a Methodist preacher lived near, hired a room for a meeting, and called in the neighbors. Next day I fell in with brother Russel, who was going to his station. So we crossed a ferry together, and continued on upwards of eighty miles, until we came to Wilmington, where I found religion low, and bigotry so prominent, particularly in the leading local preacher, that had not Mr. Russel been with me, who was stationed here, I should have been shut out. I held several meetings, and got some religious handbills on paper and silk printed, "Rules for Holy Living," which I distributed to the people of the town, and took my departure for Newbern. But this being so far north, and near the seaboard, at this cold season of the year, that I almost perished with the cold, frost, and snow; having no outer garment, and my clothing thin.

I held a few meetings in Newbern and proceeded to Washington, where I had like to have been chilled in crossing a ferry. But after getting somewhat warmed and refreshed with a cup of tea, I proceeded to meeting, where God made it up to me.

25th. I spoke at Tarborough, then at Prospect. 27th. At Sampson's meeting-house—Jones's at night; being now in North Carolina near Virginia. Hence to Raleigh, and spoke twice in the statehouse. Here the petty constable who took me up as a horse-stealer near this, did not meet me according to expectation. My appointments were not given out according to direction.

From hence I proceeded to Iredel county, to the house of a man of whom I had bought a horse, when on my way from New England to Georgia. Some people mocked him for giving me credit, saying, "You have lost your horse." But now their mouth was shut, as I paid him his demand, although he only had my word.

I visited several places around, and took my departure for Tennessee, having a cloak and shirt given to me. My money is almost out, my expenses have been so enormous in consequence of the unusual floods, &c.

In crossing the Celuda mountains the way was narrow; whilst precipices were on one side, the other rose perpendicular; which rendered it dangerous travelling in the night, had not the mountains been on fire which illuminated the heavens to my convenience.

February 14th. I spoke in Buncomb to more than could get into the Presbyterian meeting-house, and at night also, and good I trust was done. The minister was not an A-double-L-part man, but pious. Next day rode forty-five miles in company with Dr. Nelson, across the dismal Alleghany mountains, by the warm springs; and on the way a young man, a traveller, came in (where I breakfasted gratis at an inn) and said, tha he had but three-sixteenths of a dollar left, having been robbed of seventy-one dollars on the way, and he being far from home I gave him half of what I had with me.

My horse having a navel-gall come on his back, I sold him, with the saddle, bridle, cloak, blanket, &c., on credit, for about three-fourth of the value, with an uncertainty whether I should ever be paid.* Thus I crossed the river French Broad in a canoe, and set out for my appointment. But fearing I should be behind the time, I hired a man whom I met on the road with two horses, to carry me five miles in haste for three shillings, which left me but one-sixteenth of a dollar. In our speed h observed, there was a nigh way, by which I could clamber the rocks an cut off some miles. So we parted, he having not gone two-thirds of th of the way, yet insisting on the full sum.

I took to my feet the nigh way as fast as I could pull on, as intricat as it was, and came to a horrid ledge of rocks, on the bank of the rive where there was no such thing as going round, and to clamber over woul be at the risk of my life, as there was danger of slipping into the rive However, being unwilling to disappoint the people, I pulled off my shoe and with my handkerchief fastened them about my neck, and creepin upon my hands and feet with my fingers and toes in the cracks of the rock with difficulty I got safe over; and in about four miles I came to a hou and hired a woman to take me over the river in a canoe, for my remain ing money and scissors, the latter of which was the chief object with he So our extremities are others' opportunities. Thus, with difficulty I g to my appointment in Newport in time.

I had heard about a singularity called the *jerks* or *jerking exercis* which appeared first near Knoxville in August last, to the great alarm (

---

* Lost it forever.

the people, which reports at first I considered as vague and false. But at length, like the Queen of Sheba, I set out to go and see for myself, and sent over these appointments into this country accordingly.

When I arrived in sight of this town, I saw hundreds of people collected in little bodies, and observing no place appointed for meeting, before I spoke to any, I got on a log and gave out a hymn; which caused them to assemble around, in solemn attentive silence. I observed several involuntary motions in the course of the meeting, which I considered as a specimen of the jerks. I rode seven miles behind a man across streams of water, and held meeting in the evening, being ten miles on my way.

In the night I grew uneasy, being twenty-five miles from my appointment for next morning at eleven o'clock. I prevailed on a young man to attempt carrying me with horses until day, which he thought was impracticable, considering the darkness of the night, and the thickness of the trees. Solitary shrieks were heard in these woods, which he told me were said to be the cries of murdered persons. At day we parted, being still seventeen miles from the spot, and the ground covered with a white frost. I had not proceeded far, before I came to a stream of water, from the springs of the mountain, which made it dreadful cold. In my heated state I had to wade this stream five times in the course of an hour, which I perceived so affected my body, that my strength began to fail. Fears began to arise that I must disappoint the people, till I observed some fresh tracks of horses, which caused me to exert every nerve to overtake them, in hopes of aid or assistance on my journey, and soon I saw them on an eminence. I shouted for them to stop till I came up. They inquired what I wanted? I replied, I had heard there was a meeting at Seversville by a stranger, and was going to it. They replied, that they had heard that a crazy man was to hold forth there, and were going also; and perceiving that I was weary, they invited me to ride: and soon our company was increased to forty or fifty, who fell in with us on the road from different plantations. At length I was interrogated whether I knew any thing about the preacher. I replied, "I have heard a good deal about him, and have heard him preach, but I have no great opinion of him." And thus the conversation continued for some miles before they found me out, which caused some color and smiles in the company. Thus, I got on to meeting; and after taking a cup of tea gratis, I began to speak to a vast audience, and I observed about thirty to have the jerks. Though they strove to keep still as they could, these emotions were involuntary and irresistible, as any unprejudiced eye might discern. Lawyer Porter, who had come a considerable distance, got his heart touched under the word, and being informed how I came to meeting, voluntarily lent me a horse to ride near one hundred miles, and gave me a dollar, though he had never seen me before.

Hence to Marysville, where I spoke to about one thousand five hundred; and many appeared to feel the word, but about fifty felt the jerks. At night I lodged with one of the Nicholites, a kind of Quakers who do not feel free to wear colored clothes. I spoke to a number of people at his house that night. Whilst at tea, I observed his daughter (who sat opposite to me at table) to have the jerks, and dropped the tea-cup from her hand in the violent agitation. I said to her, "Young woman, what is the matter?" She replied, "I have got the jerks." I asked her how long she had it? She observed, "A few days," and that it had been the means of the awakening and conversion of her soul, by stirring her up to serious consideration about her careless state, &c.

Sunday, February 19th, I spoke in Knoxville to hundreds more than could get into the courthouse, the governor being present. About one hundred and fifty appeared to have the jerking exercise, among whom was a circuit preacher (Johnson) who had opposed them a little before, but he now had them powerfully; and I believe he would have fallen over three times had not the auditory been so crowded that he could not unless he fell perpendicularly.

After meeting, I rode eighteen miles to hold a meeting at night. The people of this settlement were mostly Quakers, and they had said (as I was informed) the Methodists and Presbyterians have the *jerks* because they *sing* and *pray* so much; but we are a still, peaceable people, wherefore we do not have them. However, about twenty of them came to the meeting, to hear one, as they said, somewhat in a Quaker line. But their usual stillness and silence was interrupted, for about a dozen of them had the jerks as keen and as powerful as any I had seen, so as to have occasioned a kind of grunt or groan when they would jerk. It appears that many have undervalued the great revival, and attempted to account for it altogether on natural principles; therefore it seems to me (from the best judgment I can form) that God hath seen proper to take this method to convince people, that he will work in a way to show his power, and sent the *jerks* as a sign of the times, partly in judgment for the people's unbelief, and yet as a mercy to convict people of divine realities.

I have seen Presbyterians, Methodists, Quakers, Baptists, Episcopalians, and Independents, exercised with the *jerks*—gentleman and lady, black and white, the aged and the youth, rich and poor, without exception; from which I infer, as it cannot be accounted for on natural principles, and carries such marks of involuntary motion, that it is no trifling matter. I believe that those who are most pious and given up to God, are rarely touched with it, and also those naturalists who wish and try to get it to philosophize upon it, are excepted. But the lukewarm, lazy, half-hearted, indolent professor is subject to it; and many of them I have seen, who, when it came upon them, would be alarmed and stirred up to redouble their diligence with God; and after they would get happy, were thankful it ever came upon them. Again, the wicked are frequently more afraid of it than the small-pox or yellow fever; these are subject to it. But the persecutors are more subject to it than any; and they sometimes have cursed, and swore, and damned it whilst jerking. There is no pain attending the jerks except they resist it, which if they do, it will weary them more in an hour than a day's labor, which shows that it requires the *consent* of the *will* to avoid suffering.

20th. I passed by a meeting-house, where I observed the undergrowth had been cut up for a camp-meeting, and from 50 to 100 saplings left breast-high, which to me appeared so slovenish that I could not but ask my guide the cause, who observed they were topped so high and left for the people to jerk by. This so excited my attention that I went over the ground to view it, and found where the people had laid hold of them and jerked so powerfully that they had kicked up the earth as a horse stamping flies. I observed some emotion both this day and night among the people. A Presbyterian minister (with whom I stayed) observed, "Yesterday whilst I was preaching some had the jerks, and a young man from North Carolina mimicked them out of derision, and soon was seized with them himself, (which was the case with many others.) He grew ashamed, and on attempting to mount his horse to go off, his foot jerked about so that he could not put it into the stirrup; some youngsters seeing this assisted him on, but he jerked so that he could not sit alone, and one got up to hold him on, which was done with difficulty. I observing this, went to him and asked him what he thought of it?" Said he, "I believe God sent it on me for my wickedness, and making so light of it in others;" and he requested me to pray for him.

I observed his wife had it; she said she was first attacked with it in bed. Dr. Nelson said he had frequently strove to get it in order to philosophize upon it, but could not, and observed they could not account for it on natural principles.

CHAPTER II.

VISIT THROUGH VIRGINIA.

I CALLED at a gentleman's house to get some breakfast, and inquired the road. The gentleman observing my tin case in my pocket, (containing my credential from the state of Georgia, and supposing me to be some vile character,) took it out and examined the contents without my consent. When he had got about half through, as he looked at me, I observed he appeared pale. He gave me what I wanted and treated me as a king.

I had not been long gone from the house before a runner on foot overtook me, and another servant on horseback, with a request that I should go back and preach. I did to many of the neighbors who were called in. The mistress deserted during the meeting, which to me she denied, until the servants affirmed that she was in the negro-house.

I observed to her that I considered her absence a slight, as they had called me back, and to make it up with me, desired she should let me know the cause of her absence. She replied she was afraid of the jerks more than of the small-pox or yellow fever.

. Next day he gave me some money, and sent a horse with me several miles; and then I took to my feet and went on to Greenville, and so on to Abingdon in Virginia. The last jerks that I saw was a young woman, who was severely exercised during the meeting. She followed me into the house. I observed to her the indecency and folly of such public gestures and grunts, and requested, (speaking sternly to make an impression on her mind,) if she had any regard for her character, to leave it off. She replied, "I will if I can." I took her by the hand, looking her in the face, and said, "Do not tell lies." I perceived by the motion of her hand that she exerted every nerve to restrain it, but instantly she jerked as if it would have jerked her out of her skin if it were possible. I did this to have an answer to others on the subject, which I told her that my abruptness might leave no bad impression on her mind.

These appointments had been given out rising of six months, with the days and hours fixed. I remarked in Abingdon, as I was dismissing the auditory, that on such a day thirteen months, and such an hour, I should be in town to hold a meeting, God willing. And I steered westerly on a circuitous route to Turswell, where I preached in a sunk hole formed by nature, to a vast auditory; being accommodated thus far by an attorney's horse. Here I saw a gentleman, a stranger, of whom I purchased a horse at a word, and proceeded across the mountains of Clinch, which were tremendously high and covered with snow, and having no outer garment. I felt as if I should freeze. However, all was made up at good meetings on the other side. So I came to With courthouse; hence to Grayson, and the lead mines; thence to New River; so to Montgomery, Salem, Fincastle, and Lexington, where I spoke in the Presbyterian meeting-house; to Woodstock, Rocktown, and so on to Newtown, where God was graciously with us. Hence to Winchester, where I spoke in the Methodist chapel, and a champion bully of an A-double-L-part minister was present, for whom the Methodist preacher's heart did ache. Next day he went from house to house among his friends, to represent me as a crazy man; but three of his pillars were shaken, one of whom replied to him, "If a crazy man will talk so, what would he do if he was in his right mind?" which seemed to confound him. I preached at Frontroyal, and crossed the Blue Ridge in the night, in order to get on to my next day's appointment. A deist was present, and on hearing me observe "that no man was a deist who would not dare to take an oath to relinquish all favors from God through Christ," he began to examine whether he would be willing, and something replied, "No, not for ten thousand worlds." Thus his foundation shook, and conviction ensued.

An A-double-L-part man who had followed up my meetings, perceiving the man to be shaken, appointed a time to answer my discourse; but, whilst attempting to answer it, forgot one of the heads of the discourse; which so confounded him, that he complained of being unwell, and concluded his meeting; and so sunk into disgrace.

I spoke in Culpepper courthouse, and then rode fifty miles, or more, to Charlottesville, near the President's seat, in Albemarle county. I spoke to about four thousand people, and one of the President's daughters, who was present, died a few days after.

Hence I went circuitously to Lynchburgh, where I spoke in the open air, in what I conceived to be the seat of Satan's kingdom.

From thence to New London, where I began speaking in the courthouse; where papa and mamma Hobson came in, and we had a gracious time. Here I fell in with brother Stith Mead, and we went on to the camp-meeting, which I had appointed last August.

March 22d. Several families came about twenty miles, and encamped on the ground, though there were but few Methodists anywhere short of that distance. The weather was chilly, the clouds appeared threatening, and the prospects before us very gloomy. However, we poured out our complaint to God, who graciously heard our cry, sent off the clouds, and gave us a beautiful sun.

23d. About fifteen hundred people appeared on the ground, and the Lord began a gracious work that day, which I trust hell shall never be able to extinguish. One soul found peace before night, and another in the night.

24th. About three thousand people attended. The solemnity and tenderness, and prospect of good increased.

25th. Sunday. About five thousand on the ground, and in general good attention. Colonel Callaway and a number of respectable gentlemen used their endeavors to protect our peaceable privileges.

Monday, 26th. About three thousand appeared on the ground; and the rejoicing of old saints, the shouts of young converts, and the cries of the distressed for mercy, caused the meeting to continue all night, until we parted on Tuesday morning 27th.

About fifty, during this meeting, professed to have found the pardoning love of God. From hence the work went home with the people and spread over the country, as may be seen from the following letters sent by William Heath, Methodist preacher, to Ezekiel Cooper, one of the Bookstewards to the Connection, and the Rev. Stith Mead to Bishop Asbury.

"Richmond District, April 4th, 1803.

"I have been in the habit of communicating to you the remarkable occurrences which have fallen in my way from time to time : but your being kept from us in the south by sickness, I have been at a loss where to direct my intelligence. Being informed you shortly will be in Baltimore, I shall endeavor to throw the following narrative in your way. But, passing over a great number of pleasing scenes which might be noticed, for brevity's sake, I shall confine myself to the giving you a list of the camp, and other meetings of magnitude, with their immediate effects ; and then in an aggregate, the consequences of the meetings will be seen on a more enlarged scale, though still much of their fruit will be unnoticed, being scattered generally over the circuits.

Dates of meetings. 1804.	Places.	Converted	Joined.
March 23—27	Bedford County,	50	
April 21—23	Campbell County,	24	40
—— ——	Goose Creek,	16	
—— ——	Lynchburgh,	16	
May 5—11	Tabernacle,	100	
——12—15	New Hope Chapel,	100	49
——17—21	Tabernacle,	150	140
—— ——	Flat Rock,	20	
—— 30 ——	Lynchburg,	50	
—— 31 June 1	New Hope Chapel,	40	49
June 3	Tabernacle,		48
—— 8—12	Charity Chapel, Pouhauta,	100	60
—— ——	Bethel Chapel,	50	
July 20—24	Leftwich's Chapel, Bedford circuit,	100	60
——28—29	New-hope,	30	19
Aug. 3—7	Bottetourt,	50	
—— 8 ——	Fincastle,	20	7
—— 1—21	Ebenezer-Chapel, Bedford	50	17
—— 3 Sept. 8	Tabernacle,	20	
—— 7—1	Oaks, Amherst,	40	13

Aug. 21—25	Brown's Chapel, Campbell,	.	.	30	12
Sept. 28 Oct. 1	Chesnut Chapel, Franklin,	.	.	10	11
1805					
Mar. 29. Ap. 2	Oarley's Chapel, Bedford,	.	.	20	13
				1036	538

"In this great and glorious work, it may be observed, that at the close of two months, I numbered six hundred converted, and five hundred and twenty added to the church. And in the six months, and that principally at the meetings, the number converted amounted to eleven hundred and seventy-six, and eight hundred and fifty joined the Methodist Episcopal church. With the preachers in the five circuits, Bedford, Bottetourt, Amherst, Cumberland and Franklin, each having one or more camp meetings, hundreds are brought to God, and into his militant church. Other denominations have shared largely the fruits of our labors.

"In this work it may be remarked, that I have baptized near one hundred adult-believers, from ten to twenty at a time; and after giving them the choice of the mode, there has not been one instance where they have chosen immersion. The blessing of God has visibly attended the ordinance by effusion; and there are but few who have joined, but what professed saving religion previous to their joining. Persecution has raged in proportion to the revival: but hitherto the Lord has helped us. And we can say with the apostle, 2 Cor. vi. 6, 'By honor and dishonor, by evil report and good report: as deceivers, and yet true: as unknown, and yet well known: as dying, and behold we live: as chastened, and not killed: as sorrowful, yet always rejoicing: as poor, yet making making many rich: as having nothing, yet possessing all things.'

"STITH MEAD."

EXTRACT OF A LETTER FROM WILLIAM HEATH TO EZEKIEL COOPER.

"Lynchburg, July 25th, 1804.

"To you, I suppose it will be a matter of joy to hear of the prosperity of Zion in these parts of the Lord's vineyard.

"The camp-meetings, which have been usual in the south and west for some years, never began with us till last spring.

"On the 23d of March, a camp-meeting was held by L. D.* in conjunction with a number of other preachers and ministers; at which fifty souls professed to find peace with God. From this the work of God spread in almost every direction, for many were awakened at this meeting, who afterwards found the pearl of great price. At the several meetings which were held at Flat Creek meeting-house, by the 16th of April, twenty-four souls professed converting grace; and the work has continued more rapid at that place ever since. Forty have joined the church there, and sixteen in the neighborhood above that have professed conversion, and planted a society among us. In the town and vicinity, from the beginning of the work in April until now, from six to twelve and sixteen, at a meeting, have professed to find the pearl of great price. So that from a class

---

* Lorenzo Dow.

of twenty members, we have now one hundred and sixty. Bless the Lord, O my soul! and let all the people magnify his holy name!

"On the 5th of May, a meeting was appointed at a place fifteen miles above us, called the Tabernacle, to be held three days; but the work was so great that it continued five days, day and night, with very little intermission: in which time one hundred were thought to have obtained true conversion. From the 12th to the 15th of May, at a place called New-Hope, five miles from town we had another meeting, which continued also day and night; at which there were about one hundred who professed to get converted: and many are daily added to our numbers. From the 17th to the 22d of May, meeting again, at Tabernacle meeting-house, at which place the people encamped on the ground, and continued preaching, praying, and other godly exercises, night and day, for the five days, in which time one hundred and fifty were thought to be savingly converted. One hundred joined the Methodist church at that time and place. From the 8th to the 12th of June, another camp-meeting was held at Charity Chapel, Powhatan, at which one hundred souls were thought to obtain saving conversion, and sixty joined the Methodist church. From the 20th to the 24th of this month, we had a camp-meeting in Bedford, at Leftwich's meeting-house, at which one hundred and ten came forward, and gave testimony of their faith, that God had converted their souls. Very many are the prayer, class, and preaching meetings, not mentioned here, at which the Lord pours out his Spirit in a wonderful manner. Considering the low ebb of religion among us, before the revival began, I can truly say, that I never saw or read of greater times. True, the times mentioned by brother Cox in his letter to Bishop Coke, in 1787, were great; but I was in the whole of that revival, as well as this, and it is my opinion that this revival far exceeds that.

"The glorious work is spreading in various directions, and extensively. It is chiefly among the Methodists: though our Presbyterian brethren are very friendly, and labor mightily with and among us. Indeed, my brother, we hope, and at times are almost led to believe, that the glorious millenium is ushering in! Proclaim at your pleasure the contents of this, or any part.

"I am, in the best of bonds, thine, &c.
"WILLIAM HEATH."

I was unwell the latter part of this meeting, from an unusual incident, but after the meeting broke up, I rode in a walk thirty miles, and lay down upon a table with a blanket and pillow, and spoke to several hundreds in the open air at night. I had been necessitated to alight several times and rest, laying upon the ground in the course of the day.

28th. I rode in great misery eleven miles and spoke to hundreds, an hour by sun in the morning. Thence to Franklin courthouse at twelve o'clock, and some were offended, but good I trust was done. In the evening I spoke twelve miles off; but was grieved with the family: could not eat with them, but next morning quitted them betimes, and went to Henry courthouse; spoke to about fifteen hundred people; and stayed with General Martin at night, where we had a good time.

30th. I started this morning an hour before day, and rode thirty miles to Pittsylvania courthouse. Here were several of my spiritual children, among whom was Polly Callaway, whom I once had pointed at whilst preaching, the first time she ever saw me, and God struck her under conviction; she ran away thirty miles to a camp-meeting, where God set her soul at liberty; and almost the whole of her father's family have been brought to God; and her brother is become an itinerant preacher. One soul was set at liberty to-day, some mocked and caused interruption, but good was done during the three meetings.

It is eight years this morning since I parted with my parents, on the errand in which I am now engaged. I still feel, "Wo is me if I preach not the gospel." Hitherto I have been preserved (through the providence of God,) by land and sea, through storms and afflictions, with the temptations of friends and foes; but the Lord hath kept me, glory to his holy name!

31st. I held meeting sun half-hour high, and then rode eighteen miles to Wilson's meeting-house; these were tender times. Eight miles hence! spoke at night.

Sunday, April 1st. I spoke at Rockingham courthouse, North Carolina, to fifteen or sixteen hundred people, who appeared in general solemn and well-behaved, considering the inconvenience of standing in the freezing air and falling snow, more than two hours. I rode twelve miles and spoke at night.

2d. I spoke in Danville to about two thousand: this was the seat of Satan's kingdom, yet I believe I shall one day see good times in this quarter. Some children were brought forward, for me to pray for them, instead of offering them up in baptism, which I had never seen before.

3d. I rode thirty miles to Halifax, Virginia, where I spoke to about two thousand, and in general good attention. A family of A-double-L-part people, without my knowledge or consent, appointed me a meeting, and, to excuse the matter, said they would pilot me a road five miles shorter to my next day's meeting. To prevent disappointing the people I complied, but on my arrival, before I entered the house, I inquired whether I might feel at home whilst I stayed? They replied, "Yes." I then observed, that I had come forty miles, and would be glad of a cup of tea or coffee, as I could not take food without them. They took their dinner, and prepared not mine, until it was time to begin meeting; but as I would suffer nothing to clash with my appointments, and finding the people talkative, I got on a table by the porch out of doors, in the dark, unseen; and with a stamp, as if I would have stove the table through, and clapping my hands at the same instant with all my might, I cried with exertion, "Hush," which caused a solemn silence among the people, and then began meeting; having told the family if my food was ready, I would take it when I had done.

When I had finished, I found it not ready and cold; and being so weary I was unable to sit up, and retired to rest, observing, I must be off betimes in the morning, and they must accommodate my breakfast accordingly, which however was not ready until I had got on my horse, neither did they procure me a pilot; thus I went twenty-three miles to Charlotte courthouse, got some breakfast, and spoke.

The above family, after I was gone, told lies about me, and one of their preachers appeared friendly to my face, but acted like them behind my back; saying, that I said, "Jesus Christ was a liar," &c. Next year when I came this way again, this family had made another appointment for me; but as it happened, before the son, who had come to meeting, delivered his invitation, I prayed to God to have mercy on those who had told lies about me, which caused shame to prevent him from doing his errand; so they had to look to the disappointment themselves.

April 5th. A Presbytery was sitting at Prince Edward, and many lawyers were here, (it being court time.) I spoke to about three thousand people, (standing upon the stocks or pillory,) on the subject of predestination and deism, showing the one to be the foundation of the other. The court adjourned whilst I spoke. I added, "A man present hath some books, which contain the essence of what I spoke, if any of you should desire to procure them." A minister (observing the attention of the great and small, and also the sale of the books) replied, that the stocks were the fittest place for me; which showed the bitterness of his heart, and procured him no small disgrace among his friends.

Lynchburg was a deadly place for the worship of God, but my friends asked, what shall be done with the profits of your Chain? which they computed at five hundred dollars. I replied, "I give the profits to build a brick chapel in Lynchburg, for the Methodists, reserving only the privilege of preaching in it, when not occupied by them, and whilst my conduct shall continue as unexceptionable as it now is."

6th. I spoke in a church, at Tarwallet, in the day-time, and at night at John Hobson's, jr., whom I called my papa and his wife my mamma. His mother, who is near ninety years of age, as I asked her if she prayed, thought, "What should I pray for unless it be to get home safe from meeting;" but in the night, whilst she meditated upon the above thoughts of her mind, reflected, "What have I been about all my lifetime? I am near one hundred years old, and never considered upon my future state." Here conviction seized her mind: she went in the morning to her son's, and desired prayer: in about a week she was brought to rejoice in God.

7th. Papa took me in a chair to Cartersville. The first time I visited this place, I sent to an innkeeper to preach in his house, who replied, as was said, he would first meet me in hell; he shortly after died.

No one offered a place, except one man a room, which would contain about a dozen; at length I got the liberty of a tobacco-shed or warehouse, where I spoke to about five hundred. One man rode into the company, and continued on his horse about two hours, until I had done; it rained so tremendously that the people, who were mostly excited by curiosity, were compelled to stay until I finished. So I left the town without eating or drinking; but now there was a stage erected for me, and I spoke to about two thousand.

I observed to the people their former coolness, and told them that would neither eat nor drink with them this time; but intended to clear my skirts from their blood. Several were brought under conviction, and since are brought to rejoice in God. I received several invitations, but would not break my word, which gave great offence.

The third time I visited this place, God gave me favor in the sight of the people: prejudice seemed to be removed, and we had a gracious time.

8th. I spoke under some shades at Powhatan, about two thousand present; we had a good time, except one drunken man, and some few took offence.

9th. I addressed an auditory on some boards, at Chesterfield courthouse, and in Manchester at night.

10th. I spoke in Richmond to about two thousand. Here I found several spiritual children, the fruit of my first visit. Here the posts of the gallery sunk two inches, crushing the bricks on which they stood, and two inches more would have let down hundreds of people upon those beneath.

11th. I returned to Cumberland to prepare my *Address to the people of Virginia* for the press.

I communicated my thoughts to papa and mamma Hobson, who, after seriously weighing circumstances, gave their advice and consent concerning my marriage.

Sunday, 15th. I came to Petersburgh; some were noisy, and some were tender in the meeting.

16th. A young gentleman carried me in a gig to Osborne church; he a few days after was thrown from the gig, and soon expired. Oh, how uncertain is life! Oh, the necessity of being always ready!

I spoke under the federal oaks to about seventeen hundred; we had a melting time. Trials I expect are at the door; the clouds seem gathering fast, and to none but a Divine Providence can I look, as an interposing friend.

I am taught to use all men as friends, and yet to put myself in the power of none, but to make God my only friend, and put my whole confidence in him; for whom else can I rely upon? The fable saith, that the snake, to oblige the porcupine, suffered him to come into his den out of the cold; the latter growing warm, began to bristle up and stir about, and the quills to prick the snake, which caused him to request the other to be gone, or else behave. He replied, "I'm well enough off, and if you do not like the place, you may seek rest elsewhere."

Brother Mallard writes thus: "I am out of hell, thank God. Christ was rebuked by Peter, and his friends thought him beside himself. Joshua thought it wrong in those who prophesied in the camp. Aaron and Miriam rose up against Moses; and John, with others, forbid one who was casting out devils in the name of Christ, because he followed not with them. And ignorant brethren cause trials, though well-meaning, beside those from false brethren, hypocrites, and backsliders." There are trials enough daily, without borrowing trouble from the morrow. All is well now, to-morrow may take thought for itself.

I spoke at Prince George courthouse, and though there were but few religious people, it was a tender time, notwithstanding it was muster-day. I rode fourteen miles, and spoke in the afternoon in Jones's Hole church to hundreds. A Quaker girl, who was excited hither, was brought under concern of mind in the meeting, and had no rest until the Lord spoke peace to her soul. The next time I saw her, she was rejoicing in God. Here I met Jesse Lee, and rode home with him to his father's, whose house has been a preaching-house most constantly for thirty years, and I suppose one of the oldest in America.

I communicated my intention to publish my journal, and apply the profit towards building a meeting-house in the city of Washington, as a gentleman had offered to give me a spot of ground for that purpose. J. L. said that he had no objection, if I told the whole truth, and gave the meeting-house to the Methodists, which was then my intention. But one of the conferences making some objection to my building meeting-houses for them, I afterwards altered my mind, and gave what I conceived to be the profits to some Methodist trustees, still in the District of Columbia, which contains ten miles square, and includes the cities of Washington, Georgetown, and Alexandria.

18th. I had meeting at Sussex courthouse; then to Jones's meeting-house, where I met five travelling preachers, on their way to general conference.

19th. Had meeting at Hall's meeting-house and Dinwiddie courthouse, and appointed a camp-meeting, to commence on the eighth of March following.

21st. I spoke at the camp-meeting ground, and next day at Brunswick courthouse, and at night at Ellis's meeting-house, to about one thousand. One professed to find peace. Ira Ellis is one of the old travelling preachers, and Drumgoole also, who live in this country. It inspires me with a sympathetic reflection when I fall in company with those who were the first in the planting the infant Methodist Church in America. I reflected how some have backslidden, others retired in oblivion, a few still engaged, and the rest gone to glory.

I spoke at Hicksford in the courthouse, and at a widow's in the night. I stood upwards of three hours in these meetings, and it was a happy time for me.

24th I rode to Jones's church, and from thence to Jerusalem, a place noted for wickedness; I spoke in the courthouse, but none asked me either to eat or drink, which was the greatest inhospitality I had met with for some time. This town was beautifully situated on a river.

26th. I held meeting at Suffolk and Jolly's chapel. Some A-double-L-part people took offence, but good, I trust, was done.

27th. I spoke at Portsmouth to more than could get into the house. Without there was disturbance, within was peace. At brother Green's also we had a good time, whilst some fell to the floor and raised the people in the street.

28th. I spoke in Norfolk and Portsmouth, and some souls were set at liberty. I refused some money, and got some handbills printed, and then had not a sufficiency left to pay my ferriage. However, some one slipped some money into my pocket, which answered the end. So I still perceive that the calls of God's Spirit and the openings of his providence go hand in hand.

29th. The Church minister and Baptist gave over their meetings, which gave me a fine opportunity of addressing the people, both in the Methodist chapel and in the church, in the latter of which one fell as in the agonies of death. I feel as if my work in this country was drawing to a close, and my heart drawn towards England. Oh, how easy some people can rest, even ministers, and see so little fruit of their labor!

30th. I rode to Yorktown, where Cornwallis was taken prisoner, and the cave to which he retired during the siege still remains, being cut on purpose for him in a rock. The effects of the siege and shot still remain. The town is since of little consequence. I spoke in the church to what I could, but I doubt if there be one white a Christian in the place. I crossed York river to Gloucester side and spoke again.

May 1st. I spoke at Mount Zion, and had a good time; saw some of brother Mead's spiritual children seven years old. Hence to Bellamy's chapel. Stood about six hours this day, but I and my horse had but little to eat till night, having travelled about thirty miles.

2d. Had meetings at Shacklesford chapel and the new church.

The Church of England was once the established religion, by law, in this state. The clergyman was allowed sixteen thou:and pounds weight of tobacco yearly as his salary from the parish. When the war commenced between England and America, the legislature of this state thought it unreasonable to compel a man to pay, and so deprive him of his natural privilege of showing his voluntary liberality; and also to compel him to pay to the support of those in whose ministry he did not believe.

Part of the clergy gave over preaching, while others, supposing the Virginians would be conquered after the above act, and their arrears made up to them, continued their attendance for a while; but after the taking of Cornwallis, they deserted the churches also, and left them vacant, which caused the legislature to permit other denominations to use them,* &c., and many scores of the best buildings in this state are now going to ruin.

3d. I spoke at Pace's meeting-house, and also in the Baptists' chapel. Benjamin Pace had borne an unblemished character as a preacher, and at length fell into a decline, which he bore with Christian fortitude and calling for his shroud and grave-clothes, dressed himself in them as some great hero on an important expedition; he then bade his wife, son, and daughters farewell, with orders to have the society notified, adding, "I am done fighting, my soul is in glory;" and with his hands fixed in a proper attitude, went off triumphant. This is a match for an infidel.

4th. I spoke four hours, lacking thirteen minutes, under the shade between two trees at Cole's chapel, to a crowded, serious, and attentive auditory. In the midst of my discourse, I observed a man at the other side of the trees, whom I considered as a backslider. It ran repeatedly through my mind to ask him before the people, if the language of his heart was not contained in these words:

> "What peaceful hours I once enjoyed
> How sweet their memory still!
> But they have left an aching void
> The world can never fill."

At length I proposed the question, after telling the congregation the cause and requested him, if it was, to give me his hand, which he did, to the surprise of the people. He was a Baptist, as I afterwards was told, and continued uneasy in his mind for some weeks, till some of his people plastered him up with the old doctrine, "*once in grace always in grace.*"

5th. I rode forty-two miles to Port Royal, and had a solemn time.

6th. I spoke in Fredericksburgh four times, and collected upwards of forty pounds for the benefit of a free school. The little boys who heard me preach, next day went all over town, spelling, "A-double-L-part—

---

* Only about three or four continued to officiate—which shows that they preached fo *tobacco* and not for *souls!*

few—elect—some—small number," &c., which diverted some, and exasperated others.

7th. I spoke in Stafford and Dumfries courthouses.

8th. I gave my last here; and spoke in a church on the way to Alexandria, where I spoke at night, and next morning.

9th. I spoke in Georgetown.

10th. I went to Montgomery, but finding my appointment not given out. I pushed on to Baltimore, making about sixty miles, and heard a sermon by night. Here brother Daniel Ostrander brought me heavy tidings, the death of my mother, the first that ever died out of my father's family. It gave me a tender sensation, but I could neither weep nor mourn, whilst these words were in my mind, "Oh! is my mother gone! is she gone, never to return!"

The last time I saw her she requested that I should come and see them once a year whilst she should live, which was my then intention. But God so wonderfully opened my way in the southern climes, that I could not find my way clear, although I had felt unusual exercise when I parted from her last, which I remarked to my friends; and also about the time of her decease, though it was near five months after she died before I heard of it.

11th. I received a letter from my father, giving me the particulars of my mother's dissolution and triumphant end; which was a little more than twelve months from the time I parted with her last. He also informed me of the death of my brother Fish, which took place a few weeks before hers. When I saw him last, he was backslidden from God. It appears he was reclaimed in his last illness, and made a happy exit.

Jesse Lee advised me to preach in the market, and published it from the pulpit, and also prepared an advertisement for the public paper, for me to preach there a second time. There was a large concourse of people at the last meeting, and near one hundred preachers present, it being now general conference time. I had come here to see if they intended to hedge up my way. Brother Ostrander informed me, that the New York conference had conversed me over, and some were minded to block up my way, whilst others objected, saying, "He does us no harm, but we get the fruit of his labor," whilst the former urged my example was bad; for perhaps fifty Dows might spring out of the same nest. So they agreed to discourage giving out my appointments. It appears that some came to this conference with an intention to have a move to block up my way at one stroke; but on seeing the southern preachers, and hearing of my conduct and success, their prejudice deserted them, and their opinions and views of things concerning me altered, (as several of them told me,) and became friendly, though before cool and distant.

Stith Mead, who was on his way from Georgia to general conference, when we met at the camp-meeting, got detained on account of the revival which then broke out, and spread as a fire on a mountain, in all directions. He wrote to Baltimore conference, and also to me, that he conceived his presence would not be necessary there on my account.

Nicholas Snethen I here heard preach in the life and power of the Holy Ghost. Oh! what an alteration in the man for the better! He once was a pleasant speaker to the ear, but little energy to the heart, until God knocked him down twice at a camp-meeting, and gave him such a oaptism as he never felt before. However, spiritual blessings may be abused through unfaithfulness to the Divine Spirit; and what need there is of our practising the apostle's caution, "If any man think he standeth, let him take heed lest he fall!"

The preachers as a body seemed unprejudiced, yet a few individuals are excepted; among whom R—— and W——, of ancient date, which I desired might be done away, and requested an interview for that purpose; but though one of them invited me to breakfast, yet they both went out before the time appointed, without acquainting the family, which caused me to feel awkward and abashed when I came.

I had felt a desire to visit Boston for some time, but never saw my way opening until now. George Pickering, who was presiding elder in Boston district, invited me to his jurisdiction, which I esteemed as a providence, expressed my gratitude, quitted Baltimore and returned to Richmond, where I put some manuscripts to press and visited some neighboring places.

I saw a man executed for the horrid crime of murder, having spoken to him through the grate the preceding day. Some trifled when this awful catastrophe was exhibited.

Papa Hobson met me here, but my appointments would not admit of my returning with him in the gig; and I had sold my horse to pay for printing, and how to get on I did not know, being unwell a day or two after; however, a gentleman who had been excited by curiosity to come near twenty miles to hear me at Cartersville, was there brought under concern; and with his servant was now on his return from Petersburgh, where he had been to purchase a coach to accommodate his family to meetings. He hearing of this appointment, delayed on his journey twenty-four hours, and then in his coach carried me home to Cumberland.

26th. I have a bad cough, which some think denotes my approaching dissolution. I feel unwell out of employ these few days past, though I have had but very few rest-days for seventeen months; but have generally preached from two to five times a day, riding from thirty to fifty miles.

Sunday, 27th. I spoke at Charity Chapel preparatory for camp-meeting. We had a shout; two found peace; and some ungenerous persons struck the negroes, who were rejoicing in God, to the shedding of blood.

Friday, June 1st. Camp-meeting commenced near Poplar Spring church, in Gloucester county. Brother Mead, who had ordered me to appoint it, did not come according to expectation. No preachers were on the ground, and hundreds of people were assembled. This, indeed, was a trial of my faith among the strange people. However, in the name of the Lord, I went up the stage and began the meeting, and besought God for a token for good; and soon a poor woman, who had come thirty miles on foot, under distress, was delivered, and clapping her hands, shouted for joy. Upon this, three or four preachers appeared. These things began to revive my heart; but a shower of rain expelled us from the woods into the church, where six or eight souls found peace. The next day was a good time also.

Sunday, 3d. Some thousands assembled, and whilst I was speaking from a stage, a storm seemed coming up, which put the people in motion, but I requested the people to be still and raise their hearts to God, if per-

f the clouds, and soon the threatening grew favor-
ent round.
 meeting broke up; about thirty found peace; a
were reclaimed; scores were awakened, and good
of the Lord.
 A-double-L-part discourse, delivered against me in
, who had heard me preach, which I think was un-

net brother Mead at papa Hobson's, who informed
Bedford county has greatly spread. Six hundred
hundred and twenty he had taken into society, and
ng on.
-meeting came on at Charity Chapel, Powhatan
as precious, but the wicked strove to trouble us.
ut five or six thousand were on the ground. The
 opposition increased. Twenty-five combined to-
flogging. They ransacked the camp to find me
me repose. This was the first discovery of their
it of the tent one was seen to cock a pistol towards
s heard, "There he is! there he is!" My friends
t. Next day I had one of the young men arrested,
ore they could be taken. The young man acknow-
promised never to do the like again. So we let

from the stage, and after that we had peace.
 ad brought to hush with only growling what should
 me on the road. I defied them to do their worst.
 id continued all night and next morning. When
 ad good reason to believe that one hundred souls
y. Some were minded I should go off in a covered
d, but with brother Dunnington went off in a gig,
d no power to hurt me. What enraged them so,
improper behavior in their striking the blacks, &c.
 spoke at friend Baker's, in whose family God hath
k.
 -suit for the dead, and sent it to Betsey M——, and
 Petersburgh.
: going, I was detained twenty-four hours behind my

 rived on the camp-ground, about an hour by sun in
 ound peace; some attempted interruption; but the
 our side. I continued on the ground until Monday
 e about sixty professed to have found peace, and
 vakened. Brother Cox wrote me that about thirty
I left the ground. Some blamed me for appointing
r, the devil's kingdom suffered loss in the Isle of
ice.
 dollars worth of books towards building a chapel;
 n Norfolk and Portsmouth; and several souls were
 tayed.

CHAPTER III.

RETURN TO NEW ENGLAND.

SUNDAY, 24th. I embarked for New-York. We had some contrary winds, horrible squalls, and calms; however, in eight days, I spoke with some friends in New-York, having quitted the vessel, and by the way of Elizabethtown came to the city.

N. Snethen is stationed here, and seems not so lively (by the account of friends) as he was some time ago. He is lately married.—Cyrus Stebbens objected to my preaching where he was stationed, though the trustees were mostly friendly. He withdrew from the connection soon after, which showed what spirit he was of.

I put my trunk on board a vessel for Middletown, and a friend took me in a chaise, near forty miles, whence I continued on foot until I came near Connecticut line. When about sixty yards off, whilst raising my heart to God to open me a way for provision, as I had but a few cents in my pocket, I met Aaron Hunt, a preacher, who told me where to call and get some refreshment. I did so, and held two meetings in the neighborhood; then came to Danbury, and pawning my watch, took stage for Hartford.

July 10th. Walking twenty miles I came to my father's house, which appeared empty. Things seemed pleasant round about; but my mother is no more. I cannot mourn—my loss is her gain. I trust to meet her in the skies, where sorrow and parting are no more. The rest of my friends were well in body, but low in religion.

I went to Middletown for my trunk, and found the plans for the contemplated meeting-house like to fall through, although six hundred dollars were subscribed. I offered them eight hundred dollars worth of books to aid therein, provided they would give me assistance in putting my journal to press. Here brother Burrows met me, and we went to Hebron, where we saw brother Wood. We agreed on a camp-meeting, to commence the last day of May following; which when known, was ridiculed as enthusiasm, to think that I could get people to go into the woods, and encamp night and day in this populous part, where elegant meeting-houses were so numerous. I was now called to another difficulty—a young horse being dead, and some money miscarried which I had sent for his keeping and a coat: my appointment had gone on to Boston, and how to do, I saw not my way clear; but here that same Providence, whose kindness I had experienced on many interesting occasions, was manifest. A letter from a motherly woman, who had never seen me but once, came to hand. in which was enclosed a bank note. This enabled me to pay what I owed and take stage from Springfield to Waltham. A paper-maker agreed, if I would pay one hundred dollars down and give him bonds for the remainder he would accommodate me; but how to accomplish this I did not know until I fell asleep at brother Pickering's father-in-law's in Waltham, when I dreamed how and where I could get the money, which I observed to P——, who replied, "A dream is a dream." I said, "True; but I intend to see the result."—I wrote to my Middletown friends and succeeded a cordingly. I spoke several times in Boston, and once on the common, where two caused interruption; but shortly after God called them to *eternity.*

Some dated their awakenings and conversions from this visit.—Thence I took stage and returned to Springfield, where I arrived about twelve at night, and lay under a haystack until day; when I called on the paper-man, with a friend I met from Middletown, and completed our bargain. I then went with the friend to Hartford, and completed our agreement with the printers and bookbinder.

I had now a tour of about six thousand miles laid off before me, to be accomplished against my return in May, and not a cent of money in my pocket; however, in the name of God, I set off on foot from my father's house, though no one knew my situation; doubting not, but that the providential hand which I had experienced heretofore, would go with me still. I walked to Hartford river, telling the ferryman my case. He carried me over, saying, "Pay when you can," (it being one cent.) I sold some books, and continued my walk to Litchfield, falling in with a wagon of Quakers, who suffered me to ride some on the way.

Thence I took stage to Danbury and redeemed my watch: held a few meetings, and came to New-York. A friend who had employed me to get him some printing done, not making remittance, I had like to have been involved in difficulty; but Providence delivered me from this difficulty also. Brother Thatcher had consented for my holding a camp-meeting in his district; but reconsidering the matter, recoiled with prohibition. Yet to prevent my disappointment from being too great, he suffered four appointments to be made for me by a local preacher, not choosing to give them out himself, considering the agreement at last conference. These appointments were given out wrong end foremost, considering the line of my journey, which caused me much more travelling. However, with a heavy heart, I fulfilled the appointments, in each of which I could but remark, with tears, that some persons had accused me with being of a party spirit, and striving to get a separation, which thing was false, and I did not expect to trouble them any more in that part, until there was an alteration and God should further open my way.

As I was going to take the stage, a man brought up a horse, saddle, and bridle for me, with orders to pay when convenient. I considered this act as Christian kindness; but Satan strove to raise a dust, as I did not make remittance very speedily, having no safe opportunity for some months.

I passed through my old circuit, the Dutchess, and saw some who retained prejudice; but I continued my journey, putting up at the inns, being unwilling to screw any thing through the devil's teeth.

When I arrived in Albany, the preaching-house doors, which had been shut in *Stebbens'* time, were now open. As the stationed preacher was out of town, and one or two others, who were expected, not coming, the people were like to be disappointed; which to prevent, gave rise to the opening, which I embraced as providential, and held a number of meetings. Here I have always found some kind friends, particularly brother Taylor.

I took my departure to Weston, where I saw Smith Miller, his wife Hannah, and PEGGY, after an absence of nearly two years.

August 31st. Camp-meeting began, and the people were entirely strangers to the quality and magnitude of this kind of meeting. Several Methodist preachers came as spectators, intending, if the meeting did well, to take hold, heart and hand with me ; but if ill, to leave it as they found it, and let the blame devolve on me. A stage being erected, I addressed the people thereon. from Luke xxi. 19. An awful solemnity came over the people : several mourners came forward to be prayed for ; and some shortly found comfort, and the Lord began to move in the camp. However, the preachers were minded we should disband to private habitations ; but I replied, "If I can get twenty to tarry on the ground, I will not go off until the meeting break up." Soon the Lord began to move among the people, and many were detained on the ground, and souls were born to God. Next day the congregation and work increased, and so in the course of the night likewise.

Sunday, Sept. 2d. I was sick. It rained, and the people were punished, by getting wet in the shower, through not coming better prepared for en campment, &c., which I was glad of, as it taught them a useful lesson against my return. It cleared up and the sun broke out, when I addressed them. Being informed of some ill designs among the youth, to bring a stigma on the meeting, and observing three companies in the woods, I got on a log in the triangle, and began relating a story concerning a bird's nest, which my father had remarked represented his family, that would be scattered like those young birds, who knew not the getting of things, but only the fruition of provision, and not parental affection until they come to have children of their own ; which remarks had made great impression on my mind. The rehearsal to them had the desired effect, and gathered their wandering minds into a train of serious thinking, and prepared their hearts for the reception of good advice. Several of them desired I should pray with them ; soon nine were sprawling on the ground, and some were apparently lifeless. The doctors supposed they had fainted, and desired water and fans to be used. I replied, "Hush !" Then they, to show the fallacy of my ideas, attempted to determine it with their skill ; but to their surprise their pulse was regular. Some said, " It is fictitious, they make it." I answered, " The weather is warm and we are in a perspiration, whilst they are cold as corpses, which cannot be done by human art."

Here some supposing they were dying, whilst others suggested, " It is the work of the devil ;" I observed, "If it be the devil's work, they will use the dialect of hell, when they come to :" some watched my words, in great solemnity, and the first and second were soon brought through, happy, and all in the course of the night, except a young woman, who had come under good impression, much against her father's will, thirty miles. She continued shrieking for mercy for eight hours, sometimes on the borders of despair, until near sunrise, when I exhorted her if she had a view of her Saviour, to receive Him as appearing for her. Here hope revived : faith sprang up ; joy arose ; her countenance was an index of her heart to all the beholders ; she uttered a word, and soon she testified the reality of her mental sensation, and the peace she had found.

About thirty found peace ; and I appointed another camp-meeting, to commence in May.

CHAPTER IV.

MARRIAGE.

When I was in Ireland, I saw the first pair that I thought were happy in marriage, or showed a beauty in their connection as the result of matrimony. I heard also of a young man, who made a proposal of marriage: the young woman, possessing piety and consideration, agreed to make it a matter of fasting and prayer, to know the Divine will on the subject; she also told a considerate friend, who gave her advice on the subject. At the time appointed they met, to return their answers upon the subject. The man said he thought it was the will of God that they should proceed, and the two women's opinion was the reverse. It was then submitted for my opinion, why I thought the young man's mind differed from theirs. I replied, "That many persons desire a thing, and wish that it might be the will of God it should be so, and from thence reason themselves into a belief that it is his will, when in fact it is nothing but their own will, substituted for God's, and so stand in their own light and deceive themselves.

It appears to me, concerning every person who is marriageable, and whose duty it is to marry, that there is some particular person whom they ought to have. But I believe it to be possible for them to miss of that object and obtain one who is not proper for them.

Some people have an idea that all matches are appointed, which I think repugnant to common sense, for a man will leave his wife and a woman her husband; they two will go to another part, and marry, and live as lawful man and wife. Now can rational creatures suppose that God appointed this match, whose revealed will saith, "Thou shalt not commit adultery."

Again, I have seen some men and women in courtship put the best foot foremost, and the best side out; and from this their ways would appear pleasing, and fancy would be conceived and taken for love; but when they got acquainted with each other's weaknesses, after the knot was tied, the ways which once appeared agreeable are now odious: thus the dear becomes cheap, and the honey is gall and vinegar; but, alas! it is too late to repent. Their dispositions being so different, it is as much impossible for them to live agreeable and happy in love together, as for the cat and dog to agree. Thus a foundation is laid for unhappiness for life. "Whatsoever ye do, do all to the glory of God," is the language of the scripture. Therefore, as Christ saith, "Without me ye can do nothing;" and as Paul saith, "Through Christ who strengthened me, I can do all things; we are to look to God for help in whatever we undertake, as all things are sanctified through faith and prayer; therefore whatsoever we dare not pray to God for his blessing upon, we have no right to pursue: it is forbidden fruit: but as there is a providence of God attending every person in every situation in life, and no such thing as mere chance, it is my opinion, if people were but resigned to the dispensation of Divine providence, instead of being their own choosers, their will resigned to his disposal, &c., that they would find his providence to guide and direct them to the object proper for them, as the calls of his Spirit and the openings of his providence go hand in hand.

I was resolved when I began to travel, that no created object should be the means of rivalling my God, and of course not to alter the situation of my life, unless a way seemed to open in the way of providence, whereby I might judge that my extensive usefulness should be extended rather than contracted.

S—— M——, of Western, came to a big meeting in the woods, and heard that crazy Dow was there, and after some time sought and found me. He accompanied me to my appointments, consisting of about one hundred miles' travel. He kept what some call a Methodist tavern, i. e. a house for the preachers, &c. One of my appointments being near his house, he invited me to tarry all night; observing his daughter would be glad to see me. I asked if he had any children! He replied, "A young woman I brought up I call my daughter." I stayed all night; but so it happenened, that not a word passed between her and me, though there were but the three in family. I went to my appointment, where we had a precious time: but whilst preaching, I felt an uncommon exercise, known only to myself and my God, which caused my mind, which caused me to pause for some time. In going to my evening appointment, I had to return by the house, he being still in company with me. I asked him if he would object if I should talk to his daughter concerning matrimony? He replied, "I have nothing to say, only I have requested her, if she hath any regard for me, not to marry so as to leave my house."

When I got to the door, I abruptly asked his wife who had been there, and what they had been about in my absence. She told me, which made way for her to observe, that Peggy was resolved never to marry unless it were to a preacher, and one who would continue travelling. This resolution being similar to my own, as she then stepped into the room, caused me to ask her if it were so? She answered in the affirmative; on the back of which I replied, "Do you think you could accept of such an object as me?" She made no answer, but retired from the room: this was the first time of my speaking to her. I took dinner; asked her one question more——— and went to my neighboring meetings, which occupied some days; but having a cloak making of oiled cloth, it drew me back to get it. I stayed all night, and in the morning, when going away, I observed to her and her sister, who brought her up as a mother, that I was going to the warm countries, where I never had spent a warm season, and it was probable I should die, as the warm climate destroys mostly those who go from a cold country. "But," said I, "if I am preserved about a year and a half from now, I am in hopes of seeing this northern country again, and if during this time you live and remain single, and find no one that you like better than you do me, and would be willing to give me up twelve months out of thirteen, or three years out of four, to travel, and that in foreign lands, and never say, do not go to your appointment, &c.—for if you should stand in my way, I should pray to God to remove you, which I believe he would answer,—and if I find no one that I like better than I do you, perhaps something further may be said on the subject;" and finding her character to stand fair, I took my departure. In my travels, I went to the Natchez country, where I found religion low, and had hard times, but thought this country one day would be the garden of America, and if this family would remove there, it would prove an everlasting blessing (as it respects religion) to the inhabitants, considering their infant state.* It lay on my mind for some weeks, when I wrote to them on the subject, though I had no outward reason to suppose they would go, considering the vast distance of near two thousand miles. But now I found she was still single, and they all willing to comply with my request, which removed many scruples from my mind, knowing that it was a circumstance that turned up in the order of Providence, instead of by my own seeking; so our bargain was drawn to a close, but still I thought not to have the ceremony performed until I should return from Europe; but upon reflection, considering the circumstance would require a correspondence, my letters might be intercepted, and the subject known, prejudice arise, jealousy ensue, and much needless conversation and evil be the result; wherefore to prevent the same, a preacher coming in, we were married that night, though only we five were present, this being the third of September, 1804.†

CHAPTER V.

TOUR TO THE MISSISSIPPI.

4th. SMITH MILLER set off with me for Natchez, early in the morning, as my appointments had been given out for some months. I spoke at Westmoreland and Augusta that day.

5th. We rode fifty miles: I spoke once on the road, and saw a spiritual daughter, who was awakened when I travelled the Pittsfield circuit.

6th. We rode fifty miles, and stayed with a family of Methodists, near the east branch of the Susquehannah river. The man was kind, but the woman was as she was.

7th. Rode thirty-four miles, and spoke at night at Sugar creek.

8th. Thirty-five miles, to Lycoming.

9th. Twenty-five miles, to Amariah Sutton's, and found Gideon Draper preaching, who was awakened when I was on Cambridge circuit. Oh! how these things refreshed my soul, to see the fruit of my labor, hundreds of miles off, years after! I spoke when he was done. He accompanied us ten miles, when I spoke again.

10th. Thirty-three miles to P—p Antisse's.

11th. Forty miles—stayed with a Dutchman, who was reasonable in his charges.

12th. Thirty-four miles across part of the Allegany mountain to Welshtown.

13th. We crossed the Laurel hills, and though we lost some miles by false direction, yet we came near to Dennistown, and stayed with a friend.

14th. We went to Greensborough, where I spoke in the evening, and then rode thirty-two miles to Pittsburg, where we arrived about the dawn of day. I found my appointments were not given out accurately.

---

* Provided they should be faithful to God—but many good things fall through for want of humble and faithful perseverance under God.
† See the Reflections on Matrimony—and you that are young, digest it well.

Sunday, 16th. I spoke in Pittsburg, and Washington.

17th. Brownsville and Uniontown, where I heard that the bishops Asbury and Whatcoat were sick, twenty-five miles off.

18th. Spoke twice in Washington.

19th. Spoke in Steubenville, in the state of Ohio. I have now been in each of the seventeen states of the Union.

20th. Spoke in Charlestown, and some were offended.

21st. Spoke to hundreds, beginning before sunrise; and then went to Wheeling. Spoke at ten o'clock to a large concourse, and so went on our journey.

23d. Spoke to a few in Zanesville on the Muskingum river. I could not but observe great marks of antiquity, ridges of earth thrown up so as to form enclosures of various forms, on which three or four might easily ride abreast. Some of these I think would contain near one hundred acres or more.

24th. Came to New Lancaster, where I spoke.

25th. Came to Chillicothe: held four meetings: some of the A-double-L-part people were offended: stayed with the governor two days. In him are connected the Christian and the gentleman. I think this state is laid off in townships, six miles square, and then into sections of one mile square, (containing six hundred and forty acres,) and half sections. The title of this is obtained from government at nine shillings English per acre, for ever, in four annual payments: or if the money be paid down the interest will be deducted. No slavery can be introduced here. There are lands laid off for schools in great magnitude: and I consider the form of the constitution superior to that of any other in the Union.

Near the Ohio river, people are sometimes troubled with fevers; but on uplands near the heads of the streams, the country is far more healthy.

Monday, Oct. 1st. I found Mr. Hodge, a Presbyterian minister, had failed in giving out my appointments. However, I fell in with the western conference, which was now sitting in Kentucky, and God was with them and the people. I saw the *jerks* in Pennsylvania, Ohio, and this state on this journey. Several of the presiding elders called me into a private room; and after some interview, we parted in friendship. Next day I spoke under the trees, nearly the whole conference being present. I thought I could discern every countenance present, and tell the Methodist from the A-double-L-part people. I never before observed that present impression would cause the countenance to be such an index to the mind, of pleasure and pain, especially in an auditory. From thence I went to Lexington, held a few meetings, and saw one whom I had known in Dublin, but he was not as happy now as he was once. I here experienced some kindness, and also spoke at Paris by the way. An A-double-L-part man being convinced that A-double-L meant *all*, caused great uneasiness among the Presbyterians. First, several preachers formed themselves into an association, by the name of the Springfield Association, and then made a will and voluntarily died, and instead of being a distinct party, sunk into union with all Christians.

Sunday, 7th. I spoke in Herodsburgh and Springfield. As I was getting up, I found my clothes had been moved during the night, which caused me to arouse the family. My jacket was found in the piazza, and all my money gone except one cent.

Thence I went to Tennessee, but found my appointments were not given out. I spoke in Clarkesville and Nashville, and many other places over the country, until I came to a brother Canon's, who had been the means of opening my way (under God) before.

Friday, 19th. Camp-meeting commenced at Liberty. Here I saw the *jerks ;* and some danced : a strange exercise indeed. However, it is involuntary, yet requires the consent of the will : i. e. the people are taken jerking irresistibly ; and if they strive to resist it, it worries them much : yet is attended by no bodily pain, and those who are exercised to dance, (which in the pious seems an antidote to the jerks,) if they resist, it brings deadness and barrenness over the mind ; but when they yield to it they feel happy, although it is a great cross. There is a heavenly smile and solemnity on the countenance, which carries a great conviction to the minds of beholders. Their eyes when dancing seem to be fixed upwards, as if upon an invisible object, and they lost to all below.

Sunday, 21st. I heard Doctor Tooley, a man of liberal education, who had been a noted deist, preach on the subject of the jerks and the dancing exercise. He brought ten passages of scripture to prove that dancing was once a religious exercise, but corrupted at Aaron's calf, and from thence young people got it for amusement. I believe the congregation and preachers were generally satisfied with his remarks.

The Natchez mission had almost discouraged the western conference, having made several trials with little success. However, Lawner Blackman and brother Barnes, finding that I was going thither, offered as volunteers and fell in with me for the journey.

Tuesday, 23d. We started from Franklin, (where I received some kindness,) and riding thirty-two miles, encamped in the woods. It rained, and apparently we could get no fire ; but some moving families from North Carolina got affrighted by some Indians, and were returning, being fearful to venture on their way. They showed us the remains of their fire where they had encamped the preceding night ; and with difficulty I prevailed on them to stay with us, until I let them know my name, which they had heard of before : they intended travelling on all night to the settlement, fearful of being massacred by the Indians.

24th. Travelled about thirty-five miles, and saw one company of Indians on the way.

25th. The post and a traveller passed us by early ; but we overtook them, and continued together to the Tennessee river. The wind was high, and none crossed except the post, and he with danger.

26th. We crossed, paying one dollar each, where was a small garrison, and some few half-breed Indians.

27th. We gained the suburbs of Bigtown of the Chickasaws. I am now beside the fire, the company laying down to rest, and our horses feeding in a cane-brake and provisions nearly out.

Sunday, 28th. Two of our horses were missing, but were returned early in the morning by a negro and an Indian, who, I suppose, had stolen them to get a reward. One of our company was for flogging the negro, which I opposed, lest it should raise an uproar, and endanger other travellers by the Indians, who are of a revengeful temper. This day was a hungry time to us. We thought of the disciples who plucked the ears of corn on the sabbath.

At length we came to another village where some whites lived, and one Mr. Gunn (who was touched under the word, when I was here before) received us kindly. We tarried two days in this settlement, held some meetings, and receiving gratis necessaries for our journey, took our departure. Having a gun with us, we killed some turkeys, which were numerous in flocks. From what we saw, there were bears and plenty of wolves and deer in these woods. The canopy of heaven was our covering by night, except the blankets we were rolled in. We kept fires to prevent the wild beasts from approaching too near. The post we saw no more. The man who was with him continued with us, and being seized with derangement for some hours in the woods, retarded our progress.

November 4th. Crossed the ground where I had the providential escape from the Indians, and arrived at the settlement of Natchez. We were glad to see white people, and got out of the woods once more. Stayed at the first house all night.

5th. Called on Moses Floyd, a preacher on Bigblack. Here brother Barnes tarried to begin his route. Blackman went with us to Colonel Barnet's, on Biopeer. Next day we went to Randal Gibson's, on Clarke's creek, and got some washing done, and there Miller stayed. Blackman went with me to 'Squire Tooley's, father of the doctor, where brother Harriman, a missionary, was at the point of death. However, he recovered. Our presence seemed to revive him.

8th. I visited Washington and Natchez, and some of the adjacent parts. Here I must observe the truth of the maxim, "Give the devil rope enough and he will hang himself." A printer extracted a piece from the Lexington paper, as a burlesque on me, which, however, did me no harm, though it circulated in most papers in the Union. He had just got his types set up before I made application for the insertion of a notice, that I should hold a meeting in the town on Sunday. This following the other, made impression on the people's minds, and excited the curious to attend meeting. When I was here before I found it almost impossible to get the people to meeting any way, and had my scruples whether there were three Christians in town either black or white. But now I spoke three succeeding sabbaths, and some on week days.

12th. This day I am twelve years old. Brother Blackman* preached a funeral sermon. I spoke a few words, and God began a gracious work. Here by Washington we appointed a camp-meeting. There is ground laid off for a college, and Congress, beside a handsome donation, hath given twenty thousand acres of ground, &c. This country is now dividing into townships and sections, and sold by government, as in the state of Ohio; and though only a territory now, yet will be incorporated into a state when the inhabitants shall amount to sixty thousand. They now had a small legislature; the governor is appointed by the President. One representative goes to Congress.

Sunday, 25th. I spoke for the last time at Natchez. I visited Seltzertown, Greenville, and Gibson Port. This last place was a wilderness not two years ago, but now contains near thirty houses, with a courthouse and jail. We held a quarterly meeting on Clarke's creek. Some supposed I would get no campers, but at this quarterly meeting I wanted to know if

---

*After many dangers in his years of itinerancy, came to his end by Providence, evidencing a remarkable foreboding.

there were any backsliders in the auditory, and if there were and they would come forward, I would pray with them. An old backslider, who had been happy in the old settlement, with tears came forward and fell upon his knees, and several followed his example. A panic seized the congregation, and a solemn awe ensued. We had a cry and shout, and it was a weeping, tender time. The devil was angry, and some without persecuted, saying, "Is God deaf, that they cannot worship him without such a noise?" though they perhaps would make a greater noise when drinking a toast. This prepared the way for the camp-meeting, and about thirty from this neighborhood went thirty miles or upwards, and encamped on the ground. The camp-meeting continued four days. The devil was angry at this also, and though his emissaries contrived various projects to raise a dust, their efforts proved ineffectual. In general there was good decorum, and about fifty were awakened, and five professed justifying faith; so that it may now be said that the country which was a refuge for scape-gallowses a few years since, in Spanish times, is in a hopeful way, and the wilderness begins to bud and blossom as the rose, and the barren land becomes a fruitful field. I crossed the Mississippi into Louisiana, and visited several settlements, holding religious meetings. I believe there is a peculiar providence in such a vast territory falling to the United States, as liberty of conscience may now prevail as the country populates, which before was prohibited by the inquisition. We got some things fixed to our minds, and procured three Spanish horses, which had been foaled wild in the woods, and had been caught out of the gang by climbing a tree and dropping a noose over the head, it being made fast to a bough, &c. We got letters from home, with information that they were well, and the work going on.

CHAPTER VI.

RETURN TO THE NORTH.

DECEMBER 16th. Our horses being tamed and taught to eat corn, by forcing it into their mouths, and we prepared with a tent and provisions, bid the settlement on the Mississippi adieu, and betook to the woods for Tombigbee, having two others in company. We had not gone far before the saddle turned on the pack-mare. She took fright, which affrighted the one S. M. rode, and they both set to rearing and jumping, which endangered his life. However, he held them both until he dismounted and they got settled. If they had got away there was little prospect of catching them again. Twenty-three miles to the Indian line, on the main branch of Homachitti, we encamped for the night, it being cloudy and rainy. We spread our tent, kept a good fire, hobbled the forelegs of our horses together, leaving a long rope dragging from their necks. Here was plenty of grass, and a cane-brake.

20th. Thirty-five miles. Encamped a little off the road, lest the Indians should steal our horses.

21st. We arrived this afternoon at Pearl, or Half-way river. The ford last year was good a number of yards wide, but now not more than five or six feet, which we knew not. A man who knew the ford, (being much among the Choctaws,) attempted to cross first and succeeded, though his horse made a small misstep; the next man's horse erred a little on the other side, but still I knew not the danger. I proceeded next, leading the pack-mare, but there not being sufficient ground for both horses, the water running like a mill-tail, carried me down the stream two feet, whilst my mare could swim but one towards the shore. She struck the bank, which gave way; however, she being an excellent swimmer and springy, made a second effort and got out. I lost my hobbles, and our tea, sugar, coffee, &c., got injured. And I being much chilled by the wet, we went on till we came to a convenient tarrying place, and encamped for the night to dry our things, &c. N. B. The river was muddy, I could not swim, and had not the mare struck the bank where she did, I must have lost my life, as the trees and brush filled the shore below.

22d. I met some people from Georgia. At night I was taken with a strong fever, but drank some water and coffee, and got a good night's rest.

Sunday, 23d. Feel somewhat better. It snowed some, and the sun hath shone scarcely ten minutes during these five days.

24th. We rode about forty miles, through Sixtown, of the Choctaws, and whilst we were passing it I observed where they scaffold the dead, and also the spot where the flesh was when the bone-picker had done his office. The friends of the deceased weep twice a day for a term, and if they cannot cry enough themselves, they hire some to help them. It was weeping time, and their cries made our horses caper well. I was informed of an ancient custom which at present is out of date among them. When one was sick, a council was held by the doctors; if their judgment was that he would die, they being supposed infallible, humanity induced the neck-breaker to do his office. An European being sick, and finding out his verdict, to save his neck crept into the woods and recovered, which showed to the Indians the fallibility of the doctors and the evil of the practice. Therefore, to show that the custom must be totally abolished, they took the poor neck-breaker and broke his neck.

25th. We came to Densmore's, agent for Indian affairs. Our provisions were gone, and with difficulty we procured relief. Some people who were dancing in a neighboring house came in to hear me talk. I held a meeting with them, and then lay down to rest.

26th. After breakfast we came near the trading road from the Chickasaws to Mobile, where we encamped near a spring and cane-brake The leaves of the cane are food for cattle, &c.

27th. We started betimes and came to the first house on the Tombigbee settlement, within four miles of Fort St. Stephen, where there is but one family, but it will be a place of fame in time. We had met the man of the house where we stayed, who told us to call. His wife made a heavy charge; we paid her, and S. M. said, "Tell your husband never any more to invite travellers to be welcome for his wife to extort." The river was high and swamp not fordable, which necessitated us to go down the river about seventy miles to the Cutoff, which is a channel from the Tombigbee to the Alabama river, about seven miles from their junction, where they form the Mobile. The island contains about sixty thousa acres, which are commonly overflowed by the spring flood, as Egypt is by the Nile. I held meetings during the six days of my tarrying in the settlement, and took my departure for Georgia, but was necessitated to keep on the dividing ridge between the streams, to prevent being intercepted by creeks. There were ferries at the above rivers. In the settlement there was not a preacher of any society. My appointments were given out in Georgia, with the days and hours fixed. In consequence of the high waters we had to lose much travelling.

January 4th, 1805. We fell in with a camp of whites, where we were informed of some whites having been murdered by Indians, and one Indian killed by a white, and another wounded. The wounded Indian was determined to kill some white in revenge. These whites had hired a chief to pilot them around to avoid the danger. But my time being limited obliged me to take the nighest cut, which was through the village where the wounded Indian lived. Here we parted from all the company, and set off by ourselves, having four hundred miles to go.

8th. We fell in with an Indian trader, who was out of provisions. We gave him some, and tarried at his habitation that night. He made us some return next day. Then we pursued our journey. This being in the Creek nation, we had some difficulty in finding our way, there being so many Indian by-paths; however, we came to Hawkins's old place that night.

10th. Our charges were eleven shillings, though I think not worth the half. We left the place about an hour by sun, having the prospect of a pleasant day before us; but we had not gone many miles before it gathered up and began to rain and sleet, which made it tremendous cold. So we stopped to let our horses feed, and pitching our tent, kindled up a fire to warm us; but the weather appearing more favorable, we proceeded on through a bad swamp, meeting two travellers by the way. At length we perceived it began to grow dark, which convinced us that it was later than we thought. We halted, hobbled out our horses immediately, (finding some grass present on the hill,) and proceeded to kindle up a fire, but every thing being so wet, and covered with sleet, and our limbs benumbed with cold, it was next to an impossibility to accomplish it. Things appeared gloomy; the shades of a dark night fast prevailing, death appeared before. In consequence of my being robbed I had no winter coat, but only my thin summer one at this time; however, at length we succeeded in getting prepared for the night. Our tent spread, which kept off the falling weather, and a good fire at the door soon dried the ground. We prepared our kettle of coffee, and partook with gratitude, and found we here could sing the praise of God, not without a sense of the Divine favor, considering our situation a little before. We lay down to rest as under the wing of the Almighty in this desert, inhabited only by wild beasts, whilst the wolves were howling on every side. Next day we passed the settlement where we considered the danger was, and continued our course till we came to Hawkins's, on Flint river; having seen an Indian point his gun at us by the way. We stayed with Hawkins a night; he was kind and hospitable, and has had some success, though with difficulty, in introducing civilization and cultivation among the Indians. First they despised labor, saying, "We are warriors;" and threatened him with death if he did not depart, (they being prejudiced, supposing him to be their enemy, as if to make slaves of them like the blacks,) and cast al the contempt on him imaginable ; but being afraid of Longknife, (i. e. Congress,) refrained from violence. However, they would not accept of tools or implements of agriculture, but would go directly opposite to his advice ; e. g., he said, scatter and raise stock : but they would live more compact. Two years elapsed with less rain than usual, causing the crops to fail ; some died with hunger. A chief asked, " Have you power with the Great Man above, to keep off the rain ?" H— replied, " No, but the Great Man sees your folly and is angry with you." H— wanted pork and corn ; the Indians, accustomed to sell by the lump, would not sell him by weight or measure, apprehending witchcraft or cheatery. A girl bringing to him a hog to sell, asked one dollar and three quarters, which they call seven chalks ; he weighing the pig gave her fourteen ; she supposed the additional seven were to buy her as a wife for the night, it being their custom to marry for a limited time, as a night, a moon, &c. Another girl bringing a larger hog, demanded fourteen chalks, which came to twenty-eight, which the other girl observing, supposed herself cut out, began to murmur, and flung down the money. But an old chief seeing the propriety of the weight, explained the matter. This gave rise to its introduction and reception among them. An old squaw receiving by measurement more than her demand for corn, laughed at the Indians who had refused to sell in this manner. Thus, measures were introduced.

I met some travellers, who showed me a paper containing the advertisement of my appointments published by brother Mead, beginning six days sooner than I appointed.

Thursday, 17th. We reached the settlement of Georgia, near Fort Wilkinson, and falling in with Esquire Cook, whom I knew, we went home with him, and had a meeting. He lent me a horse, and I went on to camp-meeting, and got there the very day I had fixed some time before.

We had a good time. Brigadier-general John Stewart and his brother, the captain, in Virginia, had agreed to join society, which the latter had done ; and as brother Mead had taken him and their wives into class, the general, to the surprise of the people, came forward in public, and requested to be taken under care also. Many had heard of my marriage, but did not credit it, until they had it from my own mouth, the particulars of which, to prevent fruitless and needless conversation, I related in public : for many said, " I wonder what he wants of a consort ?" I replied, as above, to enable me to be more useful on an extensive scale.

Hence I spoke at the Rock meeting-house, Comb's meeting-house, and Washington.

January 25th. I spoke at Scott's meeting-house, and Jones's at night. Here Smith Miller fell in with me again. In my sleep I viewed myself as at papa Hobson's with my companion, and shortly separated at a great distance, and found myself with a horse upon a high hill from whence I could espy the place where she was, although there intervened a wilderness with great rivers flooded into the swamps. I felt duty to require my presence there, and descended the hill the right way for that purpose after I had set my compass. However, I soon got into the dale, on a winding, circuitous road, where I could not see before me ; discouragements seemed almost insurmountable, yet *conviction* said I must go; *faith* said it might be accomplished by patient diligence, resolution, and fortitude; as well as some other things I had succeeded in, &c.

I had a similar dream upon this, from which I inferred that some severe trials are at hand, but by the grace of God through faith I may surmount them.

Sunday, 27th. I spoke three times in Augusta, and had some refreshing seasons. I found the first cost of my Journals would amount to between two and three thousand dollars; the profits of it I designed to aid in erecting a meeting-house in Washington, the Federal city. A person had promised me the loan of one thousand dollars to assist, if necessary, but found it inconvenient to perform: also, about two hundred guineas' worth of books were missent and not accounted for about this time. So that my prospects of pecuniary means were gloomy.

28th. Bidding farewell to Georgia, I spoke at Jetter's meeting-house, and twice at Edgefield courthouse.

29th. I spoke at the cross-roads and Buffington's.

30th. At Edney's meeting-house in the morning; at noon at Newbury courthouse, where were Quakers, Baptists, Presbyterians, Methodists, Universalists, and Nothingarians.

31st. I spoke at Mount Bethel, in the Methodist academy, to hundreds of people, and addressed the scholars in particular, who amounted to about sixty; and at night in Clarke's meeting-house.

February 1st. I crossed the Enoree, and spoke at Fishdamford meeting-house; then riding across Broad River, through danger, I spoke at Ester's at night.

2d. Spoke at Chester courthouse to many hundreds in the open air, and at Smith's at night.

Sunday, 3d. Was excessively cold; however, I rode twenty miles to Esquire Fulton's, and had a gracious time, though twice interrupted by a deist. This winter is the coldest of the four which I have spent in the south, and the oldest people say it is the severest they ever knew.

4th. Went twenty-five miles to Davenport's meeting-house; and finding a fire, around which the auditory were warming themselves, I availed myself of the circumstance for the sake of agreeable convenience, and gave them a preaching, which surprised them as a singularity. At night I stayed at a private house where I held meeting, having just got through S. to the edge of North Carolina. Here the family, either as a *put* or for convenience, were guilty of improprieties, considering I was a stranger, but God will judge between them and me.

5th. I spoke at Charlotte courthouse, but some A-double-L-part people strove to kick up a dust. S. M—r met me here again, and we were entertained at an inn gratis.

6th. I went twenty-six miles in the rain to Sandy-ridge, where we had a comfortable time, but S. M. felt a bad effect from the rain. Thence we rode to Salsbury, and I spoke in the air, as it was court-time, but in the evening in the courthouse, from Solomon's *irony*. A man, who had been careless about religion, was so operated upon, that God opened his heart to give me cloth for a winter coat, which I greatly needed.

8th. I spoke twice in Lexington, but a drunken man interrupted us, and when he became sober, he made acknowledgment.

9th. Early this morning I parted with S. M. (my father-in-law so considered) who started for Mr. Hobson's, and I rode twenty miles to Salem, and spoke to about three thousand people in the open air; in general good attention. Whilst I was speaking about our sorrows ending in future joy, it appeared like going to heaven with many, whose countenances were indexes of their sensations. I being a stranger, on entering the town, it appeared providential in my choice where to stand whilst speaking, being contiguous to an economy-house of the Moravian sisters, as, where it otherwise, they would not have heard me.

Sunday, 10th. I spoke in Bethany to about three thousand; at night at Doub's, who has the most convenient room, with a pulpit and seats, of any I have seen in the south.

11th. Stokes's courthouse, three thousand, a solemn time; left my mare, and procuring a horse, proceeded to Mr. M—'s; felt awfully, delivered my message as in the presence of the dread Majesty of Heaven, which greatly shocked the family, considering some circumstances in the same.

12th. Three thousand in the woods by Meacomb's, and good, I think, was done in the name of the Lord: at night, at Mr. Wades's, Henry county, Virginia; he gave me some cloth for over-alls.

13th. At Dr. French's, whose wife is my spiritual daughter, and sister of Mrs. Jennings.

14th. Spoke at the courthouse at night, at Henry Clarke's, but was interrupted by some drunkards. I have spoken to so many large congregations in the open air of late, and not one day of rest since I got out of the wilderness into Georgia, that I feel considerably emaciated, and almost broken down. These appointments were made without my consent and contrary to my orders, so that some of my intentions were frustrated.

15th. I feel unwell this morning, my horse is missing, things appear gloomy, but my hope is in God, who hath been my helper hitherto in trials past. Some more cloth given to me, as I am still unprepared for winter, neither have I had it in my power to get equiped with proper clothing for the inclemency of the weather, since I was robbed in Kentucky; but have the same clothes now which papa Hobson gave me last spring. Spoke at General Martin's, in the door. What is before me I cannot tell; my heart feels drawn and bound to Europe, where, I believe, the Lord will give me to see good days, in that weary, disturbed, distressed land. Lord! increase my faith, to put my confidence in thee, and feel more resigned to thy will and disposal, that when I come to die, I may be able to lay my hand upon my heart and say, "I have spent my time as I would try, if I were to do again."

Many think that ministers have no trials. I am confident this is a mistake: there is no life more trying, yet none on earth more happy. As Nancy Douglass said, "It is not the thing itself that is the trial, but the impression it hath on the mind;" for some have great disappointments and yet but little trials, whilst others with less misfortunes break their hearts with grief: therefore what a fine thing is faith in the order of God, and submission to his disposal, who can and will overrule all our unavoidable trials for our spiritual and eternal good. But, alas! where shall the wicked and careless find strength and repose from danger in the time of

dismal is the thought to have no God to rest upon, it trusteth in the arm of flesh.
; brought to me and I rode twenty miles to Watson's I spoke to a listening multitude. The bench on ly let me down out of sight of the people; recover- :rved it was a loud call to sinners to be in readiness, lower than the grave. My pilot being of an airy ling is to be given for something, and as you have ill pay thee, and pointing to him, directed my dis- ; *irony*, and concluded from Rev. xvi. 15.
:e in Danville in the open air, and then at Allen

ed by a singular dream, about one o'clock, that I :ople through my neglect; and as my sleep departed,)t some refreshment, and took my departure. Over- the road, who were going to the meeting, I was in- e being nine miles beyond my expectation, which 'e disappointed the people, the road also being intri- lreds, and also the next day at Halifax courthouse, L-part people got angry, and attempted to kick up harlotte and Prince Edward, where I spoke, and)n's, in Cumberland county, late in the evening on

say that I have grown lazy since my marriage, as ! in this country, but now could rest a day.
:t about three thousand at the Boldspring meeting- hem from the *death in the pot*, and Paul's going to The night following, my mind was much depressed, natural principles,) so that my sleep departed, and some storm was gathering, though I could not tell vould originate, and the trials come. Next day I breeding mare for a travelling one; then we pro- iiles to the city of Washington, where a gentleman)t of ground in a central place for a meeting-house. en lame from an old infirmity, I took the stage to unwilling to disappoint the people. S. M—r de.

;e in the stage, I left my cloak and walked thirty- iture disappointments. On this journey I experienced he one side friendship and favor, and on the other, without any particular provocation, but the foresight invisible world, could discover the movements of the danger of his kingdom; which reminds me of id, the devil is come down in great wrath, knowing iort.

6th. I saw one whom the Lord gave me as a spi- imond, and after visiting some others in Manchester, rgh, where I received a letter from J. Lee, that my termanded, and I must not attend it, he assigning did not like my appointing meetings of such mag- of the year being too early; and 3dly, it was too

soon after conference: but I could not in conscience falsify my engagement, seeing I was within a few miles of the ground. This meeting was
appointed some time before the alteration of the time of the conference.

Friday, March 8th. Lawson Dunnington fell in with me, and carried
me in his chair to Stoney-creek meeting-house, where the camp-meeting
was appointed, and I found two preaching stands erected, a number of
wooden cabings, tents, covered wagons, carriages, &c. The meeting lasted four days, in which time the Lord gave us extraordinary fine weather;
and although the preachers did not arrive from conference, several local
ones joined with me heart and hand in the work. About five thousand
people attended, and about thirty souls were hopefully converted to God.
Sinners were alarmed, backsliders reclaimed, Christians quickened, and
good was done in the name of the Lord. The weather at this season is
generally inclement, and was so now until we arrived on the ground,
when the sun beamed forth the warmth of his influential rays; and so
the weather continued until about three hours after the meeting broke up,
which caused some to say, I will tell J. Lee that God is able to send fine
weather in the fore part of March, as in April. These before had been
prejudiced against me. The wicked observed the weather suitable to our
convenience so extraordinary, that they said, it was in answer to prayer.
The trustees requested me to occupy the meeting-house, but I refused, lest
I should give offence, considering the countermand, but desired the local
preachers to occupy it within, and I would officiate without, so the cause
might not be wounded: hence the Lord raised up friends to aid me on
through my appointments to papa Hobson's in Cumberland.

Friday, 15th. I went in their carriage, and spoke on a funeral occasion.

16th. We went to another vicinity, where, standing on the carriage-box,
I addressed a large congregation from Solomon's *irony*. in which I showed
the contrast of a gentleman and fool *deist;* with an address to the magistrates and candidates. Here I parted with my friends, and rode to Squire
Evans's, who hath three daughters and a son, whom the Lord gave me at
a camp-meeting after I had begged them of their father; greatly to the
mortification of the daughters, who with inward reluctance attended, to
prevent their father's displeasure. I, perceiving uncommon tranquillity
and felicity in this family, desired the father to tell me how it was that his
children were so respectful. He replied: " When they are little stubs of
things, I take the switch and let them know that they must submit; so I
have but little difficulty with them when growing up."

Sunday, 17th. I spoke to about two thousand, near Hendrick's new store,
and then proceeded around the country nearly one hundred miles: spoke
at Amelia courthouse, and Chinkapin church, where the congregation was
a third larger than I had ever seen there before. It being court-time, the
auditory at Petersville church was not so large as it otherwise would have
been; however, what few there were were solemn and tender; among
whom were some of the twenty-five men who had in vain combined to flog
me at the camp-meeting. I spoke at Columbia and Fluvinna; also at
New Canton, where I found some given me in the Lord. Bidding farewell
to my friends hereabout, I started for the west on Tuesday.

26th. In company with brother Mead, but having returned my borrowed horse I was on foot, when a young gentleman, who, having finished his
studies at Philadelphia, was on his way home, dismounted, and constrained

me to ride; thus we three spelled each other alternately. When I came to Lynchburg, I found the brick meeting-house was in a fair way, and engaged thirty pounds worth of books more for its aid; had a good time, and went to New London.

Friday, 29th. Camp-meeting began at Ebenezer; the inclemency of the weather retarded many; however we continued the meeting, and God sent off, in some degree, the clouds which threatened us. Being invited to a local preacher's tent, I at first hesitated, till they agreed to give me their daughter to give to my Master, which greatly mortified the young woman, and prepared the way for her conversion. I found two young men, and another young woman, in the tent, with whom I conversed about their souls: the young woman was turbulent: I told her *Old Sam* would pay her a visit; which reminded her of my description of a character some months before, pointing to her, and saying: " You, young woman, with the green bow on your bonnet, I mean." Here conviction ran to her heart; her shrieks became piercing, and the three others also, which gathered the Christians around to wrestle with God in prayer, and he set their souls at liberty. Prejudice had been conceived in the minds of some; which was removed by my relating in public the particulars of my marriage. I bought me a new horse for forty-five pounds, and continued my journey.

Sunday, April 7th. I feel unwell, having travelled in the rain near a hundred miles expeditiously, to get on to this chain of appointments, which began this day in Abington. Here I spoke to hundreds, at eleven o'clock, in the sun; at three, at Crawford's meeting-house; thence five miles: spoke by candle-light.

8th. Arose at two, proceeded to Royal Oak, and spoke at eight. The day before, a man was buried, moving from Powhatan to Kentucky: I could but pity his disconsolate widow, who requested me to speak something over her husband. Oh! how uncertain is life! I proceeded to Wyth, and spoke in the courthouse. My horse was taken lame, so that I was constrained to leave him and borrow another, and proceed to my evening appointment, which was to begin at nine; being appointed about thirteen months. This day I had travelled seventy miles, and spoke three times. I was disappointed of near one hundred dollars, which were to have been sent to me.

9th. Spoke at Montgomery courthouse to a large auditory, and in Salem at night; having travelled fifty-five miles. I think good was done.

10th. Left my borrowed horse with a friend to be returned, and my lame one to be disposed of; but my directions not being followed, was a great detriment to me. However, I got another horse on credit for thirty-six pounds, this morning, and proceeded to Fin Castle, where I employed a smith to shoe my horse during meeting; but having no money to pay him, I was under the disagreeable necessity of making my circumstances known to the congregation, who gave me three fifths of a dollar; this being the first time that I ever had hinted for the public aid since I commenced travelling. I sold a book, which enabled me to clear up with the smith, and then went to Springfield, where I spoke at night.

A man privately asked my advice, saying his daughter shouted and fell down, which caused him to beat her, with prohibition from religious meetings. I asked him if he did not believe his daughter sincere, and feel conviction for his conduct. He answered in the affirmative. I replied that parents have no right to exercise authority in matters of conscience, further than giving advice, as every one must account for themselves to God.

11th. Lexington; the people mistook the time by an hour, which made me hurry to my evening meeting in Stantown, where I arrived about sun-set, opposite a house which I had felt my heart drawn particularly to pray for when here before. A woman now rushed out of the door, and grasping me in her arms, gave me a welcome to the house; she was a spiritual daughter of nine, and lately married to the man of the house, whose former wife with him found peace, and she shortly after died happy, though I knew not who lived in the house at the time I had preached in the street. Fearing lest my horse might have been heated too much, to prevent injury I gave him salted grog. The church being open, I sat on a table in the door, and spoke, I suppose, to some thousands.

12th. My horse, I think, is as well as usual; so I proceeded on my journey, preaching in Rocktown, and two other places, on the way.

Sunday, 14th. I spoke at Newtown, at an hour by sun in the morning, to about three thousand; thence to Winchester, where I spoke, at eleven, to about six thousand, in the woods; rode twenty-two miles, and spoke at night; continued my way to Carlisle, where I spoke twice, fulfilling appointments on the road; hence a Methodist preacher accompanied me to Tioga Point, 150 miles, in three days. This young man was laboring under some depression of mind when we met; but the circumstances of the meeting and journey seemed to help him both in mind and body. Thus in fifteen days I closed the journey of seven hundred and fifty miles; speaking twenty-six times on the way, which appointments were given out about thirteen months beforehand.

CHAPTER VII.

TOUR THROUGH NEW ENGLAND.

22d. ARRIVED back in Western, after an absence of near eight months. Peggy was not at home. Our marriage was not known in general in this neighborhood, until within a few days past. It caused a great uproar among the people.

23d. Peggy felt it impressed on her mind that I was here, and so came home early in the morning; having enjoyed her health better, and her mind also, than for some time previous to my absence. In the afternoon S. Miller and his wife came home, well, and were preparing for their journey to the Mississippi Territory.

Thursday, May 2d. I saw brother Willis, who married us, and Joseph Jewell, presiding elder of Genesee district, who came a great distance to attend the camp-meeting, and brought a number of lively young preachers with him, they having never attended one before.

Friday, 3d. The people attended in considerable crowds, amongst whom was Timothy Dewey, my old friend, whom I had seen but once for more than four years past. The wicked attempted intrusion; but their efforts were ineffectual, and turned upon their own heads, being checked by a magistrate.

Monday, 6th. We had a tender parting-time. In the course of the meeting good was done in the name of the Lord. I moved a collection for one of Jewell's young preachers, Perley Parker, formerly a playmate of mine. Here I left my Peggy on the camp-ground, within three miles of home, and proceeded on my tour, speaking twice on my way.

Tuesday, 7th. We rode fifty-nine miles, parting with Jewell and Parker by the way.

8th. Came to Albany. Here the preaching-house was shut against me, being the only one which has been refused to me for a considerable length of time : Canfield assigning, as the reason, the vote of conference ; which, however, was only a conversation concerning the giving out of my appointments, &c., lest I should be a pattern for others, and "fifty Dows might spring out of the same nest." I spoke in the courthouse, and God gave me one spiritual child.

9th. With difficulty I crossed the river, and coming to New Lebanon, saw one of my old acquaintances, with whom I held a meeting.

10th. Fire being out, I did not stay for breakfast, but rode fifty-four miles to New Hartford. My mind is under deep trials concerning my singular state and many disappointments ; but my hope is in God, who gives me peace from day to day.

11th. Came to Hartford. Found the printing of my Journals finished, and about half the books bound. I now had a trial from another source ; the two preachers with whom I had intrusted the preparation of the camp-meeting at hand had, in my absence, incurred the displeasure of the Methodists. The one, for embracing some peculiar sentiments, was suspended ; the other had withdrawn. Therefore, said brother Ostrander, the presiding elder, "If Lorenzo Dow admits them to officiate at his camp-meeting, he will have no more liberty with us." My trials were keen, for these men were in good standing when we made the agreement ; and I had no doubt but that Ostrander would fall into the measure, considering the circumstance of my not being able to consult him, for want of time, on the occasion, so I went to two meetings to explain the matter to him.

Sunday, 12th. He spoke with more life than I think I ever heard him. Afterwards I spoke, and God cut a young woman to the heart : her father came and dragged her out of meeting, and her soul was set at liberty while she was in his arms ; so I made remarks on the folly of his conduct. Ostrander, upon reflection, viewed my conduct in a different light than before, and consented, if I would give up the camp-meeting to his superintendence, that he would bring on his preachers to attend with me. This I had always expected, and advertised the meeting accordingly.

13th. Pawned my watch for an old trunk, and taking stage came to New Haven ; thence embarked for New York, where I spent a few days, and found prejudice in some minds, and in some it was removed. I received a letter with information that more books, which I expected, would fail coming ; thus I find one disappointment after another.

Saturday, 18th. I sailed to Long Island to attend a camp-meeting with brother Thatcher, and preached in the packet to about fifty friends. I also spoke at night at the camp, and then called up the mourners to be prayed for ; several found peace, backsliders were reclaimed, and Christians quickened and comforted. Bishop Asbury came up before I had got through, and the meeting continued all night.

Sunday, 19th. Whilst one was speaking on the subject of the dead, small and great, standing before God, an awful black cloud appeared in the west, and flashes of forked lightning, and peals of rumbling thunder ensued. A trumpet sounded from a sloop, whilst hundreds of a solemn auditory were fleeing for shelter. This scene was the most awful representation of the day of judgment of any thing I ever beheld.

Next day the meeting broke up. My hat could not be found, so I embarked on board one of the fifteen craft which brought passengers, and sailed forty miles in three hours and a half; and after landing at the Black Rock, one of the passengers pulled me into a store, and constrained me to take a hat. Thence I walked to Strafford, and so through New Haven to Durham, thence to Hartford, where I settled with the ferryman for a former passage, and a gentleman paid my present one, as it had taken the last of my money to redeem my watch. Thence I went to Coventry, and found my father and friends well.

Sunday, 26th. Spoke twice at Square Pond meeting-house, and once in Tolland, and the quickening power of God seemed to be present; but I soon must quit this my native land, and repair to parts to me unknown.

30th. The camp-ground was in the township of Bolton, on Andover parish line, to which lead a lead-off road, ending on this spot of ground unoccupied. This appeared providential, as we could repair to the spot of woods on the hill, without trespassing on any man's ground in this solitary place.

The neighborhood was thick settled by bigoted, federal Presbyterians, much prejudiced against the Methodists. The people were unwilling that we should get water from their brooks or wells, but held the meeting in ridicule and contempt, thinking, who should I get to encamp on the ground. However, a report having prevailed that the Indians, in their times, had a spring on this hill to which they resorted, caused a man to go in search of it; and after some difficulty, he struck upon a fountain beneath a rock, which afforded us a sufficient supply.

31st. Many people came from distant places to the ground. Satan hoisted his standard near by, as a grogman brought his liquors for sale, but was constrained by threats (when reason would not do) to give it over, the law being against him.

I opened the meeting, and had an agreeable time; the work of God began in the evening.

Saturday, June 1st. The congregation and work increase.

Sunday, 2d. Some thousands appeared on the ground; several found peace, and prejudice seemed to wear off from the minds of the people.

Monday, 3d. Meeting broke up. I had given my farewell to the people; it was an affecting time of parting with my Christian friends, many of whom I shall see no more until eternity. I observed to Ostrander, that I had caused him some uneasiness, but should trouble him no more whilst he presided in the district.

4th. About 7 A. M. I left my dear father, I know not but for the last time, and with my sister Mirza rode to the burying-ground, where my dear mother was interred. for the first time of my seeing the grave. I could not mourn, but was comforted with the prospect of meeting again. I departed to Windham, and preached under the trees, and tarried in Coventry, Rhode Island, that night, riding fifty miles without food, through want of money, to Providence, and pawned a book by the way to get through a toll-gate. I held several meetings in Providence, then rode to Norton, where Zadock Priest died at old father Newcomb's, whose wife had then no religion, but since professes to be converted, and is in society. On their ground, brother George Pickering, with eleven of his preachers and myself, by agreement, held a camp-meeting, the preparation for which was now going forward.*

This being about a mile from the place where I first attempted to preach, I related a dream to brother P., who replied, that he thought some trials were near me, but by the blessing of God I might escape, which in fact proved to be the case, for Satan's emissaries set up the grog-tents, which cost them dearly; for after that they would not hearken to reason, I showed the impropriety of corrupting the meeting, and warned the people against them, and also laid a foundation whereby they might be prosecuted, in consequence of which they were alarmed, sunk into contempt, and did not sell a sufficiency to indemnify them for their expenses. This so exasperated them, that they fell on different plans to be revenged, either by provoking me to say something that would expose me to the law, or else to get an opportunity to give me a flogging. However, God defeated their designs, and turned their treacherous intentions to the disgrace of their characters, so that they appeared as ciphers in the eyes of a generous public.

The Lord was wonderfully present with his Spirit to acknowledge the meeting; for, whilst P. was preaching, numbers fell, as if the powers of unbelief gave way, and the cry became so general that he was constrained to give over, but the work continued. The full result of this meeting will not be known until eternity. I was to have met some friends at the New York district conference, now sitting at Ashgrove, where I once had a glorious revival when on the circuit, but my wife and they were disappointed, as brother P. had made arrangements for me for about two weeks.

Monday, 10th. The meeting broke up, and the Boston friends who were the first arrived on the ground, took me in their stage-coach and carried me home with them. Here I spoke several times, and we had comfortable times from the presence of God.

. I gave near forty pounds worth of books towards the deficiency of the meeting-house, and remitted money to clear out with my printer in Hartford. I visited Lynn, where we had a precious time, though religion had been cold there for some time. I also visited Marblehead, where I saw a preacher from Ireland, who escaped with some others in an open boat at sea, from on board the ship Jupiter, as she struck against a cake of ice, and went down, with twenty-seven persons on board, among whom was a preacher with his wife and seven children. What an inestimable support must be the Divine presence at such a time as this!

---

* 1801. Camp-meetings began in Kentucky; next, North Carolina; attended them in Georgia; introduced them in the centre of Virginia, New York, Connect 'ut, Massachusetts, and Mississippi Territory 1803–4–5.

14th. The following appeared in the Salem Gazette, (where the Quakers had been martyred by religious bigotry:)

"By desire, Lorenzo Dow, an eccentric genius, whose pious and moral character cannot be censured with propriety, is to preach at the court-house, precisely at nine o'clock this morning."

I spoke to a few of various ranks, who fain would have made a laugh, but there seemed to be a restraining hand over them. This day I had five meetings, and near thirty miles' travel; at the last of them, the rabble attempted to make a disturbance, set on by some, called gentlemen; and at night broke the windows of the preaching-house, which denotes that Satan views the danger of his kingdom; and caused P. to remark, that the devil thought he had as good a right to the common, as God Almighty. This reminded me of last year, concerning two who attempted interruption and shortly after had to appear at the bar of God.

Hence to Waltham, to brother P.'s quarterly meeting. His wife is a well educated woman, of a sweet amiable disposition, and far from the proud scornful way of some. Here are four generations under one roof; i. e. her grand-parents, own parents, self, and children.

I preached on Saturday and Sunday, and called up those who would wish me to remember them, and strive to remember themselves in prayer, to give their hands: and the power of God seemed to come over all. I visited Needham and Milford, which places I had been invited to before, but Providence overruled my coming here, though I had previously put them off.

21st. Set off with P—, thirty miles to Salem in New Hampshire, and spoke from, "halting between two opinions," in which I observed, if a lamb should be led from its dam by a goat, to feed on moss, it would die.—N. B. A man was present whom the A.-double-L.-part people had been fishing for.

22d. We came to Hawke, where I met Bachelor, Webb, and Metcalf. I spoke from "Oh! thou man of God, there is death in the pot." At night I had conversation with some, and felt my work drawing to a close in this quarter.

Sunday, 23d. Spoke again to a large assembly, bade my friends farewell, and rode thirty miles to Pembroke, where I arrived about half past nine at night, and being weary, I could not stay up to supper, but retired to rest, having taken no food all day, except some sacramental bread remaining after the ceremony, which a young man observing, said, "I had got more than my share," which set some in a laughter.

24th. Rode about sixty miles to Romney, and stayed with a man, who a day or two before had joined society, and was about to charge me for my poor fare, when his wife hushed it.

25th. I went fifty-four miles to Peacham Gore, in Vermont, and stayed with a friend, where I had been before, meeting Phineas Peck, a preacher, on the road.

26th. About nine o'clock I arrived at my youngest sister's, Tabitha French, she being married and settled here in the midst of the town of Hardwicke, on river Demile; this being the first time I had seen her husband. Joseph Bridgman, my brother-in-law, and my sister Ethelinda his wife, resided about a mile hence. For this day I had a meeting, appointed some months before, which I now held, and spoke five days successively. I had sent on a chain of appointments through Upper Canada, from Montreal to the Falls of Niagara; thence to Philadelphia; but when in Hyde-park, I felt whilst preaching, a secret conviction or impulse, that my appointments were not given out, and that I must return to Western; thrice it ran through my mind. I rejected it twice, but perceiving a cloud or depression beginning to come over my mind, I yielded, and taking the left-hand road, went to Stow that night, where I found some of my spiritual children, whom God had given me some years before; spoke next day in this township on my way: in Waterbury twice, and rode to Richmond that night: next day I breakfasted in Starksborough, with a blacksmith, who once intended to flog me, but he now put a shoe on my horse, having since got religion. About twelve, I arrived at Middlebury, fed my horses, and spoke in the street; then came on to Orwell, and stayed the night with my uncle and aunt Rust, having rode forty-six miles.

July 3d. I rode sixty miles, by South Bay, Fort Ann, Glenn's Falls, and stayed at an inn; but judging from circumstances that it was necessary to watch my horses, I slept none that night.

4th. I started between three and four in the morning, and came sixty-five miles to the Little-falls on the Mohawk river.

5th. Rode forty-six miles to Western, arriving about three P. M.; found my Peggy and friends well.

Sunday, 7th. I spoke twice, and had good times: rested the 8th: rode to Camden the 9th: spoke to an attentive congregation and returned: rested on 10th; but soon shall be bound with expedition to North Carolina.

11th. I visited Floyd, by brother Keith's request: he was Peggy's spiritual father. Here many gave me their hands, if they should see me no more on earth, that they would strive to meet me in a happy eternity. I visited several other neighborhoods, as a wind-up for this quarter.

CHAPTER VIII.

JOURNEY TO NORTH CAROLINA.

Sunday, 14th. Gave my farewell to a vast congregation, under the shades at Western, when Hannah Miller, standing upon a log, bade her neighbors farewell; she being one of the first settlers in the country: and Oh! what a weeping and embracing there was between the neighborhood (of all ranks and descriptions,) and her and Peggy. After this we went to Westmoreland, taking leave of all things by the way. Here Timothy Dewey met us, who informed me that he had seen the Canada preachers, and my appointments were not given out; so that if I had gone, I must have lost one thousand miles travel; and my time being so limited: I held two meetings, and realized the propriety of the poem:

"We should suspect some danger nigh,
Where we possess delight."

When I arrived at Albany, brother Vanderlip, the stationed preacher, gave me the liberty of preaching in the meeting-house: from hence I shipped Peggy down the river for New York, myself proceeding thither by land, and settled some temporal concerns by the way.

Saturday, 27th. We met again, and heard a Baptist preach in the park just after sunrise next morning. He had a tincture of A-double-L-part-ism, yet his discourse in general was good, and blessed to the people. I spoke here in the afternoon, and also in several other parts of the city. Ezekiel Cooper, one of the book stewards, and superintendent of the book affairs, invited me to preach in the preaching-house at Brooklyn, which he also superintended: here I spoke sundry times. Said he, "I am of the same mind now concerning your mode of travelling as I was when you saw me in Philadelphia; but nevertheless, I wish never to hinder good from being done, or prevent your usefulness." He is a man of general reading and strong powers of mind.

I have been much troubled with the asthma, of late, which I suppose originated from drying up an eruption on my body by outward application, which was recommended from the idea that it might be the itch brought with me from Ireland: this reminded me of what Dr. Johnson said concerning my inward complaint.

Peggy being unable to keep up with me, I was necessitated to leave her with brother Quackenbush, and disposing of her horse, I proceeded to Elizabethtown, New Jersey. Saw T. Morrel, whose father was dying: he excused some former things to me. I rode fifty miles to Trenton, where Washington took the Hessians, which turned the gloomy aspect in favor of America.

My appointment was not given out as expected; however the preaching-house was open, and I held sundry meetings in and about this place. Then proceeded to Philadelphia, where I called and found brother Colbert, who, being superintendent, paved my way to the getting access to all the Methodist meeting-houses in and about this place, one excepted, which was in the power of a contentious party. The other houses amounted to about half a dozen.

August 14th. Elder Ware informs me that my appointments were given out through the Peninsula, which I had been informed was prevented: so after preaching at Ebenezer, I silently withdrew, and taking my horse, travelled all night, until ten next morning, when I spoke at Bethel, and then jumping out at a window from the pulpit, rode seventeen miles to Union: thence to Duck creek cross-roads, making near eighty miles travel and five meetings without sleep. These few weeks past, since the eruption was dried up, and the asthma more powerful and frequent than usual, I feel myself much debilitated.

16th. Spoke at Georgetown cross-roads, and at Chestertown at night, and next morning; after which I crossed Chester river gratis, and preached in Centerville. Here some unknown gentleman discharged my bill of fare. I spoke at Wye meeting-house in the afternoon to a few.

I inquired the cause why more general notice was not given; and was answered, that John M'C. replied, "I give out no appointments for him: I have nothing to do with Lorenzo Dow."

Sunday, 18th. I spoke in the open air at Easton, to about two thousand. The Lord was with us. James Polhemus (M'Clasky's colleague) gave out my appointments, as most of the preachers in this country also did. In the afternoon I spoke at the Trap to a large auditory, having (on account of M'Clasky's mind) concluded not to occupy the preaching-house until the trustees solicited me, to prevent wounding the cause of God.

I find that Roger Searle has withdrawn from the Methodist connection.

19th. Spoke at Cambridge, in the Methodist meeting-house, and at Foster's chapel in the afternoon: then accompanying a carriage with two sisters, we, in crossing a bridge, espied some careless people and a town. I expressed a desire to preach. And on perceiving a collection of people, and inquiring the cause, found that it was a Methodist meeting. One of the sisters knowing a man, got me introduced to preach.

20th. I had a meeting at St. Johnstown, under great weakness of body, which caused me to sit down whilst speaking, as I had puked, and was obliged to stop several times by the way. From this I was carried in a chair to Deep-creek meeting-house, passing near where G. R. was raised, who took me into society, but now thinks I am crazy. Surely, if one from such a low sphere of life, through conversion and diligence can attain to such an extension of useful knowledge, what will be the account most must give at the last day? I also spoke at Concord, Laurel-hill and Salsbury, being aided thither by carriages.

22d. Princess Anne courthouse, and Curtis's meeting-house. Near this my spiritual father, Hope Hull, was raised.

23d. I spoke under the shades at Newtown, to about two thousand or more. I gave them a mixed dose, and we had a good time from the Lord, whilst they gave me their hands to remember me to God when on the other side of the Atlantic. I spoke at Downing chapel also. On this peninsula were now C. Spry, Fredus Aldridge, and Z. Kankey, the last of whom I met. I have now seen most of the old preachers on the Continent: the greater part of them are retired into the private spheres of life. The chief of those who most opposed me have located, and are almost in oblivion, cr withdrawn, or expelled the connection, or in a cold, low, uncomfortable state of formality. Lord! what am I? Oh! ever keep my conscience holy and tender! Trials await me, and unless God support me I cannot succeed. Oh God! undertake for me. I have seen thy salvation in time past, and shall I distrust thy goodness or providence at this critical time? No; my hope is still in thee: I will hope and trust to thy providence until I must give up.

I feel my work on this Continent drawing to a close, and heart my and soul bound to Europe.

24th. Spoke at Guilford. Feeling my strength more and more to decline, without help I must depart; but hope I shall recover on my intended voyage.

· Sunday, 25th. Spoke to near three thousand at Drummingtown: good decorum, except in a few. At Onancock we had a shout. The sandy dust has been distressing for hundreds of miles, there having been no rain for near twelve weeks over this country. Vegetation and the cattle are in mourning: yet not so much here as in some parts of the north, this land being more level.

I viewed the camp-ground, and preparations making for the meeting, which I think the most convenient I have seen. Spoke at Garretson's meeting-house, and in a farm-house at night.

27th. A young woman took me in a chaise to Northampton courtyard, where I held some meetings. Being unable to ride on horseback with propriety any longer, I sold my horse, &c. at great loss. I find the grea:

have their trials as well as the small, from what I now observe in others. But "all shall work together for good to them that love God."

28th. I rode in a coachee to the camp-ground, with a family, having solicited several to attend. I found hundreds on the ground to be in readiness for the next day. I have been reading Washington's Life. What must have been his sufferings of mind during the war, particularly when retreating from New-York through the Jerseys to Trenton, and the gloomy aspect of the times—his life and property in danger, and particularly if defeated. Yet he was not cast down, but supported, and finally won the day. Here I reflected, if he, through difficulties, endured to accomplish an earthly transitory design, shall I, for a little earthly trouble, desert that which I think will turn to the glory of God in the promotion of the kingdom of Christ on earth? Though I meet with difficulties I will not despair. I want more faith: in order to accomplish the spread of the gospel, I want a greater acquaintance.

29th. By invitation from Dr. Chandler, the presiding elder, and preachers, I spoke in the afternoon on sanctification. About three thousand rose up in covenant, sundry of whom came up to be prayed for, and among them three young women, two of whom were prayerless three days before, and came with me. One of them found pardon in a few minutes, and shouted the praise of God; the other was delivered shortly; and the third, who owned the camp-ground, found deliverance that night. Thus the work went on, so that there could be no preaching until ten the next day, though meeting had been appointed for eight at night and morning. When I left the place, the rain impeded the meeting, yet it continued until Monday; and, on a moderate calculation, there was reason to believe that about five hundred were hopefully converted.

A captain sent word that I might sail with him over the Chesapeake. But the wind being high, and from such a direction that I could not be landed where I would, so I must where I could.

We sailed about one hundred miles in less than a day, to Suffolk, where I spoke at night. Our danger was great on the passage, in consequence of the sloop being old, and impossible to keep dry below decks.

Sunday, September 1st. I set off in a chair for Portsmouth, it raining by the way. However, I preached, and also in Norfolk, where two souls found peace. Next day got some temporal affairs adjusted, and returned to Suffolk, where I spoke to about one thousand, and rode on a cart, as a chair could not be obtained for love nor hired for money.

4th. Rhoda Williams, a young woman, of late under concern for her soul, was somewhat unwell, yet took me in a chair forty miles to Smith's chapel, before she alighted. Here we found a congregation of about three thousand, waiting, whom I addressed with liberty. Oh! may God remember Rhoda for good, in recompense for her kindness. We were deceived in the distance about seventeen miles, yet the disappointment was prevented.

I had twelve miles to go this evening, so I rode four in a cart, walked one, and a Connecticut pedler coming along with his wagon, carried me the remainder to Halifax, in North Carolina, where I spoke, and got a letter from Peggy.

5th. Esq. B―― sent a servant and chair with me to Ebenezer, where I addressed about one thousand seven hundred: then a friend whom I had never spoken to, said if I would dine with him, he would carry me in his chair to the camp-meeting, about twenty miles, where we arrived that evening. Thus I find God provides for those who put their trust in him.

6th. Camp-meeting came on in the edge of Franklin county. The weather was somewhat lowering, which incommoded us, at intervals. Thousands, however assembled, and though Satan was angry, and, by means of a few drunkards, strove to make a rumpus or uproar, yet I think here was the best decorum I ever saw, considering the magnitude of the assembly from this wilderness country. There were near one hundred tents, and upwards of sixty covered wagons, &c. the first day, besides carriages, &c.

Philip Bruce, an old preacher and friend, was presiding elder here. The Lord began a glorious work: it might truly be said, we had the cry of heaven-born souls, and the shout of a King in the camp. Some months ago brother Mead had agreed to appoint a train of camp-meetings through his district, the first of which was to begin a week after this in Buckingham county, Virginia, which he had engaged me to attend. But, being unacquainted with my arrangements, he took the liberty to anticipate the time, and publish accordingly, which made the two meetings clash. This brought me into a dilemma, as I was necessitated to attend them both, not only by engagement, but also to get my temporal affairs wound up, and business settled with individuals who were to meet me; and also my book concerns, as they related to meeting-houses, &c.

7th. Feeling my mind greatly exercised about what was before me, I was convinced of the necessity of attempting to force my way from one camp-meeting to the other, before they should break up, which would make a distance of about one hundred and forty miles to be travelled over in about forty hours, across a country where were no country roads, except for neighborhood or plantation convenience. I slept but little the past night, in consequence of laboring with mourners, conversation and preaching. In my last discourse I remarked my decline, my necessity of departure, and intention of sailing shortly. As I bade the people farewell, hundreds held up their hands, as a signal of their intention and desire that we should remember each other when separated, and if we never meet below, to strive to meet above.

A young man whom I had never seen before, took me in a carriage about forty miles to his brother's, where I took some tea. Then a servant, carriage and two horses, were despatched with me seventeen miles. A man, on whom I was directed to call for further assistance, pleaded inconvenience, but asked me to tarry until morning; so I took my feet and went on. Being feeble in body, I made poor headway, having the inconvenience of near eight hundred dollars in a tin box. At dawn of day, I arrived at Mecklenburgh courthouse, where a chair was not to be hired on any terms, but a gentleman who had never seen me before, on finding out my name, gave me a breakfast, and despatched a servant and two horses with me about twelve miles, (the servant carrying my luggage;) but I growing weak, and perceiving I must alight, espied a chair, which I strove to hire, though at first in vain, yet on telling them my name and situation, the mistress consented, (her husband being out,) and the son for twelve shillings carried me expeditiously ten miles, where I called, making my case known as before. The family rejected, until they un derstood my name, when a servant was sent with me six miles. Here I called again, but was denied assistance, until a female visitor said, "If you are Lorenzo Dow you shall be welcome to my horse;" and so her son went with me thirteen miles. Then I got some refreshment, but here could get no assistance further; so I took to my feet and went on as well as I could, being frequently assaulted by dogs on the road, at different periods of the night, and at length one of them made such a fuss, that the master came out with his gun to see what was the matter; and as I spoke to the dog, he knew my voice. He invited me to come in and tarry, but not prevailing, aroused a servant to get me a horse; so I mounted and pushed on, and coming to a house, hailed them up for a pilot on the road. The old man said, "Tarry till morning." I replied, "I cannot." Then he despatched several for his horse, whilst he should dress himself, which doing in haste, he forgot his small-clothes until after his boots were on. At length we started, and arrived on the camp-ground just after sunrise, where I found brother Mead and papa and mamma Hobson, with hundreds of friends, who were surprised and glad to see me, as they had despaired of my coming. There were about ten thousand at this meeting. Scores were hopefully converted to God, and the Lord was with them of a truth. I addressed the auditory as my bodily strength would admit, and settled my temporal affairs to my mind, though some in whom I had confided betrayed it.

Tuesday, 10th. I bade the people farewell, the meeting broke up, and I went home in the carriage to Cumberland, with papa and mamma Hobson.

12th. A servant aided me four miles, whence a friend helped me with a carriage to Richmond.

Sunday, 15th. Having put to the press my "Farewell to America: a Word to the Public—as a hint to suit the times," I preached in Richmond and Manchester. Then brother Dunnington, in his chair, carried me to Campbell camp-meeting; papa Hobson being with us. At this meeting a woman found peace with God, who had thought camp-meetings scandalous for women to attend. Her husband, some months previous, had felt serious impressions from some talk I had given him, and he wanted her to go to the last camp-meeting, but she to get off said, "If you or any of our neighbors get converted at it, I will go to the next." He found peace, and held her to her promise. She, as a woman of veracity came, though much to the mortification of her pride, but now the happy pair went home rejoicing in God.

Here, also, a man a hundred and three years old found peace. Another man, some nights ago, dreamed that he came to this meeting, and asked a black woman to pray for him, and that God set his soul at liberty. The dream so impressed his mind, that he could not enjoy himself until he came to see what we were about, and searching round out of curiosity, he found the very countenance he had seen in his dream. A secret impulse ran through his mind—"Ask her to pray for you?" which at first he rejected, but for the ease of his mind, secretly made the request, so as not to be distinguished by the people, thinking thus to avoid the cross. Said she, "If you will kneel down, I will." Thought he, "I shall mock the woman if I do not;" and, when on his knees, thought he, "the people are now observing me, and if I do not persevere, I shall look like a hypocrite: the cross I must bear, let me do as I will; therefore, seeing I have gone so far, I will make a hand of it." And whilst on their knees, he yielded in his heart to be the Lord's, and God set his soul at liberty. Thus, God's words are verified, which say, "*Now* is the accepted time and *day* of salvation." The devil's time is a future one; but God is immutable, and of course always ready, he being love. As saith the apostle, "God is in Christ reconciling the world unto himself." Therefore, the exhortation is, "Be ye reconciled to God;" i. e. "Give up your will and heart to God, for him to reign within." Look at the thief on the cross, and the jailer and family. Paul's was the longest in the pangs of the new birth of any related in the New Testament, yet that was but three days; though some think it must take a man two or three years to be converted. Thus, denying the freedom of the will, waiting for what they term a special call. Yet it is evident, that the Spirit of God strives with *all*, and no man will condemn himself for not doing what he believes to be an impossibility; yet many condemn themselves for acting as they do, which implies that they believe they had power to have acted otherwise than as they did, and argues the power of choice and the freedom of the human will, which every one must assent to.

I returned to the Lowlands, bidding my friends farewell, and brother Dunnington, who had accommodated me two hundred and fifty miles.

Many dear faces in these lands I expect to see no more until in a better world. A man and wife who were my spiritual children, were passing in a coach as I concluded my meeting; they took me in and carried me a distance, when brother Mead carrying me in his chair, brought me to New Kent camp-meeting. The rain kept back many; however, there were about fifty hopefully converted to God in the course of the meeting; and it may be said, "the beloved clouds helped us," as my life had been previously threatened, and the collegians, backed by their president the bishop, said they would have been upon us had not the rain hindered them. A chump of wood being flung in through the window, I leaped out after the man; he ran, and I after him, crying, "Run, run, Old Sam is after you." He did run, as for his life, and leaping over a fence hid among the bushes. Next morning I cut Old Sam's name on the wood, nailed it to a tree, and called it "Old Sam's Monument."* I asked the people publicly, pointing to the monument, who was willing to enlist and serve so poor a master. I also observed, that the people who had threatened my life, only upon hearsay accounts, were cowardly and inhuman, as I was an entire stranger to them, and their conduct against me was under cover. I said, "Your conduct is condemnable, which expression means damnable, and of course, to make the best of you, you are nothing but a *pack of damned cowards*, for there durst not one of you show your heads." These young coxcombs were mightily grated, and to retaliate, said that I cursed and swore. Many I believe, at that time, had a sense of the poor wages the devil would give his servants.

---

* The monument stuck to the tree for many months; a young man was hired to pull it down, but when he arrived on the ground and was looking at it, such were the inward workings of his mind, that he forebore to do it. The collegians, backed by their president, were held back by the rain from disturbing us at this meeting, and a few months after one of those who had a hand in and led on the van of this disturbance, had the end of his nose bit off; and another was flung from his horse and broke his neck; and several others were remarked to be followed with chastisement from the Lord.

Oct. 3d. Camp-meeting began at Old Poplar Spring church, and continued four days; several found peace, among whom was a young woman that came ill with an ague and fever, whose mother had long been praying for her conversion: she was smitten down by the power of God, but went home well in soul and body. Many say these camp-meetings are injurious to health, but I do not find ground to believe that more evils accrue than otherwise, considering the number and time. Many go home better than they came; even delicate women, who rarely would step off a carpet for twelve months, grew more healthy from that time.

I held meetings in Pace's meeting-house, and Cole's chapel, and stayed with old father Le Roy Cole. He wrote a letter to Bob Sample, one of the most popular A-double-L-part preachers in the country, who like a little fice, or cur dog, would rail behind my back. He charged his conduct with being unmanly, and said, "If Lorenzo be wrong, you ought to come and correct him to his face, or hush." He attended, heard me preach, and then said he would answer my discourse at a future period, at the same time knowing that I was leaving the country. I replied, it is hard not to give a man a chance to defend himself, and was minded that he should come out early next morning, so as not to delay my journey, and let the people judge where the truth lay. He refused, until I insisted that backbiting was unfair; however, I could not get him out before eleven. I invited the people, and we met. He spoke two hours and forty minutes, wearying the patience of the people; though I was minded that we should speak fifteen minutes at a time, alternately, which he refused, but in his talk observed, "I dare not say that Christ did *not* die for any *living* man; I dare not say he died for any who are in *hell*." And many other expressions he dropped similar to the above. I attempted to follow him as well as I could, making remarks upon the dark expressions to blindfold the people, and said the man was not honest to proceed in such an intricate way. Said I, why did he say, that "he dare not say Christ had not died for any living man ?" Because he did not know but that that man was one of the *elect*. Again, why did he say, "that he dare not say that Christ had died for any who are in hell ?" Because he did not believe that Christ died for any who are lost. This shows he does not believe that Christ died for *all*, yet he was not honest enough to acknowledge it in plain words; and he has not brought one passage of scripture in support of his ideas, only that sometimes the term *all* is limited. But, said I, it never can be used with propriety in the *Calvinistic* sense, because it always means the greater part; yet they say a *few elect*, or a small number; and I gave about thirty passages to demonstrate it. He raked up the ashes of *John Wesley*, and quitted the ground before I had done.*

Hence I rode with F. and M. Cole to camp-meeting, where the Molechites and some split-off Methodists, had done much mischief by prejudicing the minds of the neighborhood; and to avoid a quarrel, were suffered to occupy a meeting-house which belonged to the Methodists. However, the Lord was with us, and thirteen souls were set at liberty in the course of the meeting; and though there were the greatest discouragements

---

* Leaving his bible behind. The wordlings compared us to officers fighting a duel—one flung down his sword, and ran off, crying, Sword, fight for yourself!

against this meeting, yet our enemies who came as spies, acknowledged they never saw so much decorum in so large an auditory.

Leaving Hanover I came to Louisa, with brother Mead, where I attended the last camp-meeting for America. Providence was with us here. Hundreds at these meetings gave me their hands as a token of their desire that I should remember them in my absence, and that they would strive to remember me when I should be beyond the Atlantic, that God would preserve, succeed, and bring me back in peace, if consistent with His will, and if we meet no more below, strive to meet above. It was a solemn feeling thus to bid friends farewell, on the eve of embarking from one's own native country for a land unknown, and there to be a stranger among strangers. At this last meeting, in the act of shaking hands, many left money with me, which sufficed to bear my expenses to the north.

Perceiving my bodily strength more and more to decline, and my heart still bound to the European world, I was convinced of the propriety of a speedy departure, and as my wife did not arrive in Virginia, where I intended to leave her, at P. Hobson's, (for the fever breaking out at New-York, expelled her to the country, so that she did not get my letters in time,) I took the stage, and went on to New-York, about four hundred miles, in about four days and nights, not getting any rest. The season being far advanced, I suffered by cold, but got an old cloak on the way at Fredericksburg, which I once was necessitated to leave there. Arriving in New-York, I found my Peggy and friends well, and a vessel bound for Liverpool. I gave Peggy her choice, whether to go to her friends who were still at Pittsburg, waiting for a fresh in the river; or to Virginia, to P. and M. Hobson's, who had made the request; or to my father's, who had written to that purport; or to tarry with friends in and about New-York who solicited; or to go with me to Europe, the dangers of which I had set before her. She choosing the last, if agreeable to me, I engaged our passage on board the ship Centurion, Benjamin Lord master, belonging to a steady, fair Quaker.

When I was in Europe before, I suffered much from the political state of affairs, for the want of a protection, and proper credentials; but now after I had got ready to sail, only waiting for a fair wind, the Lord provided me with them. The Penny-post brought me two letters one day, and one the next, containing a certified recommendation from the Governor of Virginia, with the seal of that state; another containing an American protection under the seal of the United States, from Mr. Madison, the third man in the nation. This was obtained only on the intimation of a Methodist Preacher. A third was from the Town Clerk, Magistrates, County Clerk, Judges and Governor, of Connecticut, giving an account of my parentage, &c. &c., as may be seen in the document.

Considering my four credentials, which had so providentially fallen into my hands, I thought it advisable to have my protection perfected so as to carry authority out of the nation, and conviction or evidence on an investigation, and went to a Notary Public's office, with two substantial witnesses accordingly, viz. Nicholas Snethen and James Quackenbush. Here my descriptions were taken, proven, and certified, as may be seen in the beginning.

CHAPTER IX.

SUNDAY,* Nov. 10th, 1805, having got equipped for sailing, and my affairs settled as well as I could, considering my many disappointments, the wind became fair, we saw them hoisting sail, and from circumstances I believe the captain designed to have left us behind—so I hired a boat for ten shillings to put us on board. The sea was rough and I believe somewhat dangerous; but we reached the vessel in time, and she soon was under way. I wrote a letter for our friends, to notify them of our departure, which the pilot took ashore. Whilst writing we passed the lighthouse, the sea began to toss the vessel, whilst an ocean without bounds seemed to present itself to view, and the land to disappear. Poor Peggy went on deck to look about, and beholding above, returned with death seemingly pictured in her countenance. We lost sight of land before night; she began to grow sick, becoming worse and worse for some days, and then recovered it better than for some years.

18th. The wind blows a fresh gale. The head of the rudder was observed to be unsound; so the helm would not command the ship, which exposed us to great danger. The captain afterwards said that he suffered more in his mind on this voyage, than in all the times he had been at sea before; however, they got cordage and wedges and bound it together as well as they could, and carrying less sail to prevent straining, we weathered the voyage, Providence favoring us with an aft wind.

20th. We are now on the banks of Newfoundland, about one third of our passage. There are thousands of sea-gulls around our vessel, four land birds came aboard, one of which the mate caught and let it go. In one of the late gales it appears Peggy passed through some trials of her faith, as I heard her saying, "How much easier to rely on human probabilities, than on divine promises!" When our Lord called or set apart the twelve, he did not at first send them to preach and do miracles, but kept them with him a while, and then gave them commission to go forth with power, &c., and predicting what should happen to them in their latter days, to prepare their minds for it; and afterwards it appears, he told them what should happen to himself, which it seems they did not realize, as they had an idea of a temporal kingdom; but he informed them that what they knew not then, they should know afterwards more perfectly. Though God the Father had already revealed to Peter, that Jesus was the Christ.

After our Lord's resurrection, he renewed a promise of the Holy Ghost or Spirit, being given unto them more fully, yet commanded them to stay in Jerusalem until that time should come, and then they were to go and preach everywhere they could among all nations. and, for their encouragement, promised further to be with them unto the end of the world, &c. Now, he cannot be with ministers, unless he hath ministers to be with; and this promise could not refer to the apostles alone, as he previously predicted their dissolution: therefore, it must include succeeding minis-

---

* Mr. N. S. this day spoke against me in three different places of worship, which meetinghouses I had never been suffered to occupy. Compare this date with his oath in the Preface and his letter in the Appendix, with their dates, &c.

ters, which God in Christ would raise up to tread in the apostles' steps; and they cannot be his ministers, unless he has sent them, any more than I can be the king's ambassador, when no embassy has been committed to my charge.

Singing I once delighted in the sound of, but after my conversion abhorred it, abstracted from the spirituality, and when in Ireland almost was *Quakerized* in that sentiment; but after I saw the effects of singing in the power of faith at camp-meetings, &c., in the awakening and conversion of sinners, I was convinced of the medium, and that singing properly was a divine employment, and will be done to the approbation and declarative glory of God and our own profit.

December 3d. We have seen but three vessels on the way, one of which was the New York, of Philadelphia, which had brought General Moreau from Cadiz to America, whom I saw at Trenton ferry. The winds have been very unsteady for several days, like some people, almost in a gale and then a calm.

We are now in latitude 49 29, and longitude about 20. I hope in a few days, of course, we shall breathe the air of the European world. Surely, the nigher I draw across the mighty waters, the more I feel the work of my mission on my mind at heart, and am more and more satisfied that I acted in the will of God in coming, let what may ensue. I want to see Doctor Johnson, whom I have not heard from this year and a half. A few days now will put me in quite a different sphere of life. I shall quit the ship, and then have crosses, &c., to surmount, which I am conscious will require all the faith, zeal, wisdom, and patience, which I am possessed of, and after all must fail unless God be with me. But my reliance is on Him, the great, the strong, for strength, and as I penned before, so do I again—"I feel an uncommon exercise about what is before me." What Doctor Coke will say, I know not; perhaps there is a great providence in my sailing to Liverpool first, as I expect some have heard of me there.

This is one of the happiest voyages thus far I ever had, and my companion is a great consolation to me as a lent favor; but oh, how apt we are to under or over value the creature, and thereby lose its blessing designed by God for us! I am convinced of our privileges of walking as it were in eternity whilst in this unfriendly world—that is, the soul walking in the light of God's countenance, whilst veiled in flesh and blood.

. Whether I shall die a natural death is to me at times a query, and sometimes causes sensations of heart; but while the soul hangs on God alone it cannot suffer, properly speaking, though in this probationary state. Still, there may be outward trials, yet inward peace, which is sweet and satisfactory to the mind. Oh, what may we not attain unto if we be faithful? Religion will beget sympathy, or a feeling for the welfare of others; sin makes people dark and contracted, selfish and barbarous, but religion the reverse; and those acts of humanity, sympathy, and pity, which even the Indians and heathen show forth, who can with propriety deny but they are under the influence of *God's Holy Spirit?* Oh, that people would hearken more to the guidance within, and not put so much stress on what is handed down by tradition without evidence: then we should have more affectionate ones than we now behold among the nations of the earth. Hundreds of my American friends, I doubt not are daily praying for me.

Whilst in devotion, Peggy being called to a fresh trial of her faith in the gale, the words of our Lord to his disciples, "others have labored, and ye have entered into their labors," went with power through my mind, as on former occasions; and why have I to labor in other men's labors, unless it be to provoke them to jealousy.

There are three Methodist connections, besides the new connection, so called, raised by Alexander Kilham, viz., the English, Irish, and the American Episcopal one. The two latter I have travelled through, from centre to circumference, without their consent, and though they have done * * * * * * * * * * * to hedge up my way, yet I have travelled * * * * * * * * of them as a *body*, however much I am indebted to *individuals*, as a means under God to open my way, and give me access to the people.

Thursday, December 5th. Saw two vessels on our voyage. Late at night saw land, and afterwards passed Waterford lighthouse.

6th. Saw Wales. Had a fair wind with some gales, but all is well now. We have eaten up but the smallest part of our provisions. We shall soon be at the pilot ground, and what will then ensue is now in the womb of futurity, but I expect to see the providence of God in trials; but how, when, by whom, or what means, I know not, yet still I feel power to leave all to the Author of breath, and Disposer of all events.

When on my former visit, I was advised to go immediately on board the vessel again and work my passage back, as I should have no opening there; but, as I could not do ship-work, did not, neither could I in conscience comply. Then they warned the Methodists against me, to starve me out, and only one family received me at first; but after God opened my way, they offered to pay my passage home, if I would quit the country, and promise never to return, which in conscience I could not do. Then Dr. C. wanted me to go on a mission to some other part; I could not comply, neither in reason nor in conscience. Then the conference passed a vote to hedge up my way, whether or no, &c., &c. I may expect similar from the English conference, on whose shores I expect shortly to land, if they think me dependent; but my trust is in God.

About the time I landed in Ireland before, this passage ran repeatedly through my mind, Joshua, iii. 7, and it hath been so imprinted on my mind, that now I make a memorandum of it. Again: Isaiah, "Ye shall go out with joy," (from the * * * * * * * * * *,) "and be led forth with peace;" (of mind by the Spirit of God;) "the mountains and hills" (of difficulties and discouragements) "shall break forth before you into singing," (of salvation,) "and all the trees of the field shall clap their hands," (for joy,) &c.—Beginning of the millenium—camp-meetings.

7th. We took in a pilot, and came to anchor in a dangerous place, if the wind had blown a gale, as the tide would not admit of our going over the bar, and the weakness of the rudder would not admit of beating into the quarantine ground. We heard of the defeat of the French and Spaniards off Cape Trafalgar, by Nelson, and also of the defeat of the Austrians. Wrote to Dr. Johnson, in Dublin, to let him know of my arrival.

Sunday, 8th. Slipped our cables, and came up the river by the town;

saw about forty windmills as I sailed, and a few ships of war, and not wharves, as in America, but lock-docks, &c. The country around appears like a garden, considering the season of the year. I sent a letter on shore to-day for Edward Wilson, attorney at law, with one enclosed from his brother, John Wilson, book-steward to the connection in America. I wrote a letter to the preachers in the city, as preparatory.

11th. Wrote some letters to my friends in America. The ship-carpenters came and examined our rudder, and made reports accordingly to the officers of government relative to our state. We were exempted from quarantine, after a detention of ten days, which time passed heavily away, two miles above the town in the river, as we had a bill of health from the British consul.

December 17th, Tuesday. At five o'clock this morning the *Prodic* came on board, which made me rise and prepare to go on shore, and see what God would do for me there. I must undertake it by faith, as I know no one in town, and have heard of no friend. The captain will go on shore by sight, but I cannot see an inch before me. I had rather die, than not see Zion prosper, before I quit this kingdom. O, Lord, prepare my way, and give me wisdom in this matter, is what this morning I ask of thee.

About ten o'clock we attempted to go on shore. I heard the tolling of the bell, which gave me a solemn feeling, under a sense of mortality; when I reflected that, when at Quebec, I saw a boat come from a ship of war with something in it which at first appeared like a white chest, but as it approached nigher, I found it to be a coffin. When I first landed at Savannah, in Georgia, I retired to a solitary place for meditation, and found a yard, enclosed by a brick wall; the gate being down I entered, and beheld the humble piles of earth, under which lay the silent human dust. When in Dublin, I saw the genteel mode of burying; the hearse drawn by six horses, and coaches following: but in the west of Ireland, I espied across a dale, a company coming down, and as we drew near to each other, I saw, lying on a board, a corpse, dressed like a beggar, which they carried over an old church wall, to inter it. Thus I saw the different modes and forms, according to their rank, in every land where I have travelled. So mortality prevails and sweeps down all! This brought to my remembrance that, when in New Salem, Massachusetts, whilst riding by myself in a shrubbery pine-plain, I suddenly came to an opening, where were some graves; and one, near the path, had these words on the headstone:

"Behold, ye strangers, passing by,
As you are now, so once was I;
As I am now, so must you be,
Prepare for death, and follow me."

I saw in Ireland, also, the ancient castles, which were said to have been destroyed in the days of Cromwell: yet none could tell me when they were built. I thus reflected: "Children did exist, like myself, when playing at my father's house, who built these ancient ruins! They are gone, many generations since; and at length, Lorenzo Dow came upon the stage of action, who, after a few more revolving years, shall be seen to act here no more!" Thus my reflections flew from thing to thing, as we were landing, with the solemn tolling still ringing in my ears; but I felt consolation at the prospect, by and by, of a better world, to me unknown.

We landed from the leaky boat about a mile above the town; and glad was I to get once more on land, as the boat was constantly bailed by two of us all the way. What now? I am on shore in an old country; old in inhabitants, and old in sin; but new to me, for I never was on the English shore before.

I left my Peggy at the captain's boarding-house, whilst I went to transact some business of money matters, and deliver letters of introduction, &c. But all was gloomy. I returned to Peggy, and wandered about the town till all our letters were delivered but one, and where that should be left we could not find, until I observed the name on the wall as we stopped, pondering what to do. The man, whose name answered to the letter, observing we did not turn to go off, said, "Come in." One said, whilst he was silently reading the letter, "Dost thou know one Lorenzo Dow?" I was surprised, and, answering in the affirmative, equally surprised them.

The man said, "Tarry a night or two;" but the wife objected inconvenience; so we put up at a boarding-house, at twenty-eight shillings, British, per week, for one. We received letters from Dublin. Strove to get places for meeting. Spoke once in an A-double-L-part place; the minister was friendly to my face, but afterwards said I was crazy. We strove five times to sail for Dublin, but were forced back by contrary winds, and twice were like to be lost. The woman who asked if I knew one Lorenzo Dow, was a Quaker, and having formed some acquaintance with Henry Forshow's family, No. 40 Edmond-street, took me there one day: these were Methodists. The last time we were driven back, our hostess, having taken in so many boarders, there was no more place for us; when, before we knew it, called in to Mr. Forshow's, whose wife invited us to tarry all night; which was esteemed by us as a providence. We stayed here a few days. One evening a woman came suddenly in, and said some people were in a neighboring house, who wished to see the American. I went; and finding about twenty together, without any ceremony, singing or prayer, I stood up and gave them a preach, to their great surprise; and God fastened conviction on one woman's heart, who, the next day, with her husband, wished me to preach at their house, which I did for a few evenings, where were some Methodists of the old society, and Killamites; when, shortly after, a conversation ensued at the leader's meeting, to this effect: "What encouragement shall we give Lorenzo the American?" At the old party it was lost; at the new I was invited by vote, &c.

Part of my experience being in a magazine, which I had published to give away when in Ireland before, contributed to clear my way, &c. I spoke in Zion not many times: some were awakened, and joined society: the preacher was prejudiced. One meeting Peter Philips, of Warrington, attended, having come to town on business, and felt his mind strongly drawn to come to Zion. After meeting, as I went into the vestry to get my hat, two women came to be prayed for, being under distress of mind; the vestry was filled with people, and four were soon lying on the floor under the power of God; which some thought was faintness, and used fans, and called for water; whilst others thought they were dying, and were frightened, thinking we should be called to an account. But I told them to hush—it was the power of God; and they soon came through happy; which caused Peter to give me an invitation to his neighborhood. I asked him what they were; and told him to go home and tell his people, and if they were unanimous, I would come and preach; being then on my way to London. He did so, and they were unanimous. These, in derision, were called Quaker-Methodists; because they were so simple, using the plain language, and held class-meetings, &c.

Through the medium of Mr. Thomas W——, a local preacher, I called on the preachers of the Old Connection on my landing; he, with his brother, having got a letter from their brother in America, the Rev. John Wilson, one of the book stewards. The testimonials, letters, &c., were left for their inspection. Mr. Brown was as a cousin on my calling, according to direction. Mr. Barber seemed satisfied with my testimonial credentials; but as Thomas Taylor, one of the oldest preachers, came in, *he* wanted me to begone, not waiting to hear what Mr. Barber had to say, but interrupting him, saying, "I fear he is not settled in his *head*," &c. As I was going out, Mr. Barber put W.'s into my hand, saying, "It may be of service to you;" but I having not *then* the consent of the W.'s, laid it on the table, and went off. Through another local preacher, I called on Mr. Atmore, who wrote the Methodist Memorial. He came to the door, and said if I had not special business with him, he could not see me, and advised me to go to Mr. B——. I replied, "I have been there, and want to form some acquaintance with you;" but he shut the door upon me, without inviting me to come in. I thought perhaps there was a cause, and so called again. I met with similar treatment. I called the third time, when the children came, and said, "Call to-morrow morning." I did, and found the gate locked; so I pounded, but none could I rally, &c.

The power of God was present, as I preached twice in Warrington. Thence I went to Manchester; here I wandered about for eleven hours to get a place to lodge, but could find none, for love or money, among Christian or sinner, except one, which I thought to be a house of bad fame, and not prudent to stay in. I called on Jabez Buntin, but he would not be seen, and the public houses were full; but as I was getting passage for London, in the coach, I found a garret where I could stay, being near ten at night. I heard Jabez, and also in the morning; then I went to Brodaz Bandroom. Here, in sermon, one looking earnestly at me, said, "You are a stranger—dine with me." I did: stayed two days. A chapel of the New Connection offered. Preacher and trustees said they would be passive, if I could obtain an assembly; so I got one thousand handbills and gave them through the town. Got five hundred to speak to, and a thousand next evening, same way; as the preachers would not suffer me to publish from the pulpit my appointments, &c.

On my arrival in London, I delivered, with much difficulty, all my letters but two or three, and those persons could not be found. One place, in Monmouth-street, the woman, to whom a sum of money was sent, would hardly give me access to deliver her some money, sent from her friends in America, they are so afraid of strangers. She took the letter. I told her she must read it, and I must come in. The daughter said, "Come in;" but placed herself between me and the door, that she might alarm the neighbors if I was a robber. I stayed a few days: held no meetings. Got the king's license to stay in the kingdom, under his seal manual. Surely London is more like the city of Babylon than any other city, to fill the world with her merchandise, and answers better to that mentioned in Revelation than any other. The British appear to me to lie under an infatuation as it relates to their "wooden walls;" for the means of coming with a flotilla is doubtless more than many know, and might set their "walls" on fire: "Cursed be he that trusteth in the arm of flesh, but blessed is he whose God is the Lord." *V* is used for *w*, and *w* for *v*—*conwerted*, *conwicted*, and I *wow* I *vill*, *&c. &c.* There were many curious monuments to behold. The state of the country was such, I did not think it proper to hold forth here in meetings, it being the metropolis; and as the laws of these lands require every preacher to have a license for that purpose, obtained from the sessions, with an oath of allegiance, and two others, or be subject to twenty pounds fine; also every place must be licensed, or pay twenty pounds, and the hearers five shillings each, &c.; which things militated against me, as I was an alien, considering the times, and was a trial of my faith. I believe I ought to conform to the laws of the country which I am in, if they don't militate against the law of God and my own conscience; but if I cannot in conscience submit to it, I could not take the oath, and of course could not have the license.

I returned to Manchester—spoke in Zion's Temple, so called, belonging to the Kilhamites; but as I once spoke on A-double-L-partism, they would allow me to speak there no more. In Warrington, among the Quaker-Methodists, we had a great revival under an out-pouring of the Spirit of God, and many were gathered in, which brought many out from other vicinities, to hear and see; so that I got invitations into various places, and God was with us at Risley, Appleton, Thorn, Lymn, Preston-Brook, and Frodsham. Here, when I was first invited, before I went, Simon Day recalled my appointment, and then sent word by Musquit, that I would not be received, and must not come. I thought the errand strange, (Musquit being ashamed, did not deliver the message to me, he only came to the door, called Peter, and told him, and so went off.) I went—the meeting-house was opened contrary to my advice, as I desired to do no harm, but when the people were assembled, I dared not do otherwise than to speak to them; so I stood on a bench, not feeling freedom to go into the pulpit, as that was the object of contention; spoke twice, then the trustees were afraid. I made neither of the appointments—it was themselves; so I spoke in a salt-pan, and about twenty were struck under conviction.— The meeting-house was then opened again, but as the preacher S. D—— was so rash, he liked to have broke up the society, and kept many out until he was gone the circuit, which otherwise would have joined immediately. I visited Bolton, Hayton, Norley, Preston, and the File Country, and God was with me, opening my door step by step, and raising me up friends against times of need; neither did he suffer me or my Peggy to want in this strange land, though we asked for no assistance.

Travelling so extensively, exposed me to a fine and imprisonment, and the families that entertained me, to fifty pounds each, as my license was limited; but I dare do no otherwise than go, feeling how I could account to God; so I went in his name and he opened my way, gave me favor in the sight of the people, and access to thousands; yet I had souls for hire, almost in every neighborhood where God cast my lot, though many hard sayings were spoke, and many letters as a *bull*, sent to block up my way;

but hitherto the Lord hath been my helper, preserver, and protector, and on him I will rely for strength.

When in London, Adam Clarke treated me as a gentleman; he frequently had heard of me from America; but did not show or discover it, by his conduct, but said Dr. Coke was to preach in such a place that evening; so off I ran, as hard as I could pull, to see the little man, as he was the only one I knew in England. They were singing as I came into the meeting-house. After sermon I got one to introduce me to him; but though he first appeared friendly, as when in Georgia, yet on finding out my name, asked what I came there for; and before I could tell him, he turned to another. He shook hands, and bid all in the room farewell, except me, and went suddenly off. So I had seven miles, as it were at the hazard of my life, to walk to the opposite side of London, to my lodgings, late at night. Next time I saw him was in Lancashire; he supposed Peter to be one of the old society's official members, and Peggy to be his wife, and treated them very friendly. I asked him if he thought he should be over to the next general conference. He replied, "If the connection positively sees it necessary, and insists upon it, and cannot do without me." I saw him at the Dublin and Leeds conferences, but did not speak together, as I could not intrude myself with propriety any more; many wondered why it was that the doctor did not publish me, and make a public example of me, whilst others inquired, what for?

Mr. B—— called my hostess to account for Peggy's going into band-meeting, though she had her certificate from Elijah Woolsey, as an acceptable member on the Western circuit.

Saturday, May 3, 1806. I spoke in Preston Brook, and a prospect of good, as numbers appeared under deep divine impression. I bade them farewell for the present, and went to Warrington, where I spoke the next morning, and had a comfortable season, in the little chapel belonging to those called Quaker-Methodists, and found that about forty new members had joined them in my absence, and the prospect of good increases. Thence to Risley, where I found several had been set at liberty since I was there last. From this I went to Leigh, where I spoke to about two thousand people, at a Methodist chapel, of the old connection; and we had a powerful season. This is the first chapel of the Old Methodists, into which I was voluntarily invited by what they call a round preacher.

Monday, 5th. I spoke at Loton Common, and found a number more had been brought into liberty; we had a great display of the Divine presence. Hence I walked fifteen miles to Hayton Bridge, spoke at seven o'clock, and twice a day afterwards, for several days, and the prospect greatly increased, and several backsliders were reclaimed, and some were brought into liberty. I visited Black Rod and Carley, but I fear with little success.

Saturday, 10th. I spoke in a country village on my way to Preston, not in vain.

Sunday, 11th. I spoke four times in Preston, and attended a love-feast, of what is called by some the Free-gospellers, or third division of Methodists; and six souls gave comfortable satisfaction of being brought into liberty this day. Hence I visited the File Country, for several days; but was disagreeably disappointed of hearers, by my appointments not being regularly given out; however, I spoke to a few, here and there. In this journey I saw a woman, who preached, and I was informed that she was born three months before the time, and remained without nourishment, wrapped in flannels, in a torpid state like sleep, yet frequently moving: the natural heat was supported near a fire, and in about thirteen weeks, appearances or actions took place, such as in a child new born at the full time.

15th. The tide being out, I crossed Preston river, in a cart, at a ford three miles wide, called the Guide, and walking a few miles, in the rain, took the canal boat, and arrived in Liverpool about five in the evening, and completed the bargain for printing my journal.

I held a few more meetings in Liverpool; and had the satisfaction to find more people rejoicing in God.

Here I find that my hostess had been called to an account, for inviting Peggy to a band-meeting; although she had a certificate of her membership from America: and a number of their own members also were called to an account, for having attended some of my former meetings.

Sunday, 18th. We embarked in the Lark with Hannah Gough, the Quaker woman; who said to me, the first day I came on shore in the country, in the house where I presented a letter, &c.,"Dost thou know one Lorenzo Dow in America?" (She had seen me formerly in Dublin, but did not now recognise my person, only my voice reminded her of the name.)

Tuesday, 20th. With a light breeze from Liverpool we reached Dublin harbor, and the tide not serving to come to the wharf, I took a boat for Dunlary, where I landed about six o'clock, and hiring a jingle, came to Dublin, and whilst walking to New-street, William Thomas, the man at whose house I first lodged when in this country before, suddenly met me at the end of a street: we recognised each other's countenances, and were in each other's arms before a word was spoken on either side, and our hearts were mutually refreshed as in former days. He went with me to No. 102, where I was in hopes to have embraced my dear doctor and mamma Letitia, but the servants informed me of their having just gone out. I waited with uncommon anxiety for their return, whilst the servants went through the city in search of them.

I took tea with a very feeling sense of obligation for past favors: but still the doctor and his companion not returning, I went to Thomas-street, with William Thomas, to see his wife, and received some letters, which I was informed were from America. This pair was the first couple in whom I ever saw, as I thought, a happiness in matrimonial union. I embraced her in my arms, with a feeling remembrance of my first reception, when a stranger in this city, and but two shillings in my pocket, when all other hearts, seemingly, were shut against me; here I had an asylum, though reproved for harboring me and giving me bread. I returned and found the doctor had come home, and was anxiously waiting my return, which was near eleven at night; we embraced each other in our arms, and mamma Letty gave me a kiss and a hearty welcome. Thus I was cordially received after an absence of five years, one month, and eighteen days.

Thursday, May 22, 1806. The German church was opened to me by invitation to the doctor, before I came, but the wardens considered themselves slighted, not having been consulted; and one of them said at the leader's meeting, "If you are not willing he should have the liberty, it shall be prevented." They replied, "they had nothing to do or act concerning it." However, as I was not willing to be called a thief or a robber, I chose to come in by the door, and went to the above warden accordingly. This church belongs to the German congregation, but is occupied by the Methodists and Cooper, who belonged to lady Huntingdon's party, but now is near a Sandimanian. I held a number of meetings that were respectable and very profitable to many. Alice Cambridge, the woman who was so attentive to me when in this country before, still continues her meetings, and gave up her meetings and room to me, and another company who occupied it alternately did the same; so that my way was opened, and the quickening power of God seemed to be present at most of the meetings which I held in the above place, and at Esquire Shegog's, the barracks, and the streets, which amounted to about twenty in number.

I was invited to hold a meeting in Ranelagh, by a rich old woman, who had built a preaching-house, which she had given to the Methodists, and a door from her bedchamber opened into the gallery. Her own house not accommodating the number, she with much fuss and ado got the preaching-house open, which I refused to occupy, lest I should be esteemed a thief, but addressed them from her chamber door, and we had a good time. The doctor I found had been lately unwell in my absence, but was now recovered.

Saturday, June 7th, 1806. Having received invitations to the country, through the medium of the missionaries, G. Ousley, W. Hamilton, and others, I set off for Wicklow county in a gig, through the kindness of a backslider, whose heart God had touched. I held a meeting at New town, Mount Kennedy, by the way to Wicklow, where I found religion low. We had quickening times, though with difficulty I got the people convened at the latter place.

Sunday, 8th. I spoke thrice in the town, and once at widow Tighe's, who was prejudiced against me when here before.

9th. I gave my last, and a backslider took me in a jaunting car to Rathdrum, whence a man helped me with a horse to Cappagh, where I spoke that night and next morning, and then departed with him to Hacketstown. Here I spoke seven times in three days, having previously been invited by a man who had married one of my spiritual daughters. She, with her sister, who had married a Methodist preacher, still endured. These were the daughters of the old man who felt these words to run through his mind, whilst they talked with me back and forth through the door, when I was in Ireland before, "Be not forgetful to entertain strangers." Two others of his children God gave me for my hire now. The quickening power of God seemed to be displayed in the different meetings, and convictions and conversions were shortly multiplied; and not long after my departure, I was informed that about four-score were added to society, the most of them happy in God.

I spoke in Baltinglass, on my way to Carlow. In both places I had good times, and a preacher was friendly whom I formerly thought cool. He invited me to meet a class and attend his quarterly meeting. With the latter I could not comply. I rode on the car of my daughter, which brought me here to the colliery, where I found the missionaries praying with some mourners. Here was a big meeting appointed, which they called a camp-meeting, but I a field-meeting; there being no tents, only the open air, in imitation of America.

So I see the spirit of the revival is spreading in the breasts of the children of men. Here I saw Mr. Averill, who appeared as friendly as ever, and solicited my attendance at another meeting of magnitude, at Mount Mellick, and some other places. At this meeting I preached, and when I had done, I invited up the mourners to be prayed for; several found peace, and we had a refreshing season from the presence of God.

A Romanist interrupted the meeting, which caused many of them to run away, supposing him to be a priest. I never knew that in this our day priestcraft was so influential, and carried such a dread to the fear of man. Next morning I spoke again; the missionaries took about fifty into society. Hence we went to Castle Comber. They spoke in the street, and I beside the chapel door; having the church minister present, whose relations gave him a look whilst I was repeating what I heard an old man say in my infancy, that a minister's call was two hundred pounds settlement, and one hundred pounds a year.

Next morning I spoke again, and breakfasted with the clergyman's friends, who seemed piously inclined. Here the missionaries took about forty into society, and then we went to Kilkenny. The above priest said the missionaries were mountebanks, kidnapping the people. In this place we stayed three days. The missionaries attacked popery in the streets twice or thrice a day, and I attacked sin with A-double-L-partism in the preaching-house, which caused considerable uneasiness in the town. The mayor had a potatoe flung at his head, and also received a letter without signature, threatening that if he did not put us three out of town, his house should be pulled down on his head.

They took about thirty into society here. I bade some old friends farewell. So we departed to Moneybey, where I spoke under an ash; had a good time, though under some depression of mind. I attended two other meetings in a large warehouse. Here thirty were taken into society, and some shortly before, making eighty-two in all. William Hamilton took me in a gig to Carlow, where I spoke at ten in the morning, intending to comply with Mr. Averill's invitation, but was prevented by sudden inward illness, which flung me into spasms like convulsions. So by the advice of my friends I stayed until next day, and then W. H—n attended me in the canal boat about seventy English miles to Dublin, where I arrived about ten at night, on Sunday the 22d, and found my Peggy and friends well at the doctor's. He said he thought my complaint proceeded from a small abscess of the liver, bursting into the cavity of the belly outside of the bowels.

A love-feast being held at Gravelwalk, I was informed that a number spoke there of being quickened by my last visit. I breakfasted several times in company with William Smith, the assistant preacher. He invited me to pray in the families, and is thought by some to be one of the most popular preachers in Ireland. I find he is a great kingsman, but I am convinced that many in these countries, who have been shining lights, are in a more lukewarm state than they are aware of. I continued my meetings as before; the Lord was with us, and the revival seemed to increase, which some of the preachers, who still retained a degree of life, as they came to conference observed, and took hold with me heart and hand.

One evening, I was informed, upwards of twenty preachers were present, among whom were several of the old preachers that had treated me with coolness and neglect when here before, besides others who had been friendly. Among these was Mr. Averill, who requested me to tour the kingdom at large.

During this visit at conference time, I received not one unkind word from any of the preachers, but the reverse. Several gave me encouragement to visit them in their circuits, and also persuaded me to go into the pulpit at Ranelagh, where I had preached from the chamber-door, through the gallery into the preaching-house. Even Tobias said he believed that I was an honest man, when he read Snethen's letter, asserting in the most positive terms that I was an impostor: though he had a spat with the doctor about keeping his hat on in the meeting at prayer-time. The doctor replied, "Because I believe thou art not sent of the Lord to pray nor preach, for thou art the man that used Lorenzo ill and never repented of it. nor of the poor woman whose heart thou broke, and was the cause of her death, and her blood is upon thee." He turned off shocked and confused. This man, in the course of my absence to America, was stationed on the Larne circuit, where some of my spiritual children spoke in a love-feast, concerning the blessing of my labors to their souls, which caused him to reprove them, saying, "Let Mr. Dow alone; if you have any thing to say for God, speak it." He also has been put back on trial for some improper conduct. Thus, those who are hard upon others, find hardships to overtake themselves. In the same house where he first checked me, taking the hymn out of my mouth, &c., the doctor gave him his due in the presence of several of the preachers and people, which I could not find that any of the conference were displeased with the doctor for. Tobias's impertinency, because the doctor believed and practised some of the Quaker forms, gave rise to this.

Snethen's letter from New York to block up my way, was investigated at the leader's meeting, and unanimously acknowledged to have been written in a bad spirit, and did me no injury, but refuted itself, and so opened my way.*

About these days, Wm. Thomas, Dr. Johnson told me, had a liver complaint, which I remembered when he was taken unwell. The disorder increased to a degree of insanity, which caused him to leap out of a window, on the third floor, and yet so as only to break his thigh. After this he came to his right mind, and called off his thoughts from the world to divine subjects, and the last words he said before he expired were, *glory! glory!* He was attended by an ungodly physician and surgeon, who prohibited him seeing religious visitors, and pronounced him in a fair way for recovery after his fall; but Dr. Johnson, who did not attend him, said he would die, his liver being rotten, &c.

I put the first part of the second volume of my journal to the press, which contained one hundred and twenty pages duodecimo. Having now completed my visits and business, I contemplated a departure; saw Doctor Coke, who did not speak to me; but I had several more refreshing seasons, and embarked for England in the Lark, Capt. Williams, having my Dr.

---

* A meeting of about seventy official members, the result of which was—"Written in a bad spirit by a wicked man."

Johnson in company. The wind seemed contrary, and a prospect of a long and a tedious passage at first; however the wind came round and we were favored with only about thirty hours on the water. A doctor of a Guineaman, a passenger, treated me at first ungentlemanlike on the way. Dr. Johnson fell in conversation with several of the cabin passengers, who were Romanists, which seemed to cast some light upon their minds, and on his informing them about me, they expressed a desire that I should preach in the cabin, which accordingly I did. The Guinea doctor was the first to propose and urge my preaching, he having previously made very humble acknowledgments for his rudeness, saying to my doctor, that it had cost him a tear.

Saturday, July 12th. We landed early in the morning at Liverpool, called on Mr. Forshow, my printer, and kind host, and after giving some directions about my books, we took our departure in the coach for Warrington, and arrived safe in the afternoon; where I found my friends well, and many glad to see us, and some of my spiritual children shed tears at our meeting.

Sunday, 13th. I spoke four times: we had tender seasons.

14th. Gave my last, and many seemed to take fresh courage for the Christian race to glory, and one soul found peace.

15th. We walked to Knuttsford. I spoke in the old Methodist chapel, but there seems to be a hardiness over these meeting-houses in England, so I don't have such good times in them as in Ireland and America, or even the third division here. We came to Macclesfield, where I spoke at night, John Mee and Peter Philips being with us, having walked twenty-four miles that day.

A man being urged by his friends to read deistical writings, when dying, *cursed* those who were the instigators, and T. P.'s "Age of Reason," being in black despair. Oh! how careful people should be, what they ask others to do; for one act may cause repentance with tears in vain, without a possibility of retraction.

19th. I feel much unwell, unusual sensations which I conceive originate from the abscess, but trust by God's favor to recover.

We have visited Joseph Bradford, one of the oldest preachers of the old connection; he being a former friend and acquaintance of the doctor's. he manifested after the doctor's suggestion, that had I called on him when I first came to town, I should have had the liberty of his pulpit; the young preacher was also willing, but the trustees objected.

I have held meetings twice every day since my arrival here, and there seems a quickening among the people. This party, it seems, were once of the old Society, but driven off on account of not obeying orders which they conceived to be hard; they call themselves the Christian Revivalists. some call them the Free-gospellers; they are of the third division, (the Kilhamites being second,) somewhat similar to the Quaker-Methodists, and of the spirit of the Methodists in America.

Sunday, July 20th. My labors were equal to seven sermons. which gave me a fine sweat, that was very refreshing, and seemed to add to my health, as I felt better at night by far than in the morning, and more able to preach another sermon than I was at first. In speaking twice in the street, I addressed about five thousand. I attended a love-feast, and wrestled with mourners at night, having stood, &c., about ten hours or upwards, in the different exercises through the day. I observed, that for people to make a noise, and loud amens, &c., was irksome to me, and I would like as well to hear a dog bark, unless it came from a proper feeling in the heart, which if it did, would carry its own conviction with it; but otherwise it would appear flat, and bring a deadness over the mind. And to make a fuss and pretend feeling without possessing it, is a piece of hypocrisy, like a man possessing a vessel of water partly full, yet would say it was running over, and to prove it, would tilt the cup that it might run out. Yet if people feel the power of God, (of which I have no doubt at times they do,) to constrain them to cry for mercy or shout for joy, I can bear it as well as any one. I dare not oppose it, knowing that God communicates these superlative blessings, that others also may be benefited by it: as I have seen a general move from the conviction through one, more than from a whole sermon, which if the person had suppressed, he would have quenched the spirit of God.

I spoke sixteen times while here, which was short of six days. I think about twenty professed to find peace in that time; some backsliders were reclaimed, sinners awakened, and a considerable move in the town. Afterwards I was informed by a letter, that the revival went on increasing, so that three, five, eight, and even so many as fourteen appeared to be converted at a meeting, besides sundry who found peace the afternoon, evening and morning after my departure.

21st. I found a similar people in Stockport, who had been driven out from the Kilhamites. I held meeting with them at night and next morning, which were comfortable times.

The late society who separated at the band-room in Manchester, have been the abuse of itinerancy so much that they are prejudiced against having any at all, but think the gospel can be spread sufficiently by local preachers alone. This is a misconception.

22d. I arrived in the evening at Oldham, where also I found some of what may be called the Third division; had good times at night and in the morning.

23d. The doctor was with me all this time, and helped me some at Macclesfield; but being disappointed of a place in the coach, we set off on foot for Leeds in Yorkshire, where we arrived next day in the afternoon.

On the way we were frequently beset with rain; and the doctor having left his cloak and great-coat behind, was exposed to the weather, and being unaccustomed to be much wet with rain, having always had a good fire at home, he was now put to his shifts, (possessing a delicate constitution,) and strove to take shelter beside a wall or a rock more than once or twice; however, one time we stopped in a cottage, where he got some repose in sleep, whilst I dried his coat at a peat fire. Another time, we evaded a shower whilst resting at breakfast, yet the doctor was determined, let the weather continue as it might, he would not be the cause of detaining me, so as to break my appointments. My sympathetic feelings in pity were tried, when I saw the tenderness and danger of his constitution, when taking shelter as above.

I could but reflect on the goodness of God, in making my constitution require a great degree of exercise, according to my sphere of life and action, and also its preservation through the various changes, in different seasons, and different climes and circumstances.

From what I could collect, it appears to me that Wm. B—— ought to have launched out as a champion for God, but unbelief to trust God with his family, &c., caused him apparently to shrink. Is it not possible for a man to lose a great share of his crown? It appears that he saw the formality and danger into which the English connection were exposed, and sinking; he came out for a space, and God began to open his way, but through unbelief, the reasoning of Satan, and the solicitation of his brethren, he was prevailed upon to shrink, recant in part, and return; in consequence of which, some pious ones, who requested Christian liberty to pray with mourners, &c., and united with him to dissent, were left in a dilemma here. They were similar to the Quaker-Methodists, Free-gospellers or third-division, though most of these societies had no particular intercourse or communion together, or with each other. I suppose I was the first preacher who made them a general visit.

They held a conference some few weeks ago, to know each other's minds, and see how near they could come towards the outlines of a general union. I was invited to Leeds by some of this society; I tarried several days, but it being a particularly hurrying time in the cloth business, and the conference of the old connection sitting, I found it impracticable to get many to meeting on the week days, and on Sunday they chose to go and hear the old preachers, with whom they were acquainted. Here I saw Adam Clarke; I think I was informed, that he was acquainted with fourteen different languages. He is esteemed a man of as great letters as any of the age, and all acquired by his own industry, without the aid of college or university.

He acknowledged to me that he once was in the spirit of the great revival in Cornwall, and that he was almost ready to persecute some who objected to the work, as an "impropriety and wild-fire;" "but now," said he, "I see better!" He treated me in all respects as I might expect from a gentleman; but his mind was made up against the camp-meetings in America, as being improper, and the revival attending them, as a thing accountable for altogether on natural principles. It seemed to me, from circumstances, that he had got his mind hurt and prejudiced through the abuse of revivals, which caused him to fix his mind to one invariable rule as a criterion for direction, viz., the old system, *order;* for he seemed determined not to listen to any argument which might be adduced to solve the query. He was chosen president of the conference, as I was informed, by a great majority of votes. This was an honor he had not sought for, but accepted it with considerable reluctance.

He was an old acquaintance and particular friend of the doctor's, which opened a door for intimacy of conversation on some points—one of which was my singular way of proceeding, which he could not at all approbate on any consideration as being right; assigning as a reason, that if once generally adopted by the body, it would completely destroy Methodism in three months; therefore, he barred his mind against listening to any arguments, or making an exception to the general rule for particular cases.

This appears to me to be wrong in any person, to form their mind, hit or miss, right or wrong, to stick to the old system, as though it were infallible, or the summit of perfection. For to be thus bound up, without laying open our minds to conviction, as sincere inquirers after truth, is to kill the spirit of inquiry, and prevent the spreading of true knowledge and righteousness; and by so doing vice will continue to reign, and the grossest errors to go undiscovered or unclipt.

I heard him preach. Just before the meeting an anthem was sung, apparently without the spirit or understanding, as nothing could be heard but a dead, dull sound, &c.

The sermon was well delivered in speech, though there appeared much deadness in the beginning; but in his last prayer he grew somewhat fervent, until God began to send down his power, and there began a move among the people, when he seemed to lower, as if to ward off the move, to prevent a *noise*, which it seems the English connection in general are determined to prevent, as it appears from their conduct and publication in the Magazine.

I heard S. Bradburne. He spoke somewhat lengthy, and had the outlines of an orator; but I thought there were some *flaws* in his discourse too great for a man of his supposed abilities. For example: he insisted that a child is impure as it comes into the world, and is enlightened as soon as it is born, but not before; which would argue that a seven months' child might be saved, and one come to the full time could not, were it to die but one day before its birth. Therefore, one should suppose, according to his idea, that the being enlightened with the divine light was inseparably connected with the breathing the natural air, or receiving the natural light of the sun.

Here I also saw Dr. Coke, but so it happened that we did not exchange a word, though we met, passed and repassed each other in the streets, &c. I, being a little one, must keep my place.

I carried a bundle of my journals to the door of the conference meeting —one copy for each chairman of a district, amounting to twenty-five, and one for a preacher, who agreed to take them in. These were all refused, and returned. I sent one to the doctor's wife, which she received with acknowledgments, saying afterwards, when she had read some, that the more she read of it, the better she liked me, and had a better opinion of me than before, and that she had desired to see me when in Dublin, but was disappointed. She, by accounts, is an agreeable, plain, fine little woman, of some piety; but, if I am informed right, was not, nor is, a Methodist, though I think the rule of Methodists in Europe require marriage in society, if they do marry.

A. Clarke bought one of my journals at his lodgings at Banker's, where he had invited me to breakfast with him, giving more than the price, saying it was not enough.

30th. Leaving my doctor near Leeds, I came in the coach to Rochdale, whence I walked to Bolton, twelve or fifteen miles, where I held meeting at night by appointment, and next morning; both comfortable times.

31st. Went to Hayton, and had a good time.

August 1st. Walked to Preston, and was disappointed of my books. Spoke to a few; and next day, returning, spoke in Blackrod.

Sunday, 3d. Spoke at twelve o'clock. Went twelve miles to Leigh, so to Loton, then to Warrington, (where I met my doctor,) having spoken four times this day.

4th. Spoke here again; and Miss Mary Barford, eldest sister of Martha, who was principally educated and brought up in London, under a rich aunt, who, having no children, adopted her as her daughter, and dying, left her a large, independent fortune, being now here on a visit with her mother, gave me an opportunity of speaking closely with her concerning her soul's salvation. This night God gave her to feel the comfort of religion, and about two days after, an evidence of her acceptance. There are four in this family whom the Lord has given me for my hire, who were all careless when I visited this town.

5th. I spoke at Lymn, Appleton, Thorne, and Peter Wright's, where we had good times.

6th. At Preston Brook, and twice in Frodsham, where the Lord was with us; and after my last meeting in the evening, feeling my mind uneasy, I could not feel free to comply with various and strong solicitations to visit some new places; not even Macclesfield, from whence we received the most urgent request, but walked to Runcon in the dark and rain, and sleeping none all night, was up betimes in the morning, and finding a packet just going off, I embarked for Liverpool, where I arrived about eleven o'clock. Got my affairs arranged, cleared out with my printer and bookbinder, and contracted for a second edition of part of my second volume; then finding a boat with some passengers going to pursue a packet, I embarked in it, and overtook the vessel beyond the rock, where I got on board about five in the evening, with a positive, direct head wind for several hours. The wind at length becoming favorable, we made the lighthouse in Dublin bay, when the wind and tide would not suffer us to proceed further. Here they cast anchor, and I hired the sailors to put me ashore, and walking up by the Pigeon House, arrived at home in New-street about noon, where I found my friends and Peggy well, having been on my passage about thirty-six hours, and left my doctor behind me in England.

The British conference read N. Snethen's letter to Benson concerning me; yet it appears that it bore but little weight with them, considering its spirit, although they agreed, according to its design, to have nothing to do with me. The letter sent to Mr. Joyce, the book-steward in Dublin, was read in the leader's meeting, where it was unanimously agreed to have been written in a very bad spirit, so much so as to be its own refutation. It was also read in conference, where it was investigated, and received the same censure, which the British conference heard of, and did not scruple to mention it. It being asked if any one knew any thing against me, one replied, that it was *said* I had taken two hundred dollars in one contribution, which was false; but if it were the case, what was that to him or them, if I made a proper use of it?

I am informed by a special letter from Joseph Mitchell, dated New York, May, 1806, that N. Snethen had *located*, and that in consequence of his opposition, &c. Mr. Joyce tells me that he saw brother Beatty, a local preacher from America, come to see his friends here, who informed him, that Mr. Snethen had mostly lost his congregations, in consequence of his bitter ambition or activity in writing to Europe against me.

Monday, August 12th. This morning early the doctor arrived safe somewhat benefited by the excursion, as he thought himself, both in body and mind. His Letty had not been so long deprived of his company before for twenty-four years past. She seemed somewhat uneasy at m return without him; but I replied it would be some guineas benefit to her to learn to trust all things with God: and now her joy at his return took place of fears. I find Matthew Lanktree, my old particular friend, is appointed assistant or head preacher of Dublin. By what I can understand, he would be willing to let me have the pulpits, but the trustees were in the way. Alice Cambridge gave up her meetings always to me; and her room in Golden-lane, near Whitefriar-street chapel, is open to me, where I constantly hold meetings at eight o'clock in the evenings, so as not to clash with their hour. This room I conceive to be better filled than any worship place in Dublin.

Sunday, 17th. By invitation I took coach with two friends about sixteen miles to Balbriggen. A little deformed man behaved as if a legion of devils was in him, as on the road he would neither be still nor civil, but apparently profligate in order to irritate and ruffle me.

I saw church service performed, but never saw any thing appear so much like a sham as this ceremony in the way of religious worship; neither had I ever a greater sense of the difference between praying and saying prayers. I thought if human wisdom could have invented a machine to go by steam, to preach and pray, and say amen; and also to make the organ play, all to charm a parcel of beasts, when no human intelligence was there, it would be divine worship as much in reality, as some things which are now substituted for it.

I held meeting in a private house in the evening, and some Romanists and children attempted to make a disturbance in the street, when a sudden shower of rain dispersed them, so we had a quiet meeting, and next morning also, and I think that good was done. Hence, I returned to Dublin, and put the third edition of the first volume of my journal, to press: also "Thoughts on different religious subjects."

I continued my meetings in Golden-lane, night after night: the house was generally crowded. I also held some meetings in the barracks, and there appeared some fruit of them to my encouragement.

Sunday, 24th. I walked to the camp, and spoke in a hut built by the soldiers, in the following manner: James Ransford, my bookbinder, frequently held meetings in various places with the army. Near this they had no place but a quarry in a corn-field, and being exposed to the weather, as no person would hire them a place, he got application made to the barrack-master, (by the quarter-master-sergeant,) who gave them leave to cut sods on the camp-ground to make the wall, though the privilege had been refused for soldiers' families. They set to work by cutting a platform out of the side of a hill, leaving the back in such a form as served for a wall, with the bottom part projecting for a seat. The other three sides were raised as above with sods or turf well beaten down solid; then a kind of rafter was put on for the roof to be thatched with straw. But now they were put to their shifts to know how to complete it, as their finances were now out, having paid the irreligious for their labor, not feeling free to receive it gratis, which was offered. But about half an hour after the discouragements concerning straw for thatching, which was then dear, an officer brought them a pound note, &c. and shortly after some shillings so the house was completed, and would contain about one hundred persons. Most of the officers attended my meeting, and among them the head one

They gave good attention, and, as I was informed, expressed satisfaction, and wished that I should come again.

As I was returning I passed one, who to me appeared like a coxcomb.* I was informed that he belonged to the Stranger's Friend Society, and was sent here to preach. When he arrived and was informed that I had held a meeting, which seemed to supersede his exhibition, he broke out in a rage, and began to scold before the unconverted : saying that I was not countenanced nor accountable for my conduct ; which hurt tender minds.

I have continued my meetings at Golden-lane all this week, and once in the barrack ; and the work seems to deepen and increase.

Tuesday, September 2d. The devil viewing the danger of his kingdom, began to work in the minds of the people, and to raise confusion and disturbance. However, on my return from meeting I took a street out of my customary way, by which means I escaped the rabble, who were in pursuit ; one of whom was heard to say, " Now for the life of Lorenzo," another cried, " Mind the white hat," &c. &c. The former escaped by desperate exertion, with his coat much torn and dirtied ; the latter was secured by my friends, (after having a sharp contest between the parties,) and kept by the watchmen until morning, when the alderman, being partial, discharged him at the earnest intercession of his mother.

The next evening, some peace-officers, with others, brought swords, pistols, &c., but I retired unobserved through an intricate passage, and so baffled the mob. Another night a friend changed hats with me, so they were deceived.

My friends finding fault at my so obscurely retiring, I came off with the doctor, the usual way, and one beginning to cry for the mob, received a blow on the head, which kept him quiet. However, about half way a drunken attorney in derision, asked if we had a good meeting. To which was replied, " Yes : but thy master's servants did not like it." A friend interrogating concerning an obscene and scurrilous reply, received a blow as an answer ; for which the attorney was taken into custody, not without a torn shirt, &c.

8th. Lord Belvidere and his lady, this evening and last Saturday, attended meetings. On Thursday, by invitation I took tea with them. A Presbyterian minister present, wanted to know what A-double-L-part, in my journal meant, or who the A-double-L-part people were.

Lady B.'s sisters are under good impressions. We all came together in the coach to meeting, and on Saturday evening I took tea at his house again, and held meeting with a select party, and by his desire spoke largely on A-double-L-partism, and the 8th and 9th of Romans, &c.

Sunday, 14th. We had several comfortable meetings. I have spoken once particularly to the little boys, and have held Sunday meetings, similar to class-meetings, in which I find many who not long since were careless, now stirred up to seek religion, some of whom are rejoicing in God. My mind is strangely drawn out in exercises. and views of the present time in the political world, the state of Zion, whose walls are broken down, and how to counteract the kingdom of darkness, by expanding the travail of Zion.

18th. A general meeting of the official members of the Methodist So-

---

* His name was Murphy.

ciety in this city was held this evening, by a special call on my account. I went and made a speech to the following purport, in the loft where Tobias had once checked me. Said I, " I remember near seven years ago, to have been in this house. I have my feelings as well as other men, and am sometimes tried. There are, on a moderate calculation, near one hundred persons or more under awakenings of late, from my labors in Golden-lane. I feel it my duty indispensably, to travel as I do, and of course cannot watch over them, but desire to recommend them to your care ; yet as I fear that some of them are somewhat prejudiced against the Methodists, they will not come into class, unless they are led on by degrees. Wherefore, I wish, if any plan can be devised to meet the circumstance, that it may be adopted, knowing they will be apt to fall away, unless united in some religious body ; and I feel more unity with none, to recommend them to than you." I was then asked, " Who should watch over them ?" I replied, " One of your leaders ;" and observed, if they had any more questions to ask me, I would solve them if I could, to their satisfaction. A general silence prevailed. Then I was interrogated, if I had any thing more to say: and also repeatedly, whether I did not design to return to Dublin, and make a party ? As soon as I had replied, I retired.

A talk was held among themselves, and Matthew Lanktree, the assistant preacher, with J. Jones, was desired to tell me the next morning, which they did, viz. that they had agreed to receive any I should recommend to them, after examining them ; but could not think it expedient to have classes formed particularly at or from Golden-lane, lest it should appear too much like a party business, and they say, " We are Lorenzo's people ;" but would intermix them with the other classes, among the solid members. Oh! when will the time commence, when people shall be actuated with only purity of intention in all things, to glorify God, and not be afraid to follow his providential openings with the leadings of the Spirit, and exercise faith enough to leave the contingencies of events with him.

29th. Justice Bell, (who it appears has made his livelihood, of late years by exerting himself to bring people to the gallows) interrupted our meeting, saying, I could not talk common English, because I used the word " besom," for which he was put out of the house, getting several blows in his passage. Finding he was known to the peace-officers, &c., he cried, " Keep the peace and I'll support you," to deceive them. The next day the Rev. Mr. M'Cay, father-in-law to Lord Belvidere, with Mr. Clarke, a justice of the peace, called on Bell to inquire and demand a public apology. But he, to cloak the matter, denied the charge.

Several persons were considerably injured in the hubbub, by getting out of the window, &c. Among these was a young woman, who had a bone of her arm put out of joint ; and the next evening, absconding again, for Bell's sons were present with drawn swords, &c., she felt conviction for her littleness of faith, which she acknowledged the next day at meeting, and has since been happy in religion.

Saturday evening there was also a hubbub ; and one or two hundred persons came home with me, as an escort, almost every night, which caused a rumpus through the streets, as some were friends and some were foes ; part of which were for my safety, but the others threw stones. Sundry, on each side, were charged upon by the watch ; but the Alderman,

&c., were such poor things, that none of the disorderly were brought to trial.

Sunday, 21st. I spoke four times, being feeble in body; but could not feel freedom to attend Golden-lane at night, where Alice C———e spoke, as I felt there would be a disturbance, which was the case; and a guard of soldiers, with fixed bayonets, came to keep the peace, the watch being found insufficient.

22d. Going to a meeting, a stone, from a youth, through design, hit me in the back, near the kidney, the shock of which I felt for several days. This exhibits to view why it is that the common Irish have the name, over the world, for wicked, disorderly conduct, being kept in ignorance, and trained up in bigotry and prejudice, without the fear of God. This, to me, shows the propriety of literature for general information, and encouragement for freedom of thought on conscientiousness.

23d. Being informed of some little uneasiness in the mind of the man who lent us the house in Golden-lane, as the mob had broke the windows, &c., and escaped prosecution, I thought proper to discontinue my meetings; and so appointed my last for the next day afternoon, and a contribution to repair the injuries, &c.

24th. Spoke from Acts xx. 25, 26, 27, and had a solemn, tender time. God opened the hearts of the people, so that a redundancy was received.

The last night, a powerful mob was assembled; but as I spoke on the nature, &c., of camp-meetings, their minds were so attracted, that we met with but little disturbance during the meeting; and, as I retired through a back, intricate way, the mob lost the object of their aim, though they had a race through a number of streets. I knew nothing of this all the time, but, by a strong impulse, went into a friend's house, and felt as if in safety; and as I thrice attempted to come out for home, I felt a forbidding, unaccountable for on natural principles, which I expressed to J. Jones; and he, sending for a coach, brought me home in it, when Dr. Johnson told me what had happened in the streets. It appears that many were determined on some horrid action of violence, if we judge from their weapons and conduct.

Thus far the Lord has delivered me; though a female friend, it appears, received a blow for my sake, mistaking, in the dark, her bonnet and pelisse for my gray hat and surtout. I was unwell some few days, which prevented my going to the country; also the delay of my books, the workmen being indolent.

Mr. Parsons, the owner of the house in Golden-lane, sent me a note, expressing a desire that I should hold more meetings in it; which I accordingly occupied sundry times at five P. M., so that the rabble would not be at leisure. Justice Clark, with some difficulty, procured me the liberty of the Tailor's Hall, in Back-lane, which I occupied two evenings, at seven o'clock; but as the hour clashed with Whitefriar-street, I thought proper to discontinue, lest the last part of my conduct should seem to contradict the first. However, it appeared that considerable numbers of the fruit of Golden-lane have joined the Methodist society, by my advice to g to Matthew Lanktree, &c.*

I have been taken very unwell of late, with a convulsive affection of my

---

* See his letters in the Appendix.

belly, similar to that with which I was seized at Carlow; and my doctor said he had never before seen or heard of any person under the same affliction altogether. The disorder was somewhat keen, and very weakening, and continued, at intervals, for several days.

Matthew Lanktree sent me a ticket, with my name printed on it, and signed with his own, to admit me to the love-feast; but being somewhat weak in body, I did not think proper to attend; and also, as I might feel it my duty to speak somewhat more than would be agreeable or acceptable; which, to prevent, I might come away with a burdened mind, as most of the leading and official characters were to be there.

Several friends came to see me. A question was proposed: "Would I be willing for a petition to be drawn up, &c., to get signers, for the opening to me the Wesley chapel?" I replied: "What other people do is nothing to me; but I would advise not, as I conceive that it would be labor lost, and might raise a hubbub, by causing uneasiness, &c." I observed that when I came to Dublin, it was with the expectation of seeing a revival, and I was not disappointed: yet I believe that much more good would have been done, had I had a place to have access to the people; but those who had it in their power to accommodate me and did not, the blood will lay at their door, if good was prevented through their omission, for I feel conscientiously clear: therefore, I shall leave their conscience and their God to settle it together.

Shortly after I was interrogated by a visiter, to know if I intended to denounce judgments against the society. Another inquired of my printer if I was going to print, and call names, &c., after the manner of a pope's bull.

October 16th. This day I enter upon my thirtieth year, twenty-five of which I could reflect back; and, behold, they are gone as a dream!—and thirty years more will soon revolve, which, if I live, will bring me to the ordinary age of man. Oh! the preciousness of time! Oh! the duration of eternity!

I held several meetings at Golden-lane, as I have been detained here about two weeks by contrary winds, and waiting for my doctor.

I received a letter from Matthew Lanktree,* the assistant preacher, mentioning that about thirty, or upwards, of those who had been awakened, had joined his society on my recommendation of them to his watch care, and that many of them were rejoicing in God.

23d. The wind became fair, and we embarked with Captain Thomas, in the Duchess of York, for Liverpool. We were accompanied from the doctor's house to Pigeon House, by Mamma Letty and Sally Jones, who had procured a coach for that purpose.

Here I could but now reflect, that I sailed up this river, near seven years ago, with only five shillings and sixpence, British, in my pocket, without credentials, or acquaintance, or a place to go to; that I was a poor stranger in a strange land, having none to rely upon, but, like the fowls of the air, to trust to Divine Providence for my daily bread. This was living by faith instead of sight; and a trial of my faith it was; but God did carry me through.

Now the scene is changed. I have friends to convey me in a carriage

---

* See Appendix.

by the side of a river: I have now a wife and a daugnter, and my wiy is opening before me.

When I sailed from Quebec, it appeared to me that God chose to make use of that means to recover my health, for some end unknown to me. But now, methinks, I dimly see the end or purpose, viz. to lay a foundation for the enlargement of Zion's borders; for God works by means, and simple means answer the most noble ends: a small mustard-seed in the east will produce a great tree, and the kingdom of God is compared to it, and to a vine. I also see even some of the effects, in different respects, of my former visit, particularly in the publication of my conversion, &c., to give away, though it then took all my money, but one guinea, just as I was taken ill of the small-pox.

After about twenty-seven hours sail, we anchored in the river, and the next morning went on shore at Liverpool. I was considerably unwell on the passage, both as it related to the convulsions arising from my late abscess, or humor, &c., and the foulness of my stomach, which was the bitterest of the bitter, and set my teeth on edge, which thing I had never heard of before: this was not the effect of sea-sickness. My doctor was of singular use to me at this time.

Sunday, October 26th. We took coach and came to Warrington, where we arrived about noon, and found our friend, Peter Philips, from home. So we went to the chapel where Peter was preaching; but he, espying us through the window, told the people, and sat down in the midst of his discourse, as if just assembled. However, as we came in, the conduct of the auditory expressed their joy at our arrival. I sat down, and we had a Quaker-meeting for some time; *i. e.* silence. At length Peter spoke, and I dismissed the people. I spoke twice, and the next evening also; but I had my fears that some had not been as faithful as they should.

28th. Set off, on foot, for Macclesfield; but felt so weak in body, that I could scarcely go two miles an hour. However, Mary B——, who had heard me speak, by way of warning, concerning what I thought was coming over the country, and felt as if a witness in her own breast, concluded to have some talk with me on the subject of America, as being an asylum to those who might escape from the storm, as she had an independent fortune fallen to her from a relation, who brought her up, in London. She accordingly took post-chaise with her sister Martha, overtook us on the road, insisted on our getting in, and carried us to our destined place. Immediately after our arrival, word ran through the town, "the doctor and the American are come;" and that night there came more than could get into the house.

We tarried a few days, and found wonders had been wrought since our departure; between two and three hundred had joined society by convincement, and several strange things had taken place, among which was a dumb boy who had seen me cutting the initials of my name upon a tree, as he was passing by on crutches, came to meeting, got happy, and desired to express it to others, and was enabled so to do, in the power of speech and songs, to the surprise of the people. His father had strove to hire him to speak; had flattered, and even threatened to flog him if he did not, but all in vain.

The people carried the news to his father, that his son could talk, which he was scrupulous to believe, for joy, saying, "I must put my ear to his mouth, to be sure that the sound comes from him."

A deist also, who had been a commissioned officer, in both the navy and army, and had been in many parts of Europe and Africa, a great profligate, and a disciple of Voltaire, having heard of the American preacher, with the white hat, &c., happening to see me in the street, was excited by curiosity, or some other motive, to come to meeting; and so it happened, that whilst I related a story of a negro, who feeling so happy that he shouted the praise of God, was asked by a gentleman deist passing by, "Negro! what do you praise God for? Negroes have got no souls!" The negro replied, "Massa, if black man got no soul, religion make my body happy." The power of God fastened it on his mind that he wanted his body happy, and could not rest until he gave up his deism, and found what the negro expressed.

I visited some other places, but found my bodily strength to decay, being much agitated with the asthma or convulsions, as if nature was breaking loose, shrinking, and giving up. The people would flock out to meeting, as many or more than could get into the house before day, so that my meetings could conclude as soon as it was light.

So I visited Preston-brook; hence in a gig to Frodsham, where I had comfortable meetings. A backslidden Methodist, a sea-captain, whom I happened to lay hold of by the hair in the meeting, and putting my finger on his heart, told him my thoughts, felt the truth of my remarks, and the next morning, as soon as it was day, with a hand set out to carry me in an open boat to Liverpool, there being no flats ready. We had proceeded a few miles, when we espied a flat beating forward. The morning being calm, we strove to fall in with her on her tack, which brought us into the middle of the river, that was about a league broad. Of a sudden there came on a puff from a squall of wind, the most sudden I ever saw. We could not catch the flat, nor stem the wind, nor gain the shore. Scarcely had we turned round to run before the wind, when the squall overtook us, which seemed to raise the waves, and yet to smooth them, so as to prevent breakers. In this state the Runcon Packet espied us, and bore down to our relief. I was so chilled that I could not clamber into the vessel, but was dragged in by main force. My state was truly sensible of being attended with convulsions, the surprise of the passengers, &c.

A well-dressed female on board, was so indecent in her conduct with the captain, in the presence of the passengers, as I had never been witness to the like before. It makes me think of the state of Port-au-Prince and Cape St. François before the insurrection, and of former nations who had filled up the measure of their iniquities, like the Canaanites or Sodomites. And if this be a specimen of this country, is not the downfall of many at the door?

On my arrival in Liverpool, I found my appointment was not given out until for next evening, which gave me some rest. An A.double-L.-part man, who had in general executed his work well for my printer Forshaw, was employed to do my books, but departed from the pattern given him, and had like to have spoiled some hundreds, as he fell into a passion, and became saucy and fretful without a cause, (unless it was the subject of my writings.) I went to see him; he acknowledged the above, which made me think of Charles Wesley having once said in company,

"I can always know a C———t by his temper." One replied, "That'
a lie." C—— W—— rejoined, "Hah! Leviathan, have I drawn thee
out with a hook."

I got some more letters from America, one of which informs me that
Bishop Whatcoat is dead, and of a camp-meeting, in the little state of
Delaware, in which eleven hundred and sixty-five professed to be converted, and six hundred and six sanctified. Oh! may the flame kindle
over the whole earth.

I had a comfortable meeting in Zion chapel, and then took the canal
packet to Wigan, where Dr. J——n and brother J. Mee, from Warrington, met me. We proceeded to Hayton, where I held three meetings;
met the children, and found the work prospering.

Sunday, Nov. 9th. Spoke at night in Bolton, and next morning; and
thence returned to Warrington, through Lowton, where I had ordered an
appointment, which through mistake was given out for a wrong hour.
So I left them very abruptly, bidding none farewell, leaving my doctor
and J. Mee behind me. However, this turned for good; for, as the doctor had previously spoken of visiting this family, they would not readily
let him off. The people assembled, and the doctor spoke near an hour
and a half to their general satisfaction, which I think seemed somewhat
to raise his drooping mind.

I visited Risley with some satisfaction.

12th. Set out from Lynn, but through weakness of body was necessitated to give over, and requested my doctor to proceed to Lynn, as a gig
was waiting for us on the way. He did, and found a congregation waiting, and spoke to them with a degree of liberty, and I believe to their
general satisfaction, and some to himself.

A man of no religion living near Warrington, in a neighborhood where
I had frequently felt a desire to hold meetings, came and invited me.
A thought struck me to ask him if he had plenty of stable-room, as I had
some thoughts of getting travelling convenience in consequence of my
late weakness. He replied in the affirmative, and also added, he had a
horse and chair at my service.

November 13th, 1806. Some months ago I took tea in company with
a preacher's wife of the name of Beaumont, and gave her a camp-meeting book. They were stationed this year at Congleton, and the account
which she gave of me, caused a desire in the breasts of the official members that I should pay their town a visit, particularly after they had heard
of the revival in Macclesfield, and some of them had heard me preach.
It was tried at the leader's meeting whether I should be invited there.
Some strenuously opposed it, among whom was the young preacher.
Beaumont, the assistant, was silent. However, it was carried by a great
majority; and one told the young preacher that he had better go home
to the plough, than to talk in such a manner.

At first I had thoughts of taking Peggy with me on this visit. But
upon reflection thought best to have my doctor. So we proceeded in the
carriage to the place, where we arrived about six in the evening, and
were cordially received by friends who had sat up the preceding night,
expecting me by the coach, and were now preparing to send in search
of me.

I felt as if this field was ripe for harvest. About seven o'clock the chapel was nearly filled, and though I felt weak in body, I appointed four meetings for next day, intending to make a proper trial in the town. The people thought, surely the American intends to give us preaching enough.

14th. At half-past five o'clock in the morning, the chapel was full, and more at noon. At six the house was filled, and at eight overflowed.

15th. Had four meetings also, and the doctor went to Macclesfield, which appeared providential, as otherwise the people would have been disappointed; which was prevented to the people's general satisfaction, as far as I could learn.

Sunday, 16th. I spoke at six o'clock in the chapel, at twelve in the open air, to, as some supposed, from four to eight thousand. After Beaumont had done in the evening, I addressed the same congregation, and those members who had opposed my coming, were detained to hear, as they could not get out, which I believe removed some prejudice, as some of them heard me again.

Monday, 17th. House nearly filled at half-past five o'clock, and I invited the mourners to meet me at twelve. A number came, and Beaumont's wife took an active part in helping me to pray with them. In the evening the house was filled at both meetings as usual.

18th. Meeting again in the morning, and appointed my farewell for noon. There was a large auditory attended. At the close of the meeting I invited the mourners to come forward; about fifty distinguished themselves. I prayed with them; several professed to find deliverance. I retired, leaving a number of mourners with those who were helping me. The work spread and became more general, so that people flocked from various parts of the town to see what was the matter. The meeting continued until night, after which, two young men came after me to Macclesfield, where I was gone, and brought me the news before day, that about sixty had professed to find peace before the conclusion. Among these were my hostess, who had been a thorn to her husband for about twenty-three years, and a profligate son of the man who had been the principal cause of my coming.

Beaumont said he would rather have a noise that would blow the roof off the house than have the people all dead. These were Old Methodists, and there was no separate party at Congleton; but a great majority of the leaders, &c., were determined to leave the society if the invitation was prevented, which I knew not of till afterwards.

At Macclesfield, these Quaker-Methodists, or Third Division, who call themselves Revivalists, were hoped by the Old Methodists to have dwindled away. But now this expectation was given up, apprehending that my visits had been the means of their perpetuation, in consequence of the late great revival and large addition to their society.

On my first coming to Macclesfield, my doctor, being acquainted with Joseph Bradford, the head preacher, waited on him with the originals of my credentials, &c., letting him know that I was no party man, but kept in as close connection with the old society as the nature of my calling would admit.

He, with the young preacher, was willing I should have their pulpit, but it was objected to by the official members, which, as I was well informed, caused him to lose a night's rest. But now I received an invita-

,tion to occupy the house. I spoke twice, to about one thousand five hundred each time, and twice at the Revivalists'. Some of the minds of these were pained, and the conduct of the others reminded me of a little, fierce dog I once saw, who, to save his food, would only come when the cat was called. Oh, party spirit! when will it be abolished from the earth?

Wednesday, 19th. Came to Knuttsford in the evening, but found my appointment had not been given out according to my direction; however, I spoke at eight o'clock, and early in the morning. At the last meeting there seemed some good impressions.

My mind was distressed. I took no food in town, and but little sleep, which was on a hard seat near the fire in the kitchen, and walked off on my way before daylight, after dismissing the people, and leaving the doctor to get the chair and follow me. We arrived in Warrington as soon as we could, where I found the family; but not seeing my Peggy, I inquired where she was. Went up stairs, and found her lying sick upon the bed, just as I had seen her in my sleep the night before. She was in a nervous fever, as the doctor said, having been taken unwell the night I went away. An unconverted doctor or apothecary attended her, but whether he had done much harm or good, I know not; however, he was now dismissed, as I had the one I desired with me, who, if he were in Dublin, I should have sent for him. He the first day seemed to think the fever only a momentary thing, and in no wise dangerous; but next day shook his head as he was going to Frodsham, where he held two meetings, to the general satisfaction of the people; and returning, found the fever inflexible, which seemed to leave little grounds for hopes of recovery.

Peggy complained of great heaviness and continual sinking, like the giving up of nature; which the doctor said was the nature of her disorder, arising from a complaint in the liver, which she had been more or less affected with for many years, and was the cause (by the humor getting into the blood) of her long-continued infirmities, and particularly fainting, &c., with which she had been attacked in America, and the cause of which had not been understood.

Having several appointments given out, my present circumstances were such that I scrupled about fulfilling them, considering her situation and my own weakness, until Mary B———d requested, as doing her a favor, that I would accept the loan of a carriage, &c. In company with Peter Philips, I visited Northwich, the metropolis of the circuit, where I spoke twice in the Old Methodist meeting-house, I believe to the general satisfaction. Good was done, and some prejudice removed.

Sunday, 23d. Spoke at the forest at ten A. M. Many had to stand in the rain; but we had a shout which frequently drowned my voice.

As I was passing the Moor, I could but reflect on Nixon's prophecy of a battle to be fought in this place, in which England should be won and lost three times in one day, whilst a miller with three thumbs should hold three kings' horses; which I remarked in my discourse at Newpale at two o'clock. I was afterwards informed, that a miller of the above description now resided at the mill mentioned in the prophecy, and, moreover, that "in the neighborhood where Nixon (called the Cheshire fool) lived, it was received as a truth, and that many things which he prophted did really come to pass, and that he died of hunger in the palace of James I., according to his own prediction in his native place."

I spoke in the evening at Norley, but many could not get within hearing; so I spoke in the chapel next morning, which was nearly filled. I since hear that a good work then began. Thence to Bradley Orchard, where we had a quickening time. Also at Frodsham. From hence to Warrington, having been absent fifty-two hours, held nine meetings, and travelled about fifty miles. Found Peggy still in her sinking, low state. The first words she spoke as I entered the room were, "Where is my Jesus?"

The doctor said he had never known more powerful means used with such little effect, on account of the inflexibility of the fever. I observed the doctor to make use of the oil of tar (not the spirits of turpentine) externally on the feet, and a preparation of camphor and opium internally, which produced such a copious sweating that her clothes were necessitated to be changed twice in a night, and this successively for several days. We also used a large stone bottle, filled with hot water, kept constantly to the feet. These had the desired effect, and were the only means that seemed to give any relief to the *sinking*, as she called it, which the doctor said proceeded from the disorder in the liver approaching towards a mortification—the poisonous, corrupt humor of it operating upon the heart and nervous system, and producing this sensation; and he since has added, that he never before saw any one in a similar situation, who did not either die, or fall into melancholy, madness, or despair.

The man who had lent me his horse and chair for Congleton, had invited me to hold meetings in a large barn at Stockton Heath, where he resided. These I now attended to with assiduity in the evenings; and Mary B.'s favoring me with a seat in a carriage was no small convenience at this time, as my body was still weak, not being entirely free from the convulsions; and also attending mostly by night and day to Peggy, as we had no watchers of consequence till towards the last, and no proper nurses at this time, though the family did all in their power for our convenience; but the mistress was taken sick with the fever, and our little child taking the infection from the breast, made the house a kind of hospital at this time.

Sunday, December 6th. I held meeting last evening, and three to-day, in the Kilhamite or New Connection chapel, in Chester, where there seemed to be a considerable quickening among a barren people. J. Mallison, the preacher, is one of the sweetest, most liberal-hearted, spirited men I have seen in that connection, as in general they are too much given to finding fault with the Old Methodists.

On my return, Peggy's appearance seemed a little more ghastly to me; but the doctor replied that the inward symptoms were to the reverse.

On Tuesday the symptoms again appeared unfavorable. On Wednesday I felt an omen in my mind, as if something in our circumstances was going to turn up.

In the afternoon a spiritual daughter of mine, from Elsby, (a country place about twelve miles off,) came to see us; and it so happened in conversation, that she agreed to take our child and attend it with motherly care, they being in comfortable circumstances; and also our watcher seemed to answer so well, that I prevailed with her to give up her own employment, and attend upon Peggy till the conclusion of her illness.

The workshop being contiguous to the house, the work of both lofts, together with the noise of the children, annoyed Peggy more than she was well able to bear, which she had not complained of until now. So I determined to remove her to the house of Peter Wright, at Stretton, about four miles off, in the country, where the air was more pure.

Dr. Johnson sat up with her about fifteen nights, without taking off his clothes; neither did I change mine for three or four-and-twenty days. However, the jarring of the coach did her no injury, but in a few days some symptoms of a recovery were entertained.

She was now called to a fresh trial. I had felt it on my mind ever since my leaving America, to pay Ireland a general visit; and as circumstances had turned up, and feeling my soul bound to America in the spring, I had no opportunity until now; which circumstances I stated to to her. She said, "Go." However, I tarried a week later; we then joined in prayer. I went to Stockton Heath, spoke at night, then took coach to Liverpool, so lost my night's rest; but as no packet had sailed for two weeks, nor probably would shortly, the winds being contrary, I got my affairs adjusted, and took packet to Chester, but was disappointed in getting a seat in the mail coach for Holly Head; but another in a circuitous route presented to view, in which I was overcharged in my fare, on account of my ignorance, being a stranger. I also was deceived, as a cross coach was to take me on the road, which perhaps might be full, and so I lose my accommodation. Thus I lost the next night's rest, but had not gone twenty miles before I changed my inside to an outside passage, the cross coach being so full; and had not a man quitted the coach to accommodate me, I should have been left in the lurch. My situation was trying, it being a hundred and twenty miles, and exceedingly cold and rainy: also some young Irish officers, of the Popish religion, just from Malta, were continually my tormentors over these Welsh mountains, many miles of which I walked to avoid them, the coach being overloaded. One day as I passed a lake or pond of water, a whirlwind from a mountain crossed the road just as I had passed. I could but reflect on a providential care, when I saw the water forced many yards into the air. Took food but twice on the journey. Had not time to procure provisions, but went on board in my wet clothes, (as the packet was then ready to sail,) and took my passage in the hold with the horse, rag, tag, and bobtail, to avoid the Irish officers. Thus I continued from Saturday to Monday, when a boat double manned, by signal, came to take some out, charging treble price; adding they never were in such swells before. Pawning a note to satisfy them, it was with the greatest difficulty that I could get to the doctor's house, where Mrs. Johnson got me a cup of tea, with a hearty welcome. I lay down before the fire to dry myself, it being now Monday evening, and my last refreshment was breakfast on Saturday.

Here the hand of providence was manifest. I arrived in Dublin just before the holydays, which are kept more sacred than Sunday. At a leader's meeting, (being informed I was come,) it was broached by some who had been distant heretofore, if they should not open the Dublin houses, which hitherto had been shut against me, and it was not objected by general vote; wherefore Matthew Lanktree, the assistant or superintendent preacher, took me to Gravel-walk meeting-house, where I exhorted after sermon—thence a way opened for me to hold meeting also in Whitefriar-street meeting-house, where I spoke a number of times both evenings and mornings; then Mr. Averill, who was a church clergyman, formed me a route through Ireland, adding a kind of recommendation to this purport:

"Our Brother Lorenzo Dow has preached in Whitefriar-street and Gravel-walk meeting-houses: he travels Ireland relying on God. In the name of the Lord I wish him success, or bid him God-speed.
"*Dublin, December, &c.* ADAM AVERILL."

The man by the name of Wade, who had taken me in his gig to Wicklow, accommodated me with it on this intended journey also. It being whispered that I wanted a young man to attend me, to take care of the horse and gig, one by the name of John Fleming, obtaining his master's consent, offered. The first day we went to Drogheda, where I spoke five times in the Methodist meeting-house, and Tholsel; thence to Cullen, spoke twice—Dundalk once—mostly Roman Catholic. At Carickmacross, meeting not being appointed, I spoke in the street to a few attentives, and went to King's Court, spoke in the market-house, and stayed with Mr. Dyoss, a kind family. Thence to Baleborough, spoke in the street and in the house; so to Coote Hill, where were three houses for meeting in a row. The Methodists had invited all the Calvinists in town to come. I spoke on A-double-L-partism, which gave great offence, as it was wrongly supposed to be designedly done, and some being abashed, others exasperated—neighbors would hardly speak to each other next day. At Clones saw Wood, whom I had seen when in this country before—his friendship still remained—spoke twice—appointed when to come again; and went to Caven, a cool town—hard people—spoke twice, and also at Kilmore, in the house of ———, brother to ———, who abridged the church articles for America, when Dr. Coke was designed to come over, &c. Spoke six times in Granard, and an A-double-L-part church minister taking offence, went out—twice at Old Castle—twice at Mulengar—once at Terilspass—also at Kilbegan—then to Bracke Castle, to the house of a great man, of about three thousand sterling per annum; he thought I had an errand to his family: some of this Handy family followed me to Moate. I visited Moss-town, tarrying with Mr. Kingston in a great house, but as the family were designingly striving to retard or detain me from meeting, saying, it is too late, &c., I suddenly and abruptly left the table, found the way out of the house, and pushed off to meeting, which brought out all hands upon a jaunting car. Next morning I visited Goshen and Lisduff—held four meetings—saw the wife of the clergyman who had left the meeting; she was a pious Methodist, but got deceived in his A-double-L-partism, until the matrimonial knot was tried; and many a poor woman gets imposed upon as a cipher for a husband. Spoke twice in Longford—good times—saw Mr. Armstrong, a preacher, and I believe an excellent man. Visited Athlone; spoke twice—called for mourners, but none came forward. One who did not preach, though he had the name, said, "The people here are uncircumcised in heart and ears, and will not stoop and bow to Lorenzo." His name was Robinson. Next morning about twenty came up under the melting power of God to be prayed for—thence to Clara, where some of the Handy people were—thence to Tullamore, and several friends met me on the way, one of which was Christopher Wood. When in this country before, I felt distress and abruptly left a house of quality, where I intended to lodge, late at night—I met this man in the street and went home with him, whose wife from that time became serious; so now I had a home—had two good meetings—got the gig repaired, and went to Mount Mellick—pressed a man to send a bell-man through the town, to ring out the people, saying, "Put on the courage of a man"—he did—afterwards I found he was a Methodist preacher. Spoke twice in Portarlington—here I received the solemn news of the death of our only child—I felt, as it were, as if part of myself was gone; yet could not murmur, but felt with submission to say, "The Lord gave, and the Lord hath taken away, blessed be his name:" it is a feeling which nothing but experience can fully realize. Though our Letitia be no more seen, yet she having escaped the evil to come, with all the vain snares of this delusive world, I trust it is not long before we shall meet above, where parting shall be no more. What must have been the feelings of my poor Peggy, when in a strange land, given over to die, at least but small probability of ever meeting again—her husband and child absent—and then the news of the death of the latter to reach her ears?—Experience only can tell. Messrs. Jones and Griffin, who brought me the above news, accompanied me to Monsteverin and Athy, and talked about going to America. I visited a country place, and then to Maryborough; stayed with John Campoin, who was a happy local preacher when I was here before; but now he is in an uncomfortable state, some uncomfortable circumstances having turned up. He spoke frequently; finding fault and speaking of the faults of the Methodists, which is too frequently the case with backsliders, retailing the improprieties of others without mending their own. Vice ought to be discountenanced; but to watch others with a jealous spirit, to speak of them in a canting way, &c., argues very bad, and savours of an unholy spirit. I visited Mountrath and Tentore, where Mr. Averill lives. His conversion was as follows. His grandmother was a good church woman for the time; a church clergyman gave him a rap on the head with a cane in play, when he was six years old. He said, "Grandmother, I wish that man would never come again." Said she, "Wish God's minister would never come again!" Feeling the effect of the blow, a large bunch on his head, she was exasperated also: he desired an explanation why the man preached. She said, "To save people, but he would not except he was well paid for it." Thus, while she was explaining things to his understanding, he felt a great light or comfort to break into his mind, but could not tell the cause, nor what it was—it lasted near twelve months. He said to her, "When I am grown up I will preach for nothing." She replied, "That is a good resolution, but you will forget it." He said, "I will not." His father lost a purse of gold, and said, "The child who would find and return it, should have whatever they would ask." He found it, and said, "Let me go to college instead of my elder brother, (whom the father intended to educate,) and would not be put off."

Thus he got his education and became a church minister, but preached for hire; and one day when visiting his parish, he called on a family called Quakers. They asked, "Who art thou, the man who preaches in the steeple-house?" One said, "Don't thee preach for hire?" He said he did. Q. "Dost thou think it is right?" A. "I don't know that it is wrong." Q. "I did not ask if thou thought it wrong, but dost thou think it is right?" His youthful promise started into his mind, not to preach for hire, so he dare *not* say he thought it right, and he still replied, "I don't know it to be wrong." Q. "Art thou willing for light on the subject?" A. "Yes." So the Quaker gave him a book against hirelings, which he read with attention, and every word carried conviction to his mind. So he gave up the *curacy*, which his wife had for pocket-money heretofore; and when she observed him not go to church, she inquired the cause, and said, "What shall I do for pocket-money?" He replied, "My dear, I trust God will help me to make you out the same sum some other way," &c. He built a pulpit in his own house, and held meetings; and shortly one man professed to be converted, and know his sins forgiven, which Averill reproved him for, saying, "I don't know my own forgiven." A Methodist present said, "If you don't, I do; and if you will look for the witness God will give it you;" and soon after he felt the same sensations as when a lad, &c. His wife* left him because he dare do no otherwise than itinerate and preach without hire, being possessed of an independent fortune. So the order of providence brought him among the Methodists. One day a mob saw him coming over a bridge, and one said, "Devil split my head open if I don't do so and so to the swadler," (the Methodists being called swadlers in Ireland, in derision;) but the restraining providence of God kept them, so he passed unhurt. Afterwards that man on the continent had his head opened by a French sword, which one saw who heard him express the words, and wrote home to his friend not to oppose Mr. Averill, for he was a man of God. He (though in connection) is not confined to a *circuit*, but travels as he pleases. Also there are ten missionaries employed, though not particularly confined, but are somewhat like Mr. G. and C., &c., in New York district.

I had three church ministers to hear me, one of whom was a deist, yet continued his living in Averill's vicinity. From Durrow I went to Kilkenny, and from thence to Moneybeg, where some more conversed about America. I visited a country place, Carlow and Ballitore; here I spoke in a Quaker meeting-house. Here Job Scott died, and Dr. Johnson was born. I visited Baltinglass, Hacketstown, Tinahaly, Killaveny, Rednagh, Rathdrum, to Wicklow. Here was J. Wade, son to the man who lent me the gig, who conversed about America. He also accompanied me to Arklow and Gorey, where I spoke in the market-house; thence to Ferns and Newtown-Barry. When I was here seven years before, I was sur-

---

* She lived but a few years, during which time she caused him much trouble, sorrow, and anxiety, though he allowed her two hundred pounds sterling per annum for her support, and the daughter; and she would not see him, nor suffer the daughter to write to him, though she appeared ready to fly when she met him on the road. But after the mother's death, she returned, being young.

The wives of J. W. and George Whitefield were similar; but those three men stuck to the work, and God blessed them in it, until those objects were removed out of the way. And if a man is faithful in the way of duty, and those beings who act thus are removed and taken away, how can one in conscience and in truth call it a "LOSS?"

And those men whom God has moved by his Spirit, and called to preach the Gospel, how do they feel when under petticoat government so far as to desert the work? "Any way for the sake of peace." But remember that which God wills concerning the sphere of our action, is the only road to sure PEACE, "for the way of transgressors is hard." Therefore, out of the order of God a conscientious man cannot feel easy in his mind until he fully backslides in heart.

prised by an unusual noise, so that I could not sleep; yet I would not be scared away, knowing if the devil came he could not hurt me, but could obtain no satisfactory information relative to it, yet would sleep there no more. That family now told me that they heard the noise several days successively after I was gone, until a backslider who was then sick under the roof, was dead, being in black despair. Enniscorthy, Wexford, Old Ross, New Ross, city of Waterford, Carrick on Seur, Clonmel, Cashel, Littleton, Rosgrey, Templemore, Clesordan, Burr, Aughrim, Tuam, and Castlebar, I visited. Some of these places had received wrong information relative to my coming, which disappointments paved the way to my getting greater congregations. Gideon Ousley, one of the missionaries, met me and observed, "Yesterday a Roman priest being insufficient, got another to help him, and one with a whip and the other with a club, drove off some thousands of people like swine to market, who were attentively hearing me preach." I could scarcely believe that the clergy in this our day, could have such an ascendancy over their people. He accompanied me to many appointments to Sligo. In this journey I found numbers converted, the fruit of awakenings when here before, and many came out to hear who did not usually attend any place of religious worship; so I have access sometimes to one class of people, which was I to labor in any other sphere of life I should not. Thence to Manor-Hamilton, Violet-Hill, Enniskilen, Maguire's Bridge, Brookborough, Clones, Monaghan, Aghnacloy, Cook's-town, Cole-Island, Moy, Blackwater, Armagh, Rich-Hill, Tanderagee, Portadown, Lurgan, Moria, Lisburn, and Belfast. Here I met some of my old friends from Larne, who informed me of the expectations of the people there. I intended to visit that place ever since I came to Europe, but now could get no further down into the north. There may be the providence of God in this. Balinahinch, Downpatrick, Newry, and so to Dublin, having been gone sixty-seven days, in which time I travelled about seventeen hundred English miles, and held about two hundred meetings, in most of which the quickening power of God was to be felt, and some were set at liberty before we parted. I returned the horse and chair to the owner, satisfied the demand, left money for the doctor's books which he once had sent by me to America, and prepared for my departure. The friends who had conversed relative to sailing with me, now met and agreed that I should engage their passage.

I suddenly departed to Liverpool, feeling my work done here, and engaged the steerage of a ship for our company accordingly. Peggy was recovered, and thus the Lord was good to bring us together once more, when there was so little prospect to human probability when we parted. Many condemned me for going to Ireland when and as I did but had I tarried I could have done her no more good, as I obtained the nurse I wished for, and by going I answered a clear conscience. We went by canal to Wigan, walked to Hecton, and from thence we went to Bolton; in the mean time I visited Blackburn and another place. S when I came, the man who invited me treated me cool, by which mean I was disagreeably necessitated to disappoint hundreds of people. W came by canal to Manchester, where we met the doctor, who suddenly departed from us by coach to Chester; thence to Hollyhead, and so we over to Dublin, and I saw him no more. He is one of the kindest, human men to the poor I have seen, and I am under more obligations to him tha any I have acquaintance with in my travels. I was in hopes to have had his company to America, but here I was disappointed, as he could not see his way clear to come. Thence to Warrington, saw our friends and found them well. The society called *Quaker-Methodists*, gave me a testimonial concerning my conduct, as may be seen in the appendix. Here I met brother Shegog. We went to Knutsford, and thence to Macclesfield, where I preached the dedication sermon of the new chapel belonging to the Free-gospellers, or Revivalists. Instrumental music was introduced here in form, to draw the more people together, to get money to defray the expense of the house. I believe they got less money by so doing than they would otherwise; and of course it is a foolish thing to take the devil's tools to do the Lord's work with; it is an evil practice, and you cannot deny it.

I visited Congleton, and found more than one hundred had been taken into society since my other visit. I also visited Boslem, in Staffordshire, and many other places; also the city of Chester, and all around its vicinity. I received invitations into different parts of England, but feeling as it were my work done here, and my heart and soul bound to America, I dare do no otherwise than return, and of course durst not accept the invitations but with thankfulness, and not comply.

There are six kinds of names of Methodists in England: 1. Old Society; 2. Kilhamites; 3. Quaker-Methodists; 4. Whitefield's Methodists; 5. Revivalists, or Free-gospellers; 6. Welsh Methodists, (called jumpers,) a happy, simple, pious people, by the best accounts; besides the Church Methodists.

The old body are the main stock, as that in America; they have never had a final separation from the church. They are called protestants, but most of them are as *dissenters*, preaching in church hours, which Mr. Wesley did not allow. They mostly have the ordinances among them, though their preachers are not ordained, but say the power which qualifies them to preach, does not make a man half a minister; and if he be properly called, and qualified by God to administer the *substance* in the word to the salvation of souls, the same of course is fit to administer the *shadow* in form, and of course count the *ordination* but a *form*.*

There is instrumental music in most of the leading chapels in England. But for a lad to start up and sing away in form like a hero, yet have no more sense of divine worship than a parrot that speaks a borrowed song, I ask how God is glorified in that? If mechanism was in such perfection, as to have a machine by steam to speak words in form of sentences; and so say a prayer, repeat a sermon, and play the music, and say amen, would this be divine worship? No! there is no divinity about it; and of course it is only mechanism. And hence if we have not the Spirit of God, our worship is not divine. Consequently, it is only form; and form without power, is but a sham.

In Ireland the separation from the Church has not taken place. There is more of the ancient Methodist simplicity discoverable among them, but not as in America. I believe the plan fallen upon in these United States, and has been the most proper one for the time being, to carry on an extensive itinerancy with little expense; but what will or should be best

---

* For the sake of order

in future, may God's wisdom direct, and his providence point out? Well may the Poet say,

> "Except the Lord conduct the plan,
> The best concerted schemes are vain,
> And never can succeed."

If " the kingdom of God be righteousness, peace, and joy in the Holy Ghost," and the " testimony of Jesus be the spirit of prophecy," well may the Apostle say, " No man can call Jesus Lord but by the Holy Ghost." Again, " If any man have not the spirit of Christ, he is none of his."*

In Europe there is much more stress put upon forms, names and tradition, than in America; you can scarcely give a greater offence, than ask, " Have you any religion?" " Got any religion!" " Think I am a heathen—got my religion to seek at this time of day?" " I was always religious." What is your religion? It is the religion of my father, and he was of the religion of his father, the good old way; we don't change our religion." Suppose a man has a young horse, that will run a race—win a prize, and is a valuable animal; he wills the horse to his son, and he to his son, and so on. But the horse dies: the grandson boasts, what, have not I got a good horse? I have, my grandfather raised him, willed him to my father, who gave him to me; and I can prove by the neighbors, he ran such a race, and won such a prize. But on a close inspection, it is found only the bones are remaining. Look at the Congregationals, or Independents, Presbyterians, Quakers, &c. &c. &c., and compare them now with the history of their ancestors, and a change will be visible.†

Two or three centuries ago, perhaps, ancestors had religion, and were out of stigma, called by a name that has been attached to their form, and handed down from father to son. These ancestors living in the divine life of religion, in that divine life have gone to heaven, as Christ saith, " My sheep hear my voice, and follow me, and I give unto them eternal life," &c. But the children down have, or, bearing the same name, think they have, the same religion; but on a close reflection or inspection, there is no more divine life about their form, than animal life about the bones of the old horse; and of course, will no more carry a man to heaven, than the bones will, with whip and spurs, carry a man a journey, &c. Because bible religion is what we must have especially, for the ancients " were filled with joy and with the Holy Ghost," and " without holiness no man shall see the Lord;" but " blessed are the pure in heart, for they shall see God."

I scruple whether the funds which have been raised in England have not proved a temptation to some, though they might be turned to the glory of God, and doubtless have in many instances; yet I fear that to some, through fear, it hath proved a snare, so that they have not borne that testimony, which their conscience and judgment told them was their duty, against a growing evil; whilst others have had too much affluence and ease, and by that means have sunk too much upon their lees! God forbid it should be the case in America! Whilst a man, or body of people are simple and sincere, having frequently recourse to their first principles in

---

* Mr. Asbury is to America what Wesley was to Europe.
† And unless people have recourse to their first principles they will degenerate?

the Lord, there is no room to doubt his favor and his blessing, and these will make a happy life, and procure a happy end; and all is well that ends well, is the old proverb. But who can stand when God sets his face against them? Or what can prosper if God don't smile his approbation. The wicked may prosper for a while, but at length they will be driven away as the chaff, and their candle put out—whilst the righteous shall be had in everlasting remembrance.

CHAPTER X.

A SHORT ACCOUNT OF "ECCENTRIC COSMOPOLITE."

When Cosmopolite was on his last tour through *******, orders were sent from the "Castle," somewhere, by somebody, that he must be taken into custody; which body returning, replied for answer, that Cosmopolite could not be found*—this, more than once or twice. Moreover, the Threshers pursued him two nights and one day for a noted heretic; but he unwittingly escaped from them likewise. The martial law was now proclaimed in four counties, which made it dangerous travelling without a pass; but Cosmopolite was providentially kept in peace, and safely delivered from the whole—yet not by foresight in any human wisdom—for it was not within the reach of human ken.

"Question 22. A man from America, named ******* ***, having travelled through this country, professing himself a friend to the **********, what judgment ought this ********** to pass concerning the conduct of that man?"

"Answer. He came —————————— or any authorized to give it ——————— has not travelled as one of our people, nor as one of our friends—and we are determined that should he return, none of our ************* shall be opened to him on any account whatever."—Minutes of both countries.

He left ****** at full tide and fair wind, in an extra packet—having just stepped on board as she cast off: down came the "pursuers," and looked from the dock, while he gazed at them from the deck, and thus went out of the harbor.

Twice the consul had applied for passports in vain, and likewise solicited the interference of the ambassador, but there were no returns. Hence Cosmopolite, when he had finished his work and got ready, came away in a vessel that was fitted for the purpose; but not with design, except by Providence. Another vessel had sprang a leak, which the pursuers were searching, as Cosmopolite sailed by out of port, in the other ship.

---

* Cosmopolite was on the chase seventeen hundred miles in sixty-seven days, and held two hundred meetings—such being the distance from the people, without intimacy—and the velocity of the journey, that they scarcely knew from whence he came or where he was gone!

The fog was as a hiding-place in the hand of God—to preserve from those "Floating Hells"—while coming round Hibernia and doubling Cape Clear—for several days together!

This vessel was called the Averick—323 tons—De Cost, master—would keep half point nigher the wind than usual; hence ships at the leeward must run parallel, or cross our track to gain the weather gage, in order to bear upon us—therefore would lose time and distance. De Cost put out his lights and altered his course, and so evaded the intruders thrice—whereas the other ship which had been refused on account of her leak, was boarded twice. Thus Cosmopolite was preserved to Columbia's shores, for which praised be the Lord!

Though a stranger, the way was opened for meetings, and some good times in public—some aquaintance with the Quakers, and sailed to New-York with most of the passengers.

Cosmopolite was accused with "hush money" clandestinely, by some who were on board. On getting wind of it he had the agreement stated, and then produced the receipt to the full amount, which answered to the articles. Then he was accused of having received a present of ten pounds from the captain, which they said should have been divided with the passengers. Cosmopolite said why? was there any such agreement? They acknowledged not! yet observed it would have been but just. Cosmopolite said, he did not see nor feel the obligation—had the donation been given—which he observed had never been given; and appealed to the captain if ever he had made the gift, who answered in the negative. Nevertheless, ungenerously did some persist to make the impression that Cosmopolite was a swindler. But what is amiss here must be rectified hereafter.

Some of those people who were led by inclination or judgment to come to America, questioned Cosmopolite antecedent to their coming. Civility demanded a reply, which accordingly was given. As free agents they came for their own interest only; but meeting with some trials, bitterly accused Cosmopolite, as the cause of all their trials, calamities, and misfortunes—who could have no interest in their coming. One even went so far as to curse the day she ever saw his face, though he had done all he could to serve them. But the sin of ingratitude is one of the most abominable crimes that the heart of man can be contaminated with, and very obnoxious in the sight of heaven—evidently marked with just displeasure in righteous retributions.

Here it may be observed, that those who have fled from oppression and privation to the "Land of Liberty," are the worst enemies, and most bitter in the execrations of any on these shores, when fortune smiles upon them. But yet it is very observable that few of them are willing to return to the old world.

A certain pair, whose passage the king paid, from the old world to the new—fortune smiling on them in Alexandria—the term being expired, in contempt he quit the country, exclaiming, "the best flour in America is not equal to the mud of London." There he put his barrel of dollars in a private bank; which broke in a few days after, and he then had to turn porter, and stand in the mud, to get wherewith to support nature!

On this voyage, Cosmopolite frequently felt a foreboding of approaching trials; and a secret conviction that all was not well at the Mississippi, which he expressed more than once or twice.

He went to Virginia, by land—saw brother Mead—met his *rib* in Richmond, and then returned to New England, holding meetings and had good times by the way. But now the storm began to gather, preludes of which were seen. Hence, Cosmopolite felt he must fortify his mind—considering these omens a dispensation of preparation accordingly, from the beneficent Parent of the world!

Whilst in Europe Cosmopolite was attacked with spasms of a most extraordinary kind, which baffled the skill of the most eminent of the faculty; and reduced his nervous strength, and shook his constitution to the centre, more than all his labors and exposures heretofore—which had been from seven to ten thousand miles a year, and attending meeting from six to seven hundred times. But now his sun appeared declining, and his career drawing to a close. But the idea of yielding and giving up the itinerant sphere, was trying to Cosmopolite, seeing it was his element and paradise to travel and preach the gospel. Hence he got a stiff leathern jacket girded with buckles to serve as stays, to support his tottering frame, to enable him to ride on horseback; which the doctors remonstrated against. When that would answer no further, he took the gig and little wagon; but was obliged to sit or lay down some part of the meeting to be able to finish his discourse, mostly for seven years.

Some could or would not make the necessary distinction between voluntary singularity and a case of extreme necessity. But such a cavilling argues an ungenerous mind, and is too much tainted with "moral evil."

Cosmopolite had bought a pair of mules, which were to have been fitted to the carriage against his return; but in lieu thereof, were put in a wagon; and so broke down they were unfit for service: hence he had to part with them for about half value, to be able to prosecute his journey. The horse he had was shortly starved so as to fail, and hence obliged to part with him for one of little worth.

Shortly followed the residue—while in his decline of health. From New England he was found in the Mississippi Territory; having travelled there by land through Georgia, where he received letters of confirmation that all was not going right.

Here Cosmopolite was induced to aid two parties, as a friend between, who got him bound and would not let him go off. He offered all he had; but in vain. The circumstance was, one party owned three hundred and twenty-four acres of land, and verbally consented for the other to build a mill on it; who set up a frame without any title, and getting involved in debt, the first would not sell it to him lest they should lose it by his creditors; and he was afraid lest he should lose his labor for the want of a title. So they wished Cosmopolite to step in between them, so as to make each secure—which, without looking at consequences, he did. This was an error of his life, and he repents it once for all. However, it has been a school of an important nature to him, and doubtless will be for life.

Then went for his *rib*, by the advice and request of friends—whose friendship in the sequel consists in fair words untried, like the pine tree which appears as good timber, but upon investigation is found *rotten* at the heart.

For, after Cosmopolite had gone, in a few months, over most of the northern states, he returned with his companion to that part, and was reduced to the most painful situation imaginable, as follows:—

First, some heavy debts, in consequence of purchasing sixty-four acres of the three hundred and twenty-four; though he had but about twenty-four remaining, with the mill frame on it, having parted with about forty, to be able to work through.

Secondly: No money or flush loose property.

Thirdly: A sick companion, without house or home—this being the time when friends forsook him—all except a *deist* and his family.

Fourthly: Reputation—attacked on all sides, and in remote parts through the states—that he was revelling in riches and luxury, with a fine brick house, sugar and cotton plantation, flour and saw mills, slaves, and money in the banks, &c. &c. &c., like a nabob in the east. Whilst others made use of every thing they could that would be to his discredit—among which, some few who had subscribed for his journals and paid in advance; but not getting their books, no allowance was made for the books being lost; but all was construed, " a design to cheat, and had got the property, and gone to the Mississippi to feather his nest."

Hence the famous expression—

"The *star* which *rose* in the EAST, is *set* in the WEST."

About this time he dreamed that he was in New York, and was going from the Park to Pearl-street, in quest of J. Q's. house, when the street appeared burned and only the ruins of the walls remaining, and not a trace of his family could be found in the city—which waked him up in a tremor of horror. He told his wife that he thought they should hear something disagreeable from New York, which the sequel proved in a few days, for a letter from Mr. W . . . . . was opened in Virginia, and accidentally, or rather providentially, a friend wrote to the Mississippi, "I suppose that you have heard that J. Q. has eloped to the W. I. and taken off another man's W . . ., and also left you in the lurch with Mr. W. . . . . and J. C. T." &c. &c. &c. The whole mystery was then developed, and consequences to be read that would be disagreeable enough.

Mr. N. S. had his trial by men who had never seen his "letter," or been acquainted with Cosmopolite, nor heard any thing he had to say about the circumstance—gave judgment in Mr. N. S.'s favor, and a certificate of acquittal, only on hearing *his* own statement—though pagan Romans had the accuser and accused face to face, that he might have an opportunity for his own defence. The Jews' law did not condemn a man before it heard him.

Hence Cosmopolite had the sentence of being the agent of all the evil instead of Mr. S——; and moreover was a "sabbath breaker," having let some people have a few religious books through necessity, and not of choice, as they could not be supplied with them at any other time: therefore must have no countenance, but go on his own footing.

Cosmopolite delivered a discourse from, "As ye would that others should do to you, do ye even so to them:" First, in *person ;* secondly, in *property ;* and third, in *character :* which discourse gave great offence!

These things now came to a focus about one time, which augmented the distress of Cosmopolite. As he was fast verging towards the grave, to human appearance he could not stay long; and the thoughts of dying in this cloud, under these gloomy circumstances, were of the most painful and distressing nature. Circular letters were sent forth from the executive already, that he might rise no more; and at N. Y. it was thought and said by many that he would never dare to show his face again!

A gathering in the side of Cosmopolite for some time, now began to ripen, and, finally, burst in the cavity of the body, between the bowels and skin, and he expected to die; but, falling asleep, he dreamed that he was in a mill-race, below the wheel. The water was as clear as crystal, but the bottom and sides were a quicksand, so that there was nothing to seize hold of or to stand on, for the possibility of relief. Thus situated, he drifted with the stream towards the ocean near by, where was a whirlpool of vast depth. People were sitting on the banks, merrily diverted to see him drift, without offering any assistance. However, a little man, in white raiment, ran down to the stream, waded in up to his chin, between the current and whirlpool in the eddy, and, stooping over, reached as far as he could, seized him by the edge of his garment, and dragged him to shore: here a gentleman opened his house, and invited him to the parlor, while the lady made the necessary arrangement for his relief in food, raiment, &c.; he was then shown into a convenient room, where he was left to compose himself to rest. In the mean time, the people on the bank merrily diverted themselves, saying, "He has lost one shoe in the river, and will never be able to travel and preach again." But in the morning, to the surprise of all, both shoes were found safe in the dining-room, though the doors were shut and locked all night.

The idea of being stigmatized, and of having his ashes raked up by misrepresentation after his dissolution, was painful in the extreme; because of the slur it would bring upon religion, as the time appeared fast approaching. He cried to the "God of Jacob" for relief, and that for His name and glory's sake, to hear his prayer, that His cause might not be slandered on his account.

Thus, after spending the bloom of youth in the service of others, for Zion's welfare, to be now, in the greatest time of affliction, forsaken of friends, and turned out as an old dog who hath lost his teeth, was a feeling that cannot well be described.

"But where *reason* fails, there *faith* begins—
For man's extremity is God's opportunity."

As the last retreat, Cosmopolite retired into a canebrake, at the foot of a large hill, where was a beautiful spring, which he named "Chicimaw spring," by which he got a small cabin made of split poles, where the bear, wolf, tiger, &c., &c., with all kinds of serpents in North America, abound. This was an agreeable retreat from the pursuing foe, there to await and see what God the Lord would do.

Once he met with three animals, when going to a neighboring house, upon a by-way, which he hacked out through the cane; he told them to get out, and chinked his tins together; one took to the left, and two to the right a few feet, and he passed between, when they closed behind. He inquired if Mr. Neal had been there, having seen his bull-dogs. The family, on hearing their description, replied that they were wolves!

Being routed from this peaceful retreat, in the manner that the porcupine drove the snake from his den, Cosmopolite made arrangements to leave his *rib* and go to the states; so, by mutual consent, they parted for three hundred and seventy-one days, and he came into Georgia, having only about three dollars when he started in the wilderness from the Mississippi.

He attended a large association of Dominies in South Carolina, who were mostly strangers to him—there being not more than three members remaining of the same body when he was acquainted with them a few years before, as about five years changes the majority in each * * * * * * * * * * *, and not more than five or six spoke to him.

However, he endeavored to make clear work as he went; which, through the mercy and providence of God, was accomplished; except about subscribers, which he supplied a few months after, though he had to travel several hundred miles to accomplish it. There was a subscription which Cosmopolite had made, but part remained unpaid. He parted with his horse, which cost one hundred and thirty-five dollars, and fifty dollars in cash, with which he was let off, though he was denied the privilege of preaching in the house before he asked it. So he took to his feet, and went on to New-York, and sent for Mr. W—— and J. C. T., and shortly all the horrid consequences of J. Q.'s conduct came to view.

Some years before, Cosmopolite was in a house where the man and all his family were confined with sickness, who requested some papers to be filed, in the west, to save his land, which he had been banished from by the Catholic Spaniards, on account of his religion; and he had to take his family, in an open boat, round Cape Florida, living on game, and had nothing but Providence and his gun to depend on until they arrived in Georgia, during a space of about seven months. To oblige him, Cosmopolite took the papers and filed them; and J. Q. wished to make the purchase; which matters were executed, accordingly, all round, excepting one instrument of writing, which was only prevented by a sudden fit of illness.

Thus God sees not as a man sees: what we think for the best, may prove our ruin; and what we think for the worst, may be the best way of all! J. C. T. acted the reasonable part, on Christian principles, to bear and forbear, and wait the bounds of possibility; but Mr. W—— acted otherwise.

J. Q. had been in the habit of opening the letters of Cosmopolite, and taking out money; also, he was to have paid Mr. W—— and J. C. T.; the latter he did not pay, but the former received a *note* from J. Q. on the account of Cosmopolite, but not to the full amount; giving a receipt for money, and wrote a letter to Cosmopolite, for the " balance," to Virginia, where it was broken open, and remained on a shelf for more than a year; and was taken down carelessly by Cosmopolite, who, observing his name on it, opened it, read it, and put it in his pocket, with the receipt, as he came along.

Mr. W—— denied the " receipt," although he acknowledged the letter; but the names were in his own proper handwriting, so admitted by judges, when compared with a receipt-book.

He demanded the whole from Cosmopolite, saying the note of J. Q. was destroyed, which amounted to about two hundred and eight dollars; the whole was less than three hundred.

Cosmopolite said it was hard to pay it twice, but was willing to submit it to arbitrators, and abide their judgment; to this Mr. W—— assented; he should choose one, Cosmopolite another, and these two should choose a third, a majority of which should be final. The hour being fixed, Cosmopolite started with his, and met that of Mr. W——; and who should it be but the sheriff, prepared to take Cosmopolite to the "tight-house." Thus his situation was of the most gloomy nature; however, two men stepped up and became security for his appearance at court. This gave him time to breathe, and see what next.

The assignees to the estate of J. Q., who had died in the West Indies, offered to acquit Cosmopolite of all demands, if he would let them step into the place of J. Q., and have the transfer in his lieu from those whom it had concerned, (as J. Q. had left a demand on book against Cosmopolite improperly;) and, moreover, would step in between him and Mr. W——, and fight him in the law, giving Cosmopolite a bond of indemnity.

Cosmopolite readily consented; being paid only his expenses, but flung in his trouble; so that in attempting to favor the sick man, he neither gained nor lost, except the plague and censure, as the sick man was paid his full demand.

There is one instrument of writing which hath been paid, but was never delivered up, which, in justice, Cosmopolite should have—as Major Mills, Charles Smith, and Frances Steel, doth know!

Thus Cosmopolite was enabled to clear off with J. C. T., and leave the city in peace; while Mr. W—— was left to have his dispute decided in his own way. But what was the consequence? He was cast, having the cost of court to pay, and only got the balance. After which there was a resurrection of the note of J. Q., which he, Mr. W——, wished Cosmopolite to purchase; and for the refusal, called him all to nought, as a "scoundrel," &c. &c. &c.

Cosmopolite went as far as Boston, where he had a few books, procured him a horse and little wagon, and returned to the south, and so to the Mississippi to his *rib;* and immediately started for Georgia, through the wilderness, without bidding a friend farewell. He visited many counties, and then started for the north. Was pre-warned in dreams, which the sequel proved, at Lynchburg, Virginia. She was taken sick, brought nigh unto death, and detained two years. See her "Journey of Life."

Cosmopolite was defeated in attempting to get a small cabin here, his reputed " riches" not being adequate to surmount it.

He was taken unwell with those spasms, and lay beside a road, and probably would have died, but a doctor came along, and gave him some medicine, which flung the spasms from the nerves into the blood-vessels; and he began to amend from that time.

The Presbyterians were remarkably kind and open in North Carolina. Many of their meeting-houses were at his service, and some of their ministers he formed acquaintance with, who appeared like very pious men, with the spirit of liberality!

Thus, after long struggles, Cosmopolite got through his difficulties, into which others had involved him, after turning every way,* even to parting

---

* Though he thought of paying with a "ramskin," as the saying is—i. e. deliver up all— but Providence wrought the other way, when it came to the last extremity with Mr. W*****.

Cosmopolite sent the money to J. Q. according to agreement, but he gave his note to Mr. W*****, and kept the money, which Mr. W***** accepted on Cosmopolite's account, and gave the receipt for money accordingly!

with his horse and library ; the latter of which he had taken much pains to collect and select, having the small piece of ground left at the Mississippi, on which was the old mill frame, from which he derived no benefit, neither does he expect to, having sent a deed of relinquishment, but received no value.*

Those who are fond of retailing evil reports about absent characters with a degree of rejoicing, are a partaker of evil, inasmuch as they would consider it very hard, ungenerous, and unjust, for one to take half the liberty about them in their absence that they do about others. For the motives cannot be good, nor the spirit savor of righteousness. Therefore, if they profess friendship to the face, they are only base "hypocrites" in heart, from which, may society be delivered!

Dreams may come from the enemy—from the business of the day past—from a disordered body—propensities founded by contamination—from "moral evil"—and from God, through the medium of angels and departed saints, as forewarnings to stir up and prepare the mind for those scenes ahead, as a dispensation of preparation; which many remain ignorant of for the want of due attention, with a heart conformed to the Divine government.

Many people, from a spirit of prejudice founded on jealousy, surmise things about others, which amounts to a reality in their imagination ; and hence assume the liberty to report and circulate it as truth founded upon fact, to the great injury of society, friendship, and the innocent.

The foregoing short history of "eccentric" Cosmopolite, is given for the benefit of all those whom it may concern.

CHAPTER XI.

JUNE 9th, 1813. Leaving Peggy at John M. Walker's, in Buckingham county, Virginia, where she was confined with ———, I spoke in Charlotte county, Mecklinburg, Brunswick, Belfield, and Murfreesborough, down to Edenton, in North Carolina, at which place I was interrupted by a Baptist preacher, who gave me the lie, and brought himself into disrepute. I replied, "There were some good, mistaken men whose hearts were better than their heads."

By Elizabeth I came to the Hickory Ground, and down to Princess-Ann ; and while upon the road I heard "Jefferson's bull-dogs," so called, roaring at one of neighbor George's frigates ; which gave me awful sensations concerning the horrors of war, and the curse the world is under. On my arrival at Norfolk, I saw the smoke of cannon, and the awful scene during the battle of Craney Island.

"God sees not as man sees ; for the race is not to the swift, nor the battle to the strong," which was exemplified in that instance ; the termination being different from every calculation, both of friend and foe.

---

* Roswell V*****, who was disinterested by his influence and interference, saved some little value from the wreck.

I returned by Suffolk, where I found my old friend, Yarborough, had gone to the other world. By Petersburgh to Richmond, where I found my old friend, Stith Mead, still going on in the work of the Lord.

On my arrival in Buckingham, finding Peggy still low in health, and the people unwilling for her removal, as unadvised, I requested a ride in the gig, and the family not suspecting my intentions, we started; and, beyond probability, she endured ten miles before we stopped, as the doctor had advised the " White Sulphur Springs," in Greenbriar. Next day we reached Lynchburgh, where I was requested to preach, but Le Roy Merritt, who had been converted in this place, and came with me from the Lowlands, had been to see his friends, was now on his return, and desired to preach. I felt as if it was his turn, and gave way accordingly. He spoke with life and authority from above, and going to his station in Portsmouth, died in a few days after, with the shouts of " Victory! Victory! Victory!" in his mouth.

" Let me die the death of the righteous, and my last end be like his."
" Mark the perfect man, and behold the upright, for the end of that man is peace."

While in the Lowlands I saw some good times, and revivals of religion; but the drought, the sun, and flies, were dreadful at that time. Many streams were so dried that swine fattened upon their fish, and the want of water and food for cattle were distressing; with the addition of swarms of flies to suck the blood of man and beast.

Hiring a hack we came to the " White Sulphur Springs," in Greenbriar, where I got access to many neighborhoods where I had not been before, being a stranger in those parts. Our expenses were nearly one hundred dollars, but I did not begrudge it, considering the benefit we received from those waters. When on the way, Peggy could hardly bear her weight ten yards, but now was able to ride sixteen miles on horseback to the "Sweet Springs," where I spoke to a large and attentive audience, though the devil reigned in those parts. Lawyer Baker collared me, and threatened to break my neck for preaching; because, he said, I insulted Mrs. ———— ten years before, by saying, hell is moving from beneath to meet her at her coming: and he did it to revenge her cause. But his assertion was false. The ladies, however, took up my cause, and promised me protection. And hence his gambling comrades became ashamed, and he had to hold his peace and let me alone.

By the assistance of Providence we found the way opened to gain Fincastle, and the camp-meeting, near Salem, where I had to apologize for my " lappel coat," single-breasted, which I was reprobated for wearing. The case was this: eighteen months before, I was in distress for a coat, the winter coming on, and had not money to spare to get one. But a man owed me twenty dollars, which he could not pay in ready money; hence I must lose it, being about to leave those parts, unless I would accept a turn to a shop where garments were ready made, being brought over from England. Hence, from my necessity, and the nature of the case, originated the contended coat, the most valuable I ever wore in my life. But I soon gave it away rather than hurt weak minds, and got a sailor's blanket coat to prosecute my journey.

From thence to Blackrod in a wagon, where we had some good times. I spoke to the military in Christianburg, where they gave me a surtout.

I attended a camp-meeting one day and two nights, which appeared like a blank in my life. So I started off twenty miles on foot to my destination.

Having procured me a tackey, and parting with Peggy at the Yellow Springs, in Montgomery county, I started for the west, while she went to the east, with brother and sister Booth, in Brunswick county.

On Walker's creek I saw the greatest preparation for camp-meeting that I ever viewed in my life, being encircled with barracks all round. It was a dreadful rainy time, but from our convenience preaching went on in the tents, and all were accommodated.

I called at a house to feed my horse, where I was recognised, and solicited to stop and preach, which I did, and had a good time. The man of the house turned away circuit preaching, because they held private class-meetings, and so broke up the class.

In Abingdon I spoke three times. Exchanging my poney for another, as she was with foal, which had been kept a secret from me by the seller, I got imposed on again, as the latter had not been corn-fed, and in two days she tired. Hence, I was obliged to exchange for a third, to be able to keep up with my appointments. But this was so rough in his gait, that my state of health would not admit of keeping him. Hence, I exchanged for a fourth, having expended eighty-three dollars. I obtained one worth about forty, having but one eye.

When I started on this journey, I felt to go as far as Nashville;* but any further, a gloom seemed to overspread my contemplation on that subject. I could not tell why; yet when I arrived in West Tennessee, the cause was obvious. The Indians having commenced war, blocked up the way to Louisiana, as many were murdered in that direction.

Putting my work, improved, to press, I sent off my appointments; after which, I commenced my tour through Gallatin, Carthage, Lebanon, where I saw the wife of the "Wild man of the Woods." I strove to obtain his journal; but in that I was disappointed—though they had agreed on certain conditions to let me have it—he died in peace. From Lebanon to Jefferson, Murfreesborough, Columbia on Duck; Ricees' M. H., Franklin; Liberty, near Green Hills; Dixon county, Clarksville, Palmyria, Christian county and Russellville, Kentucky; Robinson C. H., Macminsville, Secotchee valley, Washington, Kingston, Marysville, Seversville, Knoxville, Clinton, Jacksborgh, Claiborne C. H., Rutledge, Rogersville, Greensville, Jonesborough, and Carter C. H., to Wilksborough, and then

---

* In Nashville jail I saw an Indian chief of the Creek nation, named Bob, taken prisoner by Coffee's spies. I asked him why their nation took up the hatchet against the whites, when they were paid for their friendship by the United States.

He replied, that a letter from the Great Father, the King of England, said the time was arrived to take up the hatchet. Then the governor of Pensacola sent for the big Prophet, who said if we did not take up the hatchet, our cattle would become buffalo, and our fowls like wild turkeys, and our hogs would become lizards; and likewise our dogs would become spirits and kill us, because we had whipped them. Which prophecy the governor delivered by an interpreter to runners, who quickly circulated it through the nation. Some believed it, who were credulous in the doctrine of spirits. It was through such a threefold influential source; others believed it, being disaffected to the United States; and a third, to prevent being tomahawked, as there could be no neutral in the war, and hence the commencement of hostilities.

They that observe lying vanities, forsake their own mercies. Four armies are now against them, and destruction appears coming upon them to the uttermost. But vow then who make use of religion to answer their wicked ends thereby!

Huntsville, so to James C emments, where I arrived on Tuesday evening, the 14th of December; intending to proceed immediately to Raleigh, and from thence to Brunswick, where Peggy is. But in this I was disappointed: being taken sick, was confined until Thursday, when the weather set in bad. On Sunday I spoke to several hundreds in the door-yard, and rode fourteen miles on my way; and falling in with a congregation, I spoke at night. Next day it rained, snowed, and hailed, in a distressing manner, so that I could not feel myself justifiable to pursue my journey, however anxious.

There is something peculiar in my detention here,—for I felt to hasten my journey to the utmost, and accomplish my route; but still I was prevented going further at present, though I have accomplished the essence of my visit.

More than a year ago, I dreamed that we were on the shore in the Lowlands; where about twelve o'clock at night the great ocean presented to view before without bounds, and the awful cavalry pursuers were in the rear, and destruction to the uttermost awaited us if we stayed there until day. I saw a batteau, without sails, oars, or rudder, in which I said we must embark as the only alternative, and leave the event to God; and putting in our trunk, for it was present with my papers, and all we had, Peggy stepped in, and as I shoved it off stepped in myself; the motion of which, with the wind and tide, took us out of sight of land before day. A porpoise rose and struck the gunwale of the boat, and broke in a part, which admitted the waves to dash in, and the boat began to fill. I said, "We are lost—there is no hope, but to commit ourselves to God, and hang our souls upon Him!"

Just then a fine large ship presented to view, and was immediately alongside; and seeing our danger, flung us a rope, to which we fastened the trunk, and so were drawn into the ship, as the boat just then filled and went down! There were three ladies in the cabin, who served us with a dish of warm coffee or tea; for we were wet and very much chilled. I could eat but little, from the gratitude to the great Disposer of all events for our late deliverance from the danger of the sea, and our dreadful pursuers. I asked the captain where he was from, and bound to? He said, "From Ireland—have been to the West Indies—am sailing to Jerusalem." While reflecting on the subject, and the probability that my pursuers would not hear of me for years, if ever, I awaked, all in a flood of tears! What it means, I know not; time must unfold it!

· When on my return from Europe, from an unaccountable impulse of mind I frequently said, I awfully feared that all was not right at the Mississippi; as a brother and sister-in-law had gone to that territory about the time we left America.

In Ireland, one day a person observed to me her dream, which left a tremor of horror on her mind—that I had wings, and could roam at pleasure where I pleased; at length I lit down on a certain place, and sunk into the mire—and the more I strove to get out, the deeper I sunk down in the black mire; when she waked up with a degree of horror.

Those persons in M. T. separated, by grievously sinning against the tender mercies of the Lord. Leaving Peggy in Virginia, I arrived at Claiborne county, where he had begun a mill on ground which was not his own, and got involved in debt, which caused both parties, viz. the owners of the ground and him, to desire me to act as a mediator between them; which I did, and writings were passed accordingly.

But alas! this was the beginning of sorrows to me; and proved a school, arising from a combination of circumstances, which I shall never forget.

I offered all I had, in a few days after, for a release, but in vain—they proved like blood-suckers, which stuck close to the skin. Hence I was compelled to purchase a part of the land and improvements; which involved me in debt head and ears, of several thousand dollars, which took me some time to extricate myself! But which was accomplished by perseverance, through the providence of God.

The "Rights of Man," fifth edition, being finished, I visited Fayetteville, Wilmington, Kingston, Georgetown, and Charleston; where the woman lived at the "Planter's Hotel," who had been instrumental in saving me from the hand of Baker—here I put up gratis.

I visited Sumpterville, Statesborough, Columbia, Chesterfield, Wadesborough, and several adjacent counties, to Moore; and Raleigh, Smithfield, Kingston to Newbern, and Washington; so by the intermediate places to Tarborough, and also to Nash C. H., Louisville, Williamsborough, Granville, Hillsborough, to Terswell and Person, to Warrington and Brunswick—from whence we took our departure to Petersburg, Richmond, Fredericksburg, Alexandria, Washington to Baltimore; and on the way I met Jesse Lee, who hailed me in the stage. I once saw him at a camp-meeting in Georgia—we took a walk * * * * * * *

He has been Chaplain to Congress longer than any one individual since the "True American Federal Government" was formed. I spent some time with him at Washington—he gave up his appointment for Cosmopolite in the "Big House." One night Cosmopolite, while sleeping in the room with him, dreamed, that a rat came out of the dark, and fastened on his finger, and began to suck his blood, which he, in endeavoring to shake off, had like to have sprung out of bed. Next day there came a swindler to Cosmopolite, and ingeniously duped him out of thirty-eight dollars, which he desired never to reimburse. This also was a school, and taught him the lesson—" He that will be *surety* for a stranger shall smart for it."

Mr. F. A. is sick, and perhaps is about to end his long and arduous labor. What then? * * * * * * * *

Cosmopolite heard N . . . . S . . . . . . preach from, "The Lord knoweth how to deliver the godly out of temptation, and to reserve the unjust unto the day of judgment to be punished." The Lord knoweth —not is able or willing—but *knoweth how*, i. e. the *best* way to deliver, &c.; and to reserve the unjust unto the day of judgment—not the general judgment, but some *particular* judgment in *this* world: adding, those who will not be subject to rule and order, put themselves out of the power of the magistrate, for he cannot follow them through all their intricate windings; of course they surrender themselves into the hand of God only— and hence we may expect to see some particular judgment befall them, as a just dispensation, and make a striking example of them as a warning to others!

From Baltimore to Philadelphia, and so to New York, where he saw J . . . . . M . . . . . ., who professes himself to be an "alien enemy" —who hath caused (more) uneasiness in the . . . . society, and disturbance (than Cosmopolite hath done on these shores this eighteen years*) though accountable to none in a moral or ecclesiastical point of view, for his conduct on these shores; though a man of "order," yet he has been generously used in various senses in this city; but his life shows the liberty in his country, as published by himself. However, Americans as "alien friends" there in time of peace, are used worse than "alien enemies" are here in time of war; which Cosmopolite doth know.

There Cosmopolite, with his *rib*, had to appear at the customhouse, by summons; and tell his age, parentage, birth-place, occupation, city, street, number of the house, and name of the family where he stayed before embarking, ship's name, &c., &c., &c., complexion, height, flesh-marks, &c., &c., all the answers recorded, and his name he had to sign to his testimony. This examination they passed through three times at the customhouse, then at the Mayor's Office, and also at the Alien Office; then he could not stay without the king's license, on which were certified his lodging, &c., which must not be removed even to the next door without permission, under a penalty; and the family who received him to fifty pounds fine. Moreover, he must not exceed eleven miles distance, nor preach without license from the sessions, which could not be obtained without, first, the oath of allegiance; second, to support that particular form of government; third, against Popery, or be subject to pay a fine of twenty pounds; and those who suffered meetings in their houses without a license from the Bishop's court, were subject to twenty pounds fine; and each of those who attended, to pay five shillings.

Render unto Cæsar the things that are Cæsar's, and unto God the things that are God's. For the devil ought to have his due, and God requires no more; and every thing should have justice done to it!

And to misrepresent any thing designedly, with an intention to deceive, to injure another, and thereby answer our own designs, is a "moral evil" of the deepest dye. And while the Vicegerent governs the world in righteousness, judgment must and will be given in favor of the injured. Therefore vice must not triumph over virtue; and though the "wicked may flourish like the green bay tree" for a season, the day of retribution will come at last. Consequently, all persons whose actions flow from impure and unjustifiable motives, will have only a curse and bitterness, as a just entailment at last, as the final issue of their conduct!

But innocence, uprightness, and integrity of heart, founded upon virtuous and justifiable principles, as a responsible agent to the Supreme Governor of the world, will meet his approbation; who will carry them through safely. However severe their trials and conflicts may be for a season, salvation will come at last.

Hence the propriety of "faith in God," and a "hope" in his providential hand! Likewise charity or love, which is the spirit of the gospel of Christ, should be the moving spring of all our actions, in order that we may glorify him in all our ways, by a suitable disposition of heart fitted to his government, which requires a worship in spirit and in truth, with the understanding!

---

* The example of Cosmopolite, it had been urged, would prove pernicious: but where has the effect been produced yet? Moreover the "Defence of Methodism" states the distinction between "Accidental and Moral Evil;" and shows the absurdity of saying "most good or evil," &c.—"more evil than good."

"Natural law," "moral law," and the "rule of practice," originated from the same Author.

Natural law embraces unalienable rights, which are founded upon innate principles, as life, liberty, and the pursuit of happiness, &c., from which equality originates "natural justice." Agreeable to such natural justice is "moral obligation"—"love the Lord with all thy heart, and thy neighbor (not less or more, but) as thyself,"—"and as ye would that others should do to you, do ye even so to them, for this is the law and the prophets"—or what the law of Moses, and the spirit of the prophets, and the example of Jesus Christ enjoined. "Therefore, with what judgment ye judge, ye shall be judged," and "with what measure you mete, it shall be measured to you again."

The just retributions of divine Providence have been observable in social bodies, as well as in personal and individual cases. Haman and Mordecai exemplify an instance—"he that will dig a pit for another, shall fall into it himself."

CHAPTER XII.

CONCLUSION.

The first fifteen years of my life were as lost, not being devoted to God: though more sober and steady than most at that age, which was remarked by many.

When in my sixteenth year, I became acquainted with the comforts of religion, which hath kept me out of many a hurtful snare. About eighteen I commenced my itinerant career, which is more than eighteen years since. Various are the scenes through which I have been preserved since, by land and water, in those different climes where my lot hath been cast, arising from the different customs, interests, and the prejudice of education. There is a family likeness, so there may be a family temper, and likewise a family education. Hence the various modes give rise to various prejudices; and those that predominate will infest and taint whole societies or neighborhoods, whose influence they control.

Little minds are capable of little things; and hence to see an exaltation, is apt to produce a jealousy, which when admitted begets envy: and friendship and respect degenerate into hatred, malice, and ill-will.

Every person supposes himself to be in the middle of the world, and his way to be the most right, as a criterion, and the summit of perfection. A difference of course to be an error, which should be cured. Hence he bears testimony against it with all the zeal, acrimony, and bitter censoriousness imaginable. Why? Because it varies from his views; without allowing others the same liberty that he takes, to think, and judge, and act for themselves; but all are in error who do not come to his rule, founded upon bigotry and the prejudice of education. For, the most ignorant are generally the most rude, saucy, impertinent and positive in their assertions: not knowing how to state a proposition, nor draw a right conclusion; but think that assertion is argument, and so take it for granted that it proves the point.

Those persons who have sprung out of the ashes, and have been raised in the corner, when they get into office and power, become the most important, self-exalted, imperious, and tyrannical of any persons whatever, and domineer with a vengeance over those that come within their power and displeasure,* from which, good Lord deliver the earth !†

I perceive all things below the sun to be of a fleeting nature—nothing permanent but divinity and immortality! And to feel the love of the former, brightens up the prospects of the latter; and inspires the heart with hope beyond this life !

I have not an acre of ground I call my own upon earth, and but a small pittance of this world's goods in any shape or form. But I am without house or home of my own, and but very few on whose friendship to depend.

The last seven years of my life have been a scene of trials, but they have been a school. During this time, I have not received from other people in my travels, what would bear one half of my necessary expenses, and yet there is no time nor place in Europe or America, that any person can point out, when or where I asked for a " contribution," for " myself," either directly or indirectly—though I have taken a few, made by other people, in some cases of extreme necessity, or to prevent doing harm by hurting the feelings of some well wishers, in the course of those eighteen years; but have by far declined the bigger part—perhaps ten to one.‡

The profits of my books, I derived no real advantage from, before I went to Europe the last time; and by the Journal I sunk about one thousand dollars, by engaging too many to meeting-houses, before the work was done; at one of which there happened to lack twenty-five of eight hundred; and hence twenty-five dollars in cash was demanded, and paid from other publications; so that I had but about ten dollars, when I embarked for Europe.

But hitherto the Lord hath helped and brought me through, and gently cleared my way. I feel a sweet inward peace of mind—a blessing I have never lost since I saw Calvin Wooster. What is before me I know not—trials I expect ever await me, while upon the journey of life on these mortal shores; but the anticipation of a better and happier world, attracts my mind to surmount every obstacle by " faith in Jesus," to gain that bright abode; and strive by every possible means to regenerate the earth by the knowledge of God; that " moral evil" may be expelled the world, the kingdom of Christ become general, and rule over all.

I verily believe these are the last days of troublesome times; and will continue to grow worse and worse, and rise higher and higher, until after the " fall of Babylon," which I expect cannot be far off—and the " beast and

---

* This is observable in petty understrappers ********* as well as in the black overseers in the West-Indies.

† The narrow contracted tyrant—condemned such a variety of heights—thought to be " uniform" would be for the best—and choosing his own height for the model, had an " Iron bestend" erected for the criterion—and all the longer must be " cut off" and those that were shorter must be stretched—which neither nature nor grace admit.

‡ I have now and then rode up to a house, and asked for a bit of bread and some few things of the like necessity, &c.

false prophet" be taken away; then the divine government will be acknowledged—natural justice attended to—moral obligation performed in the golden rule of practice, as enjoined by the Vicegerent of the world!

Whoever will read the xxviii. of Deut., and compare it with the history of the Jews, and our Lord's prediction with Josephus, must be at least rationally convinced of the doctrine of providence in nature and grace. And whosoever is convinced, and looks at the "signs" may discern the "times;" "for the light of the moon is becoming as the light of the sun," when compared with the last centuries, and "the light of the sun shall become seven fold, as the light of seven days," saith the inspiration of the Almighty. Then "the house of the Lord shall be established in the top of the mountain, and exalted above the hills,"—"and all nations shall flow unto it;" then "the wolf and the lamb shall dwell together," and the "nations learn war no more," for "the name of the Lord alone shall be exalted in that day," and natural evil will be expelled the world, and the earth restored to its paradisaical state "until the thousand years be ended;" whether a common thousand, prophetic or apostolic, when Christ shall reign on earth and bring his saints with him. But after the loosing of Satan, then there will be a falling away, and shortly will come the general judgment, "moral evil" having contaminated the earth *again*. And hence it is inconsistent with the nature and government of the Almighty to continue the world in being any longer: then we arrive at the "consummation" of all things.

The world is fitted to man's body, but not to the mind; the love of God is the only principle that can satisfy the mind, and make him happy. Man is ever aspiring for new and greater things. Now this principle is not wrong, being implanted by the Author of nature as an inherent principle that is innate. The evil consists in the pursuit of improper objects, objects that can never satisfy, and so become idolaters, to the neglecting the Author of all good, the privation of which is misery, as he is the only fountain of perfect and lasting happiness.

This world is man's beginning place, like a state of embryo, he being a candidate for future happiness; hence the other world is his place of destination. For "moral evil" brought "natural evil" into the world. Man is degenerate; hence the necessity of "regeneration" by the divine Spirit, called the "new birth." "The kingdom of heaven was prepared for man," not from all eternity, but "from the foundation of the world;" whereas "the lake of fire and brimstone" was never made for man, but was "prepared for the devil and his angels."

The "pleasure" of the Lord was the moving cause of "creation;" "love" was the moving cause of "redemption;" and "faith" is the instrumental cause of "salvation." But "sin," man's own act, is the cause of his "damnation."

Therefore the necessity of seeking the Lord by faith, to find that knowledge of him which will give an evidence of pardon, and bring peace to the mind.

The "divisions" of the human family into "nations," has its advantages, to cause a balance of power, and a refuge for the oppressed people.

The variety of "denominations" also in those nations have an advantage, that no one should have the pre-eminence to domineer over others in matters of "conscience" there being so little real piety in the world

Union of form and ceremony is not religion in a moral point of view, for by it, with the addition of power, the world hath been imposed upon, and taken the shell for the kernel in their awful, delusive ignorance, which hath driven men to deism and infidelity, as common sense began to wake up and see the imposition,—and doubtless will continue so to do more and more. Hence the propriety of these words, "When the Son of man cometh, shall he find faith on the earth?"

But the union of heart in the spirit of the gospel of Christ, is a necessary thing to promote peace, and convince the world of the reality of the religion of Jesus being founded in divinity, that they may embrace it by faith and "know" its blessed enjoyments.

Let brotherly love continue, for where bitter contention is, is every evil work; and instead of judging and striving for a party, and using the devil's tools with which to do the Almighty's work, strive to excel in love; evidencing your "faith in Christ by works," and bringing forth those fruits of Christianity that will be the evidence on which will turn your eternal "justification" forever, in the day of final retribution.

The glory of God should be our object, the will of God our law; his spirit our guide, and the Bible our rule, that Heaven may be our end. Hence we must "watch and pray," endure to the end to receive the "crown of life," where is pleasure without pain, for evermore.

Then the storms of life are forever over, and this journey is drawn to a close, where there is glory, and honor, praise, power, and majesty, might, and dominion forever ascribed to God and the Lamb. O! this pleasing anticipation of a future world, the hope beyond the grave!

After our arrival in New York, a combination of circumstances conspired together, whereby I was enabled to put my works to press, through the assistance of some friends, whose friendship I required. But as many of the books were sold at cost, and considerable expense attended the transportation and circulation of them, there was very little if any nett gain or profits attending the same, without counting the great attention, care, &c., attending it; if we except the pleasure and benefit of mankind, which were my principal objects in their circulation; all of which was accomplished in about seven months, and discharged.

Frequently did I attend meetings at the Asbury meeting-house, belonging to the Africans or people of color, and some other places; and departed to New Haven, where we spent a few days. It was the Fourth of July, and many were celebrating the time of independence, but in a way neither to the glory of God, nor the honor of our country; but rather savored of a spirit of ingratitude, arising from a state of insensibility of how great and glorious our privileges are, when contrasted with other nations, and what has been before. So I made some remarks upon the sin of ingratitude, and its concomitant evils prospectively, on the occasion. Thence to North Guilford and Middletown, where I found a wagon going to Hebron, having held a number of meetings by the way.

Here I received a note from N. D., of N. L., containing the following queries: 1st. Why less time in private devotion now than formerly? 2d. Whether the time spent in writing would not be better spent in private prayer? 3d. Why more conversant with my friends?

These questions reminded me of a circumstance of several vessels which were loaded with live stock, cattle, sheep, hogs, geese, &c., when several foreign vessels were off at a distance. Those things caused me to think so loud that I spoke out: "This looks like fulfilling the scripture—'If thine enemy hunger, feed him.'" "Yes," replied a bystander, "the Connecticut people are very pious in *that* respect." But books are next akin to preaching, and may benefit society when I am no more; and duties never clash.

Getting equipped with a horse and small light wagon, I proceeded to Coventry, and found my aged father, one sister and two nephews well. I stayed a few days, and visited a number of adjacent places, and had some tender times. But my mind was uneasy, and some hours of sleep departed from me when I reflected upon the state of the country, and the spirit of the times.

When in Hartford city I felt as if bewildered, and scarce knew which way to go; I left the beast to start which way he chose, feeling no inclination to go anywhere in particular. Thus in a slow walk we started and took the road west, towards the state of New York, about twenty miles, when I met an old man. I asked him if anybody in the neighborhood loved God. He mentioned a family, and escorted me to the house, where two persons lived, who were my former acquaintance when they were single. Stayed all night, had two meetings, and went to Wensted, where I was invited by John Sweet, an acquaintance whom I fell in with by the way. Had two meetings, and went to Lenox and Pittsfield, and saw some of my old acquaintance and spiritual children whom I had not seen for fifteen years. Held several meetings, and went to Bennington and spoke once. Then to Cambridge, where I had formerly travelled, but felt not free to call on any of my old acquaintance; nor have I felt free to do it intentionally where I formerly travelled the circuits, unless it so happened just in my way of travelling.

Spent about a week with Peggy's sister and brother-in-law; held several meetings, met some opposition with an A-LL-part minister, and departed to Saratoga and Ballstown springs, and held about fifty meetings in the adjacent country towns. Thence went to Stillwater and Waterford; so to Lansingburg and Troy, where Chichester proclaimed war against me before I came, assigning as the reason, "ORDER!" But they who are not conformed to moral order in the divine government, will not be able to stand in that day when all hearts shall be disclosed!

Thence to New York, where the countenances of the people were an index to the mind, during the awful suspense of the engagements at Baltimore and Plattsburgh; and also it was visible who were the friends of the country and felt interested, and those who were not; and a day or two days after, when accounts came from those two places that they had not fallen, the scene was equally reversed.*

Thence to Philadelphia, where I spent about a month. Sold my travelling convenience, and went by water in a steam-boat to New-Castle, in Delaware. Saw an old house one hundred and twenty-seven years old: held one meeting, and took stage to Smyrna; spoke once. Then to Dover, and found a distant people. Spoke four times; disturbed twice by something coming into my room in the night. Spoke to it, got no reply; interrogated the family, got no satisfaction, only found others had been dis-

---

* The countenance being an index to the mind.

turbed there before. Thence to Frederica; spoke three times, and went to Milford; where I spoke several times, and went to Georgetown; and spoke twice. So on to Daggsborough, and spoke in a church of England meeting-house, and then to Martinsville, and held two meetings. From thence to Poplartown, in Maryland; and Snow-Hill, where I spoke six times, and departed to Havertown, and from thence to Drummingtown, in Virginia. Thence I returned by Downing-Chapel, and Newtown to Snow-Hill; thence to Salisbury; and so to Cambridge, where the snow and cold overtook me. During this journey so far, I had many precious times—at the Trap, in particular, and in Eastown and Centreville, and at Chestertown, and at the head of Chester. I then returned to Smyrna, and visited its vicinity.

At the head of Sassefras, I saw Margaret Keen, whom I saw two years before in Baltimore; and who had accurately dreamed of Bonaparte's disasters, &c. &c., which had made considerable impression upon my mind. Thus, after about thirty days, I returned to Philadelphia, where I met my companion from New York, where I had left her; having travelled about five hundred miles, and held upwards of sixty meetings.

As neither of us had been in those northern latitudes at this inclement season of the year, having been seasoned to a warm climate, prudence dictated the propriety of a proper line of conduct. Having some writing to do, it was proper to attend to it; and now appeared the time. But a proper place was hard to find, where we might be retired.

Once, seemingly we had thousands of friends; but alas, a true friend is hard to find!—one who is not like the pine tree, rotten at the heart. Man is not to be trusted, unless fear, interest, or the grace of God, shall influence him! For mankind in general, are led like an animal, by inclination for the time being, without exercising judgment or reason, which should be founded in a virtuous principle! There is none but God who can be depended upon as certain; for he never forsakes us, unless we first forsake him! though some talk to the contrary, saying, David was left to do so and so, &c.

Where are my many friends now? Zion is gone into captivity; her harps are hung upon the willows; but she will yet come out of the wilderness of this world, leaning upon her beloved, terrible as an army with banners!

When travelling north and south, the difference of the country, the prejudice of the people, in their different modes of raising, both among the religious, and those who do not profess, taking the Potomac for the dividing ground, makes me think of the "ten pieces" of garment that Ahijah gave to Jeroboam; which prejudice had begun in the time of Saul, the first king in Israel, and the house of David!

When Cosmopolite was invited to preach in Congress-Hall, before the House, he spoke from these words: "Righteousness exalteth a nation; but sin is a shame to any people." He went down to the Navy-yard, and stayd at the house of James Friend. During the night he dreamed, and thought that he was in the gallery of the Capitol, which was much crowded, and the House was in session. A little, sharp-looking man came to the top of the stairs, and winked and beckoned to me, as if in great agitation; and then turned and went out. I thought I made my way through the crowd, and got out of the door, where I found a military guard around the house. Getting through them, I started towards the Navy-yard, when I saw the house arise, and fall into two parts, and burst into ten thousand atoms, and the whole was enveloped in a column of smother and smoke, which shock waked me up! I told James Friend in the morning my curious dream. Fifteen months after, as I was coming from Virginia, I called at his house; he reminded me of the dream, adding, that he had never been in the house since, without thinking of it, and feeling a degree of horror! ☞ Several months after this, when I heard of Ross and Cockburn being at Washington, I could measurably interpret my dream.

There was more blood spilt in the Carolinas, between the inhabitants, during the former struggle, than between the regular armies. There is an awful gloom gathering fast, and clouds hang over a guilty land. Wars are neither less nor more than the sword and scourge of God; not only for a nation, but as individuals also; and there are two classes who feel it heaviest here: the first is those who are of no service to God or man—viz. those who are a nuisance to society, not pursuing any useful, innocent or lawful calling, to gain a subsistence; but have corrupted society by the influence of their example, and violating the divine law, by profane cursing, swearing, lying, drinking, whoring, and lounging about the streets. This filth is in a great measure drained from our towns, and gone to the slaughter-house. The other is the mercantile class, who, through the unparalleled space of peace and prosperity, were led off by the temptation of riches and grandeur, whereby they forgot God: hence the influence of their example, to the injury of society, and the dishonor of God's government. Therefore it was necessary that those avenues of wealth should be shut up; and hence the scourge from God. Consequently we should take warning that we may be able to stand; and of course must conduct ourselves accordingly, in the duty of love to God and our neighbor; and attend to our Saviour's golden rule of practice, "As ye would that others should do to you, do ye even so to them."

After inquiring some time, I found a place in a Quaker family, where we obtained a room. Attended some of their meetings; had some very comfortable feelings while sitting in silence with them; heard some who spoke feelingly, and to satisfaction; among whom was Richard Jordan. His track I was much upon in Ireland, but never saw him until in this city: visited his house, and had good satisfaction. Peter's call was to the Jews; Paul's to the Gentiles: so there are different gifts and calls in our day, and all by the same Spirit.

Dorothy Ripley, an English woman, who hath crossed the ocean five times, is now in this city. She belongs to no religious society; but is rather upon the Quaker order. She was very kind to me, when going on my last tour to Europe. She has travelled most of the states of the Union; and also in Ireland, as well as her native country. There has been much opposition to her, from those who may be called religious bigots, who are of narrow, contracted minds; for little minds are only capable of little things. But she hath brunted the storm, and lived down much that was designed to block up her path, and make the way bitter; but God hath been with her. How many she hath been a blessing to, the day of eternity must disclose!

Theophilus R. Gates; the influence of his example is very impressive on many minds. He travels on foot, inculcating the necessity of innocency, and purity of heart, flowing from love to God and man. He belongs to no particular society, but considers that to be bigoted to a party is to have or subscribe to, and constitute one of the number of the beast.

How many more God may stir up to go the same way, I know not; but though many have prophesied of the mischief that would arise from the influence and example of Cosmopolite; yet those are not "Dowites," neither is "Dowism" planted, in a spherical point of view. But

> "Let talkers talk, stick thou to what is best!
> To think of pleasing all, is all a jest!"

Hence, O! ye bigots of

> "Different sects, who all declare,
> Lo! here is Christ, and Christ is there!
> Your strongest proofs divinely give;
> And show us where the Christians live!
> Your claim, alas! you cannot prove!
> Ye want the genuine mark of love!

The news of peace salutes our ears, and reverberates through the land: but many appear to be intoxicated with the prospects; as though the bitterness was past. However, it may be that many ere long may find that the struggle between the powers of darkness and light is not over: time must disclose it. May God have mercy on the human family, prosper Zion, and help the Pilgrims through this thorny maze to the peaceful shores, where the wicked shall cease from troubling, and the weary shall be at rest!

I saw two chairs made out of the elm tree under which William Penn held his treaty with the Indians, when treating with them for the ground of Pennsylvania, and where the city of Philadelphia now stands—not considering the mere discovery and donation of a king a sufficient title, though done as the reward of merit, for his father's services to the public.

While the New Englanders were at war with the natives, it is said to be a fact that there was no war between Penn's colony and the Indians, all the days of Penn!*

---

* It is said that a man was employed to a' end the king's fire, and keep it well perfumed, while Penn was waiting to have the accounts regularly and carefully made out and delivered, which contained the amount of arrears for his father's services—which perfume was very expensive. His majesty being present, was invited by Penn to visit him, and he would honor him with one equally costly; which invitation being accepted, Penn put the obligations into the fire—doubtless as a testimony against war. The king afterwards sent for Penn, and made him a donation of the grant of Pennsylvania.

* 102, *New Street, Dublin, 9th of 5th mo.*, 1813.

Dear Lorenzo—

This day thy very acceptable letter of March 19th came to hand, and afforded us particular satisfaction. It was about this time two years when we received the last letter from thee, and the only one since our return from England. I am now established in more extensive and profitable practice than I ever had before—indeed I think the last year exceeded any two former ones since my first commencing as physician, and I must acknowledge that I think Divine Providence made use of thee, in a particular manner, as an instrument to bring about this, to me unexpected, event. For thy persuading me to go at that time with thee to England, opened the way for my going to settle when I did at Macclesfield, where I willingly resumed my medical practice, after having striven for about seven years earnestly to decline it. My last year's business amounted, I think, to near 700*l.*, which with former years' increasing prosperity has enabled me to give some hundreds away to assist others in their distresses, and at present to have a few hundreds at my command. for the use of myself and others. But whatever I may have, either now or in future, I consider not as my own, but as a

However much these people called Quakers, are derided for ——— ———, the Protestant Christian world is indebted to them, as the means, for many of the blessings, both civil and religious, which we now enjoy under God.

stewardship put into my hands by the great and good Master, and to be unreservedly devoted to his service in whatever way and manner he may seem clearly to point out. If professors of religion would in general consider themselves only as stewards of what they possess, I think it might then be said with truth, as it was at the time of the first promulgation of the gospel, that no man counted any thing he had his own, and no member of the church felt any wants.

If any thing has gathered with me it has been providential, and not by my own seeking: by which means it is not a burden to me, as I once felt some to be.

However easy and prosperous in outward matters I seem to be, yet I think it would be far more agreeable to me to be in America, travelling along with thee—even encountering some difficulties. But this gratification seems hitherto forbidden me; and I apprehend that I shall have to abide the great thunder-storm, which I fear ere long will shake and agitate these hitherto highly favored countries. I think it will take place much sooner than most people apprehend, and in a time and manner somewhat sudden and unexpected. I believe it will try the foundations of hundreds of thousands, and the truly upright, and those free from all idolatry, be alone preserved safely through it. I suppose I shall be favored to know of its approach, and a place of safe and quiet retirement be afforded to me during its continuance. I am not afraid of my opinion being known, as I am clear of all political spirit and parties.

I heard that thou hadst thoughts of going to the West-Indies, and from thy long silence I had fears that thou hadst gone thither, and sunk under the unwholesomeness of the climate. But now I have a hope of seeing thee once more in this wilderness; for if thou art favored to visit England after her conflict is over, I have no doubt at present but that I may then meet thee there, and I hope much to our mutual satisfaction.

Thy true friend,
P. JOHNSON.

The following is the substance of a poem which I wrote down the 24th of February, two days before Napoleon left Elba for France. The first verse, for reasons, I omit. I was then under restraints on account of singularities of various sorts. By the beast and false prophet I designated Napoleon and Mahomet.—P. J.

N B. The second beast of the 13th, seems the false prophet of the 19th chapter.

  Verse 2. I sing of a glorious day near a-coming—
    The kingdom of heaven set up amongst men—
   The servants of God to his standard a-running,
    As sheep when their shepherd calls into the pen.
   The Beast and False Prophet shall first be a-reigning,
    And horrible carnage 'mongst Christians will make ;
   The servants of Jesus in conflicts engaging,
    A glorious warfare most valiantly waging,
    Their lives laying down for their Great Master's sake ;
   Their blood not these monsters' deep malice assuaging,
      Till God's blessed day in the morning.

   These tyrants alive being cast into fire,
    As shown to the Lord's highly favored friend ;
   Their armies destroy'd in God's terrible ire :
    The world's great wickedness come to its end—
   Then Satan fast bound and most firmly chained,
    Is in the abyss for a thousand years fix'd,
   A seal set upon it, he horribly pained,
   His blasphemous rage by his torments untamed.
    The cup of his punishment here is unmix'd.
   But God's righteous judgments can never be blamed—
      For he is the Lord from the morning

   The Serpent no more poor weak mortals deceiving,
    They all shall acknowledge God's heavenly law :
   His righteous commands with obedience receiving,
    The saints shall promulge without error or flaw.

Marriage, for example, was considered an ecclesiastical subject—hence no marriage, unless the ceremony was performed by a priest—otherwise, the children illegitimate of course!

The bold, firm and patient stand, which these people made with perseverance, was what broke the charm—and obtained the act of Parliament in their favor on that subject. Thank God! there never has been a spiritual court in the United States.

Also the "Act of Toleration," under King William, was another effect from the conduct of this people. Likewise the "equal rights of conscience," in our form of government, is another effect, growing out of Penn's policy for the government of his colony; requiring no particular test as a qualification to office, only a general test, viz., the belief in one God, with future reward and punishment.

Thus the lesson *he* learnt from the persecution in his time; so a little "leaven leaveneth the whole lump." May it go on throughout the world, till priestcraft and tyranny shall fall, and the nations learn war no more.

I took stage for Mellville, and arrived between seven and eight o'clock at night. Word flew over town, and soon the school-house was filled; I spoke there, and next day at Buddville. Thence to Elizabeth Port quarterly meeting, where I spoke twice, and thence to Dennis's creek meeting-house. Being disappointed of a conveyance, I went on foot; found a wagon, and so got on to Cold Spring meeting-house. Thence to Cape May courthouse, and so walked to brother Moore's. Brother Fidler carried me to Big Egg Harbor Baptist meeting-house; so to Tuck-

---

These servants, raised up by their Great Master's power,
  Shall sit upon thrones with Messiah to reign:
'Tis now of God's kingdom the glorious hour,
His blessings come down in a plentiful shower,
  There now is no suffering, sorrow, nor pain;
But Jesus's presence their heavenly dower—
      For he is the Star of the morning.

This glorious day of a thousand years' standing,
  All death shall abolish to Jesus's friends;
They rule o'er the nations with sceptres commanding,
  Their Master now makes them abundant amends.
The wolf and the lamb they shall lay down together,
  The calf and the lion in harmony meet,
The birds of the air—of all sorts of feather—
At springs of the land, both the upper and nether,
  Together shall play, and in innocence breed;
An infant shall lead the wild beasts in a tether:
      'Tis day with the sons of the morning.

But how can I sing of these wondrous matters—
  In Babylon's bastile a prisoner fast?—
My bonds are made stronger—the devil bespatters
  My soundness of mind from the first to the last.
Poor David* from home and from friends now is banished,
  As formerly happened in Saul's cruel day;
All comforts domestic entirely vanished,
The hillocks of cheerfulness thoroughly planished.
  The devil triumphant now carries the sway.
But God's loved servant, although now astonished,
      Will yet see a glorious morning.

* David means a beloved one.

ahoe and May's Landing. Then Weymouth, Fairfield Presbyterian meeting-house, Bridgetown, Penn's Neck, Salem, Sharptown, and Woodbridge, so back to Philadelphia—having been gone seventeen days, held thirty meetings, and travelled about three hundred miles.

In going to the east, Peggy was taken seriously ill. We were detained about a month in New York: Thence we sailed with Captain Howard to New London, who generously gave our passage, as did Dr. Brush his bill at New York.

Held a number of meetings, then sailed to Norwich, and spoke in the Baptist meeting-house. I hired a wagon, and came to Coventry; found my father well. I left Peggy, and visited Hebron, Stonington, (where George's ship Nimrod killed two horses, one hog, and a goose,) and Newport, Rhode Island.

My constitution is so broken, and nervous system worn down, that let me put on what resolution I may, I am necessitated to sit down every little while to rest, if I attempt to walk and go on foot.

After speaking several times in a large meeting-house with a steeple and bell, occupied by brother Webb, and where he taught school, I spoke in Bristol, where I had been near twenty years before, in the beginning of my itinerancy, and departed to New Bedford, where I had been about eight years before. I spoke several times. Designed for the Vineyard, and attempted to sail for New York; in both I was disappointed, so I returned by land. One offered a horse, another a chaise, and a third attended me to Providence, where I saw a vessel, and found two boxes of books on board. I disposed of them in the best manner I could, and after attending several meetings, and experiencing some kindness from whence I had no ground to expect it, and in other cases it turned out the reverse, I returned to Coventry. I made preparation to leave my Peggy for some time, and departed to New Haven, sailed in the dreadful gale to New York, came to Philadelphia, and visited Baltimore. I spoke in the second African meeting-house, and the one formerly occupied by old father Otterbine.

Friday, 22d September, 1815. I took stage for Carlisle; the wheel came off, and we upset; but, thanks be to God, none were materially injured. I quit the stage, and walked several miles through the mud—spoke several times—made remittance to my printer and bookbinder—assisted ten miles with a horse.

Monday, 25th. I spoke in the Dutch "United Brethren" meeting-house, near the big spring, to a simple-hearted people.

I found my father to be entitled to a tract of crown land, for service—probably will be cheated out of it, as many others are of their just rights—and as one day I myself may be also: but what is amiss here, must be rectified hereafter.

Tuesday, 26th. I rode on the coupling tongue of the wagon—came to Shippensburg—feeble in body—faith revives, that the providence of God will attend and bar my way upon this journey. But a few months will turn up something—I know not what. Things cannot continue as they are. May I be prepared for all events!

I spoke in the Methodist meeting-house—well-behaved—a few dollars to assist me on the way—the stage was full, and could not take me—Providence provided—a man brought me a horse for his brother to return

'ashington. Thus I was accommodated two hun-
ountains, while many were hurt by the upsetting
ay, about this time.
rode twenty-four miles to Kines—spoke to a few
ay to Bedford, and spoke in the courthouse.
a minister wanted his elders to agree with bonds
or life, whether he should preach or not, and killed
prevent it. Another, who was a magistrate, com-
and after sentence, asked him what he thought of
1, "I know I *have* had religion, and shall of course
can prove by the articles of our church."
iirty-five miles, and next day came to Greensburg—
told me when, &c., he became religious. Those
I cast on the water, and found many days hence;
repeatedly happen, and are a comfort to my poor
p my head above the billows.
t. I spoke three times—good attention.
to Pittsburgh—stayed about a week—spoke a dozen
ided more than could get into the house—appears a
it. Here are some of my old friends from Hiber-
was received hospitably when on my former visit
anger in a strange land. Among these are the
es.
rt Duquesne, then Fort Pitt, from the great minister
ious in the new world; and by nature, combined
be one of the greatest manufacturing towns in
seven or eight glass-works in this neighborhood,
places of worship. The turnpike-road is in a fair
d the steamboats will accommodate the west.
in body. Hence, I call it well, though threats of
the spasms, with which I am frequently attacked;
quently interrupts my sleep, and tends to weaken
s, also, which are painful and distressing to a tra-
e scrofula on my neck. The frequent speaking
mation in the organs or glands of my throat, which
at times. To walk six or eight miles in a day fa-
hirty or forty would once. Thus nature will fall
ice it was capable to resist and throw off. This I
om theory; I can know it only by experience. To
one may be reduced by exposure, fatigue, sickness,
kinds! Anxiety of mind is impairing to health;
nly real support to keep the mind in peace through
ing the journey of life. But I feel a measure of
t Disposer of events, that it is as well with me as
I that I have as much strength remaining, and can

ne to Washington just as the man was starting in
e horse, got out, and so I delivered him up. I spoke
id took stage to Middletown, where I was beset to
ing election-day. A religious bigot made a motion
c would second it. A worldling replied to him,

"Let the dead bury their dead." The same night and next day I spoke in Charleston, where Mr. Fetter lent me a horse to ride to Wheeling. Here I spoke three times, and found a Quaker family who had been kin' to Peggy when she had travelled the west with me. Here, it is probable, the great roads from the Atlantic will intersect with the waters of the Ohio, and this will be the grand place of deposit between the east and western country. Though the Alleghany, Muskinzum, Sciota, and Miami, with the Wabash, &c., intersect with the waters of the lakes of Canada, with only small portages of a few miles—connect with that round the falls of Niagara, and from Albany to Schenectady—yet the principal will be through the waters of the Mobile and Tennessee, which are connected by a portage—one of eight miles, by Coosee and Highwassee—one of thirty, from Twenty Mile creek to Bear creek—and sixty-nine, from Main river to Main river. Mobile has a tide of about one hundred and fifty miles.

Taking water with Captain Wood, I arrived at Marietta on Sunday, fifteenth, and spoke in the Methodist meeting-house to more than could get in—generally well-behaved.

Monday, 16th. This day I am thirty-eight years old. Sixteen years ago I embarked for Europe; nineteen, I was in Orange meeting, addressing the youth. Thirty-eight more, no doubt, will change my state. Above half of the "seventy-six" is gone.

Spoke, at sunrise, to about two hundred; at about nine in the two-steepled, or rather horned meeting-house; spoke several times; and also at Point or Fort Harmer.

The marks of antiquity in this western world are so conspicuous, that should New England be depopulated, the monuments would not be so visible, in a few hundred years, as what these are now. And it is remarkable, that where nature appears to have formed it commodious for a town, those ancients, as well as these moderns, fixed on the same sites in a great many places.*

What is ahead I know not; but this one thing I am conscious of, that it requires more grace to be able to suffer the whole will of God, than merely to do it.

> What now is my object and aim?
> What now is my hope and desire?
> To follow the Heavenly Lamb,
> And after his image aspire!

A young gentleman and his lady, returning from a visit to her parents, having a spare horse, I obtained the privilege of riding it about one hundred miles, visiting Gallipolis and Greenopsburg† by the way.

---

* The works of antiquity are beyond any description as yet given, that I have seen, by Morse or others. Here are two circles, including several acres each, with what is called a covered-way to the water. In one of these circles are two platforms, one of which I found to be fifty paces square, eight feet high, and three convex and one concave walk to ascend x. The earth appears to have been brought from a distance, to make the top a hard walk, like that near Natchez. There have been found brass and copper polished beyond what is common in our day, "steel bow," iron, silver, glass beads, a salt well laid in cement, flint knives, and stone axes. Also, a stone "image," large as life, denoting great antiquity.

† Here an old gentleman replied, I should not preach so; "for," said he, "it will hurt the feelings of my neighbors." Thus he interrupted two or three times. They made a collection for *me*, which was given to bear the expenses of another. At a public house, the woman charged fifty per cent more than her husband. I made some remarks upon it. It was replied, "That is nothing; for it was a customary thing in this our day." I observed, "That I liked *honest* women to maturity, and *honest* afterwards."

Thence, in a family-boat, to Portsmouth and Alexandria, where I was recognised, and embargoed to stop. So I held several meetings; saw the "mammoth orchard" of America. Thence to Limestone, where I had a meeting. Was driven ashore at Augusta; the courthouse was soon filled. After meeting the wind fell, so we departed, and arrived at Cincinnati, where I had never been before, as was the case with most of the towns on the Ohio; I found here many of my old friends, from different parts of the Union.

There was soon a large collection on the bank of the river, to whom I spoke. Was requested to stop a few days, which I accordingly complied with; and, in eleven days, held about thirty meetings in the vicinity of this place, and trust it was not time spent in vain.

I got several thousand handbills printed for distribution, and received some remuneration from those whose hearts the Lord had touched, among whom was General Taylor.

William B., one of Snethen's men, got vexed, as is said, at something I said in the market, at Baltimore, 1804. * * * *
* * * * * * "Chicimaw exshow."

The laws from Europe, tribunal in France, Spain, and Italy, to restore the order of Jesuits, which were exiled as dangerous to papistical governments; and the Inquisition, with all its horrors.

Here Lawner Blackman was drowned. I accompanied him to Natchez. He was retarded by no danger—by land, or crossing streams of water. It appears he felt ominous preludes of his dissolution; and the concomitant circumstances show that he came to his end by Providence,

"Who plants his footsteps in the sea,
And rides upon the storm."

Captain C———, of the barge Defiance, took me, in a skiff, down the river to the falls, a distance of about one hundred and fifty miles. Visited Lawrenceburg, in Indiana, which has 68,000 inhabitants, and will soon become a state. First time I was ever in this territory.

Thence to the Rising Sun, about seven at night. The people assembled before eight, and again, before day, in the morning. So I took my departure by sunrise to Vevia. Thence I spoke at the mouth of Kentucky river; held two meetings: at Madison likewise, standing on the logs to collect the villagers, which had the desired effect. Then to Bethlehem.

. November 13th. I came to Lewisville, at the Falls of Ohio, and went to distributing handbills through the town. Though I had never been there before, was recognised by many. Thus I was provided for, and gained access to the people.

On the 15th, I embarked in the United States' boats, after speaking in a fine large new brick meeting-house, and circulating subscription papers for a new edition of my works.

This river is a gentle stream, and by no means so rapid as is commonly supposed; it is rising fast. This branch of the army is going up the Mississippi to build a fort near Carver's Claim, which, by purchase and transfer from Carver's heirs, belongs to Benjamin Mun, one hundred by a hundred and twenty miles from the Falls of St. Antina to the mouth of Chippewa river, east.

16

One, who had stolen hospital-stores, was condemned to receive two hundred lashes with rods, which were inflicted while the boat gradually drifted down the current, he being tied to three guns, which were braced in a triangle. This was called running the gauntlet; but my feelings were shocked at the sight. It was performed by deserters.

I doubt if the punishment did not exceed the crime, and whether it is agreeable to the laws of the land. Punishment should be apportioned to the crime; or else how shall we make a proper distinction between vice and virtue?

One thing is observable, that for hundreds of miles on the Kentucky side, the people were dilatory at night and morning in coming to meeting, &c.; but on the opposite side the thing was quite different. The only thing, as a reason, that I could assign for this, is *slavery!*

Some of the "articles of war," by Charles the XII., were good, considering the time in which they were written; but some of the relics of priestcraft still remain, which may do for the old world, but should be expunged and kept from the new, which is reserved for a new era of new things.

The oath of honor is more binding to the soldier than any other, in most cases.

Sunday, 19th. The time on board is something solitary, though the officers are jovial and civil to me; yet this is not the kind of company I want, though they render themselves as agreeable to me as they can.

This evening, while at camp on shore, by the request of some of the officers, I stood on a log and lectured the cantonment: good decorum.

Col. H. had some *paddled*, but not striking hard enough to please him, were ordered to take a turn—about a dozen; one stretched, and a cat drew by the tail across his back; others disgraced by their hats, and called "pioneers."

Thursday, 23d. Arrived at the cave, formerly inhabited by Mason's band of robbers; it extends one hundred and twenty feet back, with proper proportions, sixty feet wide at the mouth, and twenty-five in height. I cannot well describe the music on the water from the cave.

Spoke at the Red-banks. Quit the boats at the mouth of Cumberland river; embarked in a boat from that river going to trade with the Indians up the Arkansas. At the mouth of the Ohio I embarked in a keel-boat, and descended the Mississippi to New Madrid, in Missouri Territory.

The earthquakes here made awful distress among the inhabitants, as may be seen by the following letter:

New Madrid, Territory of Missouri, March 22, 1816.

DEAR SIR:—In compliance with your request, I will now give you a history, as full in detail as the limits of a letter will permit, of the late awful visitation of Providence in this place and its vicinity.

On the 16th of December, 1811, about two o'clock, A. M., we were visited by a violent shock of an earthquake, accompanied by a very awful noise resembling loud but distant thunder, but more hoarse and vibrating, which was followed, in a few minutes, by the complete saturation of the atmosphere with sulphurous vapor, causing total darkness. The screams of the affrighted inhabitants, running to and fro, not knowing where to go, or what to do—the cries of the fowls, and beasts of every species—the cracking of falling trees, and the roaring of the Mississippi, the current of which was retrograde for a few minutes, owing, as is supposed, to an eruption in its bed—formed a scene truly horrible. From that time until about sunrise, a number of lighter shocks occurred; at which time one still more violent than the first, took place, with the same accompaniments as the first, and the terror which had been excited in every one, and, indeed, in all animal nature, was now, if possible, doubled. The inhabitants fled in every direction to the country, supposing (if it can be admitted that their minds were exercised at all) that there was less danger at a distance from, than near to, the river. In one person, a female, the alarm was so great that she fainted, and could not be recovered. There were several shocks in a day, but lighter than those already mentioned, until the 23d of January, 1812, when one occurred, as violent as the severest of the former ones, accompanied by the same phenomena as the former. From this time till the 4th of February, the earth was in continual agitation, visibly waving, as a gentle sea. On that day there was another shock, nearly as hard as the preceding ones. Next day, four such; and on the 7th, at about four o'clock, A. M., a concussion took place, so much more violent than those which had preceded it, that it is denominated the *hard shock*. The awful darkness of the atmosphere, which, as formerly, was saturated with sulphurous vapor, and the violence of the tempestuous, thundering noise that accompanied it, together with all the other phenomena mentioned as attending the former ones, formed a scene, the description of which would require the most sublimely fanciful imagination. At first, the Mississippi seemed to recede from its banks, and its waters gathered up like a mountain, leaving, for a moment, many boats, which were here on their way to New Orleans, on the bare sand, in which time the poor sailors made their escape from them. It then rising fifteen or twenty feet perpendicularly, and expanding, as it were, at the same moment, the banks were overflowed with a retrograde current rapid as a torrent; the boats, which before had been left on the sand, were now torn from their moorings, and suddenly driven up a little creek, at the mouth of which they laid, to the distance, in some instances, of nearly a quarter of a mile. The river, falling immediately as rapidly as it had risen, receded within its banks again with such violence, that it took with it whole groves of young cotton-wood trees which ledged its borders. They were broken off with such regularity, in some instances, that persons, who had not witnessed the fact, could be with difficulty persuaded that it had not been the work of art. A great many fish were left on the banks, being unable to keep pace with the water. The river was literally covered with the wrecks of boats; and, it is said, that one was wrecked, in which there was a lady and six children, all of whom were lost. In all the hard shocks mentioned, the earth was horribly torn to pieces; the surface of hundreds of acres was, from time to time, covered over, of various depths, by the sand which issued from the fissures, which were made in great numbers all over this country, some of which closed up immediately after they had vomited forth their sand and water, which, it must be remarked was the matter generally thrown up. In some places, however, there was a substance somewhat resembling coal, or impure stone-coal, thrown up with the sand. It is impossible to say what the depth of the fissures, or irregular breaks, were; we have reason to believe that some of them were very deep. The site of this town was evidently settled down at least fifteen feet, and not more than half a mile below the town there does not appear to be any alteration on the bank of the river; but back from the river a small distance, the numerous large ponds, or lakes, as they were called, which covered a great part of the country, were nearly dried up. The beds of some of them are elevated above their former banks several feet, producing an alteration of ten, fifteen, to twenty feet, from their original state. And lately, it has been discovered that a lake was formed on the opposite side of the Mississippi, in the Indian country, upwards of one hundred miles in length, and from one to six miles in width, of the depth of from ten to fifty feet. It has communication with the river at both ends; and it is conjectured that it will not be many years before the principal part, if not the whole, of the Mississippi will pass that way. We were constrained, by the fear of our houses falling, to live, twelve or eighteen months after the first shocks, in little light camps, made of boards; but we gradually became callous, and returned to our houses again. Most of those who fled from the country in the time of the hard shocks, have since returned home. We have, since their commencement in 1811, and still continue to feel, slight shocks occasionally. It is seldom, indeed, that we are more than a week without feeling one, and sometimes three or four in a day. There were two this winter past, much harder than we have felt them for two years before; but since then they appear to be lighter than they have ever been, and we begin to hope that ere long they will entirely cease.

I have now, sir, finished my promised description of the earthquake—imperfect, it is true, but just as it occurred to my memory; many of, and most of, the truly awful scenes having occurred three or four years ago. They, of course, are not related with that precision which would entitle it to the character of a full and correct picture. But, such as it is, it is given with pleasure, in the full confidence that it is given to a friend. And now, sir, wishing you all good, I must bid you adieu.

Your humble servant,
ELIZA BRYAN.

The Rev. LORENZO DOW.

P. S. There is one circumstance which I think worthy of remark. This country was formerly subject to very hard thunder; but for more than a twelvemonth before the commencement of the earthquake there was none at all, and but very little since, a great part of which resembles subterraneous thunder. The shocks still continue, but are growing more light and less frequent.—E. B.

The vibration of the earth, shook down trees; thousands of willows were snapped off like a pipe stem, about waist high, and the swamps became high ground, and high land became the low ground, and two islands in the river were so shaken, washed away and sunk, as not to be found.

After speaking once, I descended to the Iron Banks, acres of which had been shaken down, the effects of which were awfully impressive! Being very high, some trees, the tops just above water; others just ready to fall and slide off.

There are many sawyers in this river, i. e. trees fastened by the branches or roots in the bottom of the river, which saw up and down, by virtue of the pressing of the water; whilst others are so firm as not at all to yield to the current. Those things make it dangerous going at night or in the fog.

We lay by two nights and one day; the wind and fog being our hindering cause.

New Madrid had been designed as the metropolis of the New World, but God sees not as man sees—it is deserted by most of its inhabitants; the upper Chickasaw Bluff does not wash like the others, and probably will be fixed upon one day as a proper site for to convene the portage up and down the river, which now is inconvened by the Indians owning the soil, or the inundation of the water.

Our boat got aground near this bluff, but two men coming along in a canoe, helped us off—then we struck a planter and split and hung the boat—which with difficulty was got off and mended, so I quit her, paying my fare, and took to another.

There are but few inhabitants for several hundred miles,—Indians, or whites degenerated to their level! There are natural canals from the Mississippi to Red river, and so to the sea, far west of Orleans. The map of this country is but little understood—ten companies are now surveying the public military land.

At length I landed at Natchez, obtained several letters, and not finding any friends, I embarked in another boat, after paying my fare; and on the 20th of December, I arrived in New Orleans, having changed from one boat or canoe to another, thirteen times.

Thus by the providence of God, after many restless days and nights, I got to my journey's end—stayed about a month, mostly at the house of Captain William Ross, who was flour inspector of the port, and at whose house I was treated as a friend, in Europe, when I first landed in a strange land! May God remember them for good!

My books, through the delay of the binders, did not come in time for me, I only got a few—took steamboat, ascended to Baton Rouge—visited St. Francisville and several places in Florida; thence to Woodville, Liberty, Washington, Greenville, Gibson Port, Warrington, Natchez and many country parts—saw some of my old acquaintance—bought me a horse and thought to return by land; sold him again, being unable to endure the ride; so I went down the river, visiting such places as God gave me access unto. On the island of Orleans, I find the influence of the clergy is going down-hill—many of the people came to some of my meetings.

Mr. Blunt requested me to preach at his wife's funeral. She told when she should die, and pointed out the place where she chose to be buried. But few men feel the union in the bonds of nature more than he did.

I baptized twelve, by request, showing that water was not the essential point—but the answering a good conscience—the ancients used water. I availed myself of the opportunity to impress the subject of inward religion home to the heart—without which we could not be happy in time nor eternity. We had a solemn tender time, and I trust profitable to some souls.

About the twentieth of March, I arrived in New Orleans, to take shipping for the north—none for P., so I engaged my passage to New York—the captain runaway with my passage money and things, which left me in the lurch.

Governor Strong sent to the governor here to have a "Convention" to, &c.—deep laid scheme! Thank God, it did not succeed—could not give up the ship.

Governor C. invited me to dine—observed how many of his colored people were religious, and the satisfaction he took in hearing them sing and pray at devotion at night. One who was not religious caused more trouble on the plantation than all the rest.

His Excellency gave me the privilege of a court-room, to preach in, when I was here several years ago, and also at this time.

April 11th. I was over the ground where thousands were killed and wounded on one side, and but six or seven on the other! Surely it is plain that the great Being has a hand to attend, and superintend human affairs, to eventuate the same.

In the night I could not sleep—went down to the shipping. Captain Toby generously gave me a passage. After I had been on board his ship, took up a roundabout way, called at a house—he was there; thus the hand of providence guides by the way we have not fully known.

On the 12th, embarked—several days to the Balize, and from thence went within a few miles of the "Tropic Line"—saw the Bahamas, had but few fair winds, but many contrary, and high seas—vessel pitched much and leaked a good deal—preached numbers of times on the way—32 people on board; arrived safe about the 12th May, went to Philadelphia, returned to New York, and so to Coventry, and found my Peggy and father still on these mortal shores. Thence I got me a horse and wagon, and with my Peggy came to New York—went to P.—came back, and am now visiting through East Jersey—and verging towards my fortieth year; the day of my life is advancing away fast, and the evening shades come apace; the night of death draws near, and now to be in a state of readiness is my chief concern—so I may not be called from the stage of action unawares—but fully prepared for the scene.

*Whether those infirmities with which I am afflicted may necessitate and compel me to leave the field for want of bodily power to continue, I know not: to "lay up treasure on earth, is not my desire"—nor yet to be a burden to my friends: but the prayer of Agur, for " neither riches nor poverty"—for

> "Man wants but little here,
> Nor wants that little long."

In a few weeks I expect to start for the west again, but where I may be this time twelve months, is very uncertain with me; whether in England, Sierra Leone in Africa, West Indies, or New England—or eternity; but the controversy with the nations is not over, nor will it be, until the Divine government be reverentially acknowledged by the human family.

---

* October 4, 1816. I have just returned from a tour through Genesee, Vermont, New Hampshire, and Connecticut, to Philadelphia—found the spirit of inquiry increasing, and heard of revivals among four different Societies—saw three of my sisters whom I had not seen for eight years. Left my companion at my father's until my return in the spring. Here judged by man, but which must and will finally be decided by the judgment of God only

END OF THE JOURNAL.

CHAIN OF LORENZO.

AFTER I had found religion, I began to reflect on my experience, and perceiving that I felt a love to *all*, though I had been taught that God only loved a *few*, which he had given to his Son,* I could not reconcile the two ideas together, how my love should exceed the love of God : and feeling within myself that I stood in danger of falling into sin, and consequently into condemnation, I could not reconcile it with the common idea, that if a man once obtained religion he was always safe, let him do as he would. This put me upon examining the scriptures for myself, and comparing past ideas therewith : and on examination of the same, I could find no promise that any should be saved, but *those who endure unto the end.* On the other hand, the Bible seemed to correspond with my feelings, that there was danger, being full of cautions; and there is no need of caution where there is no danger. The more light and knowledge a person hath, and commits a crime, the worse it must be ; because he sins against the more light. Therefore, any sin is greater in a professor of religion than in a non-professor, seeing he sins against the greater light.

If the sin is the greater, of course the condemnation and punishment must be proportioned ; as Christ saith, "He that knoweth his master's will and doeth it not, shall be beaten with many stripes ; whereas, he that knoweth not his master's will, shall be beaten with few." Therefore, if the sinner, who never had religion, deserves to be damned for actual transgression, why not the professor, upon the principles of impartial justice.

Now, it appears to me that this doctrine, *once in grace, always in grace,* is inseparably connected with the doctrine of particular election, and re-

---

* To talk about an eternal covenant between the Father and the Son before all worlds, a bargain that Christ should have a certain number of mankind, which some call the *elect*, is a contradiction in terms, and a piece of inconsistency. For, first, a covenant is a contract made between two parties, and there cannot be a covenant without two parties.

Therefore, to say that the Father and Son made a covenant, would be to adopt the idea that there were two divinities, which would divide the Godhead, and of course argue two Gods. But the Bible authorizes us to believe in one God and no more.

Again, if the Father and Son made a covenant, there was a *time* when they made it, and if so, then there was a time *before* they made it; consequently it was not made from all eternity, unless we suppose eternity began at the time when they made it, which is inconsistent, because *eternity* implies unbeginning *time*.

Again, this covenant cannot be a *new* one if it be so old, and a new covenant of works made with Adam but six thousand years ago, cannot be called an *old* one. Therefore, to term the *oldest* covenant a *new* one, and the *newest* the *old* one, is a piece of inconsistency, like putting the cart before the horse, and you cannot deny it. For, there is *no* account of such a *covenant* in the Bible, between the Father and the Son, but "between God and his *people*," to whom Christ was given for a covenant, &c.

probation; and to deny the latter, and to hold to the former, to me appears inconsistent. For, if a saint cannot be punished in proportion to his conduct, then he is not accountable; and if he be not accountable, then not rewardable; and if neither rewardable nor punishable, then his salvation or damnation does not turn upon his actions, *pro* nor *con*, but upon the free electing love of God. Therefore, God will have mercy upon whom he will, and whom he will he passeth by. Thus, they appear connected, like two links in a chain. And it appeareth moreover, that the doctrine of particular election leadeth to Universalism. For, according to the above, we must suppose that God decreed all things; if so, God being wise. *whatever* he hath decreed, he must have decreed it **right**; consequently nothing cometh to pass *wrong:* then there is no sin, for it cannot be sin to do right. If then one shall be damned for doing right, why not all? And if one be saved for doing right, why not all? according to the rule of impartial justice. Again, this doctrine of election saith, *all* that were given by the Father to the Son, in the covenant of grace, will be saved; none that Christ died for can be lost. The Bible saith, "Christ gave himself for *all*," (1 Tim. ii. 4, 6. 1 John ii. 2;) and A-double-L does not spell *part*, nor *some*, nor *few*, but it means *all*. Well, now if all Christ died for will be saved, and none of them can be lost, then Universalism must be true, and you cannot deny it.

And now it appears furthermore, that Universalism leads to deism; for, if all are saved, none are lost, and of course no future punishment. Therefore, the threatenings in the Bible must be false, like a sham scarecrow hung up in the fields to represent what is not real. And if the threatenings be false, the promises are equally so; for, while the promises are given in one scale to encourage virtue, the threatnings are put in the opposite one, to discourage vice. To deny the one, disallows of the other, and of course breaks the chain of the Bible, and thereby destroys its authority; consequently, ye cannot suppose with propriety that it came from God by divine direction; but rather, that it was hatched up by some cunning politicians, to answer their political designs, to keep the people in order; and that it has been kept on the carpet ever since, by the black and blue coats, to get a fat living out of the people. "Away with the Bible," says the deist, "I will be imposed upon by that no more, but I will go upon *reason;* for, whoever came back from the other world, to bring us news from that country about heaven or hell, or exhibited a map thereof?"

Now, if I denied the Bible, I should of course deny miracles and inspiration; for, if I admit of them, I must in reason admit of the propriety of the Bible.

But no one who denies inspiration and miracles, can prove the existence of a God. There are but six ways to receive ideas, which are by *inspiration*, or one of the *five senses*. Deny inspiration, there are but the five ways; and matter of fact demonstrates, that a man by these outward sensitive organs, can neither hear, see, smell, taste, nor feel God. How then can we know him but by a revelation in the inward sense. "Why," saith the deist, "the works of nature proclaim aloud in both my ears, 'there is a God.'" But I deny it according to your scale of reasoning, for you deny miracles; and yet you say, what has been once, may be again. Now, if there was a miracle once, there may be one again. It so, then there may be such a thing as revealed religion, for that is but miraculous. But, if there cannot be a miracle again, that is an argument there never was one, and of course denies the works of creation. If there was no creation, then there is no Creator. For, it must have been a miracle to have spoken the world into existence, and to have formed intelligent beings. Therefore, if there never was a miracle, then there never was such a thing as creation; consequently, the works of nature do not speak forth a Divine Being, for his hand never formed them. But they argue, that matter is eternal, and that all things come by nature; for it is evident, that if *nought* had been *once*, *nought* had been *now;* for *nothing* cannot put forth the act of power and beget something: yet it is self-evident that something does exist; therefore, something must have existed eternally. Then saith reason, if all things come by nature, then nature is eternal; and when forming from its primitive chaos, into its present position by congelation, brought forth mankind, beasts, and vegetables spontaneously; something like the mushroom growing up without seed, or the moss growing on the tree; and are kept on the stage by transmigration, like the caterpillar, transmigrating or turning into a beautiful butterfly, or the muckworm into a hornbug. Thus, nature assumes one form or shape for a while; then laying that aside, takes up another. In confirmation of this idea, it appears, that one race of animals, or beings, goes from the stage, and another comes on the carpet. For instance, the bones of a certain animal found in different parts of the continent of America, demonstrate there was a race of beings once, called the mammoth, which, as far as we know, are now extinct. The Hessian fly, which was discovered a few years since, near where the Hessian troops encamped, and from thence took its name, is supposed to have been brought by them from Hesse; and since, this insect has greatly spread over New England, and destroys the wheat. I have made much inquiry, but cannot learn that it is found in the country from whence the Hessians came. From this, one may infer and argue, that it is an animal come on the stage within late years, as it appears some other insects have done. In further confirmation of this idea, and which stands opposed to the account given by the Bible, "that all animals were drowned except those with Noah in the ark," we find, that although it is natural for us to conclude, that all animals would generate and be found on that part where the ark rested, yet the racoon is peculiar to America. This, then, is a new species of animal, and we may say the account cannot be admitted that all other parts were drowned. But again, in confirmation of revolutions in nature we perceive, that even if scripture be true, once giants did exist, but now they are apparently extinct. On strict examination, it appears that earth and shells congealed form marble, and wood when put into certain lakes of water, becomes stone.

The turf bogs in Ireland, which are found on the tops of the highest mountains, or in the valleys, miles in length and breadth, and scores of feet deep, evidently appear to have been vegetables washed together by some singular cause, or awful deluge; whole trees, with ancient artificial materials, being found many feet below the surface. I likewise was informed of a spring in that country, by putting bars or sheets of iron therein, they would be converted into copper.

On my way from Georgia, I could not but observe great quantities of shells, which to me appear to belong to the oyster, some hundreds of miles from any salt or brackish water, and it is quite improbable they could have been brought by human art, considering the vast quantities found in the savannahs or prairies to Tombigbee, and thence to the Natchez country and in the Chickasaw nation. It evidently appears likewise, that this western country was once inhabited by a warlike, informed people, who had the use of mechanical instruments; and there are evident marks of antiquity, consisting of artificial mounds and fortifications, &c., pronounced by the curious who have examined, to have been deserted long before the discovery of America by Columbus. One of these mounds, a few miles above the Natchez, covers about six acres of ground, forty feet above the common level, on which stands another, forty feet high, making in all eighty feet. Great numbers of these artificial mounds, fortifications, and beds of ashes, are to be found, extending from the western parts of Georgia, to the Mississippi, and then northward with the waters of said river, to Lake Erie, &c., all which denote that it once was a populous, and since is a forsaken country, which neither history nor tradition hath given us any information of. Therefore it appears, that greater revolutions have taken place in this terraqueous globe, than many imagine; and herefrom we might suppose, that the earth had stood longer than six thousand years calculated from scripture—and with the Chinese assent to their boasted ancient histories, &c.*

Thus I shall be an atheist instead of a deist; but I cannot be one or the other according to reason; for if there be no God, nature depends on chance, and this earth would be like a well-stringed instrument, without a skilful hand to play upon it; or a well-rigged vessel, without mariners to steer her : for every thing that hath not a regulator, is liable to go to ruin; and if all things depend on chance, then by chance there may be a God and a Devil, a Heaven and Hell, saints and sinners; and by chance the Saints may get to Heaven, and by chance the sinners may go to Hell.

It is evident in reason, that as a stream cannot rise higher than its fountain, so confusion can never produce order; for the effect cannot be more noble than the cause : consequently, if confusion had been once, it must have remained. But as the stars keep their courses without infringing on each other in their different revolutions, so that the astronomer can calculate his almanacs years beforehand, it is evident there is such a thing as order; and to suppose this order to have been eternal, would be arguing that the earth has stood forever as we now behold it; and to suppose that the earth has forever had its present form, is to suppose that there has been an eternal succession of men, beasts, and vegetables, and that to an infinite number; (for if the number be not infinite, how could the succession have been eternal?) and yet to talk about an infinite number, is a contradiction in terms, for there is no number but what may be made larger, by the addition of units; but that which is infinite cannot be enlarged. Again, if there has been an eternal succession of men and beasts, by the same rule there has been an eternal succession of days and nights, and years likewise. It must be allowed that infinite numbers are equal, for if one number be smaller than the other, how can it be said to

---

* This "*fine linked* Chain" hath *two hooks* and a Swivel—*Flattery* and *Despair*—" it is so *because* it is so, BECAUSE!"

be infinite? Well, if infinite numbers be equal, and if there hath been an eternal succession of years, and days and nights, we must suppose that their infinite numbers are equal. And yet to allow there hath been as many years as there hath been days and nights, is inconsistent, seeing that it takes three hundred and sixty-five to compose one year; and if the number of years be less than the number of days and nights, the number cannot be admitted to be infinite: consequently the succession cannot have been eternal; therefore it must be, there was a time when years began. If so, we must admit the idea, that there is something superior to nature that formed it, and thus of course an Almighty regulator, that with wisdom must have constructed and preserved this system; and this power and regulator must be self-dependent, for no power could exceed it for to be dependent on, and of course self-existent, of course eternal, according to the foregoing; and this eternal, self-existent, all-wise, regulator, is what we term God, and what the Indians term, the Great Man above.* Various are the ideas formed concerning this God. Some acknowledge one Supreme Being, but disallow of what is called the Trinity, saying, how can three be one? Answer: As rain, snow, and hail, when reduced to their origin are one, (water,) and as light, heat, and color are seen in one element, (fire,) and as the Atlantic, Pacific, and Indian oceans compose but one; so, if in natural things, three can make one, why may we not admit the idea with reason, that three can be one in things supernatural and divine, &c. What is meant by God the Father, is, that eternal Being that is everywhere present. What is meant by Christ the Son, is the manhood of Christ, being brought forth by the omnipotent power of God, as the evangelists relate;† and that manhood being filled with the divine nature, of course he would be God as well as man, and man as

---

* "Causeless causator."

† "Here I trust I may be permitted to say, with all due respect for those who differ from me, that the doctrine of the *eternal Sonship* of Christ is, in my opinion, antiscriptural and highly dangerous; this doctrine I reject for the following reasons:

1st. I have not been able to find any *express* declaration in the scriptures concerning it.

2dly. If Christ be the Son of God as to his *divine* nature, then he cannot be *eternal:* for *son* implies a *father;* and father implies, in reference to *son, precedency in time,* if not in *nature* too. *Father* and *son* imply the idea of *generation;* and *generation* implies a time in which it *was* effected, and *time* also *antecedent* to such generation.

3dly. If Christ be the *Son* of God, as to his *divine* nature, then the *Father* is of necessity *prior,* consequently superior to him.

4thly. Again, if this *divine nature* were *begotten* of the *Father,* then it must be in *time,* i. e. there was a period in which it *did not* exist, and a period when it *began* to exist. This destroys the *eternity* of our blessed Lord, and robs him at once of his Godhead.

5thly. To say that he was *begotten* from all *eternity,* is, in my opinion, absurd; and the phrase *eternal Son* is a positive self-contradiction. *Eternity* is that which has had no *beginning,* nor stands in any reference to *time. Son* supposes *time, generation,* and *father,* and time also *antecedent* to such generation. Therefore the conjunction of these two terms *Son* and *eternity* is absolutely impossible, as they imply essentially different and *opposite* ideas.

The enemies of Christ's divinity have, in all ages, availed themselves of this incautious method of treating this subject, and on *this ground,* have ever had the advantage of the defenders of the Godhead of Christ. This doctrine of the *eternal Sonship* destroys the *deity* of Christ; now if his deity be taken away, the whole gospel scheme of redemption is ruined. On this ground, the atonement of Christ cannot have been of *infinite* merit, and consequently could not purchase pardon for the offences of mankind, nor give any right to, or possession of, an *eternal* glory. The very use of this phrase is both absurd and dangerous; therefore let all those who value *Jesus* and their *salvation* abide by the *Scriptures*"—*Dr. Clarke*

well as God—two distinct natures in one person;* and it is no more inconsistent with reason, to acknowledge that he came as above, than to acknowledge a miracle for the first man's origin; which idea in reason we must admit, for there cannot be an effect without a cause; and as men

* We read, "No man hath seen God at any time." 1 John iv. 12. But Christ saith to Philip. "He that hath seen *me*, hath seen the *Father*." John xiv. 9. Again, "I in *them*, and *Thou in me*," John xvii. 23; i. e. the invisible manifestation, as Paul saith—"Christ in *you*, the hope of glory." Colos. i. 27.—Again, "*We* will come unto *him*, and make our abode with *him*." John xiv. 23. In this the Christian feels God to be his *Father, Redeemer*, and *Comforter*. And supposing the word *Trinity* is not to be found in the Bible, or *Persons* the plural, yet there are manifestations, and people should be careful not to quarrel too much about *names, forms*, or *words*, but seek for essential realities.
We read, *Heb.* i. 1, 2, "God hath in these last days spoken unto *us* by *his Son*, by whom also he made the worlds;" or as *John* i. 1—4. He existed as the *Word*, visible manifestation or Son of God; as by an act of the mind a thought is begot, so this manifestation might be said to be begotten by the will and power of God, though some query it does not appear to be written whether he existed as the *Son* or only as the *Word* until he was *manifested in the flesh*.

The first covenant, the covenant of works, was made with us in Adam, we being in his loins; he was our federal head and representative, and God required him to keep a moral law of innocence for us in himself, &c. Adam fell from his innocent happiness, and we being in his loins, fell with him. Well, says one, would not God be just to have damned us for Adam's sin? Answer: A punishment should never exceed the transgression, and of course, we deserve not a personal punishment for that which we were never *actually* guilty of; but as we were *passive* in the action, should have been passive in the suffering: of course, as we fell in Adam's loins, should have been punished in his loins, and of course have perished in his loins. Adam and Eve only were actually guilty, and of course they only deserved an actual punishment, which I believe would have been just in God to have inflicted; but to punish his posterity with a personal punishment, for that of which they were never personally guilty, would be representing God as unjust, by making the punishment to exceed the crime, which would exceed the bounds of moral justice. I therefore argue, that as the punishment should be proportioned to the crime; if a Mediator was not provided, we should have perished by being punished in Adam's loins; and if we had, then God's declarative glory must have been eclipsed, he not being actually glorified in our personal salvation or damnation. In further demonstration of this idea, I argue, that as every title to any blessing was forfeited by Adam's fall, they could never have been enjoyed, except they were purchased, (for if they could there was no need for him to purchase them for us, &c.) Our temporal lives being blessings, they came through the merits of Christ; of course, if it had not been for Christ's merits we should not have had this blessing, and of course should have perished in Adam, as we fell with him as above. But we read that Christ was a lamb slain (not from all eternity) from the foundation of the world, though not actually slain until four thousand years after; meaning that God made a revelation of his Son to the ancients, who were saved by faith in a Messiah which was to come, the same as we are saved by faith in a Messiah which hath come eighteen hundred years ago, &c., as Christ said, "Abraham rejoiced to see my day; he saw it and was glad." John viii. 56, Rom. i. 19, 20, to ii. 14, 15, Gal. iii. 8. Job was a heathen, yet observe his faith, Job xix. 25, 26.

Observe, as the first covenant, the covenant of works, was made with us in Adam, he being our head and representative, &c.; so the second covenant, the covenant of grace, was not made between the Father and the Son, as some do vainly think, (there is no mention of such a covenant in the Bible,) but was made with us in Christ, he being given to the people for a covenant, &c. Isaiah xlii. 6. and xlix. 8.

God had a sovereign right to make the first Adam and require his obedience; and when he fell, he had the same sovereign right to raise up the second Adam as he had the first—and to require his obedience. But, says the deist, there would be no moral justice to make the innocent suffer for the guilty. Allowing it, what then? If the innocent suffer voluntarily, who can be impeached with injustice? For instance, if I break a law, and the penalty is, pay five pounds or take the lash; if I cannot advance the money, I must take the stripes. But a gentleman steps up and voluntarily suffers the loss of five pounds out of his own pocket: nobody can be censured with injustice. At the same time the law, having full satisfaction, would have no further demand—and of course I should be extricated from the punishment. So Christ our second Adam, our second head and representative, was raised up to heal the breach that Adam made. For this purpose he stepped right into the shoes of the first Adam, between that law of moral innocence, that Adam was required to keep for us, and kept it even as Adam was required to keep it. How did he keep it? First, by a passive obedience, having no will of his own, abstract from what that law required. Secondly, by an active obedience—doing what the law did require, during the thirty-three years which he resided in this vale of tears. And thirdly, by voluntarily laying down his life to suffer in our lieu, what we must have suffered do exist, it is evident there is but one way for them to generate in nature: if so, who did the first man and woman generate from? To suppose that they came by nature, is to suppose the earth brought them forth spontaneously. If so, take the inhabitants from an island, and it would produce them again; but matter of fact saith it will not. Then if nature hath not changed, it never brought forth people; for if it had, it might again do so; and if not, a miracle hath taken place in nature. What is meant by the Holy Ghost, is the Spirit of God proceeding from the Father, through the mediation of the man Christ Jesus, down to the sons of men; the office of

---

in Adam if he did not do it. Observe—it was not the divinity of Christ that suffered, but the manhood. And where the Bible calls Christ the Son of God, it does not allude to his Godhead as God, but manifestation: as we read (Gal. iv. 4. Heb. x. 5. and i. 5, 6. John xv. 13. and x. 18,) that he was made or born of a woman, (who was the first in the transgression,) and made or born under the law, as no man came into the world as we are informed Christ did, &c. Luke i. 35. But says one, Prove that he did it voluntarily. Very well—Christ saith, "Greater love than this hath no man, that he lay down his life for his friends;" and, "I lay down my life for the sheep." Again—"No man taketh my life from me—I have power to lay it down, and power to take it again."

Now, if no man took Christ's life from him, then their nailing him to the tree did not cause him to die; if not, then it must have been something else—and of course the sin of the world. Again—we read that Christ was heard in that he feared—and that he pleased not himself, but gave himself a ransom. Heb. v. 7. Rom. xv. 3. 1 Tim. ii. 6. Luke xxii. 42. and Heb. xii. 2. "He, for the joy that was set before him, endured the cross, despising the shame, and is set down at the right hand of the throne of God," &c. Again—he said in the garden of Gethsemane, "Not my will, but thine be done," &c., which certainly argues that he had a human will; and when he thus gave up voluntarily, &c., we find that the sin of the world was laid upon him, and caused him to cry out, "My soul is exceeding sorrowful, even unto death," (and he never spoke extravagantly,) and the agony of his mind caused the very blood to gush through the pores of his skin, and run down like drops of sweat; and by his dying so much sooner than malefactors do in general when crucified, the governor appeared to have been astonished, and marvelled if he were already dead; and could hardly believe the account till he had called the centurion and had it from his own mouth, &c., Mark xv. 41—45. I herefrom infer, that as no man took his life from him, and as he died out of the common course of nature, that something out of the course of nature killed him—which must have been the sin of the world. And when he had suffered so much as what was necessary to suffer, even unto death, the law which Adam broke had full satisfaction on him; and having full satisfaction, it had no further demand. On the third day, the Divinity raised the humanity from the dead, by which means life and immortality are brought to light by the gospel: and glory be to God!

We read nothing about John the Methodist, nor John the Presbyterian in all the Bible, but we read of John the Baptist; but what did he say? He saith, (John i. 29,) "Behold the Lamb of God, which taketh away the *sin* of the world."

Observe, the *sin* of the world was the sin of Adam, as he was the representative of the world, and Christ the second Adam, John says, took it away. How? By atoning for it, &c. Now if John preached up that Christ took away the *sin* of the world, then all John's people ought to preach it up. And if he took it away, then it does not lie upon us; and if not, then we do not feel the guilt, only the effect, which is the evil corrupt nature instinct within, &c., and not the guilt: this is the truth, and you cannot deny it.

Thus, you see the *first* covenant of works was made with us in our first head, and the second covenant with us in our second head, (Christ.)

According to Isaiah liii. 6, "*all* we like sheep are gone astray, &c., and the Lord hath laid upon him (Christ) the iniquity of us *all*."

Observe, John did not say the *sins* of the world, but *sin*, the singular; and the prophet Isaiah doth not say *iniquities*, but *iniquity;* which must have alluded to the fall of man. Therefore the plaster is as large as the wound, and you cannot deny it. We read, (Rom. v. 18,) "therefore *as* by the offence of one judgment came upon *all* men unto condemnation—*even* so (not *uneven*) by the righteousness of one, the free gift came upon all men unto justification of life." Observe, the words *justification* and *regeneration* are not synonymous, as some use them, but are of different meanings. Regeneration signifies to be born of the Spirit of God; i. e. to be purified within by its inspiration, and to become holy and Godlike, &c. But justification signifies to acquit and look upon as free from guilt. And now if the free gift from God by Christ, came upon all men unto justification of life, I herefrom would infer, that God hath justified all men by the death of his Son, i. e. acquitted them from what is called the guilt of original sin, and looks upon them free therefrom as they came into the world.

which Spirit is to instruct mankind, and purify and prepare them for the enjoyment of God in glory.

If I deny there was such a person as Christ on this earth eighteen hundred years ago, I should deny three things: first, our dates; second, all sacred, and, third, the greatest part of profane history, which historians in general would not be willing to give up. If I allow there was such a person as Christ, I must acknowledge his miracles too, for the same histories, sacred and profane, which mention his person, relate his miracles; and to deny his miracles would be giving the histories the lie, and of course destroy their authority. If I allow his miracles, I must allow his sacred character also; for it is inconsistent with reason to believe that God would aid and assist a liar or an impostor to do the mighty deeds which we are informed Christ did.*

---

* There is an inward feeling of the mind, as well as an outward feeling of the body. For instance: sometimes my mind is calm, yet I feel pain of body; at other times, my body is well, and I feel pain of mind—remorse, guilt, fear, &c.—which are not feelings of the body, but in, or of the mind, which feelings are as perceptible as the wind blowing upon the body, and you cannot deny it. Again—a man walking along, spies the wild beast of the forest, and feels his hair to rise, and his flesh to crawl upon his bones. What is the cause of this feeling? It must be the fears in his mind, originating from a view of his danger; and perhaps, likewise, he may feel the powers of his limbs in a measure to fail, and sits down under the shock. Now, allowing the above, why should it be thought strange, if people were to fall under the mighty power of God operating upon the human mind?

But, says one, it is inconsistent with reason to adopt the idea that God will work in this form. But I say, Hush! There cannot be a law without a penalty, and we know that we are accountable to God for our moral conduct, for we feel it in our own breasts; and when we do wrong, we feel misery, and, living and dying therein, shall carry our misery to eternity with us, as death only separates the soul from the body, but doth not change the disposition of the mind.

Again—through the medium of organs my spirit can convey an idea to the spirit of another, and make him angry or wrathful, or please him with novelty, and make him laugh and feel joyful. If so, then spirit can operate on spirit, as well as matter upon matter, and convey ideas, and you cannot deny it. If so, why not the divine Spirit operate on the human mind, and give an inward conviction, &c., of right and wrong? If we are accountable unto God, then we are rewardable or punishable according to our behavior and capacity; and of course a day of account must take place, when these rewards and punishments must be actually given. From this I argue there is such a thing as moral evil and good, or vice and virtue, and of course there is a road to shun, and a particular one in which we ought to walk; therefore it is necessary to have a guide. And now the question arises, What guide is necessary? Some say the Alcoran; but there is more proof for the belief of the writings of Moses than for those of Mahomet. Moses got a whole nation of people to believe that he led them through the Red Sea, by drying it up before them, &c. He likewise got them to erect a monument in remembrance that they actually saw it, viz., to kill the paschal lamb, and eat him with bitter herbs, and walk with their staffs in their hands on a certain night of the year, which monument is now standing, and has been annually observed among them for some thousands of years, though for near eighteen centuries they have been scattered as a nation. Now, it is evident, the most ignorant people could not be imposed upon, and made to believe that they saw a river dry up, if they never did see it dry; and likewise to erect a monument of stone in remembrance that they saw it, if they never did. But Moses left this proof of his mission, which the other did not; therefore there is more reason to credit him than Mahomet, and you cannot deny it.

Another says, Reason is the surest and only guide. This I deny; because the greatest divines, so called, disagree; as you may find that, out of about three hundred and seventy denominations, thirty-one take the scripture to prove their doctrines by, yet out of these thirty-one, neither two agree with regard to their religious tenets or opinions. Yet one says, I am right, and you are wrong; another, No, you are wrong, and I am right. Here steps up a deist, and says, All religion is counterfeit; and the reason why they so disagree is, because no consistent system can be formed on the Christian plan. Answer: Your objection proves too much, and is not solid. For, first, to say all religion is counterfeit, is inconsistent; because counterfeit religion implies a false one, and there cannot be a false one except there be one to falsify; and if there be one to falsify, before it is falsified it must be genuine. Therefore to say all religion is false, is proving too much, and just argues that there is a genuine one, as there cannot be such a thing as falsehood without truth, of course counterfeit is the opposite of genuine.

If there be no such thing as inspiration, how could the prophets foretell future events out of the common course of nature? Some people say the prophecies were written in prophetic language, after the things took place. But that is unreasonable to suppose; for if they were, they were written as late down as what the New Testament dates back; and if so, then both Testaments came on the carpet about one time. How could you impose the one Testament on the learned people without the others, seeing their close connection? But as the Jews acknowledge the Old Testament and disallow the New, I therefrom argue, that the Old Testament was written some time previous to the New—of course, previous to the things being transacted which were predicted. It must, therefore, have been by divine inspiration. But, says one, the word revelation, when applied to religion, means something immediately communicated from God to man; that man tells a second, the second a third, &c., &c.; *it is revelation to the first only*, to the rest it is mere hearsay. And if the Bible was revealed once, it was not revealed to me; to me, therefore, it is hearsay. Answer: Allowing the above, yet if a man tells me it is revealed to him that my father is dead, &c., and the same spirit which revealed it to him accompanies his words with energy to my heart, then it is revelation to me as well as to him, and not bare hearsay. Consequently, if the same Spirit which dictated the writing of the Bible attends the same with energy, then it is not hearsay, but revelation, because we have a divine conviction of the truths therein contained. And the sincere, of different persuasions, find something in the Bible to attract their attention, above any other book; and even the deists, when conscience begins to lash them, find something in

---

Again—reason alone is not a sufficient guide without revelation; because, when reason was to determine the number of gods, she said there was about thirty thousand. And in this our day, the men of the greatest acquired information and strongest powers of mind, who deny revelation, (of whom some doctors and lawyers, &c., may be included,) disagree in their ideas on divine things, and that which is in connection with them, as much as the ministers and preachers; whereas, if reason was a sufficient guide, I suppose they would agree and come into one particular channel, &c.

Some say the Bible is revelation, but deny that there is any in this our day, saying the Bible is sufficient without the influence of God's Spirit. Observe, I believe in the scriptures as much as any person, &c. But with regard to the influence of the Spirit, I believe it is strictly necessary; for supposing I was to cast a look at the print and paper, what would be the benefit, except I realized the truth of what is contained therein? And how can I realize it but by the influence of the same Spirit which dictated its writings? Surely we read that no man can call Jesus, Lord, but by the Holy Ghost; and that the natural man understandeth not the things of the Spirit, for they are spiritually discerned. Romans viii. 9. 1 Corinthians, ii. 11, 12, 13, 14, 15, 16—xii. 3. Rev. xix. 10.

Why is it that the men of the greatest natural and acquired abilities get to be deists? They say it is reason, and that the more weak and ignorant part embrace religion. This is pretty true, viz.: their reason makes them deists. And why? There are certain ideas which must be taken through certain mediums, in order to have a right and just conception of them, and otherwise, would cause a person to run into absurdities. For instance: I heard of a blind man, who hearing persons talk about colors, informed them that he thought he could describe what the color of red was like, viz., *the sound of a trumpet*. This absurdity, that red was like the sound of a trumpet, originated by attempting to catch the idea through the medium of the ear. Equally absurd would be the idea of sounds, if taken through the medium of the eye, which only can be taken through the medium of the ear. So these deists attempt to conceive just and accurate ideas of revealed religion by natural reason, which leads them into an absurdity, and causes them to conclude that it is imagination, deception, or hypocrisy, in those who pretend to it: whereas, if they would conceive of it through a different channel or medium, viz., the inward sensations or convictions of the mind, &c.—if they would give due attention to the same, as sincere inquirers after truth, they would feel the Spirit of Truth bearing witness to, or of the truth, to convince and correct, &c., and their deism would flee away. Oh, may God cause the reader to reflect on what I have just observed, and turn attention within your breast, and weigh the convictions of your mind for eternity!

the Bible to attract their minds, of the truth of which, the conduct of a number to be found on this continent might be adduced.

Neither can I believe all will be saved; for in Mark iii. 29 we are informed of a certain character, which hath never forgiveness, but is in danger of *eternal damnation*, which they could not be in danger of if there be no such thing. And in Luke xvi. we read (not a parable, but a positive matter of fact, related by Christ himself, who knew what was transacted in eternity as well as in time) concerning a rich man, who died and went to hell, and there was a separation between him and the good place; and if one be lost, Universalism is not true. We feel in our breast that we are accountable to God; and if so, we are rewardable and punishable according to our behavior and capacity; and of course a day of account must take place, when the rewards and punishments are given. Some say we have all our punishment here. In reason I deny it, for the benefit of religion is to escape punishment; and if so, none have punishment but the vicious. But as many of the virtuous have suffered the most cruel, tormenting, lingering deaths, as may be said, for years, in matters of tender conscience, while others have lived on flowery beds of ease, and thus die; from this I argue that the punishment is to come hereafter.*

If all go to heaven as soon as they die, it being looked upon as a piece of humanity to relieve the distressed, would it not be right for me to end all the sorrows of those I can, who are in trouble? And does not this open a door to argue that murder is humanity, thereby sending them to heaven? But, says one, I will acknowledge future punishment, but it is not so long nor so bad as it is represented by some; for we read of the resurrection, when all mortal bodies shall be raised, and of course become immortal and spiritual; and corporeal fire and brimstone cannot operate on spiritual bodies, and of course the punishment is but the horror of a guilty conscience. And the word *forever*, frequently in the scripture, being of a limited nature, it may be inferred the punishment is not eternal. Answer: Allowing that the punishment is only the horror of a guilty conscience, (which will bear dispute,) yet I think that horror to the mind will be found equal to fire and brimstone to the material body; for frequently I have been called to visit people on sick-beds, who have told me that their pain of body was great, but their pain of mind so far exceeded it as to cause them to forget their pain of body for hours together, unless some person spoke particularly to them concerning it. Again—

---

* Can I suppose those thinking powers which constitute the soul, and make us sensible, active, and rational, and prevent the corporeal body from returning to its mother dust from day to day, will cease to exist when I am dead, or fallen asleep, or gone into a state of non-entity, by annihilation? Nay, I rather must believe this immortal doth still exist. I say immortal, because I do not see how those qualities can be subject to decay, considering their nature, though I acknowledge, whilst acting upon organs, there may be heaviness, in consequence of mortality, which is the effect of sin, but when disembodied shall appear in their strength. And as a proof of future existence of this thinking power, I ask, Why is it that so many well-informed people shrink at the thoughts of death, seeing it is the common lot of all mankind? I ask, Is it barely the thoughts of dying which makes them turn their attention to various objects to divert their minds from reflecting? Nay, but a conviction of the realities of an awful eternity. Again—if a limb of mine be dissected or taken off, does that depreciate an eighth or sixteenth part of my soul? Nay, I am as rational as ever. Therefore if my soul can exist without a part of the body, why not exist without the whole or any part of it? I have known men, who have lost their limbs, feel an itching, and put down their hand to rub. I ask, What was the cause of that sensation, seeing the leg or foot was gone?

you know what horror you have felt for a short space for one crime. Now, supposing all the sins that ever you committed in thought, word, or deed, in public and in private, were set in array before you, so that you could view all of them at one glance, and, at the same time, that conscience were to have its full latitude to give you the lash; would not the horror which here causeth people to forget their temporal pain, while there is hope, be worse than fire to the body, when hope is for ever fled? For when hope is gone, there is no support.

And the idea that the punishment is not eternal, because the word *forever* sometimes in scripture is of a limited nature, I think will not do; because the duration of certain words is bounded by the duration of the things unto which they allude. For instance, "The servant shall serve his master *forever*," in Moses's law. The word *forever* was bounded by the life of the servant. And where it relates to mortality, it is bounded by mortality; of course where it relates to immortality, it is bounded by immortality, and when it relates to God, it is bounded by the eternity of God; and as we are informed in several parts of scripture, after that mortality is done away, that the wicked shall be banished forever from the presence of God, the word *forever* and the word *eternal* must be synonymous, having one and the same meaning as endless, being bounded by the eternity of God, and the endless duration of the immortal soul, &c. Matt. xxv. 41, 46. 2 Thess. i. 9. Rev. xix. 3. Judges vii.

And observing the doctrine of particular election and reprobation to tend to presumption, or despair, and those who preached it up, to make the Bible clash and contradict itself, by preaching somewhat like this:

" *You can and you can't—You shall and you shan't—You will and you won't—And you will be damned if you do—And you will be damned if you don't.*"

Thus contradicting themselves, that people must do, and yet they cannot do, and God must do all, and at the same time invite them to come to Christ.

These inconsistencies caused me to reflect upon my past experience, and conclude that the true tenor of the Bible did not clash, of course that a connected chain should be carried on through that book, and the medium struck between the dark passages, which literally contradict, and reconcile them together by explaining scripture by scripture; and by striving so to do, I imbibed what here follows: 1st. That election is a Bible doctrine, but not an elect number, for I cannot find that in the Bible, but an *elect character*, viz: " Him that becomes a true penitent, willing to be made holy and saved by free grace, merited only by Christ." And on the other hand, instead of a reprobate number, it is a reprobate character; namely, " him that obstinately and finally continues in unbelief, that shall be cast off," &c. Thus any one may discover that it is an election and reprobation of characters instead of numbers, and you cannot deny it. But the following scriptures demonstrate undeniably, that God, instead of reprobating any, is willing to receive all: 2 Pet. iii. 9; Ezek. xxxiii. 11; 1 Tim. ii. 3, 4; 2 Cor. v. 19. 2dly. That Christ, instead of dying only for a part, the prophets, angels, Christ, and the apostles, positively affirm that salvation by his merits is possible for all: Gen. xxiii. 14; Isaiah liii. 6; Luke ii. 10; John iii. 16, 17. 3dly. That the Holy Spirit doth not strive with a part only, as some say *a special call*, but strives with every man according to the hardness of his heart, while the day of mercy lasts: John i. 9 and xvi. 8, (compare vi. 44 with xii. 33.) Again, there is a gospel for and an invitation to all, and you cannot deny it: Mark xvi. 15; Matt. xi. 28. Again, there is a duty which we owe to God, according to reason, conscience, and scripture; and there are glorious promises for our encouragement in the way of duty, and awful threatenings in the way of disobedience, and you cannot deny it: Prov. xxviii. 13; Matt. v. 2 to 9, vii. 24—28; Isaiah i. 16—20; Ps. ix. 17. And now to affirm that a part were unconditionally elected for heaven, and can never be lost, what need was there of a Saviour? To save them from what? And if the rest have no possibility of salvation, who are benefited by Christ? Or what did he come for? Not to benefit the elect or reprobate, but to accomplish a mere sham, or solemn nothing. This reminds me of a story I heard concerning a negro, who had just returned from meeting. His master said, "Well, Jack, how did you like the minister?" "Why, massa, me scarcely know, for de minister say, God makey beings, calla man; he pickey out one here, oney dare, and givey dem to Jesus Christ, an' da can't be lost. He makey all de rest reprobate, and givey dem to the devil, da can't be saved. And de devil he go about like a roaring lion, seeking to get away some ob Christ's, and he can't. De minister he go about to get away some de devil's, and *he can't;* me don't know which de greatest fool, de preacher or de devil."

It is evident that the devil and the damned in hell do not believe in the doctrine of eternal decrees, for it is the nature of sinners to strive to justify themselves in evil, and cast the blame elsewhere. This is evil practice, therefore came from an evil source, and consequently from the devil. When Adam fell, and God called to him, he cast the blame on the woman. God turning to her, she cast the blame on the serpent. God turned to him, and he was speechless. Now if he had believed in the doctrine of decrees, does it not appear evident that he would have replied, "Adam was not left to the freedom of his own will; he was bound by the decrees, and we have only fulfilled thy decrees and done thy will, and thou oughtest to reward us for it?" But he was speechless, and knew nothing of such talk then; therefore it must be something that he has hatched up since—as saith the poet:

"There is a reprobation plan,
   Some how it did arise,
By the predestinarian clan
   Of horrid cruelties.

"The plan is this: They hold a few,
   They are ordained for heaven;
They hold the rest accursed crew,
   That cannot be forgiven.

"They do hold, God hath decreed
   Whatever comes to pass;
Some to be damned, some to be freed—
   And this they call free grace.

"This iron bedstead they do fetch
   To try our hopes upon;
And if too short, we must be stretch'd—
   Cut off, if we're too long.

"This is a bold serpentine scheme,
   It suits the serpent well;
If he can make the sinner dream
   That he is doomed to hell.

"Or if he can persuade a man
   Decree is on his side;
Then he will say without delay,
   This cannot be untied.

"He tells one sinner, he's decreed
   Unto eternal bliss;
He tells another, he can't be freed,
   For he is doom'd to miss.

"The first he bindeth fast in pride,
   The second in despair;
If he can only keep them tied,
   Which way he does not care."

It appeareth by the rich man's desiring his five brethren to be warned, lest they come to hell with him, &c., (Luke xvi.,) that he did not believe their states to be unalterably fixed by God's decrees; for if he did, why did he request their warning? saying, "if one arose from the dead, they would repent," &c. It appeareth likewise that if God hath decreed all things, that his decrees are as ancient as his knowledge; as his decrees are generally argued from his foreknowledge, and that he foreknows it will be so, because he hath decreed it, &c. This opens a door to argue, that there was a time when God was ignorant and knew nothing. For a *decree* is an *act* of the *mind*, and there cannot be an action without there being a *time* when that action took place. If so, then if God hath decreed all things, it must be that there was a *time* when God passed those decrees; and if so, then there was a time when the decrees were *not* passed; and if God did not foreknow any thing until he decreed it, then there was a time when God knew nothing. This is the truth, and you cannot deny it.*

And now to talk about God's foreknowledge, or decreeing all things *from* all eternity, appears a nonsensical phrase; because to say *from* (as the word *from* implies a place of starting) all eternity, implies eternity had a beginning; and as some use an unmeaning expression to convey an idea of unbeginning time, for the want of language, it is nonsense to attempt to build an argument thereon. For as it is argued in the foregoing that God is eternal, we may admit with propriety that he possesseth all the attributes that are ascribed to him; and yet it is not inconsistent to say that the first thing ever God made was *time*,† and in time he made all things, and probably the angelic creation was previous to men.

Now, many attempt to make God the author of sin: but sin is not a creature as many falsely think; *it is the abuse of good*. And to say that God, who is good, abuses good, is the highest blasphemy that we could impeach the Deity with; therefore he cannot be the author of it, consequently it must have come from another source. Now we must admit the idea that there was a time when there was no creature, but the Creator only: and declarative glory could never redound to God; except that finite accountable intelligences were created, (for what should declare his glory,) his justice nor goodness could never be shown forth in rewards and punishments, except such accountable beings were made; and of course must have remained in solemn silence: therefore, declarative glory could never have redounded to God. But, that he might have declarative glory, arising from his attributes,† by intelligences, it appears that angels were

---

* Whatever is, or exists abstract from God, is finite. How or what God conceives or knows of himself, or the manner of his knowing, I shall not attempt to fathom till the day of eternity. But relative to his knowledge, as it concerns his creatures, I think the term *infinite* improper, for he can know no more than what hath been, is, and will be, (for there is no more to know,) which are only finite in any and every sense whatever. Therefore to attempt to build an eternal covenant, by arguing or attempting to conceive his infinite knowledge, is a contradiction. For first, the term *knowledge* implies a power of perception, to know and comprehend the existence of qualities, or things, &c.; therefore in this sense, when you speak of the knowledge of God relative to creation or his creatures, in the sense they speak, you must necessarily *bound* God's knowledge by finity. I now refer only to the act or circumference of the act, not to the power or capacity, for only God is infinite; of course to apply the word infinite, &c., to argue great knowledge, is a contradiction; and you cannot deny it, because there cannot be an *infinite* finite.

† Eph. i. 3, 4, 5. God hath blessed *us* with *all* spiritual blessings *in* Christ, (*not out of him*,) according as he hath *chosen us in him before* the foundation of the world, that we should be *holy and without blame* before him in love. Ver. 9 and 10 hath reference to building up Zion in Christ, not in the Un'versalist's sense, but upon *earth*, &c.

‡ Rev. iv. 11. "*Thou* hast created *all* things, and for thy *pleasure* (or glory) they *are* and *were created*."

created; and we must suppose they were all happy, holy, and good at at first, seeing this is the nature of God, (as all argue, from the Christian to the deist.) As likeness doth beget likeness, and every cause produces its own effect; and as we are informed, that the devil sinneth from the beginning, and that some kept not their first estate, but left their own habitation, and sinned, and were cast down to hell, &c. (2 Pet. ii. 4, Jude 6, Rom. iv. 15, 1 John iii. 4, 8;) and as we read, where there is no law there is no transgression; it must be that the angels had a law to keep, and power sufficient to keep or break the law; or else, how could they be accountable? And if they were not, they could not be rewardable; and if not, then not praise nor blame worthy. But says one, allowing that God did make such pure, intelligent, accountable beings, and had a sovereign right to demand their obedience, seeing they were dependent; what should induce a *holy being* to sin against a holy God, especially as there was no evil in him or them, nor yet any to tempt him? Answer: Suppose I were walking along in meditation in a great field: of a sudden I cast a look forward, and can see no end to it: it would be natural for me to stop and look back the way from whence I came. So, in my opinion, the angels were looking into futurity: they could discover no end to eternity, and it would be natural for them to reflect on time past. They could remember no time when they had no existence, any more than I can. This would open a door for self-temptation to arise in thought, "How do we know but we are eternal with God? and why should we be dependent on him, or be accountable to him?" In order to find out whether they were dependent or independent, the only method was, to try their strength, by making head against the King of heaven, by a violation of his command.

Now, *evil* is the abuse of *good*, and the first abuse of *good* was the origin of *evil*, and as their commandment was good, the evil consisted in the abuse of it; and the natural consequence of breaking the same, would be to convert them into devils—as the consequence of murder is death. From this we may see, that God made THE devil, but he made himself A devil. Now, it appears to me impossible for God to show the devils mercy, consistent with the principles of reason and justice; for I may sin against my equal, and in the eyes of the law, the crime is looked upon as a trifle: the same crime against a government would forfeit my liberty, if not my life. Thus, the magnitude of a crime is not looked upon according to the dignity of the offender, but according to the dignity of the offended: of course, a finite being sinning against an infinite God, there is an infinite demerit in the transgression; of course justice demands infinite satisfaction. A finite being can make finite satisfaction only, although the crime demands an infinity of punishment. A finite being cannot bear infinity of punishment at once; therefore the punishment must be made up in duration, and of course be eternal, that it may be adequate to the crime.

But, says one, Why was not a mediator provided for fallen angels, as well as for fallen men?—Answer: It was impossible, in the reason and nature of things; for when mankind fell it was by the action of one, and they multiply. So the Godhead and manhood could be united, as in the person of Christ. But not so with the devils, for they were all created active beings, and each stood or fell for himself, and of course was actually guilty and therefore must have actual punishment, except a mediator was provided; which could not be, for the devils do not multiply; therefore the

Godhead and the devilhood could not be joined together. But supposing they could, yet, says Paul, without the shedding of blood there can be no remission, and spirits have no blood to shed: and upon this ground it appears, that the devils' restoration or redemption must fall through.

The scripture saith, Rom. ix. 11, &c. "The children being yet unborn, having done neither good or evil, that the purpose of God according to election might stand, it was said unto her, the elder shall serve the younger; as it is written, Jacob have I loved, and Esau have I hated," &c. Any person by examining Genesis xxv. 23, and Mal. i. 1, 2, may see that Paul's talk doth not mean their persons, but that undeniably it must be applied to their posterity. And to apply them the other way, as though one was an elect, the other a reprobate, on purpose to be damned, without a possibility of escape, is a plot of the devil, to blindfold mankind by a multitude of words without knowledge: for no such inference can be drawn from that passage, that Jacob was made for salvation, and Esau for damnation. But observe, it must be applied to their posterity: see Genesis xxv. 23. "And the Lord said to Rebecca, two nations are in thy womb, and two manner of people shall be separated from thy bowels; and the one people shall be stronger than the other people, and the elder shall serve the younger." Which came to pass in the reign of King David, when the Edomites were brought into subjection to the Israelites, (2 Sam. viii. 14, 1 Chron. xviii. 13;) and that passage, "Jacob have I loved, and Esau have I hated," was not spoken before the children were born, but hundreds of years after they were dead, by Mal. i. 1, 2. Now, cannot any person who is unprejudiced, plainly discover, that the word "Jacob" here means the Jewish nation, which God saw fit to exalt to high national privileges; because Christ was to come through that lineage, &c. And as to "*Esau have I hated,*" the word *hate* in scripture frequently means loving in a less degree, &c.: for instance—Christ saith, except a man *hate* his father, mother, and his own life also, he cannot be my disciple—the word *hate*, here means loving in a less degree, as we are to love God supremely; and lent favors in a less degree, as belonging to him. So the passage "Esau have I hated," meaneth, that God did not see fit to exalt the Edomites to so high national privileges as the Jews; yet they were the next highest, for their land was given to them for a possession, which the Jews were not permitted to take from them, as they were going from Egypt to Canaan, (Deut. ii. 4, 5;) and that passage (Heb. xii. 17) which saith, that "Esau was rejected, and found no place of repentance, though he sought it carefully with tears," we must not therefrom infer, that it was God who rejected him, because he was a reprobate, but his father Isaac.

Take notice, at a certain time Esau went out a hunting, and on his return home, being at the point to perish with hunger, came into Jacob's tent, and desired refreshment; but Jacob attempted to make Esau's extremity his opportunity to grow rich, and to cheat him out of his birth-right for a mess of pottage; and Esau, rather than starve, promised to give it up; and who can blame him, considering his distress? All that a man hath will he give for his life, saith Satan: this is the truth, and you cannot deny it, (Gen. xxv. 30, &c.) But there is no account that ever Jacob got the birth-right; but by Esau's continuing with his father, and being so rich on Jacob's return, it appears that he lived with his father, and was heir to the inheritance. Jacob got not any thing from Esau; but Esau got a present from him. After this, Isaac was determined to bless Esau, and commanded him to get venison for that purpose; and while he was going for it, Rebecca told Jacob to kill kids, &c., and he should get the blessing. He saith, " I shall get a curse instead of a blessing." She said, " The curse be on me," &c., and it appears as though she got it, as it was the means of her losing her idol's company during her lifetime; for there is no account of her being alive at his return. Scarcely had he told the lies to Isaac, and withdrawn, &c., but Esau came in, and thereby blind Isaac perceived the deception in full, and began to tremble exceedingly, by which Esau perceived what had passed, and immediately lifted up his voice and wept, and sought after repentance; not in himself, (for he had done nothing to repent of,) but in his father Isaac. But Isaac would not take back the blessing, but said, Jacob is blessed, and shall be blessed, (Gen. xxvii. &c.) From this loss of the blessing, some people think Esau was reprobated and damned: but Paul saith, (Heb. xi. 20,) " By faith Isaac blessed Jacob and Esau concerning things to come." Some forget to read that Esau was blessed as well as Jacob, though not in so great a degree, and how could he be blessed by faith if he were reprobated? (Gen. xxvii. 39, 40.) Esau was blessed with four things; the first two were like a part of Jacob's, viz. the dew of heaven, and the fatness of the earth—thirdly, by his sword he was to live—and fourthly, when he should have the dominion, he was to break Jacob's (or Jewish) yoke from off his neck, which came to pass in the reign of Jehoram, the son of Jehoshaphat. 2 Chron. xxi. 8—10. And now to show the inconsistency of thinking that Esau served Jacob the younger, it doth appear that Jacob served Esau; and moreover, that Jacob had no religion when he attempted to cheat and lie, that being contrary to the spirit of Christianity. But it appears that he got converted afterwards, when on his way to Padan-aram; he lay to rest in the woods, and in the night he had a vision, in which he saw a ladder, the top reaching to heaven, &c. Now, as the ladder had two sides, it represents the Godhead and manhood of Christ, and the rounds, the different degrees of grace. If Jacob had been pious, doubtless he would have realized the presence of God being there to protect him from the wild beasts; but his expression, " the Lord was in this place, and I knew it not," argueth ignorance. Secondly, he adds, " it is no other than the house of God and gate of heaven;" which is the language of young converts. Thirdly, he made a vow, if God would give him food to eat, and raiment to put on, and bring him back in peace, that God should be his God; which certainly implies, that he did not serve God before as he did afterwards. (Gen. xxviii. 16.)

Observe, first, Jacob served Esau, was afraid of him, and ran from home twenty years, through scenes of sorrow, and had his wages changed not less than ten times—Secondly, when he set out to return, his past conduct created such fear in his breast, that he dared not see Esau's face until by messengers he inquired, " May I come in peace ?" And understanding that Esau with a body of men was coming to meet him, his sleep departed from him. He divided his host in two bands, and wrestled all night in prayer; and such fear surely denotes guilt. Thirdly, he sent a number of messengers with presents, and a message to Esau, calling him lord, as if himself was the servant. Fourthly, Esau bowed not at all; bu

Jacob bowed not once, nor twice only, but seven times; and then cried out, "I have seen thy face, as though I had seen the face of God." Now if Esau was a reprobate, how could his face have been as God's? Nay, it would have been as the devil's. But as they had a joyful meeting together, like two Christian brethren, that had been some time absent; I therefore conclude, that Jacob saw the image of God in his brother Esau; and in that sense, Esau's face might be said to be as the face of God, and in no other. And as the general tenor of Esau's conduct was not so bad as some part of Jacob's conduct, I therefrom conclude, that Esau died in peace; and if ever I can be so happy as to get to glory, I expect to meet Esau there as well as Jacob. (Gen. xxxii. and xxxiii. &c.)

If I believed all things were decreed, I must suppose that Pharaoh did the will of God in all things; seeing God decreed all his thoughts, words, and actions: and the *will* being the determining *faculty*, it must be, that whatever God *decrees*, he *wills:* therefore Pharaoh did the will of God, according to that doctrine, and you cannot deny it. If the scripture be true, then Pharaoh doing the will of God, according to that doctrine, must be saved, according to the intimation of Christ, that whoever doeth the will of God is his brother, sister, and mother. Observe, if all Pharaoh's conduct was decreed, he did as well as he could, and Peter as bad as he could. According to that doctrine, then, which is the most praise or blame worthy? Again, if God decreed Pharaoh's conduct, did he not decree it right; and if so, could it be wrong? If not, there was no sin, consequently no punishment; unless you say a man is punishable for doing right. Again, if God decreed Pharaoh should do as he did, why did he command him to act to the reverse? Does he decree one thing and command another? If so, then you make God's *decrees* and *commandments* clash; for according to that doctrine, God's *revealed* will is that we should *obey:* and his *decreed* will is that we should *disobey.* Thus you make out that God has *two wills* right opposite to each other, which makes God *divided* against himself. Christ intimates that that which is *divided* against *itself*, cannot stand. If so, then Deity being divided, must fall, and of course the works of nature sink, and go to ruin. Thus we see the inconsistency of dividing and subdividing God's will.

There is no account of Pharaoh's heart being more hard than others, until he became hardened; but it appeareth from Rom. v. 19, 20, that the hearts of all people are alike hard by nature. Well, saith one, what is the meaning of that scripture, "For this same purpose have I raised thee up, that I may show forth my power in thee. And I will harden his heart, and he shall not let the people go," &c. Answer: The Lord raised Pharaoh up. Up from what? From the dust unto a child, from a child to a man, to be a king on the throne, that he might show forth his power in him. And he has raised up you, and me, and all mankind, for the same purpose; viz. to show forth his power in us. If it be not for that, what is it for? We read in several places that the Lord hardened Pharaoh, and yet that Pharaoh hardened himself: how could that be? God do it! and yet Pharaoh do it! We read that the Lord afflicted Job, and yet that Satan did it, (Job xix. 21. ii. 7;) and that the Lord moved David to number Israel, and yet that Satan did it, &c. (2 Sam. xxiv. 1. 1 Chron. xxv. 1;) and that Solomon built the temple, and yet tells how his many workmen did it. Thus we see there is a first cause, and a second cause; as saith the poet:—

"No evil can from God proceed,
'Twas only suffered, not decreed;
As darkness is not from the sun,
Nor mounts the shades till he is gone."

Reason saith, tha, mankind are agents or else prophets; for they can foretell some things, and then fulfil them :* this is the truth, and you can.

---

* Matter, when it is moved by another cause, cannot stop of itself, and when stopped cannot move of itself. But as we have the power of action, (the same as I give out my appointment months before hand, and then fulfil it,) it is evident that we are prophets or else agents. To adopt the idea of prophecy, you will not; and if not, you must acknowledge agency, which material substance without thinking power doth not possess. From this I argue that there is something in man abstract from matter, which is spirit, which some call the soul, and which makes him *sensible* and *rational*, &c. And to suppose the soul to be a part of God is inconsistent, because God is completely happy, as is acknowledged from the Christian to the Deist. Therefore, if my soul was a part of him, I should have one continued stream of happiness.

But as I have frequently felt unhappy in mind, I herefrom argue that my soul is spirit abstract from God.

Some people have an idea that the souls of infants come right pure from the hand of God by infusion into the body, and that the body being of Adam's race, pollutes the soul, and causes it to become impure, just as if the body governed the mind. Allowing the above—When did God make the soul of the child that was born yesterday? Why, says one, within the course of a few months past. Hush, I deny it; for the Bible says, Gen. ii. 1, 2, 3, that God finished the heavens (that is, the starry heavens) and earth, and all the *host* of them, and then God rested from the works of the creation on the seventh day—he hath not been at work in creating new souls ever since. Therefore your idea that God makes new souls daily, falls to the ground; and you cannot deny it, if the Bible be true.

But, says one, their souls were made in the course of six days.

Where then have they been ever since? Laid up in a storehouse in heaven? If they were, they were happy; if so, what kind of a being does this represent the Almighty, especially if connected with the opinion of some who suppose that there are infants in hell not more than a span long!

First, God made Adam happy in Paradise, and these infantile souls happy in a storehouse; then when Adam falls, prohibits adultery, and at the same time previously decrees that they shall commit it to produce an illegitimate body; and he to help them on to perfect the illegitimate, takes one of these pure souls, infuses it into the body, and the body pollutes it, caused it to become impure, and is now a reprobate for hell-fire. Thus you see some people represent God as making souls pure and keeping them happy some thousands of years, then damning them for a sin they never committed! And now the difference between this *Being*, if any such there be, that dealeth thus with his creatures, and *Him* that we call the *devil*, I leave you to judge. God help you to look at it in the scale of equality, and see whether the above be right or wrong!

But, says one, where do you think the soul comes from?

As Adam was the first man, I must suppose, from reason and scripture, he got his soul right from God, as there was no other source for him to derive it from; but Eve was tak n out of Adam, and there is no account of her receiving her soul right from God; and if not, I must suppose the whole of her was taken from Adam, and of course she got her soul from him as well as her body. And as we read that the souls of Jacob's children (Gen. xlvi. 26) were in Jacob's loins, and came out, &c., I herefrom infer, that they were not laid up in a storehouse in heaven, but came by natural generation from the parents, as well as the body.

Well, says one, estimate the value of the soul, (by mechanism.)

First, some people prize a thing according as who made it: if one mechanic made it, they prize it so much worth; but if another made it they would prize it higher, because it was made by a more perfect workman. If we prize the soul by this standard, it must be considered as valuable, because it was made by the perfectest of the perfect, and the wisest of the wise, him that cannot err, *God Almighty*.

Secondly, some people value a thing according to its duration. If the soul be valued on that ground, it must be prized high; for it being spirit, it is immortal, and must endure as long as eternal ages pass away.

Thirdly, some people prize a thing according to the ease of it; if the soul be prized on this ground, it must be esteemed as valuable, for a certain time, it is said, five millions were offered to any one who would contrive a machine that would perform perpetual motion, and yet none have been able to do it; yet in the construction of the case of the soul, which is the body, there is more wisdom discoverable than all the wisdom of the mechanics, in all the machinery on the face of this terraqueous globe.

not deny it. If so, then it may be said with propriety, that the Lord hardened the heart of Pharaoh, and yet that Pharaoh hardened himself, even as mankind are hardened in this our day, &c.

Observe, first, the Lord called to Pharaoh by favor, and gave him a kingdom. Secondly, the Lord called by commandments, and Pharaoh would not obey, by saying, "I know not the Lord, neither will I let Israel go." Then the Lord called, thirdly, by miracles, but Pharoah reasoned against them in a diabolical way, by setting the magicians to

If the case is thus wisely and beautifully made, how valuable must the soul be which the body is made to contain!

Fourthly, some people prize a thing according to what it costs: if the soul be prized according to this medium, it must be valuable, for if any smaller ransom than the blood of Christ could have purchased immortal souls from the curse of a broken law, doubtless God would have accepted that offering. Some people say that one drop of Christ's blood is sufficient to cleanse a soul, which idea I condemn, because the magnitude of a crime is not looked upon according to the dignity of the offender, but according to the dignity of the offended; therefore a finite being sinning against an infinite God, there is an infinite demerit in the transgression, and justice demands infinite satisfaction. But a finite being can make finite satisfaction *only*; therefore there needs a mediator between a rebel *creature* and the *Creator*, which could be formed no way but by the two natures being joined together, that is to say, the *finite* and the *infinite*, or in other words, the *Godhead* and *manhood, or Divinity veiled in humanity.*

But here comes up a deist, and says, Hush, Lorenzo, it is inconsistent to adopt the idea that divinity and humanity can be joined together, as you talk, in the person of Christ. But I say, hush; for it is no more inconsistent with reason to adopt the idea that divinity and humanity can be joined together, than to adopt a former one which is self-evident, viz. that spirit and matter can be joined together and form a man, which idea, how it is, I cannot comprehend; yet self-evident matter of fact puts it beyond all doubt, that spirit and matter are joined to form man, and you cannot deny it—and of course the idea that divinity and humanity can be joined together in the person of Christ, may be admitted according to reason. The manhood being offered up under an infinite influence of the *Divinity*, the sacrifice would be of *infinite* merit according to the transgression and the demands of justice. But to return—I cannot suppose that Christ would have done any thing superfluous for man's redemption; and of course, that one drop of his blood is sufficient to cleanse a soul or save a world, is inconsistent, as though a considerable part of what he did was superfluity, &c. And of course in atoning for what is called original sin, I must believe that nothing needless was done; if not, then Christ did no more than what was necessary; and if so, the idea that one drop of his blood, &c., to cleanse a soul, is inconsistent. And if the demerit of one transgression demands infinite satisfaction, then the atonement made for that would be a sufficiency for all the world, or ten thousand times as many: for what greater satisfaction could be made than that which is infinite? Therefore, the human nature being offered a sacrifice by the influence of the Divinity, for the *sin* of the world, which was the sin of Adam, the sacrifice or ransom in some sense may be considered as infinite, it being offered under an infinite influence of the Divine Spirit; therefore, the satisfaction would be according to the transgression, and of course, in doing that, there would be a sufficient provision for all the actual sins of men, considering the nature of it, and how unbounded it is. Therefore, the soul, when prized according to what it cost, must be considered very valuable.

But again, fifthly—some people prize a thing according to the scarcity of it. If a thing is very plenty, they would give so much for it; but if it were more scarce, they would give much more, &c. So, immortal souls are plenty, and yet very, very scarce, for each man hath but one, each woman hath but one. O sinner! if thou lose thy soul, thou losest thy all, thou hast nothing left. God help thee to consider seriously, and stimulate thee to improve thy time (which is on the wheel) for eternity accordingly!

The soul, which we perceive governs our body, (as the body without the soul is a lifeless lump of clay,) we find from experience hath a memory, which is the power of reflection or recollection, to call past things to remembrance, &c. Again, it hath an understanding, which is a power to comprehend and realize things as they are; again, it hath a will, which is the power of choosing and determining.

We also have passions, one of which is *love*, inclining us to that which appears delightsome. Anger is another passion, which implies dislike or opposition to a thing that is odious in our minds. Also we have fear when danger we behold. Also joy, when pleasure or happiness we possess. There are five outward senses by which we distinguish objects or qualities; these are inlets of knowledge to the mind, and only through them can we receive ideas, (except by inspiration, which is an inward conviction wrought by another Spirit.) These five senses are, hearing, seeing, tasting, smelling, and feeling.

work. Then, fourthly, God called by affliction; and Pharoah made a promise to obey God, and let the Jews depart, if the affliction might be removed: but when the judgment was removed, Pharoah broke his promise. Therein he was to blame, and you cannot deny it. For, by breaking his promise, his heart would naturally become harder, like metal when melted it is tender, and when grown cold is harder than before, and of course requires a hotter fire to melt it again. So it required a heavier judgment to operate on Pharaoh; and God would send it, and Pharaoh would promise and break them, till ten afflictions passed away; and when the first-born were slain by the Lord, and yet by evil angels, as David in the Psalms tells you, Pharaoh was shocked, and let the Jews depart. He pursued them, and God permitted him to be taken in his own folly, and drowned in the Red Sea. Thus, we find how God hardened Pharoah's heart, and yet how he hardened himself by disobedience; and so in this our day it may be said, that God hardens some, and yet they harden themselves, as follows:—First, God calls by prosperity or favors, and yet many enjoy them without a feeling sense from whom they flow. Secondly, God calls by commandments; an inward monitor, telling what is right and what is wrong. But some do not give attention thereto, which, if they did, they would hear the voice more and more distinctly, till at length it would become their teacher. Thirdly, God calls by miracles; the operation of his Spirit, perhaps, under preaching, or some other cause, and they have thought, "If I could always feel as I do now, I should soon be a Christian: or, if all my companions would turn and serve the Lord, I would gladly go with them to heaven." But through inattention, those serious impressions, which I call miracles, soon wear off. A miracle is something done out of the common course of nature, by the operations of the power or Spirit of God. Therefore, O reader, it was not the minister who made you have those feelings, but the power of God. Therefore, in some sense, you have been called upon miraculously, and you cannot deny it. Fourthly, God calls by affliction; and when people are taken sick, and view death near, they make vows and promises, and think how good they will be if God will spare them and raise them up. But when they are recovered, they, Pharaoh like, too soon forget their promises, and break their vows, and hereby become harder than before, and can do things without remorse, which once they would have felt the lash of conscience for. And that preaching, which once would make impressions on their mind, strikes their heart and bounds back like a stone glancing against a rock. This character is what may be termed a *gospel-hardened sinner*. Thus, you may discover that this plan clears the Divine character, and casts the blame on the creature, where it ought to be cast. Whereas, the opposite would cast the blame directly on God, if he decreed it so. This is the truth, and you cannot deny it. Although Christ hath promised once to draw *all* men unto him, (not to drag, for bait draws birds, yet they come voluntarily,) yet he never promises to draw them a second time, but on the other hand positively saith, "My spirit shall not always strive with man." And again, "Because I have called and ye have refused, but ye have set at nought my counsel, and would none of my reproofs, I also will laugh at your calamity, and mock when your fear cometh." "Ephraim is joined to his idols, let him alone." And the language of a reprobate is, "The harvest is past, the summer is ended, and we are not saved."—Jer. viii. 20. Prov. i. 24, 25, 26. Gen. vi. 3.

As the Lord requireth a right sacrifice in the path of revealed duty, those who, like Cain, bring a wrong offering, the fruit of the ground, instead of the firstling of the flock, like Abel, must expect, like Cain, to be rejected, (Gen. iv. 7;) for God saith, "Behold, I have set life and death before you, choose you this day whom ye will serve," &c. (Josh. xxiv. 15.) "One thing is needful, and Mary hath chosen the good part." We do not read God chose it for her. This is the truth, and you cannot deny it. Even, as we read in John iii. 19, that "this is the condemnation, that light has come into the world, and men love darkness rather than light," &c. Oh! reader, prepare to meet thy God!

Objection: Hath not the potter power over the clay, of the same lump to make one vessel to honor, and another to dishonor?

Answer: A potter never makes any vessel on purpose to destroy it; for, the most dishonorable one in family sickness is as useful as the honorable teacup in time of health. Neither doth God make any on purpose for destruction, but all mankind are useful, if they get the spirit of their station, and fill up that sphere for which they are qualified. For, without servants there can be no masters; without subjects, no rulers; without commonalty, no quality; and any one may observe that David was elected or set apart to be king, Jeremiah and Samuel to be prophets, &c.; and any discerning eye may easily discover that Paul's election (Rom. ix.) was not an election to future happiness, but of temporal advantages. And yet those not so positive, but that the privileges might be forfeited and lost by sin, as you may find, 1 Chron. xxviii. 9, 10: "If thou serve him with a perfect heart, and with a willing mind, he will be found of thee; but if thou forsake him, he will cast thee off for ever." (Deut. xxx. 15—19.) Moses's dying declaration was, that the children of Israel must obey, and if they would, all needful blessings they should have, but if rebellious, should be cursed and scattered, &c. This is a truth and you cannot deny it. And observe Paul, when talking about the clay and potter, alludes to Jer. xviii., where the prophet was commanded to see the potter work, &c. And then God says, verse 6th, "Cannot I do with you as this potter, O house of Israel?" &c. Again, verse 7th, "At what instant I shall speak concerning a nation or kingdom, to pluck up, pull down, or destroy it; if that nation against whom I have pronounced, turn from their evil, I will repent of the evil I thought to do unto them. At what instant I shall speak concerning a nation or kingdom, to build or plant it, if it do evil in my sight, that it obey not my voice, then will I repent of the good wherewith I said I would benefit them."

Now observe, if God be unchangeable, as Paul saith, God cannot lie, then he is bound by his immutability, or the law of his nature, to perform his promises to the obedient, and his threatenings against the disobedient; and this is the truth, and you cannot deny it.

Objection: Bible language is, "I will," and "you shall;" and the promises are "yea and amen," without any *ifs* or *ands*.

Answer: To take the *promises* without the *condition*, is a practice of Satan, (Luke iv. 10, 12,) which he made use of to our Lord to get him to fall down from the battlement of the temple, and thereby tempt God, and presume on God, because of the promise which the devil intended he should think to be *unconditional;* and so bear him up in the way of *dis-obedience.* Whereas, our Saviour knowing the *path of duty* to be the way of *safety,* replied, " It is written, thou shalt not tempt the Lord thy God." For in the way of *obedience* there is a *promise* of preservation, and in the way of disobedience a *threatening* of destruction. This is the truth, and you cannot deny it. Therefore, to cut these two little letters *if* out of the Bible, which make such a great significant word, is wrong, seeing it is so frequent in scripture. Frequently there are conditions *implied* in the Bible, though not *expressed;* for instance, David, when at Keilah, (1 Sam. xxiii. &c.) inquired of the Lord whether Saul would come down, and the men of the city deliver him up, and the Lord answered in the affirmative. Here is no condition expressed, yet there is one implied; for David left the city and fled to the wilderness; so Saul came not down, neither did the people deliver him up. Again, God said to the Ninevites, by Jonah, " Yet forty days and Nineveh shall be overthrown." Now, if you say all threatenings are without conditions, you give God the lie; for the city was spared in consequence of their believing God, and turning from their evil ways; Jonah iii. 5—10. This is the truth, and you cannot deny it. Again, Ezek. xxxiii. &c. There is a condition implied and explained undeniably, though not so fully expressed at the first, concerning the righteous and wicked man, which you may read at your leisure. This is the truth, and you cannot deny it.

Objection: Says one, " God will have mercy on whom he will have mercy," &c. Answer:

" God will have mercy on whom he *will,*
Come think you who they be?
'Tis every one that loves his Son,
And from their sins do flee:—

'Tis every one that doth repent,
And truly hates his sin:
'Tis every one that is content
To turn to God again.

And whom he will he *hardeneth—*
Come think you who they be?
'Tis every one that hates his Son,
Likewise his liberty:—

'Tis ev'ry one that in sin persist,
And do outstand their day;
Then God in justice leaves them to
Their own hearts' lusts a prey."

Objection: " *My* people shall be *made* willing in the day of my power," says one. Answer: That is home-made scripture; for the Almighty doth not so speak, but King David (Psa. cx. 3) speaks to the Almighty: " Thy people shall be willing in the day of thy power." He doth not say, they shall be made willing; the word *made* is not there, neither has it any business there. Again: those little words in italic letters were not in the original, but were put in by the translators, to make what they thought to be sense in the English language; and those little words, *shall be,* are in italic letters—of course, put in by the translators: now, I leave them out, and in lieu thereof put in the word *are,* and then read it, " Thy people *are* willing in the day of thy power." Now is the day of God's power, and now his people are willing; they are always a willing people. It is the reprobate character that is unwilling that God's will should be done.

This is the truth, and you cannot deny it. (Matt. vii. 24-26.) Objection. Christ did not pray for all mankind, &c. Answer: That's a lie—see John xvii. 9: first, Christ prayed for his disciples; secondly, (ver. 20,) for those who should believe on him through their word; and, thirdly, for the whole world, (ver. 21-23:) thus, "That the *world* may *believe* that thou hast sent me." Again: that the *world* may *know* that thou hast sent me; and this doth not mean A-double-L-part. Objection: Paul says, (Rom. viii.) whom God foreknew he predestinated, called, justified, and glorified, &c. Here is no condition expressed; of course, it appeareth that he glorified all that he justified, called, and predestinated, and foreknew, &c. Answer: If that be taken just as it stands, without any conditions whatever, it will follow that Universalism is true, or else that we are all reprobates; for God foreknows one as much as another, in every sense of the word, and, of course. foreknows all mankind. And now, if all that he foreknows he predestinates, calls, justifies, and glorifies, without any condition, in any shape or sense, it undeniably argues the universal salvation of every son of Adam. This is the truth, and you cannot deny it. Or else, if you take the apostle unconditionally, as he speaketh in the past tense, then no more can be glorified. Therefore *we* are all reprobates; and you cannot deny it. But it is my opinion that Paul is only rehearsing a catalogue of states, as they take place in succession. And to take any particular part of the Bible, in the face and eyes of twenty scriptures more, any doctrine thereby may be proved: and thus we find, by such means, have sprung up the many sentiments in the earth. People, desirous to get to heaven in an easier way than God hath pointed out, will hew out an opinion of their own—a broken cistern, that can hold no water—and will twist and bend the scriptures to their sentiment; and sometimes will have to grind the same, and put it into a press and press out a construction of their own. But this will not do. Scripture must be explained by scripture, and that according to reason, so as not to make it clash, but rather correspond with, true Christian experience.

Objection: We read, "As many as were ordained to eternal life believed." Answer: True; but the word *ordained*, signifies, set apart as a minister for his office: thus Jeremiah was set apart a prophet. And David saith, "The Lord hath set apart him that is godly for himself." (Psa. iv. 3.) And there is no account of any being set apart for the Lord's self, but the godly. No man is godly, or godlike, but the believer; therefore, none are ordained, or set apart for heaven, but those that believe. Besides, the Acts of the Apostles were written some time after the things took place, and, of course, are all written in the past tense. *Ordained* is in the past tense, and so is *believed*; and there is no account of the one being prior to the other. But it may be said, as many as believed were then ordained to eternal life; as none are ordained, or set apart for eternal life, but the saints. No man is a saint except he believes; for "he that believeth not is condemned already," saith Christ. Therefore, as soon as one believes, he is free from condemnation, and, of course, set apart for heaven, and not before—he being in Christ now by the act of faith. Now observe: Peter talks about elect *in* Christ, not *out of him*. Paul saith, (2 Cor. v. 17,) "If any man be in Christ he is a new creature," &c.; and (Rom. viii. 1) saith, " There is *now*" (not yesterday or to-morrow) " no condemnation to them which are in Christ Jesus; *who walk not after the flesh, but after the*

Spirit," &c. ; which implies, there *is* condemnation to those who are not in Christ, but walk after the flesh, and not after the Spirit. And Paul saith, " They which have not the Spirit of Christ, are none of his." (Rom. viii. 9.) And John saith, " He that committeth sin is of the devil." (2 John, iii. 8.) And again : " No man can call Jesus Lord, but by the Holy Ghost." " But as many as are *led* by the Spirit of God, they are the sons of God."

Query. If all things are decreed right, is it not evident that there is no no such thing as sin or guilt ? For it cannot be wrong to fulfil right decrees. Consequently, there can be no redemption, for there is nothing to redeem them from: consequently, if mankind think they have sinned and are redeemed, their thoughts must be a deception, and are imaginary ; and, of course, their praising God for redeeming love is folly, for they praise him for that which he never did. Now, supposing this imaginary, false, mistaken idea, that they " had been sinners and were redeemed," was removed, and they so enlightened as to discover that nothing, according to right decrees, had ever taken place wrong, &c., how would the heavenly host be astonished to think they had been deceived! What silence would immediately ensue !

Some people hold to a falling from grace, which I think is wrong ; for, say they, if we were always to be in the light, we should grow proud ; therefore, it is necessary that we should have a darkness. to make us feel our weakness and dependence. From this, it appears that they think a little sin is necessary for the perfecting of the saints ; and you cannot deny it. Now, to hold a thing necessary, implies *holding to it :* the same as I think doing duty, or perfection in love, to be necessary, therefore, I hold to it. Thus you see they hold to a falling from grace, which I think wrong. Yet I adopt the idea that a man *can* fall from grace according to *conscience, reason, and scripture,* which idea some people think to be dangerous : but I think it is not naturally attended with such bad consequences as the other ; for if a man thinks he is safe, he is not apt to look out for danger ; whereas, if he thinks there is danger he is apt, like the mariner, to look out for breakers. Again : supposing I have religion, I think I can fall so as to perish everlastingly. Here is another man, with the same degree of religion, believing *once in grace always in grace.* Now, if my idea of the *possibility* of falling, &c., be false, his sentiment, if true, will certainly reach me ; so I am as safe as he. But supposing his doctrine to be false, and mine true, he is gone for it, and mine will not reach him.

So you see I have two strings to my bow to his one. This is the truth, and you cannot deny it. Now, reader, observe : as I heard of a seine on Rhode Island which caught a shoal of fish, and, for fear of the escape of some, a number of seines encircled the enclosed, so that they could not escape, and if any did escape the first or second net, the others should catch them, &c. So you may plainly discover, as I have linked the above doctrines, if some of my ideas are false, the other ideas, as so many seines, will catch me. *Once in grace always in grace ;* or *Predestination,* or *Universalism,* or *Deism* with *Atheism.* But if they are false, those characters are gone, if they have nothing else to depend upon but principles ; yet I still may be safe. This is the truth, and you cannot deny it.

Again it it evident, in reason's eye, that the more light a person hath, if he abuse the same, the greater is the sin and guilt. Therefore, in justice, the condemnation and punishment must be proportioned, according to the saying of Christ, " He that knoweth his master's will, and *doeth* it not, shall be beaten with many stripes ;" whereas, he that committeth things worthy of stripes, and knoweth not his master's will, shall be beaten with few stripes. Thus you see it is required according to what a man hath, and not according to what he hath not. As we read, every man is to be *rewarded according* to his *works*, or the deeds done in the body. (Rev. xxii. 12, and xiv. 13: Luke xii. 47, &c.)

Now scripture proof that a man may fall from grace, runneth thus: "If any man *draw back*, my soul shall have no pleasure in him. The backslider in heart shall be filled with his own ways," &c. Now if a man were in a high pillory, it would be nonsense for one to cry out, "Hold tight, stand and hang fast, for if you fall it will hurt you," if there be no danger of his falling, and more so if there be not a possibility of it. If so, then how much greater nonsense, for an almighty God to give us his will, with many cautions as needless as the above, there being no danger nor even a possibility of danger. And yet he, like some passionate parents who say to their children, "If you do so and so, I'll whip you—I'll burn you up—I'll skin you and turn you out of doors," &c., and yet have no intention to perform the threatenings, but do lie to them. Just such a character some people seem to represent the Lord in. When he cautions as follows: Gen. ii. 17, "In the day thou eatest thereof thou shalt surely die ;" serpent-like, say they, (Gen. iii. 4,) " Ye shall not surely die." But it is evident that God is in earnest in the following threatenings: Rev. xxii. 19, "If any man shall take away from the words of the book of this prophecy, God shall take away his part out of the *book of life*, and *out* of the *holy city*," &c. There is no account of a *sinner's* having a part in the *book of life*, or *holy city*, but the saint; for it is holiness that gives the title. Heb. xii. 14. Again: "Hold fast, that no man take thy crown," &c. Rev. iii. 11. "Be thou faithful unto death, and I will give thee a crown of life," and "he that endureth to the end, the same shall be saved." Rev. ii. 10. Mark xiii. 13. Jude tells us of some "whose fruit withereth, twice dead, plucked up by the roots." Now it is evident that a sinner is but once dead, then these must have been once alive in the scriptural sense ; or else how could the fruit wither, or they be twice dead and be plucked up by the roots? Ver. 12. Again: there is as in unto death, which we are not commanded to pray for, (compare 1 John v. 16, 17 with Hebrews x. 26 to 31.) Again: Peter tells of some that have forgotten that they were purged from their old sins, and even escaped the pollutions of the world, through the knowledge of Christ, &c., and yet are again entangled therein ; and saith he, "it had been better for them not to have known the way of righteousness, than after they have known it, to turn from," &c., (2 Pet. i .9 and ii. 20, &c., to the end.) How could they have forgot that which they never knew ? Again: (Heb. vi. 4 to 7) what higher attainments can one have than are here mentioned ; and (2 Pet. iii. 17, &c.) "if any man thinketh he standeth, let him take heed lest he fall." 1 Cor. x. 12, Rom. xi. 20, 21, Heb. iv. 1. Observe, there were six hundred thousand Jews, all well, active men, &c., which came out of Egypt with Moses, and one was in as fair a way for Canaan as another ; and God promised as positively to carry them to the promised land, as ever he promised to carry the saint from earth to heaven: only four got through the wilderness. Aaron and Moses died on the mountains, and Caleb and Joshua reached the desired country. But all the others it appears were once favorites of heaven, from Paul's talk, (1 Cor. x. 3, 4, &c.) as he saith, "they all drank of Christ, the spiritual rock," &c., "and yet some of them tempted him," &c., ver. 9, "and thus they all by sin fell in the wilderness." And Paul addeth, moreover, that these things happened unto them for examples, and were written for our admonition, ver. 11. Now what need of saints being admonished, if there be no danger of losing the spiritual land of rest? Paul was afraid of falling, ix. 27. But observe, though God had promised to carry the Jews to Canaan, &c., yet there was a condition implied. Numb. xiv. 34 : "And ye shall know my breach of promise.". There was a condition implied, though not fully expressed before. Gen. xvii. 8, 28, xiii. 50, xxiv. 25; Heb. xi. 2; Exod. iii. 16, 17, &c.; Lev. xxvi. 27, 28, &c. Hark! "If you will not for all this hearken unto me, (saith God,) but walk contrary unto me, then I will walk contrary unto you also in fury, and I, even I, will chastise you seven times for your sins." Now if all things are decreed right straight forward, how could the Jews walk contrary to God? And if not, how could God walk contrary to them? God help thee to consider this, if there be no condition implied; and likewise Exod. xiii. 17; Numb. xiv. 21, 22, 23, 24, &c. "Because those men, which have seen my glory and miracles which I did in Egypt and in the wilderness, and have tempted me now these ten times, and *have* not *hearkened* to my voice, surely they shall not see the land which I sware unto their fathers," ver. 34. God help you to take warning by the Jews, for it is evident that according to the words of Moses, (Deut. xxviii.) that great blessings were promised, if the nation would obey, and curses in consequence of disobedience, which ideas were confirmed in the dying speech of *Joshua*, (xxiv. 20,) which was fulfilled, according to the book of Judges. When it went well with the Jews, we find they were serving God; but when they did evil, God sold them into the hands of their enemies. God help thee to compare the promises and threatenings in Deuteronomy with the book of Judges, &c. and observe God's dealings thenceward, and apply that to Matt. vii. 24 &c. And observe the gospel, for we are to take warning by God's dealings with the ancients, and square our lives accordingly; because to judgment we must come, and be judged with strict justice, and receive sentence accordingly. Either "come ye blessed," or "depart ye cursed," (Matt xxv. 34, 41, &c.) Now observe, if I am guilty I must have pardon here and then if my life from the day of forgiveness brings forth good frui from a holy heart, it is right; consequently the reward must ensue accordingly. But if I turn, and willingly love sin again, my conduct flowing from that evil desire, thus living and dying, my sentence must be accordingly agreeable to the principles of true justice. This is the truth and you cannot deny it. Read attentively about the good and evil servants, from Matt. xxiv. 46 to 48, &c., and xviii. 23, &c.

Observe, Paul exhorts Timothy to war a good warfare, holding *fast* and a *good conscience*, which, saith he, "some having put away concerning *faith*, have made *shipwreck;* of whom is Hymeneus and Alexander,' (1 Tim. i. 19; John xv.) Christ saith, "I am the true vine, and m Father is the husbandman; every branch in me that beareth not fruit h taketh away, (observe, he could not take them away unless they were there;) and every branch that beareth fruit, he purgeth it, that it may bring forth more fruit." "Now ye are clean, through the word which I have spoken unto you." Observe, a sinner is not clean, but filthy. But if these were made clean through the word of Christ, as just mentioned, then they were saints, and you cannot deny it. Ver. 4: "Abide in me, and I in you. As the branch cannot bear fruit of itself, except it abide in the vine, no more can ye, except ye abide in me. I am the vine, ye are the branches," &c. Ver. 6: "If a man abide not in me, he is cast forth as a branch, and is withered," &c. Observe, a sinner is not compared to a green tree, but a dry; this could not wither except it were green, and a branch once withered, it is hard to make it green again, &c., but they are gathered and burned. Verses 7, 8: "If ye abide in me, and my words abide in you, ye shall ask what ye will, and it shall be done unto you; herein is my Father glorified, that ye bear much fruit, so shall ye be my disciples." Ver. 9: "Continue ye in my love." Now ye may see that the five little letters that are herein enclosed, which too many people overlook, and which fixes the sense of a great many scriptures, running parallel through the Bible, &c., viz: "if and eth." Now the Bible runneth thus: *if* ye do so and so, I will do so and so; and *if* ye do so and so, I will do so and so, &c. And again, "ed," past tense, we find but little in the Bible. But the scripture, instead of making a yesterday Christian, it maketh a present, every-day Christian. Thus, he that *believeth, heareth, seeth, understandeth, knoweth, pursueth, watcheth, hath, enjoyeth,* and *endureth.* This is the truth, and you cannot deny it, for the Bible doth not inquire what I was yesterday, but what I am *now?* Objection: Christ saith "my sheep *hear* my voice; they *follow me,* and shall never perish, neither shall any man pluck them out of my hand," &c., (John x. 27, 28.) Answer: Here the saint is represented by the similitude of a sheep, hearing and following a shepherd; and observe, the promise is made, as before observed, to a certain obedient character, and here the promise is to those that *hear; hearing* doth not mean stopping your ears, or being careless and inattentive; but it implieth giving strict attention to the object which requireth the same; and *following,* likewise, doth not mean running the other way, but a voluntary coming after. Therefore, there is a condition implied and expressed in this passage, viz: *hear* and *follow,* and the promise is to that character. Of course a backslider doth not imitate it, and of course cannot claim the promise but what he may perish; may *turn away,* according to Ezekiel xxxiii. 18. "When the righteous [man] turneth away from his righteousness, and committeth iniquity, he shall even die thereby," &c.

Objection: The death there spoken of is temporal. Answer: I deny it, for the body will die, whether you sin or not; and God when he meaneth the body, doth not say the soul, but positively declares, "the soul that sinneth, it shall die," chapter xviii. 4.

Objection: But the righteous man there spoken of is a self-righteous man. Answer: I deny it, for he is pronounced a righteous man by God himself; and how can he be righteous, in the judgment of God, without saving faith? God doth not call a wicked man good, nor a good man evil; yet you say that him that God here pronounceth righteous is only self-righteous—a Pharisee. Oh, scandalous for any man to twist the scriptures thus! Now look at it in your own glass; self-righteousness being wickedness, we will style it iniquity, and the man an iniquitous man, and then read it, "when an iniquitous man turneth away from his iniquity, and committeth iniquity, for his iniquity, &c., shall he die." Read the above twice over, and then sound and see if there be any bottom or top, according to your exposition. Leaving your shameless construction, I pass on to answer another objection, which may be urged from Romans viii. 38, 39, where Paul saith, "I am persuaded that neither death nor life, nor angels, principalities, powers, things present or to come, nor height, nor depth, nor any other *creature*, shall be able to separate us from the love of God," &c.

Observe, though Paul speaks of a second cause not being able to separate us from the enjoyment of God's love, yet he does not say but that *we* may separate ourselves by disobedience, which is sin. Sin is not a creature, as some people falsely think; but sin is a non-conformity to the will of God. If you still say that sin is a creature, I ask you what shape it is in, or what color it is of, or how many eyes or wings it hath, or whether it crawls like a snake? Paul doth not term it a creature, but agreeth with St. John, where he saith, "Sin is the transgression of the law, and where there is no law, there is no transgression;" and being not without law to God, but under the law of Christ, the Christian still feeleth himself conscientiously accountable unto God, and you cannot deny it. 1 John iii. 4; Romans iii. 20—iv. 15; 1 Corinthians ix. 21, for we read, not that a good man falleth into sin every day, and still is in the way to heaven, being a child of God, but to the reverse. 1 John iii. 8, "He that committeth sin, is of the devil." John viii. 8, "Whosoever committeth sin, is the servant of sin;" verse 36, "If the Son therefore shall make you free, ye shall be free indeed." Romans vi. 18, "Being then made free from sin, ye became the servants of righteousness;" verse 20, "For when ye were the servants of sin, ye were free from righteousness;" verses 22, 23, "But now being made free from sin, &c., for the wages of sin is death."

Any person, by reading Psalm lxxxix., may plainly discover that the promise made therein to David, as in the person of Christ, was not altogether without condition, by comparing the promise from verses 19 to 20, &c., to 38. From that, either there is a contradiction in the Psalm, or else a condition must be allowed; for one part saith that, "His seed and throne shall endure for ever," and another part, "Thou hast cast his throne to the ground," verses 36, 44, &c. But, observe, most people when quoting this Psalm to prove once in grace always in grace, read thus, verse 33: "Nevertheless, will I not utterly take from them, nor suffer my faithfulness to fail," which is a wrong quotation. He does not say in the plural, he will not take it from *them*, but in the singular, will not utterly take from *him*; that is, from Christ Jesus, as David frequently represents Christ. Compare this Psalm with 1 Chronicles xxviii. 6. 7. and 1 Kings ix. 4 to 9, where undeniably you will find the condition.

Objection: "I have loved thee with an everlasting love," and. "He that believeth hath everlasting life." Answer: The life there spoken of is the love of God, which is called everlasting, because it is his eternal nature, which all those that believe enjoy; yet God, being holy, cannot behold iniquity with allowance, and of course his justice cries against it, and demands satisfaction. It must be, that if I lose that life, that the nature of it does not change, but returns to God who gave it, by my out sinning the day or reach of mercy, &c. But, says one, can a man sin beyond the love of God, or out of the reach of mercy? Answer: We read that God loved the world, and yet that there is a sin unto death, which we are not commanded to pray for when one committeth, John iii. 16, 17; 1 John v. 16. Those who may read the above, that have enjoyed the comforts of religion in their own souls, when they are faithful to God they feel his love, and enjoy the light of his countenance; and a mountain of trouble appears as a hill, and he surmounts it with delight and cries in the poet's language:

> "Give joy or grief, give ease or pain,
> Take life or friends away,
> But let me find them all again
> In that eternal day."

They feel the truth of Christ's words, (John viii. 12,) "He that followeth me shall not walk in darkness, but shall have the light of life." But when they let down their watch, their strength departs, like Sampson's when shorn, and their enemies get the better. A hill of trouble appears as a mountain, and they feel like one forsaken; and, on reflection, conscience lays the blame not on God, like the doctrine of decrees, but on them, and they have no peace until they repent and do their first work, viz., to go to God as a criminal, and yet as a beggar, broken-hearted, willing to part with the accursed thing; then they find the Lord to lift upon them the light of his countenance, and their peaceful hours return. They take their harps from the willows, and cry, like the ancients, "Our soul is escaped as a bird from the snare of the fowler; the snare is broken, and we are escaped."

Query: Who ever fell from grace? Answer: We are informed (1 Samuel xv. 17) that when Saul was little in his own eyes, God exalted him to be king over Israel; and (x. 6) when Samuel anointed him, he said, "The Spirit of the Lord will come upon thee, and thou shalt prophesy, and shalt be turned into another man," &c. Verse 9, we read, moreover, that God gave him another heart, &c., and what sort of a heart God gives, I leave you to judge. And God seemed to prosper Saul while he was humble, xiii. 12. It appeareth after two years that his heart got lifted up with pride, and the Lord sent him to utterly destroy the Amalekites, and all things belonging thereto, according to the commandment by Moses; but Saul rebelled, and committed a sin thereby, which was as the sin of witchcraft and idolatry, xv. 23. After this the Spirit of the Lord departed from him; and afterwards Saul murdered himself in the field of battle. And we read, no murderer hath eternal life abiding in him, and that murderers hereafter shall be shut out of the holy city, xvi. 14, and xxxi. 4; 1 John iii. 15; Revelation xxii. 15. But, saith one, was not David a man after God's own heart, when committing adultery and murder? Answer: No, for God hath not the heart of an adulterer nor a murderer. And again—no murderer hath eternal life abiding in him, 1 John iii. 15. And supposing David was a man after God's own heart when feeding his father's sheep, that is no sign he was when committing adultery and murder, any more than if I were honest seven years ago, and then turned thief, am honest still because I was once; this is the truth, and you cannot deny it. But observe, the Lord was displeased with David, being angry with the wicked every day; and there is no account that the Lord put away David's sin until he confessed it, &c., 2 Samuel xi. 27—xii. 13; and all backsliders, who sincerely repent, may receive pardon as David did, &c. But yet there is no scripture that saith they shall be brought to repentance irresistibly, whether they will or not; for God will have volunteers for heaven, or none at all, Revelation xxii. 14–17. We cannot with reason suppose that a king would choose an enemy as an ambassador with an embassage to rebels, but a friend. Neither can we suppose, with propriety, that God or Christ would call an enemy—a child of the devil—to go and preach and do miracles, but a friend. Yet we find in Matthew x. that Judas, with the others, was positively called, and commanded to preach, and had power to raise the dead, heal the sick, and cast out devils, &c. And the twelve went out, and returned, &c. It speaks of them collectively, but not individually, doing miracles, till after Christ's resurrection. Chapter xix., Peter saith, " *We* have forsaken all, (not *I*,) and followed thee ; what shall we have, therefore ?" Christ answereth, (verse 28,) " Verily, (or certainly,) I say unto you, that ye which have followed me in the regeneration, when the Son of man shall sit in the throne of his glory, ye also shall sit upon twelve thrones, judging the twelve tribes of Israel." Now, I ask, how they could follow Christ in the regeneration except they were regenerated, i. e., born again ? Doth it not mean Judas for one, seeing there were twelve apostles, twelve thrones, and twelve tribes—a throne for each ? But it appeareth that the thrones were promised on conditions of overcoming, (Revelation iii. 21,) and that Judas forfeited his title by disobedience, &c. But, saith one, I thought Judas was raised up for the very purpose to betray Christ, and was always a wicked man. Answer: Many people think so, through the prejudice of education, and set up their opinion for the standard, and attempt to bend the scriptures to it; but that will not do, for truth will stand when error falls, and of course our tenets should correspond with the Bible, which doth not say that Judas was always evil. But Christ conveys an idea to the reverse, when referring (John xiii. 18) to Psalm xli. 9, where David is speaking of Judas, as in the person of Christ, and saith, " Mine own *familiar friend, in whom I trusted*, which did eat of my bread, hath lifted up his heel against me." Here Judas is not only styled Christ's friend, but his familiar one, in whom he trusted. Now, can we suppose, with propriety, that Christ would be familiar with the deceitful, and put confidence in them ? No, methinks he would have set a better example.

Objection : Christ says, John vi. 70, "Have I not chosen you twelve, and one of you is a devil ?"

Answer: Sometimes Christ spoke as man, and sometimes as God, and God frequently speaks of things that are not as though they were. For instance, (Rev. xiii. 8,) we read that Christ was a Lamb slain from the foundation of the world, and yet he was not actually slain till four thousand years after.

Again, God said to Abraham, " I have made thee a father of many nations ;" when he was not the father of but one child, Ishmael. So Christ, foreseeing, as God, that Satan would enter into Judas, spoke it, as if it was in the present tense, though it was not really so for some time after

There was more trust put in Judas than in the other apostles, he being made treasurer. We have repeated accounts of Peter, James, and John sinning; but no account that Judas did, until six days before the Passover, John xii. Mark xiv. 3. When our Lord was in the house of Simon the leper, which appears to be Judas's father's house, a woman came in to anoint Christ, &c., and it appears that Judas felt a *thievish*, covetous disposition arise, and from that no doubt he was called a *thief*, and had the bag, for he was never called a thief *before;* and Christ gave him a gentle rebuke, and it appears that Judas got affronted, by his complying with a suggestion of Satan. Satan was not really in him yet, only tempted him. And going out the same day, he made a bargain, (John xiii. 2, and Mark xiv. 10,) like some ministers, saying, "What will ye give me, and I will deliver him unto you," &c. Some people make scripture, and say, whom Christ loves, he loves to the end, (to the end of what?) There are no such words in the Bible. In John xiii. 1, we read thus: "When Jesus knew that his hour was come that he should depart out of this world unto the Father, having loved his own which were in the world, he loved them unto the end"—namely, the night in which the sacrament was instituted—Judas being present, &c., received the sop, *after* which Satan entered him, verse 27. And now it may be said, in the full sense of the word, that *he* was a *devil*, and *not before*, unless you allow of his being one before, and another entering into him now—and so making a double devil of him—and what sort of being that may be, I cannot tell.

Objection: I think if Judas had *regeneration*, or was ever a friend to Christ, as you talk from Matt. xix. 28, 29, and Psa. xli. 9, that he is gone to glory. Answer: No, he has not; for Christ affirmed, "Wo to that man, it had been good for him that he had never been born," Mark xiv. 21; Luke xxii. 21, 22. Again, we read Judas murdered himself; and no murderer hath eternal life abiding in him. Objection: I do not think one that is *given* to Christ can be lost. Answer: Then you do not believe the Bible, for we read (John xvii. 12) that Judas was *given* to Christ, and yet he is lost, and styled a son of *perdition*, which means a son of destruction; and, (Acts i. 24, 25,) when the eleven surviving apostles chose Matthias to fill up Judas's sphere, they prayed thus: "Thou, Lord, which knowest the hearts of all men, show whether of these two thou hast chosen, that he may take the part of this ministry and apostleship, from which Judas by transgression fell," &c. Now, if Judas were always a devil, (which could not be, for there must have been a time when he began to be one,) why would they choose a good man to fill up a devil's place? Observe, there were twelve parts of the ministry, and the apostles were persons accountable to God. Judas fell by transgression, for where there is no law there is no transgression. Now, what did he fall from? An old profession? To fall from an old profession, is no transgression at all: for transgression is sin, which implies the violation of a known law; of course, falling by transgression, implies losing something which is valuable, by misconduct, &c. This is the truth, and you cannot deny it. "But," says one, "I do not like your talk, for you destroy my comfort; and it is a discouraging doctrine against getting religion, if one thinks they can lose it after they get it." Answer: I might on the other hand, or in another case say, that it is discouraging against getting money, or buying this farm, or that horse, for perhaps it may be squandered, lost, or die; therefore, I would not try for them. What would you think of the man who would stop and be negligent at such objections? People temporally do not term such things discouraging, so as to flee; and methinks none will make that reply, but those who live and plead for a *little* sin: one leak will *sink* a ship.

Objection: Solomon was a wise man, but did many wrong things, and yet wrote Ecclesiastes afterwards; from which we may infer, no doubt, he is happy. Answer: Solomon no doubt was a *wise* man, above all the kings of the earth, and yet became the greatest *fool* by abusing his wisdom; for, after that God had done so much for Solomon, Solomon turned and committed sin, and, according to the Mosaic law, was worthy of temporal death in *five* respects. First, he made an *affinity* with Pharoah, king of Egypt; secondly, took his *daughter* to be his wife; thirdly, made *affinity* with Hiram, king of Tyre; fourthly, fell in *love* with *heathenish* women, who turned his *heart* from God; fifthly, fell into *idolatry*. He had *four* gods that he worshipped himself, and *others* for his *wives*. When Solomon was young, we read the Lord *loved* him; but now he was old, we read the Lord was *angry* with him, and he is angry with the *wicked* every day. The Lord endeavored to reclaim Solomon; first, by mercy, and then by affliction; and raised up three adversaries for that purpose. But Solomon would not hear, but went on a step further, and attempted to *kill* Jeroboam, who arose and fled to Egypt: and as the scripture leaves Solomon, he died in that state, with *murder* in his heart, as he attempted to slay the *innocent;* and "no *murderer* hath *eternal* life *abiding* in *him*." And there is no account of Solomon's repentance, but that he died in his sins; and our Lord intimates, that if we die in our sins, where he is, we cannot come. And David's dying words to Solomon were, "If thou seek the Lord, *he* will be found of *thee*; but if thou *forsake* him, he will cast thee *off* forever." Solomon sought the Lord, and the Lord *appeared* to him *twice;* afterwards he forsook God, and there is no account of his return, as before observed: and as for believing that Ecclesiastes was written afterwards, I no more believe Solomon could write when he was dead, than I believe I could. To evade this answer, and say Solomon wrote it when he was old; I reply, it is no more than any old man that swears and gets drunk can do, to cry out vanity of vanities, &c. when their lives are burdensome. But what makes the beauty of Ecclesiastes is, to see that a young man could cry out *vanity*, which is so contrary to *nature*, when nature is so fond of it. As for the book of Proverbs, any person may discover they were written before the building of the temple, by turning to 1 Kings iv. 32, &c., and before much of his wickedness. You need not say, that I *said*, that Solomon is gone to hell. I did not affirm so; but I take Solomon where the scripture doth, and leave him where the scripture doth, in the hand of a merciful God; asking, since the Bible is so particular to mention all the *good* conduct of Solomon, and then his *bad* conduct, if he repented, why was not that put down? Turn to the history of Josephus, and it leaves Solomon, if possible, in a worse situation than the Bible doth, &c.

Some people blame me for holding to perfection, and at the same time they hold to it stronger than I do; and moreover, for not holding to the *final perseverance* of the saints; which assertion I think is wrong, for I think there is danger of *falling* away—therefore, I hold to *perseverance* and hey cannot deny it. But they hold, a man *cannot* get rid of sin. Here, therefore, they hold to *persevering* in sin, and they hold to a falling from grace of course. This is the truth, and you cannot deny it. Some have heard ministers pray to God, that the people might be sanctified from all sin, and then told them that they could not get rid of all sin. This was a clash. People frequently feel good desires from God to get rid of " all sin," (James i. 17,) and yet think they cannot obtain the blessing, so pray in unbelief for it. We read, that whatsoever is not of *faith* is *sin*; therefore, if I hold with them, I should pray thus: " Lord, save me from part of my sins now, and at death take them all away," &c. But this doth not correspond with the Lord's prayer, which commandeth us to pray that God's *kingdom may come*, and his *will* be done, &c., as in heaven, and we be delivered from *evil*.

The kingdom of God, we read, is not meat and drink, but righteousness, peace, and joy in the Holy Ghost. And Paul saith, this is the will of God, even your sanctification; and if a man be delivered from all evil, there is no sin left. And what is the benefit to pray for it, if we cannot have it? But in obedience to the commandment to pray for deliverance from evil, Paul besought God to sanctify the Thessalonians wholly, and to preserve their whole spirit, soul, and body blameless, unto the coming of Christ, (1 Thess. v. 23;) and again, verse 16 to 18, he commandeth them to rejoice evermore, pray without ceasing, in every thing give thanks, for this is the will of God in Christ Jesus concerning you. Matt. v. 48, Christ saith, "Be ye perfect, even as your Father which is in heaven is perfect;" i. e. for a man in our sphere, as perfect as God is for God in his sphere. Again, " Be ye holy for I am holy." Again, "The commandment is to love the Lord with all our heart, soul, body, mind, and strength, and our neighbor as ourself," &c. And blessed be God, the promise is equal to the commandments, for God hath bound himself by a promise, (Ezek. xxxvi. 25,) " Then will I sprinkle clean water upon you, and ye shall be clean; from all your filthiness, and from all your idols will I cleanse you, a new heart also will I give you," &c. Again, (Psalm cxxx. 8,) the promise is, that "Israel shall be redeemed from all his iniquities." John viii. 12, Christ saith, " He that followeth me shall not walk in darkness, but shall have the light of life." And again, God hath promised by the hand of Moses, thus: " I will circumcise thy heart, and the heart of thy seed, to love the Lord with all thy heart," &c., and thy neighbor as thyself. And Paul speaketh of the oath and promise of God, two immutable things, in which it is impossible for God to lie. Now, if God cannot lie, then he cannot do all things, especially that which is contrary to his nature. If so, then the above mentioned promises are equal to the commandments, and God is bound by the law of his nature to perform the same. This is the truth, and you cannot deny it.

Objection: David saith, " There is none righteous, no, not one." Answer: True, yet we read about *righteous* Abel, and Lot's righteous soul, (2 Pet. ii. 8. Matt. xxiii. 35.) Objection: Solomon saith, " There is no man that sinneth not." Answer: True, but John saith, " He that is born of God doth not commit sin." Objection: Paul saith, " I am carnal, sold under sin;" yet he was a saint. Answer: Paul addeth elsewhere, " that the carnal mind is enmity against God, and is not subject to his law, neither indeed can be, and to be carnally minded is death." Again, "Christ came to save sinners, &c. of whom I am chief." Now to take these expressions together just as they stand, you might prove that Paul was one of the worst of men, in the way to death, and at the same time one of the best apostles, in the way to life, &c. Though Paul saith, I am carnal, sold under sin, yet it cannot be that he was speaking of himself, as a holy apostle; but was describing or rehearsing the language of one under the law, as you may see, Rom. vii. 1: "I speak to them that know the law," &c. But chap. viii. 1, 2, Paul saith, "There is therefore now no condemnation to them which are in Christ Jesus, who walk *not* after the flesh, *but* after the Spirit, for the law of the spirit of life in Christ Jesus hath made me *free* from the law of sin and death." And now, if Paul was made free he could not be groaning under bondage at the same time, unless you can reconcile liberty and slavery together. Paul saith in one place, "I robbed other churches." Now to take this passage just as it stands, you might prove that Paul was a robber; if so, would not the government hang him if he was here, as they hang robbers, &c.

And to take any particular passage you may prove almost any doctrine, if it be not taken in connection with the context, or general tenor of scripture. But as the Bible doth not plead for sin, but condemneth it, commanding us to be holy in heart and life, &c., therefore we should not plead for sin as though we loved it, and rolled it under our tongue as a sweet morsel, but should be *scripturians* or Bible men; for Paul telleth the Romans, to whom some think Paul made allowance for a little sin, inferring it from the 7th chapter; but, by the by, they should remember that Paul talketh thus, "being justified by faith, we have peace with God," chap. v. 1: vi. 18—22, he saith, "Being made free from sin," &c. and being now made free from sin, &c. Well, says one, what next? Answer: Any person by reading the epistles of John may find a sufficiency of proof to convince any candid mind that the doctrine of Christian perfection in love, is a Bible doctrine. Query: How far can a man be perfect in this life? Answer: A man may be a perfect sinner by the help of Satan, and you cannot deny it. Now, if a man can be a perfect sinner, why not a perfect saint? Shall we not allow as much power to God to perfect his children in his own nature, which is love, as the devil has power to perfect his in sin? &c. But, says one, answer the former question, and likewise, who ever attained what you are talking about? Very well: I'll tell you; I think a man cannot be as perfect as God, except it be for men in our sphere, as God is for God in his sphere; for *absolute* perfection belongs to God alone; neither as perfect as angels, or even as Adam before he *fell*, because I feel the effect of Adam's fall; my body being mortal is a clog to my soul, and frequently tends to weigh down my mind, which infirmity I do not expect to get rid of until my spirit returns to God. Yet I do believe that it is the privilege of every saint, to drink into the spirit and nature of God: so far as to live without committing wilful, or known, or malicious sins against God, but to have love the ruling principle within; and what we say and do, to flow from that divine principle of love within, from a sense of duty, though subject to trials, temptations and mistakes at the same time; and a mistake in judgment may occasion a mistake in practice—I may think a man more pious than he is, and put too much confidence in him, and thereby be brought into trouble. Now such a mistake as this, and many other similar ones I might mention, you cannot term sin with propriety; for when Eldad and Medad prophesied in the camp, Joshua mistaking in his judgment, thinking they did wrong, occasioned a practical mistake, requesting Moses to stop them, &c., which was not granted. Observe, one sin shut Moses out of Canaan, of course one sin must have shut Joshua out. But as God said, Joshua wholly followed him, and *wholly* not being *partly*, and as he entered Canaan from that circumstance, I argue that a mistake following from love is not imputed as a sin. Again, as we are informed that Christ was tempted in all respects like as we are, Heb. iv. 15, yet without sin, and *can* be *touched* with the *feeling* of our *infirmities*, &c. Again, as we are commanded, James i. 2, to count it all joy when we fall (not give way) into divers temptations. And if the devil, or wicked men tempt me, and I reject and repel the temptation with all my heart, how can it be said that I sin? Am I to blame for the devil's conduct? I can no more prevent my thoughts than I can prevent the birds from flying over my head; but I can prevent them from making nests in my hair.

Some people expect purgatory to deliver them from sin; but this would, methinks, make discord in heaven. Others think that death will do it. If death will deliver *one* from the last of sin, why not *two*, why not all the world by the same rule? So Universalism will be true, and death have the praise, and Jesus Christ be out of the question? But death is not called a *friend*, but is styled an *enemy*, and it does not *change* the disposition of the mind. All that death does is to separate the *soul* from the *body*; therefore, as we must get rid of the last of sin, either here or hereafter, and as but few in America allow of purgatory, I suppose it must be here. If so, then it is before the soul leaves the body, consequently it is in *time*, of course *before* death. Now the query arises, how long first? Why, says one, perhaps a minute before the soul leaves the body. Well, if a minute before, why not two minutes, or an hour; yea, a day, a week, a month, or a year, or even ten years before death—or even now? Is there not power sufficient with God, or efficacy enough in the blood of Christ? Certainly the scripture saith, all things are now ready; now is the accepted time, and behold now (not to-morrow) is the day of salvation. To-day if you will hear his voice. Remember now thy Creator in the days, &c. And there being no encouragement in the Bible for to-morrow, now is God's time, and you cannot deny it, &c. Observe examples: "By faith Enoch walked with God (not with sin) three hundred years, and had the testimony that he pleased God," Gen. v. 22. Heb. xi. 5; and Caleb and Joshua wholly (not partly) followed the Lord, Numbers xxxii. 11, 12. Job likewise, God said, was a perfect man, and you must not contradict him; and though Satan had as much power to kill Job's wife, as to destroy the other things, (as all except Job's life was in his hands,) but he thought he would spare her for an instrument, or a torment, Job i. 12—22, and ii. 9, 10. David was a man after God's own heart, when feeding his father's sheep, not when he was committing adultery, 1 Sam. xiii. 14, and xvi. 7—11, 2 Sam. xii. 13. Zacharias and Elizabeth were both righteous before God, walking in all the commandments, &c., blameless, Luke i. 5, 6. Nathaniel was an Israelite indeed, in whom there was no guile, &c., John i. 47. John speaking of himself, and those to whom he wrote, says, "Herein is our love made perfect, and perfect love casteth out fear." 1 John iv. 17, 18. Aga n, of the seven churches of Asia, five had some reproof, but two had no reproof at all, Smyrna and Philadelphia; why not if they had a little sin. The latter was highly commended, (Rev. ii. 8, 9, and iii. 7,) and so on, &c.

Query—Must we not get rid of all sin before we go to glory? Do not we feel desires for it? Did not God give us those desires? Does not he command us to pray for it? Should we not look in expectation of receiving? God help thee to consider without prejudice the above impartially, as a sincere inquirer after truth, let it come from whom it may, intending to improve conscientiously, as for eternity: Amen. Says one, do you think a man can know his sins forgiven in this life, and have the evidence of his acceptance with God? Answer: We are informed, that Abel had the witness that he was righteous, Gen. iv. 4, Heb. xi. 4. Enoch had the testimony, v. 5. Job said, "I know that my Redeemer liveth," (Job xix. 25,) and "though he slay me yet will I trust in him." David said, "Come unto me all ye that fear the Lord, and I will tell you what he hath done for my soul." "As far as the east is from the west, so far hath the Lord separated our sins from us." Psalm lxvi. 16. Peter said, (John 21,) "Lord, thou knowest that I love thee." John saith, "He that believeth on the Son of God hath the *witness* in himself," 1 John v. 10. Matt. i. 21, "Jesus shall save his people" (not in, but) "from their sins." Again, (John iii. 8,) "the wind bloweth where it listeth, and thou hearest the sound thereof," &c.; "so is every one that is *born* of the spirit." The wind, though we do not see it, we feel and hear it, and see the effects it produces,—it waves the grass, &c. So the Spirit of God, we feel it, it gives serious impressions, and good desires within our breast for religion. Again, we hear it—an inward voice telling what is right and what is wrong: and the more attention one gives to the inward monitor, the more distinctly they will hear the sound, till at length it will become their teacher. Again, we may see the effect it produces—some that have been proud and profligate, get reformed and become examples of piety; which change, money could not have produced, &c. Says one, I will acknowledge the ancients could talk of the knowledge, but inspiration is now done away; therefore, it is nonsense to expect any such thing in this our day. Answer: We read (Jeremiah xxxi. 33, 34) of a time when all shall know the Lord from the least to the greatest. Now, if there hath been a time past, when people have known God, and a time to come when all shall know him, which time is not yet arrived, (Isa. xi. 9, Heb. ii. 14;) why may not people know him in this our day? Nature has not changed, nor God; and if matter still can operate on matter, why not spirit upon spirit? Some people are so much like fools, that they think they are not bound in reason to believe any thing except they can comprehend it. This idea centres right in atheism; for the thing which comprehends, is always greater than the thing comprehended: therefore, if we could comprehend God, we should be greater than he, and of course look down upon him with contempt; but because we cannot comprehend him, then according to the above ideas we must disbelieve and reject the idea of a God. The man who so acts, supposes himself to be the greatest, he comprehending all other men or things, and of course he is God; and many such a god there is, full of conceit.—Observe, I can know different objects by the sensitive organs of the eye, ear, &c., and tell whether they are animate or inanimate; and yet how my thinking power gets the idea, or comprenends the same through the medium of matter, is a thing I cannot comprehend; yet it being such a self-evident matter of fact, I must assent to the idea, &c. But, says one, who knows these things in this our day? Answer: The Church of England prayeth to have the *thoughts* of their *hearts* cleansed by the *inspiration* of God's *Holy Spirit;* and with the Church of Rome, acknowledgeth what is called the Apostle's Creed, a part of which runneth thus: "I believe in the communion of saints, and in the forgiveness of sins." Again, the above ideas are in the Presbyterian Catechism, which saith, "that the *assurance* of God's love, *peace* of *conscience,* and joy in the Holy Ghost, doth accompany or flow from justification, adoption, and sanctification in this life," (not in the life to come.)

Agreeably to the above, the Baptists, when going to the water, tell how this *assurance* was *communicated* to their *souls,* and when, &c. The Quakers likewise acknowledge that the true worship is in spirit, (not in the outward letter,) and in truth, (not in error;) and many other proofs might be brought, but let one more suffice, and that is in your own breast. You feel the witness and reproof sometimes for doing wrong; now why may we not, on the principles of reason, admit the idea of a witness within likewise of doing right; also of pardon from God through Christ, and acceptance. And now I have as good a right to dispute whether there were any such land as Canaan, as you have to dispute revealed religion; for if I credit it, it is by human information, and you have as strong proof about revealed religion. And such proof as this in other affairs, in common courts of equity, would be allowed, and you cannot deny it.

REFLECTIONS

ON THE

IMPORTANT SUBJECT

OF

MATRIMONY.

' Marriage is honorable in all, and the bed undefiled. But whoremongers and adulters God will judge."—Heb. xiii. 4.

VARIOUS are the opinions with regard to the subject before us. Some people tell us it is not lawful for men and women to marry, and argue thus to prove it: " It is living after the flesh; they that live after the flesh shall die, (by which is meant separation from God;) therefore they who live together as husband and wife shall die." Now the premises being wrong, the conclusion is wrong of necessity; for living together as husband and wife is not living after the flesh, but after God's ordinance : as is evident from Matt. xix. 4, 5, 6—" And he answered, and said unto them, have ye not read, that he which made them at the beginning, made them male and female, and said, for this cause shall a man leave father and mother, and shall cleave to his wife; and they twain shall be one flesh? Wherefore, they are no more twain, but one flesh. What therefore God hath joined together, let not man put asunder."—In these words Christ, our great lawgiver, refers to Gen. ii. 24; which at once proves, that the *paradisaical* institution is not abrogated. From the beginning of the world until the words of the text were written, people lived together as husband and wife, and had divine approbation in so doing; as is easily proven from the word of God. Some people have an idea that we cannot be as holy in a married as in a single state. But hark! " Enoch walked with God, after he begat Methuselah, three hundred years, and begat sons and daughters." (Gen. v. 22, Heb. xi. 5.) Now if Enoch under that dark dispensation could serve God in a married state, and be fit for translation from earth to heaven, why may not another person be equally pious, and be filled with " righteousness, and peace, and joy in the Holy Ghost" under the Gospel dispensation, according to Rom. xiv. 17?—But admitting it is right for common people to marry, is it right for the *clergy* to marry? Answer: I know that too many think it is not, and are ready to conclude that whenever " a preacher marries, he is backslidden from God;" hence the many arguments made use of by some to prevent it. When I hear persons who are married trying to dissuade others from marrying, I infer one of two things: either that they are unhappy in their marriage, or that they enjoy a blessing which they do not wish others to partake of. The Church of Rome have an idea that the pope is St. Peter's successor, and that the clergy ought not to marry. But I would ask, if it was lawful for St. Peter to have a *wife*, why not lawful for another priest or preacher to have one ? But have we any proof that Peter had a wife ? In Matt. viii. and 14, we read as follows : " And when Jesus was come into Peter's house, he saw his *wife's* mother laid, and sick of a fever." Now how could Peter's *wife's* mother be sick of a fever, provided he had no wife ? And as we have no account that Christ parted Peter and his wife, I infer that he lived with her after his call to the apostleship ; according to Rom. vii. 2, for " the woman which hath an husband is *bound* by the *law* to her *husband* so long as he liveth ;" now if Peter's wife was " bound" to him, how could he go off and leave her, as some people think he did ? The words of the text saith, " marriage is honorable in all." But how could it be *honorable in all*, if it were *dishonorable* in the *priestly order ?* For they form a part, of course are included in the word A-double-L. In the first epistle written by St. Paul to Timothy, (iv.) we read thus : " Now the spirit speaketh expressly, that in the latter times some shall depart from the faith, giving heed to seducing spirits and *doctrines of devils ;* speaking lies in hypocrisy ; having their conscience seared with a hot iron ; *forbidding* to *marry* and commanding to obstain from meats, which God hath created to be received with thanksgiving of them which believe and know the truth." Observe, forbidding to marry is a doctrine of devils; therefore not of divine origin ; of course not to be obeyed, for we are under no obligation to obey the devils ; but in opposition to them, to enjoy all the benefits of divine institutions. Marriage is a divine institution, therefore the benefits of matrimony may be enjoyed by them that believe and know the truth. Having briefly, but fully shown that matrimony is lawful, I shall proceed to elucidate the words of the text. In doing which I shall,

First. Show what matrimony *is not*.

Secondly. What *it is*.

Thirdly. Point out some of the *causes of unhappy marriages*, and conclude with a few *words of advice*.

Resuming the order proposed, I come, in the first place, to show what matrimony is not.

1st. Two persons, of the same gender, dressed in the garb of the sexes, deceive a magistrate or minister, and have the ceremony performed ; which is no *marriage*, but downright wickedness, which some have audaciously been guilty of.

2d. There are certain beings in the world in human shape, and dress in the garb of one of the sexes, but at the same time are not properly masculine or feminine ; of course not *marriageable*. They enter into matrimonial engagements with persons of one of the sexes, and the formal ceremony is performed. This is not matrimony, but an imposition ; forasmuch as the design of matrimony cannot be answered thereby.

3d. Sometimes a banditti catch two persons, and compel them ceremonially to marry at the point of the sword, to save their lives. But this is not matrimony, for it is neither sanctioned by laws divine or human ; neither are they obligated by such laws to live together.

4th Some men have a plurality of women, but they cannot be married to them all : if the first marriage was lawful, the others are not ; " for two," saith He, (not *three*) " shall be one flesh." Moreover, when two persons enter into marriage they promise to forsake all *others*, and be true to each other while they both shall live; therefore are not at liberty to have any thing to do with other persons.

5th. Sometimes persons who are married, without just cause leave their companions, take up with another person, and live with him or her. This is not matrimony, but adultery; and all such persons may expect to meet with God's disapprobation in eternity; "for such shall not inherit the kingdom of God."

6th. Two persons living together as husband and wife, and yet feeling at liberty to forsake the present and embrace another object at pleasure—this is not matrimony but whoredom; and "whoremongers and adulterers God will judge." Yet we may here observe, in many parts of the world the political state of affairs is such, that two persons may live together by mutual consent as husband and wife, where there is no formal ceremony performed, and yet be justified before God; which was the case with the Jews, (instance also if some were cast away upon an island;) but this is not the case in America, except among the colored people, or heathen tribes, as will be more fully shown under the next head, in which I am to show—

Secondly, What matrimony is.

Some people believe in a decree, (commonly called a lottery,) viz. that God has determined, in all cases, that particular men and women should be married to each other; and that it is *impossible* they should marry any other person. But I say *hush!* for if that be the case, then God appoints all matches. But I believe the devil appoints a great many; for if God did it, then it would be done in wisdom, and of course it would be done right; if so, there would not be so many unhappy marriages in the world as there are. If one man steals or runs away with another man's wife, goes into a strange country and there marries her, did God decree that? What made God Almighty so angry with the Jews for marrying into heathen families? and why did the prophet Nehemiah contend with them, curse them, pluck off their hair, and make them swear that they would not give their daughters to the Ammonites, &c., as we read in the xiiith chapter of Nehemiah, if he appointed such matches? Again: why did John the Baptist exclaim so heavily against Herod for having his brother Philip's wife? If it was necessary, he could not help it; therefore John talked very foolishly when he said it was not lawful, for that was to say it was not lawful to do what God had decreed should be done. Notwithstanding I do not believe in lottery, (so called,) yet I believe* that persons who are under the influence of divine grace, may have a guide to direct them to a person suitable to make them a companion, with whom they may live agreeably; but this can only be done by having pure intentions, paying particular attention to the influence of the Divine Spirit within, and the opening of Providence without; being careful not to run so fast as to outstrip your guide, nor yet to move so slow as to lose sight thereof.

But to return. Marriage consists in agreement of parties, in union of heart, and in a promise of fidelity to each other before God; "forasmuch as he looketh at the heart, and judgeth according to intention." (1 Sam-

---

* I apprehend that every person who is marriageable, and whose duty it is to marry, there is a particular object they ought to have; but I believe it possible for them to miss that object and be connected with one that is improper for them—one cause of so many unhappy families. There is a providence attending virtue, and a curse attending vice.

xvi. 7.) As there is such a thing as for persons *morally* to commit adultery in the sight of God who never *actually* did so, (Matt. v. 28,) so persons may be *married* in his sight who never had the *formal ceremony* performed. Observe: marriage is a divine institution; was ordained by God in the time of man's innocency, and sanctioned by Jesus Christ under the gospel—he graced a marriage-feast in Cana of Galilee, where he turned water into wine. (John ii. 1.) Now, that marriage consists not barely in the outward ceremony is evident; for this may be performed on two persons of either sex, and yet no marriage; for the benefits resulting from marriage cannot be enjoyed through such a medium. If matrimony is the formal sentence, who married Adam and Eve?, and what was the ceremony by which they were constituted husband and wife? But if Adam and Eve were married without a formal ceremony, then something else is matrimony in the sight of God: of course it must be an agreement of parties, as above. Yet it is necessary to attend to the laws of our country, and have a formal ceremony performed, which is the *evidence of matrimony!* For we are commanded to "be *subject to every ordinance of man*, for the Lord's sake." (1 Peter ii. 13.) St. Paul saith, "Let every soul be subject unto the higher powers, for there is no power but of God; the powers that be are ordained by God. Whosoever, therefore, resisteth the power, resisteth the ordinance of God; and they that resist shall receive to themselves damnation." (Rom. xiii. 1, 2.) Moreover, without this outward evidence it cannot be known who are married and who are not; so that men could leave their wives and children to suffer; deny they ever engaged to live with such women; and, having no proof thereof, they could not be compelled by any law to provide for such women and children. Once more: unless the law is complied with, the woman cannot be considered as his lawful wife, (for what makes her his *lawful* wife is compliance with the law,) and of course the children are not lawful: then it follows they are adulterers and adultresses; else fornicators and fornicatresses; their children are illegitimate; and, after the death of the man, the woman and children cannot *heir* his estate if he dies without a *will*.

Question. If two persons contract for marriage, and have pledged their fidelity to each other before God, are they justifiable in *breaking* that marriage contract?

Answer. If one has acted the part of an *impostor*, told lies, and deceived the other, this is not *marriage*, but an *imposition;* of course the person so imposed on is justifiable in *rejecting* such deceiver! But if they both make statements in *truth*, are acquainted with each other's characters, dispositions, practices, and principles; and then, being in possession of such information, *voluntarily* engage before God to live together as *man* and *wife*, unless something wicked, more than was or could be reasonably expected, transpires relative to one or the other of the persons so engaged, the person who breaks such contract cannot be justifiable before God! For I think I have clearly proved such contract to be marriage in his sight; and Christ saith, "Whosoever shall *put away* his wife, except it be for fornication, and shall marry another, committeth adultery;* and whoso

---

* Now it appears, furthermore, that the Jews considered a mutual contract, as above, marriage and sacred; as is evident from Deut. xxii. 22–28, "If a damsel that is a virgin be betrothed unto a husband, and a man find her in a city and lie with her, then ye shall bring them both out unto the gate of that city; and ye shall stone them with stones that they die

marrieth her which is put away" (for fornication) "doth commit adultery." (Matt. xix. 9.) From this passage it is evident that, for the cause of fornication, a man may put away his wife, marry another, and yet be justifiable in the eye of the divine law. Moreover, if a man puts away his wife for any other cause, she is at liberty to marry, but he is not. This I think is what St. Paul meaneth in 1 Cor. vii. 15: " But if the unbelieving depart, let him depart ; a brother or sister is not under bondage in such cases ;" *i. e.* they are free from the law, for that is what they were bound by ; of course at liberty to marry again, for the innocent are not to suffer for the guilty. Admitting the above to be correct, how many such adulterers and adultresses are there in the world ! And what a dreadful account will thousands have to give in the day of eternity for the violation of their most sacred promises ! But one is ready to say, " I was not sincere when I made those promises." Then you dissembled to *deceive*, and *told lies** to *ensnare* the *innocent*—like the devil when he transforms himself into an angel of light ; and the greater shall be your damnation : " for *all* liars shall have their portion in the lake that burns with fire and brimstone." (Rev. xxi. 8.) Many men will work a hundred schemes, and tell ten thousand lies, to effect the most devilish purposes ; and after their ends are answered, turn with disdain from the person deceived by them, and make themselves merry to think how they swept the pit of hell to accomplish their design.

Thirdly, I am to point out some of the causes of *unhappy marriages*.

Here I would observe, that divine wisdom hath ordained marriage for several important ends—1st. For the mutual happiness of the sexes in their journey through life, and as a comfort and support to each other. 2d. That *souls* may be propagated agreeably to the Divine will, capable of glorifying and enjoying him for ever. 3d. As the man without the woman or the woman without the man, is not in a capacity to provide for a family, divine wisdom hath wisely ordained their mutual aid, in providing for, instructing, and protecting offspring as guardian angels who must give account ; besides the reason assigned by St. Paul, 1 Cor. vii. But to return, I would observe—1st. Too many marry from *lucrative* views ; their *object* is not to get a suitable companion who will sweeten all the ills of life, but to get a large fortune, so that their time may be spent in idleness

---

the damsel because she cried not, being in the city, and the man because he humbled his neighbor's wife." Now observe : the woman is styled a virgin, and yet a man's wife, because she was betrothed—that is, engaged to him by solemn contract. Take notice : the punishment inflicted on such as broke their marriage contract was death ; whereas there was no such punishment inflicted on those who were not betrothed ; as you may read in the same chapter, ver. 28. 29. Why this difference in their punishment ? Answer : Because the crime was aggravated by the violation of the marriage contract. God is the same in justice now that he was then ; and crimes are not less under the gospel than they were under the law. " Let them that read understand."

In the gospel as recorded by St. Matthew, this is further verified, (Matt. i. 18. 19, 20,) as exemplified in Mary the mother of Christ, and Joseph ; for, before they came together, she is styled his wife, and he her husband. This is the truth, and you cannot deny it. Strange to think what numbers in the world, for the sake of human flesh and a little of this perishable world's goods, will persuade their friends or children to sin against God by breaking their marriage contract ! The devil can but tempt, but mortal men compel ! I am here speaking of contracts where there is no lawful objection.

* A man (I do not say a gentleman) in the west sought the destruction of an innocent and, to accomplish his designs, "wished that heaven might never receive his soul nor the earth his body, if he did not perform his contract ;" and afterwards boasted of his worse than diabolical act. But God took him at his word ; for he was shot by an Indian, and rotted above ground !

at they may make a grand appearance in the world ; sup-
perty will make them honorable. This being the leading
irect their attention to an object, which, if it was not for pro-
erhaps be looked upon by them with contempt, and profess
gard for the person while the property is the object of their
rhaps the person is old; the ideas are—" This old man or
: live long ; then all will be mine, and I shall be in such
that I can marry to great advantage ;" forgetting that there
le in the world just of their own opinion ! The contract is
n marriage is performed, there is a union of hand but *not*
consequence of which they are not happy together. The
nding out the deception, wishes a reversion in vain, which
sensibly feel ; for sin hath its own punishment entailed to
1e curse of God follows such impure intentions. I appeal
1ave married from these incentives, whether these things
1d. Some people take *fancy* for *love ;* they behold a person
uld almost take to be an angel in human shape, (but all is
;litters,) through the medium of the eye become enamored,
itil the object of their fancy is won. *Beauty* being but skin
or age soon makes the rose to wither ; they are then as
1ted as the miser who thought be had ten thousand guineas
: after counting them over every day for twelve months, the
y which means he discovered his gold was only tarnished
1rse it lost its value in his estimation. So when beauty
dation of happiness being gone, and seeing nothing attract-
it is not uncommon for an object more beautiful to be sought.
uch a thing as for persons to marry for love, and yet be un-
say marry for love ? Yes—but not their own love ; only
r parents or friends. For instance, two persons of suitable
dispositions, &c., form attachments of the strongest nature,
y pure motives, are united in heart, and enter into the most
ments to live together during life ;* the parents being asked,
to give their daughter, without any sufficient reason for
In the next place, they strive to break the marriage con-
by the two young people. Perhaps the man has not pro-
o please them, for worth is generally (though improperly)
1e quantity of property a person possesses ; instead of his
principles, his practices, &c. In order to effect their wishes,
they can invent is pushed into operation, (and it is fre-
se that family connections, and even strangers interfere,
usiness so to do ; but fools will be meddling) to change the
, and make bad impressions on the same with respect to the
fections ; they strive by placing their diabolical optic to her
1er view every thing in the worst light they possibly can ;
things if she will break it off—(" all these things will I
1ou wilt fall down and worship me," said the devil once ;)
ce the black seal of reprobation upon her if she fulfils her
Here the mind becomes as a " troubled sea which cannot

---

say the bargain should be conditional, thus—" If my parents love you
ll have you." This just proves the point in hand, that they must marry
ve and not their own

rest;" she is at a loss to know what is duty—she loves her parents, also the man to whom her heart has been united—her affections are placed, her honor is pledged—she spends restless nights and mournful days to know how to decide! Critical, but important period! Her present, and perhaps eternal peace depends upon the decision! After many struggles with her own conscience, at length through powerful persuasion she yields to the wishes of others—betrays her trust, breaks her marriage contract, deserts her best friend, and pierces herself through with many sorrows.* Does this decision give peace of mind? By no means! She is pained at the very heart, and flies to some secret place to give vent to the sorrow she feels. Follow her to the lonely apartment—behold her there as pale as death—her cheeks bedewed with tears! What mean those heavy groans? What mean those heart-breaking sighs? What mean those floods of briny tears poured forth so free, as if without consent? She was torn from the object of all her earthly *joy!* The ways of God "are pleasantness, and all his paths are peace," but she finds nothing save sorrow in the way and path which she has taken—therefore she is not in the way in which she ought to have gone. Another man pays his addresses to her; by no means calculated to make her a suitable companion—but he has large possessions; and this being the object her parents and friends have in view, they do and say all they can to get her to consent. But parents should remember, that they can no more love for their children, than they can eat and drink for them. Through their entreaties she is prevailed on to give him her hand, while her affections are placed on another. Thus she marries for the love of her parents: they having laid a foundation to make her unhappy while she lives; and may I not say, more than probable to procure her future misery? For how can she be happy with a man whom she does not love? "How can two walk together except they be agreed?" Where there is no agreement there can be no union, and where there is no union, there can be no happiness. As the parents are not so immediately concerned therein as the child, they act very improperly in over-persuading their child to marry. For if she is unhappy in such marriage, she will have cause to reflect on them, and place her misery to their account; while she waits for the hour to come to end her existence, and terminate the misery which she feels! Marriage was intended for the mutual happiness of the sexes—for the woman was given to the man to be "an help meet for him." Gen. ii. 18. Marriage is an emblem of that union which subsists between Christ and his Church, Eph. v. 32. Solomon saith, "Whoso findeth a wife, findeth a good thing, and obtaineth favor of the Lord."—Prov. viii. 22. Again, "a prudent wife is from the Lord," Prov. xix. 14. I therefore conclude that a happy marriage is the greatest blessing and consolation which can be enjoyed on this side of eternity, next to the love of God in the soul. Of course an unhappy marriage is the greatest curse which is endured on this side of hell, next to the horrors of a guilty conscience.

Quitting this, I pass on to observe that many people make themselves

---

* If the woman is *under* age, she my perhaps be justifiable on that account: but if she of age, it argues imbecility; for she has as much right to act for herself, as her parents have to act for themselves: of course should have a judgment and soul of her own! If the man is altogether in herself, she proves at once she is not to be confided in; and I would pronounce that man blessed who has escaped a woman of so mean a principle—for such thing has scarcely been known among heathens.

unhappy after marriage. I shall first notice some things in the conduct of men; secondly, in the conduct of women; thirdly, point out some complex cases. First, It frequently happens that wicked men pay their addresses to religious women; and, in order to accomplish their desire, pretend to have a great regard for piety, promise to do all in their power to assist them on their way to heaven, and call God to bear witness to a lie that they will be no hindrance to them, &c.; and many go so far as to put on the outward garb of religion, that they may the more easily *betray with a kiss!* But shortly after marriage the wolf sheds his coat, and openly avows his dislike to the ways of godliness, and either directly or indirectly declares that his wife shall not enjoy the privileges of the gospel. Here the wife is convinced of the insincerity of his promise, which makes her doubt the sincerity of his affection for her; the house becomes divided, and the foundation of their future misery is laid; and it will be a mercy of God, if they are not a means of peopling the regions of the damned, and at last go down to the chambers of death together. Secondly, Some men pretend to respect their wives; the wife looks up to her husband as her head for protection, and, as a reasonable woman, expects *him* to redress her grievances. But, alas, how is she disappointed! For he approbates that in others which he could prevent without any loss of property or character, and appears to delight in her misery. Instance those who have religious wives, and suffer drinking, swearing, frolicking, gambling, &c., about their houses. Is it not natural for such women to conclude their husbands have a greater regard for such wicked beings than themselves? If so, how can my husband have that regard for me which he ought to have? And what becomes of that scripture which saith, "So ought men to love their wives as their own bodies: he that loveth his wife loveth himself," Ephesians v. 28. Again, (Colossians iii. 19,) "Husbands, love your wives, and be not bitter against them." Thirdly, A great many men stay away from home *unnecessarily*, spend their time in drinking, &c., expending their money in the taverns, which ought to go to the support of their families, while their wives have not the necessaries of life, and are laboring night and day to keep their children from starving. Thus many families are brought to disgrace and misery by the wickedness of husbands. But one is ready to say, I provide well for my family, and am I not at liberty to go and come when I please? Yes, as far as is *expedient*, but no farther, if you do not wish to forfeit your wife's confidence. I ask, What must be the feelings of a woman left in such a case, when she knows her husband has no lawful business to detain him from home? What conclusion can she more rationally draw than this? My company is disagreeable to him, therefore he is determined to have as little of it as possible. The society of others is more pleasing to him than that of his family; therefore he seeks pleasure abroad. Here grounds are given for her to suspect his virtue; and it is very common for women to think such men have their *misses* from home, which is too often the case. Reflect, for a moment, what must be the sensations of a delicate woman, to hear that her bosom friend lies intoxicated among the swine in the streets. I am certain, from observation, that no woman can be happy with a drunken man; therefore I am bold to say, wherever you see such a thing, you see an unhappy family; and, except such persons repent and get forgiveness, they will assuredly be damned, however rich, honorable, and wise they may be, for St. Paul ranks drunkenness among the works of the flesh, and positively declares, "They who do such things shall not inherit the kingdom of God," Galatians v. Therefore I would advise all young ladies, if they wish to be happy in time or eternity, to avoid such young men as hanker about the taverns, and have not respect enough for their own characters to raise them above the level of the beasts; for beasts do not get drunk. They who get drunk when young, are apt to be sots when old. Moreover, a great many sins flow from that of drunkenness, a few of which I shall here mention. First, It brings on disorders to their destruction; which, second, Prevent their usefulness as worthy members in society. Third, Shortens their days, which is a species of murder, the most heinous of all crimes. Fourth, A bad example before others. Fifth, Procures a family scandal. Sixth, His money is laid out for that which is worse than if thrown into the fire; which, seventh, Prevents his usefulness as a charitable man. Eighth, Is a breach of God's law. Ninth, Quenches the divine Spirit. Tenth, Exposes his family to want. Eleventh, Liable to bring a burden on the country. Twelfth, Deprives him of the power of reason; which, thirteenth, Makes him liable to injure his friends, and commit every horrid depredation. And such men as will get drunk, and then abuse their wives, do not deserve the name of *men*, for they have not the principle of men, but may be called the devil's *swill-tub* walking upright: such deserve a dose of eel-tea. Now, take notice, a man of good principles thinks as much of his word as his oath, therefore will be true to his engagements, and will fulfil that promise, made before witnesses, "to forsake all other women, and keep to his wife only, so long as they both shall live, to live with her after God's holy ordinance." Now I ask, Is adultery God's ordinance? No, for he forbids adultery, Exodus xx. 14. He who breaks his most sacred engagements is not to be confided in. Matrimonial engagements are the most sacred; therefore he who breaks his matrimonial engagements is not to be confided in. Fifthly, Some men have an unhappy temper—are morose and peevish—and though their wives do all they can, or as they may, it is impossible to please them. They are easily angered, and view a mote until it looks as large as a mountain; one word brings on another, and at length they proceed from words to blows, until they become so large that one bed cannot hold them both. Many of our eyes and ears have been witnesses to this shameful conduct; the jarring string of discord runs through all the family; they live like devils incarnate; and if a person happens to be in the family who has never been used to such conduct, would he not be almost led to think he had gotten into the territories of the damned? What is here said of the man is applicable to a great many women. A wounded bird will flutter.

God has placed the man as governor in th family, and he is styled, "the head of the woman," Ephesians v. 23. Now there are some women, though they promise to "live after God's ordinance," are not willing to do it, but wish to be head themselves. Whatever is to be done, they must give directions; the man durst not bargain without leave, and if he does, his wife's tongue runs as though it would never stop. What does it argue? It argues great straight I, and little crooked *u;* that the woman thinks herself possessed of great wisdom, and her husband ignorant in the extreme, and sets him aside as a mere cipher. But so far is this from being a trait of wisdom, that it proves the reverse; for a wise woman will reverence and obey her husband, according to Eph. v. 22, 23; 1 Peter iii. 1. Moreover, it argues self-importance, to see people climbing to the high seat of power, where they have no business. Self-importance flows from ignorance. If the man is a man of sense and spirit, he is not willing to give up that which properly belongs to him, viz., the rein of government, and of course the contest which began in words frequently ends in blows. Thus many women, by assuming to themselves a prerogative which does not belong to them, make unhappy families. Women, by indulging a mean opinion of their husbands, become ashamed of them; but this can happen in no case where there is not a want of information and judgment. If you stoop in marrying him, do not indulge the thought that you added to his respectability; never tell him, "you lifted him out of the ashes," for it will be hard for you to extricate yourself from this difficulty. "If you stooped of necessity, because you could get no one else, the obligation is on your own side. And if you could get a better companion, why did you marry him? If you stooped of choice, who ought to be blamed but yourself? Besides, it will be well to remember when you became his wife he became your head, and your *supposed superiority* was buried in that voluntary act." There are many young women, who, in order to marry well, appear very mild, very affectionate, and very decent in their persons, houses, &c., frequently using an air of affectation, and speaking with faltering voices. Some young gentleman, wishing to get a companion of this description, offers his hand to one of these "jackdaws dressed in peacock feathers;" the nuptials are celebrated, her wishes are answered, the cloak is laid aside, and she soon appears what she is in reality. The innocence of the lamb is lost in the fierceness of the lion—the affection of the dove in the cruelty of the ostrich, and the cleanliness of the sheep in the filthiness of the swine. These properties are bad in the abstract, but far worse when they meet together. Filthiness is the fruit of laziness. Go to the house where a lazy woman bears rule; examine the floor, the furniture, the bedding, the linen, the children, and, last of all, herself, and see what an agreement throughout the whole; every thing is out of fix, and if she is a professor of religion, you may, without erring far, form a rational judgment of the state of her soul, from the appearance of her body. Laziness is inconsistent with the gospel of Christ, and with the spirit of Christianity; for St. Paul told the Thessalonians to note such "a man, and have no company with him, that he may be ashamed," 2 Thess. iii. 14. Moreover, a lazy Christian is as great a solecism as an honest thief, a sober drunkard, a chaste harlot, or a holy devil.

But it may be asked, What are the evils which accrue from dirty houses, &c. I answer, 1st. If a gentleman or lady visits you, they have no appetite to eat or drink in your houses, and what are your feelings when you are certain of the cause? 2d. They can have no satisfaction in your beds, they smell so offensive, and are so infested with hungry *night walkers*, which thirst for human blood. 3d. The very disagreeableness of the air, causes them to wish to make their escape, lest they should be seized with putrid or malignant fevers, which might terminate in death. 4th. Many diseases originate therefrom, which are productive of the most fatal consequences to the family. 5th. Thereby you transmit a curse to your children; for the children, in common, pattern after their parents, and as they do with you, so will they do when they get to themselves. "Therefore," says one, "take care of the breed." There is no excuse sufficient to justify those who are able to work and live in dirt, where water is plenty, and may be had for nothing. Therefore, I would advise all persons who value their health, to shun such places as they would a city where the plague is in full rage. Now, if a man is thus *taken in*, how can he be happy, provided he has never been accustomed so to live? And if he has, by seeking a woman from whom he expected better things, he clearly evinces his dissatisfaction in *that* manner of life. But finding out the deception, he has no heart to work; takes to drink to drown his sorrow. Here we behold another cause of family misery, or unhappy marriages. 6th. It sometimes is the case, that the wife, for want of due consideration, as it relates to his constitution and *inclination*,* treats him as a *husband* with *neglect*; which makes a bad impression on his mind that is not easily erased, but tends to wean his affections from her, and exposes him to the temptation of others; till she becomes a burden, and he wishes her out of the way as a *rival*. Thus, she is blind to her own happiness, and procures her own destruction.

Quitting this, I pass on to the third thing under consideration; in which I am to point out some complex cases, in which either party may be guilty. And 1st. That odious practice of talking about each other in their absence, and endeavoring to expose each other's faults to the world. If they are one flesh, he that exposes his wife, exposes himself also. How then can the family be respectable? This comes to her ears, and she feels disposed to retaliate, and presently the whole neighborhood is filled with things which ought never to have been known, only to themselves. Men and women both have their foibles; therefore ought to overlook each other's faults, and put the best construction possible on each other's conduct, and exercise that charity which thinketh no evil. Therefore, should never unnecessarily expose each other's faults, but support each other's character as far as truth and propriety will admit. St. James saith, "The tongue is full of deadly poison, and sets on fire the course of nature." Need we wonder then if it sets on fire whole families where it is not curbed? 2d. Sometimes it is the case that one of them has been married before. I'll say the woman. Her present husband treats her well, but if at any time she gets crossed, she cries out, "Ah, I once had a husband, he did not treat me as you do; there never was such a man as he was, but he is gone now." And as apt as not tell fifty lies about his goodness before she stops: and more than likely her present husband is better than the first ever was. Now, it is very certain that this makes a bad impression on the mind, and if it is not done purposely to hurt feelings, the best apology which can be made for such conduct is *weakness* or *ignorance*. Whatever women or men think in such cases, if they value their peace, they should keep their thoughts in their own breasts. For a small needle may occasion a great deal of pain if stuck in the heart. And, "Behold! how great a matter a little fire kindleth." Such a line of conduct as the above, cannot but chill the

* See Dr. Clarke's Commentary, 1 Cor. vii. 2, beginning at the words, "In the Jewish constitutions," and ending with the word "sense."

affection of your companion towards you: of course, as he esteems or disesteems you, so his treatment towards you will be.

2d. There are instances of one or the other's having a parent or child who comes to live in the family:—the other treats the person ill; this touches in a very tender part; feelings are hurt; at length it is productive of bad consequences, the evil seed is sown, it springs up, it becomes a great tree, it bears abundance of fruit, and yields a never ending crop of misery. 3d. *Jealousy,* which is sometimes founded in truth, and sometimes in error. However, jealousy is such, properly or improperly founded; and where it takes place, all conjugal affections are destroyed; for confidence once lost can hardly ever be regained.

1st. I would advise all young people, male and female, to get religion; by which you will be better qualified to do your duty to your God and yourselves, being under the influence of Divine grace. If you keep an eye single to the glory of God, you may have a guide to direct you to a person, such as will make you a partner, who will be willing to share with you in all your sorrows. Do not look so much at *property* nor *beauty* as *good sense, virtue,* and *piety.* Avoid as much as possible the company of such as are not afraid to sin themselves; knowing that if it is in their power, they will lead you into that gulf of iniquity which has swallowed up thousands:* " evil communications corrupt good manners," (or rather good morals, as is intended;) and "a companion of fools shall be destroyed." Get a person who will love you from a *sense of duty* to God. This foundation, if beauty and fortune fail, standeth sure; and then you need not fear that *such* a companion will desert you in the day of trouble. If you both love God, it will be impossible for you not to love each other. This being the case, you may always have a paradise at home, and be more happy in each other's company, than with any other person beneath the canopy of heaven. As many of our young friends have been called from time to eternity before they had time to settle themselves in the world, it ought to be a warning to you not to put off your return to God until you get married; for before that time comes you may be numbered with the dead, and lie down between the clods of the valley; and if without religion you are cut off in the bloom of youth, how soon will all your earthly joys come to an end, and an eternity of misery commence! But if you get and keep religion, whether you marry or not, it shall be well with you. If you marry such a person as I advise, when your companion dies you may have a well-grounded hope, that the ever-faithful companion of all your cares is gone to rest in "Abraham's bosom;" and after serving God together in time, you may spend an eternity of pleasure together in praising God and the Lamb.

2d. I would advise such as have companions, to consult each other's happiness, both as it relates to *time* and *eternity.* As husbands, love your wives; and as wives, see that you reverence your husbands; try and

---

* Perhaps some will say, "The subject is too plain and tends to hurt delicate feelings!" But let it be remembered that it is not more plain than important. And delicacy must give way to propriety, when truth and matter of fact demand it. Moreover, some delicate people have prejudices which are founded in error, and yet, when matrimony is treated plainer in romantic novels, will greedily relish and digest it! Observe, they exhibit characters which nowhere in real life exists, and yet young minds are too frequently captivated, and thereby form an idea —————; and must of course be disappointed, and consequently made unhappy, perhaps for life. This is one of the many evils of novels to society.

find out each other's dispositions, consider your own *weakness*, and think not any thing too hard to be done by you to render each other happy, (save the giving up of your conscience.) If heaven has blessed you with a good companion, esteem it as the greatest temporal blessing which can be enjoyed, and be very careful not to abuse so good a gift; remember that eternal things are connected therewith, and if you misuse your companion you will have to render an account to God for the same; for "God will bring every work into judgment, with every secret thing, whether it be good, or whether it be evil."*

If you have a bad companion, you made your own *contract*, or at least consented thereunto; therefore, make the best you can of a bad bargain; and avoid every measure, as far as possible, to answer it in the eternal world, which might tend to make you more unhappy. If you have religion, walk with Zacharias and Elizabeth in all the ways of God *blameless*. If you have no religion, your own consciences testify that all is not well with you, and God himself is witness to the many promises you have broken: therefore, it is high time for you to begin to think more seriously on your latter end, for many of you are past the meridian of life; your sun is going down in death: others hover around the shores of time—but one step between you and the bar of God! With others the the sun of life will go down at noon—eternal things depend upon life's feeble strings! Heaven lost, is lost forever! Careless man! Prayerless woman! Why will you die? Are you greedy of eternal pain? What harm did God ever do, that you are determined not to be reconciled to him? Are you so in love with sin, that you will risk the loss of heaven, and the torment of hell for a momentary enjoyment? O! be wise—seek salvation—fly from the gathering storm! Believe in Jesus Christ, and thou wilt be saved. So shall you enjoy peace in life, tranquillity in death, and crowns of victory in eternity. Serious consideration is the first step in matters of religion, with a fixed resolution to avoid whatever you discern to be wrong; having your mind in a studious frame of inquiry after God's will, to do it. Never lie down to rest without committing yourself into the protection of kind Providence; and as you awake, give thanks to the hand that has kept you. Thus begin, spend and close every day with God; then he will be thy father and thy friend in Jesus Christ.

Most evils prevalent in society have their origin from the influence of example, by which children are contaminated, and the seeds are sown in the prejudice of their education, to the great injury of themselves and others, beyond any possible calculation.

The poor *opinion* which mankind entertain of each other, and the little *confidence* they are pleased to place in strangers, as well as acquaintance,

---

* Never put your property out of your hand to be dependent on your children; for they will not feel nor do with you as you with them when children! The son that must be hired ... to reform will deny .... the loan of a horse; the old man must walk on foot; and is used and wished out of the way as a piece of useless lumber!

Set no example before your children but what is worthy for them to copy after; but use your united parental influence to preserve their morals, and stimulate them to noble principles. Mothers particularly are bound by the strongest obligations, however few may realize it, to preserve the chastity and virtue of their daughters; for on this, in a great measure, depends much of their welfare for time, if not for eternity—as a woman without a character, is like a body without a soul of course female education ought not to be neglected.

exemplify the truth which shows the corruption of their very raising. For example: the two first things generally taught to children in their infancy, is to be *deceitful* and *lie*. The mother is going out, the child cries to go too; the mother *promises* to bring the "*pretties*," with no intention to perform. The child is deceived and disappointed, and confidence is forfeited. " I will whip, &c., if you don't hush," but the child is not influenced, knowing the *scarecrow*.

Thus being taught to *deceive* and *lie*, he becomes expert at the trade, and then must be *whipped* for the very thing the parents have taught him; whereas if the example had been good, and all foolish, wicked, and evil improprieties were discountenanced by a proper line of conduct, then a blessing would be transmitted to posterity according to the promise, and as exemplified by Abraham.

It is a rarity that young women go the leeward with a broken * * *, provided the seeds of modesty, innocence, and virtue are sown in the mind at an early age; whereas those mothers who do not watch over their daughters as " guardian angels," are apt to let them run at random. Hence many get their ankles scratched, if no more! Fathers and sons may also take a hint.

The *tyranny* of parents, as well as too great liberty, is equally pernicious; also their being divided in their family government—likewise backbiting, flattery, &c.

But remember the day of retribution, and conduct yourselves accordingly! For *first* impressions are most durable, therefore the propriety and necessity of beginning right to end well. As the consequence of starting wrong, you will forever continue in error.

Hence the propriety of " *consideration*," and a proper exercise of "*judgment*," as rational creatures, who need *divine assistance*, for which we should look accordingly.

ANALECTS

UPON

NATURAL, SOCIAL, AND MORAL

PHILOSOPHY.

GENERAL WASHINGTON, in comparing those days of ignorance, when people tamely submitted to the galling yoke of tyranny and priestcraft, with modern times, when men take the liberty to suspect the propriety of the creed of "*passive obedience and non-resistance,*" dropped the following reflection: "But this seems to be the age of wonders, and it is reserved for intoxicated and lawless France, *for purposes of providence far beyond the reach of human ken*, to slaughter her own citizens, and disturb the repose of all the world besides."

When we reflect on past occurrences, on the awful revolutions of the present day, and those big events now probably at the door, any person who thinks for himself, and is not callous to all important things, must feel a degree of interest.

It is a self-evident matter of fact, that there has been, and there still is, a great deal of deceit, oppression, and consequent misery in the world.

It is equally certain, that there is such a thing in the world as "*natural evil.*" And natural evil must be the effect or consequence of "*moral evil,*"* otherwise all our ideas of *goodness* and *justice* are chimerical. It therefore may be taken for granted, and our own experience and observation will justify the conclusion, that all things are not right in the present condition of the human family. To be a little more particular, I will for a moment consider man in an individual, social, and moral capacity.

First, *Individually.* One seeks to take care of himself only, as charity is said to begin at home. And as long as self is served, he may make pretensions to friendship, but when interest ceases the case is altered.

Again: one is a poor outcast, perishing in the streets, while another is revelling, having more than heart could wish; but because of the trouble, will not give the stranger an asylum or afford him wherewithal to allay his hunger, not expecting a reward. One is in trouble, another is merry at his distress. One commands, because it is his pleasure, and another must obey, however hard and imperious the command. One claims the country for his own, and all the others must pay *him* for the privilege to live in it, or else suffer banishment. One hath thousands, gained by the labor of others, while another hath not the assurance of a day's provision,

---

* Gen. iii 17. Rom. v. 12.

nor money to procure the coarsest raiment, much less the promise of a friend in the day of adversity.

Secondly, *Socially.*—There is a body of men called *gentlemen,* or *nobility.* There is another grade called *peasants.* The first will possess the country, and feel and act more than their own importance; while the latter are put on a level with the animals, and treated as an inferior race of beings, who must pay to these lords a kind of divine honor, and bow, and cringe, and scrape.

The will of one must be the *law,* and it must be the pleasure of the other to obey; and it is the policy and interest of the former to keep the latter in subjection and ignorance. For if they were permitted to think, and judge, and act for themselves, they would overthrow their rulers.

Here the question will arise, how such *differences* came to exist among men? Another question also arises, Can the *motives* of men who thus conduct themselves in the world, be " just and good ?"

A third question also arises: If men be actuated by motives in their objects and ends, and in particular in their actions and dealings with their fellow-men, who can doubt whether there be such a thing as " *moral evil*" in the world? Every purpose must be weighed and willed in the heart, before it is acted out. Of course, to take from another his substance without his consent, or giving him an equivalent, is contrary to every rule of equity.

Thirdly, *Morally.*—Some people invade the divine rights by prescribing " *articles of faith,*" and *binding* the *conscience* of man in all things of religion, under the most severe penalties that human ingenuity could invent.

When we reflect, therefore, upon the actions of men, taken as they stand in relation to one another, we are led to inquire how they may comport, first, with our " personal rights;" secondly, with our " social rights;" and, thirdly, with our " moral rights," as established on the " law of nature."

OF THE LAW OF NATURE.

I here would observe, that all our *rights,* whether personal, social, or moral, are the *graces* of the Governor of the universe, and established by him primarily in the great and universal " LAW OF NATURE."

It is a self-evident truth, that all men are born *equal* and *independent;* and as individuals, are endowed by their Creator with certain inalienable rights, among which are life, liberty, the use of property, the pursuit of happiness, with the privilege of private judgment.

These principles being admitted, it will follow, that as the wants or necessities of mankind and their duties are equal, so their rights and obligations are equal also. Hence our rights, duties, and obligations are the same in each and in all.

The " rights of man," when applied to an individual, are called " personal rights;" considered as he stands in relation to his fellow-creatures, they are called " social rights;" and considered as he stands in relation to his Creator, they are called " moral rights."

OF PERSONAL RIGHTS.

Personal rights are those benefits or privileges which appertain to man in *right* or by virtue of his *existence*. Of this kind are all the intellectual rights, or rights of the mind; and also all those rights of acting as an individual for his own comfort and happiness, which are not injurious to the natural or personal rights of others—of course the rights of the mind, religious liberty, freedom and independence, cannot be taken from a man *justly* but by his own consent; except only when taken by the laws of the Creator, who gave them, or when forfeited to society by some misdemeanor.

The human family, which is divided into nations, is composed of individuals. And, as a whole is composed of parts, and the parts collectively form one whole, of course in their individual capacity they are naturally free and independent, and endowed by their Creator with certain inalienable rights and privileges, such as life, liberty, pursuit of happiness, and the right of private judgment in moral duty, &c. They are equal and independent in their individual capacity. This is called the "law of nature," established primarily by the Governor of the universe. Of course, differences and distinctions are rather the result of art, in which the order of things is inverted, and by which mankind are deprived of their personal and just rights, than of any natural modification of things. And hence the "nick-names," or unmeaning and empty titles in the old world.

Such distinctions arise, therefore, from a self-created authority, or an usurped authority, which of course must be considered as an unjust tyranny. For any thing given by the God of *nature* only, can be remanded by none but him alone; consequently, for one to take it from another without his consent, or without giving an equivalent, is to deprive him of his personal rights, and must be an infringement upon natural justice.

All men may be considered thus equally free, and independent in their individual capacity; but when taken in a social capacity, they are certainly *dependent* on each other. And none more so than those who consider themselves the most independent; because the Governor of the universe hath determined, as we see in the order of nature, that health and laziness cannot dwell together. So man must not be a Stoic nor a machine, but an active being. Therefore, the laws of nature are fixed, that self-interest shall be a stimulus, or moving spring to action. Hence, there are some things which man cannot do, or subsist without, such as food, water, &c. &c., consequently, self-preservation is called the first law of nature, in point of duty.

But there are some, yea, many things which we cannot perform ourselves, and are, of course, dependent on others for their assistance and help. Such is the case in different operations of mechanism, agriculture, and commerce. All of these are mutually connected, and dependent on each other. Therefore, if I derive advantage from others, why should not others derive some benefit from me in return? This is equal and right, and of course it is just and proper. If, therefore, I withhold that advantage which I could bestow on society, it is an infringement upon natural justice. Of course, we must account to the Author of nature, for the neglect or abuse of those natural, or personal and social privileges, bestowed by him, and enjoyed by us.

OF SOCIAL RIGHTS.

As a whole is composed of parts, and the *parts* collectively form one whole, so to judge correctly of social principles we must view them as they apply naturally, individually, collectively, and prospectively.

As our personal rights are the same, so are our obligations the same. And hence our rights and obligations are naturally and necessarily reciprocal.

To derive the benefit of society collectively and individually, there is need for general rules, for the regulation of the whole. And how shall general rules be formed, but by general consent? It is, therefore, our true interest as individuals, to be involved and connected with such regulations, as may be formed for the benefit and safety of our personal rights; and such as prudence dictates, as necessary to guarantee them from usurpation.

Our personal rights, privileges, and obligations, being *equal*, we have each, as an individual, a right to claim a voice in the formation of those general rules; and *personal duty* arising from the law of nature calls upon us collectively, to act our part as individuals: and there would be an infringement upon *natural justice*, to neglect the right of suffrage.

Social rights, are those which appertain to man, in right of his being a member of society. Every social right has for its foundation some personal right pre-existing in the individual, arising from the law of nature; but to the enjoyment of which his individual power is not, in all cases, sufficiently competent. Of this kind are all those which relate to security and protection.

From this short review it will be easy to distinguish between that class of personal rights which a man retains after entering into society, and those which he throws into the common stock as a member of society.

The personal rights which he retains, are all those in which the power to execute, is as perfect in the individual, as the right itself. Among this class, as is before mentioned, are all the intellectual rights, or rights of the mind; consequently, religion and the privilege of private judgment, are some of those rights.

The personal rights which are not retained, are all those in which, though the right is perfect in the individual, the *power* to execute them is *defective*. They answer not this purpose. A man by the law of nature has a personal right to judge in his own cause; and as far as the rights of the mind is concerned, he never surrenders it. But what availeth it him to judge, if he has not the *power* to redress? He therefore deposits this right in the common stock of society, and takes the arm of society, of which he is a part, in preference, and in addition to his own.

Society grants him nothing. Every man is a proprietor in society, and draws on the capital as a matter of right.

From these premises, a few certain conclusions will follow.

First: That every social right grows out of a personal right, and is founded on the law of nature; or, in other words, it is a personal right exchanged agreeably to natural justice.

Secondly: That civil power, which is derived from society, when applied to the body, is called *political*, but when applied individually is called *civil authority*. This power when properly considered as legal authority, is made up of the aggregate of that class of the personal rights of man, which becomes defective in the individual, in point of power, and auswers not his purpose; but when collected to a focus, becomes competent to the purpose of every one.

Thirdly: That the power produced from the aggregate of personal rights, imperfect in power in the individual, cannot be applied to invade the personal rights, which are retained in the individual, and in which the power to execute is as perfect as the right itself, without intruding on natural justice; seeing the rights are personal only and can concern nobody else.

Thus have we seen man traced as a natural individual, to a member of society; and observed the qualities of the personal rights retained, and those which are exchanged for social rights.

Those principles, when digested and properly applied, show the origin and foundation of the only true and proper fountain of government, which is, properly speaking, the personal social compact. Because mankind, in their individual capacity, are equally free and independent, by the law of nature, as established by its Author. Therefore the facts must be that the individuals themselves, each in his own personal and sovereign right, entered into a compact, not with a government, but with each other to produce a government.. And this is the only mode in which governments have a right to arise, and the only principles on which they ought to exist, or possibly can exist agreeably to *natural justice*.

It is a self-evident fact, that the *people* are the original and only true and proper source from whom a government can be deduced, and spring into existence, on just and equitable principles, agreeably to the law of nature, because the people existed before any government came to exist. Of course society, on social principles, have a right to three things:

First: To form their own government.
Secondly: To choose their own *rulers*.
And thirdly: To cashier *them* for misconduct.

Hence it follows, first, that the authority of rulers is only delegated authority. Secondly, that *they* are accountable to the *fountain* from whom they derived it. And thirdly, that they are not to serve themselves, but society, *whose servants they are*, and by whom they are employed and paid for their services.

OF MORAL RIGHTS.

Moral rights are the personal privileges to think, and judge, and act for one's self in point of moral duty. This is the more plain and clear, as no one is concerned but God, the judge, and the individual man, as a responsible agent.

For what right hath any one to meddle with that which does not concern him?

Moral duties are the result of moral law, which is the Divine prerogative alone; and man hath no right to invade the moral duty of another, for this is the right of the Divine government. No man, therefore, nor set of men, have a right to infringe upon or bind the conscience of another. Man, therefore, as a rational creature, must be *convinced* before he can be *converted*, in order to act consistently, as an agent accountable to the Supreme Governor of the universe. Consequently, a submission of will to a compulsory power, in matters of religion, in repugnance to the dictates of tender conscience, is nothing but an empty show, a piece of hypocrisy, without any mixture of moral goodness or genuine virtue.

All natural religious establishments, or " churches established by law," have been a curse to mankind and a pest to society. Vice and corruption in religion are encouraged and upheld, and virtue lies depressed. If a man, from a principle of duty, would support religion voluntarily, by being compelled to do it he is prevented the opportunity of showing the virtue of his heart, and the influence of his example is lost. If his religion be different from that "established by law," his conscience is bound, and he is prevented from supporting his own religion by taking away from him that which he would give to his own minister, for the support of those in whom he does not believe. Law-religion will cause people to be hypocrites, but cannot cure them of error. A man must be convinced in his judgment, by evidence to his understanding, before he is converted in his heart. Of course, to form articles of faith, for people to subscribe to under severe penalties, is not founded upon common sense, nor on equitable principles. For it supposes people capable of believing without reason or evidence—is contrary to the "law of nature," and repugnant to natural justice, inasmuch as all men are free and independent in their individual capacity, and of course their rights and privileges are equal—to think and to judge, and also to act for themselves, in point of moral duty, and in all matters of opinion in religion.

Suppose that one man believes in one God; another believes in ten: what is that to the first? "It neither picks his pocket nor breaks his leg;" of course, why should he persecute him? Persecution is contrary to natural justice, inasmuch as it assumes a power which no mortal man can claim, it being the Divine right only to judge in such cases. But, nevertheless, moral duty, from pity and a concern for his welfare, may excite a man to strive to convince another for his good—to shun his errors and find the happy road.

Universal right of conscience is given by the Author of nature, who is the moral Governor of the human family; and such liberty of conscience ought to be established in every land.

Intolerance assumes to itself the right of withholding liberty of conscience; toleration assumes the right of granting it: both are despotisms in their nature. Man worships not himself, but his Maker; and liberty of conscience, which he claims, is not for the service of himself, but of his God. In this case, therefore, we must necessarily have the associated ideas of two beings; the mortal, who renders the worship, and the immortal Being who is worshipped.

Toleration, therefore, places itself not between man and man, nor between church and church, nor between one denomination of religion and another, but between God and man—between the being who worships, and the Being who is worshipped; and, by the same act of assumed authority by which it tolerates man to pay his worship, it presumptuously and blasphemously sets itself up to tolerate the Almighty to receive it.

Suppose a bill was brought into any legislature, entitled "An act to tolerate or grant liberty to the Almighty to receive the worship of a Jew or a Turk," or "to prohibit the Almighty to receive it," all men would startle and call it blasphemy: there would be an uproar. The presumption of toleration in religious matters would then present itself unmasked.

But the presumption is not the less, because the name of *man* only appears to those laws; for the associated ideas of the worshipper and the worshipped cannot be separated. Well may one exclaim : " Who then, art thou, vain dust and ashes, by whatever name thou art called, whether an emperor or a king, a bishop or a state, or any thing else, that obtrudest thine insignificance between the soul of man and its Maker? Mind thine own concerns. If he believes not as thou believest, it is a proof that thou believest not as he believeth, and there is no earthly power can determine between you."

With respect to what are called denominations of religion, if every one is left to judge of his own religion, there is no such a thing as a religion that is wrong. But if they are to judge of each other's religion, there is no such a thing as a religion that is right; and, therefore, all the world is right or all the world is wrong. But with respect to religion itself, without any regard to names, and as directed from the universal family of mankind to the Divine object of all adoration, it is *man bringing to his Maker the fruits of his heart;* and the grateful tribute of every one is accepted—"like as a father pitieth his children, so the Lord pitieth them that fear him." He looketh at the heart, and judgeth according to intentions—" of a truth is no respecter of persons, but in every nation he that feareth God and worketh righteousness, is accepted with him." It is required of a man according to what is given him, whether one, two, or five talents; and " he that knoweth his master's will, and doeth it not, shall be beaten with many stripes;" for "where there is no law, there is no transgression;" "sin is the transgression of the law." Man is under a moral law—the law of the mind—of right and wrong. There is a moral duty, and a moral obligation on the part of man to perform that duty. If he does not perform it he falls under condemnation; which he is conscious of, for not acting as well as he knew how : hence the propriety of the words, " 'This is the condemnation, that light has come into the world, and men love darkness rather than light, because their deeds are evil." Man is a rational agent, actuated by motives; his actions are deliberate, and his motives of two kinds, *good* and *evil :* one is called *moral good,* the good principle existing in the mind ; the other is called *moral evil,* because the spirit of the mind is bad, and the intention of the mind is to do wrong, which motive is not right, nor agreeable to natural justice and moral obligation. Because, as all men have equal rights and wants, so their duties and obligations are equal in their social capacity, as established in the law of nature by the Creator and Governor of the world. Of course there is need for a definite rule by which to measure our duties towards each other; because if our rights and obligations are the same and equal, then we are to expect no more than we can justly claim, or would be willing to bestow, agreeable to that which is just and equal ; and hence the command, which is agreeable to the law of nature, " Love thy neighbor as thyself," which is always agreeable to the moral law, and corresponds with the rule, " As ye would that others should do to you, do you even so to them; for this is the law and the prophets;" or what the law of Moses and the prophets, and Jesus Christ taught, which ought, therefore, to be the leading principle of every heart, and the rule of the spirit and conduct of every one in practice, in our actions and dealings with mankind in all things whatever.

Here the *moral law,* and the *law of nature,* and the *rule of practice,* a...

correspond and harmonize together in securing the "social rights, obligations, and duties of man, which have the Almighty for their author, to whom man is accountable." Of course man ought to be actuated by noble principles, conforming himself accordingly, seeing his eternity depends upon it.

But to deprive man of the right to think, and judge, and act for himself, in point of moral duty, is an infringement on the Creator's government, as well as on natural justice, and contrary to every rule of right, and is attended with complicated misery to the human family. It creates broils, animosities, and contentions in society; and raises a domineering spirit in one, and a spirit of resentment and resistance in another; and thus more blood hath been shed, in consequence of such a line of proscription and practice, than from all other sources put together, and hath been attended with more apparent cruelty and misery to mankind, than all other things whatsoever. Therefore, such national establishments of religion are well styled the "whore of Babylon," or the "mother of harlots and the abominations of the earth." The *mother* must be the old $w****$; and if she be a *mother*, who can her *daughters* be but the corrupt established Protestant churches which came out of her, and have not forgot to tread in her steps of persecution towards those who differ from them in opinion? And hence they are said to be "drunk with the blood of the saints and martyrs," which God, as a just governor, will cause to be visited on them in their turn; that the earth may revert to its original and proper Owner, and the inhabitants know that His kingdom is over all.

OF GOVERNMENTS.

From what authority shall one person or a body of men, have power and exercise a command over others?

It must be obtained in one of these three ways. 1st, It must be the gift of the Creator and Governor of the universe—or 2dly, it must be delegated by the people—or else, 3dly, must be *self-created* or *usurped*.*

OF DIVINE DELEGATION.

First, With regard to that authority, which is said to be the *gift* of the Creator, and derived from the Governor of the universe as his delegated power. It hath not for its foundation or support, either Scripture or common sense.

Before any conclusion can be admitted, certain facts, or first principles, or data, must be established or admitted for its confirmation.

The error of those who reason by precedents drawn from antiquity, respecting the rights of man, is, that they do not go far enough into antiquity. They do not go the whole way. They stop in some of the intermediate stages, of a hundred or a thousand years, and produce what was then done, as their precedent. This is no authority at all. If we travel still further into antiquity, we shall find a direct contrary opinion and practice prevailing. And if antiquity is to be authority, a thousand such authorities may be produced, successively contradicting each other. But if we proceed on, we shall at last come out right—we shall come to the time when man came from the hands of his Maker.

---

* By the Creator's 'law of nature,' is man a cosmopolite or the local property of another?

What was he then? 'MAN!' Man was his high and only title, and a higher cannot be given him.

We have now gone back to the origin of man and to the origin of his rights. As to the manner in which the world has been governed from that day to this, it is no further any concern of ours, than to help us to make a proper use of former errors, and suitable improvements upon ancient history. Those who lived a hundred or a thousand years ago, were then moderns as we are now. They had their ancients, and those ancients had others, and we shall be ancients in our turn. If the mere name of antiquity is to govern in the affairs of life, the people who are to live a hundred or a thousand years hence, will be as much bound to take us for a precedent, as we are to take as a precedent those who lived a hundred or a thousand years ago.

The fact is, that an appeal to antiquity may prove any thing, and establish nothing. It is authority against authority, still ascending till we come to the divine origin of the rights of man at the creation. Here our inquiries find a resting-place, and reason finds a home. If a dispute about the rights of man had arisen at the distance of a hundred years from the creation, to this source of authority they must have referred—and to the same source of authority we must now refer.

The genealogy of Christ is traced to Adam. Why not trace the rights of man up to his creation? The answer is, that upstart governments, through ambition founded in moral evil, have arisen and thrust themselves between, to unmake man, and trample upon all his precious rights, to keep him in profound ignorance, that they may be served at his expense.

If any generation of men ever possessed the right of dictating the mode by which the world should be governed forever, it was the first generation that existed; and if that generation did not, no succeeding generation can show authority for so doing. The illuminating and divine principle of the equal rights of man, (for it has its origin from the Maker of man,) relates not only to living individuals, but to all generations of men succeeding each other. Every generation is equal in rights to the generation which preceded it; by the same rule that every individual is born equal in rights to his contemporary.

Every history of the creation, and every traditionary account; whether from the lettered or unlettered world, however they may vary in their opinion or belief of certain particulars, all agree in establishing one point—the unity of man. By which I mean, that all men are of one degree; and consequently, that all men are born equal, and with equal natural rights; in the same manner as if posterity had been continued by creation instead of generation. The latter being only the mode by which the former is carried forward; and consequently, every child born into the world, must be considered as deriving its existence from God. The world is as new to him, as it was to the first man that existed, and his natural rights are of the same kind.

The Mosaic account of the creation, whether taken as divine authority, or merely historical, fully maintains the unity or equality of man. The following expression admits of no controversy. "And God said, let us make man in our own image. In the image of God created he him; male and female created he them." The distinction of the sexes is pointed o it, but no other distinction is implied. If this be not divine authority, it is at least historical authority, and shows the equality of man so far from being a modern doctrine, to be the oldest upon record.

It is also to be observed, that all the religions known in the world, are founded, as far as they relate to man, on the unity of man, as being all of one degree. Whether in heaven or hell, or in whatever state man may be supposed to exist hereafter, the *bad* and *good* are the only distinctions. Nay, even the laws of government are obliged to slide into this principle, by making degree to consist in crimes and not in persons.

This is one of the greatest of all truths, and it is our highest interest to cultivate it. By considering man in this light, it places him in a close connection with his duties, whether to his Creator, or the creation, of which he is a part; and it is only when he forgets his birth or origin, or to use a more fashionable phrase, "his birth and family," that he becomes dissolute.

The distinction of the sexes only, is mentioned at the creation of man. Hence, the MAN was considered as the head of his family; and so established by the law of custom, which gave rise to the simple patriarchial government.

But so far are the scriptures from justifying the idea that monarchy is the "delegated power of God," that they speak directly to the reverse.— They inform us that the Jews were the peculiar people of God, and "they desired a king to reign over them, to be like all the nations round about," after they had been a commonwealth for several hundred years. And a king they obtained, as a judgment for their moral evil; and he proved a scourge for their national sin.

Thus, "the nations round about" had kings at an early period. The Israelites also desired to have one, and a king was given them as a judgment. We may therefore conclude, that monarchy had its origin in some wisdom which was not divine.

Here it may be observed, that the wisdom of God, in his dispensations to nations and people accomplishes many great ends with very few simple means—hence when one "social compact" is removed, in justice, for sin, a way is then opened for another as a matter of mercy. This was manifested in the overthrow of Babylon, for the relief and return of the Jews to Jerusalem, to rebuild the temple. So also, Saul was removed for a better man to reign in his stead. Hence if there be kings, it is better to have good men than bad ones. Therefore the Christians were commanded to pray for them, as well-wishers and friends to mankind, who wished for peace in the land.

It could have been no difficult thing, in the early and solitary ages of the world, while the chief employment of man was that of attending flocks and herds, for a banditti of ruffians to overrun a country, and lay it under contribution. Their power being established, the chief of the band contrived to lose the name of robber into that of monarch; and hence the origin of monarchy and kings.

Those bands of robbers having "parcelled out the world," and divided it into dominions, began, as is naturally the case, to quarrel with each other. What at first was obtained by violence, was considered by others as proper and lawful to be taken, and a second plunderer succeeded the first.

They alternately invaded the dominions which each had assigned to himself, and the brutality with which they treated each other, explains the original character of monarchy; it was ruffian torturing ruffian. The conqueror considered the conquered, not as his prisoner, but his property. He led him in triumph, rattling in chains, and doomed him, at pleasure, to slavery or death. As time obliterated the history of their beginning, their successors assumed new appearances, to cut off the entail of their disgrace, but their principle and object remained the same. What at first was plundered, assumed the softer name of revenue, and the power originally usurped, they affected to inherit.

The career of Nebuchadnezzar, Alexander the Great, Julius and Augustus Cæsar, Mahomet, William the Conqueror, Cromwell, and Bonaparte, with their concomitants, are enough to exemplify the propriety of the remarks already made.

Monarchical government, when considered as the delegated power of God, supposes an hereditary succession; and of course the *will* of the monarch, with his successors, must be binding, not only on the present generation, but also on those which are to come. To suppose that the *will* of those who existed once, but are *now* dead, can be binding on the generations yet to come, is ridiculous. One is *out* of the world, and the other not *in* it, and of course they are two *nonentities*, which can never meet in this world, and therefore can by no means form obligations for one another, agreeably to natural justice. Moreover, the government is for the benefit of the people, and not the people for the government. Hence, it must be calculated so as to answer every purpose of government. But monarchy is not calculated so to do, but by the aid or assistance of an aristocracy, an additional oppression, whereby the generality of the people must be kept in fear and profound ignorance, by tyrannical laws, to prevent the "spirit of inquiry," the "liberty of speech," and of the "press;" which shows that their works are bad, and that they "love darkness rather than light, because their deeds are evil!" Of course it is not the most excellent way; because it supposes one man to have more sense and wisdom than all the nation besides—whereas hereditary succession is as liable to have a fool as a wise man for a governor; and more so, when degeneration is rendered certain by confining their intermarriages exclusively to royal blood.

The more this subject is investigated, the more the absurdity of it will appear. It is inconsistent, both with scripture and common sense. It is contrary to every principle both of moral goodness and of natural justice. It cannot stand the test of a comparison with the *moral law*, the *law of nature*, or the *rule of practice*.

OF THE POPE'S POWER.

If the progressive power of the pope, and the almost incredible height to which it grew, the summit appearing so stupendous with a pompous show, be compared with the "law of nature," and the character of the Almighty, the idea of monarchy or tyrannical power as being the delegated power of God, will sink into contempt.

Moral obligation and duty having great influence on the mind and practice of man, religion was made use of as a tool to answer the purposes of ambitious and designing men. Hence the origin of "religion established by law." But in order to accomplish the end, the charge must be committed only to an ingenious few, who are fitted and qualified for the purpose by every possible instruction; while all the rest must be kept in the greatest possible ignorance, that they may be the more manageable.

The executors of the work being ingeniously qualified, and the minds of the people prepared, a deception might easily be practised where none were permitted to think, and judge, and act for themselves. Hence the origin of the pagan heroes, and mythology, and oracles, and priests.

Under tyranny and oppression, which prohibit liberty of conscience, and bind the people in eternal ignorance, the mental powers of men are so impaired, and their moral faculties so darkened, that reason will not do its office. And hence mankind became credulous to a degree, which in this enlightened day is hardly to be believed.

Constantine the Great, in order to secure the influence of Christian ministers in his favor, and thereby establish his unbounded power, in and over the Roman empire, abolished paganism, and established Christianity as the national religion. And from thence the ministry became a species of trade and traffic down to this time.

Every valuable and important institution is capable of abuse; and not any thing more so than religion: but there is a distinction to be made between the thing itself and the abuse of it. Religion is a good thing; but from one small abuse of it may originate important consequences. Constantine, in order to accomplish his own purposes, erected the image of the Saviour on the cross, and carried it in the front of his army, to lead on the van of nominal Christians. The image of the Virgin Mary found its way to follow after; and hence all the abominations of images, &c., &c., in the Christian church.

As might have been expected, from the temptation of gain and grandeur, arising out of the "religious law establishment" of Constantine, many of the heathen priests and others became professional Christians, either for the name, or for the "loaves and fishes." Of course, "moral evil" took the lead, and the Church, so called, went on the road to ruin.

In those days of yore, when people were taught that the will of a tyrant should be considered as the delegated power of God, and reverentially obeyed accordingly; few pretended to think and act for themselves, except the true worshippers of God, who acted from conscientious motives. The multitude were sadly imposed upon. The bare say-so of the priest was received as Divine truth, and impostors became influential, and were respected. It was difficult to cope with popular opinion, which was founded in long established habits—backed by civil, and supported by ecclesiastical authority; till at length, the power of the established clergy became more respectable and influential than the civil authority, and began to take the lead, and bear rule accordingly; domineering over those who had been their promoters, until affairs were entirely transposed; so that the civil law and authority were only used as tools by the ecclesiastics, to answer their own ends, as the priests were formerly used to support the tyrannical power of ambitious usurpers.

Credulous people, still chained by despotism and ignorance, retained their old prejudices. With them tyranny was humanity, and was reverenced as the delegated power of God. And if a priest should say that a "horse was a cow," or a "ham of bacon was a fish," he must not dispute it; but must believe the say-so of the priest, in opposition to his own senses.

At length, one was exalted above his fellows, and as an expression of his power and dignity, was styled, "Bishop of Bishops, or Universal Bishop," and claimed all the world for his own, so that no king or potentate could reign but by his consent, as he was to be considered the successor of the Apostle Peter, who was constituted the Vicegerent of the Almighty upon earth. Thus the right to determine all disputes, and to bestow crowns and kingdoms at pleasure, and to make new laws, &c., &c., were his pretensions to mankind, as exemplified in the affairs of Poland—"And all the world wondered after the beast." Infallibility, which belongs to the Almighty alone, was ascribed to this great one by all his adherents.

The crown of France possessed by Henry IV., was adjudged to Rudolph, his competitor, by the power and decision of the pope, who also claimed the kingdom of Spain as the patrimony of St. Peter, by virtue of some old deeds which he pretended were lost.

The claim not being disputed, a tax or annuity was the result. Hence the origin of "Peter-pence," known in different countries to a late day.

The titles of "Most Christian Majesty," and "Most Catholic Majesty," were the result and donation of this self-claimed vicegerent power. Also "Defender of the Faith," was another spurious gift from the same self-claimed authority, as a reward for merit in writing a book in favor of the vicegerency, by Henry VIII. of England.

The crown of England was adjudged to the king of France, unless King John would comply with the vicegerent's requisition; which was done to save the kingdom.

The idea became so popular, that the sanction and confirmation of this "spurious" vicegerent was necessary to make good and valid any kingly authority, that the king of Denmark sent to Rome, to obtain the blessing of confirmation, in and over his kingdom.

The son to the emperor of Russia posted off to Rome also, to be confirmed in what he expected to inherit by virtue of his father. And, "The world wondered after the beast!"

A law of "Inquisition" was enacted by the ecclesiastical court, to destroy heresy,—that is, all who dare to think, and judge, and act for themselves.

The art of printing was considered witchcraft, and the inventor was punished as a wizard, and his colleague only escaped by proving it to be mere mechanism.

A gentleman who taught the present theory of astronomy, was adjudged to die for heresy, because he apprehended the earth to be like a ball, when the pretended vicegerent affirmed it to be like a table upon legs; and a recantation was necessary to save his life. And all who believed in the antipodes were excommunicated by Pope Gregory VII.

Difference of opinion was heresy, and the consequence was recantation or death. And doubtful cases were put to the torture, to compel them to give evidence against themselves.

If a man should speak the truth, it would be considered and construed as a libel, if in opposition to popular and common received opinion; and the greater the truth, the greater the libel or heresy, of course.

Many dead bodies were raised, and their coffins *chained*, to prevent them from giving *leg-bail*, while they were excommunicated and "cursed" to eternal misery, with "*bell* book and *candle* light," and then consigned to the flames as culprits, or "heretics,' who were to be burnt alive. What a pompous show, what a farce and a mockery of common sense!

The fallacious ideas that "tyranny is the delegated power of God," and that ignorance is necessary for the welfare of society, are now happily excluded from the United States, and ought to be banished out of the world.

THE DAWN OF LIBERTY.

The bishop's power, arrived at its zenith, had so intoxicated him that he fell asleep. This spurious vicegerent, who was so charitable as to give crowns and kingdoms not his own, to obtain money and popularity from his courtiers, and enlarge his own power and influence, bestowed *two things* more than formerly, which began to awaken up "common sense." The first was countries of which he had never heard; and, secondly, pardons, not only for sins past and present, but also for *those which were to come*. The first laid the foundation for enterprise. It excited inquiry after true philosophic information, and improvements in the arts and sciences. The latter paved the way for the discovery of truth in divinity.

One quarter of the world, by the wisdom of the Creator, for the benefit of rising generations of man, for several thousands of years had remained an uncultivated wilderness. A land, magnificent for its stupendous and lofty mountains—its numerous and extensive rivers—its expanded lakes, or inland seas, with a soil superior to that of any country in the ancient world, is discovered. A new world appears—the theatre, designed by the Governor of the universe, for the display of some important and grand design worthy of himself.

Tyranny had unmanned the people; but the spirit of enterprise and discovery being excited, and the countries which might be discovered being conferred upon the fortunate adventurer by the spurious vicegerent, which was considered sufficient to give a good title to any discovered countries, many thousands embarked in the undertaking. Supported by this authority, they considered not the countries only, but the people also who inhabited those countries, as their property, and treated them as an inferior race of beings, dooming them at pleasure both to slavery and death. Such was the degraded state of the human mind! So much was an universal revolution wanting for the amelioration of man!

On the other hand, the selling of pardons, or granting indulgences for sins to come, opened a door for all manner of vice, so offensive to virtuous minds, as to excite a spirit of detestation and abhorrence. And "common sense" awoke from its lethargy, and paved the way for what is called the "reformation." Martin Luther bore testimony in Germany against the pope. And the pope, in his turn, poured out "bulls" with fury. Their disputes, aided by the art of printing, produced an almost universal reflection among the people, attended with a spirit of inquiry and research after truth. And thus, after a sleep of several hundred years, the people were awakened, and began to think and judge for themselves. But common sense had become so much blinded by the darkness of ignorance, that she only "viewed men as trees walking!" And such were the prejudices of the people of the old world, that there was not a place found among them, where the rights of man could be peaceably enjoyed, agreeably to the law of nature.

Mark the wisdom and goodness of the supreme Governor of the world, that the discovery of America was so long delayed; and that at length it happened at such an important era of the world.

The two grants of the vicegerents, viz., that by which unheard of countries were given away, and that by which indulgences for sin were given to purchasers—were both conferred about the same time; and the discovery of America, and the reformation in Germany, followed very shortly after the same period of time—all of which co-operated in effecting a revolution in the theories both of astronomy and divinity. The earth was no longer considered by thinking men as a *table upon legs*. The vicegerency was treated with contempt, as being an imposition upon mankind, and the bishop was soon stripped of one third of his dominions. But, nevertheless, the spirit of persecution still prevailed among the different sects, until the innocent Quakers appeared in the days of Fox. It could not be otherwise; it will ever attend all law-religion. John Calvin was the cause of M. S. being put to death for mere matters of opinion, and Melancthon justified him in it. Martin Luther wrote to the magistrates to punish some who differed from him, which afterwards gave great uneasiness. Hence, many thousands, who were waked up, "flew to the wilderness of America," hoping there peaceably to enjoy those rights bestowed upon them by the God of nature. But the spirit and prejudice of education, so deeply rooted, was hard to be eradicated. Hence, some who had fled from the intolerant hand of persecution became oppressive themselves, and others in turn had to suffer. Four Quakers were put to death, merely for indifferent matters of religion. And from the old idea, that religion could not be maintained unless upheld by civil power, those who had come hither to enjoy their opinions began to form religious establishments by laws of their own. At length, however, they were better informed, and their progeny better taught, which laid a foundation for the investigation of the rights of man, and the more perfect knowledge of the law of nature.

As virtue and religion and the arts and sciences have gone hand in hand together, so dissipation and destruction succeed each other. These things are observable in the rise and fall of the five succeeding nations—the Jews, Babylonians, Medes, and Persians, Greeks, and Romans—who succeeded each other in their turns.

Persecution drove the first settlers to America, and oppression pursuing them still, gave rise to the spirit of inquiry. All that energy of soul with which man is endowed by the God of nature was roused, and they were determined to enjoy as much of nature's law as by their exertions they could secure. From this sprung the outlines of our national character.

As ignorance and severity are necessary for the support of tyranny, to keep the people in awe, so light and information are necessary to cut the sinews of tyrannical government, and bring mankind into the exercise and enjoyment of their proper rights and dignity, agreeably to the law of nature, to the moral law, and to the rule of practice, as established by the Governor of the universe.

The laws, prejudices, and ignorance of mankind had been such, that there was not a place in the ancient known world, that admitted the revolution to begin, which was necessary for the emergency of man.

No place was so ripe—no part in the natural world so fitted, as America. Because of its infancy, the people would hear instruction, as a child who wishes to acquire a perfect education. But those of the old countries of monarchy, imagined themselves to have arrived at the summit of political perfection: of course there was no occasion for further inquiry. Religious bigotry was also another great hindrance, which, through the prejudice of church and state, had mighty influence. Besides, the minds of the people were so degraded, and the moral faculty was so debased, they were not prepared to act with that prompt and deliberate firmness which was required in so great a work. From all these considerations, such persons who had the clearest heads and best hearts which those days afforded, fled to America. Determined not to receive things as matters of fact on the bare say-so of others, when repugnant to common sense, (they were men, and had the spirit of inquiry,) they took the liberty to think, and judge, and act for themselves. And as that was not admissible in the old world, they had energy and enterprise enough to come to the new world and enjoy their opinions. Thus the spirit of independence in embryo migrated with our ancestors when they emigrated to this happy land.

One thing is worthy of observation, which, though of small beginning, produced noble consequences. William Penn, the celebrated Quaker, in his regulations for Pennsylvania, contrary to the practice in all other countries, required no particular test, or religious opinion, as a qualification for office, but encouraged all societies to settle in the state, making all equally secure, and eligible to any office and dignity which their worth and virtue might deserve.

The persecution of the Quakers in Massachusetts, was the effect or relic of prejudices brought from the old world. But the death of those four innocent sufferers, tended in its consequences to check religious bigotry, and it lowered away.

The various opinions which emigrated were a check upon each other, and laid a foundation for a mutual forbearance, which was exemplified by Providence and Rhode Island!

Lord Baltimore also, who was a Roman Catholic, being provoked to jealousy, became liberal towards emigrants of different opinions, and gave them encouragement to settle in his colony. And since the revolution, the oppressive tobacco laws have been repealed both in Maryland and Virginia, which put the established clergy on a level with other denominations. New Hampshire and Vermont have likewise laid aside the clerical yoke.. But Massachusetts and Connecticut retain a tincture of the old W——; which is a departure from the law of nature, and a violation of moral obligation, and an infringement upon natural justice! Though some of their laws have been modified in a small degree.

And the liberal spirit of Penn, so agreeable to the law of nature, the moral law, and the rule of practice, prevailed in the land, until the law of nature, established by the Governor of the universe—that is, an universal liberty of conscience, was established.* This done, nothing fur-

---

* By the confederation in the constitution of the federal government.

ther is wanting, but that the moral law of love should be written in every heart, "Thou shalt love thy neighbor as thyself;" and the rule of practice be seen in the conduct of each and every individual, "As ye would that men should do unto you, do ye even so unto them," that golden rule of practice, which was the law of Moses, the spirit of the prophets, and the injunction of Jesus Christ.

Before all things can be right in the human family, the moral law must reign in all parts. Before that can exist universally, the law of nature must be revived and restored, to reign in all nations; and that it may be so, the rule of practice must be attended to from *principle;* because they are connected with, and mutually dependent upon each other. Therefore, there is need for a general reform in the world, both in the head and heart. For the whole head is sick, and the whole heart is faint; from the crown of the head to the sole of the foot, is full of wounds, bruises, and putrefying sores.

The discovery of America after her dormant state, with the concomitant circumstances attending it, began to cast great light on the dispensations of Divine Providence, and shed a new lustre on the aspect of human affairs.

The spirit of the gospel, or the moral law of love, the law of nature and the rule of practice, have begun to revive, and some are running to and fro, and knowledge is increasing. But all things are not right yet, nor can they be, until the personal, social, and moral rights of mankind are restored. When this is done, there will be an end of tyrannical power, and established religion will cease, and universal liberty of conscience will be enjoyed in the love of the Creator, and of mankind. Then the "wolf and the lamb will dwell together, and there will not be any more war."

The Almighty had long borne with the nations of the earth, but now his controversy has begun, and happy will it be for those who are prepared for the storm.

It is a matter of rejoicing with the upright in heart, that they have an asylum in the day of trouble. But where will the wicked and proud oppressors hide their guilty heads? The day of vengeance is near, and the *five swords of the Almighty* are so visible in the earth, that no considerate man can deny the hand of God—destructive insects, earthquakes, wars, pestilence, and famine. Though people account for these things on natural principles, yet nature emanated from the *power* of God, and is still under *his* control, which, to the discerning eye, is visible in all *his* works. Hence the words of General Washington are pertinent to the case in hand: "But this seems to be the age of wonders, and it is reserved for intoxicated and lawless France, *for purposes of Providence far beyond the reach of human ken,* to slaughter her own citizens, and disturb the repose of all the world besides."

OF FORMS OF GOVERNMENT.

We have no instance of an elective monarchy established upon proper social principles. To avoid perpetual civil commotion, it has been found necessary to make the electors hereditary. Of course, to confine the right of suffrage, in the most important of all elections, to a few overgrown individuals.

An hereditary monarchy is both dangerous and absurd. And an absolute monarchy, where an individual is endowed with both legislative and executive authority, is still much more to be feared. He that is not accountable to anybody for his conduct, should be intrusted by nobody. Besides, hereditary monarchy, in any form, runs an equal risk to have a fool as a wise man for a governor; and more so, considering the effects of limited intermarriages.

An aristocracy may secure to the counsels of state a larger fund of information; but at the same time, it places the people under many tyrants instead of one. Besides, as they must also be hereditary, and be supported by entailed property, they are *disqualified* for legislative and executive, and even for judicial trust, inasmuch as the law of nature is violated in their very raising. They have become unnatural brothers, who consider their brethren as beings of an inferior grade and rank to themselves: and of course, from the spirit of their education, they are contaminated with prejudices and partiality, which wholly *disqualify* them to judge with equity and humanity agreeable to the law of nature.

Democracy, in small and petty societies, may apply and answer many valuable purposes to mankind, as in days of old, where the whole voice of the people could be obtained, or at least all of those concerned. But in a large and extensive country, it would become too unweildy. But as the law of nature on social principles makes them equally interested and entitled to a voice in the formation of those *prudential rules* made for the regulation of the *whole*, a *representative form of government* presents itself as most appropriate to answer every purpose. By this method the voice of the people is made over to their representative. And hence, there is a personal and social compact, agreeable to the law of nature; which may be made to suit the greatest nation. And provided the world of mankind were more enlightened, it might forever exclude the necessity of an appeal to war. Wars are neither more nor less than national quarrels; and when both parties are sick and tired of the contest, they settle their differences through the medium of a convention of delegates. Why not take this course in the first instance, and spare human blood?

This mode of government will best guard the people against tyrannical imposition of both church and state. The representation being only for a limited time, and the delegate then returning to his former sphere, and becoming a private citizen, he of course feels the effect of his own legislation as a member of society. This exchange of public for private life, like the ebbing and flowing of the sea, will tend to keep things pure, so that the affairs of the nation may at all times bear investigation. Moreover, it stimulates people of all classes to search after truth and to communicate knowledge. And the interest of the commonwealth is made secure, whilst the rights of individuals are safely guarantied, and sacredly kept by chosen men in trust, who, as faithful executors, must give account.

RIGHT OF PROPERTY HELD UNDER MONARCHS.

In monarchical governments, in cases of rebellion or treason, the real estates are forfeited to the monarch, and the widow and fatherless child are turned out of doors, and the poor culprit himself suffers death. Now, considering the punishment to be proportioned to the crime, the conclusion must be, that the *land* properly belongs to the monarch; otherwise why disinherit the wife and children, seeing there is no natural justice in making the innocent suffer for the guilty? But as *real estates* are made hereditary in a particular branch of the family, and subject to forfeiture to the crown in cases of rebellion or treason, it is manifest that they must have been derived from the government, and are only held during good behavior. Of course all lands originally were considered crown lands, no doubt made so by conquest or usurpation, and then parcelled out to a few, who should hold them as tenants to the crown. These tenants had their tenants also—and thus the whole was dependent on the will and pleasure of *one* individual.

OF REPRESENTATION.

All men being considered free and independent in their individual capacity, but dependent in their social capacity, the rights of each are equal. The first, by virtue of existence; the latter, by virtue of being a member of society. Our personal and social rights being equal, neither of them can be taken from us but by our own consent, without infringing upon natural justice, except only when forfeited to society by some misdemeanor, or taken by the laws of the Creator who gave them. Our rights being equal, so are our privileges—of course our rights, privileges, duties and obligations are the same in each and all. Therefore, the neglect of the right of suffrage in any individual is a violation of social duty—that is, a breach of one of the obligations we owe to society. By neglecting our social duties, we involve ourselves in a violation of natural justice, which requires a proper use and improvement of those social blessings, conferred upon us by the Supreme Governor of the world, who will hold us accountable for the neglect of every relative duty. These are considerations not sufficiently weighed by many. All are deeply interested in them, though many remain ignorant of it. And to excuse ourselves by concluding that these things do not concern us, though our well-being is deeply concerned, is all of a piece with the supposition, that the *will of a tyrant* is the order of Providence and the delegated power of God.

As individuals and as members of society, we have a right to claim a voice in all public deliberations, and to see to it that we have justice done us; because our social rights grow out of our personal rights. Our own power as individuals, not being equal to our wants and necessities, we exchange a part of our personal rights for social rights, by casting a part into the common stock by delegation; and hence our power and will are made over to our representative, and we take the arm of society of which we are a part for our protection, in addition to our own. So that society grants us nothing; but we draw on the capital as a matter of right. Hence, it is self-evident that social or civil distinctions can be founded only on public utility, agreeable to the rules of equity.

NATURE AND DESIGN, AND ENACTION OF LAW.

Social rights when protected by general rules and applied to a nation or people as a body, are called political; but when applied to individuals, are called civil. Hence the distinction between political and civil law.

The end of all political associations is the preservation of the natural and imprescriptible rights of man; and these rights are liberty, property, security, and resistance of oppression. The people are essentially the source of all sovereignty. Nor can any individual or body of men be entitled to any authority which is not expressly derived from them. Civil liberty consists in doing whatever does not injure another. And the law is an expression of the will of the community for individual instruction.

The law of course ought to prohibit such actions only as are hurtful to society, and to impose no penalties, but such as are absolutely and manifestly necessary for the welfare of society.

And all citizens have a right to concur, either personally or by their representative, in the formation of those general rules, which might be properly enough called the law of prudence.

The general rule, or the law of prudence, should be the same to all, whether to punish or protect. All being equal in rights, are equally eligible to all honors, places, and employments, according to their different abilities, without any other distinction than that created by their virtue and talents.

OF THE LAW OF NATIONS.

Here it is proper to remark, that there is frequently a misapplication of terms, which gives improper conceptions, leading the reader or hearer to ascribe effects to causes which could never produce them. And so setting out in error, they must forever continue to be wrong. Thus, says one, "Reason teacheth me this or that," when the information was derived through the channel of tradition. Again, "Nature works" so and so, when there is no principle in nature to operate it; but is wholly the effect of art, or the works of nature's God.

To ascribe that to nature which belongs to art is certainly wrong, and leads to confusion! Every effect should be ascribed to its original and proper cause, in order to come at the true knowledge of things as they are, or as they should be in a relative point of view.

Islands, for example, may originate three ways. First, From nature's God; Secondly, From nature herself; Thirdly, From art. Thus, the island of Great Britain was formed by nature's God, at the creation. The island of New Orleans, near two hundred miles in length and about twelve in breadth, was formed by nature; the flood-wood and mud washing down from the Missouri and other rivers into the Mississippi, having formed this island, and divided the water that was once an arm of the sea, making Lake Ponchartrain and Tuckepaw Bay. And an artificial island is formed at New York for the erection of a battery, at the junction of the two rivers.

I have now hinted at our rights, as existing by the law of nature, established primarily by our Creator, as we individually stand related to each other; and also at the law of nations, which is improperly called the law of nature, and is evidently the effect of art; and such as prudence dictates as necessary for general rules, for the regulation of the whole, and may with greater propriety be called the law of prudence. These las being received in some degree among the nations, are therefore called the law of nations. And indeed it might be well if they were received more generally among the human family.

RECAPITULATION.

We have derived from the God of nature certain inalienable rights. It is necessary to have those rights guarantied against an usurper. Civil government is therefore necessary. Prudence dictates the propriety of delegating to suitable persons so much of those rights as may be necessary for the formation and execution of that political machine which is called government.

Government, when formed, is under obligations to act only for the public good and general welfare. And the principles of natural justice and moral obligation will sanction the same, when considered in relation to the moral Governor of the world.

By way of explanation, from what hath been observed, as one of the whole, I have certain personal rights which cannot be taken from me on the principles of natural justice, without my consent. I am naturally interested in their security, and of course prudence requires my consent. I give it, and by virtue thereof I have a right to expect and claim, in conjunction with others, certain privileges at the hand of my government—that is my bounty, viz. protection of my person, character, and property, and peaceably to enjoy without interruption the use of my liberty, and the privilege of seeking happiness in an innocent way : that is, where no man's right is invaded, nor the public peace disturbed. I have also the right and privilege of private judgment in matters of opinion and moral duty in the things of God and eternity—things which can concern no one but myself.

A CONTRAST.

Let the foregoing reflection be contrasted with the present state of the world, and we shall distinctly see that all things are not right in the world, and of course that there is need of a great and general reform before the head and heart, the motives and conduct of men will correspond with the moral law, the law of nature, and the rule of practice. And it will be well to remember that all men are accountable to the Supreme Governor of the world, not only for their motives and conduct towards each other, but for their disposition of heart towards him, whether they be rulers, subjects, or citizens, if they would meet the approbation of God upon their souls. Let them therefore take heed how they suffer considerations of interest or popularity to lead them astray, lest they sell their eternal peace for a transitory object. Upstart governments may take heed and tremble. and so may all oppressors and workers of iniquity, seeing their eternity is at stake !

OF PUNISHMENTS.

It is the certainty of punishment, more than the severity of it, that will have the greatest effect upon mankind. Vigorous laws, properly apportioned to the nature of crimes, and well and faithfully executed, are best for the well-being of society. But as the degrees of punishment must bear some analogy to the circumstances of the crime, so the heinousness of the offence, with its magnitude, must be taken into the account, to judge properly what degree of chastisement shall be inflicted in any case. Very few, if any, persons should be punished with death, because it is taking that which cannot be restored. And to take that from another, which we did not bestow, and which cannot be restored, is running near to the precipice of doing unnatural justice.

An innocent person being suddenly cut off, is injured irreparably beyond all possible calculation; for his eternity may depend upon it. But the variations of crimes are so great and numerous, that a variety of punishments is necessary to meet every case; hence the penitentiary system presents to view, as proper for the subject, by admitting of degrees, both of time and solitude.

The institution is humane, both in its nature and consequences. The culprit is prevented from further injury to society, and has opportunity for reflection—and by learning or improving some trade, he may become a useful member of society—and if innocent of the charge, may yet be restored to his privileges, which has been exemplified in several cases.

In many cases, the judge or jury, from strong presumptive proof, may believe a man accused to be guilty of the charge, and, as a dangerous man to society and to his neighborhood, would feel free to send him to the penitentiary, when neither the crime nor the evidence would justify them to take his life. Hence, under sanguinary laws many offenders would escape through humanity.

A few plain rules, properly enforced, will prove of more consequence than tyrannical barbarity or despotic cruelty. This is self-evident, to those who reflect on the various modes of family government.

Those parents who threaten much, and perform but little, and promise some and do nothing; but, by fits and starts, deal out blows without rule or reason, and then only when in a pet or passion; have children who have no confidence in what they say. For their inconsistencies they are cordially despised by their children, who wish to get from under their government. And such children become mere pests to society. On the other hand, such parents as use few words, and are firm, who act deliberately, perform their promises or threats, are generally blest with obedient children, who afterwards are a blessing to the community.

The design of punishment is,—1st, to reform the person who suffers it—2dly, to prevent the perpetration of crimes, by deterring others—3dly, to remove those persons from society, who have manifested by their tempers and crimes that they are unfit to live in it.

The reformation of a criminal can never be effected by a public punishment, for the following reasons:

First—As it is always connected with infamy, it destroys in him the sense of shame, which is one of the strongest outposts of virtue.

Secondly—It is generally of such short duration, as to produce none of those changes in body or mind, which are absolutely necessary to reform obstinate habits of vice.

Thirdly—Experience proves, that public punishments have increased propensities to crimes. A man who has lost his character at a public whipping-post, hath nothing valuable left to lose in society.

Pain has begotten insensibility to the whip, and shame to infamy; there, added to his old habits of vice, probably beget a spirit of revenge against the whole community, whose laws have inflicted his punishment upon him, and hence he is stimulated to add to the number and enormity of his outrages upon society.

Therefore public punishment will harden the heart, and tend to qualify a man to be a nuisance to society, and a pest to mankind. For a man who hath neither moral virtue, nor a good character, nor property to influence his actions and conduct, hath nothing to lose by misconduct but his soul, the company of his friends, and his liberty and life.

Hence the punishment should be fitted to his case, and the degree to the nature of his crime, which the law of equity requires. The difference of crimes and the variations are such, that the penitentiary system seems best fitted to it, and appears the most suitable, on the principles of humanity and common sense, to answer the purpose.

First—It admits of degrees both of time in the duration, and also in the confinement.

Secondly—It prevents the stupefaction, or insensibility to every sense of shame, or duty and moral obligation and character, which the ignominy from the pillory or whipping-post beget—and also it prevents the resentment or desire to revenge the public infamy.

Thirdly—It prevents his bad example from corrupting society, and gives him no opportunity of injuring others, were he disposed to do it.

Fourthly—It gives him time and opportunity for reflection and repentance; and must naturally prove a stimulus to the mind. The loss of friends and their company, the loss of liberty, the idea of which is more painful than the thoughts of death, and the hope of regaining or being restored to them again, which is so animating and pleasing, have a powerful operation and influence upon the mind to produce a reformation. And he may yet become a useful citizen by his trade: the injured also may be indemnified, and likewise the public expenses paid.

The practice of hanging for horse-stealing, under the idea of proportioning the punishment to the crime, is to suppose that a man is of no more value than a horse, degrading mankind down to a level with the brutes.

The frequency of public executions and gibbets in Great Britain, tend to harden the people, and contaminate the human mind. It eradicates those soft principles of nature, implanted in the human breast by the Creator, which are so visible in childhood, until they are erased by a long course of evil habits. Thus people becoming hardened, are qualified for every evil work, so as to sport with death, and scoff at damnation—and hence the many pick-pocket robberies, and other evils which transpire while viewing the awful scene of execution, and which, if detected, would expose them to a similar fate.

There are upwards of one hundred and sixty offences which are punishable with death, according to their code of criminal laws.

Now to consider this subject properly, there appears not that distinction observed between vice and virtue, which the nature of the case admits and requires to be made for the welfare of society;—and of course, if the human mind is not properly informed, and impressed with just views of right and wrong, good society cannot be cultivated, and the world will remain as a bedlam under the curse of ignorance. For according to the fountain so will be the stream. Hence if the principle be bad, the fruit must be bad also. Therefore the axe must be laid at the root, and the rubbish, dissipation, and darkness, arising from ignorance, must be removed. General information must be promoted, and proper ideas implanted and cultivated in the mind, that people may practise virtue from principle, as rational agents, who must give account.

The propriety and importance of a good and early education, is not considered by many. But let it be remembered, whatever is learned in youth, remains fixed for life; whereas what old people learn, is like writing on the sand, which is washed out by the first rain. Therefore bend the tender mind, like a young branch, the way you would have it grow, otherwise it will be hard to effect by art, what would become easy and natural, if timely performed.

Provided we are not to be governed on such principles as ignorance and terror compose, then we must insist on the opposite theory, viz. general information and proper motives; such as are noble in their nature, and calculated in their consequence to promote the welfare of society. And every one must strive to do his part, both in cultivating and practising the work.

This subject, properly digested, shows the propriety of inculcating the doctrine of first principles—our relation to God and man. Without this, how shall people judge of natural justice and moral obligation? Or how perform their moral duties? In proportion to the ignorance of the people, vice and imposition have ever abounded—whilst on the other hand, in proportion as light has shone, true dignity of soul has appeared in a line of virtuous conduct, natural justice been attended to, and the moral government of the Supreme Being acknowledged. In proportion as any nation or people have been just and good, so prosperity has attended them, whilst the arts and sciences have flourished. But when their conduct has been reversed, though God may have borne with them for a season, the day of their visitation has come at last!

OF POLITICAL EXISTENCE.

God, as the Creator and supporter of man, hath a right to govern his creatures and prescribe the rule of their actions. Man, as his creature, has a right, and it is his duty and privilege to obey. In eternity people must be judged and rewarded as individuals only. But in this world, as we exist socially, we have social privileges, which are called political; and national political privileges abused, become a political evil: and a political evil must be cured, or it must become remediless. And as these privileges are for time only, when abused, the personal rights of mankind are infringed upon, contrary to the law of nature, and natural justice calls for a remedy. Of course there must be a reform, or else an overthrow! It is perfectly consistent with propriety to demand the former—the latter is the just visitation of a righteous Judge! The first is a duty which is in our own power—the latter always a just dispensation of the Almighty. As it is nowhere said that nations in their political capacity shall be judged in futurity, political evils must be punished here.

Therefore, when a government is overgrown in tyrannical power and wickedness, dissipation, luxury, and oppression abound, and unheard of cruelties prevail. All manner of debauchery, drunkenness, and revelling, with other concomitant vices and evils, so great and so many abound, that it may be said "moral evil" reigns triumphant in the land, and virtue cannot be found; justice is trampled upon, moral obligation is despised, and mankind become like bedlamites, and the doctrine of atheism is the order of the day.

Hark! Let reason ask, Does it not seem to comport with the moral government of the Supreme Being, who is just and wise, to overthrow such political existence, as being unworthy, and thereby open a door for another such an one as will secure to the people the enjoyment of their rights, agreeable to the order of things, and acknowledging his government, live agreeable to the moral law, the law of nature, and the rule of practice?

If all our ideas of good and evil, of right and wrong, are not chimerical, we must answer in reason, that it would be *just* to overthrow them as a social and political body, as unworthy of their privileges; and it would be a mercy to the people and to rising generations, by some revolutions to be restored to their just rights.

The history of the Egyptians, from the time of Joseph to Moses, with their conduct towards the Jews, and the overthrow of the Egyptians, with the consequent deliverance of the Israelites, the former being necessary for the accomplishment of the latter, are examples of this truth. How just and merciful, and yet how wise are the dispensations of divine providence, in the social and political existence of human affairs!

The history of the Jews, from the time of Moses to the present day, is a further continued example of the same. And taking moral good and evil as the rule or criterion by which to judge of expected dispensations, according to Deuteronomy, xxviiith chapter, any considerate man may foretell the probable fate of any nation. The present state of the Jews is a living and standing monument of the dispensations of divine providence. The overthrow of Babylon, as unworthy of a political existence, was just; and yet it was a mercy to the Jews, whose deliverance was connected with it. And the same observation would equally apply to the rise and fall of kingdoms and empires in different countries and ages of the world; provided we had light and information enough to view the hand of the Lord. For these things happen not by accident or chance, neither do they spring up from the dust, but they happen under the wise and superintending hand of the providence of God. And these things will continue until universal rights, obligations, and duties are universally regarded, and his kingdom rules over all.

OF THE SPREAD OF THE GOSPEL.

To judge correctly of things we must view them as they ought to be, as they are now, and then inquire how they became so.

First. The gospel was commanded by Jesus Christ to be preached to all nations, and to every creature, promising to be with his heralds to the end of the world. When the persecution arose about Stephen, the brethren were scattered, and were travelling abroad preaching the word. The blessing of God attended their labors, while the apostles still abode at Jerusalem. Hence the command and promise for the spread of the gospel was not confined and limited to the twelve disciples, but extended to all the ministers of Jesus Christ through all ages to the end of the world. Therefore if all things were right, the gospel would be received in all lands and in all hearts. But it is not so; a small part only of the world hear and enjoy the heavenly tidings, and that in a very dark degree.

In Asia, which contains, as is computed, five hundred millions of people, what darkness and ignorance prevail! But a few, very few, have even the outward preaching of the gospel; not even excepting those countries and parts of Europe and Africa, as well as Asia, which are contiguous to old Jerusalem, where the gospel was first propagated and substantiated. Turkish darkness and Mohammedanism triumph, and the name of Christian is held in contempt. Of 120,000,000 of Christians, nominally so called, in Europe, how few have just and proper notions and ideas of things pertaining to religion! Far the greater part are almost as ignorant, even of the doctrines of Christianity, as the Indians of America, and of experimental religion they are as ignorant as the Hottentots at the Cape of Good Hope! Of seven or eight millions of people in North America, though most of them have the Bible or Testament in their houses, how many are unacquainted with experimental religion, and even ignorant of the very first principles of the doctrines of Christ! though America is favored with the greatest share of common learning among the common people of any nation in the world, probably as three to one. Yet how dark and ignorant still! What selfishness prevails, and how little is natural justice regarded in social life! How little is *moral obligation* considered in the various transactions and concerns of life!

How few are living for eternity, and conducting as they expect to answer at the bar of the Supreme Judge! In short, how few attend to the moral law, "*to love the Lord with all their heart, and their neighbor as themselves;*" and to the law of nature, which coincides with the rule of practice, as "ye would that others should do to you, do ye even so to them!" Yet this is "the law and the prophets," and is sanctioned by Jesus Christ.

Until the gospel is preached to all mankind, there is somebody who *ought* to preach that does not; and there are grand causes, enough to provoke the God of love to anger towards those who hold the people in the darkness of ignorance by cruel and wicked laws!

Query.—How happens it that Mohammedanism rooted Christianity out of the eastern world?

Doubtless Christianity was abused, perverted, and so corrupted that the substance was lost in the shade, and the name of the thing only remained. Hence Mohammedanism, which admits of no idolatry, was preferable; therefore the nominal Christians, who were not worthy of a political or social existence, having forfeited their right and privilege by sin, were justly scourged, deprived of the gospel, and removed out of the way, that a better '*ism* might follow.

These ideas will "justify the ways of God to man." When a social existence is forfeited by abuse, the people constituting it stand in the way of their betters, and of course the Being who "gave, hath a right to take away," and bestow it on such as are more worthy. Justice is then administered to the former and mercy to the latter. And that people who possess the most moral virtue, or will answer the best and most noble purpose, are the most preferable. Therefore, to remove the vicious out of the way, as being hindrances to righteousness, is good. Of two objects, goodness and wisdom will prefer and choose the best, to answer a good and important purpose, and accomplish a noble end. Hence of two '*isms* supported by the arm of human power, one is old in evil and very bad;

the other young and more hopeful; and therefore it is consistent with wisdom, justice, goodness, and mercy to prefer the latter.

Many people talk about the plans of the Almighty! If man was *perfect* in wisdom he would need no plan; and that which argues imperfection in man will not, cannot argue perfection in the Deity. Therefore such expressions are perfect nonsense, if brought for any thing more than a comparison or illustration.

Morally speaking, whosoever is *right* must be *just;* and whosoever is right and just, must be good; and whosoever is right and just and good, must be wise; and whosoever is just and righteous and good and wise, must be most NOBLE, in the superlative degree. Therefore we must unite these ideas of justice, righteousness, goodness, and wisdom in the moral character of the Almighty, in order to have any proper conceptions of his moral government and of his noble dispensations to the social bodies of mankind.

Some people, to exalt his justice, destroy his goodness and mercy, and represent him a mere tyrant; others speaking to exalt the power of God, destroy his justice and mercy; another exalting his mercy, destroys his justice. Thus they split up the Almighty into parts, ascribing to him certain ideas which they call attributes, formed in their own conceptions. And by extolling his power, or his mercy or justice, improperly bear false testimony, and give the Almighty a character which is far from the truth, as manifested either in his dispensations or the written word. For instance, says one, "God is *all* mercy, he is *so* good." If he be all mercy, where is his justice? A governor is so good as to be all mercy, and therefore will pardon every culprit, and will suffer none to be punished, however dangerous to society. Thus the innocent must suffer, and the guilty escape and go free! Now to let the guilty escape and the innocent suffer, without any possible remedy, exhibits the executive power as possessing neither mercy nor justice nor goodness in his procedure; and of course he cannot be right or noble in his nature or dispensations. A being without mercy, who is unjust and not good, but destitute of every right and noble principle, and is not in possession of any true and genuine wisdom, is the picture of the very devil himself.

But the true character of Jehovah, or the manifestation of God in Christ, is uniformly consistent with itself, agreeable to the principles of justice, and righteousness, and goodness, and wisdom, and mercy,—mercy to proper objects of mercy, for to let the innocent suffer and the guilty escape is an unjust tyranny. But mercy is always dispensed consistent with, or agreeable to, the principles of true justice, when administered by the Most High. If a person hath sinned, pardon without repentance could never excite gratitude; therefore it would be a thankless act, or favor, bestowed upon any culprit who remained impenitent. Religious privileges are the graces of God, and, as a wise Governor, he expects and requires a proper use of them. Some people abuse these privileges by stealing a power, without a right, which is assumption; and a power possessed without a right is an unjust tyranny. Now here is an abuse of social rights; and the innocent must suffer, by being oppressed and deprived of their rights, who have not merited such treatment at their hands. Natural justice is infringed upon, and the government of the Almighty is despised. God is said to be "jealous for his glory, and will not give it to another." Therefore, for the honor of his government, and the mercy of the injured, justice demands the removal of such power. And such removal would bring mercy to the injured, justice to the guilty, and honor to his own moral character.

As natural evil is the effect or consequence of moral evil—as nations have flourished in proportion to their virtues, and as judgments have pursued them on account of their wickedness—hence, " angels sinned, and are reserved under chains of darkness to the judgment-day to be punished." Sin drove Adam out of Paradise; sin brought destruction on the antediluvian world; sin was the cause of the overthrow of Sodom and Gomorrah.

Of the Canaanites God said, " The iniquity, &c., is not yet full." He had a right to demand their obedience, and to dispose of their lives in any manner he chose. God waited and bore with them near five hundred years as a political body, and then destruction to the full overtook them as a nation. Sin brought calamities on the Jews as a nation, and they are a standing monument thereof to this day.

Again, as political evils in social bodies, consequent upon moral evil in them, bring national destruction, so a social repentance and political reform are necessary to avert the judgments of God, which threaten impending danger over a guilty land. The case of Nineveh is a striking example of the dealings of God with a sinful and repenting people. The Jews frequently experienced deliverances in their social capacity, when a reform and repentance took place among them. If ten righteous persons had been found in Sodom, the place would have been spared for their sakes. Isaiah said, " Except the Lord had left unto us a small remnant we should have been as Sodom and Gomorrah!" Jesus Christ calls the righteous the " salt of the earth." And if it were not for the righteous that now are, and those that will be in succession, it would be inconsistent with the moral character of the Almighty, and the nature of his moral government, to continue the world in existence.

The Jews were to attend three feasts in a year—Pentecost, Tabernacles, and Passover—by the special command of God. All the males who were twenty years of age and upwards, were to appear thrice annually before the Lord, in one congregation at Jerusalem, which would leave all their borders defenceless, and exposed to an invading foe. Their enemies, in their absence, might have laid their country waste, and captivated their wives and children, unless restrained by the providence of God. Here would be a trial of faith, and a proof of Providence, who, for their encouragement, promised that their enemies should not desire their land at such times, which argues the superintending hand of Providence over nature and over human affairs. The fourteenth chapter of Ezekiel is pertinent to the same point of doctrine. When a nation or people had forfeited their political existence by sin, the sword of the Lord, either beasts, famine, sword, or pestilence, was drawn for their extermination; "though Noah, Daniel, and Job stood before me, saith the Lord, they should deliver neither son nor daughter, but their own souls." The escape of Lot from the overthrow of Sodom, and, by the warning of Christ, the escape of the Christians from the destruction of Jerusalem, are striking examples of salvation, and remarkable proofs of the providence of God.

OF GOD'S REPOSITORY.

There was but one generation between Adam and Noah, inasmuch as Methuselah, the oldest man, connected them both in a line. Again, Shem connected Noah and Abraham, from whence a connect-chain down through his posterity was transmitted, recording the dispensations of divine Providence.

God, as a wise and good being, we may apprehend, has actions and ends worthy of himself—hence, the righteous Disposer of events, and the universal Governor. What he doeth must be right, just, good, and wise. And hence, righteousness, justice, goodness, and wisdom, reigning together, goodness will bestow mercy where it can be done agreeable to justice; and wisdom and righteousness are perfect and will not err, for here is perfect and complete harmony in the attributes of God, in every case whatever. The fewest means are employed to accomplish the most important and noble ends, in the display of his justice against the impenitent, and in his warnings to rebels. Hence privileges revert to the objects who were injured, whilst the greatest possible good and mercy are extended to future and remote generations of mankind.

Moral evil being universal in a social capacity, there was no moral virtue but in individuals, and hence the necessity of virtuous society. Therefore, as every thing must have a beginning, Abraham, the fifth life from Adam, Methuselah, Noah, and Shem, having come in between, to connect the chain of tradition, by having a personal acquaintance with each other, until the invention of letters should furnish a record. Abraham lived in Chaldea, feared the Most High, and was enjoined to quit that part of the country, and come to the land of Canaan. And God made a "covenant with Abraham." Christ was on the side of God. The nature and object of the covenant was holiness, which Abraham was to "receive, practice, teach his family, and transmit to his posterity."

Faith was the condition on which the promised blessings were depending, and circumcision was the seal; and the blood of Christ, to which it looked forward, and which was comprised in the blessings, was to purify the heart, through the faith of Abraham, which was in fact the faith of the gospel.

The eternal covenant between the Father and Son, to divide the world between Christ and Satan, is nowhere to be found in scripture; but the covenant with Abraham was real. The covenant was frequently intimated, but never confirmed, until it was actually done with Abraham.

The apostle calls it a "man's covenant;" yet as Abraham was brought into it by faith and obedience, so must we, for we are to be "justified by faith," and "without faith it is impossible to please God." "He that cometh to God, must believe that he is, and that he is a rewarder of them that diligently seek him." Hence, in this manner of seeking through faith, there is a moral conformity to the whole will of God, from the heart, which necessarily implies resignation and dependence. Of course there is an agreement between the will of the creature and the will of the Creator, at which time and place the blessing of pardon and holiness is given by Christ, and received by the suppliant, which is the new covenant of grace written in the heart, and a confirmation of the covenant made with Abraham.

Thus Christ is the meritorious cause of our redemption. But faith is the instrumental cause of our salvation.

"Abraham believed God, and it was counted (or imputed) to him for righteousness." Thus Abraham was justified by faith, and he was called the friend of God. And Abraham was circumcised, and the males of his household also, which was the beginning of the Church of God, established by faith upon earth, as a spiritual, personal, social compact.

From the family of Abraham originated afterwards what was called the "congregation of the Lord," and the "church in the wilderness," through whom the oracles were transmitted to posterity. As bad and as rebellious as the Jews were, God chose the best people the world furnished at that time, to prove and show his mercy and display his justice, in a visible and providential manner, to bring about universal righteousness, as a precious seed in reserve, and as a repository for himself, to be manifested as a standing and living monument and credible proof through all ages of the world, as a reasonable evidence against infidelity. To this day, in Hindoostan, there are found black and white Jews. One class of them is called *children of Israel*, from the ten tribes; the other is called *Jews*, from the tribe of Judah.

On account of "national sin," the ten tribes were permitted to separate, and become a distinct nation.

The Lord promised them his blessing, and an establishment and a sure house, if they would fear, obey, and love him. But they did not, but were vain idolaters, until they became unworthy of a political existence. So the justice of God removed them into captivity by the Assyrians, who scattered them into all countries; and of course they carried the writings of Moses and the prophets with them.

And it proved to be a mercy to succeeding generations, who thereby had their minds impressed and prepared with expectations of the Messiah to come, as the Saviour of men, which was remarkably exemplified in the language of the woman of Samaria, who said, "when the Messiah cometh, he will tell (or teach) us all things."

The writings of Moses, and the Psalms, and the prophets, which were dispersed and conveyed by means of the ten tribes, who were scattered all over the then known world, prepared the way for the dispensation of the Gospel; and the spread thereof, from the persecution which arose about Stephen, is an incontestable proof of its authenticity. As they were scattered at such an early period, and were a people who were held in detestation among the nations of the earth; which is also the fact at this very day, there was not the same temptation to counterfeit, alter, and impose, as there might otherwise have been. And moreover, if they were disposed to do it, there was not the same opportunity, considering the enmity between those at Jerusalem and those of the Samaritan mountain, and the dispersed. Besides, the great number of copies which they must have had among them, must have enabled any one who chose, to detect an attempt at an imposition.

And although twenty-six false Christs have appeared in different ages of the world, the folly of each quickly became manifest; for error and falsehood can never become truth. But the true Messiah, although ne met with every opposition, and although he appeared not in any worldly pomp or grandeur, and although his gospel was contemned, and every method used that human ingenuity could invent, to abolish and destroy it out of the world, it still stands unshaken. And why, unless it had its foundation in Divinity? Truth will bear investigation, and carry its own conviction with it, when properly understood. And hence we have sufficient cause to be thankful for the repository which Divine Providence hath favored us with, by transmitting the account of his former dispensations for our perusal, reflection, and benefit, inasmuch as we may become the heirs of the inheritance, through the covenant of grace, which by faith are partakers of the happy realms in the paradise of God.

God is declared to be a Spirit. His worship is required to be of that nature, viz. in spirit and in truth, i. e. in the heart and really! For he is said to be "the God of Abraham, the God of Isaac, and the God of Jacob!" Thus making a discrimination among men, and confining his spiritual favors to his faithful worshippers. Thus also Paul declares that all are not Israel that are of Israel; neither because they are the seed of Abraham, are they all children. They must become spiritual children by an action of faith, under the influence of love divine, inspiring the heart with peace and joy, running through all their conduct. Or as the scriptures declare, "If ye are Christ's, then are ye Abraham's seed, and heirs according to the promise." Or, as said Christ, "If ye were the children of Abraham, ye would do the works of Abraham." "Abraham rejoiced to see my day, and he saw it and was glad:" for "before Abraham was, I am." John viii. 56, 58. Compare Genesis xvii. 1, 8, 14. Rom. iv. 9 to 13, &c. Galatians iii. 6. to 15. shows 1st, Abraham is called "the father of the faithful," and the "heir of the world."

Secondly. Abraham was justified by faith, while in uncircumcision; and to him was made the first* promise of the Messiah to come, "In thy seed, (Christ) shall all the families of the earth be blessed." "Abraham believed God, and it was imputed to him for righteousness." "Now it was not written for his sake alone, that it was imputed to him, but for us also, to whom it shall be imputed if we believe on him that raised up Jesus our Lord from the dead, who was delivered for our offences, and was raised again for our justification," Rom. iv. 23 to 25.

Thirdly. The promises of the blessings in Christ the seed, are by faith, through which the blessings of the seed are to be received and enjoyed; and hence,

Fourthly. "If ye be Christ's, then are ye Abraham's seed, and heirs according to the promise." Galatians iii. 29.

Thus the true light of moral virtue came by revelation, and is enjoyed by divine inspiration operating on the heart, which all men are under the restraining influence of, in a greater or less degree, until the day of their visitation be past. But when they become incorrigible, they are unworthy of a social or political existence. Hence, said Jesus, "O Jerusalem! Jerusalem! how often would I have gathered thy children together, as a hen doth gather her brood under her wings, but ye would not. Behold, your house is left

---

* The thing was intimated and hinted, but never confirmed till the time of Abraham. Gen. iii. 14, 15, was not a promise, but a threatening against the serpent. "I will put enmity between thee and the woman, and thy seed and her seed; it shall bruise thy head, and thou shalt bruise his heel."

unto you desolate, and ye shall not see me henceforth, until ye shall say, Blessed is he that cometh in the name of the Lord." And they were destroyed and dispersed, like the ten tribes, abroad among the nations of the earth, by the Roman army; like as a curse for disobedience, entailed on them to this day.

The abuse of moral privileges, by luxury and dissipation, tends to sink the human mind into brutality, and destroy every principle that is kind, noble, generous, and humane. The present state of the natives of Africa and America, are striking examples, and show to what a low ebb the moral faculty can be reduced. We see them prefer a toy or trifling trinket to useful arts. In them we see every unkind disposition indulged towards their fellow-creatures, and strangers considered as enemies; so that almost every family becomes a village, and every village becomes a nation. And these are almost continually at war, destroying each other, so as to prevent their population from extending.

"The love of money" is said to be "the root of all evil." The spirit of it is "moral evil," and the effect is "natural evil," as the necessary consequence entailed. The "love of money" led the nations of Europe to enslave and destroy the poor blacks of Africa, and the miserable Indians of America. And within the space of three centuries, they have destroyed and enslaved together, as many of those unfortunate creatures as now exist in those two quarters of the world. Nine millions have been enslaved from Africa, which is computed to contain twelve millions of inhabitants. And an incredible number also must have been slain. The Spaniards in South America, enslaved and destroyed alone, twelve millions—besides the millions which fell in the isles, of which Hayti itself contained 3,000,000. But the superintending hand of Providence, which overrules the actions of men and devils, will no doubt bring good out of evil. Most of those unhappy wretches, after being in slavery a term of time, will be affronted at the idea of being sent back to their native shores; and many are rejoiced at their situation, miserable as it is, and express gratitude that by this means they have found the faith of Abraham, in the gospel of God's dear Son, to bring them the peace and joy of the kingdom. And why should it be incredible to believe, that one day the gospel shall return to their native shores, and spread through Afric regions, and that wilderness blossom like the rose?

The natural abilities of the European and the African, perhaps admit of improvement equally alike. Yet while one is now rising to its highest excellence, the other is but a little superior to the brute beasts. Doubtless it is the providence of God, attending the improvement of one, while the other is justly visited with the entailment of ignorance, stupidity, and sloth; whilst moral evil fills their hearts, and governs all their actions.

America, adorned and enriched with some of the most lofty mountains, extensive rivers, natural canals, and numerous fresh inland seas; situated between two oceans, nearly divided in the centre, and yet connected by a narrow isthmus; enriched with almost every species of valuable treasure in the bowels of the earth, as if to invite the foreign emigrant to pay a friendly visit; nevertheless, lay undiscovered for several thousand years, as if reserved for the era when "common sense" began to awake up from her long slumber. As if the Creator's wisdom and goodness had a "new world," in reversion for a new theatre for the exhibition of new things.

Here a new philosophy, both in nature and in divinity, was to be taught and embraced. False notions respecting the figure of the earth, and the spurious vicegerency, were both to be rejected together. The doctrine of "passive obedience and non-resistance" was then to be suspected, and to go down the hill. There seemed to be no place in the political world, nor any part of the natural world, that admitted of the change to begin so thoroughly as in America. The state of the country, and the prejudices of the people, were both favorable for it.

And these things are the result, which are worthy of reflection:

First. All religious opinions are protected, and universal rights of conscience established; and also a government of representation, which is elective only.

Secondly. The dirty slave-trade, in which almost all Eurpoe, as well as America, was engaged, is now forever at an end—no nation protecting it. And in those countries where slavery exists, they are used more humanely than formerly; and instead of death for mere trifles, the penitentiary system is adopted.

Thirdly. The spirit of inquiry, and the spirit of missionary, is prevailing, together with the translation of the scriptures into so many new languages. Bible societies are forming, to disperse the holy scriptures. Priestcraft is falling, and the power and influence of the established, corrupt, and wicked clergy, is broken, and tumbling down. Crowned heads are going out of date. The whole world is in commotion, and peace is taken from the earth. The animal creation is proving a scourge, in many parts, to the human family. The wars may be considered as the sword of the Lord; as if "the devil had come down in great wrath, knowing that he hath but a little time." This brings scarcity, which produces famine; and famine will bring plague, which already prevails in many parts of the world. Besides, such general and repeated shocks of earthquakes, so that sixteen cities were destroyed, in a very short space of time, in South America. Thus, so many extraordinary things as have transpired of late, and are transpiring, have not been known in the annals of history. And there never was a time, except the era which gave our Saviour birth, that was so pregnant with important things as the day in which we live.

May not the *seventh trumpet* now be sounding, and the *seven last plagues* be pouring out? Is not the harvest of the earth ripe for the reaper with the sharp sickle? Then we should swell the cry, "Thy kingdom come—send forth more laborers into the harvest." Is not the "vintage of the earth ripe also to be gathered, and cast into the wine-press of the wrath of Almighty God?"

Are not all the governments of the old world tyrannical, and repugnant to the law of nature? Is there any government in the world, except America, that is framed so as to admit of *amendment?* Being contrary to the law of nature, and not admitting of amendments, are not those governments, in their very first principles, of a pernicious kind, and of an incorrigible nature, founded in moral evil, so as to perpetuate the same, without any possibility of redress? Why ought they to exist? By what right can they exist? Are they worthy of an existence? Does not injured innocence cry against them for redress to the Governor of the world, whose tender care is over all his works? Does not justice, in the law of nature, demand a satisfaction against them? Would not mercy be extended from the divine Governor to the injured, by undertaking their cause, and restoring to them their rights, which are unjustly withheld by those civil governments? Do not these reflections lead the mind necessarily to conclude, that a powerful and just Judge will undertake the cause of the oppressed, and overwhelm the oppressors with an everlasting destruction?

SUMMARY REVIEW.

The *law of nature* is that relation which man originally stands in to his Creator, and to his fellow-creature.

In this state all men are equal, and naturally free and independent, in their individual capacity, and endowed by their Creator with certain inalienable rights, as life, liberty, enjoyment of property, pursuit of happiness, and the privilege of private judgment. In these they are equal and independent, as much as if there was no other person upon the earth but the individual himself alone. But when taken in a social capacity, they are dependent upon each other. The king is dependent on his subjects, and the governor on the governed; the master on the servant, and the servant on the master; the blacksmith upon the carpenter, and the carpenter upon the blacksmith, and both of them upon the farmer for their bread; and the farmer, in his turn, is dependent on them for his mechanism. Thus social privileges are reciprocal; being connected mutually, they are necessarily dependent upon each other.

A hermit's life, in solitude, is the most independent of any; and yet what could he do in sickness? He would then be dependent upon others for their assistance, to do that for him which he could not do for himself. Therefore, the idea of social independence is a solecism, which has no place in common sense.

As a whole is composed of parts, and the parts collectively form one whole; so the human family are, and must be considered, socially related, and collectively dependent upon each other.

Hence, our rights and necessities being equal, so are our obligations and duties likewise; and, therefore, considering the rights of man as an individual, they are called *personal rights;* considering them in his relation to his fellow-creature, they are called *social rights;* and considering them in his relation to his Creator, they are called *moral rights.*

Personal rights are by virtue of existence, as life, liberty, and all the intellectual rights of the mind; of course, religion is one of those rights, as also the pursuit of happiness, &c.

Social rights are by virtue of being a member of society; and as one of the whole, who is interested in the security of those personal rights against usurpation, he hath a claim, in conjunction with others, for protection of his person, property, and character. The right itself is good and perfect, by virtue of existence; but is imperfect in point of power, both in each and all, in their individual capacity. And hence the power, which is called *government*, is made up, or composed of, all those rights which are surrendered by the individuals themselves, and cast into the common stock, for the better regulation of the whole; which is made up, or consists of, the aggregate of those rights, which, though perfect in the individual personally, yet, socially, answer not his purpose, for the want of power. And, therefore, for the want of personal power for the security of personal rights, the right, imperfect in power, is surrendered, and cast into the common stock; and so the arm of society, of which he is a part, is taken in preference, and in addition to his own. The aggregate of those rights, imperfect in power in the individual, is surrendered to trustees in trust, as the delegates of the people, to act as their representatives, for the benefit of the whole. This delegated power is called *government*, and can never be applied to invade those rights retained, which are sufficiently perfect in the individual, and, for their proper exercise, need no political strength. Of this kind are the rights of life, limb, liberty, and all the intellectual powers, or rights of the mind, as study, pursuit of happiness, private judgment, &c. These things can never be invaded by the power of the government, without infringing upon natural justice, because the power delegated is to be applied for the benefit and welfare of the people, and not to oppress, domineer, and tyrannize over the people, and make them miserable.

These observations show the origin of government, and the necessity of a constitution, to point out what may and what may not be done; to make the rulers responsible for their trust and conduct, and to secure the admission of improvement, as experience may point out wherein the constitution is defective; and all the laws which are founded upon this, as a charter given to the delegates, or trustees, in trust, should be an expression of the will of the people. And those laws should be as few as is possible, consistently with the nature and state of things; and should be founded on such principles of justice as will admit of the greatest humanity in the suppression of vice, in the maintenance of equity, and in the promotion of virtue in the land. Therefore, a proper distinction between vice and virtue should be made, and punishment fitted and apportioned to the nature of crimes. Torture, barbarity, and every thing which has a tendency to harden mankind, should be cautiously avoided. Private revenge should be discountenanced by civil law; and the abuse of servants ought not to be passed over with such impunity as it is in many parts of the world; but there ought to be some restriction upon masters, so that justice may take place in the administration of corporal chastisement. Ought not a responsibility be secured in this as well as in any other exercise of authority? There is something here which deserves to be seriously weighed, when we reflect on the universal rights of man.

Moral rights are the result of *moral law*: and, as a creature dependent upon the Supreme Governor of the world, who enjoins the obligation and prescribes the law, and rule of practice, man has a *right* to obey, by attending to the law, and by keeping the rule. Human governments have no right to interfere by assuming a power to tolerate man to pay his devotion to his God. For before any human government existed in the world, there was a compact between man and his Maker, which cannot be altered by any human laws. Therefore, all laws ought to be made in conformity to this pre-existing compact; otherwise they do mischief by making encroachments upon the rights of conscience, and cause confusion in society by creating broils and animosities; consequently, all denominations of religion should be protected in the peaceable enjoyment of their rights. And universal rights of conscience ought to be established in every land, agreeable to the Creator's law, primarily established by him.

Rights imply privileges; and a privilege implies duty, when taken on the ground of the law of nature, or the moral law, or the rule of practice. Duties imply obligation ; therefore, if by the law of nature, one is favored with the rights of equality and independence, it is his duty to enjoy, maintain, and improve them. If it be my right to enjoy life and liberty, it becomes my duty to preserve and improve them. If I have a right to enjoy property and pursue happiness, it is my duty to do it properly. And also in matters of private judgment, in matters which concern me, it is my duty to investigate and judge rightly. Why is it my duty to maintain my equality and independence, to preserve my life and liberty, and to enjoy property and pursue happiness, and also to judge in matters of moral duty? Equality, independence, life, liberty, property, happiness, and the things of private judgment in moral duty, are the gifts of the God of nature, and designed by him to answer a purpose worthy of himself. Therefore, to neglect them, is to treat them with indifference ; and to be indifferent is to undervalue them ; and to undervalue such important gifts, is to undervalue the Giver ; and of course to treat him, not with neglect only, but with a degree of contempt also : because our all is connected with it. Not only our eternity hangs upon it, but also, all the things of time ! And hence the omission or neglect prevents our accomplishing that noble purpose for which we were designed by the Creator. Therefore we infringe upon the law of nature, by departing from her rule, which is the law of God ; and violate our moral obligation to the Most High, who, as a righteous judge, will call all people to an account, and reward them, each individual, according to the deeds done in the body.

Consequently, our equality and independence is given us, as individuals, that we may be capable of thinking, judging, and acting in an individual capacity, and not to be accountable for the misconduct of others, but live in conformity to the moral law of love. Hence, life is the gift of God, which is our right to enjoy ; but man has no right to destroy it. To destroy our life, is to infringe on nature's law, and violate the obligation we are under to nature's God. Of course also, as means are necessary to be used for the preservation of life, they must be attended to accordingly. Liberty, also, is one of our rights, but it must not be abused, but used agreeably to natural justice and moral obligation. The pursuit of property is a right, and becomes a duty, that we may not be dependent on others, but have wherewith to help ourselves, and to afford assistance to a fellow-mortal in distress. Man was designed by his Maker to be happy, and the pursuit of happiness is enjoined upon him, and it is his duty to promote the same in others. Hence the object and the right, and the means and the duty, are all connected and stand in relation to each other. The duty demands the use of the means to improve the right to obtain the object—happiness ! This duty is a moral obligation, because enjoined by the moral Governor of the world.

Consequently, all the intellectual powers of the man, are called upon, and employed to act as a rational creature, who must give an account: the understanding to collect evidence, that it may judge correctly ; the memory to reflect and recollect, for the benefit of the judgment ; the will to consent only to what is right, agreeable to his best judgment: for man is led by inclination sometimes contrary to his judgment, and then he comes under condemnation, of which he is always conscious in a degree, conformable to his judgment.

Man is required to act as a rational creature, and to act from proper motives, and of course to act from a well-regulated judgment. And that the judgment may be correct, the understanding must be well and properly informed. This implies a duty to search for truth, and weigh every evidence, and give it just and proper weight, in order to proceed righteously, as for eternity.

Moral evil is an improper motive or bad principle at heart. So says Christ—"He that *looketh* on a woman to lust after her, hath committed adultery with her already in his heart;" the *desire* being indulged, and the consent of the mind being given to a thing contrary to a better judgment, against the law of nature. Sin is a transgression of the law; and the will of God is the moral law. By going contrary to it, a person must forfeit what I choose to call his *infantile justification*, mentioned Romans v. 18—20; and thus goes out of the divine favor by his own personal sin, into personal condemnation and the kingdom of Satan, and is led captive by him, at his will.

Hence, there must be a personal repentance for personal sins; and a moral conformity to the will of God, to be reinstated in the divine favor, as one of the divine family. This conformity is through "the door—the way" to God, which is Christ. Here is pardon and peace to be found in such conformity, and faith, or what may be termed an assent or conformity to the proper moral evidence—evidence given to the mind (but not to the bodily sense) is the power by which it may be done. This act of conformity is the *act of faith*, which is *imputed* for righteousness. Thus, a man is *justified* by *faith*, and hath peace with God, through our Lord Jesus Christ. Being *justified* by *faith* from the guilt of his own sins, and having peace with God through Christ, he has a sensible love to God from obligation, and a sense of the love of God towards him, in the gift of Jesus Christ, by whom he hath acceptance, and for the Holy Spirit through the same divine channel, from whom all blessings flow.

After justification by faith from the guilt of his own sins, he is required to prove his love to Christ, by *walking in the light, and keeping his commandments*. Hence the commandment is to "Love one another"—"Love your enemies"—"Do good to them that hate you"—"Pray for them that despitefully use you and persecute you."

Again: "Thou shalt love the Lord thy God with all thy heart, soul mind and strength, and thy neighbor as thyself;" which implies that from the heart we should devote our whole soul, body, and substance, with all our time and talents, to the glory of the Most High, which is a resignation to the will, disposal, and service of God only: and hence thou shalt "Love thy neighbor as thyself." Who is thy neighbor? Thy friend, enemy, acquaintance, and stranger, and whosoever is in distress, no matter who. He is God's creature, and thy brother by the law of nature; and the moral law commands to "love thy neighbor as thyself;" and also enjoins the rule of practice, "As ye would that others should do to you, do ye even so to them." Thus Moses, the prophets, and Jesus Christ, teach the same doctrine. Hence, the moral law and the law of nature, and the rule of practice, on the principles of *equity* and *obligation*, are a *unit!*

Therefore, said Christ, "If ye love me, keep my commandments." And one command is, "to do good to those who are our enemies," and "Love thy neighbor as thyself." The conduct of the Samaritan towards the man who fell among the thieves, is enough to prove who our neighbor is. The Samaritans were taught to consider the Jews as enemies, and hence the woman questioned Christ why he asked her for water.

The Samaritan proved a nurse, a servant, and a benefactor, by providing an asylum, and taking him to the inn, paying the expenses, without expecting any reward from man. And the command was, "Go and do thou likewise." But "if a man doth not love his brother whom he hath seen, how can he love God whom he hath not seen?" Again, "If a man seeth his brother stand in need, and give not wherewithal to supply his wants, how dwelleth the love of God in him?" Therefore, we are commanded to "love in *deed* and in *truth*, and not in *word* and in tongue only." Consequently, to say "be ye warmed and be ye clothed," and like the priest and Levite, pass by on the other side, with perfect neglect or composure, is a departure from the law of nature, and the moral law, and the rule of practice, seeing our rights and wants, duties and obligations, are equal in both laws and in the rule!

We are to prove our faith and love to Christ, by walking in the light and keeping his commandments: and hence the injunction, "As ye have received Christ Jesus the Lord, so walk ye in him." And thence our actions flowing from faith and love, are the evidences or fruits of faith. Hence said James, "show me your faith without works, and I will show you my faith by my works." Then he makes mention of two, who were justified by *works* flowing from *faith*, and adds, "as the body without the spirit is dead, so faith without works is dead also." Therefore, we conclude that a man is justified by *works*, and not by *faith only.*

Let it ever be remembered, that faith will never be called in question in the day of judgment; there will not be any need for faith then, because Christ, who then will be our judge, will have given up the mediatorial kingdom to the Father, and faith will be brought to sight. But the virtue of all our deeds will then be put to the trial, what spirit they were of; and mankind will be "rewarded according to their works," or "the deeds done in the body, whether they be good or bad!"

Those who "put away the evil of their doings, and wash in the fountain for sin, and have made their robes white in the blood of the Lamb," having continued to take up their cross daily, and follow after him by denying themselves, will stand acquitted; but "those who will not have Christ to reign over them," but lead a life of rebellion—the non-conformity disqualifies them for a divine inheritance, hence there must be two classes of different states and dispositions of heart. And, of course, on the principles of moral justice, they must have different sentences and rewards from a righteous judge. How then can it be said to them agreeable to truth, in that day of final retribution, "Come, ye blessed of my Father, inherit the kingdom prepared for you—For I was an hungered, and ye gave me meat; I was thirsty and ye gave me drink; I was a stranger, and ye took me in; naked, and ye clothed me; sick and in prison, and ye came unto me and visited me; inasmuch as ye did it unto one of the least of these, ye did it untome"—provided they have never been in the spirit of doing such things to the people of Christ, for his sake?

The rights and obligations of all men are equal; and so their exposures, and dangers, and necessities, and reverses of fortune; and hence the golden rule of practice, "As ye would that others should do to you, de ye even so to them,"—for the objects of distress are the representatives of that Lord Jesus—therefore as they are sent to prove our love to Christ, a cup of cold water, in the name of a disciple, given to one of his little ones, shall not lose its reward;" and when done from duty and love to Christ, will be so acknowledged by him in the day of judgment, and is as acceptable to the Lord as if it had been done to the person of Christ. For "God looketh at the heart, and judgeth according to intentions;"—therefore "he that confesseth me before men, him will I confess," said Jesus, "before my Father and his holy angels!"—"And for every idle word that man shall speak, he shall give an account thereof in the day of judgment,"—and "by thy words thou shalt be justified—and by thy words thou shalt be condemned." Matt. xii. 36, 37.

Therefore man is called to devote all his time, soul, body, and substance, to the love and service of the Lord Jesus Christ in this world, if he would stand acquitted in the day of account! Of course, objects of distress are to be attended to, and not barely those of our own household, though they ought not to be neglected; but objects of charity should be sought out. I do not say, that such as are able to work, and will not, should receive, nor the man that will take your charity to buy spirits and get drunk—because to give to such, instead of its being a charity, is paying for their idleness and wicked conduct, and encouraging them to persevere in evil. But it would be better to give to ten *impostors*, than to deny one real object of *distress*. Therefore remember the good Samaritan, "Go and do thou likewise," if you profess to be a follower of Christ, lest you hear the sentence, "depart;" with these piercing words—"I was sick, hungry, thirsty, a stranger, naked and in prison, and ye neither visited, nor fed, nor gave me drink, nor clothed me, nor took me in; inasmuch as ye did it not unto one of the least of these, ye did it not unto me —depart ye cursed, into everlasting fire, prepared (not for man, but) for the devil and his angels." Matt. xxv. 41, 42, 43, and 45. For those only "who have washed their (not Christ's) robes, and made them white in the blood of the Lamb, will stand before the throne of God." Rev. vii. 14, 15, Isaiah i. 17, Zech. xiii. 1. Therefore attend to the two laws and the rule!

CONCLUSION.

Personal rights are by virtue of existence. Social rights, by virtue of being a member of society. Moral rights, by virtue of moral obligation to the moral Governor. Equality and independence being the law of nature, from them government should spring by delegation and representation. But from assumption sprang tyrannical governments. And "religious establishments by law," founded on ignorance and false moral obligation, were imposed on the world, to answer the purposes of ambitious usurpers. Hence arose the papal power, as man was not suffered to think, and judge, and practise for himself: but the *nonsense* of others must be believed before his own *senses*; which produced the seas of blood, which flowed by the intolerant hand of persecution! At length light broke in! Common sense waked up, and embraced a new theory of philosophy, both in nature and divinity! The old world being chained, did not admit of a general and thorough reform: hence America was the only place, both in the political and natural world, that opened a fair prospect for a beginning. And such as began to think, and to judge, and to act for themselves, and felt the spirit of independence and equality of man, which is the law of nature, arose from their depressed state, and felt the spirit of enterprise. They fled to the wilderness of America, pregnant with the spirit of freedom in embryo, in their emigration, which then laid the foundation, and still marks the outlines of our national character. Moral virtue came by revelation, and is enjoyed by inspiration in the heart, called " restraining grace." Hence the necessity of a moral social compact. Abraham and his successors formed the beginning of the true Church of God; through whose succession the promised Messiah came. The Jews are a standing monument of the just dispensations of divine providence. Justice, when administered in the removal of societies corrupted through moral evil, who are incorrigible, and unworthy of a political existence, proves a mercy to rising generations. And such revolutions will continue, until it appears whose right it is to reign, and His kingdom come, and reign over all! The sword of the Lord is drawn out; and the five scourges of the Almighty are abroad in the earth; and O! that the people would learn righteousness!

A cause of a cause, is the cause of the effect also which that cause produces. And hence, those who injure others by slander or misrepresentation, are responsible for all the consequences attending it; and must answer it before the Supreme Judge of the world!

By what right or authority may one person, or a body of men, raise a persecution against another? It is not authorized in the records of Christ, either by his commands or his example. And of course, such a right or power was never delegated or sanctioned by him. Man could not bestow the right, because he does not possess the authority to do it; unless it be *assumed*, which is an *unjust* tyranny.

Persecution, for differences of opinion and modes, &c., in religion, is an antichristian spirit; and is contrary to every rule of right, and repugnant to every moral obligation; and of course it is a violation of the law of nature, as well as of the moral law, and of the rule of practice. Of course, natural and moral justice must condemn it.

Those people who usurp the liberty to attack the absent character of others, in an unjust manner, to weaken their influence by destroying their good reputation, and sinking them into contempt in public estimation, rejoicing at their misfortune and calamity, as if a very great victory was gained, do not know what spirit they are of! It would be well for such persons to study the law of nature, with the moral law, and reconsider them by comparing them with the rule of practice, examining their own spirit and conduct, and then see how they agree and comport together, according to love and union, which are enjoined by the gospel of Jesus Christ. For if the practice flows from an unjust and an unhallowed spirit of jealousy, from ambition, pride, and self-will, the soul is surely destitute of that heavenly principle, that noble mind, which was in Christ; and which was designed to reign in the heart and practice of his followers, to be made manifest in their spirit and tempers; and shine forth in their example continually. And hence they are to be called " The light of the world," and as a city set on a hill, which cannot be hid. And it would be proper for such persons as those to attend to Luke xi. 35th, with the context, and Matt. vii. 2, &c., as a looking-glass.

Therefore, " let all those who name the name of Christ, be careful to depart from iniquity," and never take the devil's tools, with which to do the Almighty's work.

But said one, "Master, we saw one casting out devils in thy name, and we forbade him, because he followed not us." Why do you forbid him?—"He followed not with us." Wherein does he differ? "In name, mode, and opinion." But do you believe he is a good man, and that the essence of the matter is in him? "O yes, but he followeth not with us." Take care! forbid him not!

The lowest sense in which one can be supposed to "cast out devils in the name of Christ," is to be instrumental in the hands of Christ by preaching the gospel, to the awakening and conversion of sinners from the errors of their ways, to serve the living God. Now, if such fruit evidently appears, and it be manifest that the pleasure of the Lord prospers in his hand, who durst set himself up as inquisitor-general? and as the accuser, witness, judge, and jury, to condemn such as being nothing but *shameless intruders and most daring impostors?* But "he followeth not us!" Hark! hear what the Master saith: "Forbid him not; for there is no one who *shall* do a miracle in my name, that *can* readily speak *evil* of me; for he that is not against you, is for you."

It is not enough barely to say, I will let him alone; for there is no *neuter* in this war! Therefore, if you are a follower of Christ, you must prove your love to him, according to your ability: "For he that knoweth to do good, and doeth it not, to him it is sin." And in the day of final decision, you will hear the sentence, "Inasmuch as ye did it *not* unto one of the *least* of these, ye did it not unto *me*. Depart," &c.

Consequently, that the cause of Christ be not hindered, but that his gospel take a universal spread, instead of being actuated by a shortsighted, mean, sinister, low, contentious party spirit, we should have a heart full of love to God and man, to expand the mind with that "charity which never faileth, and thinketh no evil, but suffereth long and is kind, is gentle, and easy to be entreated." And look at the universal or most extensive good; and encourage such means and institutions, as are most likely to accomplish the most noble ends and purposes to mankind. And hence, not like the Jews, who long looked with expectation for the Messiah, and when he came, rejected him; or, as some others, who pray to God to revive his work, and send forth more laborers into the harvest, then oppose both the work and the means which the wisdom of God is pleased to make use of to accomplish it. God doth work and accomplish great and important ends, by simple means, which are noble and worthy of himself, to exhibit his finger, hand, or arm of power and wisdom to mankind; whilst his mercy and goodness is magnified, and his justice displayed to the most ordinary understanding. And thus, "out of the mouths of babes and sucklings. God will perfect praise!"

The apostle rejoiced that the gospel was preached; and even if Christ was preached by those who were of a different ******** he did rejoice. Therefore, forbid not those whom God hath sent to preach the gospel of his dear Son, lest you be found fighting against God, and it cause you tears of sorrow and repentance when it is too late. For the *cause* is the Lord's, and the eternity of mankind is connected therewith, and hangs upon it; and "he that sees the sword coming, and blows not the trumpet —the man is taken away in his iniquity, but his blood or soul is required at the watchman's hand!" Therefore, "the gospel is to be spread into all nations, and preached to every creature;" and the ministers, i. e. servants, should " be instant in season, and out of season, to reprove, rebuke, exhort, with all long-suffering,"—and swell the cry, " Thy kingdom come," that " more laborers may be sent into the harvest," "and many run to and fro, and knowledge be increased;" that people may be informed, and turn from their idols ; " Satan be bound, that the nations be deceived no more ; but the house of the Lord be established in the top of the mountain, and exalted above the hills, and all nations flow unto it ; when the wolf and the lamb shall dwell together, and the leopard shall lie down with the kid. The watchmen shall see eye to eye ; and the knowledge of the Lord shall cover the earth as the waters do the sea. When they shall not hurt nor destroy in all the holy mount ; the nations learn war no more: when the light of the moon shall become as the light of the sun ; and the light of the sun shall become seven-fold, as the light of seven days." And then the vice of superstition, and the barbarity of ignorance and tyranny will hide their deformed faces, being swept with the besom of destruction from the human family.

Natural evil is the effect or consequence of moral evil. And ignorance, superstition, and tyranny, with impositions and wicked laws, have been, and still are the chains by which social privileges are curtailed. They are the means, also, which have brought what is called natural, as the necessary consequence of moral evil, upon society, in the different ages and nations of the world, which hath been and still is such a *curse* to the world of mankind !

General information and the spread of moral virtue, are a necessary antidote to such obnoxious principles ; that the moral faculty may be repaired, and peace and righteousness reign in every clime.*

While inventions are increasing, and the arts and sciences are improving, it may not be amiss for all the well-wishers of Zion to watch the openings of Providence, for the furtherance of truth, and the spread of knowledge valuable to society among mankind. And, provided some suitable point should some day be taken on the *Isthmus* which connects the north and south of the *new world*, now probably held in reversion, as a mercy to rising generations, to be a theatre for great things to be displayed, worthy of its Author, and there should be the proper arrangements made for the spread of the true knowledge through the whole world ; how long a space could be required to circumnavigate, and circumfuse such knowledge of the *Causeless Causator*, as would inspire all nations with sensations of gratitude to the Redeemer of mankind ; whose commandment we have for our encouragement, " Go ye into all the world, and preach the gospel, and lo I am with you !"

Buckingham County, Virginia,
August 21, 1812.

---

* The constitution of the United States was framed by a delegated confederation, who were chosen by the people for that purpose. The constitution, when framed, was recommended by the confederation to the different states ; each of which voluntarily received it by their own proper legislative and sovereign authority, whose officers were chosen by the people for that purpose—all of which procedure is agreeable to natural justice, arising from the Creator's law of nature ! Which shows the federal union deduced from democratic principles, which exhibits the difference between six and half a dozen, each state reserving to itself the power to govern its own policy ; which shows that Congress cannot legislate a slavery in the south, or upon the Yankee law religion in the north ; of course they are state instead of national crimes, existing before we became a nation, when under the k**7 !

A JOURNEY

FROM

BABYLON TO JERUSALEM:

OR, THE ROAD TO PEACE.

The *Journey of Life* is an important theme. All mankind are equally interested in it, and the happiness or misery of every individual necessarily depends upon it.

Time may be considered as the *road*, and every *day* may be compared to a *mile*, cutting off some part of the distance!

Eternity is the country to which all are travelling, and sleeping or waking they progress with unremitting speed.

Childhood and youth is the *morning of life;* the perfection of manhood is the *meridian;* and the declension of age, may be called the *evening shades*, when the sun is lowering in the western sky, and sable glooms prevail!

The experience of grace should be connected with the journey of life, as in eternity there are *two* places of destination, the *states* of which are very different both in their nature and enjoyment—one being attended with ineffable pleasure, the other with weeping, wailing, and gnashing of teeth!

As one of the human family upon the great journey of life, travelling the road of time to eternity, I am now upon the way. More than twelve thousand miles are already gone over. The morning of life is passed away—the clock strikes twelve—and the evening shades will soon come on apace.

Are all these things a fancy and but a dream? Can imagination only suggest all this as credible? Impossible! *Life* and *existence* are more than *fable*.

Hearing, seeing, smelling, tasting, feeling, with talking and walking, are things which cannot admit of proof: being *self-evidence* they do not admit of doubt.

Sensible existence excites reflection, whence *inquiries* come. Cast a look in different directions, and behold, Nature, with all her parts, and their relative concomitants, presents to view, in an impressive and august mode! The *mind*, which constitutes the *man*, is ever an *inquirer*, in search after truth, when properly employed upon a noble theme. Sensations of different kinds excite their peculiar inquiries; and the mind, on reflection seeks for names, fitted to the nature of things, intending to employ them in its investigation of *causes* and *effects.*

An *inquirer,* observing *day* and *night, seed-time* and *harvest, summer* and *winter, months* and *years,* to succeed each other in their turn, finds himself asking this important question, Where am I, and whence the origin of all these things?

Truth, sometimes, is *self-evident,* and can admit of no doubt, being an object of *sense ;* but at other times, truth is more *latent,* and can only be inferred from circumstantial things. In the first case, the evidence received is positive *knowledge ;* but the latter is only *faith,* in the solution of queries. Hence the difference between the terms, *knowledge* and *faith.* The first refers to things *present,* which are grasped by sense ; the latter alludes to *absent* things, which always admit of dispute.

The *sun,* in the centre, and all the *host* around, both of a first and second order, and their eclipses and conjunctions, are calculable to a mathematical demonstration. Hence, a few degrees east and north of the metropolis of Columbia, in the third planet from the sun in rotation, on the terraqueous theatre of human existence, Inquirer found himself, and commenced his career: first, in *sensible existence ;* and then in *reflections,* in search after *truth !*

The sensation felt on beholding a compound of various and different reflections of those rays of light, sometimes visible in the clouds opposite the sun, is termed *color ;* and, under certain shades and figures, is called *beauty :* the power to behold them is called *sight.*

The sensibility by which we discern the qualities of nutriment, arising from the different shapes of particles, exciting the sensations of bitter, sweet, sour, &c., is called *taste.*

The power by which we discern odors, whether good or bad, is called *smell.*

The vibration of the atmosphere, when striking upon the ear, is called *sound,* and the power to discern the sound is called *hearing.*

And the power to discern objects by the touch, is called *feeling.*

These things, being objects of sense, give immediate knowledge, which, of course, is *self-evidence,* and cannot possibly admit of doubt. But the *origin* and *cause* of all those things remained a *secret ;* which gave Inquirer great uneasiness, in painful suspense, from conviction of interest in the important relation of things ; and nothing short of a solution of the query could give him proper satisfaction on the subject.

"Is it possible," says Inquirer to himself, "that these things are so ? Have I an existence which shall continue here but for a limited period ; and then must I moulder to dust, and become food for worms, and have only a name remaining above-ground ?" Solemn reflection ! Awful thought !

But to soothe those sensations, which give uneasiness, the study of nature presents itself, to call off the mind from moral contemplation to natural investigation.

REFLECTIONS ON NATURE.

The *canopy* of nature appears to shut down in a concave form, through the limitation of sight ; while the water exhibits a convex shape, through the globular form of the earth. Thus the large and lowermost parts of a ship first disappear, as she sails from the coast; but the uppermost parts, which are smallest, first appear as she returns to the shore.

The *mind* makes the man, and is connected with its *casket;* which, being corporeal, confines him to the earth, as a prison, through the power of *gravitation;* which principle prevails in all material things, and is called *attraction of gravitation.*

This prison, to which man is confined, revolves, with almost incredible swiftness, in an *annual* revolution, at the rate of more than sixty thousand miles an hour, whirling its inhabitants, imperceptible of motion, more than a thousand miles in the *diurnal* revolution on its own axis at the same time.

The different kinds and grades of beings are so many, and so nearly related to each other, from the most intelligent creature to the lowest animated matter, that the exact line of distinction between the *animal* and *vegetable* commonwealth is difficult to be determined.

The *ourang-outang* appears to possess the organs of speech in his formation; and yet, for some cause, he is deprived of that faculty, though he differs from man, in anatomy, in the lack of the *pan* of the knee only.

The *sensitive-plant* has some of the appearances of animation; while some of the *sea-fish* scarcely exhibit life of any kind. Some are in *shells*, located, growing upon rocks; others, called *sun-fish*, and *Portuguese men-of-war*, are floating on the water, or near the shores, &c.

The *perch*, in embryo, has been known to produce more than twenty-eight thousand at a time, and the *cod* upwards of three millions.

Eight thousand different kinds of insects, and six hundred species of birds, with the various animals on land and in the water, of so many different shapes, forms, and sizes, with natures so diverse; and yet abundance of food is suited to the demands and situation of the whole : all of which exhibits a parental, tender care, marked with wisdom, goodness, and power, displayed through every part of universal nature. But the *origin* and *cause* of all those things still remained a query with Inquirer, whose research for important truth could not pass over things so interesting, with a stoical indifference.

The sun, near a hundred millions of miles from the earth, is but a step, in comparison of the distance to one of the *fixed stars*, which is allowed by philosophers to be so immense, that the velocity of a cannon-ball would require at least seven hundred thousand years to reach from one to another. Admitting it; and that seventy-two millions of those stars are within the sphere of astronomical calculation: moreover, admitting each star to be a sun like ours, in the centre of a *system*, with an equal number of planets of a first and second order, and each planet to be a world, with as great a variety of beings as inhabit this earth : what must be the aggregate number of the whole ! And what, or who, could be the author, and upholder, governor and provider, of this stupendous display? was the Inquirer's question still.*

MISCELLANEOUS REFLECTIONS.

The *five senses* of the body being avenues or inlets of knowledge to the mind, the things of nature may be examined, contemplated, and reasoned

---

* See the " Chain." **Causeless Causator.**

upon, but never to satisfaction. Although inferences and conclusions may be drawn from causes to effects, yet there remains a *hungering* in the mind, which continues unsatisfied until a proper object can be found, which is perfect both in its nature and degree; which alone can afford moral consolation.

Should the sun be annihilated, the effects produced by him would cease; and what would be the consequence but unbearable frost and perpetual night? The rays from the sun, but an inch in diameter, when brought to a focus, are equally unbearable, producing a flame. What a strange dependency on the sun, whose benign rays are wisely dispensed and withheld, in such a proportionable manner, as to answer every purpose! Surely this declares an overruling Hand!

From these circumstances, the sun is deified by many in the heathen world; yet we have not evidence that he can quicken an inanimate substance, and cause it to possess the power and principle of *sense* and *reason:* for the Being who is capable of such power and generous donation, must possess the principles of all *innate* substance, and, in the nature of the case, must be an Omnipotent Author.

Hundreds of *comets*, in their various orbits, with all the *heavenly bodies*, move in rotation, and have no infringement in their conjunction; but each, in order, keeps its course, and harmonizes with the whole!

Could a drop of water, or a grain of sand, go out of existence, but by the will of its Author, by the same rule, the whole fabric of nature could annihilate itself, and sink into a state of nonentity!

If every thing which had a beginning must have an end, then that which had no beginning can have no end; consequently, if nature *exists* by emanation, from the will of its Author, by the same rule, it must continue to exist, or go out of being, but when agreeable to his pleasure.

Those people who plead for the perfection of nature, independent of its Author, saying, "nature does this or that," as luck, fortune, or chance would have it, &c., necessarily ascribe omnific power and omniferous principles to matter. And this would argue the omnipotence and omnipresence of nature, abstract from its Author also, inasmuch as there is a bond of union throughout the whole; which bond of union prevails as far as nature is explored and understood, as the laws of electricity and magnetism exemplify on this globe, and as the laws of gravitation manifest throughout universal nature!

But to ascribe those powers to nature, is not to make a proper distinction between *mind* and *matter;* moreover it imputes effects to causes which could never produce them.

Matter, when moved by another cause, cannot stop of itself; and when stopped it cannot move of itself. Hence matter when put in motion is always indebted to some other cause.

Consequently those heavenly bodies which play in their different orbits, harmonizing together, have not existed forever in their order, but must have emanated from a higher Cause, who prescribed their spheres and gave them their laws dependent upon himself as their author and support. Of course the *Causeless Causator* must be considered as the centration and bond of union throughout the whole of universal nature; otherwise how can man account for any thing in nature, even how a particle of sand or a drop of water cohere together!

MORAL INQUIRIES.

Inquirer feeling a hungering in the *mind*, and being unsatisfied on various accounts, went to a school in the environs of *Babylon*, in order to be taught.

The tutors, with their ushers, who constituted masters of different grades, taught doctrines which may be inferred from their expressions, such as "seated upon a *topless* throne"—"an eternal decree"—"go down to the bottom of the bottomless pit."—"from all eternity a covenant was made"—"an *infinite* number"—"boundless space"—"the creature man is an *infinite* being."

Thus by *starting* wrong they must forever continue in error. Those expressions being contradictory, must be considered as nonsensical, and hence they ought to be turned out of doors as beneath contempt.

For how if a throne be *topless* can one be seated on it? If a decree be passed, there was a *time* when it was done; if so, how could it have been eternal? If the pit be *bottomless*, where is the bottom? If the covenant was made, there was a *time* when they made it, consequently a time before they made it; if so, how could it have been eternal, unless eternity is to be dated *from* the period of making that contract? as 'from' implies a starting place, or place of beginning. An infinite number to be enlarged by units! Space, which always implies limitation, as the space of a mile, the space of an hour or a day, &c., and yet is boundless! as some say. And man a creature *infinite* when he is limited! He had a beginning, which may be considered as the *first* and beginning end. From thence the time down to the other end, where he is *now*, may be calculated and measured to a mathematical demonstration. His futurity is a nonentity to him, and at best can only be a subject of faith.

Hence those masters gave but little satisfaction to Inquirer, on the all-important subject which still specially occupied his attention in his researches after truth.

OF HIEROGLYPHIC BABYLON.

As men journeyed from the east, in the days of Nimrod, the mighty hunter of men, they came to a plain in the land of Shinar, on the river Euphrates, where they built the memorable Babylon, which was begun in that of Babel. In this great city stood the celebrated temple of Belus, denoting the religion of the land.

Babylon was enclosed with a wall of brick three hundred and fifty feet in height, and eighty feet thick. The bricks were taken from a ditch afterwards filled with water to add to the strength of the place, the circumference of which was not less than sixty miles. It was four square, with twenty-five brass gates on a side, making one hundred in all. From each gate there was a street leading across the city from gate to gate, so that the streets intersected each other at right angles, and divided Babylon into five hundred and seventy-six squares, besides the spaces for building next to the walls, which were defended by several hundred towers, erected upon their summit.

Now there was a very wise prince, of age and experience, who reigned over Babylon; his name was Jupiter, and he was the author of the *wine* of Bacchus, which wine is *moral evil*. With this wine the people of Babylon were stupidly intoxicated, so as to be almost insensible to those important things in which all are greatly interested. And there was a great confusion of *tongues*, insomuch that there was not less than seventy-two languages, which have since increased to more than one hundred and twenty.

There were many things in the environs of Babylon, more than could be well enumerated, which were very troublesome and painful, and which are called *natural evils*, all of which are the effect or consequence of moral evil. For this was the cause of their introduction into the world.

There were also certain associations, which may well be denominated the *schools of Babylon ;* so great the influence of their example and the progress of their pupils.

Men of ability and spirit, being intoxicated with the wine of Bacchus, volunteer their services, pleased with the idea of becoming masters in those schools; which, by the by, is considered as an important distinction, constituting them great and mighty men!

The first is the *military-school.* Here is taught the art of war. Its object is fame and glory. Although it is attended with such horrors as tend to harden the heart, yet many weak men are so infatuated as to be delighted at the sight.

The second is the *dancing-school.* Here is taught the important art of hopping and jumping about, at a signal made by a BLACK man, who as their captain, with his noisy instrument directs their movements, whilst they turn their backs and faces to and fro, without either sense or reason, except indeed it may serve to show fine shapes and clothes. But consumptions are dated, and serious impressions are driven away!

The third is the school of *lawyers.* The nature of this association will be discovered by the following lines:

> "Should I be lawyer, I must lie and cheat,
> For honest lawyers have no bread to eat.
> 'Tis rogues and villains fee the lawyers high,
> And fee the men who gold and silver buy."

The fourth is the school of *music,* intended to divert the mind, and touch the passions, and is admirably calculated to be a substitute for penitence, and the prologue to forbidden indulgences.

In the fifth is taught the art of *dress.* This is intended to hide deformity, and please the eye; to gain a fanciful pre-eminence, and wear the bell as first in fashion, glorying in their shame. For dress was ordained in consequence of sin, and may be considered as a badge of fallen nature.

The sixth is the school of *quacks.* These have had success in imposing on the ignorant by high-sounding words. But the poor deceived sufferers at length detect the imposition, and die—to warn their survivors not to partake of their follies.

In the seventh is taught the fascinating art of *theatric representations.* This is called a very moral institution by its advocates, who affect to consider it very corrective of every species of vice. But the matter of fact sufficiently proves that the theatre is best supported when vice most abounds.

The eighth is an establishment for the promotion of *polite literature.* Here lectures are given upon the barbarity and folly displayed by the writers of the Old and New Testament, and on the sublimity, beauty, elegance, taste, and morality which are everywhere found in a choice collection of romances and novels. This establishment is exclusively intended for privileged orders; such as have been distinguished by wealth and idleness, and such as had rather feel than think.

The ninth is a very extensive institution, having many united colleges, in which are taught the various arts of picking pockets, picking locks, stealing, highway robbery, house-breaking, &c. And the progress of those pupils who are instructed in these various branches is really prodigious.

There is also a department, an appendage to the former, where is taught the art of preparing and using false weights and measures, the method of raising false charges, of managing extortion, the excellent art of overbearing and over-reaching in bargains, and the making of others' extremity their own opportunity to be well served at their expense.

The eleventh is furnished with male and female instructors, for the improvement of tattling, backbiting, lying, &c. Here also astonishing progress is made by all the pupils of both sexes.

The twelfth is a school for match-making. And, considering the motives which seem to govern most people on the subject of marriage, and the many unhappy families which are formed, it would appear that the wine of Bacchus furnished the stimulus, and Cupid and Hymen the only bands of union. But this is a private establishment, and their lessons are secretly given.

The thirteenth is the university of grandeur. Here pompous show, empty titles, impudent flatteries, haughty oppression, vain ignorance, pampering luxury, and wanton revelling, are effectually taught. This establishment is the most popular, and scarcely a family can be found in all the precincts of Babylon, which is not ambitious to obtain a finishing touch to the education of their children in this grand university.

In this great city is erected the "temple of Belus," called, "church established by law." This is a towering building, exalted almost to the lowering sky, intended by its stupendous height to domineer over the consciences of all the people. And so imperious are the priests, that the "temple of Belus" could never be reared but where the wine of Bacchus greatly abounds. The rites of this temple are very pleasing to Jupiter, the supreme god of the city, who is called the "prince of this world," reigning in Babylon over "the children of disobedience," without control. So much for mystical Babylon.

Inquirer, having observed all these mysteries, still looking at causes and effects, was convinced that there was such a thing as an overruling Hand, who superintended the affairs of life, and governed in wisdom and goodness, as well as in mercy and justice, and mighty power.

He perceived, also, that there were many things in Babylon which were opposed to the nature of this supreme Ruler, and therefore could not be right, nor by any means spring from the same original fountain, and consequently must have proceeded from a different source. And lo! whilst sorely grieved at the condition of the deluded citizens of Babylon, an angelic voice called his attention, inviting him to take a survey of a much more glorious city.

OF JERUSALEM.

This city is called Jerusalem, and is the glorious habitation of the moral Governor, against whom the prince of this world had revolted.

and set up his kingdom in Babylon. Jerusalem is situated in the *new earth*, where there is no sorrow nor pain, neither frost nor chilling winds, but all is delightful and tranquil, and the inhabitants have pleasure for evermore.

Jerusalem is six thousand miles in circumference, and fifteen hundred miles in height, with a *window* which extends all round the city, through which the *light* shines out from within to a vast distance, even to Babylon, so that people may see how to travel the road to Jerusalem.

There were twelve gates to the city, with an angel at each gate, to wait upon the heirs of salvation; and on the gates were written the names of the twelve tribes of the children of Israel. The wall of the city had twelve foundations, and upon them were written the names of the twelve apostles of the Lamb.

The houses of the city are of gold, the wall of jasper, and the foundations between the gates were made of precious stones.

The first foundation was a jasper, which is the color of white marble, with a light shade of green and red; the second, a sapphire, which is sky-blue, speckled with gold; the third, a chalcedony, that is, a carbuncle, and of the color of red-hot iron; the fourth, an emerald, and is of a grass-green; the fifth, a sardonyx, red, streaked with white; the sixth, a sardius, which is a deep-red; the seventh, a chrysolite, a deep-yellow; the eighth, a beryl, a sea-green; the ninth, a topaz, which is pale-yellow; the tenth, a chrysoprase, greenish and transparent, with gold specks; the eleventh, a jacinth, which is a red-purple; the twelfth, an amethyst, a violet-purple.

The twelve gates are twelve pearls; each of the gates is of one pearl. The streets of the city are pure gold, and transparent as glass.

The city hath no need of the sun, neither of the moon to shine on it; for the gates will not be shut by day, and there is no night there.

In this city there is a throne belonging to the great King; round about it is a rainbow, and four living creatures, four-and-twenty elders, sitting upon thrones, clothed in white, with crowns of gold upon their heads. Next to those were the saints, and then the angels encircled the whole, of which two hundred millions were but a part, and they are of different orders, as the cherubim and seraphim, archangels, &c.

From the throne proceeds a river, clear as crystal, which is the water of life, and those who drink it will never thirst.

This "city was prepared originally for man, from the foundation of the world," in the order of things, as primarily established by the Creator, in his moral government.

OF MORAL EVIL.

When all things were inane, and nature but in the sphere of nonentity, and all was dark and void, yet then existed the Causeless Causator—the great Author of dependent beings.

A cause of a cause is also the cause of the effect which that cause produces. This will hold in law, in nature, and in grace, upon logical principles, and yet the introduction of moral evil cannot impeach the divine character.

First, in law, a man is considered responsible for all his conduct. Hence, if in attempting feloniously to shoot a fowl, he kills a man beyond, the action being evil, he is accountable for all the consequences thereof.

In mechanism, the effects produced by the most remote cog, are dependent upon the first moving cause of the machine. And hence, the first moving cause produces the effects in a direct succession.

In grace, it is the same thing. Moral virtue, the good principle, comes from above, and not from nature. Hence its effects, of which man's free will is one, are of grace, as the original and moving cause; and it is equally as necessary for the same cause to continue to operate, in order to produce a continuation of the effects, as it was to put it in motion at the first. Otherwise, the effect and cause would cease together.

But a free agent can act freely, not on the principles of mechanical necessity, but upon that of volition, the necessary result of free agency, and the very quintessence of moral ability. Admitting this—for upon what principles can it be denied, it being self-evident?—then, if the order of things be inverted, in consequence of a wrong act, intentionally done by a free agent, under those free circumstances, the consequence of this invention must have its original and proper foundation in the agent as the author, from whom the act, and consequently the effect, flowed. On these principles moral evil could be introduced, without impeaching the divine character, and includes the ideas, that all the goodness in all beings, whether in nature or in moral agents, comes from the good Being who is the author of all goodness; and sin, which is not a creature nor a principle of nature, but the base transgression of the law of the righteous Ruler of the universe, of course, the base act of the agent who wills it, primarily originated in the abuse of moral power or agency, in a revolt against the Creator's government.

"Sin is the transgression of a law," "and where there is no law, there can be no transgression." Hence follows the associated ideas of a compact between the governor and the governed; the will of the one is the law, which the others have capacity to obey. A law implies a penalty, and of course a time of judgment and retribution; hence the trial is a limited period only, and not eternal, both as it relates to angels and man.

Here we see the propriety of the following words: "Angels—kept not their first habitation, but sinned—are cast down—reserved under chains of darkness, unto the judgment of the great day, to be punished." "The devil abode not in the truth, but sinneth from the beginning," &c.

All things were good when they emanated from their Author's hand. Thinking spirits, without earthly bodies, never sleep, but must for ever be in contemplation. Before this world existed, there were not so many things for the mind to ruminate upon. Looking forward into futurity, or viewing in retrospect, they could behold no end; neither could they remember a time when they had no existence. Hence, if tempted at all, it must have been self-temptation; and the first act of disobedience must have destroyed their innocency, and brought misery upon them, even a forfeiture of their Governor's favor, and his consequent displeasure, who is a righteous Judge, and cannot approbate a revolt against his government.

Those spirits who constituted themselves devils by sinning, do not multiply, but each, being actually guilty for himself, deserves a personal punishment for his crime.

OF MAN'S FALL.

But with the human family it was far different. Man contained a vast posterity, *seminally*, which must have perished in his loins, had they been immediately subjected to a punishment proportioned to their crime; as they sinned and fell seminally only in their first *head!*

Jerusalem was prepared for man when he was commanded to multiply, before he transgressed. And as a state of trial must be limited, doubtless man would have been translated; otherwise the earth would have been overrun with people, as none would have died, neither would there have been any miscarriages, provided man had never sinned.

Man was neither mortal nor immortal before the fall, but may be considered as a candidate upon trial; for, according to his conduct, so should be his fate.

The *death* with which he was threatened was absolute and unconditional, but not *eternal* in the common acceptation of the word *eternal death*. Otherwise, how could man be saved, seeing the threatening was irrevocable? Neither was it *temporal death*, seeing that was denounced afterwards, and Adam actually lived more than nine hundred years. If temporal and eternal death were both implied absolutely and unconditionally, man must have lost half of himself, viz. his body! For, as the resurrection came by Jesus Christ, through the gospel, he dying a temporal death, must have lost his body, and as his soul was doomed irrevocably to eternal death, how could there have been a re-union or an escape?

But thanks be to the Supreme Ruler of the world, it was not so! as is manifested in the unspeakable gift of Jesus. The death was spiritual, and was executed as the entailment, as soon as he ate. For he immediately lost his communion with his Maker, being guilty, having lost his innocence by the violation of his law. The tree was good--the evil consisted in the abuse of it—which was a moral evil.

Temporal death was pronounced afterwards in mercy, and he was driven from paradise—" lest he should partake of the tree of life and live forever"—become an immortal sinner, eternally chained to this world of wo! St. Paul, in enumerating the blessings in Christ Jesus, includes temporal death expressly; and in his conclusion says, " all are yours:" which argues that *temporal death* was denounced in consequence of *sin*, that life and immortality might be brought to light through the gospel in mercy to mankind, and man again have a chance for Jerusalem, a better opportunity than before; because, " If a man sin, we have an Advocate with the Father, even Jesus, who is the propitiation for our sins, and not for ours only, but also for the sins of the whole world," so that by grace we may repent, and find pardon for our personal crimes; whereas the paradisaical law knew no forgiveness.

Thus, the prince of this world introduced the wine of Bacchus into the moral world, so far, that even the natural world is affected with it; and hence the confusion both in the natural and moral world, with all the calamities, curses and miseries—from the elements, from vegetable and mineral agents, and from the malicious designs of men against each other: all combining in ten thousand different shapes and forms, to destroy the peace of the world, as *hieroglyphic Babylon* abundantly exemplifies, and which may be more fully seen in every quarter of the globe.

Natural evil is the effect of moral evil, or is consequent upon it, as a curse or penalty entailed by a righteous and just Judge! Hence, man should learn the lesson, "having no continuing city here, we should seek one to come!"

OF THE NEW BIRTH.

Justification by faith is what God does *for* us, through the death of his Son; but *regeneration** or the new birth, also called sanctification, is what God does *in* us by the operation of his Holy Spirit. The first work is pardon, the latter is purity. One is to forgive, the other is to make holy.

Man by *nature*, though free from guilt, is not *holy*. Holiness is not an innate inherent principle of parentage, but must be received by an operation of the Holy Spirit. And hence, "Ye must be born again;" as happiness is only consequent upon experiencing this change of heart.

A transitory object can only produce a transient pleasure; for the effect cannot exceed the cause which produced it. Therefore, the enjoyment must perish with the using, and both must cease together.

Of course there can be no permanent fruition of the things of time, for all of them are very uncertain, and at furthermost *death* will end the whole, and how soon that may come, who can tell?

Here, then, the aspect ends; and with this reflection peace is marred, and the mind is overspread with a gloom! Consequently to enjoy *perfect* happiness and solid peace, there must be some lasting fountain which can afford it. And where can such contentment be found but in Divinity? Every other enjoyment must fail. Many things will satisfy the body, as food, drink, &c.; but there remains an aching void within, the world can never fill.

The love of God shed abroad in the heart, which is comfort from the everlasting fountain, and never will run dry, is fitted to man's necessity, and is called the "kingdom of God within," which is "righteousness, and peace, and joy in the Holy Ghost." It is the moral image of God, which Adam lost, and which we must receive in order to be happy, called Christ within, the hope of glory, and is the earnest of the saints' inheritance. And hence the distinction between the *outward* manifestation of Christ in the days of his flesh, and the *inward* revelation by his Spirit.†

---

* *Regeneration* is the opposite of *degeneration*.

† The *soul*, which constitutes the man, (the body being the case, or mechanical part for certain purposes and ends, which, with the soul, was derived from the parents, as Levi paid tithes *in* Abraham,) is not a particle of the *Deity*; but must be considered as spirit in the abstract. Divinity cannot be ignorant or suffer both in a moral and temporal sense, as do the human race.

Conscience appears to be the result of *judgment*; and judgment is the conclusion of the *understanding*. For, according to the evidence afforded to the understanding, conclusions are formed and fixed in the mind; which conclusions universally modify the judgment. Hence, if the understanding be misinformed the mind is deceived, and the judgment will be wrong of necessity. Of course, in point of duty, the understanding being dark, the judgment cannot be sound and clear, and consequently conscience may be silent and not speak at all, being "seared as with a hot iron;" or it may be defiled and tell lies, and prove not to be a sure guide.

The Mahometan's conscience will not allow him to drink wine, from an error of his judgment, in consequence of a misinformed conscience, while the conscientious Christian feels

OF REPENTANCE.

Repentance implies three things. First, a conviction for sin. Secondly, a forsaking of sin. And, thirdly, a confession of it, as a penitent.

First. A man cannot repent of a sin which he never committed. Of course, he must be convinced of his *crime* before he can feel *sorrow* for it.

Secondly. If a man sees his error, and still persists in it, he of course loves and delights in it; therefore, he is not sorry for it; consequently he does not repent of it; for, if he did repent of it, he would forsake it with abhorrence and detestation.

Thirdly. A penitent would make restitution if he could. And, at least, there is a hearty confession, and a sincere desire for pardon and restoration; which causes the soul to hunger and thirst after the *salvation* of the Lord, as the chased hart panteth for the cooling water-brook!

Such have the promise of salvation; for where there is a moral conformity to the will of God, they meet his approbation, and, of course, adoption; and hence enjoy his favor, as one of the divine family: "for there

---

bound in duty on some occasions to drink it. And thus conscience guides people directly opposite to each other in point of moral duty, and two opposites cannot be right; of course conscience is not a sure guide, which argues the necessity of a *regulation*.

The conduct of persecuting Saul, who lived in all good conscience, obtained pardon, because of his ignorance; and loving Paul afterwards exhibited a very apposite disposition and conduct towards the same people, from similar conscientious motives.

But the Spirit from above will direct no man wrong; being the spirit of truth, it will tell no lies; neither can it be defiled, or "seared with a hot iron." Whereas the conscience of man, without the aid of divine influence, is liable to every species of error.

Hence, the necessity of attending to the light from Jerusalem, and to walk by the light which shines from above.

Conscience, like a nose of wax, may be put into any shape, through the influence of example and the prejudice of education. And this is one reason why there are so many opinions in the world. Conscience having yielded to inclination, vain imaginations bear the sway.

Inclination, through temptation, leads one way, while a better informed judgment dictates another. Here follows a *dialogue* in the mind. The evil must consist in giving the consent of the mind, contrary to the dictates of a better judgment. And hence, a consciousness of self-condemnation.

One among the many reasons wherefore the world is so given to idolatry, is that through the darkness of the human understanding the moral faculty is weakened, and men are prepared to be satisfied with ceremonies, modes and images, as substitutes for purity of heart, and pure spiritual worship. And thus religion, instead of being considered a *moral principle* to be cultivated in the *heart*, was at length thought to consist in *name* and *form* only; until nothing but images and ceremonies entirely made up the gods and the devotions of such idolatrous worshippers.

Even the Jews were so much inclined to be satisfied with things outward, that in the absence of Moses they made their calf, in imitation of the ox-god of Egypt.

Hence, the ceremonial-law was "added because of transgression." Which ceremonies, however, were so modified, as to be directly opposite to those in use among the heathen.

The heathen kept the first day of the week, the Jews the last. The heathen seethed the kid in its mother's milk; the ceremonial law said, "Thou shalt not seethe a kid in its mother's milk," &c.

As man cannot have a proper conception of a being whose very existence is infinite, eternal and immense, expressions which imply something incomprehensible—as man can only judge by comparison from anology—there was need for the *Causeless Causator* to manifest himself in a character suitable to man's capacity; that man, as a rational being, might worship him in spirit, with the understanding, agreeable to the principles of truth.

Hence the necessity of a Jesus Christ! both his outward manifestation, and the inward revelation to the heart, by inspiration! This *inward revelation* corresponds to the *outward manifestation* as a witness thereto.

The will of God is a secret, known only to himself; except so much only as he is pleased to reveal; reason could not find it out or fathom it, but by the aid of inspiration.

A monarch requires the obedience of his subjects to serve himself, but God requires the submission and obedience of his creatures, that he may benefit them that they may be wise and happy. And this is the proper intention of all divine worship.

is no condemnation to them who are in Christ Jesus, and walk not after the flesh, but after the Spirit." Because *spiritual* things take the lead; the flesh, the contrast, is given up; as much as a man turns his back to the north, when he travels with his face to the south.

Here, then, is repentance, which needeth not to be repented of; for it is the work of the Lord, begun by the operation of his Holy Spirit. From light cometh sight; from sight cometh sense; and from sense cometh sorrow; which causes resignation, and dependence on the arm of the Lord for salvation.

But the sorrow of the world, which needeth to be repented of, worketh death, *i. e.* misery: because it causes a fretting against the dispensation of the Lord, and procures no relief, but makes bad worse; and brings the soul under condemnation, and, finally, into despair and endless wo!

OF FAITH.

There is a distinction between *knowledge* and *faith*, which ought to be observed. Knowledge is the evidence of *sense*, and always refers to things present, *i. e.* within the present grasp and possession of the senses. But faith always refers to things which are absent, and not within the sphere of the senses: and hence, "faith cometh by hearing."

Faith and knowledge are both derived from evidence; but the evidences are different. One is *self-evidence*, being an object of sense; the other is *circumstantial evidence*, being inferred from circumstantial things.

Self-evidence is sensible knowledge, which can admit of no *doubt;* but circumstantial evidence is always *uncertain*, and, consequently, is only a subject of faith.

Evidence must always be agreeable to the nature of the subject. In arithmetic, it must be numerical; in courts of law, it must be human testimony, under certain regulations and modifications; and in divine things, we need divine evidence, in order to obtain a moral certainty.

The subject of *creation* is a doctrine of *miracles* and *faith;* and so is Christianity, which many condemn, as an unreasonable thing. But the reverse is atheism. For whatsoever is produced out of the common course of nature, by the immediate power of God, must be considered a *miracle*. And such is the doctrine of creation. And yet it is a subject of faith only, not of knowledge. We did not see it; of course, we do not know it; and yet we believe it. We have not human evidence of it; for who saw when the work was performed?

But to deny the doctrine of miracles, is to to deny the work of creation, and, of course, the Creator also; because it was the *act* which gives the *character*. Hence, we must say with Paul, "By" (or through) "faith we understand that the worlds were framed by the word of God."

The difference between *sense* and *reason* may be discovered, by considering, first, the nature of a *spirit*, having the power and use of reason, without a fleshly body; then, secondly, that of an *idiot*, who has the *five senses*, without the power of reasoning; and then, thirdly, that which would be the probable result of the two properties concentred in one complex object, and, of course, possessing the united powers of sense and reason, or the *seven senses*, if you will.

Some deny any sense but the *bodily senses*, and plead for the perfection of these. But the question may be retorted, Whether either of the five bodily senses are so keen as either to *hear, see, taste, feel,* or *smell the Deity*? If not, how can He be known, unless by the inward feeling of the mind? The body cannot feel grief, nor joy, nor anger, &c.: these emotions are peculiar to the mind. Hence, there must be an inward feeling of the mind, which may be considered as the sixth sense; and common sense may be considered as the seventh.

Common sense is that principle and power by which men can discern, understand, and judge of matters, agreeably to the truth and propriety of things; which requires the art of reason, and is common to mankind.

That which is obvious to sense, we know: hence, we do not say that we *believe* snow is white, but we *know* it.

Whatsoever the senses grasp is *self-evidence* to us; which knowledge is positive, and cannot admit of doubt. Self-evidence, when derived through the avenues of bodily sense, is called *sensible;* but when it exists in the mind, without the body being particularly considered, it is called *moral evidence.*

But *faith* is derived from circumstantial evidence, and refers to absent objects and things future, but never to things present, except where a degree of knowledge from self-evidence gives the assurance to faith, so that " we see and know in part ;" but what remains, is embraced by faith in things future : and hence, " we stand, and walk, and live, by faith."

There are degrees of faith, according to the degree of evidence, which are distinguished by different names, according to the things to which they relate ; as *historical faith, faith of heathens, faith of devils,* &c. &c.

The lowest degree of faith is *conjecture ;* the second is *opinion ;* the third is a *firm belief.*

Conjecture is an inclination to assent to the thing proposed; but is slight or weak, by reason of the weighty objections that lie against it.

Opinion is a more steady and fixed assent ; when a man is almost certain, but he still has some fear of the contrary remaining with him.

Belief is a more full and assured assent to the truth.

Belief is the assent of the mind to any truth or proposition, no matter what the arguments or propositions may be. If we admit the evidence, we give our assent, and receive it as a truth ; and hence, we believe it. But if we reject the evidence, which is only circumstantial, we do not assent to it, nor believe it ; of course, we are unbelievers in the thing.

Self-evidence, which is knowledge, is irresistible ; but circumstantial evidence is not. A man may continue in unbelief two ways: first, through a careless indifference ; and, secondly, he may wilfully reject proper evidence.

Hence, unbelief is avoidable ; otherwise, how or why should he be commanded to believe, or be condemned for unbelief, or not believing.

Here, then, is the proof or trial of man, on which depends his eternity !

He is not adequate, by his natural ability, to keep the *Adamic* or *paradisaical law* of works, which requires a perfect obedience. Through the frailty of fallen nature, man cannot do it. Therefore, " by the deeds of the law shall no flesh be justified," that it may be by *grace,* through faith in the Gospel.

Man can believe, if he cannot work. He can admit the truth, by an assent unto it, and receive it, when the Spirit of truth reveals it unto him. By giving assent heartily, he admits it, and thereby receives it ; and this is an act of faith. This act is right: and it is the lowest and only act that man could do, that is right. And hence, this act of faith is accounted or imputed unto him for righteousness. Of course, the penitent soul, who feels condemned by the moral law, which he has broken, and thereby forfeited his infantile justification, feels the need of a Redeemer or Saviour. Hence, the Saviour, as offered in the Gospel by the Spirit, is gladly embraced: here the soul finds a resting-place: even the virtue of that *name* inspires the soul with the evidence of pardon and peace, whereby he can rejoice with joy unspeakable, and full of comfort, which is the earnest of the saints' inheritance. A degree of faith and hope attends repentance.

The Ninevites had a degree of faith and hope, which, by repentance, brought salvation.

The judgment of God hung over the city for *moral evil*, which they were ignorant of: faith coming by hearing, and hearing by the word of God.

The word of God was preached unto them; and they believed God, and said, "Who can tell but the Lord will be gracious?" They fasted, and humbled themselves: which shows that they were saved; first, from their carelessness; secondly, from their practices; and, thirdly, from the destruction denounced.

A soul believes there is a God, and that salvation is necessary, or it would never seek for it: also, there must be a degree of hope, or else the soul would feel no heart to seek, but must sink into despair.

"Without faith it is impossible to please God." Faith is the way to come—"For he that cometh to God, must believe that he is, and that he is a rewarder of them that diligently seek him."

All the blessings of God are attained only by faith in Christ.

First, to apprehend there is such a blessing attainable; and then seek in fervent expectation: believing, first, that God is able to give the blessing; secondly, that he is willing to bestow it; thirdly, that he will give it, because he hath promised it, saying, "Whatsoever ye ask, believing that ye receive, ye shall have." Here claiming the blessing by faith. Fourthly, claiming it *now*, as now is declared to be the acceptable time, and day of salvation: to-day, if you will hear his voice,—"Come, for all things are *now* ready,"—God is in Christ reconciling the world unto himself—therefore be ye reconciled to God. We love God because he first loved us—he *first loved* us, before we loved him. We need not do something to pacify God, to make him willing to receive us. He is willing already; the hindering cause is on the side of the creature—his *will* being *opposed* to the will of God—as Christ saith,—"O Jerusalem, Jerusalem! how often would I have gathered thy children together as a hen doth gather her chickens under her wings; *but ye would not.*"

Knowledge, as before explained, being the effect of self-evidence, is therefore a sensible or moral certainty; which of course cannot admit of doubt: a man can testify no further than he knows.

A man who hath felt conviction, can testify, as a witness of it, and give evidence to that truth. So one who hath experienced pardon, i. e. witness of justification by faith, can justify, saying, "We know in whom we have believed"—because to him faith has been brought to sight—he has the inward divine witness to the sixth sense of the soul; and the testimony corresponds with the demands of his seventh or common sense, whereby he is able to give a rational account of it to others.

The man who has experienced the blessing of sanctification can testify what he knows, and no further; so the glorified Enoch and Elijah can testify what glorification is, for they know it; but we do not; and yet we firmly believe it and hope for it. Yet when we obtain the same state of enjoyment, faith will be brought to sight, and hope to the fruition, and these two will then cease, being swallowed up in the knowledge and enjoyment for ever.

Then let every inquirer, who wishes to escape to Jerusalem, from the overthrow of Babylon, strive in earnest for salvation, in fervent expectation of the blessings of pardon and purity. And if you cannot believe as you would, believe as you can—"Lord, I believe, help thou mine unbelief." And if you cannot pray and seek as you would, pray and seek as you can—resigning, submitting, and depending upon his bounty for deliverance; and never rest, until you find the Lord precious to your soul. Christ was in earnest for thee: O be in good earnest for thyself;—and may God for Christ's sake speed you on the way.

OF HOPE.

A hope of future glory is composed of desire and expectation, predicated upon faith and repentance; which were produced by a divine conviction in the mind of the reality of the invisible world, through the operation of the Holy Spirit of God.

Conviction being thus wrought in the heart, the consequence to such as persevere, is a reformation; a forsaking of sin, and a conformity to the will of God—who is ever ready to receive and forgive returning penitents, for Jesus' sake,—where the mind finds a resting-place, and the inquirer a home.

A man may desire a thing which he never expects to enjoy; of course he has no hope of it, but is in despair. Again, a man may expect a thing which is not desirable; and hence he does not hope for it, but is under a dread on that account.

Hence neither a desire nor an expectation, considered abstractly, can constitute a hope: they must be taken in conjunction, in order to remove the dread, avoid despair, and afford a consolation in the mind.

The Christian hopes for heaven and glory. His hope is composed of desire and expectation. Heaven he desires, being convinced it is a desirable place. He *expects* to get there, because there is a prospect before him. He has *repented*, and is forgiven. He enjoys a sense of the divine favor, and feels the evidence of pardon by the witness of the Spirit of God in his soul; which witness is righteousness, and peace, and joy in the Holy Ghost; which is styled the "assurance of faith and hope." For the aspect is animating, and the prospect is cheering whilst looking through hope, the perspective, by which we look into another and a better world.

Hence, said one, "Mark the perfect man, and behold the upright; for the end of that man is peace." Another, "Let me die the death of the righteous, and let my last end be like his." "For the righteous have hope in their death."

OF CHARITY.

Charity consists in something more than giving away a few old worn out clothes to a beggar. For thus saith Paul: "Though I give all my goods to feed he poor, and have not charity, it profiteth me nothing."

"And though a man had all knowledge and all faith; so as to remove mountains, and talk like an angel; and have not charity: he would be only as sounding brass, and a tinkling cymbal."

Charity does not consist in name, nor in outward form; but is a suitable disposition of heart, which is begotten by the Spirit of God. And hence those who are endowed with this precious grace are said to be born of God, and are called new creatures. They are new in many respects; first, they have new views and discoveries of things; their judgments are new, and so are their motives and desires, as also their objects and ends.

The term charity is frequently misapplied, and thereby abused. Hence, says one, "I have no charity for such and such persons—but such and such are very charitable." In the first case, faith or belief is intended, and in the latter, kindness.

For a bountiful act is an act of kindness, but every act of kindness is not an act of charity; because it does not always flow from a charitable motive; but often from pride, ostentation, and vain-glory.

As the religion of Christ is summed up in one word, love; to say, I have no charity, is to say, I have no religion: for there can be no religion without charity, which is love; which principle causes its subjects to attend to the moral law, in point of duty—"Thou shalt love thy neighbor as thyself." Secondly, the law of nature, which considers the equal rights, wants, duties, and obligations of man: and thirdly, the rule of practice, which is, "as ye would that others should do unto you, do ye even so to them;" for the law of Moses, the spirit of the prophets, the example of Jesus Christ, concur in enjoining them upon all mankind.

Hence the importance of charity. And the idea of a Christian without charity, is a complete solecism; like an honest thief, a chaste harlot, or a holy devil.

"Charity never faileth," being the divine, eternal principle—but "suffereth long and is kind"—suffereth wrong rather than do wrong; and instead of "being overcome with evil, overcometh evil with good"—by returning good for evil.

"Charity—thinketh no evil," i. e. is not jealous and evil-eyed, surmising evil; but "hopeth and believeth all things"—for the best, by making proper allowances, and putting the most favorable construction upon men and things, that the nature of the case will justly admit of.

But charity is not a fool; she must have legs to stand upon—knowing that justice should be done to every thing; and hence desires that God and man, and all beings should have their due—and feeling determined to render the same to every creature, she is ever ready to act in every case agreeable to the moral law, the law of nature, and the rule of practice.

And upon this disposition hangs the eternity of man; seeing he is to be rewarded according to the deeds done in the body.

OF FASTING.

"Then shall they fast in those days," which words of our Lord concerning his apostles and followers, came to pass in the gospel dispensation, as exemplified in the Acts of the Apostles, and in Paul's writings.

The practice of fasting, and the benefits derived by it, are exemplified in the cases of the Ninevites; of Queen Esther in the deliverance of the

Jews from Haman, who was executed upon his own gallows which he had prepared for Mordecai; and in the case of Daniel.

Our Lord mentioned a kind of devil which was to be expelled only by fasting and prayer.

God does not require murder for sacrifice. A person instead of fasting may starve, and injure his health; while others do not fast at all, but in attempting to avoid one extreme, run into the other.

Jesus fasted, and afterwards hungered. Daniel fasted three full weeks, and says, "I eat no pleasant bread," which implies a degree of abstinence, and bread of a coarser kind.

A person who lives to the full, would find it for the health of his body, as well as his soul, at times to use a degree of abstinence, from a principle of duty. And, moreover, by being acquainted with a degree of hunger, he would the better sympathize with others, who are objects of charity and in distress.

Fasting is enjoined; but there is no general rule laid down how often, or to what degree it shall be performed. The reason is obvious: because the states and situations of men are so various, that no general rule could be laid down to suit every case. One is confined with sickness, as much as can be done for him to take the necessary food for the support of life, while others are strong and in full health.

Thus, as things and circumstances vary so much, no general rule is laid down, only the duty is inspired to fast; but man, as a rational being is required to act according to his judgment, and clear his conscience.

The prince of darkness is more busy to buffet and tempt the mind upon our fast-days than at any other time, to prevent the exercise of faith. But as "the kingdom of heaven suffers violence, and the violent take it by force," we should spend more time in private devotion then, than what we commonly do.

OF PRAYER.

The prayer of the profligate for damnation is an abomination to the Lord, and it is a mercy that he does not take them at their word. The prayer of the hypocrite is wrong, and his hope shall perish.

Some are like the Gadarenes, who prayed Christ to depart from their coast. Others only say their prayers as a parrot says his borrowed song, without as much form as the ox, which kneels when he lies down; but, like the hog in the stye, fall down, and before they get half through, the devil lolls them to sleep! Thus they satisfy themselves by saying prayers, and asking God to save them from their sins, when they do not consent to part with them.

But the commandment is, to pray without ceasing, which is called mental prayer, being the language of the heart properly disposed towards God to do his will; and let one lay down with such disposition of the heart, and wake up any time, and appeal to the inward testimony, he still feels the same disposition to do his Maker's will.

In order to live in this frame of prayer, it is proper and necessary to attend to ejaculatory prayer, like Abraham's servant, when he went to seek a bride for his master's son, as all things are sanctified through faith and prayer. We need God's blessing upon all things we do, and all things should be done to the glory of God. Therefore we should ask his benediction on all we do; and such things as cannot be done to the glory of God, in the name of Christ Jesus, we have no right to perform; for we are not authorized to take the devil's tools to do the Lord's work with, and of course all engagements upon which we cannot look to God with a degree of expectation for his blessing to attend them, are forbidden fruit, with bitterness at the bottom. We ought not therefore to touch the accursed thing.

Private prayer was the custom of the patriarchs, prophets, Christ, and the apostles.

Jesus said, "Enter into thy closet, and shut to thy door, and pray to thy Father who is in secret, and thy Father who seeth in secret shall reward thee openly," &c.

When you retire, don't hurry it over as a burden, and feel satisfied with the mere performance, like the schoolboy, who repeats his lesson as a task; but look in expectation, believing, first, that God is able to bless me now; secondly, that, being unchangeable, he declares his willingness, and now is the accepted time; thirdly, if you are ready, close in now, and take the promise, and prove the veracity of God. "Whatever ye ask, believing, that ye receive, &c., ye shall have; for God cannot deny himself, neither can he nor will he deny our faith."

Also there is public prayer; even if but two or three meet in his name, he is with them.

OF WATCHING.

"What I say unto you, I say unto all, *Watch*," was the injunction of the Saviour of men to his followers. And hence the duty of watching is obligatory upon all mankind; and there is a positive necessity, as every Christian feels and knows from experience, to attend to this important duty of watching, by reducing it to practice, considering the dangers and difficulties of this transitory and unfriendly world, which is so full of flattery and deceit, that nothing can be depended upon as permanent here below, but snares and temptations accompany every lane of life.

As temptations generally come in through the medium of thought, there is need to watch over our thoughts, and keep our minds composed and solemnly stayed upon God; otherwise the soul will be as a ship, which, having slipped her cables, is liable to be carried away by the tide, and stove against the rocks. Examples also should be watched over, lest we corrupt society by our misconduct.

Children should be watched over, from an early period, in a tender manner, and diligently restrained from apparent evil.

Our weaknesses demand that a double guard be placed at every weak place, that we be not overtaken unawares, by any sudden or unforeseen event.

The world, the flesh, and Satan, should be watched against with unwearied diligence.

First, the world. The riches and cares of this life are both captivating and deceitful; the mind being overcharged, the soul is surfeited, and hence disqualified for devotion. Therefore, says one, "save all you can, and get all you can, and give all you can, that the things of this world may prove a blessing, and not a curse."

Watch against the love of the riches of this world, against the spirit of the world, and also the practice and fashions of the world, by not conforming to those which are wrong and improper; but be transformed by the inward renewing of the mind, and so have the adornings of truth and virtue.

The "lusts of the flesh, the lusts of the eye, and the pride of life," must be watched against and conquered.

The devil, called the "prince of this world," will flatter the imagination with promises which he never can perform, endeavoring, by vain allurements, to attract from the path of holiness. And, moreover, he will exhibit all the difficulties and trials of the cross of Christ, to deter the traveller from the happy road to Zion, saying, "mercy is clean gone, the day of grace is passed, of course there is no hope," and thus strive to drive the soul to despair, and, if possible, to suicide. But those thoughts should be resisted, with a hope in the merits of a Redeemer for acceptance with God; for while the desires remain, the spirit strives, and of course mercy may be sought and found by conformity to the will of God, depending upon his Son for salvation.

The tempter, also, after pardon is received, strives to destroy all our confidence in God, by reasoning in the mind, so as to give way to doubt, and be filled with unbelief; for this abiding witness in the soul is to be kept by a constant exercise of faith in God, under the operation of his Spirit; and hence it is obvious that this mental exercise is the reaction of the soul upon God. Therefore, a person heavenward bound, is as one rowing up against the stream; by diligence, there is progression, but if the exertion stops, the boat will float with the tide. So we must diligently keep our minds as we ought, continually looking to God, and depending our all upon him. When people backslide from God, it is not by giving away to great sins at first, but gradually, little by little—from an omission of a thing of small beginning, until conscience is lulled to sleep, and enormities can be committed without remorse. Hence their fall from their steadfastness is so gradual, as to be almost imperceptible; and when they are become poor, and blind, and naked, they still are ready to conclude that they are rich, and increased in goods, and have need of nothing, and like Samson, though shorn of his strength, and wist it not, they go out as at other times, but fall an easy prey to his conquerors. *Thus many strong men have fallen!* Therefore we should remember the caution to "shun all the appearance of evil." For it is easier to keep out of a snare while one is out, than to get out after we once get in.

Instead of reasoning with the tempter, we should betake to the stronghold in prayer, knowing that the devil cannot counterfeit the love of God, and a delight to do his will. For those sensations come from God alone.

Watch for opportunities for meetings, private devotion, family instruction, reading the scriptures, and strive to get all the good you can, and extend all the good within your power to others, which Christ will consider as done to himself, and will so acknowledge it in the day of judgment, if they flow from a spirit of obedience and love to him.

Watch for the hour of death! People are taken by him suddenly and unawares.

In such an hour as ye think not the Son of Man cometh! Blessed are those that are found watching. But those who say in their heart "My Lord delayeth his coming; and are eating, drinking, quarrelling, and sleeping," &c., such will be taken by surprise ano appointed to their portion with hypocrites and unbelievers, where will be weeping and gnashing of teeth.

Watching without prayer, or prayer without watching, is of no account. For they are mutually connected and dependent on each other. Hence, being joined by the God of grace, that which God hath joined together, let not man put asunder. For if one is a drunkard habitually, and prays to be kept from it, and yet will not be guarded nor watch against it, what can his prayer avail? And on the other hand, if one will watch but not pray, the resolution is soon broken, in consequence of the want of power to cope with the temptation and evil habit. Then we must watch and pray, that we enter not into temptation."

Sometimes watching and praying will not avail and make headway against the foe; then fasting or a degree of abstinence must be used; as our Lord said, "This kind goeth out by fasting and prayer."

And the spirit of prayer, which is the spirit of devotion, is the spirit of Christ, the enjoyment of which is a blessing. And those people, even if it be but the husband and wife who meet together thus, have the Lord Jesus with them!

OF THE NIGHT OF DEATH.

Death! What is it? Dying, simply considered, is but the changing of states! To leave the prison and prison-yard; the body, the house of clay, which confines man to the terraqueous ball through the power of gravitation. The laws of nature being reversed, what scenes present to view! Man, who was an inhabitant of time, is now disembodied and become an inhabitant of eternity! How great those realities now, which once were viewed but darkly through the glass of faith!

How dreadful and terrific to a guilty mind! What awful horrors must seize the condemned soul, who hath sinned against a righteous God!

Those who love the Lord, and feel the powers of the world to come, whilst inhabiting the house of clay, and live for eternity, by denying themselves and taking up their daily cross, and so follow after him in order to be his disciples—how soon will all the scenes of life be over, and their eternity commence! Then those important realities will be more fully understood which now at best are faintly known! But soon we shall be unveiled to see as we are seen, and know as we are known.

As it relates to the agonies of death at the time of our departure, pain of body is generally gone, at or near the last moments. The greatest pain most universally subsides, some few hours if not some days before the dissolution. In scripture the death of the righteous is called sleep. Hence, "Stephen fell asleep," &c. &c. Now the last sensation in slumber, before the senses are locked up in sleep, are very sweet and agreeable; and by the same parity of reason, if we have the due preparation in the mind, why not possess an agreeable exit at the hour of death?

Death is called the king of *terrors*, and is justly said to be a terror to kings. But why? The *sting* of death is personal *sin;* and the strength of sin is the law; for sin is the transgression of the law, which is the revealed will of God; and hence the soul comes under the divine displeasure, and the person is afraid to appear before a righteous judge, being conscious of self-condemnation.

A person with a bee in his hand might be afraid of it; but if the *sting* be pulled out and is gone, why should the man fear? So, if the sting of death be removed by the pardon of all personal sin, then being restored to the favor of God as one of his family, all dread must be removed and terror be gone: what then should one have to fear? There must be a joy in God, and a rejoicing in the prospective hope of eternity, from possessing an earnest of their inheritance in the kingdom of God.

Thus the Lord gives suffering grace in a suffering day, and dying, or *supporting* grace in a dying day!

OF HELL AND PARADISE.

Neither *hell* nor *paradise* is the eternal home of any beings, or their place of final destination at the consummation of all things. But rather they are the intermediate states and periods of time, which departed souls inhabit between the dissolution and the resurrection of the body, before the general judgment.

The souls of mankind do not sleep in the graves with their bodies until the resurrection, but exist in a separate state, in a *sensible* manner.

St. John saw the souls of those who were beheaded for the testimony of Jesus, under the altar; and the rich man's body was entombed in grandeur; yet we read of him, "In hell he lifted up his eyes," &c. "Saw Abraham—and cried, and—said unto him—I am *tormented*"—" Lazarus is *comforted ;*" which cases evince the realities of future sensation.

The term " *hell*," or *hades*, is to cease at the consummation of all things, when all the dead must be given up, and the " *lake of fire*" receive those who are doomed to it, and *hell* and *death* be cast into the lake; which shows that *hell* is something distinct from the *lake*. And hence the former will be swallowed up of the latter, like yesterday in the following time, when this day commenced.

The idea of a *purgatory*, or restoration from hell to heaven, is a delusion.. For, that Christ did not go to the *lower inhabitants* to preach repentance to the damned, is evident from what he said to the thief on the cross, "To-day shalt thou be with me in *paradise.*"

And the prediction, "Thou wilt not leave my *soul* in hell, nor suffer thine Holy One to see corruption," was a prophecy of David, concerning the resurrection of Christ: so that he should not corrupt, according to the common lot of human nature before the re-union of the soul and body!

OF THE DAY OF JUDGMENT.

At the consummation of all things, the states of all mankind will be made perfect, and become complete, and not before.

The idea of right and wrong supposes two sides to a question, with certain consequences entailed on the principles of moral equity. Hence, the subject must presuppose a governor and the governed, with *laws* from the former as governor, to regulate the latter who are the governed; and laws imply penalties annexed; and of course a judgment, that justice may reward or punish, as the case may require.

Consequently, upon those premises the conclusion must follow, seeing mankind are conscious of a right and wrong, that a day of judgment must take place, in which the world shall be judged in righteousness. And hence the beauty of the expression—" God hath appointed a day to judge the world in righteousness by Christ Jesus;" who, as man, knows what allowance to make for human infirmities; but as God he cannot *err*, as some of our finite judges do.

Christ, the Judge upon his throne! The mediatorial office being then given up.

The angels—called the clouds of heaven, of which two hundred and two millions are but a part. And all the dead from the days of Adam to that time, from the king upon the throne to the beggar upon the dunghill, both great and small, with those who will then be alive, must appear in the grand assembly, not as curious and idle spectators, but as responsible creatures, who must be judged and rewarded according to the deeds done in the body, and receive their sentence accordingly, whether it be good or evil, and it will be done according to sound justice. The devils also, who are reserved under chains of darkness unto that day to be punished, will appear to receive their doom.

And such will be the Majesty of the Judge upon the throne, that the terrestrial heaven and the earth will flee away, and the books will be opened, and the witnesses will appear.

First: The book of nature, in which the wisdom, goodness, and power of the Supreme Governor of the world may be read.

Secondly: The book of God's remembrance will be opened. Mal. iii. Rev. xx.

Thirdly: The book of Conscience: and these two will exactly tally.

Fourthly: The book of Truth; and those who have the written word will be judged according to it. And, fifthly, the book of Life will be opened, and happy are they whose names are written in that book.

The witnesses: "Thus saith the Lord, I will be a swift witness against the adulterer, and false-swearer, and such as oppress the hireling in his wages, and turn away the stranger from his right, and fear not the Lord of Hosts."

Angels who were our guardians will be witnesses; and so will the saints of God, and particularly his ministers. The devils also will be witnesses, and so will companions in sin and wickedness, witness against each other. Yea, so plain will naked truth appear, that none will deny the facts, but must acknowledge their sentence to be just.

Jesus Christ being appointed heir of all things, shall judge in righteousness. The kingdom of heaven being prepared for men from the foundation of the world, which first was attainable by obeying the paradisaical law; and after the fall, the law of faith was substituted through a Redeemer. But the "lake of fire and brimstone" was prepared for the devil and his angels, primarily, but not for man, who is an intruder there; and hence the danger of eternal damnation! Mark iii. 29.

The righteous, who are justified by faith in this world, i. e. have received the pardon of personal sins by conformity to the will of God, and then have proven their obedience and love to Christ by keeping his commandments, and walking in the light; these, in that day of final retribution, will not only stand acquitted, but will receive a reward, not of debt but of grace, called "a crown of glory which fadeth not away."

Thus faith is brought to sight. What was a subject of faith once, has now become a subject of knowledge.

The righteous are "heirs of God and joint heirs with the Lord Jesus

Christ," who said, "to him that overcometh, will I give to sit with me in my throne." Hence the sentence, "Come, ye blessed of my Father, inherit the kingdom prepared for you from the foundation of the world; for I was an hungered, and ye gave me meat; I was thirsty, and ye gave me drink; I was a stranger, and ye took me in; naked, and ye clothed me; sick and in prison, and ye came unto me and visited me: inasmuch as ye did it unto one of the least of these, ye did it unto me."—"Well done, good and faithful servant, enter thou into the joys of thy Lord!"

But to the opposite characters, who had the power, means, and opportunities of improving, but did it not, being opposed to the moral government of the Supreme Governor of the world, those rebels must receive their deserts on equitable principles, which sentence will be, to depart into the lake of fire "prepared for the devil and his angels."

The righteous, the joint heirs with Christ in his throne, will judge angels by acquiescing in the will of God, and say amen to his justice, when he pronounces upon the devils their final doom.

Three ministers appear. The first preached for money and popularity. The second preached from contention, or backslid after his labors were attended with a blessing. The third preached from conviction of duty, in the spirit of love to Christ. What will be the difference of their reward at the day of retribution?

The first delivers his Lord like Judas, and must go with him to his place, which is purchased with the reward of iniquity. The second comes forth, saying, "Lord! Lord! I taught thus and so, and cast out devils in thy name!" But hark! "Depart from me, ye workers of iniquity."

The third, whose principle was love and duty to Christ, will shine forth as the sun in the firmament forever.

OF PROVIDENCE IN NATURE.

There is no such thing as accident in nature—as accident or chance, or chance, commonly so called, in which neither the hand of God directs or superintends, any more than there can be effects without causes, or nothing can produce something.

Nature hath received her laws from God, on the principles of mechanical necessity, still subordinate to, and dependent on himself, who is the centration of universal nature, and can alter or suspend those laws at pleasure. And hence the doctrine of miracles and providence.

There is such a thing as a primary law of nature, and also a law of a secondary result of the first. The first, as primarily established by the Creator in his works; the latter, as the necessary consequence of art or habit, by the power and agency of man.

When Hezekiah had departed from God, sickness overtook him, with the message, "Set thine house in order, for thou shalt die," &c. The king's tears and prayers denote his repentance. Then God, who knoweth how to resist the proud, and to give grace to the humble, sent the message. "I will add unto thy days fifteen years." The sentence was reversed, and as a token, the sun went back ten degrees in the dial of Ahaz. Yet means were used for his recovery.

St. Paul, after it was revealed to him that there should not be the loss of any life, only the ship, said to the soldiers, as the sailors were about to flee away in the boat, "except these abide in the ship, ye cannot be saved!"

Hazael inquired if his master would recover, and received for answer, "he may recover, but God hath showed me that he will surely die;" i. e. according to the common course of things in the order of nature, he might recover; but God saw the intention of Hazael to reverse the order of nature by art, and thus he died an unnatural death.

Man sins without permission, by stealing the time, and assuming the liberty and authority to do it, which is not prevented. For should man be prevented irresistibly from sinning, he would cease to be that creature of a noble mind, for which he was designed by his Maker, as a responsible agent, who might be capable of a reward.

God permits some of the effects of man's designs to take place, by withdrawing his restraining hand, as exemplified in the instance of Job, when the hedge round about him was removed.

Man can appoint, but God, in wisdom and mercy and justice, can disappoint, having ways and means and ends worthy of himself, both in the furtherance and accomplishment and reward of virtue, and the correction or chastisement and punishment of vice!

Afflictions to the righteous are, from the grace of God, in mercy, to wean their affections from the love of the creature, to feel dependent upon the Creator. For some people cannot bear prosperity; they would be as ships with great sails, having no ballast. Sometimes God designs to glorify himself in us, by our sufferings, to prove our graces, for the conviction of others; and again to prove us, and thereby qualify us to be as instruments of usefulness to others, in some particular sphere of action in his church; to labor from experience as well as theory. But above all, the saints are tried, that they may become meet subjects for Jerusalem, the city of the great King.

OF SPIRITS GOOD AND EVIL.

It is obvious that not only the angel of the covenant, Jehovah, the Lord Jesus Christ, who being appointed heir of all things, attends and superintends the affairs of nations and individuals, but that created angels also are employed in the important affairs of man, as the general tenor of scripture will authorize us to believe both in the Old and New Testament.

Evil angels appear to have a monarchy among themselves: Beelzebub the prince of the devils—The devil and his angels—My name is Legion, for we are many. "Then goeth he and taketh seven other spirits more wicked than himself," which argues degrees of wickedness, even among the devils. From the principles of moral evil, evil spirits are always ready to go upon evil errands, like a dog when his master unchains him. This is exemplified in the case of Job. Before the hedge was removed, Satan had no power to touch Job; but when God removed the hedge, Satan went to work—and yet he had his boundaries even then.

Satan is said to be the messenger of, and to have the power of death. God is said to have slain the first-born of Egypt by sending evil angels among them. When the spirit of God had departed from Saul, an evil spirit from the Lord came upon him. Paul was "buffeted by the messenger of Satan."

For moral evil, "God shall send them strong delusions, to believe a lie;

that they may be damned, because," &c. This is exemplified in the case of Ahab, king of Israel. God sitting upon his throne, and all the host around, said, " Who will persuade Ahab to go up to Ramoth Gilead, that he may fall there ?" None was found to go, it being contrary to the nature of a good angel to go upon a bad errand. At length one appears, saying, "I will go and be a lying spirit in the mouth of all Ahab's prophets." The Lord replied, "Thou shalt prosper and prevail—go and do it." Thus Ahab was deluded and fell in battle, because he let Benhadad go, whom he should have slain; and the Lord said, " Because thou hast let go out of thine hand a man whom I appointed for utter destruction, therefore thy life shall go for his life, and thy people for his people," as the sequel proved.

Thus Benhadad, Agag, and the Canaanites lived longer than was the will of God they should; while others do not live half their days, but die sooner than is the revealed will of God they should; for some take their own lives, and the lives of others, when it is the revealed will of God, "Thou shalt not kill."

Then that we may have angels to guide or bear us away, as Lazarus did, and, as the patriarchs, be gathered to our people above, let us lead the life of the righteous, that we may die their death, and our last end be like theirs. " Mark the perfect man, and behold the upright, for the end of that man is peace!"*

---

* Grace is a gift or favor conferred upon an unworthy object. Debt implies an *obligation*; but God is under no obligation to his creatures. Of course whatsoever he bestows must be free unmerited grace.

The kingdom of heaven prepared for man from the foundation of the world, was grace. Man by grace was at first placed in a state of trial in paradise, under a law of works, which law saith, do and live; or, as Paul saith, " If a man keep the law, he shall live by the law." But the moral faculty is so impaired and dark since the fall, that man is not adequate to keep the paradisaical law; and therefore, as says the apostle Paul, " by the deeds of the law shall no flesh be justified in the sight of God, that it may be by *grace* through faith in Christ Jesus."

Hence the law of faith, requiring righteousness by grace through faith, is fitted to the capacity and situation of fallen man. Man being capable of believing, his faith, instead of works, may be imputed to him for righteousness, and thus he may be justified through faith in Christ. And so the law of faith is brought in as the condition of his salvation; and thus he may arrive at last at Jerusalem, which kingdom " was prepared for man from the foundation of the world;" and be admitted according to the original order of things, by man's free will concurring with the commandments, in the established order of God.

The lake of fire which originally was prepared for the " devil and his angels," was never designed for man. Consequently, if man goes there, it is by stealing the time, and assuming the liberty to sin; and thereby inverting the established order of things, contrary to God's appointment; for God appointed his creatures to serve him, but never gave them permission to sin—on the contrary he positively forbids it. Therefore, by violating the moral order of God, these rebels disqualify themselves for the kingdom of God, and are thereby fitted for the lake of fire. And moral justice demands the execution.

All the favors of God are grace, but more particularly those in Christ Jesus, as a Redeemer and Saviour.

As all title to every favor was forfeited by sin, man could not make atonement for his crime, but must remain condemned by the law which he has violated, and stand exposed to all the dire consequences, which at the least must be privation, unless there be a ransom! Hence " Christ was delivered for our offences, and rose again for our justification. He suffered, the just for the unjust, that he might bring us to God." " God so loved the world he sent his Son, that the world through him might be saved." " No man taketh my life from me; I have power to lay it down, and to take it again." " Greater love than this hath no man, than that he lay down his life for his friend; and I lay down my life for the sheep" "He was wounded for our transgressions," and " the Lord hath laid upon him the iniquity of us all."

We read of the seven spirits of God, referring to the different operations.

First, The enlightening grace of God, which is saving in its nature—saving mankind from their natural darkness, by " enlightening every man who cometh into the world."

OF THE RESURRECTION.

The identity of matter cannot be annihilated, but it possesses the innate principle of immortality. For, if one particle of water could be annihilated, the whole fabric of nature might, on the same principle, sink into a state of nonentity. Matter may be changed, as it relates to time, place, and quality; yet there may be certain innate principles of matter, the identity of which can never become a part, or the properties of any other body.

Supposing a person to be dead, and eaten by a fish, which fish is eaten by a man. *Query:* Could the second person have any of the real particles of the first; and if so, who of the twain will possess them at the resurrection, as both cannot have it?

"A corn of wheat cast into the ground remaineth alone, except it die." The corn upon the stalk is not the same kernel that was sown, but rather is some of the innate principle of the corn which was sown, and is brought to perfection. "It was sown a natural body, it is raised a spiritual body; sown in weakness, raised in power; this mortal shall put on immortality, that mortality may be swallowed up of life!"

Mortality implies subject to decay. Matter may be changed, as it relates to shape and form, &c., but still it doth exist, though in a different mode and situation. And the innate principle of the identity of man cannot be changed to become the property of another; then each will retain his own, though the skin, and flesh, and blood, the coarser matter, which is supposed to change every seven years upon the living, be set aside as acquired, yet the original man remains, the other being the dregs. "But it doth not yet appear what we shall be, but this we know, we shall be like him, for we shall see him as he is." "We now see and know but in part, then shall we see as we are seen, and know as we are known!"

Secondly, Restraining grace, by which man is distinguished and prevented from becoming mere devils incarnate, through the principle of moral evil, which principle is restrained by the grace of God, and saves from those consequences which otherwise would follow.

Thirdly, justifying grace, i. e. an act whereby God, for Christ's sake, pardoneth all our sins; which is salvation from the condemnation of sin, as well as from the love and reigning power and dominion of sin.

Fourthly, The infusion of the spirit, or sanctifying grace of God, by which man is saved from his privation, and from the nature of sin.

Fifthly, Comforting, supporting, and heart-cheering grace, which saves from the gloom that otherwise would surround the mind.

Sixthly, The grace which leads, guides, and instructs into necessary truth, and into practical duty. And—

Seventhly, The peace and joy of the kingdom, which brightens up the prospect of eternity, and inspires the mind with hope beyond this life, which foretaste is the earnest of the saints' inheritance of another world, and is called "righteousness, and peace, and joy in the Holy Ghost."

As it takes two to make a bargain, so grace, or the operation of the Holy Spirit, requires the concurrence of man's free will in order for him to experience salvation from his sins. For man is not to be saved *in* his sins, but must be saved *from* his sins. Hence the propriety of the caution, "Quench not the Spirit," lest it be said in the language of Stephen, "As your fathers did, so do ye always resist the Holy Ghost," and so destruction come upon you to the uttermost. And God says: "Because I have called and ye have refused, and set at naught my counsel, I therefore will laugh at your calamities, and mock when your fear cometh." "Ephraim is joined to his idols, let him alone." And then the heart's reply: "The harvest is past, and the summer is ended, and I am not saved." And the consequence is, to receive the sentence: "Depart into the lake of fire, prepared for the devil and his angels."

OF THE LAKE OF FIRE.

The lake of fire, originally prepared for the devil and his angels, into which the wicked will be cast, at their final doom, which is the second death, and burns with fire and brimstone, is dreadful to contemplate.

A bar of iron heated, when touched with brimstone, will run down like melted lead. Supposing a person to be confined, and yet not consumed, how awful is the thought!

In this life, time is divided by days, and months, and years, but in eternity, where years shall cease to roll, how will time be then described? Suppose a damned ghost should inquire of Beelzebub the time? Beelzebub replies, "Eternity!" After a period equal to ten thousand years, multiplied by the number of sands, the waves, the drops, the stars, and then the twigs, and spires of grass, and doubled over ten thousand times, and multiplied again; still the reply would be eternity! without pleasure, and without slumber, and without end!

A trial implies a limited accountability, at the end of which, judgment and justice will take place, and prove final. Therefore, in the original established order of man, his end was heaven, his will concurring; but, by non-conformity, he inverted his own order and destination, whereby he disqualified himself for the fruition, being contaminated with moral evil, and is so hardened as to be incorrigible, and hence confirmed in his vicious disposition of heart, so as to become as the lower inhabitants, and a fit subject for that region only. For any being, being put into a place or situation for which it has no disposition, the state would afford it no pleasure; not being agreeable to its nature, it could feel no union or satisfaction in it, but would rather depart to a place more suited to itself, and be with beings more congenial to its nature. And hence it appears, that the very damned would be in more torment, was it possible for them to get to heaven in their own nature, than to remain in their damned state!

Therefore, man must be born again, while the Holy Spirit strives to change the heart by grace, or else remain incorrigible forever, and continue unhappy of course!

OF THE HEAVENLY JERUSALEM.

Though we say God filleth immensity, yet that is no argument why we may not suppose, with propriety, that there is some particular place, where the effulgent glory of God is more displayed to the view and admiration of his creatures, than in any other place? Enoch and Elijah were translated; they cannot be everywhere, of course they must be somewhere. The body of our Lord was finite, of course it does not fill immensity; it is not everywhere, of course it must be somewhere, from which we may infer a located heaven; and on the other hand a located lake of fire and brimstone!

How different those places, and also the states, and situations, and dispositions of those inhabitants!

The hundred and forty and four thousand sung a song which none could learn but they themselves, although there was such a great multitude out of all nations, kindreds, tongues, and people, which no man could number, who were redeemed from the earth by the blood of the Lamb, unto God, and joined in a song of acknowledgment and thanksgiving.

The situations of individuals are different, universally varying from each other in a greater or less degree, which must vary their experience and enjoyments, and of course the degrees of their reward in the other world, which is to be prepared according to the deeds done in their body, and this taken in conjunction with their various talents, and the different dispensations they were under.

Of the millions of different complexions and physiognomies, no two are exactly alike in the whole creation. So also experiences, varying from the different dispensations, will differ in the same universal degree. Different tempers of mind, and natural dispositions of heart. Different states of the body, health, and sickness. Different circumstances too, riches and poverty. Different periods of existence, long and short life. Different abilities, whether natural or acquired. Different situations, whether in good or bad society. Difference in the opportunity, power, and means of acquiring information, and doing acts of brotherly-kindness and charity, or being confined to solitude, as objects of want and distress!

From the nature of such diversity of cases, their rewards must vary beyond description, when it is done in equity, agreeable to the deeds done in the body. Hence the expression, "There are many mansions in my Father's house." So St. Paul, when speaking of the resurrection, "those who are Christ's at his coming"—"every one in his own order"—compares them to the sun, moon, and stars, which differ from each other in glory, or magnitude.

The smallest difference there, between two saints, will be greater than the greatest difference possibly imaginable upon earth, between the greatest monarch and the lowest peasant. And yet the infant, the smallest cup, will be perfectly satisfied, being brimfull of the joys of the kingdom of God.

The memory, which is now impaired by the fall, being clogged with a disordered, mortal body, will then be liberated and repaired, being arrived to maturity. Paul compares this life to childhood, and that to manhood, saying, "When I was a child, I thought, and understood, and spake as a child; but when I became a man, I put away childish things." "We now see as through a glass, darkly, and see and know but in part; but when that which is perfect is come, then that which is in part will be done away, then shall I see as I am seen, and know even as I am known." The act of praising God then, for redemption here in time, proves the retention of the power of recollection, and hence why not see, and know, and recollect our friends again? seeing that no power of the soul, which is of utility here, will ever be diminished hereafter, but greatly strengthened and enlarged.

Consequently, the longer our stay below, with proper faithfulness, and the greater our conflict in the Christian warfare, when we shall have overcome by the blood of the Lamb, the soul will be the more enlarged and capacitated for a greater enjoyment in the realms above. Because the greater the trials and conflicts, the greater the deliverance and salvation; which experience must excite proportionate sensations of gratitude. For God designs his dispensations, whether merciful or afflictive, to prove our obedience, that we may receive a reward at his hand as grace, but not of debt, agreeable to our improvement.

Vessels may vary in size, whether a pint, a quart, or a gallon; fill them, and each will be perfectly full, according to its degree: so the infant will be as perfectly happy as its capacity can admit and enjoy, but those who live to the age of fifteen or twenty years pass through proportionably more trials, and must feel a heart of gratitude accordingly. If so, then look at the old soldiers of the cross; and those who have "turned many to righteousness, shall shine as the stars for ever and ever." There to see, not only the first, oldest, most patient, strongest, meekest, and most perfect men of old times, but all the patriarchs, prophets, apostles, and martyrs of the Lord, with all who depart this life in his favor, and join the general assembly and church of the first-born, where they obtain joy and gladness, and sorrow and sighing shall flee away, and all tears shall be wiped from all eyes, and peace and joy shall for ever flow. There the blessed shall have correct judgment of things, and view the expanded works of God with admiration and wonder.

Therefore as God sees and knows what will be best for each and all, and in infinite wisdom grants or withholds the things of this life, we ought to be resigned to his gracious and wise dispensations, knowing that whatsoever is withheld is for the best, seeing that "no good thing shall be withheld from them who walk uprightly; but all things shall work together for good to them who love the Lord"—"For as a father pitieth his children, so the Lord pitieth them who fear him"—"For the eyes of the Lord are over the righteous, and his ears are open to their prayer, but the face of the Lord is against the wicked"—"And the Lord knows how to deliver the godly out of temptation." Then, as "trials work patience, and patience experience, and experience hope, and hope maketh not ashamed, because the love of God is shed abroad in the heart"—"Our light affliction, which is but for a moment, shall work for us a far more exceeding and eternal weight of glory"—"For the sufferings of this present world are not worthy to be compared with the joys which shall be revealed." Consequently, by "enduring unto the end in the ways of righteousness," we shall have all to hope and nothing to fear, for such have the promise of a final salvation; and such, in their last moments, shall be enabled to say with one of old, "I have fought a good fight, I have finished my course, I have kept the faith, and am ready to be offered, and the time of my departure is at hand; henceforth there is laid up for me a crown of glory, which fadeth not away, which God the righteous Judge will give me at that day; and not only me, but also to all those who love his appearing."

Considering the way, the nature, the means, the end, accomplished by creation, redemption, and salvation, the subject is worthy of God himself, and his creatures ever will have ground and cause of adoration, which never can wax old.

CONCLUSION.

From the conviction brought to my rational understanding by the divine evidence in my own soul, I am convinced and fully satisfied of the following things as facts:

First, That there is such a thing as natural evil in the world.
Secondly, That there is such a thing as moral evil also; and,
Thirdly, That natural evil is the consequence of moral evil.

Fourthly, That the new birth is not a chimera, but a divine reality, on which hangs the blissful eternity of man.

Fifthly, That Jesus Christ is more than a creature, and is the only way to God as a Saviour of men.

Sixthly, That repentance, faith, hope, and love, are experienced by the people of God.

Seventhly, That salvation is of grace, man's free will concurring, which is necessary in order to be justified here, or stand justified hereafter. But man's condemnation is of himself, by revolting against God's moral government.

Eighthly, That the knowledge of pardon is attainable here—the witness, first, of our own spirit, a consciousness of it, and then the divine evidence, by the operation of his Spirit, which witnesseth with our spirit, and gives the confirmation of it, which,

Ninthly, Is the kingdom of heaven opened in the soul, and is the earnest of the saints' inheritance, and inspires the mind with the assurance of hope beyond this life.

The destruction of Babylon is inevitable ; for the wicked must be overthrown, which they are conscious of upon serious reflection, and in the hour of danger being alarmed, like poor Volney upon the lake.

But the righteous have hope in their death, arising from the assurance of faith in Christ Jesus.

From more than twenty years' experience of the truth of the revelation of Christ in the heart, as the foundation and essence of all religion, I feel a satisfaction in resting my eternal all upon him ; and by persevering in obedience to God, to my life's end, depending on his Son as my Saviour, I believe he will receive me when I die, together with all the Israel of God, who persevere to the end, into that blissful state, where we shall unanimously join to sing the following lines :

And let this feeble body fail,
 And let it faint or die,
My soul shall quit this mournful vale,
 And soar to worlds on high ;
Shall join the disembodied saints,
 And find its long-sought rest,
That only bliss for which it pants,
 In the Redeemer's breast.

In hopes of that immortal crown,
 I now the cross sustain,
And gladly wander up and down,
 And smile at toil and pain ;
I suffer on my three-score years,
 Till my Deliverer come,
And wipe away his servant's tears,
 And take his exile home.

O what hath Jesus bought for me !
 Before my ravished eyes
Rivers of life divine I see,
 And trees of Paradise ;
I see a world of spirits bright,
 Who taste the pleasures there ;
They all are robed in spotless white,
 And conquering palms they bear.

O what are all my sufferings here,
 If, Lord, thou count me meet
With that enraptur'd host t'appear,
 And worship at thy feet ?
Give joy or grief, give ease or pain,
 Take life or friends away,
But let me find them all again
 In that eternal day !

Oh, ye professional people of God, Zion bleeds ! her walls are broken down ; therefore bestir yourselves, and let not a hypocrite be found in the gate. But, if ye love Christ, put on Christ, and prove your love by walking in the light, as he is in the light, and keeping his commandments. Adorn your profession by your life and conversation, remembering how many it is to be feared have stumbled into ruin, over the misconduct of the professors, who have wounded the cause of religion more than the writings of the deists. Get all the good you can, and do all the good to the souls and bodies of men within your power, for the Redeemer's sake, who will acknowledge the whole in the day of judgment.

But oh, ye rebels in heart, take warning! for time grows old, and the judgments of God are abroad in the earth. Fly, escape for your life! Attend to the light of grace; seek Jesus, and take the high road, and tarry not in all the plain, that you may escape the final overthrow of Babylon, and have peace and happiness for ever at Jerusalem.

A DIALOGUE

BETWEEN THE

CURIOUS AND SINGULAR.*

Curious. FRIEND *Singular*, how and where have you been for a long time?

Singular. If you are *Curious* to know, I have been in different parts, and striving through grace to do as well as I could.

C. That is well; but it is a great thing for one to say he does as he ought.

S. True—but nevertheless we should act at all times, and on all occasions, as in the immediate presence of God—as the ship on the ocean, let the course of the wind be as it may, the ship's head is aimed for the port of destination, so we should conduct for eternity, as one who must give account.

C. What makes you so *singular* in your looks, dress, and conduct, from everybody else?

S. As it relates to my looks, no two persons are exactly alike. And even your looks are peculiar to yourself, and no one is just like you. And as it relates to *dress*, if *yours* were flung into a heap with others, you could pick out your own from all the rest. And with regard to singularity, I am conscious I am never singular, merely for singularity sake.

C. Why do you *act* and travel in the manner that you do? What are your *motives* and *reasons* for so doing?

S. My *motives* are the glory of God in the salvation of immortal souls! My *reasons* are a consciousness of duty to my God and my fellow-mortals —for I wish for peace of mind!

C. Do you suppose that all mankind are in the wrong, and none are right but you?

S. I suppose many are right in many things; and all are liable to err —some are more right than others. And as it relates to myself, no man should be our pattern further than he follows Christ. Also proper behavior should vary according to times and circumstances.

C. Then I suppose you conclude you are the most right; and how is it that none have found out so right a way before?

S. We are given to understand that there are various gifts in the Christian church; and yet all by the same spirit—and every man in his own order, at the coming of Christ. Of course we should have the spirit of

---

* These dialogues are founded upon circumstantial facts.

our station in the church of Christ. And this sphere of action I believe to be mine; in it, God gives me inward peace; out of it, I believe I should lose my usefulness to others.

C. Then you are for an inspired ministry, and a spiritual church. What do you think of all the religious societies; are not some of these "The Church of Christ?"

S. To style one sect "The Church of Christ," is to save that party at the expense of all the rest; and of course savors of religious bigotry, tyranny and superstition—as the preceding ages have horribly exemplified.—Whereas the book of truth informs us, that "God is no respecter of persons, but in every nation he that feareth God, and worketh righteousness, is accepted with him," and shall join in the song of salvation, with the society above, "out of every nation, kindred, tongue, language, and people." Of course there may be bad and good people among all sects.

C. Suppose all Christians should do like you, there would be no form or order in the world, and of course, confusion would come in at the door.

S. To say "if *all* should do like me," you might as well say, on the same principles, where would be the carpenters if all were blacksmiths? It is no just mode of reasoning. As the different branches of mechanism are necessary for society, so these different gifts are necessary as the eye, hand, and foot, &c., to constitute one perfect body; as a whole is composed of parts, and the parts collectively form one whole. As to confusion—what is termed confusion with and by men, may be order with God, who sees not as men see.

C. In what do you believe and preach?
S. I believe in the deity of Jesus Christ.*

---

* It being both idolatry and blasphemy to give divine honors to a mere creature, Jesus Christ must be viewed in a more noble light.

Eternity, immensity, and *infinity,* are words we have heard and can repeat; but who can fix any definite meaning to them? Though they are in common use, yet they are words fit only to be applied to the Deity, and ought not to be applied anywhere else; for they cannot be otherwise used without palpable absurdities, and nonsensical contradictions And such abuses have too long been existing in the world already!

An infinite, eternal Being of immensity! What can man know of Him, the Causeless Causator, but by revelation, inspiration or manifestation?

How can man worship his Maker with his understanding, provided he be in the darkness of ignorance, so far, as neither to know nor understand any thing about it?

The world by wisdom know not their Maker. He is a Spirit, and is spiritually discerned. "What man knoweth the things of man, save the spirit of a man which is within him?" And how shall a man know the mind and will of his Maker, but by revelation?

If the Maker of man be a spirit, how shall his will be revealed, so as to be understood, but by inspiration?

Should his voice be heard from the sky, over the whole world, who could bear the sound? The clash of ten thousand pieces of artillery redoubled, would be comparative silence! Well might the Jews at Mount Sinai request Moses should speak to them, the voice of the Lord being so dreadful in their ears. The human family is so numerous, and their cases so many and so various, and their languages so different—as twenty in New Orleans—that there could not any thing be heard distinctly, but all would be nonsense and confusion.

Hence the tender care and goodness of God, the Maker and Governor, over man his creature, in sending the influence of his Holy Spirit, to operate upon the mind and guide man upon the road to Jerusalem; so that without terror he may be enlightened to understand his Maker's will, and inspired with evidence and conviction on the all-important subject.

The Angel of the Covenant, was not a created angel; but was termed Jehovah, which name the Jews consider as implying all the divine attributes; and therefore will not speak it, lest it should not be done with suitable reverence; and so take this majestic name in vain, and not be guiltless. And hence they will write it only.

The word Lord, printed in small capitals in the Old Testament, should be Jehovah; which the Jews understand to imply the divinity of the Messiah, to be manifested in the world as the Saviour of men.

C. Do you feel willing to depend your everlasting welfare on Jesus Christ?

S. To see one malefactor put confidence in another, who is under the same condemnation, to save him, exhibits great faith; and also a noble opinion, as exemplified in the instance of Calvary. To trust in a creature to save me, I cannot; but to trust in Christ, according to the gospel, gives me peace, and brightens up the prospects of eternity before me.

C. But supposing Christ was a deceiver; then he was only an impostor, and of course you are under a delusion.

S. The worst of opposers to Christianity admit that Christ, as man, was a good man; of course no real good man will be a deceiver: if so, he was no impostor. Therefore, according to this admittance, his religion may be genuine and real. Again, it is too uncharitable to suppose and conclude, that all who have died so happy and triumphant in the love and religion of Jesus Christ were under a delusion. And if it be once admitted that it was a reality with even but one instance, the point is gained.

C. How do you know that there ever was such a person as Jesus Christ upon earth?

S. Observe the account of Josephus, of Pilate to the Senate of Rome, our dates, with other histories, as well as scripture. Also, the many circumstantial proofs, as the letters of Pliny to Trajan, which Christian opposers admit to be genuine; with the many efforts to root out Christianity from the earth in vain! Christianity has, does, and will prevail!*

C. Admitting that Jesus Christ did exist, and was a good man, yet the resurrection may be fabulous, and Christianity of course a deception.

S. On the *resurrection* and *ascension* of Jesus Christ turns the whole affair. That the body was entombed and missing, all agree.

C. The body of Christ being gone from the vault, possibly he played the *possum*, and only feigned himself to be dead, and deceived them, and at night made his escape; and hence a false report was circulated that he was risen from the dead.

S. Nay, such talk will never do! Consider the loss of blood from the thorns, the scourge, and nails, &c. These wounds so long undressed must have terminated in dissolution. Again, the orders were to break his legs, but when they saw he was dead, they forebore to obey, lest

---

Whatsoever God, the Causeless Causator, does, is done in and through Jehovah—the Lord Jesus Christ, who is called the Son of God.

Thus—He existed in the beginning as the Word—"I am." God hath appointed Him heir of all things—by whom he made the worlds—by him all things were made, and without him was not any thing made that was made.

Man was in the hand of Christ before moral evil was in the world. And when man fell he still was in the hand of Christ, who called unto him in the cool of the day—which exhibits the beauty of those words,—"God so loved the world, that he sent his Son into the world, that whosoever believeth in him should not perish, but have everlasting life—for God sent not his Son into the world to condemn the world, but that the world through him might be saved." Hence, "We love God, because he first loved us. No man knoweth the Father save the Son, and he to whom the Son will reveal him."

Christ is the manifestation of God, through and from whom the Holy Spirit proceeds, to enlighten by his quickening influence, and guide, comfort, and sanctify mankind.

Thus there is an inward manifestation, by a revelation of Christ in the heart; corresponding to the outward manifestation given in the days of his flesh!

And it is not possible that any man should sincerely pray to God to be taught by him, and if he hath a Son, to reveal him, in his heart; and not find a solution of the query to his own satisfaction.

* There is divine witness in my own soul.

they should be exposed to ridicule for breaking the legs of a dead man to prevent him from running away. And yet to put it beyond all doubt that Christ was dead, one of them up with a spear and run it through his heart; which puts it beyond all dispute he was really dead. Moreover, consider for a moment, a cell or prison hewed out in the centre of a rock, and there in prison confined, with a stone door, so large and weighty that three females thought they could not roll it away; and this door confined and sealed, and also a military guard placed to keep the same with all safety, and if any thing was amiss, must pay the forfeit with their lives! Hence, is obvious the natural impossibility of such deception, imposition, and escape.

C. But the apostles stole the body of Jesus Christ, and hid it, and then propagated a lie, that it was risen and ascended.

S. It was naturally impossible for such a thing to exist, if we, in conjunction with the foregoing circumstances, consider that the apostles could have no access to the vault; second, no temptation to steal the body; third, they were not moneyed men to bribe the guard; fourth, though an individual may be bribed, yet I do not recollect to have read, or heard of a whole guard being bribed; fifth, it was death under the Roman law to sleep on guard; sixth, if the guard had been sleepy, the natural conclusion is, they would have set or lain on the stone door, or contiguous to it, so that no one could approach without giving alarm. Now, for the seal to be broke, and the stone removed, without waking the soldiers when in such heaps and piles, would argue an unnatural sleep, and of course a miracle. Therefore, to obviate the idea of one miracle on one side, you must admit and argue one on the other side; of course your argument proves too much, like the Indian's tree, which was so straight it leaned a little over the other way. What is a miracle, but something unnatural, providentially?

C. But the vault was undermined by the apostles, and the body taken away through a subterraneous passage!

S. Nay, but it would have taken a longer space of time to undermine the vault by digging through a rock, than the space of time the body was in the tomb.

C. Some other body arose, and not the body of Christ.

S. Nay, for man before was never there entombed, of course none could arise therefrom but the body of Christ.

C. The account *contradicts* itself. "For as Jonah was in the belly of the whale three days and three nights, so shall the Son of man be in the heart of the earth," whereas he was not in the vault seventy-two common hours.

S. We should not contend for *words*, but seek for *facts*, of course take people as they mean. The Jews did not divide time as we do, into twenty-four hours; but the daylight into twelve hours, and the night into watches. Our time begins and ends at midnight, but the Jews at sunset. "The evening and morning were the first day." Any circumstance which we express by day, or include any part of what *we* call the twenty-four hours, in their mode of expression included the day and night. The body was entombed before sunset on Friday, continued there on the Jewish sabbath, (our Saturday,) which ended at sunset. The third day had commenced before the body arose. Therefore, take their meaning according to their mode of expression, and the account will hold good, and of course may be received and held as sacred truth.

C. If the resurrection of Jesus Christ be real, who saw him after he arose?

S. The apostles and hundreds of others.

C. If faith in his ascension be so necessary for salvation, why do we not have better proof thereof than the say-so of a few poor fishermen?

S. A fisherman can tell the truth as well as any one else, and of course relate what he saw. Reasonable evidence should be considered and received as proof to a reasonable mind. Therefore, if in the most consequential cases, even between life and death, two or three substantial witnesses, where there is no evidence to the reverse, are considered sufficient; then the evidence of the fishermen may be credited as reasonable and proper testimony.

C. They did not believe their own testimony, and of course were not sincere.

S. Look at the circumstance impartially. They could not be prompted by either honor or lucre to bear such testimony, but to the reverse; their personal safety would be in jeopardy thereby. The only reason they assigned for their testimony was *duty ;* and they evidenced their sincerity therein by perseverance, and sealing the same with their *blood.* What greater evidence can we desire?

C. Why did not Christ ascend in the view of all the inhabitants of Jerusalem, and so have city testimony, instead of a few individuals?

S. Admitting he had ascended in the view of all the people of Jerusalem, that would not have mended the matter, for the people of Rome, who then exceeded three millions, might have made the same objection;— " Jews we know to be deceitful, why receive it only on their say-so?" And if all people then living had beheld the sight, we were not living, and of course we might make the same objection. " Why receive it on the say-so and tradition of our forefathers; why were we not favored with the sight?" Thus, to satisfy an unreasonable mind, Christ must come a second time, to die, rise, and ascend, and then you might upbraid God with cruelty to his Son. Thus, the objection leads to error, being only founded in error, and of course is an unreasonable objection, and plead for but by unreasonable men. There is not a circumstance of antiquity so well authenticated and substantiated with concomitant circumstances, as the resurrection of the Lord Jesus Christ; of course, if we are not to give credit to the same, we must bid adieu to every thing which we have not personally *sensible* evidence of!

C. What do you think about the *covenant* made between the Father and the Son from all eternity?

S. From, implies a starting place, as the American Independence was dated *from* the year 1776; so of course, if your covenant (which is not to be found in scripture) be *from eternity,* then eternity is to be dated from the *time* of making that contract or bargain, in which God, you say, gives the major part of mankind to Satan, and only leaves a few for his Son.

C. What next?

S. Moral evil, *moral good,* accidental (or providential) evil, accidental (or providential) good, natural evil, natural good!

C. What is the difference?

S. Moral good implies good motives—a pure intention to do good only. Here is virtue in the *mind!*

Moral evil, evil motives, an intention to do wrong, to commit that which is not agreeable to right rectitude, but repugnant to equity and the law of righteousness, by following the *inclination* contrary to the dictates of a better *judgment.*

Accidental evil, evil consequences unforeseen, and unavoidable, of course, can be accounted for only on the doctrine of providence. "Is there any evil in the city and the Lord hath not done it?" Not *sin*, but afflictions and calamities, &c.

Accidental good, which can be ascribed only to a superintending Providence, as exemplified in the instance of Joseph. Moral evil in them, but providential good resulted to him. All ye who love and trust in God, be resigned, remembering it is written, "In all thy ways acknowledge thou him, and he shall sustain thee." "For thou wilt keep him in perfect peace whose mind is stayed on thee"—*God.*

Natural good, good comparatively; as the difference of dispositions, &c. Some dispositions are more sweet, even, and agreeable, than others. Not that one is more holy by nature than another, for all are alike by nature fallen; but the difference of disposition is rather arising or occasioned by the various differences of connection between the soul and body, effects produced from parental sensations.

Natural evil, such evil as will accrue or follow us whether we be good or bad, not as the effect of our own conduct, but the necessary consequence of the fall, as headache, toothache, &c. In children, some things which some call sin, is only natural evil; but not moral evil, until they come to mature years to act from motives, and are capable of reflection for themselves.

C. What about the doctrine of justification?

S. There are four distinct justifications* spoken of in scripture.

C. What are the differences?

S. The first is infantile justification, acquittance from Adamic guilt by the gift or merit of Christ. The second, adult justification by faith, i. e. acquittance from the guilt and condemnation of personal sin. Third, justification by faith and works together, after pardon. Fourth, justification by works in the day of judgment, without faith, but only as the evidence, or fruits of it. As "every man is to be rewarded according to the deeds done in the body;" evil deeds, moral evil, will have a bad reward; but good deeds, moral good, (flowing from the love of God, through faith, which purifies the heart in this life,) shall there and then in the day of judgment have a good reward, "For God hath appointed a day to judge the world in righteousness, by Jesus Christ."

Thus by Christ, God was pleased to create the world; and secondly, by Christ to redeem the world; and thirdly, by Christ to judge the world in righteousness. "And shall not the judge of all the earth do right?"

Compare Heb. i. 2. John i. 3. with iii. 16, 17. Acts xvii. 31.

C. What state are infants in by nature? Pure as Adam when he came from the hand of his Creator, or as graceless as devils?

---

* Justification signifies acquittance with approbation.

S. Neither. Adam was made, or created in the image of God; but he lost it by sin, and of course it must be restored by divine inspiration, or infusion, and all who have divine nature must receive it by inspiration. Man is but a man, and can propagate his own species only: he cannot propagate divinity, any more than a stream can rise higher than its fountain, or an effect be more noble than the cause which produced it; for holiness is not an inherent principle of parentage, but is derived from God only.

Devils receive no favors from the hand of God, which cannot be said in truth of infants; but, "as judgment came upon all men to condemnation, by the disobedience of one; even so the free gift came upon all men to justification of life," "by the obedience of one, Christ Jesus." Rom. v. 18.

C. What about justification by faith?

S. We nowhere read about "the robes of Christ's imputed righteousness," in all the Bible: of course it can be found only in the imagination of those who talk and tell about a "covenant made between the Father and the Son from all eternity," as if they were there present, and heard the bargain made, and were personal witnesses to the affair.

We read that "Abraham believed God," and his faith was counted, or imputed to him for righteousness.

Here observe—God spoke to Abraham, and it was Abraham's duty to give credit to the Divine testimony. Abraham did so, and acted consonant therewith. This act of faith (which was an act of the mind) was right, and Abraham was justified in it; his faith, i. e. the act, was counted or imputed to him for righteousness!

C. Why was the act imputed to him for righteousness?

S. Because the *principle* and *act* were right, and it was the lowest and only act that he could do that was right, in consequence of the fall; and he was liable to mistake in judgment, and from thence to err in practice. Therefore by the deeds of the Paradisaical law, shall no flesh be justified, that it may be by grace, through faith. And hence, the law of faith is fitted to man's necessity. Christ is the *meritorious* cause of man's redemption, but faith the *instrumental* cause of man's salvation. So God can be just, and the justifier of him that believeth; as the equitable Ruler and Governor of the world, who judgeth in righteousness. Rom. v. i—4.

C. Have we any account of any more being justified by faith?

S. Yes. Rom. v. 1, "Being justified by faith, we have peace with God through our Lord Jesus Christ."

C. Why need an adult be justified by faith?

S. Because he hath forfeited his infantile justification, by his own personal sin, by not acting and obeying at all times the light of grace.

C. How am I to be justified by faith?

S. Submit to the righteousness of God; for in the act of submission there is dependence implied, and where there is dependence there is reliance, and where there is reliance there hope springs up, as the fruit or effect of faith.

C. Am I to merit salvation by my own works? or shall I sit on the stool of do-nothing?

S. If one should tell another to pull up milling-stalks one day, he would give him a thousand dollars, he cannot say he has merited the thousand dollars, for he has not earned it: therefore he will not claim it on the principle of his own merit, but by the other's grace and promise! Therefore, we are not to sit on the "stool of do-nothing," but up and do the will of God, for, " Blessed are they who do his commandments, that they may have right to the tree of life." All we have we received, and of course we owe the whole: therefore, we have nothing that we can call our own: consequently after we have done all, we cannot bring God into debt. Hence we must say, we are unprofitable servants, because we can do no more than is our duty to do.

C. What about justification by faith, and works after pardon?

S. We must prove our faith and love to Christ by keeping his commandments and walking in the light, the duty to our fellow-mortals according to our ability and opportunity, so we should act the part of the good Samaritan, "doing as we would be done by"—also, suffer, as well as do the will of God; and thus, " by *works* shall *faith* be made perfect," and " a cup of cold water, *given* in the name of ——— shall in no wise lose its reward."

A man who hath a wife like Peter, and is called to preach, must undertake it by *faith;* the practice is *work*. Thus his works flow from faith, as all Christian works should do, and we should then be justified in them; as Christ said, "No man hath forsaken houses, wife, &c. for my sake and the gospel, but he shall receive an hundred fold, (i. e. ten thousand per cent,) in *this present world*, besides the promise of the life to come."

Thus he is "justified by works, and not by faith only," James ii. 24; and so, "He that endureth to the end shall be saved," saith the Lord Jesus.

C. What about justification by works in the day of judgment without faith, but only as the evidence or fruits of it?

S. Matt. xii. 36, 37. We are given to understand, that " for every idle word, man must give an *account* thereof in the day of Judgment," and "by thy *words* thou shalt be *justified*, and by thy *words* thou shalt be condemned!!!" It is nowhere said in all the Bible, that *faith* shall be called in question in the day of judgment, but only our deeds, works, &c.

Therefore, our own past sins must be pardoned, and after pardon our conduct flowing from the love of God will meet the Divine approbation. Thus the moving principle being good, the conduct flowing from it is good; hence the judge will say, " *Well* done, good and *faithful* servant, enter thou into the joy of thy Lord." But remember, the Judge will tell no lies, of course he will not pronounce them good, unless they are so in a moral point of view; for God looks at the *heart*, and judges according to *intentions*. He will not pronounce them faithful unless they are so in reality. Therefore, prepare to meet thy God!

C. Friend Singular, are the Christian's robes *his own*, or Christ's? Can a Christian lose them?

S. Rev. vii. 14 and 15. " These ——— have washed *their robes*, and made them white in the blood of the Lamb." T-h-e-i-r does not spell CHRIST, therefore the robes were their own. Chap. xvi. 15. " Blessed is he that *watcheth* and *keepeth* his (not Christ's) garments, lest he walk naked." Why pronounce him blessed for keeping his own garments, if he could not lose them?

C. I thought our own robes were only as filthy rags!

S. Admitting that our own robes were as filthy rags, what would be the cause of such filth but sin? And what can it argue but the need of a washing or a change? Justification by faith is what God does *for us* by the death of his Son; but regeneration is what he does *in us*, by the operation of his Holy Spirit. The first is the *pardon* of our sins, the latter is the *sanctification* of our nature to God.

C. Where and how are our robes to be cleansed?

S. Zech. xiii. 1. We read that "a fountain is opened to the house of David for sin and uncleanness;" and in the first chapter of Isaiah and 16th verse, "Wash you, make you clean; put away the evil of your doings from before mine eyes; cease to do evil; learn to do well." By the command, "Wash you, make you clean," &c. certainly cannot mean to sit still on the stool of do-nothing.

C. Have we any account in all the Bible that somebody got to heaven in their own robes by washing them?

S. Hark! *These* are they which came out of great tribulation, and *have washed their robes and made them* white in the blood of the Lamb; therefore are they before the throne of God. Rev. vii. 14, 15.

C. But do you not suppose that if I am one of the *elect;* if I get drunk, cheat and steal, that as Jesus Christ was temperate, honest, and benevolent, my sins will be *imputed* to him, and his acts of righteousness will be *imputed* to me, and be as acceptable to God for me, as if he did it?

S. No: for Jesus Christ did not come to save his people *in* their sins, but *from* their sins.

C. How am I to be saved from my sins?

S. By hearing, obeying, and partaking of the Spirit of God; for such as *hear* and *obey*, are pronounced *wise*, and except ye partake of the spirit of God, ye cannot be happy, for God is the only fountain of lasting happiness.*

C. It is hard to give up reason to faith!

S. What is sound reason but good sense improved? And for matter of fact to be embraced or admitted, is not repugnant to sound reason. And the gospel requires you to believe nothing but what is truth.

C. I admit the idea of a God, but not of miracles or inspiration.

S. To smell, see, taste, feel, or hear God by the bodily senses, you cannot; and if he be not revealed to your mind, how and why do you admit or believe he exists?

The existence of a world is not the effect of nature, but of God's power. To deny the doctrine of miracles is to deny the work of creation; because, to create is an act of divine power, and to deny the work of creation is to deny the Creator, because the *act* gives the *character*. Hence you must be an atheist. Again: as nobody was present when God made the world, we have not so much as lawful or human evidence to adduce. Of course the subject of creation is a doctrine of miracles, revelation, and faith.

C. Will not the doctrine of Universalism do?

S. We read of some who have never forgiveness, but are in danger of eternal damnation, Mark iii. 29.

C. "Christ preached to the spirits in prison."

S. True; viz. "while the ark was preparing." But said God on that occasion, "My Spirit shall not always strive with man," but during the

---

* Rom. viii. 9 and 14.

three days that the body of Christ was in the vault, his soul was not among the lower inhabitants, for he said to the thief on the cross, "To-day thou shalt be with me in Paradise;" and the passage in Acts, "Thou wilt not leave my soul in hell," &c., was only the accomplishment of what the Psalmist saw prophetically of the reunion of the soul and body, before the body putrefy. Hell is not the eternal torment of the damned, but is the intermediate space of time which passes between death and the resurrection, as yesterday swallowed up in following time as to-day commenced.

The "lake of fire and brimstone" is to be the place of their torment, (into which hell will be cast, or lost,) originally "prepared for the devil and his angels." A bar of steel heated, with a roll of brimstone added, will run down like melted lead! If this be but a comparison, what must be the reality?

C. What about the doctrine of once in grace always in grace?

S. Though we read that "none can pluck them from the hand of God, or any creature separate them from the love of Christ," &c., yet we do not read but what they may go off themselves, and separate themselves, by their own sins, from the love and favor of God.

N. B. If a man can believe himself but everlastingly elected unconditionally, and then fall into disgrace, he might be a dangerous man. How? The human law will not deter him from his deep-laid scheme, and the law of honor will not influence him, and the divine law cannot punish him; of course he may be a dangerous man, as he can give no assurance of fidelity. Thus this doctrine hath a baneful influence on society, by destroying moral obligation.*

C. Friend Singular, I must soon leave you; have you any pertinent advice to give?

S. Friend Curious, as you have asked many questions, I would here remark, that contempt, when defeated, begets wonder and admiration, which, through prejudice, degenerates into envy; which last, when indulged, begets malice and revenge, the most baneful and detestable of all dispositions contaminated with moral evil. Therefore remember that report is as the rolling snowball, enlarging as it goes; but do you be cautious neither to add to nor rejoice at the misfortunes of others, nor busy yourself in circulating *reports*, lest it cause you shame or tears afterwards, when it is too late to prevent the consequence which may follow, but live for eternity by "watching unto prayer."

---

* It is the *sister* doctrine of the pope's "indulgences," that is, pardons, not only of sins past and present, but those which are to come, by giving ten shillings and sixpence to the cardinal!

HINTS

ON THE FULFILMENT

OF

PROPHECY.

SEEING we have arrived to an important period of time, in which the whole world appears to be convulsed in a political, commercial, and religious point of view, I am led to think the prophecies are fulfilling, and induced, for the benefit of the Christians, if by any means it can be a help to them, under God, in the approaching calamities, to send the following abroad.

It is rational to admit that the most important things would be the most proper objects of prophecy; for to prophesy of things less consequential would be less noble, and of course less interesting. Consequently, the most extraordinary things would be the most proper subjects for prophecy, because they would be more interesting to the welfare of society.

Marcus, or Napoleon Bonaparte, having become an extraordinary character, it is not unreasonable to admit him with his coherents, or concomitants, to be found in scripture prophecy; if so, it is for our benefit, in whose days the prophecies are fulfilled: consequently, it is our duty to examine and see, that we may derive the benefit intended thereby.

The most plain, natural, literal, and easy interpretation and fulfilment, is generally the best, and surest not to err; therefore, in casting a few short hints, I shall follow this plan, which I hope the reader will peruse with attention, and a mind suitably affected God-ward.

The woman spoken of in Revelation xii. 1, in heaven, clothed with the sun, a crown of twelve stars upon her head, and the moon beneath her feet, may refer to the militant church—her being clothed with the sun, to divine righteousness; the stars, to the apostles and succeeding ministers; in heaven, the favor of God, and heavenly places in Christ Jesus, (Eph. ii. 6;) the moon, the world beneath her feet; her cries, the spiritual groans and travail of the church for her prosperity; and the child, Christ Jesus—not to be considered there in his person, but in his kingdom; and the great red dragon, elsewhere called the devil and Satan, seeking their destruction, must be so interpreted as to make common sense—therefore, to be considered as a wicked being in the spiritual world, and yet having concerns in the human world, interfering in human affairs, and having government over such as will be led by his diabolical influence.

Therefore, the seven heads and ten horns, and seven diadems, or crowns, which belonged, not to the horns, but to the heads, which belonged to the dragon, must or may be literally applied to "Rome pagan," without any thing twisted or far-fetched.

The seven heads being applied to Rome pagan, we find just so many different forms of supreme government to exist, viz.: 1, kingly; 2, consular; 3, dictators; 4, tribunes; 5, decemviri; 6, triumviri; 7, imperial. And a diadem, or crowns, which denote supreme authority in prophecy, is applied to each of them in succession; but nothing is here said about the power of the horns, for these were united then under those heads, particularly the last.

Here, observe, the civil, military, and ecclesiastical authority was at their disposal; consequently, being under diabolical influence, were led agreeable to the will of the dragon, or devil, as far as God permitted; hence the church was persecuted, as in the person of Herod against the child Jesus, when the children of Bethlehem were slain; and various other instances which might be cited, as the ten persecutions, &c.

The dragon is spoken of as in actual existence, and no mention is made of his rise and ascent, as is of the beast. But why? Because, when John wrote, he was in actual existence,* whereas the two beasts were to come in future.

The woman exhibits two flights: the first, she *fled*, the second, she *flew*. The first implies, as it were, on foot; but the second was as on eagle's wings into the wilderness. The first and second places are not the same, though the wilderness may be considered the same wilderness state. The first place is that side of the Danube next to England, which received the gospel, &c., and protection was given. The second place I apprehend to be America. The dragon poured out a flood after the woman, and the earth helped the woman, &c., which by commentators is admitted and acknowledged as applicable to human governments, giving religious toleration and affording protection. If so, the prophecy, however much it may have been fulfilled as it relates to Europe and the east, is more perfectly fulfilled under the American government. For, instead of a "law religion" for a national church, by the establishment of one sect, and the rest only "tolerated," universal "right of conscience" is established, agreeable to the "Creator's law of nature," which comports with the divine government.

The first *beast* which is spoken of in Rev. xiii. 1, 2, &c., rising out of the sea, is literally applicable to *Rome papal*, without any thing twisted or far-fetched.

· The ancients supposed Europe to be an island; hence, in prophecy it is styled the *sea*, to distinguish it from Asia the main, which, in prophecy, is styled the *earth*.

The papal authority is well known to have begun in Europe; and now observe a primary cause.

---

* One of the Roman emperors carried the dragon in his colors. After the empire was divided into the eastern and western, the Turks overran and occupied Constantinople, so called from Constantine. But more will be said of the Ottoman empire, which must be dated from 606, the year that Mahomet took to his cave, and the pope was styled "universal bishop."

Constantine the Great,* who ascended to the imperial dignity in Rome pagan, filled up the last stage of that existence; and hence is styled the "tail of the dragon," and said to "draw a third part of the stars of heaven, and cast them to the earth." How? By abolishing paganism, and establishing Christianity as the national religion! Hence, a flood of honor, riches, grandeur, and popularity, proved an inducement to many, who were called and compared to stars, (Rev. i. 16-20;) being influenced first by noble principles and heavenly-mindedness, but were now attracted and cast to the earth—that is, become earthly-minded, and answered the purpose of an ambitious, designing man: hence popery, being now in embryo, sprang into existence about the year 606, for the pope was then styled "Bishop of Bishops," or "Universal Bishop;" but it did not arrive to full perfection till about 1077.

Though this *beast* is said to have *seven heads*, yet no *crowns* are ascribed to them, but to the *ten horns;* whereas, with the dragon it was otherwise; which shows that this prophecy is more recent, viz. not barely after the division of the empire into what is called the eastern and western empires, but when it was so divided as to have ten separate and distinct governments—as ten crowns are ascribed to the ten horns; which was really the case since the division, but not under the pagan Roman emperors, or prior.†

This beast, though *no* crowns are ascribed to him, seeing the ecclesiastical authority took lead of the civil, yet "a name of blasphemy" is said to be "upon his heads;" that is, assuming the title and prerogative of God, and lording it over the consciences of men, which is blasphemous in the full and highest sense. "And the dragon gave him his power, and seat, and great authority." Observe the transfer here. The papacy exercised that civil and ecclesiastical power which was exercised by the supreme government in Rome pagan; which transfer the reader must keep in mind.

About the year 1077 he comes to his full power. He excommunicates the emperor, ascends the throne, and begins to reign without control.‡

Here it is remarkable that Mr. Wesley, in the year 1754, calculated the end of the "forty and two months" of this beast, (chap. xiii. 4, 5,) to the very *time!*—1810; which was fifty-six years previous: also, John Fletcher made a calculation in every respect like the above. After which the second beast should appear, "coming up" gradually, and yet progres-

---

* From this image-Saviour on the cross in his army, began the image-worship in the church; first Christ, then the Virgin Mary, &c.

† Constantine the Great died in 337, which was the time of the tail of the dragon. Shortly after, the empire was divided into the eastern and western empires; and in 355, Rome was plundered, and immediately after, it appears, the *ten horns* began to exhibit their crowns as follows: 1st. Huns, in Hungary, 356; 2d. Ostrogoths, 377; 3d. Visigoths, 378; 4th. Franks, 407; 5th. Vandals, 407; 6th. Sueves, 407; 7th. Burgundians, 407; 8th. Herules and Rugians, 476; 9th. Saxons, or Britons, 476; 10th. Longobards, 526.

‡ The seven heads of this beast are said to be seven hills; and yet one of them was *wounded.* Hence it is evident, that the heads are more than the seven hills of Rome, because a mere hill could not be so wounded. Four of the hills have been used by the popes, &c., which may imply four heads in succession, viz. 1st. Cælian had on it the Lateran; 2d. The Vatican, with St. Peter's Church; 3d. The Quirinal, with the church of St. Mark and Quirinal Palace; 4th. The Esqueline Hill, with the temple of St. Maria Maggiore: here I add Bonaparte's pope in the church of St. Maria Major, for the 5th and 6th. The reader must keep in mind the transfer to London. But the seventh head is yet to come, and that from the bottomless pit, (Rev. xvii. 8,) which future time must exhibit.

sively, "out of the earth," viz. Asia, and exercise all the power of the first beast that was before him. Thus, we discover a continuation or succession, in order, from pagan Rome to papal Rome, so to our day. (Rev. xii. 3—xiii. 1, 2, 11. Compare xvii. 12.)

Bonaparte went to Egypt; thence to Palestine, which was in Asia: he there rose to eminence mentally; for it was there, it appears, that the *grand design* was concerted. He retreated, and returned to France, where he actually and really brought it into execution: first, by seizing the civil authority, and using the ecclesiastical to answer his designs; and, though a degree of toleration was allowed, yet he remodelled popery, and made a pope to accomplish his own intentions.

A part of the agreement was: first, the pope should issue no bull within Bonaparte's jurisdiction without his consent; second, should ordain any man to office that Bonaparte should appoint, upon producing a certificate from one priest that the man was sound in the faith; third, the education of children was taken from all except married persons; fourth, a priest should take nothing from the people, but receive a salary from the revenue—a rector eighty pounds, and a curate fifty pounds. Thus the establishment was more nominal than real, and tended to make the priestly office contemptible to a man of letters.

The pope began to grow too strong in power to answer Bonaparte's designs. Accordingly, in 1809, he passed an edict that on the first day of January, 1810, the pope should be stripped of all civil power and influence, and remain only a limited ecclesiastic, and that Italy should be annexed to France as a French province, and Rome become the second city in the empire. Upon this the pope excommunicated Bonaparte, under the authority of God Almighty, Paul and Peter—disappears; but he is taken under military arrest: and so *he* is fallen.*

Again, Joseph Bonaparte passed an edict in Spain, that all ecclesiastical power, of every name, grade, and nature, except what was in the throne, should cease the same day, viz. January, 1810. Since which the Inquisition has been abolished, in a measure, and also in Portugal, &c.

Some attempt to find fault, because scripture prophecy does not point out the year and day; but let it be remembered, that when the prophecies were written, our mode of computing time was not in use; therefore, it must be exhibited in emblems to answer the substance.

Many persons suppose the ten horns spoken of, (Rev. xvii. 12,) referred to the horns or governments of Europe supporting the papal authority, but the idea is founded in error; because these horns are said to have *no* kingdom as yet, but received power, which was delegated to act in conjunction with the beast. Hence, it is evident that this must be applied and considered as the same horns that were in Rome pagan, then Rome papal, but now under the influence of the second beast, which exerciseth all the power of the first beast that was before him.

Henry the Eighth, of England, who was styled the "Defender of the Faith," when a papist, shook off the papal power, and retained the kingdom and title in his own hand; which shows that the kingdom was his

---

* The "forty-two months" then ended—having lost his power, which was given him in 1143, when he wore the triple crown—three of the ten horns of Daniel. The same year the power of choosing a pope was taken from the people, and lodged in the cardinals alone. The intermediate time was just 666 years, which was the number of the beast.

and not the pope's. This was applicable also to all those governments that acknowledged the papal power: but these kings have no kingdom, and yet they are kings in name and authority ; which shows that the prophecy is applicable to the present state of Europe thus far, and nowhere else.*

King George's coronation oath was to keep down popery by his armies and fleets ; and yet we find that the popish religion is established in Canada by his royal assent and authority, which the reader must keep in mind ; second, the last life-guards that the pope had, previous to his banishment by the order of the council of five hundred, (when Bonaparte was upon the Italian expedition,) were Englishmen, and for which they received medals from the pope ; third, the last relicts of *old* popery, where the inquisition law remained in force, viz. Spain and Portugal, the British are now, and have been, giving their aid thereto with all their might ; which argues, that as they are the last who are fighting for the *old* dregs, they necessarily step into their shoes, and merit a transfer.

Babylon, mentioned in Revelation : the term is borrowed and transferred from Babylon of old to Rome ;† consequently, when Babylon sunk in the east she rose in the west. If a transfer be admitted once, if need be, it may be admitted again with propriety, without any thing twisted or far-fetched.

Now I ask, where can a city be found, the destruction of which would cause such a general cry and lamentation, &c., to commence, and effect the whole world, as is described in the eighteenth chapter of Revelation, from the 10th to the 19th verses inclusive ; which the reader must pay attention to.

Rome, in the political and commercial world, has scarcely a name, and her destruction could not produce such a general lamentation. Therefore we must look for some other city of a like description, the destruction of which would be universally felt. London may be styled the "mother of trade," having her concomitants mediately or immediately throughout the world in every place of trade ; of course her fall would produce such an effect ; therefore a transfer thither may be admitted with propriety.

Again ; England having been a province under the civil government of Rome pagan, and under the influence of Rome papal, is, consequently, one of the "ten horns ;" therefore we must look for a union under the second beast, that the prophecy may be completely fulfilled throughout the whole.

What does this argue ? And what times are we to expect at hand ?‡

---

* Bonaparte's kings have received power, but not a kingdom.
† We read not only of Babylon, but also of the "whore of Babylon," styled the "mother of harlots," which is supposed to mean the Romish Church. If she be a mother, who are her daughters ? They must be the corrupt, national, established churches that came out of her. If so, what of those governments that support them ? But oh ! the cry of national sins ! Are not Connecticut and Massachusetts in possession of a quadroon, or some of the tincture ? See the conduct of the clergy !
‡ The Prince of Wales, heir apparent to the crown, is supposed to be on good terms with Bonaparte ; hence an expectation, on the death of the present king, that the clergy and Protestant nobility will make a stand against the prince wearing the crown. It is also worthy of remark, that the king suffers him to hold no commission higher than a colonel, when his younger brother, the duke of York, was commander-in-chief. Mrs. Fitzherbert, his miss, is of the Romish religion, and of one of the bitterest families, who has such influence, that he may well be styled the "Petticoat Prince." Here observe his politics. But since is delegated by the . . . ., with the regency.

The affairs and arrangements exemplify a mutual understanding in those modern scenes —which may be seen, comparatively, with a squint.

It was observed that the woman fled into the wilderness; that is, those countries northwest of the Danube, where the gospel had not been received before; but when she had the wings as eagles, I must believe America to be the place referred to in prophecy.

Reason 1st. The first settlers of New England, &c., evidently came for conscience' sake; and many others have come hither for the sake of peace and liberty, from the intolerant hand of persecution and oppression.

Reason 2d. The earth helped the woman, which by commentators here is allowed to signify civil government. Therefore whatever toleration has been given in Europe, it is not equal to that in America; for they have some kind of national established religion, which tends to bind the consciences of men and restrict their privileges, in consequence of which virtue is oppressed and vice triumphs.

But not so in America: all are protected, though none established; that if a religion be false, she shall not have the civil sword to uphold her; and if genuine and true, shall not be persecuted nor depressed.

Reason 3d. The eagle and stars are in our banners of liberty. America may well be styled a wilderness, naturally, when compared to the old world, and considering our infancy.

Reason 4th. Whoever believes in a providence must acknowledge a particular providence of God in the separation, preparation, and independence of the United States, when compared with the affairs of Europe. A whole is composed of parts, and the parts form the whole; therefore, the particular providences compose the general providence, as much as the individuals compose a family: of course the term general providence without the particular providences considered and implied, is a great swelling phrase without meaning; it is like a half dozen of ciphers, which make an appearance but count nothing. Therefore we must admit a providence, or be atheists, and suppose nothing could put forth the act of power and beget something; and that something jumped together and formed men and things, and so argue that effects may be produced without causes.

I would advise such as wish to be profited by reading history, to become well acquainted with the history of their own times and country, and view the providential hand of God in our deliverance and preservation. One instance only out of many I will now hint. The first time the British invaded Charleston, South Carolina, it was expected they would attack them in the rear; but the preventive was afterwards discovered to be the water rising some feet higher than it was wont to do—thus the place was saved. Also, when every man's hands seemed to hang down, except the great Washington, when the American cause appeared so gloomy and desperate, the night the council of war was held at Trenton, relative to the attack on Princeton. Also, Cornwallis to deliver his sword to the son whose father was in that tower, of which he was the constable. And even when on the verge of falling into the general commotions of Europe, God has kept us by his providential hand, more than once or twice, beyond human probability.

There is such a thing as national privileges, of course national blessings, which, when abused, generally become national sins—which merit national judgments, that must be poured out for punishment in this world, unless there be a national repentance; for we shall not be judged at the bar of God as nations, (for nations will then cease to exist,) but as individuals, and punished accordingly; but national sins must be punished here, seeing it cannot be done hereafter.

General Burgoyne in the course of his defence, when on his trial, made the following remark:—"I once thought the Americans were in the wrong, but now I am convinced that nothing short of the overruling hand of providence could unite the hearts of three millions of people so perseveringly to stand or fall together, as was exemplified in the case of the Americans."*

The Jewish commentators observed, if the Messiah did not come by such a time they need not expect him, which time has long since passed. They caused a large council of their most learned Rabbies to meet at Amsterdam; the result of which was, after twelve months sitting, that the Messiah had come, but to them was unknown. This is one step towards their conversion to Christianity. The Jews, who are prohibited from being landholders among all nations except America, have expressed great faith in Bonaparte ever since he was a general, to be their restorer to Palestine.

In 1806, about one 1,000 of their most learned Rabbies were ordered by Bonaparte to meet him at Paris, where he proposed about fifty questions, which they solved to his satisfaction. He then directed them to form for themselves a Sanhedrim, or Grand Council, such as they formerly had at Jerusalem, though abolished ever since the destruction of that city by Titus.

There are about 9,000,000 of Jews within Bonaparte's jurisdiction, who have the blessing of Abraham—money.

The second beast, which came out of the earth, Rev. xiii. 11, is said to "cause fire to come down from heaven in the sight of men, and to erect an image to the first beast."†

The angel spoken of, (Rev. xiv. 6, 7,) "flying through the midst of heaven, having the everlasting gospel to preach," &c., I doubt not made his appearance at Moorfields, about 1739, the concomitants of which are now publishing their creed, contained in that text.‡

Again, the angel, or extraordinary messenger, with his assistants, proclaiming the fall of Babylon, will be known in his time, 8th verse.—Also, the one warning the people of God to come out of Babylon, both literal, spiritual, and practical, will be known also; and such another threatening for the omission of compliance is not to be found in all the Bible—9th to 11th verse.

It must be observed by all who study this book, that what John describes

---

* The present war is only an appendix of the former—a continuation of those opposite principles in theory, brought to the test. But where does "natural justice" lay?

† It is said when Bonaparte was in the East, he told the Mahometans that he was greater than Mahomet; could ascend above the clouds, and cause fire to come down from heaven on a wire in their sight; which he effected like Dr. Franklin with a kite; which they did not account for on natural principles, and therefore admitted it to be the power of God: also, t is said he offered a reward to that one who would make the greatest improvement in galvanism: not Calvinism.—*Image*; imitation or likeness: whether this should be taken literal or moral, time will determine; but I here add an *imitation* of the popes, which a friend writes to his correspondent from Europe to America, thus: "A popish catechism hath been published in France, under the sanction of Napoleon, pronouncing all to be heretics, and in a state of damnation, who are not of their communion.

‡ It was there and then that the present great revival of religion first began. Observe, "Judgment must first begin at the house of God" also!

relative to the two beasts, &c., he viewed first in heaven, and afterwards fulfilled upon the earth, and a clear distinction must be kept, otherwise our ideas will be confused, or else the subject will appear as tautology.*

I have no doubt but we have arrived towards the closing of the sound of the trumpet of the sixth angel, and the commencement of the seventh, and also the pouring out of the seven last plagues. And however much the earth, or political, civil, religious, and Christian world, may now be convulsed or confused, I apprehend worse times, as it were, are at the door; and what has passed for the last twenty years, only as a few drops before a shower, in comparison to what is to come. I therefore entreat all, into whose hands these hints may fall, to take timely warning, and particularly the true Christian, that he may have suffering grace in the day of evil,† and be preserved as the seed of the gospel, and found in a state of readiness against the coming of our Lord and Saviour Jesus Christ, and be counted worthy to have a seat at the marriage-supper of the Lamb, when the Bride shall make herself ready. There is more contained in these words than many are aware of—and who is ambitious to meditate our privileges—as it relates to the "hundred and forty and four thousand."

As it relates to the states of Great Britain and France, I would make the following remarks:—Let the reader imagine four thousand *gun-boats*, three thousand five hundred of which are sufficient to carry two hundred thousand men and all their naval stores, and three thousand five hundred field-pieces; five hundred prames, carrying from twenty to forty guns each, with forges for *heating shot;* thirty-six sweeps or oars to each boat, together with sails: these may be sunk, and thereby preserved from decay, and raised at pleasure, and also fastened together with great convenience and expedition by means of spring-bridges, composed of ropes, which would enable the whole force to disembark, as though marching on parade. A wind which would be fair for these to go from France to England, which is but thirty miles, and take but about five hours, would be precisely against the British *fleet;* and a calm would do the same. If thus once on the British coast, they would be out of reach of all the king's navy, for on that side of England next to France, for seventy miles in length, a ship of war cannot get within half a dozen miles of the shore, but the *flotilla*, drawing but about twenty-two inches of water, would there be screened, and could choose their place of landing.

The British, in 1807, did not make their boast of being able to bring above seventy thousand men to any given point in twenty-four hours, provided the French should land. It was ascertained that Bonaparte had a map of London, with the number of every house and street that was worth plundering, to distribute among his officers; also to confiscate the estates of the nobility to be distributed among his army; so put an end to the war, and make gentlemen of his soldiers! What a powerful temptation! In 1805, when he was called off to Germany against the Rus-

---

* Compare Rev. xv. 1, with chapter xvi. 1, and then read from chapter xiii. 11, to the end of the fifteenth chapter, (for heaven) and the following ones to the twentieth, as fulfilled (on earth.)—This may serve, in a measure, as a key to an inquiring mind.
† "Blessed are the dead that die in the Lord, from *henceforth*, saith the Spirit," &c Why? They rest from their labors, and their works follow them. Observe, this denotes something extraordinary, which should be remarked by the Christians of those times! I here would refer the reader to Mr. Wesley's comment on Rev. xii. 12, xiii. 1, 3, then xvii. 10 xiii. 11 and 15; and the catalogue after xxii. or at the close of his notes.

sians, he told his lads it had been his intention to have given them a dinner in London at such a time; but being called off, he would give them a suit of clothes in Vienna at such a time—which he performed.

Shortly after this, Mr. Pitt, viewing the state of the country, with his last words cried out—" O my country! My country!" and expired.

The British, though ridiculing the idea of Bonaparte's breaking over the " wooden walls of old England," and saying he never designed to come, yet made great preparations to meet him. Besides the regular army in England, and two hundred thousand in Ireland, they balloted eight hundred thousand militia. And all the carriages, carts, wagons, &c., of whatsoever name or nature, were numbered, and also the draft horses and boats; beacons were erected on every high hill, composed of combustibles to give warning with fire by night, telegraphs to give intelligence by day, which would give information one hundred miles an hour; then all hands must turn out.

Here observe, Bonaparte was again called off from attempting the invasion in 1806 to Prussia, and since to Spain, &c. But now look at the present state of Europe, and behold *poor** Britain has to stand it out single-handed all alone! borrowing money at five per cent to carry on the war, the taxes being only sufficient to pay the interest of the national debt,† &c. A hint at the taxes must here suffice—1st, on every pound of hide; 2d, on every month of the tan works; 3d, on every pound of leather; again, six shillings for a dog, and half a guinea for every hound; half a crown for wearing a hat, in which you must have a stamp, or be subject to lose your hat and be fined; five guineas for a riding-horse; and five for a two-wheel carriage, &c. &c.

Whatever geographers may say of the *poor* Irish, for poverty, of which I have seen none to exceed the truth, yet the people are in a more deplorable situation in England, being dependent on foreign trade; whereas, the Irish live more on potatoes, which they raise, and of course are not so much affected by the times. And were I to have my choice, to be a *slave* in America, or one of the laboring people in England, I should, without hesitation, prefer the former, with this condition, let me chose my master; for then I would be *sure* of getting something to *eat*.

The king being head of the church, must be considered in a measure as *sponsor;* yet there is not less than sixty thousand prostitutes in the city of London, that are licensed by the crown. I forbear to mention what I know to be the truth relative to the country towns, leaving the seaports out of the question; but would advise the perusal of " Simpson's Plea for Religion," and see the corruption of the church and state, &c.

---

* Then it turned afterwards on America, now reversed. What next?

† The national debt was contracted in the reign of Henry VII. and amounted to £1,430; in 1697, two hundred years after, to £5,000,000; 1755, fifty-eight years, £72,000,000; 1776, twenty-one years, to £123,000,000; in 1786 increased to £239,000,000; 1796 to £360,000,000 sterling, and 1816 to about one thousand millions for England, and two hundred millions for Ireland; and their annual expense £70,000,000; £11,000,000 more than their income. What an augmentation in the reign of George the Second, and it may end with George the Third! Hence the solemn address of the " Plain Man" to George II.: ' It will come in the days of him that shall come *after* thee!"

Query—If 35,000,000 came to a premature end in the East Indies, under the administration of two—and the combination of 1792 was from George,—100,000,000 in his reign *untimely*—and if each person contains twenty-eight pints of blood, how much would be required to float the royal navy?

of Great Britain, particularly that edition published by John Hagerty, of Baltimore, as a spurious work under that title was published by the bishops of England, after God took Simpson from the evil to come, just as the bishops were going to call him to an account before the ecclesiastical court for that work, which it was expected would have resulted in the loss of his life.

Some have supposed the eighteen letters of his (Napoleon Buonaparte) name divided by three, and added together, will make the number of the *beast*, which is 666. Another author calculates 665 kings prior to him, and that he completes the number of 666. But my opinion is different from theirs, and should rather apply it a different way, or wait for future time to unfold it.

The legion of honor, so called, of which a legion of life-guards is the shell, or shadow of the substance, or essence of that honor. I therefore, here remark, though a legion is no positive definite number, yet a certain author calculates a perfect legion thus: six thousand privates; a captain to every ten men; a centurion to every one hundred; and one officer to every one thousand; which would make a complete legion to consist of 6666; which would make 666 officers: that would be just the number of the *beast!*

When I take a view of Bonaparte's movement—1st, relative to the Jews; 2d, as it relates to the papacy; 3d, his politics; 4th, his confederation of ten; 5th, his military manœuvres; 6th, the relation of affairs in the east, in succession with his movements—I am led to meditate the time near, when the *seven last plagues*, under the seventh trumpet, are to be poured out, and particularly the two, one on the *seat of the beast*,* the other on the Euphrates, which denotes the Ottoman empire.

Russia, which rose in lieu of the "eastern empire," whose emperor is now styled the "emperor of the east," while Bonaparte is styled "emperor of the west," and is at war with the Turks. Again, it is evident that Bonaparte has a large number of men in his employ in Persia, to teach them *his* art of war. For a moment reflect on the present state of the world; England has eight hundred thousand militia; two hundred thousand in Ireland; two hundred thousand seamen, besides what may be occupied in standing armies at home and abroad. Again, view France, as it were the whole nation as one cantonment, with three millions of militia and one million in standing armies; all Russia put in military requisition, amounting to seven millions; and the Turks putting that empire in a similar state, by order of the Grand Seignior, who is about to take the field in person.

These things, when taken in conjunction with the state of Europe, a few years ago, and what it is now, with the probable consequence of what is at the door, denote something impressive indeed, and ought to stimulate every thinking mind on the continent of America to prize their privileges, and improve them accordingly; for where can a country be found with peace, plenty, and religious liberty, but these United States? And

---

* Which vial brought darkness on his kingdom—the woman took this advantage to seat herself upon the beast, i. e. establish her maritime claims as "queen" of the ocean and "mistress" of the seas—having no rival, "shall see no sorrow." Rev. xviii. 7; but her interest will clash with theirs, which will beget opposition, and cause them to consolidate. See Revelation, chapter xvii. 16, 17. Council at Paris.

how soon we may be called to trials, is in the womb of futurity. As I do not believe that a country was ever given up to the sword and destruction, wherever pure religion was on the progression, therefore, we need to pray for peace, that we may be kept from the deluge of the old world, which is fast progressing. And should the Euphrates, or Turkish empire receive an overthrow, as other nations of late have fared, we should know exactly the time of the church; and it is not improbable but Bonaparte will avail himself of the prejudices of the Jews to answer his own design, who amount to nine millions in his jurisdiction; and in doing this, in the establishment of them at Palestine, it will cut up the Turkish empire, afford him money, men, and a half-way house to the Indies. Thus, the "Euphrates would be dried up, that the way of the kings of the east might be prepared." Rev. xvi. 12.* I add no more, only give a recapitulation of the subject, &c.

1. The woman, the church, persecuted, and the child, Christ, not in his person, but in his kingdom.

2. 1st. She fled to the north of Europe. 2d. Flew to America.

3. The devil or dragon governing the seven heads of Rome pagan, the last of which was imperial; under whom the ten horns were united in subjection.

4. Constantine the Great is the tail of the dragon, and by the change of the religious national establishment, corruption creeps into the church; Popery is begotten, in embryo; 606 appears; come to the full, 1077.

5. The ten horns NOW have their crowns.

6. The first beast out of the sea (Europe) with seven heads is the Papacy, but no crowns are ascribed to them, because the ecclesiastical authority took the lead of the civil.

7. The dragon had only seven crowns, but here are ten, which shows that the dragon and the beast are not one.

8. The dragon transferred his power to him—i. e. from Rome pagan to the Papacy, &c.

9. Five heads are fallen, viz. Cælian, Vatican, Quirinal, Equiline, and Bonaparte's pope.

10. "The beast is not," and "Babylon reigns queen." Here, observe the transfer from Rome to England, as a *city* compact, and "queen of the ocean."

11. The safety under "the wooden walls of old England,"—Stepped into the shoes of old† Popery; (to distinguish it from Bonaparte's new-

---

* The Jewish "Sanhedrim" have acknowledged Lewis XVIII. yet those "ten horns," or kingdoms, who are indebted to the "woman" for their crowns, may find it their interest to dispute her claims, and "agree to give their power" to the exiled, as a proper person; and adopt a similar continental policy to dispute her claim, which, when effected, would astonish the world, and produce the lamentation—Rev. xvii. 16 to 18. xviii. 9 to 19.

† For the last relics of old Popery, the British are now fighting, viz. in Spain and Portugal, where the inquisition law only remains in force; while the king of one is a captive, and the other fled from his kingdom to Brazil, the British authority uphold what the Popes have contended for. If so, do they not step into the shoes, and necessarily merit a transfer as above? Moreover, now they have reinstated him again, for he is gone to Rome. Wesley said the sixth head would be with or under the government of Babylon, though not with the power of his predecessors?

The Pope, after his return to Rome, passed high encomiums on the Prince Regent, for the services the royal power had afforded the Papal cause; and especially for receiving the Pope's Legate, i. e. right-hand man; which the Pope said had not been received in England before, for two hundred years modelled Popery) and reigning as a queen, styling herself, "empress of the seas!" intoxicated joy at Napoleon's downfall. Rev. xviii. 7.

12. Distinction between—1st, The dragon; 2d, The first beast; 3d, The second beast; 4th, Babylon; 5th, The power of Babylon; and 6th, The false prophet.

13. The second beast comes out of the earth, Asia, and appears at "the end of the 42 months of the first beast; which was 1810." As Mahometanism and Popery rose in one year, 666. And "the beast and false prophet will be taken and destroyed together." So the fifth and sixth angels pour out from their vials the plagues on the seat of the beast and the Euphrates, or Rome and the Ottoman empire, at no great distance asunder—xix. 20. and xvi. 10—12.

14. Bonaparte's movements with the Jews, &c.

15. The temple built at Jerusalem. The two witnesses prophesy 42 common months, and then slain; after which a tenth part of the city fell, and 7000 slain, (70,000 in all,) the rest (63,000) repent and give glory to God.

16. "Three unclean spirits, like frogs; 1st, came out of the mouth of the dragon; the 2d, out of the mouth of the beast; 3d, out of the false prophet.

17. Out of the mouth of the dragon. Paganism opposed to the true God. Atheism,* &c., which is the result of the "Heathen Mythology." The Illuminati, formed from Voltaire, who said, "Jesus Christ began the conversion of the world with twelve men, but I with six will banish Christianity from the earth." And by striving to reduce nature to its first principles, think proper to destroy every thing out of the way, even to the removing of father and mother as obstacles to the fruition of their object, so that no rival shall be in the way. This society was as a powdermine in France, and when Fayette and others went home from America to France with the flame of liberty, they took fire and blew up the French monarchy. Remarkable to tell—Robert Fleming, on the first Sunday of the last century, preached a sermon on the prophecies, in which he calculated the French revolution to the very year; which sermon was published about ninety years before. Also, one observed that the massacre at Paris by Louis XIV. would be visited on (his grandson) Louis XVI. by the hand of God.

18. The "legion of honor."—As all societies must have grades, from the "apprentice to the Grand Master," so we must conceive of Bonaparte's† "legion of honor;" and the legion of life-guards as the shell to the

---

* Antichrist is generally applied to the Papacy by commentators, but it will not apply there better than to any other sin, but is an unscriptural explanation, for John saith, "he that denies the Father and Son is Antichrist," 1 John ii. 22; but the Papists do not deny either, but confess both.

† The intoxicated joy at his downfall—a viceroy appointed for America as a consequence—a rod laid up for a while—but how long before these words may be exemplified: "The beast which thou sawest, was, and is not, and shall ascend out of the bottomless pit:" the ten horns transfer their power to him, he being the eighth, and may constitute the seventh head of the first beast, adding a peculiar degree of, and a new and singular character and title, at his last rise from the abyss—xvii. 8. The second beast of chap. xiii. 11. whose kingdom is darkened, xvi. 10, appears to be the false prophet of the xix. 20—who at his last ascent, after destroying Babylon, will go to the Holy Land, slay the two witnesses, xi. 7—having erected the image to the first beast, xiii. 14—which the angel warns against, xiv.)—and prepares the way for the battle; the last that will ever be fought, verse 20—xv. 14, o 16, inclusive; compare with xix. 19, &c.

essence of that honor. Moreover it appears by his suppressing the liberty of the press, and restricting the number of the printing presses, as though this was to sink Europe into its former darkness and ignorance ; like Voltaire's society, though on a different plan : of course is the " unclean spirit," like the frog out of the mouth of the beast.*

19. Out of the mouth of the false prophet ; after the Euphrates or Ottoman empire is dried up, Rev. xvi. 12 to the 16th inclusive, read and compare with chap. xix. from the 11th verse to the end of the chapter. Awful, but important !

20. The dragon or Satan is bound in the other world for 1000 years, but we know not the time ; Christ comes to reign on the earth 1000 years ; if a prophetic thousand, (a day for a year,) it would be 365,000 ; again, as one day is with the Lord as a thousand years, and a thousand years as one day, it may be 365,000,000 of common years.

Considering the present agitated state of Europe, and the East, where can we calculate for peace and safety unless in America ?

There are about 15,000,000 of men under military requisition ; and God's controversy with the nations will not cease until they learn righteousness.

Therefore it stands all true Christians in hand to look to God, that our rulers may be influenced aright, and have his wisdom to guide them ; that we may be kept in peace, and from falling into the general commotion and calamities of Europe and the East.

The Spirit of God teaches his followers to pray according to the pattern given ; (i. e. the Lord's Prayer) which saith—" Thy kingdom come,"—which implies that every obstacle, as a hindrance to the spread of Christ's kingdom, must be removed. Therefore, those ecclesiastical establishments which bind the consciences of men, and prevent the spirit of free inquiry, must be shaken as a rope of sand. Also, those civil or monarchical governments, which uphold those religious national establishments, must be torn down ; seeing they are mutually dependent on each other.

The peace of nations is dependent on the laws of nations. Custom makes law ; when certain customs which are the laws of nations are infringed upon, the public peace is disturbed, and commonly settled with powder and ball ; which shows that the laws of nations are dependant on the martial law, and supported thereby.

The martial law is dependent on the civil law, for it is put in execution by the same, as the military act, by the magistrate's command.

The civil law is dependent upon the ecclesiastical, for our rulers are admitted into office upon oath. An oath is a sacred thing, and is connected with the moral law, which shows that religion is the foundation of civil

---

* The constitution of the federal government, and the proceedings of Congress, may be providential, as it relates to American citizens receiving conferred honors and titles, &c, from other governments, to preserve us as a nation from falling into the general calamity. Query—It is possible that some are connected with *****, and should they be convicted of the reception as American citizens, it would run them hard as being guilty of treason—therefore, to save their **** would wish for a back door to plead that they were not American citizens, &c. Miss or Mrs. *********'s young Bonaparte, with his throne and imperial retinue may be ****** embryo ! Remember, an egg may hatch a serpent ! and if people sleep now, they will awake then !
———in France twenty being prohibited from meeting together is like——— !

government, particularly ours; therefore, all persons who oppose religion, strike at the public safety, by sapping the very foundation of civil authority; of course, advertise themselves to be public enemies. Again, any person who does not believe in religious sentiment, (the ideas of our future rewards and punishment,) does not believe in things sufficient to constitute an oath; therefore for such person or persons to take an oath, would be to act a sham, and perform a solemn nothing, also a mocking of common sense; and any persons who thus would act should be considered as deceitful hypocrites, and dangerous to society, because they trifle with things most sacred to answer their sinister designs, and cannot feel such oath binding upon their consciences; of course can give no assurance of fidelity to the public. Hence it is evident that all who give or receive a drink of grog for a vote, do no better than give or receive a trifling bribe; therefore they are trifling persons, and consequently are not fit for freemen, much less for rulers, seeing they take such improper measures to answer their own designs, which shows they are not men of principle nor veracity, but may be influenced to swerve from the path of justice by designing men, and let the guilty escape, and make the innocent suffer. Therefore, watch the conduct of people, and look out for men of noble principles, that there may be practice accordingly, good society cultivated, and justice appear in our land: be guarded against office-hunters, who would become worse than a nuisance to society.

All rulers ought to be men of information and veracity, and influenced by noble and virtuous principles, as guardian angels for the public safety and welfare, who must render an account. They being, as it were, trustees for the welfare of society, are accountable to God and men for their conduct, having derived their power and authority from the same, and of course are praise or blame-worthy, according to their motive and conduct. Truth will bear investigation, and carry its own conviction with it, when properly understood. But error says hush to the spirit of inquiry; wishing truth to lie dormant, and herself unsearched, to appear gay to every glancing eye. Therefore, our freemen ought to look well to the choice of their rulers, as it relates to society, as sponsors for what is to come.

ON THE MINISTRY

How shall one person know, and be able to determine and judge, whether it be the duty of another to preach or not?

There are but three evidences by which he may be able to judge and determine concerning him on that subject. 1st, Divine evidence in his own soul; or 2dly, by the fruits of his labor; or 3dly, the witness of his word with power.

How shall one know whether it be his own duty to preach or not? Says one, leave it to your brethren to determine. But if they have not the proper evidence by which to judge, are incapable of forming a correct judgment; of course may err, to his great injury; therefore, there should be further investigation beyond those who are incomptent to be judges.

Search the Scriptures!

The Scriptures do not say whether he, as an individual, shall go or stay.

If God wills the thing and requires it at his hand, there is no counselling against the Lord. And if it be not his duty, no man nor any body of men, have a right to tell or command him to go.

There is no rational evidence that wicked men are called of the Lord to preach. Those who feel the call enjoined upon them, by obeying the divine convictions in their soul, they feel quietness and peace, and joy in God, by walking in that way. But the rejection of duty brings pain and wo!

As there are various gifts in the Christian church, and yet all by the same Spirit, how shall a person know and determine what place and sphere is his? Answer—he must get the spirit of his station, and then he will feel the witness, and have the testimony that he pleases God. The opening of providence corresponds with the calls of the spirit, when and where to go.

But some people who are too much bigoted to a mode of their own, had rather good would not be done at all, if it does not come in their own way, agreeably to their preconceived notion of the thing—if we may judge of their conduct in opposing the instruments which it pleases God to use, as means to accomplish it. But the words of Gamaliel, Acts v. &c., are apropos to such as forbid others, because they act not with them!

DOW'S LAWSUIT.

Supreme Court.
P. & H. A. Richards
vs.
Lorenzo Dow.

This was an action brought by the plaintiff against defendant, in a plea of trespass on the case, in which is claimed damages for an unnecessary detention of water from the said plaintiff's mills by the said defendant. The jury in this case consisted of the following gentlemen:

Elisha Waterman,
Asa Roath,
Joshua Maples, jun.,
Jacob McCall,
Bishop Burnham,
Ebenezer Howe,

Matthew Brown,
Julius S. Hammond,
Thomas H. Wilson,
Abial Roath,
Henry Brown.

Being eleven, the number agreed to by the parties.

CHARLES LATHROP, *Clerk.*

January 30th, 1829.

ESTABLISHMENTS.

1, Dow's,
2, Baker's,
3, Scholfield's,
4, R. Palmer's,
5, Smith's fulling-mill,
6, G. Palmer's.
7, Giles Turner's.
8, Peter Richard's.

PLAINTIFF'S WITNESSES.

Esquire Hurlburt.—Distance from factory to pond, 1711 rods; to Giles Turner's, 235; to G. Palmer's, 163; to Smith's, 170; to R. Palmer's, 130; to Scholfield's, 526; to Baker's, 280; to the pond, 207.

Baker's pond, small; Scholfield's larger, dam small, perhaps from eight to ten feet high; considerable surface of pond; perhaps fifteen or twenty acres. R. Palmer's pond long, narrow, dam not high; does not recollect how high. Smith's pond small, dam not high. G. Palmer's pond small, dam low. Turner's pond small, dam low; no large streams running into the principal ones; has noticed them on plan; first small, second largest; it cannot differ much from thirty years since; Lester first built his grist-mill; cotton-factory been built within five or six years; oil-mill never run; before the purchase of Lester's small dam; since enlarged; did not grind; formerly went there to mill; cannot say whether every year or not; mills above occasionally dry; the Fox mills;

has been to Dow's dam two or three times since he built it; cannot say whether as much water in the stream below as before; thinks more power necessary to move the present machinery than formerly; thinks, in the course of the year, as much as formerly run to Richard's mill; does not know whether more or less in the dry season; 1827-28, wet; more wet through the year of '27 than '26; Dow's dam accumulates much more water than formerly it could have done; the surface in the basin is much larger than formerly.

Hasam Browning.—Dow's dam raised considerably, thinks four feet; dam very tight when he saw it; has frequently been there; been acquainted about twenty-five years; cannot tell how much land flowed by the new dam; trees killed; large pond, say one mile or over long; half or three quarters of a mile wide, generally speaking; in August, 1827, ninth day, found water shut up; very little leak from the dam or flume; if any had been let out that day, must have been early water, about three feet above old dam; never been there since to examine; had seen it when the dam was building, which thinks was in 1826; was a wasteway to the old dam, and when the pond was filled they would raise the gate and let it off in freshets; were some holes, thinks two, in the old dam; never saw the body of the water in the pond before; tight n atch whether he ever saw so little in the stream below; saw the dam while building; went there with Joshua Baker, and saw them wheeling the dirt; afterwards went and saw it after finished; went with Cleveland; knew the old dam leaky; been there to mill; just above Dow's dam, apparently an old dam; never saw the time but that there was water in the ditch; behind the old dam, in very dry time, and water much drawn off to grind, thinks dry. R. Palmer's grist-mill pond long; has sometimes seen the water rather low; then has been obliged to wait for grinding; in a very extreme dry time, guesses all the mills have been in want of water; as much runs down the stream as before, only what is reserved; since Dow's dam has been built has not waited at R. Palmer's, because very wet seasons.

Asahel Otis.—Former dam quite old; leaked some; Dow has raised the dam; made a nice one, very durable; thinks dam finished in 1827; in the fall blowed away the rocks; thinks the bottom of the sluiceway about four feet higher than the old dam; has been acquainted with the old dam ever since a schoolboy; old dam always pretty much the same; leaky; thinks pond would embrace a mile square; never formerly came up to the road into twenty rods; deep pond; an island in the middle; has seen half an acre dry; 1827-28 have been wet seasons; in 1826, till last of July, very dry, then wet; no leak to this pond; dam very tight; old and new dam abut against a ledge; old sluiceway would let off when up to a certain pitch; so it does now above four feet higher; thinks the dam about five feet higher than before; has been to Dow's mill formerly; frequently, when he could get no grinding, used to clear out the ditch; Mr. Miner used to invite his neighbors to dig out, thinks a little spot of two or three rods lower than the ditch, and where it stood; Palmer used to grind when Miner did not; there is another stream running into Palmer's pond; it has been so low that they ground very little; does not think that there is any more water discharged here in the dry season than formerly; has never known Dow's mill want for water since

Dow owned it; frequently did before; does not, as he thinks, grind as much as was ground seven years ago; does not know that in 1826 there was a want of water at this or any of these mills; did not think there was; has known the old dam more than forty years; pretty much the same as remained, only it grew rather worse.

Nathan Comstock, jun.—Commenced business in 1812 where he now lives; recollects the Lester mill about thirty-one years, and that before Scholfield came into these parts; grist-mill did not take so much water as the Lesters' does; when the water run over the factory dam, it came in too great quantities at a time; the water that was wasted at Lester's dam was equal to nearly as much as is necessary to operate the machinery; water might be a day or two coming from Miner's dam; said the cotton-factory stopped year before last; cannot tell at what time of the year; always been occupied since he has known it; when the Richards' factory stopped, thinks the other mills stopped on the stream at Richards'; thinks part of the same race-way in part; can't tell; race-way about the same; thinks the side built up a little higher than before; thinks the Richards' mill has occasionally stopped, in a very dry time, before Dow built his dam; not very certain.

James Comstock.—Has known Lester's mill about thirty years, situated very near Richards' mills; has been accounted as permanent a stream as any they had among them; two last seasons been very wet; as near as he can recollect, they have stopped at Richards' some days; thinks there would have been water enough the two last seasons; cannot tell whether the water wasted at Lester's would have been sufficient to carry the factory wheel; large; does not know as he ever knew Lester's mill stop for any length of time for want of water; four years since Richards' factory got a going; can lay up much more water than formerly; thinks the old race-way nearly as formerly; Richard's grist-mill where Lester's was; thinks would not vary; thinks there would have been enough for the grist-mill if it had not been used for the factory; thinks not enough to carry Lester's grist-mill.

Amos Comstock.—Known Lester's mill, say twenty-five years; some times wanted water; but considered very dry when stream lacked; occupied in W. Comstock's mill for the last two years; all that is retained has not come along; two last years has been present; has been a lack of water for several days summer before this last; he stopped one whole day and two or three days in part; dry time when stopped; frequently stop their mill because not water to carry both; doubtful whether there would have been enough to carry Lester's mill; does not know whether he ever knew all the factories and mills stopped for want of water.

Burrell Thompson.—Dow's dam higher than the other; this very tight; the old one not very tight; plenty of water for grinding at Dow's; sometimes not constant millers there; believes they had set days, thinks one day in a week; was such a time, but cannot tell how long it continued. Can't tell whether Dow's pond generally ran over; can't tell how much more it flows now than formerly; thinks does not flow twenty rods farther towards the road than formerly: has risen on his land, can't tell how far nor how deep; perhaps from two to three feet; thinks in the fall of the year, the set days for grinding; cannot tell exactly; thinks one of Miner's sons tended; was a Latham tended; after crossed the stream did not particularly observe; has known the water very low; rare that grinding could not be had; should not think there was more water run down this stream in the dry season in consequence of Dow's dam.

J. Hartshorn.—Mill stopped on the 24th of July, 1827, one quarter of a day; 25th one quarter of a day; 6th day of August, one quarter of a day, 7th whole day; 11th whole day; from 11th to 13th had a heavy rain and stopt; grist-mill had no water; should say could not be considered a dry time; factory built in 1823; commenced operation 12th April, 1824; 1825 or '26 had a dry season; afterwards more wet; thinks there would have been enough water if it had come in the natural stream; if it had come as formerly thinks it would not have been as likely to stop; thinks stopped more this season for want of water than before; forty-five persons employed; great inconvenience to be interrupted parts of days. Richards' dam completed in the spring of '27; old dam did not lay up as much water as this; unusual quantity of water came down at the time of the heavy rain; does not know whether owing to that cause or not; operations of factory suspended in '25 and '26. Flume six feet in width, depth six feet, quantity of water under the gate opens one and a half or two inches, since the dam finished by Richards; more water than before; good deal of water ran by of which he had not the benefit, wasted; don't know how much water was required at the old mill; factory now takes more water than the grist-mill. Peter Richards understood went to Mrs. Dow; don't know any thing about an application to purchase the water above; Mr. Richards sent him to request Mr. Miner to let the water down; purchased the right of Mr. Miner for fifteen dollars. In the dry season of 1825-6, can't tell how long the water had been held back; had rather pay a little than keep it back; one of the dams below would retain the water more than three or four hours; great advantage to the mill-owners be low if they could control the dam; can't say whether the entry on the book was made the same day, or day after; don't recollect whether the notes at the bottom were made when the others were, or not.

James C. Andrew.—Works in the factory; July 24th, one quarter of a day; 25th, same; August 6th, one quarter of a day; 7th, whole day; 11th, whole day; between the 7th and 11th, 25 persons in the mill; stoppages inconvenient; does not recollect how much they have stopped in previous seasons.

Joshua Baker.—Dow's dam raised in the fall of '26; does not know but that he worked on it in January; four and a half feet higher than the old dam; two and a half or three feet head raised; retains one third more water; in the summer of '27 rather held back; had some considerable grinding; winter ground only one day in the week; last of July or August '27, thinks it did not run out the sluiceway much; recollects once the water came out freely, soon after the suit was brought; ran two or three days; lowered it down to the old dam; thinks drew it down to nearly the level of the old dam; Dow not at home when the suit was brought; ran out of the waste-way before; for a fortnight previous thinks the water had run over the waste-gate; frequently went to Miner and got liberty to hoist the gate; water discharged only at the waste-gate and flume; no stream below Dow's and his mill which enters; Dow did not keep back from him; when they grind at Dow's he can saw; main flume plank had sprung, and to repair it was the object of taking off the board; two plank sprung; had a miller very generally in the summer; set days began in the fall and continued in the winter; never knew Dow stop the stream except when repairing; has known all the mills pretty much stop; did in dry times; has owned his mills thirty years; been the custom for each one to retain until he had occasion to use; often asked Miner to accommodate him; no more dry than formerly; no disadvantage to him; thinks very little difference as it regards Lester's mill; cannot say, thinks sluiceway finished after suit was commenced.

Nathan Comstock, jr.—Went to Miner; understood he refused to grind; went up, asked Miner to grind; he refused; demanded the water. Miner said he had water in the pond; pay him he would let it come; asked him twenty dollars. Richards said he would give him a five dollar bill; proposed to open the flume; finally gave fifteen dollars.

Robert Comstock, Depo.—Occupied a mill below Uncasville Factory; went to Dow's pond and Richards', a day or two before the suit. In consequence of the dry weather and detention of the water in Dow's pond, Uncasville Factory stopped.

Daniel Lester.—Son of the former owner; built a little over thirty years; tended part of the time; used to lack some for water; only in a dry time; has known it stop; present canal a little larger than formerly; does take more to carry this factory than old gristmill, what ordinarily run in the stream. Don't think at all times the water that run in the stream would carry the factory. His father used to collect the water in the night; formerly let it come as they had occasion to use it.

Edwin Baker.—Stoppage of the factory in the summer of 1827. July 24th part of the day; 25th same; August 6th one quarter; 7th whole day; 11th whole day; kept a meteorological journal. 7th of August, Comstock and Richards were up to the Dow dam.

DEFENDANT'S WITNESSES.

Gideon Palmer.—Acquainted with the stream; knew Lester's situation, small dam; temporary to turn water into the ditch; above could put down a plank and raise considerable water; could operate his mill with little water; $2\frac{1}{2}$ inches when he saw it; considerable grain in the mill; could grind but little. Just above this pond a little brook puts in; about a quarter of a mile another stream puts in; Giles Turner's mill in '27; from 12 to 14 feet high; into that pond a little stream from the east; on the west side one or two small streams; above his pond a considerable of a stream; Smith raises about four feet; above this is a small stream which empties in. The Fox mill-seat; Elder Palmer and Eells; head about four feet, twelve feet head and fall; pond a mile or more long; channelway running from the dam to the upper end; whole distance across the marshes thinks fifty rods when pond full; stream, considerable one empties into the pond; Scholfield's pond considerable large; raise four and a half or five feet of water; does not recollect any year in which there has not been a complaint of want of water. At Dow's mill about the time of lowering his sluiceway; of great advantage as he thought. Has bought the water at the Fox mill-seat; thinks the dam very beneficial if properly used; much safer thinks in high freshets; if it should be shut down and kept tight would be of great advantage. Brother Reuben's pond large; necessary that the oil-mill should be kept in operation. Fore part of August, '27, his brother wished to repair; went to help him on Tuesday; then turned the water into a particular channel; secured the bottom part Tuesday afternoon; repaired the dam up along; Thursday night put up another plank; held the water until Saturday afternoon; thought the water came down in the usual quantity; run faster than he expected; thinks July and first of August dry; has heard no complaint from the owners above; never knew that the lower proprietors had any claim upon the proprietors further up the stream; Mr. Lester's grist-mill frequently stopped for want of water; the detention of the water at Elder Palmer's pond and not at Dow's; when put down first plank rarely any running water below; as it rose leaked a little more. Fore part of the month of August, began to repair on Tuesday; on Wednesday supposed there would be a want of water; cannot tell how much higher this dam than the old one; droughts operated considerably on the springs.

Elder Palmer.—Should agree with the testimony of his brother generally; thirty-three years has known the stream, excepting four years in the mean time; knew of Lester's building his mill; did not much business at it except in dry season; the one occupied by him has had an extensive custom; very durable; more so than at Lester's; for seven years past or more; business managed differently; Rogers built a machine factory; that failed and then turned into a cotton mill; then run all day; prior to that time had used it for customers. When Richards' folks began, workmen went to Richards'; his factory burnt in March, 1825— knew the privilege twenty years before he was interested in it. All retained supposed he was obliged to submit to it. Has been acquainted with the stream thirty years. Cannot say whether the present establishment requires more water than the gristmill; his gristmill did not want water long. Miner's pond and his are the only two natural ponds; Lester's mill frequently had not water enough in the morning. Do not think the stream impaired. In the summer season has more water than formerly. Cannot say whether the water was stopped at Dow's dam when he repaired. Monday or Tuesday after his repairs, saw Richards and Comstock returning. Privileges have not been injured. Have always considered themselves independent of Miner's pond. Thinks at present more water requisite to carry the factory than did the old mill. Thinks it would take twenty-four hours for the water to go from Dow's to Richards'. While his dam was repairing water continually flowing. Advantages—detaining freshet water—reservoir: gave him to understand (i. e. Richards and Comstock did) that they had been to Dow's; all stopped below till he has started; thinks the time he was repairing his mill the usual quantity of water came down; and that the lack of water at Richards' factory in August, 1827, was occasioned by the not using his dam.

Cushing Eells.—Owned the property several years, never there but once. Thinks the alterations beneficial; should think it beneficial to the factory below.

H. Miner.—Owned the mill between twenty and thirty years. As soon as the pond is full, runs round; gravelled the dam; if as much grinding, as much water runs; tended the mill for Dow, and does now: Peter Richards wanted to get the water. None of the proprietors claimed a right to open his dam while he owned it; at his own dam once stopped, could only grind about a bushel. Dam, say fifteen feet; pond is increased; covers five or six acres more than formerly; supposes —— ground one day in a week, in the fall, or fore part of the winter, or in the winter. When they ground but one day in the week, plenty of water. Richards wanted the water; talked of knocking down the flume; gave him fifteen dollars for letting the water go; always the practice to raise a pond, and no one ever interfered with him til! Richards; returned home a week or fortnight after the suit brought.

John Vallet.—Acquainted with the water privilege, i. e. Dow and Baker's; have always calculated upon a scarcity of water in the stream once a year. Used to go to Fox's mills pretty much in the last resort for grinding. Thinks Dow's improvements beneficial to all. Elder Dow has not to his knowledge withheld the stream. Dam, before Dow had possession, sometimes leaky. Waste-gates could sometimes be raised; then put down boards; used to stop the dam as had occasion. The stoppages in the dam to reserve the water.

Branch.—Came in May before last, in 1827. Mill required more water in 1827 than now. No such lack of water as required him to stop his wheel. Never knew Dow withhold his water intentionally. Pond fifty rods, say twenty wide. Never stopped all his machinery.

Scholfield.—Did not know about the stream prior to April. Mill principally furnished by the Miner pond. A stream runs into his pond; operated one carding machine, sometimes not so fast as he could wish. One time, was the week before the water came on; suffered no inconvenience.

Abel Bissel.—Concerned in an oil-mill. Did but little business except when the water was plenty. Improved Scholfield's establishment three or four years. Lacked water, thinks in the fall of 1825. Thinks if Dow operates his mill, beneficial to all. Thinks the custom to the mill would cause this to discharge more water than Miner's could. In Aug., '27, thinks there was a miller regularly employed and constantly attended.

Giles Turner.—Should agree substantially with the Palmers as to the effects of Dow's improvements at the head of the stream. Something was said to him about paying Mr. Miner. Mills below have occasionally wanted water. Eells's establishment, as far as he knows, could do more or less business every day, although there has been a leakage. Those at the lower part of the stream have smaller dams; never claimed a right to control others; had some acquaintance with the Lester mill; often wanted water; although ground a little every day. Fore part of the season of 1827, wet; July, and fore part of August, not.

THE CONFESSION.

According to the best of my knowledge and belief—I confess that I think Owanico, principal sachem of the Mohegan tribe, to be the same as Onecho, the son of Uncas—was a blood connection of the great Sassious, principal sachem of the ancient Pequot Indians!

That Uncas was made a princely sachem by the white men. That Owanico, on the 11th of December, 1698, gave a deed of land to Thomas

Stanton, of Stonington; that the said Stanton sold it to Lieut. James Harris, a noted land speculator, who sold it to Joseph Otis; and the said Otis sold it to Wm. Mynard; and the said William left it by heirship to his son Jonathan, who conveyed it by deed to his son, Capt. Jonathan Mynard, jr., who conveyed it by deed to his son Henry; and the said Henry Mynard conveyed it to me—with all the cows and hogs, &c. &c., by deed—as recorded in Montville.

There were four mortgages on the premises; the last was mine. In my absence, there was a decree of court, that if I did not pay the others, I must be cut off by a "foreclosure." Hence, I confess, I did not want the property—so I concluded to offer it to Peter Richards, for less than the value of my mortgage on the face!—As the said Peter and son were preparing great water-works below, on the same stream, near six miles off; as I thought that they would wish for a fountain, as a reservoir for a dry time; so I confess that in good friendship I offered the same, as I saw no way for them to be supplied with *sure water* otherwise.

But the said Peter differed from me in opinion, and declined the offer, as if he felt no interest seemingly. So I was obliged to take the deed myself or lose my claim!

After this, with some hands, had the trees and bushes cut down, at the outlet of "Oxonoxo" pond, on said premises—to see how the appearances were, and the location of the situation, also.

On the east side, there is a high pile of rocks, from the summit of which may be seen the ocean, three light-houses, several islands, vessels sailing, &c., and retiring down, you have all the romance of the wilderness, bordering on the solitude of monastic hermitage!

On the west side of the stream is another pile or ledge of rocks, forming a promontory!

One pile of rocks is considered good for building-stone, of superb quality, that may be rolled down with ease and convenience; and the other may be easily split into flag or flat stone, according to wish; and also some "fire-stone," enough for several hundred buildings, near at hand.

The pond in front—a dale in the rear, or down the stream southeast, towards the Thames—with excellent springs of water, convenient to the establishment—and other things in appearance, as "chalk clay," "iron ore," &c.

This place has about twenty feet, press and fall, of water; and according to computation, from testimony in court, "a mile square," twelve feet deep, more than 300,000,000 cubic feet, might be applied to the use of machinery.

There was a mill erected here, about one hundred and twenty years ago, kept in use for the neighborhood ever since; and said to have been the first erected in this part of the country; and of course must have been the oldest on the stream by occupancy.

There are eight dams below mine; the last but one belongs to the Richardses—lying on the road from Norwich to New-London; and six betwixt theirs and mine.

From rocks on each side, at the outlet of the pond, a wall for a permanent support might be connected with them at the ends—being about seventy-five feet asunder—from side to side!

This wall being raised sixteen feet high, connected with the two rocks at the ends, would admit of a trench in front for boards to be set perpendicularly, with two thicknesses, so as to break joints, that water nor eels should find a way through the dam, when completed : hence, the old dam being about forty feet above or higher up the stream than the wall, the concave was filled with earth—wet down, to make it permanent and solid around the boards ; and from the old dam to the new wall, which wall was eight feet thick.

The rock on the west side might be so reduced as to admit of a sluiceway for the pond floods to escape from the pond, and so vent itself, without danger of being washed away by ice and freshets. And moreover, double the quantity of water would be retained of the spring freshets, and reserved for a dry season, without injury to anybody, but beneficial to all parties concerned or any ways connected or interested in the water privileges on the stream.

I went to Mr. Richards, and attempted to describe to him the advantage that might be taken of the situation by improvement, thinking it would be for his interest as well as mine ; and if he would aid therein, should share the benefit. I confess that I did go to him this second time, and made this second offer—whether right or wrong, it was well meant by me.

But the offer was declined by him : so I undertook the erection of the dam alone, with the intention of raising it higher than the old dam, to detain more water. For I had no idea of giving offence to any one ; nor did I think that such an act could injure any one, seeing all the water which I expected to detain, was only that which would run off in the spring of the year, without doing anybody any good ; and at a season, too, when there would be plenty of water for all concerned.

But Mr. Richards wrote me a curious kind of letter, or at least it seemed so to me, of which the following is a copy.

New-London, 11 *Oct.* 1826.
Rev. LORENZO DOW,

Sir—Understanding that you are repairing or rebuilding the dam to your Miner pond, without knowing or pretending to know your intentions as to the structure of it, we deem it a friendly duty to advise you, that you have no legal right to raise the dam in the least degree above what it has heretofore been, and that you have not the right to hold back water or to let it off at your pleasure to the injury of those who improve mill-seats below you. We would presume that you have no unfriendly intentions, nevertheless we consider it our duty in this friendly manner to advise you as above, what we have no doubt is law on this subject ; and to add, that we shall endeavor to maintain our own rights, and should you raise your dam above its former height, or hold back, or let off water, otherwise than for your own necessary and fair purposes, and we are injured thereby, we shall hold you liable for all damages.

We are, very respectfully, your obedient servants,
P. & H. A. RICHARDS.

So I called on him for an explanation ; when, I confess, I talked my Lorenzo talk, very plain.

Among the rest, if I mistake not, I think I said, "If you sue me for

damage, and the law will give you my property, without an equivalent—
if you can afford to receive it so, I can afford to let you have it for nothing"
—or words to that point—this being the third time of my calling, and I
think it was the last.

In Nov. 1826, I went to the West and South, and was gone till about
the 16th or 17th of Aug. 1827.

About Dec. 20th, 1826, the sluiceway was blown out, the dam finished,
and the gates shut down, and pond filled and run over, without any harm
to anybody. The mill ground for the neighborhood, one day in the week,
which supplied the neighborhood for the winter. But in the spring there
was a miller all the time, every day, until late in the fall, so that there
should be the usual flow of water as heretofore, steadily grinding for customers as they came to mill.

Before this property fell into my hands, the water has been so low, that
I have been under the necessity of sending out of the neighborhood a distance to obtain grinding for my family. For it appears that almost from
time immemorial there has been a scarcity of water in a dry season, there
being no stream that runs into the pond in a dry time, above-ground ; still,
the pond has been known, before it came into my possession, to rise a foot
in a few days, from springs, when the gate has been kept shut—the water
being, as is said, about fifty feet deep.

All those who are concerned in the water privileges below me, except
the Richardses, admit my dam is no injury to them or their water privilege ; but most of them admit it rather, of the two, to be a benefit than
otherwise !

Mr. Peter Richards called on my wife in my absence, and requested
extra water to be let off, over and above the usual quantity, to keep his
factory with a steady supply, which is very different from a mill going
occasionally, for customers, at my mill ; and it was at Lester's mill, before Mr. R. put up the factory there—which mill was about "thirty odd"
years standing, only.

But as there fell a torrent of rain, Lucy concluded that Mr. R. was
supplied with water; and hence, things remained as they were, until
Elder Palmer, wishing to repair his flume, drew his pond as low as possible, and stopped all the water he could, by corking it with moss, &c.,
which dried Mr. R.'s big factory right up, and they had to stop.

Mr. R. then called on Lucy a second time, and *demanded* the gate to
be hoisted, as his *right*, to have water over and above what the miller let
off by grinding.

I confess that I suppose that she talked some of her "Lucy talk," as
she, instead of playing the hypocrite, is very apt to let off ; and, according to her statement, said that she was glad there were some men, viz.
the Thames Company, who had honor and honesty enough to procure a
fountain of water at their own expense.

So he told her what he would do ; and he did it—namely, commence
suit.

The overseer of the factory, in the fall of 1826, told me that it yielded
a profit of twenty-eight dollars per day, after paying every expense, and
allowing ten per cent interest on the whole capital of sixty thousand dol
lars also.

Now, after my return home about the 16th of August, 1827, to find my property under an attachment of two thousand dollars, was a thing that I little expected ; and to find myself to be so *bad* a man, so mean and wicked, was a thing that I little dreamed of.

The power of fancy must have been very great, when some have believed the *say-so* of the doctors, or of the priests, in opposition to their own senses!

So, thought I, is it possible that I have been at home, and have given such instructions, as some say? No! Where was I when I wrote those instructions laid to my charge?

I was from home when the dam was finished, and wrote nothing about it, by way of instruction, while absent.

But I must confess that I am *convicted* and fould *guilty*, in the eye of the law, of what I here call "Villany detected"—matter of fact to the contrary, notwithstanding; for, to come to the nicety of the case, it is my candid opinion that the dam erected by me, was never any real injury to any one below me. Neither do I think that Peter and H. A. Richards ever had one hogshead of water detained by me, or from having it when they wanted it, and that would have been beneficial to them, had my dam been out of the way.

Now I confess, that after my return from the west, the Messrs. Richards came to see me, and, as they intimated, to settle with me.

But I replied, that I had got nothing to settle with them, for I owed them nothing, neither had I any claim against them, and, of course, had nothing to settle. But if they wished to talk about water, provided the suit was withdrawn, and the cost paid, I was ready to meet them on fair ground ; but while they had a rod shaking over my head, I had nothing to say.

This, Peter said, he was not disposed to do ; for he supposed the law was on his side.

What this law was, I then knew not; for it was not to be found in the *statute book*. But I knew the common old custom ; and the privileges I had bought were handed down, through seven hands, between the Indians and myself.

But times turn. A "new law" must be brought in!—the dawn of a new era begins to appear! One must be favored, and the other depressed!

The privilege of the water, according to custom, which had remained undisputed, not only for "fifteen years" last past, (before Peter began the trouble to claim more water than heretofore,) but for an hundred years anterior to that, was in peaceable possession, by occupancy, one hundred and sixteen years in all.

The suit was commenced three months sooner than was necessary for suing timely for court ; whereas, if they had wished to meet me on principles of reciprocity, they would have waited one week longer, when I should have been at home.

But I suppose they wished to establish a principle, and to see the same exemplified as the law of the land ; and if they did not, no doubt others would.

So the case was appealed up from the county to the superior court ; and in the January term, was put over to October, 1828, when there were so many criminals to be tried, that it was put off till January, 1829; keeping me in suspense by detention, and cutting across all my other arrangements—giving me cost, vexation, and trouble enough.

Being in New Orleans, I had to return back on a fool's errand to attend court for nothing; and such was the conduct of the case during eighteen months.

But the struggle came on at last, with a strong fend-off. The agony is over, and brought forth both a mountain and a mouse!

Now, thoughts being involuntary, I confess what came into my head like a dream, viz. that the office of the county court "bench" being somewhat vacant, an appointment is made for a gentleman of very high standing, as a *counsellor at law*, to fill; but it was not accepted till *after* the late decision; which, if it had been anterior, might have prevented his assiduity on the trial.

Young Mr. C. appears to possess a good delivery at the bar.

My friend Hungerford, made a speech to the point, as I thought, considering circumstances. Here I was called from court to attend meeting, which prevented my hearing the two other gentlemen, viz. Lyman Law, who was my attorney, and Calvin Goddard, who was on the other side. Judge Hosmer was on the bench. The *anti's* were all around, whispering that his honor would give me the case, because I was a *mason;* and were watching for signs, as they have since confessed. Such is the delusion and fanaticism among them!

I applied to the Hon. Calvin Goddard for his plea; but he gave me to understand that he could not help me to "make a book."

I applied to Mr. C., who only furnished me with a short extract, which is annexed, in the trial, with such official documents as I could procure.

An *h*-Englishman, from Wales, by the name of John Dolbeare, a brass-founder, emigrated to America with his wife, whose *coat of arms*, according to *heraldry*, exhibits the family once to have been the *fourth family* in the kingdom of Great Britain. The personal estate inventory was about seventy-five thousand dollars, besides a vast amount of real estate, after his decease.

They had twenty-four children—twenty-two sons, and two daughters. The twenty-fourth child, named George, was given to a gentleman, in appearance, for he had a hat and coat covered with gold-lace, and came from a place called Pogwunk. This son George heired the estate of land in this part of the country.

In 1698, one of the established ministers preached an *election* sermon, (not Calvinistic, but political election,) for which he was to have "two hundred acres of land," "bounded by water," "be the same more or less," *i. e.* fifteen hundred acres; which location was made between Oxoboxo pond and Bozrah lake; and being divided between two clergymen, the preacher kept the south half, and sold it to one Livingston, whose widow sold it to James Harris, the land speculator; he sold it to John Dolbeare, of Boston, whose twenty-fourth child, George, came into possession of it by heirship.

This George was considered a great man in his day, having four sawmills, and much land.

He sent to London for a gun, with his name engraved thereon; and to make a trial with his gun, he shot down a fine beef, and gave it to the poor, saying, "Dress, and eat;" so they took it away.

Having heard *decrees*, or *predestination*, preached, he concluded that it was of little account for us to go to meeting, if all our destinies were fixed; and so he made himself scarce from the pew!

Now, this George had a son by the name of George, whose partner was named Margaret, and was called "Aunt Peggy;" but she was of an unhappy turn of mind; it was impossible for any one to meet her humor—she forever working by the rule of *contrary*.

George, jr., hired the gun, for the namesake engraved; and so it descended to his son George. But Aunt Peggy stole the gun, and sold it for two dollars, which was a grief to the Dolbeare family; and the gun went the rounds while George was absent. But when he came home, the gun being put into his hands at a shooting-match, he kept it, and carried it off, which was construed a *trespass*. So the said George was taken up, and tried before H. Browning, Esq., and condemned for a *trespass*. But George went to Indiana, and carried off the gun with him!

Now, the twenty-fourth child had six children—three sons and three daughters; one of whom married Mr. Guy Richards, of New London, the father of Peter, whose son, H. A., is mentioned in this case.

Now it must be mentioned, that Peggy lived a widow many years, and then married again to a Mr. W., whom I shall call Mr. Wrong.

With spite she cheated her children; got married, and went off: but the race of human career must have an end.

I remarked to my family, that it appeared to me that they would, ere long, hear that Aunt Peggy was taken sick. I went to Boston; returning home, I told Lucy that I thought Aunt Peggy would be willing to see her for the first time.

On our arrival we found she was sick; she then wished to see her children, and to make them some remuneration for the injury done them.

I advised them to have nothing to do with any thing she had, remarking, there would only be a curse attending it; and feeling her time near, I quit home for about two weeks, till I *felt* she was dead. I then returned home.

Judge T. wrote her will, without being candid enough to say it was of no account, but showed it to Mr. W., and put him in train to possess the whole, as Mr. W. had been much in law, and never had been known to lose a case, because he could always *prove* what he undertook!

By going away I escaped the Sunday trap business; and to get out of the clutches of Mr. W., it came into my heart to do with him as God dealt with the Hebrews in the wilderness, viz., give him all he would. I went, inquired, gave, let him dictate, and take all he wanted, and passed receipts; after which, I remarked that I thought his race short and swift, and his judgment sure, and if he died the common death of men, I was mistaken. He stayed a few months only; * * * * *
* * * * under circumstances solemnly and awfully impressive!

Aunt Peggy had her will while she lived, but was prevented it when she died.

M. Dow, of Norfolk, England, turned his thoughts to the wilderness of America. His son T. came over; and his son William Dow, the grandson, was buried at Ipswich. He had four sons, who spent one night in conversation, and dispersed to seek their fortunes. One was heard of no more; one came to Voluntown and settled; one to Plainfield, and the other, Ephraim, settled in Coventry, on lands bought of the Indian sachem, Joshua.

Ephraim married the daughter of Humphrey Clarke, of Ipswich, from whom my father was named, and lies deposited by the side of my mother in my native place. She was the daughter of James Parker, the son of Joseph Parker, whose parents came from England, and were murdered by the Indians; himself, with the other children, escaped the Indians, by hiding in the grass and brush, still in plain sight. One was an infant, which the sister had dropped from her arms; Joseph picked it up, and as the child happened to be still and quiet, they were not discovered.

Joseph died at the age of ninety-four years, having possessed the first house ever built (by one Rust) in Coventry. It had port-holes through hewn logs, for fear of Indians in that day, and was standing since the days within my recollection.

Here, then, according to tradition, were the descendants of Lord Parker, of Macclesfield, England, who is said to have descended from one of the natural children of King Charles II., who, in circumlocution, is said to have descended from William the Conqueror; and, pray, who was he? Why, the son of a w****!

Thus we may all trace back our origin to the ashes from whence we sprang—"dust thou art, and unto dust thou shalt return."

Whether my "coat of arms" be a *star*, a *basket*, or a *broom*, hereditary from my forefathers, what is that to me? If I inherit their vices, I am none the better for that; nor any the worse, if I imitate their virtues. Virtue nor vice can be hereditary in a moral point of view. The *effect* of vice or virtue may, but not the principle, personally; for natural evil is not a moral evil. By giving loose to passions evil in nature, and going beyond the bounds of rectitude, it becomes a sin—moral evil. It is your own act, involving motives, which give character to the action. Reason and judgment should then be called into the account, by proper exercise. Hence the doctrine of the cross, and self-denial, following Christ in the regeneration, by the spirit of his grace, to escape condemnation for personal crime.

Some thought the water from me to R. would take but a few hours to run; but when the gate was hoisted a little extra, (about three feet long and four inches high, which, in court, some said was five feet long and one foot high, which judgment was not correct,) it took about twenty-six hours to reach them, which is the best evidence I have on the subject of its velocity. This letting off was, first, to blow out the sluiceway rather more to my mind; the second time, to secure a plank that was sprung; third, to measure the land by survey that was overflowed, so as to estimate the damage, and remunerate the owners.

There is another privilege on the premises, but it would be a trespass to improve it, as the law now stands. What clashing of interest and trammelling of property by this something called *law!* But it is a poor wind which blows nobody any good. It makes better fishing for lawyers.

Whilst we were standing by the family vault of her great grandfather, which was one hundred years old, by the date there engraved—"John Dolbeare, 1725,"—along came our friend Lafayette, following the masonic and procession of citizens to Bunker Hill, from Boston statehouse—June 17th, 1825.

Thus "all flesh is as grass, and all the glory of man as the flower of grass; the grass withereth, and the flower thereof fadeth away."

The Hebrews were forbidden to reap the corners of their fields, or to return after a sheaf when forgotten, or to glean their fields, for it was for the stranger, the fatherless, and the widow; neither were they to glean their vineyards, for what was left should be for the needy; they might enter their neighbor's vineyard and eat grapes, but not to carry any away.

The stranger, the fatherless, and widow, with the poor, were not to be oppressed, nor be unfeeling, nor bowels of mercy shut up; but were to remember that they once were strangers, and in bondage, in Egypt.

They were interdicted oppressing each other by trading, either in buying or selling. And if a man be unfortunate in worldly affairs, or, by age, infirm, thou shalt relieve him. Humanity and mercy was the law of Moses, as well as justice.

In my experience on the journey of life, I find that man, by nature, is a democrat, as it relates to himself; but when taken in relation to his neighbor, he seems to be a tyrant. As though power constituted right. And hence he will too often make them feel it.

Several times have I *known* the walls of the *tight-houses*, called prisons, in the old world, but have been released, because they found no cause of punishment. To be arrested in my own country, I have been no stranger to such treatment; for do as one may, they will have those who will oppose them.

At Charleston, S. C., the circumstances were painful and distressing. A few months passed over; and whilst those who had me in their power are gone, having reduced me to a level with the world, "all but," yet I have been permitted to see good days in the land of the living, since most of them have been sleeping under ground.

I was called to account in Philadelphia, but a receipt in full produced my discharge, which, anterior, had been attained. In New York, by two claims, from the mismanagement of one who had gone off and died, I was brought into trouble, by those who used authority, when I ought to have been discharged; but the justice of my case was made to appear in a way beyond my ability, and deliverance came to my relief.

At Troy, twenty years after a contract was made and paid by me, and afterwards paid a second time, I was arrested, before a congregation of four or five thousand persons, to make me pay it a third time. To avoid the vexation—after going to attend court, in the dead of winter, on a fool's errand, more than a hundred miles, the law having altered the time of court a month sooner—I gave what would procure an exchange of receipts, "from the beginning of time to the end of the world." But an attorney, whom I had never seen nor employed, stepped forward as a *friend* at the time of the court, and some years after wrote me his bill, and also sent it to an attorney in ———, to make me pay it, (and there

was no escape,) twenty years from the first payment from my hands
See his bill of items:

Retaining fee, warrant attorney, and filing,	$2,68.5
Do. special bail for two, and copy and filing,	43
Notice of retaining 19, do. special bail 19,	38
Do. plea notice for 5 fair copy, copy to file and copy to serve,	1,52.5
Do. affidavit to put cause over February term for 5 and fair copies	75
Court fee taking same, 12, clerk reading and filing affidavit, 12,	25
Writ of sub. 25, do. ticket for 3 and copy,	80
Brief for trial, 75, trial for attending court on notice, $2,00	2,75
Brief on M to put one cause, and me and rule to put over cause,	2,37.5
Augt. of M 100 copy, cost 25, notice of tax, 19, tax, 25, attend. 25,	1,94
	$13,88.5
Counsel retaining fee,	5,00.
Counsel fee at term,	5,00
Received the amount of the within.	$23,88.5

October 31, 1828.

When in Europe I was pursued by the king's officers, both in England and Ireland, who were set on by those who sought to do me harm, by misrepresenting me to the government, to appear loyal, and to remove one whom they thought was in their way; but when I went back, twelve years after, where did I find the calumniators?

Twice have I commenced suit myself, not with the design ever to let it come to trial, but from the necessity of the case—of all evils, to avoid the greatest. Hence they were withdrawn, and I paid the cost; yet, perhaps, it would have been better, if I had not commenced the suits at all.

I have had various suits commenced against me, attended with much trouble and cost. I ever aim to pay all my just and honest debts as soon as I can, for it is ever more satisfactory to me to pay a debt, than to make it; and people sometimes, by suing, are kept out of their money longer than if they had used lenity. It is not a good thing to make debts; but sometimes people are unfortunate, although they have every prospect at the time.

But to oppress the poor and the unfortunate is not good; it is not doing as we would be done by, in the like circumstances; it is a violation of that golden rule of practice—love thy neighbor as ———!

Looking forward to the day of retribution, I have felt much more peace, sweet peace, to err—if indeed it was an error—to show lenity, to "forgive my debt" and lose it, than to attempt to recover it by the tyrannical hand of oppression. For I remember the saying of Him, who is all-powerful, "That which ye measure to others, shall be measured to you again." I had rather attend to the direction, feel peace, leave it with Providence, meet his approbation, and thereby insure his protection, than run the risk of losing his favor and the protecting hand of peace.

To injure another, because we can, is not good, either in his person, or property, or character. For power and confidence should never be abused.

Whoever will reflect on the Jewish economy—not merely the ceremonies of the law, but the rule of practice, as it relates to the stranger, the poor, and the unfortunate—will see a principle which Jesus Christ enlarged upon, by precept and example, on which the "law and the pro phets" were built. For it is a plain case, throughout the general run and tenor of the good Book, that virtue shall not go unrewarded, nor vice unpunished. This may appear enthusiastic. But it is my creed in times of exigency, when no human power can relieve, and all is shut up and dark.

"Where reason fails, there faith begins"—"For man's extremity is God's opportunity." Hence, "Cast thy bread upon the waters, and thou shalt find it after many days."

"In all thy ways acknowledge thou Him, and He shall sustain thee." For He will keep those in peace whose mind is stayed on Him. Read Psalm 91.

Had I been brought up behind a counter, to buy and sell at my own price, and, as an indulged child, to have my own way, or in any other located, limited, and secluded sphere, I should have had but little knowledge of the world; and, of course, been ill qualified to calculate how to meet the contradictions and opposition of a crooked and perverse world, that may well be termed "omnifarious."

But my parents, by example and precept, taught me when young to respect those I stood in relation to, and, hence, to respect myself.

At about fifteen, divine grace was my theme of pursuit. At eighteen, I went into a wide world, seeing, as I started, while viewing the rocks and trees, my mother looking till I got out of sight.

But oh, the scenes, the trying scenes, in the vicissitudes of life, till now, in my fifty-second year! But if I am the man, as stated in the writ, the several paragraphs and the figures interspersed, then it is time that I should confess judgment and be confined, that I may trouble the world no more!

The term *villain*, in these days, is perverted from the sense and mode in which it was formerly used, in the days of the feudal system, when it meant a tenant in servitude, or vassal, which was the landlord's property in that day.

And if a man now owns land, with a water-stream on it, and must not improve it, or alter the situation of it, but by the will and consent of another; then he becomes a vassal, or villain, and tenant at will, for the other. He must not build a new dam, great or small, but by the consent of the one below, if he has machinery, although miles off, and others intervene; nor stop a leak in his dam, nor make a leak, nor raise the dam, nor lower it, but must keep it stationary, for the convenience of the one below, at your own expense, though you do not wish to use it at all. Thus it is like "cap in hand," or "your humble servant"—virtually, like the ancient villains in vassalage; in its degree, according to the feudal form, "my master," which principle is reviving and travelling very fast in the country—this seizing on the outlets of streams, and monopolizing two elements, earth and water!

P. S. Cost, &c., in the aggregate, about two hundred dollars; but what the whole cost was, on the other side, I don't know.

How soon I may be sued again, I do not know; but I acknowledge myself *conquered* and found *guilty, in the eye of the law!* And although I once thought myself a free man, I find that I was mistaken. I am only a villain—vassal—tenant at will—a gate-tender for others at my own expense! And that is not all—*I cannot help myself!* Farewell, sweet freedom! My property I cannot call my own! Brother gate-tenders look out!

TO THE INHABITANTS OF CONNECTICUT.

FELLOW-CITIZENS,—

From a sense of duty to myself and to the public at large, involving the interest and welfare of generations yet unborn, I am constrained to address you on a very interesting, but painful subject, arising from circumstances beyond the power of my control; as the power of redress for relief is only to be found there by the voice of your representatives, in their legislative capacity.

The principle of law, on the subject of water, as it now stands, involves awful consequences, when considered as a precedent, introduced and adopted, to become the governing principle of the country, as the supreme law of the land.

Supposing, for instance, the intended dam on the Shetucket river, above Chelsea Landing, should go into operation—what must be the consequence, as the principle called law, now stands?

It would give a favored *few* complete control over one eighth part of the water in this state, by computation, involving the tributary streams.

For if a man has a water privilege on his premises, he has no right to improve it by building a dam on it for machinery, if there be any mill or factory below; although the dam should be no injury to any one, but rather, a very great advantage to all; but still it would be actionable, for it is considered a crime, in point of law, to do a man a favor without his consent, equally as to do him an injury.

To build a dam, to lower a dam, to tighten a dam, or to make a leak in a dam, or to raise a dam, if there be machinery below, is actionable; you must let it remain as it was, stationary.

One has all the right; the other has no right. One is privileged, the other depressed. One is master, the other a servant. One is "My lord," the other, "Obedient and very humble servant"—"cap in hand." One has all the privilege; the other is deprived of all—not allowed to improve the water equally on his own land; although nobody in the least degree is injured, still it is a crime, unless you obtain the consent of the big man below—whose works may be ten miles off—and a dozen dams intervene; and should all above and below him acknowledge it to be a real benefit to them, still he could prosecute and obtain damage and cost, by this *something*, called *law*,—as exemplified in the late decision at Norwich.

If a citizen has a spring branch on his farm, he is liable to be prosecuted even for stopping water, by damming the stream for a hog-wallow or goose-pond; or, by the same rule, for detaining it falling from the eaves of his house.

Hence the doctrine of equal rights, &c. Privilege is done away, seeing a man is not allowed to improve his own water power and privilege equal to his neighbor; when his neighbor suffers no injury or possible harm by it.

This doctrine being admitted, and the principle of it adopted for law farewell forever to the privileges which our fathers fought and bled to obtain, and then transmitted to us their children. If the fence of a farm be down for a season, my neighbor interdicts my repairing it because he claims the privilege for his hogs, &c., by the same mode of reasoning.

The darkness of the feudal system seems to threaten our borders—an "embargo" being in the land.

Thus the one who is privileged to have the ascendancy over his neighbor, is like a "lord," and should he sell his possession he would sell the privileges with it; and the other is only as a vassal or a kind of "tenant at will," without any way for redress, the statute law being lame on the subject.

Here then I would suggest the propriety of getting a petition from a considerate public, to present to the general assembly, for a redress of grievance, to obtain some special acts of legislation, to protect us in the peaceable possession and enjoyment of our freehold estates in fee simple—with all the privileges thereto belonging—that we may be protected from the imposition and tyrannical hand of oppressors; and thereby prevent the introduction of darkness—the darkness of the feudal system—a favored few being suffered to monopolize two elements, in this land!—by *ex post facto-ism.*

LORENZO DOW.

April 25, 1829.

APPENDIX.

GREAT BRITAIN.

Warrington, April 16th, 1807.

To the Church of God in every place:

This cometh in behalf of Lorenzo Dow, itinerant preacher of the gospel of God our Saviour. We, the undersigned, ministers and members of the people called Methodist Quakers, late in connection with the old body of Methodists, do testify, that although his appearance among us was in much weakness, many suspicions, good and evil report, his word was with power and the Holy Ghost sent down from heaven. From the time we have been favored with his labors, he hath conducted himself on all occasions, in prosperity and adversity, as one whose sole aim is the glory of God and the welfare of mankind, far beyond his strength, in labors more abundant, travelling night and day for the accomplishment of his vast desire to preach the gospel of the kingdom to many perishing for lack of knowledge; and we are witnesses his labor hath not been in vain in the Lord. Many of the stones of the street have been raised to be sons and daughters of Abraham—backsliders reclaimed, and many of infidel principles shaken. From the impressive manner of his life, many, sunk into Laodicean ease, have been stirred up to glorify God with their body, soul, and substance, whom we trust and pray will remain stars in the church militant, and afterwards form one part of his crown of rejoicing in the day of the Lord. Amen.

Being about to depart from this to his native land, we pray that the guidance of the same holy hand, which through a train of divine providences cast his lot among us, may conduct and protect him over the great deep to the American shores in peace and safety. Amen.

R. Harrison,
Richard Mills,
W. M'Ginnis, } *Preachers.**
Peter Philips,
G. Brimelow,

Dublin, October 18th, 1806.

My dear brother Dow:

As you are about to leave this city, I send you this small testimonial of my esteem and love, as it may on some occasions open your way among strangers.

* Also signed by upwards of one hundred persons more

I had but few opportunities of attending your meetings; when I did, I had no doubt of the divine blessing attending your ministry. On other occasions I have had the fullest proof, that although you were confined in your place of preaching, the word of the Lord was not bound, but became the power of God to the salvation of many precious souls. I suppose not less than thirty of these have, on your recommendation, joined the society; several of whom are rejoicing in God, and living to his glory in newness of life.

When you formerly visited Ireland, I witnessed the power of God attending your ministry in several instances, and I rejoice in the continuation of his grace to you. From all I have seen and heard respecting you, I acknowledge the hand of God, who is now, as formerly, abasing the pride of man in the instruments by whom he works.—See 1 Cor. i. 26—29.

I have no doubt of your candid attachment to the Methodists, in affection and interest, as well as doctrine. I believe your aim is to spend and be spent in bringing sinners to the Lord Jesus, and do therefore cordially bid you God-speed. May you have many souls given you in every place, to form your crown of rejoicing in the day of the Lord! May the eternal God be your refuge, and protect you, and your dear wife and little one, is the prayer of
Your affectionate brother in Christ,
MATTHEW LANKTREE.*

Rev. LORENZO DOW.

Dublin, April 21st, 1807.

MY DEAR BROTHER DOW:

I was in expectation of hearing from you ever since your departure. At present I must be brief. Whatever be the ultimate result of the emigrating spirit which is at present moving so many of our dear friends to leave us, I cannot tell; this I know, we already feel in a distressing way its painful effects—our hands hang down, and our enemies rejoice. May the Lord interpose, and order it for our good!

I cannot unravel the providence which prevented brother Joyce from proceeding along with you. I fear he was not in the will of God.

With respect to the fruit of your labors, the general testimony of all I have conversed with has been, that the Lord has owned your ministry in various parts of Ireland. My desire and prayer for you is, that you may feel the Lord's presence, and the power of God with you more fully than ever. I would thank you for a few lines before you leave England. My love in the Lord Jesus to sister Dow, and all our friends who accompany you.
I am your affectionate brother in Christ,
MATTHEW LANKTREE.

MR. Dow, Liverpool.

My dear wife sends her love to sister Dow and you. The class under her care is going on well in general.

---

* Superintendent preacher of the Methodist society in Dublin.

APPENDIX.

New York, November 16th, 1805.

MY UNKNOWN FRIEND:

Having received information from Mr. Kirk, respecting your situation and supposing you to be a proper person, from your influence in the Irish connection, I take this opportunity, the earliest that offers, to write to you, by the way of Liverpool, on a subject in which our brethren are deeply interested. Mr. Lorenzo Dow has embarked again for Europe, better furnished perhaps for success than when he was with you last. His confidence of success must at least be very considerably increased, having succeeded so well in deceiving or duping so many of the preachers in the American connection. I hope that our brethren in Europe will unanimously resolve to have nothing at all to do with him. There is the greater necessity of this, as it appears to me, that if you should suffer him to have any access to our people, it would not only do us an injury, but him also: for such is the nature of his plan, or system, that he estimates truth and right, not so much by principle as by success. If he should not make immediately for Ireland, please to use your ability to put the English on their guard. I expect he embarked for Liverpool. If he did not take such grounds as to lead our people into an acquiescence, and even approbation of his measures; if he did not affect to act as a Methodist, I should say nothing about him. But as an itinerant plan may indirectly lead to imposture, it stands us in hand to be very cautious to distinguish between the true and the false itinerant: the lines of distinction should always be kept very clear between the Methodist preacher and his *ape*. I am sorry, my dear friend, that we can give you no better specimen of the fruits of Methodism in this country. Alas! alas! shame! shame! It shall be published in the streets of London and Dublin, that Methodist preachers in America, have so far departed from Wesley and their own discipline, as to countenance and bid God-speed to such a man as Mr. Dow; the last person in the world who should have been suffered to trample Methodism under foot with impunity or countenance. His manners have been clownish in the extreme; his habit and appearance more filthy than a savage Indian; his public discourses a mere rhapsody, the substance often an insult upon the gospel: but all the insults he has offered to decency, cleanliness, and good breeding; all his impious trifling in the holy ministry; all the contempt he has poured upon the sacred scriptures, by often refusing to open them, and frequently choosing the most vulgar sayings as a motto to his discourses, in preference to the word of God—all this is as nothing in comparison. He has affected a recognizance of the secrets of men's hearts and lives, and even assumed the awful prerogative of prescience, and this not occasionally, but as it were habitually, pretending to foretell, in a great number of instances, the deaths or calamities of persons, &c.

If he makes converts as an apostle, he will not meet with your interference; but I have this confidence in my elder brethren, that as the disciples of the great Wesley, whom they have known in the flesh, they will make a public stand against this shameless intruder, this most daring impostor.*

Grace and peace,

NICHOLAS SNETHEN.

To the Rev. MATTHIAS JOYCE,
Dublin, Ireland.

A true copy: The original is in Mr. Joyce's possession.

JOHN JONES.
P. JOHNSON.

CONTINENT OF AMERICA.

State of Virginia, Richmond District, 4th Feb. 1806.

DEAR LORENZO:

I expect you will be surprised and disappointed on the arrival of this letter, without complying with your request—" send on your manuscript." I do assure you it is not for want of inclination, but the want of time to collect the materials of such a work—the vacancy wherein I flattered myself (when with you) I could occupy in the business you required. On my arrival at Lynchburg and New London, from the state of things I was continually on the push. I went so far as to take with me the scattered accounts, in order to select therefrom, but could not take nor make time, so as to be composed for such a work; but, as I cannot comply with your request in that, I will enclose to you " Dr. Jenning's Vindication of Camp-Meetings," and "A short account of a Camp-Meeting in North America."

I received yours from New York a little before you embarked for Europe, together with your companion's inclusive, and doubt not but that you have had the prayers and well-wishes of numbers of your American brethren and friends, as well as myself, for your health and preservation at sea, and safe landing in Europe, and also for your friendly reception and usefulness among our European brethren.

We are informed in Scripture, that we should " render to all their dues;" and if you have yours, it cannot be denied that your ministerial labor, amidst your indefatigable exertions has been, and still remains a blessing to hundreds and thousands; and as I have been much in your company for the term of about four years, I have tracked your way in Georgia as Presiding Elder of the District there, as also in Virginia; and have had an opportunity of forming a considerable judgment, and am conscious that many stubborn infidels will praise God in time and eternity, that they ever heard the sound of your voice. Yet sensible I am that you

---

* An "intruder" is a bad character—but a "shameless" one must be callous to all delicate and important feelings. An "impostor" is a bad character—a "daring" one is worse;—but the "most daring" is in the superlative degree—which charge is unfounded—as Cosmopolite has given an honest account of himself at all times, to all persons, and in all countries wherever he hath been—whether in Europe or America, from Quebec to New Orleans; and the foregoing history is a simple relation in miniature for the correction of error, the wel fare of Zion, and those whom it may concern. This, with Dr. C * * * threatening me with Lord Castlereagh, &c. gave rise to my pursuers, and afterward to advertise me in the minutes of the conferences, both in England and Ireland!

have many enemies, and not confined to the irreligious alone. Yet, for my own part, (although your manner has been much out of the common order,) that piety and extensive usefulness, as an instrument to pull down Calvinism and Deism, and that accompanied with visible and sudden awakenings on the consciences of sinners, and which has terminated in (as I believe) the sound conversion of many, has ever been a motive in me to bear with your apparent irregularities, and to encourage, by every possible effort consistent with propriety, rather than to "forbid one so evidently casting out devils in the name of the Lord;" and withal, one whom I consider to be orthodox in doctrine and a friend to the cause of Methodism.

Had you been with me the camp-meeting following at Kingswood Chapel, in Amherst circuit, the first of November from Friday until Tuesday, you would have discovered on your arrival a much better prospect than we saw by the first appearance at the Marquest Road in Louisa. Providence so ordered that the week preceding which was the quarterly meeting at Keys, the weather was wet and cold, and attended with snow, which in all probability moved the brethren to fortify themselves. So they marked off the ground, and felled trees, and built seven small houses, covered with boards, and snugly filled in with mortar. Six out of the seven had fire-places, with doors hung on hinges and fastened with a wooden button; and one of these house-tents was set apart wholly for the ministers. On my arrival Thursday evening I collected those who were on the ground, at the sound of the ram's horn. Sung a millenium hymn, and joined in prayer for God's blessing on the meeting; and a melting time we had, which I received as an omen of good to come, at the commencement of the meeting next day. If ever I felt an earnest of good to come, I felt it at my arrival on that ground; and though we had fewer preachers and people than usual at such meetings, the Lord was with us in majesty and great glory. Sinners were awakened and converted, insomuch that it was adjudged not less than sixty souls obtained saving conversion at that meeting, and many were engaged for, and I trust obtained the blessing of sanctification, and forty were admitted into the church. Satan here, as at other meetings of the kind, showed his disapprobation at our breaking down his kingdom. A man threatened to break my neck: another fired off a pistol or gun. On Sunday evening I read the law, "Ten lashes on his or her bare back, well laid on." The work from this, as from other camp-meetings, spread in every direction. One wagon company from near Lynchburg, a distance of thirty miles, had occasion to stop on their return near a tavern, and being all on fire singing the praises of God, several young people came out to the wagon, and being taken by the hand by those in the wagon, were helped in; and, being touched to the heart, they professed religion before they parted: God's blessing appeared with them as with the ark in the days of old. The meeting at the Marquest Road, terminated in the conversion of about thirty souls, and a spread of religion therefrom. The meeting at Reedy Church, Carolina, the week before, was like the bread on the water. I am informed all the sinners in the wagon from Richmond, obtained religion before they got back to town, and a work took place in Richmond therefrom which proved the happy conversion of many, and added many to the church. The interview you had with Robert Sample, the Baptist minister, has (as I am told) greatly weakened his influence, and opened the eyes of the people. The discerning worldlings, I am told, burlesqued Mr. Sample as follows: two officers were represented on the field of battle, and one being found too weak, dropped his sword and ran off, saying, "Sword, fight for yourself." I suppose you recollect Mr. S. went off before you were done, and left his book.

The meeting at Roper's Chapel, in New Kent, where our opposition was greatest, has been wonderfully blessed. Two of the old lady's daughters converted, who granted us the privilege of the camp-ground, and many others. Some of those daring opposers have been severely scourged since. Old Sam's monument yet sticks to the tree. It was a providence sure enough that it rained, as we agreed; as I am told since, the collegians at Williamsburg, backed by their president the bishop, say, had it not rained they would have been upon us: so the beloved clouds came and helped us. The work is going on in a lively degree about Roper's yet Our preacher, the magistrate John Saunders, who was afraid to befriend us at that time, writes me since thus: "When you appointed our camp-meeting some time last summer, so weak was my faith, and so hardened did I believe the people in our neighborhood to be, that it was a query with me whether one soul would be converted at it; yea, I feared (although I can truly say I was a friend to the institution) that through the wickedness of the wicked, it would be productive of more harm than good (accidentally.) But oh! the depth of the riches both of the wisdom and knowledge of God! How unsearchable are his judgments and his ways past finding out! May light ever shine on that day that the camp at Roper's commenced! Whenever you see Doctor Jennings of Campbell, please present my compliments to him, and inform him that if there was but one of his pamphlets in the world on the subject of defending camp-meetings, I would willingly, gladly give its weight in gold for it, rather than see it no more."

I am now just from the Virginia conference, at Norfolk. The bishops Asbury and Whatcoat were well, and we had a time similar to a camp-meeting. Preaching went on by night and day in both towns, and souls were awakened and converted; and although Satan raged, some spat in the faces of the ministers, and one minister had his nose rung, they bore it with Christian fortitude, and I trust one hundred souls were converted during the time. Glory to God in the highest, peace on earth, good-will to men! My respects to sister Dow. The Lord bless you both, and bring us all to glory, prays your brother and friend in Jesus,

STITH MEAD.

VICISSITUDES;

OR THE

JOURNEY OF LIFE.

BY PEGGY DOW.

"A virtuous woman is a crown to her husband: but she that maketh ashamed is as rottenness in his bones."—*Prov.* xii. 4.
"Who can find a virtuous woman? for her price is far above rubies.
The heart of her husband doth safely trust in her, so that he shall have no need of spoil.
She will do him good, and not evil, all the days of her life."—*Prov.* xxxi. 10, 11, 12.

NEW YORK:
R. WORTHINGTON, 750 BROADWAY.
1881.

VICISSITUDES, &c.

I was born in the year 1780, in Granville, Massachusetts, of parents that were strangers to God; although my father was a member of the Church of England, and my mother had been raised by pious parents, of the Presbyterian order. But, whether she had any sense of the necessity of the new birth and holiness of heart, I cannot say; for she was called to a world of spirits when I was but five months old, leaving behind six children, two sons and four daughters, my eldest sister being about fifteen years old. My father married in about six months after the death of my mother; and, although the woman that he married was an industrious, good housewife, yet he lost his property, and was reduced very low, by the sinking of continental money; and the children were scattered as a consequence. My eldest sister married when I was six years old; and she prevailed on my father to give me to her, which accordingly he did; and I was carried into the state of New York, and saw his face no more.*

My tender heart was often wrought upon by the Spirit of God, and I was at times very unhappy, for fear I should die, and what would become of my soul! I was early taught that there was a God, a heaven, and hell; and that there was a preparation necessary to fit me for those mansions of rest, prepared for all that are faithful until death. My heart often mourned before God, young as I was, for something, I scarce knew what, to make me happy. I dared not sleep without praying to God, as well as I knew how, for many years. My sister's husband being a man not calculated to gain the world, although they had no children, I was raised to labor as much as my strength would permit; and perhaps more, as my constitution was very delicate from my birth. But the Lord was my helper, though I knew him not by an experimental knowledge, yet I had a fear of him before my eyes; and he that taketh care of the young ravens cared for me. From the time that I was six years of age until I was eleven, my serious impressions never left me; but from twelve to fifteen I was mixing with those that were unacquainted with God, or the things that pertain to the kingdom of heaven. My mind was taken up with the vanities of this present world, although my heart was often tender under the preaching of the gospel, so that I could weep and mourn; yet

---

* The summer past, in my journey to the east, I met with a half-brother, whom I had not seen for twenty-seven years—and with whom my father died: and also was at one of my sisters, whom I had not seen but once for twenty years. She being nine or ten years older than myself, was able to inform me of some particulars concerning my mother's death, which were a consolation to me

I did not seek the Lord in earnest to the saving of my soul. At the age of fifteen, the Lord laid his rod upon me in taking away my health, which was not restored until I was seventeen. In that time, I was much afraid I should be called to pass the dark valley, but the Lord was pleased to restore me to health again in a good degree; and at the age of nineteen, I set out to seek my soul's salvation, through many trials and difficulties. The Methodists' preaching and zeal were new in that part of the country where I lived at that time; and my sister's husband was very much opposed to them, so that it made my way very trying; but I was determined, come what might, that I would take up my cross and follow Jesus in the way. I was willing, and gave up all my young companions, and all the diversions of which I had been very fond—such as dancing, and company that feared not God; and the Lord, who giveth liberally, and upbraideth not, gave me peace and consolation in him. My sister and myself joined the first society that was raised in that part of the country, at a neighborhood called Fish Creek, about four miles from where we lived; where we attended preaching and class-meeting once a week. And the Lord was very precious to my soul in those days.

About that time, my brother-in-law was brought to see himself a sinner, and embraced religion; and we were a happy family, although but three in number. We often felt like heaven began below, Jesus precious to our souls! The preachers made our house their home, at that time, and it was my delight to wait on them. I felt as if I could lie at their feet, and learn instruction from their lips. My chief delight was in going to meeting, and praising and singing praises to my God and Saviour. We had preaching once in two weeks in our neighborhood. But few attended for nearly two years; yet the preachers continued to preach, and that in faith, and the Lord heard and gave them their hearts' desire. They formed a little class, consisting only of seven; my brother and sister, two other men and their wives, and myself, composed the society in the place where I lived. We had class-meeting and prayer-meeting every week at the beginning; and it was but a few months before the Lord burst the cloud, and the work broke out, and sixty or seventy were added to the number. We had precious times of the out-pouring of the Spirit of God. If we met only for prayer-meeting, oftentimes our meetings would last until twelve and one o'clock, and souls would be so filled with divine love, that they would fall prostrate on the floor, and praise Christ their King! So we continued to love like children in one family, for two or three years, when some difficulties took place; however, none were turned out of society. O! how sweet it is for brethren to dwell together in unity—but how often doth the enemy of mankind make use of that most destructive weapon, *division*, to destroy the fallen race of Adam!—O that Christians would make a stand against him; and live and love like children of one family—that the world might say, "See how these Christians love one another!"

After this, I lived in love and union with my brethren for two years or more; and enjoyed the privilege of preaching and class-meetings, and had many precious seasons to my soul.

About this time, "camp-meetings" began to be introduced into that part of the country, and were attended with the power of God, in the conversion of many precious souls!

e was one about thirty miles from where I then lived;
aw attended it, where he met with Lorenzo Dow, on
; and invited him home with him, to preach at our
d sent on the appointment a day or two beforehand,
ight get notice. And as he was a singular character,
us to see and hear him. The day arrived, he came,
rowded, and we had a good time. I was very much
ad heard such strange things about him.
o my brother-in-law's, but did not come for several
intments to preach twice and thrice in the day. How-
e, and tarried all night. The next morning he was
miles from our house; and little did I think that he
marrying, in particular that he should make any pro-
to me: but so it was, he returned that day to dinner;
ı with my sister, concerning me, he inquired of her
essed religion. She told him the length of time. He
rhether I kept wicked company. She told him I did
that I had often said, "I had rather marry a preacher
, provided I was worthy; and that I would wish them
ful to souls." By this time I happened to come into
ked me if I had made any such remarks. I told him
ed me if I would accept of such an object as him. I
but went directly out of the room—as it was the first
to me, I was very much surprised. He gave me to
should return to our house again in a few days, and
conversation with me on that subject; which he did,
eting ten or twelve miles from where I lived. He re-
ning, and spoke to me on the subject again, when he
ld marry, provided he could find one that would con-
; and preaching the gospel; and if I thought I could
him, and give him up to go, and do his duty, and not
have his company more than one month out of thir-
free to give his hand to me; but if I could not be
bor in the vineyard of his God, he dared not make any
; for he could not enjoy peace of mind in any other
he I must weigh the matter seriously before God,
ke such an engagement, and conform to it; and not
o as to prevent his usefulness to souls. I thought I
y a man that loved and feared God, and that would
tue and religion among his fellow-mortals, than any
lt myself inadequate to the task, without the grace of

Yet I felt willing to cast my lot with his; and be a
lrance to him, if the Lord would give me grace; as I
uld, if I stood as I ought—and I accepted of his pro-
ı on his way to Canada, and from thence to the Mis-
ınd did not expect to return in much less than two
dence spared, and the way should open for a union of
eturned, we would be married! But would strive in
ı in all others of such importance, to lay it before the
eted by him, as far as we could judge, and not rush
state, that so much concerned our happiness in this

world and the next. As I doubt not many engage
matrimony, without once considering its importance
they lay themselves under to each other, to do all in
the silken cord not prove a chain of iron.

He left me, and went on his way to preach the g[o]
and from thence to the south, and was gone for nea
returned; he left an appointment for a camp-meetin
some of the preachers, on his return, which he fulfi
ber the fourth, we were joined in the bands of m
evening. There was not any present but the fam
who performed the ceremony. Early in the morni
Mississippi territory, in company with my brother
to remove to that country if he should like it, as L[e]
appointments, previously given out, for four thousan

I expected to continue to live with my sister, as
and was much attached to me, or seemed to be so
Lord ordered it otherwise. My Lorenzo was gon[e]
before he returned to me. My brother-in-law was p
try, and intended to return to it with his family, i[n]
husband was preparing to go to Europe, in the fa[l]
stayed with me about two weeks: and then started
me with my sister. They were preparing to remov
July; this was in May, and my Lorenzo was to me[e]
country, where they were to carry me; and from t
New York, and they continue on their journey to the
But he went on as far as Vermont, and held a numb
he saw his sisters that lived there; and then feeling
to Western, where I then was, he gave up the inte[r]
nada, and came back, prepared to take me to New
intended to embark for Europe.

We stayed a few weeks in Western, until my b
temporal concerns settled; and then, after bidding m
in the Lord farewell, we set off for New York, a
who went the same road we were going, eighteen or
Lorenzo held several meetings, and stayed two or
and then bid each other farewell, expecting to meet ag[ain]
or two years. But the providence of God did not f[ar]
ference of the enemy of mankind prevented; for w
and could I have foreseen what awaited my unfortun
try to which she was bound, the parting would have
ing. But it is happy for us that we do not know w
the great Master knoweth best how to prepare our m
lation, while we travel through this world of wo. (
sorrowful and afflicting, but it was light when compa

We left Westmoreland, and went down to Albany
some acquaintances, and stayed for several days at t[h]
lor, and were treated as if we were their children.

Now my sphere of life was altered. It was the
so far from home without my sister; she was like [a]
knew no other. My heart often trembled at what [I]
continually among strangers; being so little acquai[nted]

the world, it made me feel like one at a loss how to behave, or what to do.

Lorenzo was very affectionate and attentive to me. He left me at Albany with sister Taylor, who was going down to New York in a sloop. As I was very much fatigued by riding on horseback, he thought it best for me to go down with her, by water; while he went by land, rode one horse, and led the other. He arrived in New York perhaps four-and-twenty hours before me. I went on board, for the first time that I ever was on the water, except to cross a ferry.

It made me somewhat gloomy to be on board the vessel among strangers, while going down the river to the city of New York, as I had never been in such a place before. However, we landed about ten o'clock at night, where I met Lorenzo, who had been on the look-out for some time. We went to a friend's house, that had been very kind to him in days past, who then belonged to the Methodist church. I felt much embarrassed, as I had never been in the city before. We stayed in New York several weeks, and had some precious meetings. Here I became acquainted with some kind friends, who were to me like mothers and sisters; whilst Lorenzo left me and went to fulfil some appointments he had made in Virginia and North Carolina, and expecting only to be gone five or six weeks; but was detained, contrary to his expectation, near three months. In that time the fever, that was common in the city of New York, broke out, and I went with Mrs. Quackenbush to the country, about forty miles up the river, to a brother Wilson's, where she carried her children to go to school. Here I stayed several weeks. They were people of handsome property; but the more we have the more we want, as has been observed by many. And I think it will hold good almost without exception; for they were much engaged to gain property, as if they had only bread from hand to mouth. I was a stranger, and many times I felt as such, but the Lord gave me support, so that I was tolerably cheerful in the absence of my companion. Before he returned, I went back to New York, where I stayed until he came; and prepared to sail for Europe, which was some time in November. We obtained a protection from our government, when leaving the country for England. It was necessary to have witnesses to prove that he was the Lorenzo Dow that was identified and intended in the documents which he had obtained from the United States of America. Consequently he got N. S. and J. Q. to go before a notary public, and certify that he was the same Lorenzo Dow referred to in the documents. Mr. N. S. gave in under oath, that "he knew him from his youth * * * * * * * * holy gospel!" And about the same time he wrote letters to Ireland and England, to make his way narrow in those countries. And no thanks to him that it did not bring Lorenzo into the greatest distress and difficulties that a man could have been brought into. But through the mercy of God it was otherwise overruled.

He gave me my choice, to go with him, or stay with friends in America, as there were many that told us I might stay with them, and be as welcome as their children; and strove to prevent my going to a land where I would find many difficulties and dangers to encounter that I was unacquainted with, and could not foresee. But I chose to go, and take my lot and share with him of whatever might befall us. Consequently on the 10th of November, 1805, we set sail from New York for Liverpool, in old England. We embarked about 10 o'clock, with a fine breeze. They spread their canvass, and were soon under way.

Lorenzo came into the cabin, and told me to go on deck, and bid farewell to my native land! I did so—and the city began to disappear! I could discover the houses to grow smaller and smaller; and at last could see nothing but the chimneys and the tops of the houses; then all disappeared but the masts of vessels in the harbor. In a short time nothing remained but a boundless ocean opening to view; and I had to depend upon the Providence of God. I went down into the cabin, and thought perhaps I should see my native land no more!

The vessel being tossed to and fro on the waves, I began to feel very sick, and to reflect I was bound to a foreign land; and, supposing I should reach that country, I knew not what awaited me there. But this was my comfort, the same God presided in England that did in America. I thought if I might find one real female friend, I would be satisfied.

I continued to be sea-sick for near two weeks, and then recovered my health better than I had enjoyed it in my life before.

We were twenty-seven days out of sight of land. The vessel being in a very bad situation, we had not been at sea more than five or six days, before the rudder began to fail; so they could not have commanded her at all, if the wind had been unfavorable. The weather was very rough and stormy; but through the mercy of God, the wind was favorable to our course, so that we reached safe our place of destination.

When we arrived in the river at Liverpool, we were not permitted to land, until they could send up to London, and get returns from there, as our vessel came from a port subject to the yellow fever; on that account, we were obliged to stay in the river for ten days, before we were permitted to come on shore.

I never saw a woman for thirty-seven days, except one, who came along side our vessel, to bespeak the captain as a boarder at her house, when he should come on shore.

I strove to pray much to God to give us favor in the eyes of the people, and open the way for Lorenzo, to do the errand that he came upon; and to give him success in preaching the gospel to poor sinners. The prospect was often gloomy. Lorenzo used to say to me, keep up your spirits—we shall yet see good days in Old England, before we leave it, as the sequel proved.

We went on shore the twenty-fourth or fifth of December. Lorenzo had a number of letters to the people in Liverpool. Some were letters of recommendation; others, to persons from their friends in America.

We went with the master of the vessel to a boarding-house, where I was left until Lorenzo went to see what the prospect might be, and whether he could meet with any that would open the way for him to get access to the people. After giving out all the letters but *one*, he returned to me; having been two or three hours absent without any particular success.

The house that I tarried at was a boarding-house for American captains; and the women that were there, were wicked enough! My heart was much pained to hear my own sex taking the name of their Maker and Preserver, in vain! O! thought I, shall I never meet again with any that love and fear God? Lorenzo intended to go and find the person that the last letter was directed to, and told me I might either stay there or go

e to go with him, rather than be left with them any long-
it night, and we had not much to depend upon, without
'rovidence. We started, but could not find the person
However, at last, as we were walking, Lorenzo looked
and happened to espy the name that he was after; ac-
it up to the door, and gave a rap, and were admitted.
letter. There was a woman from Dublin, who seeing
igers and foreigners, began to inquire of Lorenzo, for
merica; and shortly after this, she asked him if he had
nan by the name of Lorenzo Dow. Not knowing that
country could have any knowledge of him, it was very
He told her, that was his name, and she was as much
irn. She had seen him in Ireland, when he was there
; but did not know him now, as he had had the small-
seen him, which had made a great alteration in his ap-

ie house invited us to tarry all night; but the woman
ons. They were Friends, (Quakers,) and told us there
dy just across the street that kept a boarding-house,
e accommodated with lodging for the night. And as it
iat late in the evening, the man conducted us thither,
l permission to stay.
l little to depend on but the openings of Providence, he
reland, and take me to his friends, and leave me there;
to that country, and had returns from his old friend Dr.
invitation from him to bring me, saying that I should
is house as long as we chose, while Lorenzo pursued
i Ireland and England. Lorenzo went and procured a
: channel, in a packet, to Dublin, but we did not sail for
we had to stay in Liverpool for some time. Our board
wo guineas a week, which was bringing Lorenzo very
. At last we got on board of the packet, with our little
e provisions for the voyage; but the wind proved unfa-
'ere driven back into the port of Liverpool again; and
for no less than five times in succession.
friend that we met at the Quaker's, had introduced us
iple who were Methodists, where the woman was a very
; this opened the door for acquaintance, and we went
s.
hat we were boarding with, told us we could not stay
er, as her house was full; so we must go elsewhere.
re went on board of the packet, and put to sea, we had
: than two or three hours before the wind blew a gale.
at they could not see their hands before them on deck,
how soon we might be cast on rocks or sand-banks, and
r. There were some on board who, before the storm
n very profane in taking the name of their Maker in
hey saw and felt the danger that they were in, they were
as any persons could be!
wonder that people would or could be so careless and
saw no danger; but when the waves began to roll, and

the ship began to toss to and fro, they were struck
horror !
My husband and myself lay still in the birth, and
in that Hand that could calm the roaring seas ;
composed. At daylight the captain made for the p
and about eight or nine o'clock in the morning, we
but as we were coming in, under full sail and a st
large ship, of the African trade, that was lying at
we ran foul of her, but through mercy were preserv

The weather was very rainy ; the streets were m
ed through the mud for a considerable distance ; th
beyond description ; but my Lorenzo cheered my
that the Lord would provide, which I found to be tr

We went to Mr. Forshaw's, the people that we
the friend that we saw at the Quaker's, the first ni
pool. When my good friend, Mrs. Forshaw, now
was touched with pity for me, as I was very mud
told Lorenzo that he had better leave me with h
through the country, until the weather was better,
to Ireland in the spring ; which invitation we we
Oh ! how the Lord provided for me in a strange lan
to depend on but Providence !

My Lorenzo left me at her house, and proceeded
he was gone about two weeks. But previous to thi
his way, so that he had held a number of meetings
woman had been brought to see herself a sinner,
of her soul.

I was at this time in a state of * * * * * * * * *, ar
wnat depressed ; but the Lord gave me favor in th
and they were very kind to me while he was g
meetings and preaching, which was very refreshin
ought to bless God that I had found the same religi
I had experienced in my own native land. I was
distressed in mind, for fear my husband should
strange land. But he returned to me at the time I
had several invitations to other parts of the cou
which he accepted.

I left Liverpool with him for Warrington, where
a man that came to Liverpool on business. This n
there was such a person as Lorenzo in the country
had done his business, as though he wanted to go to
ed about for some time, when he at last went into a
longed to the people called Kilhamites, (where Lor
to preach,) and found a congregation assembled to l
preaching, during which the people were very sol
many were much wrought upon, this man invited I
rington, where there was a little society of people
ists, and that the meeting-house should be opened to
found them a very pious people. We stayed there
he held meetings two and three times in the day ; w
good work in that place, and many were brought

Peter Philips, the man that invited Lorenzo there, and his wife, were very friendly to us, and their house was our home ever after when we were in Warrington.

A widow lady who lived there, had three daughters, one of whom lived in London, and the other with her. She came out to hear Lorenzo preach; and one day, after meeting, she came to Peter Philips' to see us, and was very friendly. Lorenzo asked her if she had any children. She told him she had three, and that two were with her. He inquired if they professed religion. She told him that one of them had made a profession, but she feared that she had lost it; but that the youngest never had. He requested her to tell them to come and see him; but the mother insisted that he should come and see them, and he then could have an opportunity to converse with them at home. He did so; they both became very serious, and came to his meetings; and although they had been very gay young women, they would come up to be prayed for in the public congregation. The result was, they both got religion; and the youngest has since died happy in the Lord. The eldest came down from London on a visit to her mother's, where my Lorenzo saw her, and he was made an instrument, in the hand of God, of her conversion to Him. She was one of the most affectionate girls I ever saw.

We stayed in and about Warrington until May; in which time Lorenzo had openings to preach in different places—more than he could attend; and the Lord blessed his labors abundantly to precious souls!

In May we returned to Liverpool, and prepared to cross the channel to Ireland. We had a very pleasant voyage, and arrived in safety. We found our kind friend, Dr. Johnson, and his family, well; and we were received with affection by many. The preachers that were in Dublin, were very friendly, and I felt much united to them. We were invited to breakfast, dine, and sup, almost every day. But my situation being a delicate one, it made it somewhat * * * * * to me! The friends were as attentive to me as I could have wished; for which may the Lord fill my heart with gratitude!

Lorenzo stayed with me for some time, and then went into the country, where he held many meetings, and the Lord was with him. After which he returned to Dublin, and, with the doctor, he went over again to England. I stayed with Mrs. Johnson until his return, where I expected to continue until I should get through my approaching conflict, if it was the will of the Lord to bring me through. I felt in tolerable good spirits; and although I was many hundred miles from my native land, yet the Lord gave me favor in the eyes of the people. My wants were supplied, as it related to my present situation, abundantly.

Lorenzo stayed in England for six or eight weeks, and then returned to me, to be with me in my approaching conflict. He was very weak in body, but continued to preach two and three times in the day. He got some books printed, which enabled him to prosecute his travels through England and Ireland.

While he was absent, a woman had spoken to a doctor to attend me when I should want him, which was not agreeable to my Lorenzo. But having gone so far, it was thought by those that employed him, that it was best not to employ any other; and I, being unacquainted with the manners and customs of the country, was passive. My Lorenzo was much hurt;

but I was not sensible of it, as much before as after. If I had been, I should not have suffered it to be so; but we are often mistaken in what will be best for us.

The time arrived that I must pass through the trial, and my Lorenzo was at the doctor's. But those that attended on me would not suffer him to come into the room where I was, which gave him much pain. I did not at that time know how much he was hurt; but after my child was born, which was on the 16th of September, between three and four o'clock, he was permitted to come in; he had a white handkerchief on his head, and his face was as white as the handkerchief. He came to the bed, and took the child, observing to me, that we had got an additional charge, which, if spared to us, would prove a blessing, or else one of the greatest trials that possibly we could have to meet with. I expect Lorenzo passed through as great a conflict in his mind, as he had almost ever met with. The Lord was my support at that time, and brought me safely through. The friends were very kind to me, and supplied my wants with every thing that was needful; and in about two weeks I was able to leave my room. My heart was glad when I viewed my little daughter: she was a sweet infant. But oh! how short-lived are earthly joys! We stayed in Dublin until she was five weeks old; and then Lorenzo, with myself and our little one, embarked on board a packet for Liverpool. The weather was rainy, and tolerably cold: there was no fire in the cabin. There were a number of passengers, men and women, who thought themselves rather above the middle class, who were very civil to us. But I was so much afraid that my little infant would be too much exposed, that I neglected myself, and probably took cold. We were two nights and one day on board the packet. We got into Liverpool about ten or eleven o'clock, where I was met by my good friend, Mrs. Forshaw. We went to her house, where we stayed a day or two; and then took stage for Warrington, about eighteen miles from Liverpool, where we arrived on Sunday morning. Our friends, Peter Philips and his wife, were at meeting. Lorenzo went to the chapel. The people were very much rejoiced to see him. They had been concerned for us, as they had not heard from us for some time. Many of the friends from the country came to see us; while Lorenzo had meetings, in town and country, two and three times in a day; and the Lord was present to heal mourning souls.

Dr. Johnson came with us from Ireland. He was much engaged in helping to bring souls to the knowledge of the truth, and was, I trust, made an instrument of good to many. Lorenzo and the doctor travelled into various places in Lancashire and Cheshire, with some other counties, and many were brought to see themselves sinners, and seek their souls' salvation.

The people in that country seemed to feel much for me, and manifested it by numberless acts of kindness. For, instead of having to sell my gown for bread, as Lorenzo told me I might have to do, when we were in America, there was scarcely a day but I had presents of clothing or money, to supply myself with whatever I needed. Oh, how grateful ought I to be to my great Benefactor, for all his mercies to unworthy me!

My little *Letitia Johnson*, for so was my child called, grew, and was a very fine, attracting little thing. I found my heart was too much set upon it, so that I often feared I should love her too well; but strove to give myself, and all that I had, to my God.

Lorenzo was in a very bad state of health, which alarmed me very much. I often cried to the Lord to take my child or my health, but spare my dear husband! The thought was so painful to me, to be left in a strange land, with a child, so far from my native soil. The Lord took me at my word, and laid his afflicting hand upon me.

Lorenzo and the doctor went to Macclesfield, and expected to be gone a week, and left me at Peter Philips', where I was taken sick, the day they started, with the nervous fever, but kept up, and nursed my child, until two or three days before they returned. I thought I had taken a very severe cold, and should be better, but grew worse every day.

The friends were very kind to me, particularly Mary Barford, a young lady of fortune, who had got religion through the instrumentality of Lorenzo. She attended me two and three times a day. After I got so as not to be able to sit up, she hired a girl to take care of my child. My fever increased very fast, and the night before Lorenzo got to Warrington, I thought I was dying, and those that were about me were very much alarmed, and sent for a doctor; he came, and administered something to me. He said I was not dying, but that I was very sick. The next morning Doctor Johnson and Lorenzo came; they found me in bed. The doctor thought perhaps I had taken cold, and it would wear off, after giving me something to promote a copious sweat. But when he found that the fever continued to rise, he told us to prepare for the worst, for it was a nervous fever, and that it was probable it would carry me to a world of spirits.

I had continued to nurse my child for more than a week after I was taken sick, which was very injurious to her. The doctor forbade my suckling her any longer, which gave me much pain. They were obliged to take her from me, and feed her with a bottle. My fever increased, and rose to such a height, that it was thought I could not survive many days. The doctor stayed with me, and payed every attention in his power, for twenty days and nights. Lorenzo was not undressed, to go to bed, for near three weeks, nor the doctor for nearly the same length of time.

My kind friends gave me every assistance in their power. They came from the country, for many miles distant, to see if we were in want of any thing that they could help us to. May the Lord reward them for their kindness to me in the day of adversity. Our dear friend, Mary Barford, used to come every day two or three times to see me, and administer to my necessities; and many others came also. She was a precious girl, and although she had been raised in the first circle, would go into the houses of the poor, and supply their wants, and nurse and do for them like she had been a servant. Although Lorenzo was so broke of his rest and fatigued by night, yet he held meetings almost every day, some of which were a considerable distance from town; and as he was weak in body, our friend M. B. frequently hired a hack to convey him to his appointments and back, so that he was with me the greatest part of the time.

I was very much reduced, so that I was almost as helpless as an infant.

There was a chairmaker's-shop adjoining the house, and the room that I was confined in being most contiguous, the noise of the shop, together with that of the town, was very distressing to me; likewise the family was large, and the house small, so that it was very uncomfortable. We were under the necessity of having some person to sit up with me every night, for my fever raged to that degree I wanted drink almost every moment. The light was not extinguished in my room for six or eight weeks. My poor child was very fretful; the girl that nursed it would get to sleep and let it cry; this distressed my mind, and it was thought best by my friends to get some person to take it to the country, to be nursed there.

To be separated from my child was very painful to me; but as my life was despaired of by my friends, and as I myself had not much expectation that I should recover, I strove to give it up, knowing it would be best for the child, and for me also.

There was a woman from Cheshire, who lived about ten miles distant from Warrington, that had no children. She came to see me, and offered to take my baby and nurse it, until I should die or get better, which was agreed to; so they made ready, and she took it. But oh, the heart-rending sorrow that I felt on the separation with my helpless little infant! Language cannot paint it! But the Lord was my support in that trying hour, so that I was enabled to bear it with some degree of fortitude. I was anxious to get well and return to America; but little did I know what awaited me on my native shore. My disorder affected my mind very much. Likewise I was very desirous to see my sister that raised me once more in time. She was as near to me as a mother. We had heard that they had arrived safe in the Mississippi territory, and were like to do well.

At times I was very happy; and then at other times my mind was very gloomy, and sunk, as it were. The doctor said that he never saw any one's nerves so affected that did not die, or quite lose their reason for a time. But I retained my senses and recollection as well as ever, although it seemed that I scarce slept at all.

As I was surrounded with noise, the doctor thought it would be better for me to be removed to a friend's house in the country, who lived about four miles from where I was. Accordingly they hired a long coach, and put a bed in it, and then a man took me in his arms and put me in. The doctor and Lorenzo got into the coach with me, and carried me four miles into the country, to a friend's house, where I had every attention paid me that I could wish for, and from that time I began to mend and recover. This was about Christmas.

Lorenzo felt a desire to visit Ireland once more before he returned to America, as he wished to make arrangements to return in the spring; and if he did not go to Ireland in a short time, he could not go at all. I was at that time so low that I could not get up, or assist myself so much as to get a drink of water; and it was doubtful whether I should recover again or not.

He told me what he felt a desire to do, but added, that he would not go unless I felt quite willing. I told him the same merciful God presided over us when separated, as when we were together; and that he would provide for me, as he had done, in a strange land, through my present illness, and wished him to go and do his duty. Accordingly he hired a young woman to come and stay with me night and day.

He had to preach at a place about two miles from where I was at night, and told me perhaps he should not return that night, and if he did not, he should not return to see me again before he left that part for Ireland. However, I thought he would return to me again before he left England; but he, to save me the pain of parting, did not return as I had expected, but took the coach for Chester, and so on to Holyhead, in Wales, there to embark for Dublin. He left the doctor to stay with me until his return, which he did, and was a father and a friend to me in his absence.

Although I felt willing for him to go and blow the gospel trumpet, yet my heart shrank at the thought of being left in a strange land, in my present situation, being so weak that I could not put on my clothes without help, and my sweet little babe at a considerable distance from me, and among strangers. But the Lord was my support, and gave me strength to be, in some considerable degree, resigned to the will of God.

Lorenzo went on the outside of the coach, exposed to the inclement weather, and to the rude insults of the passengers, until he got to Holyhead, where he went on board a packet for Dublin, when he was both wet and cold, and was for four-and-twenty hours without food. But when he got to Mrs. Johnson's, he found her, as ever, a friend indeed. He stayed there until he got recruited, and then commenced his travels; whilst I was left behind, to encounter the most trying scene that I had ever met with.

My strength gradually increased, so that I was in a few weeks able to sit up and walk about the room. The people that I was with, were as kind and attentive as they could be: may the Lord reward them. But the doctor thought it would be best for me to go to another neighborhood, as a change of air and new objects might contribute to my health; and I should be nearer my child, which was a pleasing thought to me. We got into a carriage, and went to a friend's house, eight or ten miles, where I had been invited and sent for. We stayed a week or more, and then we went to another place, within two miles of my child, which I expected to see and clasp to my bosom! O how short-lived are all earthly enjoyments! I did see my sweet little babe once more! The woman that had her, brought her to see me; and my heart leaped with joy at the sight. The innocent smile that adorned her face—O how pleasing! I wished very much to keep her, but the doctor would not consent that I should undertake to nurse her. He said I had not recovered my strength sufficient to go through the fatigue of nursing. But He that gave it, provided for it better than I could. He saw it best to transplant it in a happier soil than this; for in two or three days, the flower that began to bloom was nipped by the cold hand of death, after a short illness of perhaps two or three days: my tender babe was a lifeless lump of clay, and her happy spirit landed on the peaceful shore of a blessed eternity.

They kept me in ignorance of her sickness, until she was dead. I could not tell why my mind was so much distressed on the account of my child. I inquired of every one that I could see from where she was; but they would not tell me of her danger, until she was dead. I was then about four miles from her, where I had gone the day that she died. A kind sister walked that distance to let me know that my little Letitia was no more, lest some one should too abruptly communicate the heavy tidings; as my health was not yet restored, and it was feared that it would be attended with some disagreeable consequences. I was much surprised to see sister Wade come, as I had left her house only the day before. The first question I asked her was, How is my child? She made me no reply. It struck my mind very forcibly, that she was no more! I requested her to tell me the worst, for I was prepared for it. My mind had been impressed with a foreboding for some time! She told me my child was gone, to return no more to me! I felt it went to my heart, in sensations that I cannot express!—It was a sorrow, but not without hope. I felt my babe was torn from my bosom by the cruel hand of death! But the summons was sent by Him that has a right to give and take away. He had removed my innocent infant far from a world of grief and sin, perhaps for my good; for I often felt my heart too much attached to it; so much that I feared it would draw my heart from my duty to my God! O the danger of loving any creature in preference to our Saviour! I felt as one alone: my Lorenzo in Ireland—my child was gone to a happier clime! I strove to sink into the will of God; but the struggle was very severe, although I thought I could say, "The Lord gave, and the Lord hath taken away, and blessed be the name of the Lord!"

The day that my child was carried to Warrington, to be interred in the burying-ground of the Quaker-Methodists, about ten miles from where she died, I felt as though I must see her before she was consigned to the dust to be food for worms. They had to carry the corpse by the house that I was at: and my friends opposed it so warmly, urging my present state of health as a reason, that I thought perhaps it would be best, and strove to compose myself, and use my reason, and resign my all into the hands of the Lord. It was a severe struggle, but the Friend of sinners supported me under all my afflictions.

They carried my sweet little Letitia, and consigned her to the tomb, there to rest until the last trump shall sound, and the body and spirit be reunited again; and then we shall see how glorious is immortality!

I wrote to my Lorenzo the day that our child died. He did not get it, but wrote to me, and mentioned that he wished to see me and the child; which opened afresh the wound that had been received; but he got the news by way of Mrs. Johnson. He wrote to me that he intended to return to America in the spring; which I was very anxious for. My health began to get better, so that I was able to walk two miles at a time, as walking was very customary among the people in that country. I felt a desire to return to Warrington, which I did in a canal boat, and was kindly received by my good friends and benefactors, Peter and Hannah Philips, with many others that had contributed to my comfort, while afflicted with sickness and distress. I stayed in the town of Warrington for several weeks, with my friends, and was frequently at the little chapel, where my sweet little infant's remains were deposited. I often felt a pleasure of the sweetest kind in contemplating that my child had escaped all the vanities and dangers of this treacherous and uncertain world, for the never-fading glories of paradise, where I hoped, when life should end, I should meet her to part no more: notwithstanding, I felt the loss very sensibly.

I wrote to Lorenzo from that place and received an answer which was calculated to console my heart, and comfort me under my present affliction. He desired me to meet him in Liverpool, on the 1st of March, which I did. I went by the way of Fordsham, in Cheshire, down the river in a large flat, with a man and his wife who were employed to bring the rock for making salt. The river had been frozen considerably, and was full of ice; and when the tide came in it appeared very alarming to me. But after a little the boat got under way, and we had a tolerably pleasant sail down the river to Liverpool, where I met with Mr. and Mrs. Forshaw, my kind friends that had succored me in days past, when I had no one to depend upon on that side of the great ocean! They still were, as ever, friendly. Here I stayed until near the middle of March, when Lorenzo returned from Ireland, which made my heart rejoice.

We left Liverpool in a canal boat for the country, and visited several towns, where Lorenzo preached to numerous congregations. The people were remarkably attentive. There was a pleasant prospect opened before him, and he received more invitations to preach in different parts of the country than he could attend.

There had a number of people determined to come from Ireland to America with us; and were accordingly to meet us in Liverpool in April. Consequently, we had but a few weeks to stay in and about Warrington. I had become so much attached to the friends, that it was truly painful to part with them. Our friends came from various parts of the country to bid us farewell; and we had sweet and melting times together, not expecting to meet again until we should meet in a blissful eternity.

We left Warrington for Lymn, where Lorenzo preached, and bid the people farewell. They were much affected. We parted with a hope of meeting in a better and a happier world. From thence we went to Prestonb-rook, where Lorenzo preached again another farewell. It was a precious time to many. From thence to Fordsham: the people flocked around him with the greatest affection, for there the Lord had blessed his labors in a peculiar manner to the souls of many. He preached to them for the last time, and bid them an affectionate farewell, while they were bathed in tears, seemingly as much pained as though they were parting with a parent.

From thence he went to Chester, the most ancient city, perhaps, in that country, except London. He left me to come in the coach a few days after, whilst he visited the country adjacent. Accordingly, I met him on the day appointed, and we stayed some time in Chester. It was a great curiosity, as it was built on the most ancient construction, being walled in quite round, and the outside of the wall very high. There was a trench dug on the outside, and it was walled up from that. The top of the wall was wide enough for a carriage to pass, with a breastwork sufficiently high to prevent any thing from falling over, and upon the inside was another similar.

The antiquity of the houses, and the nobleness of the public buildings, struck me with a solemnity that I cannot express. My thoughts ran to times that had gone by, when those who had laid the foundation of these walls were animated with life and activity! Where are they now? They have gone to a world of spirits—and we must shortly follow them; and those that take our place, will wonder at the labor of our hands in like manner.

The country is truly delightful that surrounds the city of Chester. I was in the spring when I was there, when every thing wears a pleasing appearance.

The people were hospitable and kind, at least they were so to me. We left Chester for Liverpool in a little sail-boat, and the river was something rough. There was a number of passengers, which made it quite unpleasant; but we arrived safe in the evening, where we met our friends from Ireland, that intended to come to America with us. Lorenzo had made the necessary preparations for the voyage, and he had chartered the cabin and the steerage for the accommodation of passengers, at a lower rate than he could have got it if there had been but two or three.

The first ship that he engaged to transport us to our native soil, sprang a leak as she was coming out of dock. She got injured by some means, and had to unlade, and get it repaired, so that it delayed her sailing for some time longer. But as we were in readiness to leave the country, Lorenzo met with another, where he could obtain accommodations at a better rate. He accordingly made a bargain with the captain for a passage in her; and every thing being prepared for our voyage, on the sixth of May we hoisted sail and weighed for America, which gave me a very pleasant sensation; after having been in England and Ireland about eighteen months, and experiencing many kindnesses and favors from the people; and that Lorenzo was made an instrument in the hand of a gracious God, in bringing many precious souls to the knowledge of the truth.

On the first day, in the morning, we had a pleasant breeze, but a fog springing up, it was something gloomy for several days; but by that means we avoided the ships of war that were very numerous on the coast of England; and Lorenzo and myself had no legal passport from that country, the law being such that aliens were much put to it to travel in that kingdom, particularly those that were in Lorenzo's capacity, such as preachers. They must first take the oath of allegiance to the king of England, and get a license to preach, or they were subject to a fine for every sermon they should preach, of twenty pounds each. Every house must be licensed also, or the man that owned it was subject to a fine of twenty pounds; and every person that heard preaching there, was likewise liable to pay five shillings! But Lorenzo, in the first place, could not take the oath that was requested, to obtain that license. He thought as he had left his native land, not to gain worldly honors or applause, he could still trust that Providence who had guided his course through the great deep, and brought him through many dangers and difficulties in his own country; so he strove to do his duty, and leave the event to God.

We had a very pleasant voyage, except the passengers were generally sick, for more than a week, except my husband and self. I was never better in health in my life; but they recovered their health and spirits after a few days, and we had some very good times on board. Lorenzo preached to the people on Sundays, and we had prayers night and morning, when the weather would admit. We had plenty of the necessaries of life to make us comfortable.

We were near six weeks on our passage. Some time towards the last of June, we saw the long-wished for land of America, which I so earnestly desired to behold once more. The beautiful country and town of New Bedford, in Massachusetts, presented to view, where we landed, and were kindly received

The people that professed religion were chiefly Quakers, and those who styled themselves Christians. Lorenzo held several meetings in the town, which were very satisfactory to many.

After staying near two weeks in New Bedford, Lorenzo, with nearly all the passengers that were in the ship, went on board a packet for New York; and left me to come round with the other women in the ship, to Virginia, and meet him in Richmond.

We parted, and I had to stay nearly two weeks before the ship sailed; they were taking out the lading, and preparing her for a fresh cargo when they should arrive in Virginia. It was about the time that the ship Chesapeake was fired upon by the British. We sailed from New Bedford about the first of July, and had tolerable pleasant weather, though we were lonely, not having any company but us three women. We got into Chesapeake Bay at evening, and passed one of the armed vessels belonging to the British, and expected them to have stopped us, as it had been reported that they were in the habit of requiring the captains of American vessels to pull down their colors to them, or else firing upon them. However, we passed unmolested, except that they hailed us; but it being dark we got by. Sister Wade was very much alarmed; but I felt so much of the spirit of independent America, that I did not wish my country's flag to be disgraced in our own waters. In the morning we came into Hampton Roads, where we anchored and stayed several days, in sight of the British ships of war, while the captain took a boat and went to Norfolk to seek for a cargo.

We were in a very unpleasant situation, as we had no one on board that we could place any real confidence in; but Providence provided for us, and we met with no insults from any. The captain returned at night, and the next morning we set sail for City Point. The day was delightful, and the scenes that surrounded were truly pleasing. The river seemed by the bends to be enclosed in on every side; and the banks to be covered with all the beauties that summer could produce, which gave my mind a pleasant sensation, when I reflected that it was my native country—my beloved America! But little did I know what awaited me in my native land!

We sailed on very pleasantly through the day, and about eight or nine o'clock we arrived at City Point. The ship was in the river, until her lading was brought down from Richmond in lighters. The weather was getting very warm, and we were obliged to stay on board until we could get an opportunity to go to Richmond, which, by land, was not more than twenty-five miles; by water it was, perhaps, twice as far. And here time passed away very heavily, until the master of the ship went up to Richmond on business, and hired a hack to return; consequently we embraced the opportunity, when it returned, to get a seat in it to Richmond, leaving our trunks and other things to be brought up by the boats that were to bring down the lading for the ship.

We bid farewell to the ship, where I had been confined the most of the time for near three months; and it was a happy day for me, although I was in a part of the continent that I had never been in before. I felt as though I could kiss the ground: but my companion, Mrs. Wade's mind, was occupied in quite a different way—she was thousands of miles from her native land, while I was breathing my native air.

We arrived in Richmond about one or two o'clock, and stopped at the "Bell Tavern," strangers to all that we saw. However, I had received a direction where to go, and make myself known; which I did, at a brother Foster's, and when they learned who I was, received us very kindly; but it was a severe trial, it being the first time I had been obliged to call on friends, without any one to introduce me. But the Lord provided for me, and I found many friends in that place: we stayed there some days.

Brother Wade and Lorenzo came and met us, and the latter held several meetings, and we had good times with the brethren. There I saw the girl that brother Mead has since married.

Lorenzo had bought a span of mules before he went to Europe, and they were to be broke for a carriage by the time he should return; but they were taken and put into a wagon, and so broke down that they were unfit for use. He had paid eighty pounds for them just before he left the continent; this was the beginning of trouble to him.

We obtained the loan of a gig from one of our friends, to carry us up as far as Cumberland, to Mr. John Hobson's, who had been a great friend to Lorenzo in days that were past and gone, and still appeared to be such. Here he traded off his mules with a man, for a horse and gig not worth half the money that he paid for them; but he could do no better, as we were under the necessity of going to the north, to make ready to go to the Mississippi, where my relations had gone, and I was very anxious to go. But oh, the heartfelt sorrow they were the cause of to me and my companion after!

We left our friend's house, and started for the north. As we had written to my sister in the Mississippi, on our first arrival in America, but had got no answer from them, I felt very desirous to hear from her, as she was as a mother to me in my infant days—I loved her dearly.

We went through New London and Lynchburg, where we met with many friends, and attended a camp-meeting in Amherst; from thence to New Glasgow, where Lorenzo preached at night. We stayed at an old gentleman's house, who was very friendly. Thence we continued our journey to a camp-meeting near Georgetown, where we stopped and stayed until the meeting broke up. Our horse was at some person's place, to be kept, and I expect got nothing to eat; for we only went from the camp-meeting to Leesburg, and from there to another little town, which was two short days' travel, but before we reached there he tired, and Lorenzo was obliged to trade him away for an old horse that was not worth but a little more than half as much! However, he answered our purpose, so that we got on to New York, where I met with some friends that I had seen before; which were the first faces that I had met with for two years that I had ever beheld before, which gave me much satisfaction!

We stayed at New York for several weeks, and then started for New England, to visit Lorenzo's father. I had never seen him, nor any of the family, except one sister: it was a very great cross to me: but we arrived at his father's some time in September, and were joyfully received by our father, there being none of the family with them, except one daughter and one grandson. There my Lorenzo could contemplate the days of youth; for that was the place of his birth, and of his rambles in childhood: the place where he first sought the path of righteousness—the way to peace and true happiness, in this world and that which is to come: the house where his honored mother had taken her flight to a happier clime—where once he had enjoyed her company, with the rest of the family; but now were separated hundreds of miles asunder!

Lorenzo held several meetings in the neighborhood, and had tolerable solemn times: but the society that he once belonged to was quite gone! Some had died, and others had moved away, while others had gone back into the world, and lost their love to Christ and his cause, which made him feel very awful! His father was a worthy old man, a kind friend, an affectionate parent—he was every thing that was good in his family. I thought I could have done the part of a child for him, if I might have the privilege; but I felt a strong desire to see my sister in the Mississippi.

We went to Tolland, where Lorenzo had sent an appointment to preach at a Methodist meeting-house, and I did not expect to return to his father's any more; but Lorenzo's sister from Vermont coming down to her father's, we returned, and stayed two or three days longer.

Lorenzo sold his gig and horse to a preacher, and bought his brother-in-law's horses to return to New York, where he had made an engagement with a man to make him a light wagon, which was to be ready on his return for the south.

We left his father's on horseback, after bidding them farewell: but as I had not been accustomed to travel in that mode for a long time, it was very fatiguing to me, so that I could not endure it; and when I got within about forty miles of New York, I was obliged to go by water the remainder of the way, while Lorenzo rode one horse and led the other. He arrived there some time before me, and had gone to the country, about ten or twelve miles from the city to preach, but he returned that night. We stayed a week or more until our wagon was ready for us to start; then bidding our friends farewell, proceeded on our journey.

Lorenzo had given out appointments all the way to Virginia, and had tolerable hard work to keep up with them; we had to travel nearly one whole night over the mountain from Fredericktown to the Potomac river, which we crossed about two o'clock in the morning.

Lorenzo's appointment was some distance the other side of the river; we lay down, and as soon as it was light we started again, and reached the courthouse just as the people had assembled. I went to a friend's house, while Lorenzo preached to the people. After meeting we went on to the next appointment, where he preached again at night also: and so continued on our journey, until we arrived in Virginia. Lorenzo preached every day, once, and twice, and three times; and when we arrived at Winchester, he preached twice to large congregations. From thence we went to a camp-meeting, where I saw brother Grober, a presiding elder, whom I had been acquainted with a number of years ago, which was very satisfactory to me.

We left the camp-ground in the morning for Staunton, where Lorenzo had an appointment at night. It was threatening to rain in the morning when we started, and about twelve o'clock it began, and rained almost as fast as I ever saw it: we were in an open wagon, and I was wet through and through, as it continued to rain excessively all the afternoon. When we arrived at Staunton it was almost dark, and the people had assembled for meeting; Lorenzo had not time to take any refreshment, but went and preached in his wet clothes. We were received with coolness by the family that we stayed with, although he was acquainted with them before—but that is nothing uncommon; man is so changeable in his nature, that we may find him at one time all friendship, and perhaps the next day he is as cool as need be. Hence I have found it necessary to strive to take it as it comes; to be thankful for friends, when I find them, and to be satisfied when I have them not.

It was on Saturday night that we got to Staunton, and Lorenzo intended to stay until Monday morning. On Sunday morning brother Wade came from New London to meet us, and carry me home with him; and Lorenzo had calculated on leaving me at Hobson's, in Cumberland, while he went to the Mississippi territory; consequently he thought it best for me to go to New London with brother Wade, who was anxious for me to go and stay with his wife a few months, as she was a stranger in this country; and my coming to America in company with her made us like sisters indeed. It was a trial to my mind to part with my companion for nine or ten months; as I did not expect to be with him but a few days, even if I went on to Cumberland with him, as he then must leave me, and start for the country where my sister lived: accordingly we parted, and I went home with brother Wade. This was on Sunday, and he was to leave Staunton the next morning. My spirits were very much depressed; but I did not know what laid before me. I arrived in New London in safety, and was kindly received by sister Wade, and had got tolerably composed, when I received a letter from Lorenzo, which gave me an account of the imprudence of my sister that lived in the Mississippi—but it was in so dark a style that I did not comprehend it fully, as I could not believe that she would be guilty of such enormities. I thought some one had charged her without grounds: that was some consolation to me, as I hoped it was not true. I was in hopes that he would come through New London, and give me a more full account of the circumstance; but he could not, consistently with his arrangements. I was in great distress of mind on her account, as she had been a great professor of religion, and the cause must suffer by her falling so *foully:* and the disgrace attending it was almost unbearable. Brother Mead and his wife came through New London on their way to Georgia, and brought the news that Lorenzo was not coming through that place, which made my heart almost sink within me. I felt as though the trial was more than I could bear—but this was but the beginning of sorrow.

I stayed at brother Wade's for more than two months, and was kindly treated by him and his wife, and many others; and had many good times in meeting with the children of God, to worship him. The letter that I had received from Lorenzo, in Cumberland, had stated that my sister had been guilty of very improper conduct, but that she was penitent. But when Lorenzo got to Georgia, he received a letter from brother Blackman, stating that she had escaped from her husband with a young man, and had gone over the line into the Spanish country, to elude the displeasure of their connections. It was then an undeniable fact that she was really guilty—and Lorenzo wrote to me from Georgia a full account of the circumstance, which gave me the severest wound that I had ever felt. To have heard of her death, O how much more preferable!—but I had no other way, but must submit. My dear sister, that lay so near my heart had strayed so widely from the path of rectitude—it was such a heart rending affliction, I thought it was almost more than I could bear! It appeared impossible that she could be so far lost to her own honor, and the love that she had manifested to the cause of God, and the prosperity of Zion, as to be guilty of such an atrocious crime. But so it is, that some who make the greatest show of religion, wound it the deepest. So it was in this case. She had professed to have experienced the blessing of religion for many years; and was as much opposed to any thing that had the appearance of *imprudence* in her own sex, as any person that ever I knew. She was married, when young, to a man that was inferior to her, in point of talents, and was not calculated to get the world, as the saying is, as much as many others—and she possessed a very proud spirit, together with a very quick temper; and he not having as mild a disposition as might be, they were unhappy in their union, which was attended with many disagreements. He was subject to intoxication, and that was frequently the cause of much misery between them! I was witness, many times, to such conduct on both sides, that gave me the greatest pain of any thing that could have befallen me. I often would beg my sister to say nothing, but her turbulent disposition was such, that I have thought she would almost suffer death, rather than submit to any one.

They lived in that way for many years. She was very industrious, and strove hard to live; but he was negligent, and often spent more than he made. They removed, when they were first married, into the state of New York, about ninety miles from the place of their nativity, where they lived five or six years; she had religion at that time, and he opposed her very much, as she had joined the Baptist church before she left New England; but after leaving her Christian friends, and having so much opposition, she had lost her religion almost entirely, and became like the rest of the world. At that time the Methodists came into the neighborhood, and she became acquainted with them, and would have joined their society, but her husband would not permit it—but she attended their meetings, and was much engaged at that time. My brother-in-law took it into his head to remove to Fort Stanwix, on the Mohawk river, within seventy or eighty miles of the line of Canada, and she backslid again, not having any to converse with but those that were unacquainted with God or themselves! O how prone we are to forget the obligations we are under to our Saviour, notwithstanding it is on his bounty we live, and we are indebted to him for every mercy that we enjoy! She continued to live in that careless way for several years, until I was, perhaps, eighteen years of age, and the Methodists found her out again, and I got under distress for my soul: and she was stirred up again, and I believe had religion. My brother-in-law opposed us with all his might. They had got in a tolerable good way before this, and there was a prospect that they might live comfortably, as to the things of this life; but he possessed such an uneasy disposition, that he could never be satisfied unless he was trading, and he had but a poor talent for that business. He sold his plantation, that he could have made a comfortable living upon, to a man that was a sharper, on trust, and took no security—the man sold his property, and cleared himself, without making any compensation for the land. This was a very great affliction to my sister, as she had made every exertion for a living that a woman could do, and strove in every way she could to prevent his selling his place—but all to no purpose. He carried on a great stroke at drinking, and spending his time for nought: she was harassed and troubled on every side, not enjoying that satisfaction in religion she had formerly done—it made her truly wretched! I strove to comfort her in every way I could. We supported the family by our labor, weaving, spinning, and sewing, and any kind of work that we could do.

This continued for more than twelve months, and then he took a little farm of about fifty acres of land, with a comfortable house for a small family, that suited us very well; the rent being small, he could have lived as well as need be, if he would have been industrious. He was of a turn that was rather indolent and careless, but my sister and myself kept the family in tolerably comfortable circumstances.

It was at that time that the Methodist preachers came into the neighborhood, and preached the gospel to poor lost sinners. My heart was wrought upon, and I set out to seek the salvation of my soul. My sister heard the pleasing sound with gladness, but my brother-in-law was violently opposed to them, and strove in every way that he could to prevent us from going to meeting; but I felt determined to seek the Lord with all my heart, come what would, and strive to save my soul. It was near twelve months before I or my sister joined society; but at last we broke through and joined the people called Methodists—and I have never seen the time that I was sorry that I cast my lot with them; but I have often lamented that I did not live nearer to the gospel rules that they teach.

After we had joined society, my brother-in-law became somewhat more softened, and let us have more peace, and would sometimes go to meeting; but he still continued to go on in the same evil practice of spending his time in the most unprofitable way—but the preachers and people that feared God ceased not to pray for him, and at last he was brought to see his situation, and the danger of living in sin, and set about the work of his own salvation; and I doubt not but he experienced the pardon of his sins. O the joy that was felt on this occasion! we had, as it were, a heaven begun below! He became a new man, and providence seemed to bless us on every side; and we continued to enjoy the consolations of religion for several years, and the Lord prospered us in all our undertakings until after I was married; and they started for the Mississippi, and my husband and myself parted with them: we were coming to New York, and from thence to sail for Europe.

They went to that country, and it appeared they left all the prudence that they ever possessed behind them; for when they arrived, he, it appeared, thought he could launch into building mills, not counting the cost that he must be at, but calculating that Lorenzo, when he returned from his tour in Europe, would pay all expenses—he ran into debt for land that had a mill-seat upon it, and began to erect a mill.

Some people were much pleased with them, as they appeared to be engaged in religion. My sister was very much respected by the people, both religious and irreligious—but O the danger we are exposed to while in this world! She was possessed of good natural abilities, and considerable acquired knowledge, and was the last person I should have thought would have conducted in the way she did; but we have need to watch and pray, lest we enter into temptation. She had lived with her husband for twenty years at least, and I never heard or knew any thing laid to her charge of that nature, before or after her marriage—and she had been a guide to me in my youth, and I suppose, possessed as great a sense of honor as any person I ever knew. But—how it was I cannot tell—she fell into a snare of the enemy, and became a prey to the most unaccountable of all vices. There was a young man, that was of a most abandoned character and principle, that was taken into the family, that she was fond of by some means; and there was a criminal intercourse between them for several months before it was discovered. She was in society, and thought to be very pious, but at last it was mistrusted by some, and a plan laid to detect them, which was accomplished. When it was proved upon her, she gave some marks of penitence, and her husband would have made friends with her; but when the devil gets the advantage of poor infatuated mortals, he makes the best improvement of it in his power So it was in this case; for I expect her sorrow was but slight, if she was in the least affected with sorrow—for as soon as she found that Lorenzo and myself had returned to America, she laid every plan to make her escape with that wretched young man into the Spanish country, which she effected, and left her husband in a state of mind almost frantic: he had more affection for her than I once thought him capable of. He went after her, and strove to get her to return, but she would not. I do not think there ever was as permanent a union between them as was necessary for happiness. O the misery of many that are joined in the holy bands of matrimony: for the want of due consideration they rush into that state, and are wretched for life.

When she completed her wicked plan, information was communicated to us—my Lorenzo had left me, and started for that country. No one can paint the heart-felt sorrow that I experienced on receiving the information. I felt as though I was deprived of almost all my earthly comfort. I felt I could not believe it possible that she could have acted in that miserable, disgraceful manner; but it was even so! Many have been the nights that I have wet my pillow with tears upon her account, but all to no purpose. O that it may be a warning to me to watch and pray, lest I enter into temptation! Lorenzo went on, and found my poor brother-in-law in a wretched state of mind, and every thing that he had was in a ruinous condition; and furthermore, they had run so deeply in debt that it was impossible for my brother-in-law to extricate himself from it. He had made a contract with a couple of girls for a tract of land that had a mill-seat upon it, and began to build a mill, without a title to the land! When Lorenzo came, he wished Lorenzo to assist him to procure the land, that he might not be in danger of losing his labor. Lorenzo felt a very great reluctance to engage in any thing of the kind, but by the persuasion of friends he was prevailed upon to make a contract with the girls for the land, and likewise paid the old man for his labor, as he desired to return to the state of New York. There was considerable less than one hundred acres, with a log-cabin upon it. He paid a very enormous price, which was a great disadvantage. As Lorenzo was not a man that felt a freedom to have much to do with the world, except when he could not well avoid it, after he had got the place, he scarcely knew what to do with it. The mill was not finished; there was a dam and mill-frame, but the dam had broke, and it was uncertain whether it could be made to stand, as the banks of the stream that it was erected on were so subject to wash in times of high water. There was a man who thought he could make it stand. Lorenzo made an offer to him of the place; if he would take it, and make a mill upon it, he should have one half of the mill. Accordingly he undertook, and repaired the dam, so that it sawed some that winter. He intended to tear up the old foundation, and build entirely on another plan—and was to have the use of the old mill until he should get the other finished.

People in that country appeared anxious that Lorenzo should come to that part of the world, and get a residence; they talked that they would assist us in any thing we needed; and as Lorenzo thought that it might be best to prepare for sickness, and for whatever might befall us, he concluded to come for me and bring me with him to that country. I had felt a great desire to go to the Mississippi, before my friends had conducted themselves in that wretched way, but now I felt a reluctance to going, for it appeared to me that I could not hold up my head in the place where my own sister had disgraced herself and me. My heart recoiled at the thought of being a mark, as I knew I must, for people to look at, and say, that is a sister to such a woman; and she had been guilty of an odious crime. But as my Lorenzo thought it would be best for me to go, I made no objection. He returned in June to Cumberland, in Virginia, and we started for the North, and went on to New York, where we stayed a few days—and from thence to Albany, where Lorenzo left me, and continued to journey on to his father's in Connecticut, being gone six or seven weeks.

I stayed in Albany part of the time, and Troy, and I also went to see my brother, that lived near Schenectady. He did not profess religion, but was friendly to it. I stayed there a few days.

There was a camp-meeting within eight or ten miles, where I expected to meet Lorenzo: my brother and his wife went with me to the place on the commencement of it, and there to my great joy I met my companion, with many others of my acquaintance, that I had been acquainted with many years before. The meeting was attended with good to many—we stayed until the close, and then we went with some very kind friends to Troy, who gave Lorenzo a good suit of clothes, and were as affectionate to us as people could be.

My brother-in-law, who came from the Mississippi, had been to the place that he left when he removed to the South; was at the meeting, and came down to Troy after us, as Lorenzo was to let him have some books on the account of his labor in the Mississippi: he did so—but this was not the end of trouble to us. It gave me inexpressible pain to see the man that I thought had been the cause, in one sense, of the destruction of my poor sister; for he had been an unkind husband in the days that were past. Although I could not excuse her, yet I believe, if he had done as he ought, she never would have become what she did. But they were not equally yoked together: he had some good traits in his character, but he was indolent, and a bad economist, consequently kept them behindhand. She was industrious, and would have managed well, if she had been united to a man that would have stood in his place, and made her known, and kept hers—for she possessed a turbulent disposition. But he was neither a good husband, nor a good manager: that made her fret at him, and he would not take it from her. Thus it was a means of their living a considerable part of their time in discontent: but after they both

1, they lived more agreeable, until they removed to the
fell in with that young man who proved her ruin.*
our friends at Troy, after getting a small wagon and
at little we could get together, and started across the
ern waters, in company with a young man that came
⁊, and a brother Valentine, from the state of New York,
that country. We travelled with as little expense as
e state of Pennsylvania, and struck the Ohio river at
e stayed for near two weeks, at a Quaker's, who was
‿orenzo strove to get a passage in a flat-bottomed boat,
tly took horses, carriages, and produce, with families
remove to that country—but he could not obtain one
ı horses, consequently he was under the necessity of
rough by land : he met with a person who was going
ı a loaded barge to Natchez. They engaged to carry
ks, and other baggage. These people were friendly
:d the boat that Lorenzo had engaged my passage in.
ady to sail for some time ; accordingly Lorenzo left me
ı that came with us from Europe, to go down the river
he went on by land. I felt very gloomy to be left
ıd to go on board a boat with a company of men, with-
ı companion.

Wheeling were very kind to me while I stayed there,
ıe, which gave me much satisfaction. They provided
ssaries for the voyage, such as sugar, and tea, and other
:omfortable, for which may the Lord reward them.

:ling between one and two weeks after Lorenzo left
he people who owned the boat sold it to a couple of
ıia, with all that appertained to it ; but they made a
to go in the boat. This was a very trying time to me :
ed the boat, when Lorenzo applied for me to go down
ıakers, and they promised Lorenzo to take good care
ı that had bought the boat was quite of a different ap-
he was in a gentleman's garb. The young man that
ıs a hand to help work the boat. We went on board
.rge was laden with flour and cider, and various kinds
for the Natchez. There was a small cabin with two
or four persons might sleep tolerably comfortable.
l to rest at night : and there was a small vacancy be-
ıd the other part of the boat, where they had run up a
re they could cook provisions. In this gloomy situation
for the Mississippi, where I knew I must meet with
I should reach there.

time when we started, was very low, and we made
for many days together. I could not set my foot on
boat, with none but men, and those of that class who

:umstances, which correspond and hang together like a chain of
vas a combination of Deists, one of whom was a physician, who
the family, through the object of temporal gain, (they being a fami-
ho owned the mill-seat,) and to bring a stigma upon the cause of
iderably over forty years of age at this time of her life

neither feared God nor man, though they, for the most part, treated me with civility. None can tell how disagreeable such a situation is, but those who have passed through something similar.

We left Wheeling about the last of October. The boat stopped at Limestone, in Kentucky, for part of one day and a night. There Lorenzo had some acquaintances; and when they found out that I was on board of this boat, some of them came down to see me, and invited me to go on shore and stay the night, which I accepted with thankfulness.

I had some hope that Lorenzo would arrive there before the boat would start in the morning. Oh! how anxiously I looked out for him! But he did not come; and I had to go on board the boat very early in the morning, and continue on my journey with a very heavy heart. My mind was much depressed; the prospects before me were dark, when I should reach my place of destination; and the weather was uncommonly cold for that climate and season.

After being confined on board of a boat for six weeks, we reached the mouth of Byopeare, about twelve miles from Gibson Port, which was forty miles from Natchez. We left the boat, myself and the young man that was with me, and took our things to a public house; but that was ten or twelve miles from the place that we wished to get. I had never been in that country before, but Lorenzo had several times; and hence I had some grounds to expect I should find some friends, as many of them had manifested a desire that I should come to that country. But my sister had conducted in such a manner, that it made my way difficult; and how to get to the neighborhood that I wished to go to, I did not know.

However, brother Valentine, who came with us from the state of New York, travelled by land with Lorenzo as far as Limestone, and then put his horse on board of a boat, and worked his passage down to the same place that I was at. I landed at night, and he came in the morning; so that I was provided for. We left our things at this public house; and I rode the horse, while he and the young man walked about twelve miles through the mud. This was about the 12th of January. We stayed at Gibson Port that night, about four miles from the place where my sister had lived, and brought such a stain on the cause of religion. We were all strangers; but Lorenzo had written to some friends that we were coming; and, furthermore, he had requested them, if I should arrive before him, to take care of me until he should come.

We left Gibson Port, and went to the neighborhood of the mill, to the house of Samuel Cobun. He did not profess religion, though he was very kind and humane; but he had two sisters that were members of the Methodist church. He had no wife living, and they lived with him to take care of the family. They had been friends to my sister, when she first went to that country. They received me, apparently, with affection, which was a consolation to my heart; for I expected to meet with many a cold look, on the account of my poor unfortunate sister, and I expect I did; but I do not blame them, as it had given them so much pain: but I could not help it. However, I stayed at Mr. Cobun's until Lorenzo came; as those that professed religion seemed not to take much notice of me. When Lorenzo left me at Wheeling, he went on through the state of Ohio, Kentucky, and Tennessee, and so on through the Indian country to the Mississippi territory.

A man, who was a Methodist, and preached, and who had appeared very friendly to Lorenzo in days that were past, Lorenzo had written to and requested, that if I should reach there before him, that he would permit me to stay with him until he should arrive. But he did not seem very anxious that I should stay at his house. He came over to Mr. Cobun's, which was six or seven miles, to see me, and requested me to come and see them—as though I had been fixed in a comfortable situation, with every thing that I needed. But it was quite the reverse with me; I had neither house nor friends in that country, without the people chose to befriend me. I was a stranger, in a strange land, and in the neighborhood where my nearest relatives had conducted very improperly; and I expect that was one cause why the friends kept so distant. However, the family that I was with was very kind. I went once to this friend's house, before Lorenzo arrived, which was somewhere about two weeks. I stayed there one night, and then returned to Mr. Cobun's, where I stayed until Lorenzo came to me.

The winter had been uncommonly severe, and he had a very distressing time through the wilderness; but Providence had brought him through in safety, which was a matter of rejoicing to my poor heart.

The cloud that had been gathering for some time, grew darker and darker, so that we scarcely knew which way to turn, or how to extricate ourselves from the difficulties that my imprudent friends had brought us into on every side. They had run in debt to merchants, making the impression that when Lorenzo came from Europe he would pay all. There were some that had befriended them on Lorenzo's account; these he felt it was his duty to compensate, which he did. My brother-in-law had made a contract with some people in that country for a tract of land, on which was a mill-seat; and without any title whatever, before we returned from Europe, he went to building a mill, which involved them still deeper in debt. After Lorenzo returned from Europe, and went to that country, which was nearly twelve months after, finding him in such a distressed situation, he, out of pity, stepped in to assist him as a kind of mediator, when they cast the whole burden on his shoulders, which proved a heavy one to Lorenzo.

We arrived there in January. We had a couple of tolerably good horses, and a small wagon, and some money; but we were under the necessity of parting with them, and what little money we had was soon gone. The old mill-frame, which was all that was done to the mill, Lorenzo let a man take on such terms as these—that he might undertake to build a mill if he chose, without any more expense to Lorenzo; and if he could make one stand, Lorenzo should be entitled to one half.

We stayed with a family near the mill-frame, from March until July. In this time I was taken sick with the fever that is common in that country, on the day that Lorenzo had resolved to prepare to start for Georgia, and my life was despaired of. The people that had appeared so desirous that we should come to that country, forsook us; and had not the man that was styled a *deist*, and who first received me into his house, befriended us now, I know not what I should have done. His two sisters, Elizabeth and Ann Cobun, were friends indeed. Ann stayed with me, day and night, for about three weeks; and then we were under the necessity of removing from this house somewhere else. But where to go we could not tell.

However, Mr. Cobun gave us permission to come and stay at his house as long as we chose ; but I was so low at that time that I could not sit up at all. They sewed some blankets together over a frame, similar to a bier to carry the dead, and putting a bed upon it, laid me thereon, and two black men conveyed to his house, which was, perhaps, a mile.

The next day Lorenzo was taken very ill also. There we were, both confined to our beds, unable to help each other to as much as a drink of water. At that time Lorenzo could not have commanded one dollar, to procure so much as a little medicine.

This was a trying time ; and when the storm would be over we could not tell. But the Lord supported us under these distressing circumstances, or we must have sunk beneath the weight. Forever praised be the adored name of our great Benefactor, for all his mercies unto us!

My fever began to abate, but Lorenzo grew worse ; and it was doubtful which way it would terminate with him. Oh ! the anguish of heart I felt at this trying juncture ! I was still so low that I could not sit up but very little, nor walk without assistance ; and we were altogether dependent on others for the necessaries of life. Lorenzo appeared to be fast approaching to eternity ; but after some weeks he began to gain a little, so that he was able to ride a few miles at a time. We then removed to brother Randal Gibson's, where we stayed a few days. I was still unable to work, as I then had the common fever and ague, which kept me very weak and feeble. After staying there for some time, perhaps two weeks, we returned to friend Baker's, near the mill. Lorenzo held meetings as much as he was able, and perhaps more ; and, although he was so weak in body, and depressed in mind, he did not slack his labors, but preached frequently sitting or lying down. There was a young man, who died about six or seven miles from where we then were, desired Lorenzo should preach at his funeral. He was still very feeble, but wished to be of some use to his fellow-mortals the few days he might have to stay in this world of wo.

He started soon in the morning to attend the funeral, and brother Baker went with him. This was on Sunday. He preached to a crowded congregation, with considerable liberty. The people were tender and attentive. After the conclusion of the ceremony, he started to return to brother Baker's, where he had left me. He had rode but a few miles before he was suddenly taken ill, and would have fallen from his horse, if friend Baker had not seen that something was the matter, and being active, he sprang from his horse, and caught him before he fell to the ground. As it happened, they were near a small cabin, that was occupied by a man who professed religion. They conveyed him into it senseless ; and so he continued for some time. When he came to himself, he was in the most excruciating pain imaginable. They gave him a large quantity of laudanum, which gave him some little relief; but he could not be removed from that place.

Brother Baker stayed with him until nearly night, and then came home. I had become very uneasy in my mind on his account, as he did not return according to my expectation. When this friend came and told me Lorenzo's situation, my heart trembled lest I should be called to relinquish my claim, and resign him up to the pale messenger. It made me cry mightily to God to give me strength to say, "The will of the Lord be done!" I had no reason to doubt, if the great Master saw it best to remove him from this region of pain, he would be conveyed by angelic hands to the realms of peace and happiness, where he would have to suffer no more pain and affliction, either of body or mind. But it was a task too hard for me to accomplish, without the immediate assistance of the Friend of sinners.

I slept but little that night, and early the next morning, the friend at whose house Lorenzo was, came with two horses to take me to him. When I arrived there, I found him in a very distressed situation; he could not be moved in any position whatever, without the greatest pain; he could lie no way, except on his back, and in this position he lay for ten days. The disorder was in his left side, and across his bowels. I was apprehensive it would terminate in a mortification, and others I believe were of the same opinion. One day we thought he was dying, the whole day; he was unable to speak for the greater part of the day. My mind was in such a state of anxiety as I had never experienced before; however, that appeared to be the turning point—for the next day he was something better, and continued to mend slowly, and in a few days he had gained so much strength as to ride about a mile to a quarterly meeting: and a precious time it was to me, and many others.

O what an indulgent Parent we have to rely upon! May my heart ever feel sensations of gratitude to that God who hath cleared my way through storms of affliction, and various other difficulties.

I had not recovered my health fully at this time. The people, it appeared to me, were almost tired of us in every direction. I was unable to labor for a living, and Lorenzo was so feeble in body that he could preach but little; consequently we were entirely dependent on others for a subsistence.

We continued in the neighborhood where Lorenzo had been sick, and that of the mill, until the first of January, and then we left that part for a friend's house, twelve or fourteen miles off; their house was small, and family large, which made it very inconvenient to them and us, although they were very kind and friendly.

Our situation at this time was truly distressing—we scarcely knew which way to turn. Lorenzo concluded it was best to strive to prepare some place as a shelter from the storms that appeared to have come to such a pitch, as not to admit of rising much higher. Sickness and poverty had assailed us on every side; and many, such as had professed to be our friends, forsook us in that country as well as in the states. It was circulating through many parts that we were at that time rolling in riches, surrounded with plenty.

The old mill-frame (for it was never finished) had made such a noise in the world, that many had been led to believe that we possessed a large plantation, with an elegant house, and other necessary appurtenances, together with two or three mills, and a number of slaves, besides money at interest. Whilst this was carried from east to west, and from north to south, and the people supposing that Lorenzo had ranged the wide fields of America, and also of Europe to gather up worldly treasure, and had gone to the Mississippi to enjoy it, would of course make a very unfavor able impression on their minds, as it related to his motives in travelling in such an irregular manner as he had done.

We were, as I observed before, in quite a different situation—without house or home, or any thing of consequence that we could call our own.

There was a tract of land, lying in the midst of a thick cane-brake, on which was a beautiful spring of water, breaking out at the foot of a large hill, which some person had told Lorenzo of: the soil belonged to the United States, and the cane was almost impenetrable, from thirty to forty feet high; and likewise it was inhabited by wild beasts of prey, of various kinds, and serpents of the most poisonous nature. Notwithstanding these gloomy circumstances, Lorenzo got a man to go with him to look at it, to see if it would do for an asylum for us to fly to, provided we could get a little cabin erected near the spring. After he had taken a survey of the place, he concluded to make a trial, and employed a man accordingly to put up a small log-cabin within ten or twelve feet of the spring, which he did, after cutting down the cane for to set it—a way was made through from a public road to the spot, so that we could ride on horseback or on foot. We obtained a few utensils for keeping house, and in March we removed to our little place of residence, in the wilderness, or rather it appeared like the habitation of some exiles;—but it was a sweet place to me—I felt I was at home, and many times the Lord was precious to my soul.

There was a man who had resided in Philadelphia, and by some means had got involved in debt, and left there to reside in this country. He had a wife and one child: once he had belonged to the Methodist society, and then backslid; but after he came to that country he was brought into trying circumstances, which brought him to reflect on his present situation; and meeting with Lorenzo at this time, there began some intimacy between them on this occasion: after this he wished to return to Philadelphia for a short time, and wanted some place for his wife to stay at while he should be gone; consequently he requested us to let her stay with us at our little cabin, which was agreed—she came, and this made up our little family. She was a peaceable, friendly woman, and we spent the time quite agreeably; although we were left by ourselves for days together, Lorenzo being frequently called from home to attend meetings, and to procure the necessaries of life.

The people were much surprised when they came to our little residence, how we came to fix on such a lonely place as this to retreat to!—This is a proof, that experience teaches more than otherwise we could learn : we had felt the want of a home in the time of trouble and sickness. This was a pleasant retreat to us: the wilderness appeared almost like a paradise to me. There were but two ways we could get to our neighbors, the nearest of which was more than half a mile, and the way so intricate, that it would be almost impossible for any one to find it, or get through either place in the night.

We stayed there for near four months; in that time Lorenzo preached as much as his strength would admit. We were sometimes very closely run to get what was necessary to make us comfortable; yet I felt quite contented. I had, in a good degree, regained my health; so that I was able to labor, and I strove to do all I could for a living, although my situation was such, that I could not do as much as I wished; but the Lord provided for us, beyond what we could have expected. We did not know how long we should stay in that place; we had no other alternative but to stay there, until Providence should open some other way.

The man that had left his wife with us, and started for the city of Philadelphia, went as far as the falls of Ohio, and got discouraged, and getting into a boat, he returned to us in the cane: there we had an addition to our family, this man, and his wife, and child. The chief of the burden fell to my lot, to do for them and ourselves, which Lorenzo thought was too much for me to go through with—and the man seemed not to give himself much concern about it. His wife was in a situation that would require more attention than I should be able to give. We thought it was best to make our way to the states, if possible, as we had been defeated in almost every thing that we had undertaken in that country. Accordingly, Lorenzo made some arrangements to prepare to leave it. He let the man that was with us have possession of the house and spring, and what little we had for family use, as it relates to housekeeping, and took a horse for the intended journey. We left the peaceful retreat of the spring, where I had enjoyed some refreshings from the presence of the Lord, and were again cast on the world, without any thing to depend upon but Providence. However, he had never forsaken us: his power and willingness to save all that trust in him was still the same; and as he had promised that he would be with us in six troubles, and in the seventh that he would not forsake us, so it proved in the end. We left the little cabin on Sunday morning, to attend an appointment that Lorenzo had given out, twelve or fourteen miles distance from there, on horseback, where we arrived in time. He preached to an attentive congregation. This was about six miles from Cobun's, where we had found an asylum in days that were past. We left the place where the meeting was held, and started for Mr. Cobun's, but we lost our way, by taking a foot-path that we supposed was nearer, and wandered in the woods until almost night, before we came to the place that we were in pursuit of: but at last we got to the place, where we met with sister Cobun, and with brother Valentine, who had been back to the state of New York for his family, and had arrived here a few weeks previous.

We did not intend to stay in the country any longer than we could make the necessary arrangements for our journey through the wilderness to Georgia. Lorenzo turned every way that he could, to obtain what was necessary, and had got all ready to start, our clothes and every thing being packed up, when we concluded to attend a camp-meeting about six miles from the neighborhood of the old mill-frame, and then continue on our journey: but Providence seemed not to favor our intentions at that time, for I was taken sick, and unable to travel; consequently, Lorenzo was under the necessity of leaving me behind, and going through without me—but he stayed for several weeks longer, until I had in some degree recovered my health. He had made some preparations for me to be provided for in his absence. Brother Valentine had erected a small log-house, on public ground, near the mill-frame, and contiguous to the little tract that Lorenzo still retained, of perhaps five-and-twenty acres. This house, in conjunction with the sisters Cobun, he obtained from Mr. Valentine for us to reside in, while he should take a tour through the states.

He had let another man have a part of the right that he still held in the mill, if ever it should be made to do any business; consequently, this left him but one fourth, and that was in a state of uncertainty whether it would ever be of any use to him, which the sequel has since proved to be the case.

About this time my poor unfortunate sister finished her career, and was called to a world of spirits, to give an account of the deeds done in the body. I felt very awful when I first heard the news—but I considered that we had done all in our power to bring her back to the paths of rectitude. Lorenzo had seen her three times: the first, on purpose—the second, on the road—the third, she came to meeting thirty miles to see me, but I was not there—and strove by every argument to prevail on her to come to us, and forsake the ways of vice and strive to seek her soul's salvation, and we would strive to do the part of children by her. But she would not—alleging that she could not bear the scoffs of her acquaintance. When Lorenzo found that she was determined to stay with the person that she had apostatized for, he told her to read the counsel of Jeremiah to Zedekiah, on their last interview, and look at the sequel, and make the application, at which she wept as they parted. This was the last time that he ever saw her; she was taken sick shortly after, and died in a strange land, without a friend to drop a tear of compassion over her in her last moments! The person that had been her seducer went on like one distracted—his wickedness and evil conduct, no doubt, stared him in the face, when he reflected that he had been the cause of one, who had once enjoyed the Divine favor, losing that blessing, and falling into sin of such an enormous nature as she had been guilty of—and I know not but he might have been the cause of her sudden departure; but I leave that until the day when the secrets of all hearts shall be disclosed!

She was interred in a lonely place, where, perhaps, in a few years, the spot of earth cannot be found that contains her ashes.*

O that this may be a warning to all that may peruse this short account of the fall of one that might have proved a blessing to society, and a comfort to her friends, if she had kept at the feet of her Saviour, and attended to the dictates of that Spirit which teaches humility.

I was much afflicted on account of my poor sister—she had lain near my heart: but I was enabled to give her up, knowing that she was gone to a just tribunal, and her state unalterably fixed. What remained for me to do, was, to strive to make my way safely through a tempestuous world, to a glorious eternity.

Lorenzo had made the necessary preparations for me to stay with the sisters Cobun, and for him to take his departure for the states, not expecting to return in less than twelve months. This was something of a cross to me, as he was still considerably afflicted in body, and, to appearance, would never enjoy health again. But I was supported under it, so that I

---

* The foregoing unfortunate circumstances, are necessarily involved in the thread of those vicissitudes, which are connected in the narrative in order to be explicit—seeing the circumstances were generally known, but in many respects greatly misrepresented, through the prejudice and ambition of some, to block up the way and destroy the reputation of Lorenzo, by unfavorable impressions on the public mind. Many, through false modesty and pride, are willing to claim relationship with some, because they are considered in the higher circles of life; which they would be ashamed of, if it was not for their money—as worth is generally estimated according to a man's property, agreeably to the old saying, "Money makes the man." Whereas, what am I the worse for others' vices, or better for their worth and merit, if I have no virtues of my own?

felt in a great measure resigned to this dispensation also. I was supplied with what I needed to make me comfortable.

I had joined society when I first came to this country, within a mile of the place I then lived. I lived in great harmony with my two companions that Lorenzo had left me with, while he had gone to visit the states once more. I attended meeting regularly every week, and had many precious times to my soul. I had some trials to encounter, but the Lord was my helper, and brought me through them all. I was desirous to return to some part of the states, if Providence should spare Lorenzo, and he should again come back to me in safety.

He left me in October. I spent that winter and the next summer, as agreeably as I had done such a length of time in almost any situation that I had been placed in for several years; at the same time these people that had pretended a great deal of friendship to us in former times, were quite distant. However, this affected me but little, as I had learned in some degree this lesson, that our happiness does not depend on the smiles or frowns of the world; but we must have peace in our own breast, or we can find it nowhere else.

I lived quite retired from the world, with a few exceptions. I seldom went out but to meeting; there I found most peace and consolation. Thus, I continued to spend my time, until the period that Lorenzo was to return.

I received a letter from him, to meet him about twelve miles from where I then was, where he had sent an appointment to preach. This was pleasing intelligence to me, as I had then been separated from him for near twelve months.

I went the day before the time appointed for him to arrive at the place, and the day that he came I was again attacked with the ague and fever, which I had never escaped for one summer while I was in that country. The ague had left me, and the fever was tolerably high, when it was observed by some of the family that Lorenzo was come! My heart leaped for joy at the sound of his name. We met, after having been separated for twelve months and six days. I felt some degree of gratitude to our great Preserver, that he had brought us through many dangers and difficulties, which we had met with during our separation.

We intended to return to the states, as soon as we could get prepared. There was a large congregation attended to hear Lorenzo preach; and it was a solemn, melting time among the people. After meeting we started for the place that I had made my home in his absence. Although I was quite unwell, in consequence of having a fit of the ague the day before, we rode twelve miles, in company with several friends that had come from the neighborhood to meet him.

It was then ten o'clock before we reached our destination: however, we were very much rejoiced to have the privilege of joining our hearts and voices in prayer and praise to that God who had prolonged our lives, and brought us to meet again on mortal shores. The next day I had a very sick day—the ague came on more severely than it was the day that Lorenzo came back. He wished to make ready to leave the territory, and I was anxious to go with him, as I could not enjoy health in that country. I made use of some means to get rid of the ague, and it had the desired effect so that after a few days I got something better, and in about two or three weeks I was able to start on our journey through the wilderness to Georgia.

Lorenzo had intended to have stayed longer than he did when he returned, and had given out a chain of appointments through the country; but reflecting that the winter rains might come on, and make it impossible for me to get through the long and tedious wilderness that we had to travel—consequently, he attended but one or two of these appointments, and recalled the rest, and started for Natchez, where we got what was necessary for our journey, and from thence we made the best of our way to the wilderness, although our friends expected us to have returned and bid them farewell, and I myself expected to have seen them again before I left that country; but it was otherwise ordered, for I saw them no more, and I do not know that I ever shall, until we meet in eternity. May God help us so to live, that we may join the blood-washed throng, in the mansions of endless day.

We reached the outskirts of the settlements of Natchez on the third day after we left the city. It was something late in the day before we left the last house inhabited by white people, and entered the vast wilderness. This was a new scene to me, such as I had never met with before. My heart trembled at the thought of sleeping out in this desert place, with no company but my husband: however, a little before sunset we came to a place where we could get water and plenty of cane for our horses. There we stopped for the night, built a fire, and cut a quantity of cane to last our horses through the night: after that we prepared our supper, which consisted of coffee and hard biscuit, which we had brought from the settlements with us. We had no tent to screen us from the inclement weather, but we had blankets on which we slept, which made us tolerably comfortable when the weather was clear. We lay down, after having prepared a quantity of wood for the night; but it was a gloomy night to me, it being the first time that I ever had been in the like circumstances; and to look up and see the wide extended concave of heaven bespangled with stars, without any covering, it was truly majestic. Yet to consider we were in a lonely desert, uninhabited by any creature but wild beasts and savages, made me feel very much alarmed, and I slept but little, while Lorenzo was quite happy and composed; as he observed, he had never been so well pleased with his situation in travelling through this wild unfrequented part of the country before; and this was the tenth time that he had passed through it, in the space of nine or ten years!

We met with no molestation through the night, and as soon as day dawned we started on and travelled until late breakfast time, when we stopped, struck up a fire, and prepared some refreshment, and fed our horses, and then continued on our journey.

We travelled near forty miles that day. It was quite dark before we got to Pearl River, which we had to cross in a ferry-boat, and stay at a house, such as it was, that belonged to a half-breed, during the night. I was very much fatigued, but rested tolerably well.

In the morning we started by ourselves soon after we had got some refreshment, and travelled on through the day until towards evening, when we met a company of Indians, who had been preparing their camp for the night. This struck me with some considerable dread, and to add to that we had to cross a dreadful slough, called by travellers, "Hell Hole."

This place consisted of thin mud, so that horses, after they were stripped of saddle and harness, could swim through; and then it was necessary that some one should be on the other side, so as to prevent them from running away. But we had no one with us to assist, and we could not tell what we should do: yet so it happened, that the Indians had made a temporary bridge of poles and canes to get their horses over, which served for us to get over upon also.

We were then under the necessity of preparing for the night, as it was almost sunset, and we were not more than half a mile from the Indians' camp, which was quite alarming to me; but there was no alternative, there we must stay. Accordingly Lorenzo made a good fire, and provided a plenty of cane for our horses, and made ready our little repast; by this time it was dark. We then lay down to try to compose ourselves to rest, but my mind was too much occupied by gloomy reflections to sleep, while I could hear Indians' dogs barking, and the horses' bells jingle, although it was a beautiful night. The moon shone through the trees with great splendor, and the stars twinkled around; and if my mind had been in a right frame, it would have been a beautiful prospect to me, but I was so much afraid, that it quite deprived me of any satisfaction, while Lorenzo would have slept sweetly if I had not been so fearful, and frequently disturbed him. I longed for daylight to appear; and as soon as it dawned we started and travelled a long and tedious day, still in this dreary wilderness. We expected to have got to a man's house, living on the Chickasaw River, who had an Indian family, before night. Accordingly we came to a creek, which Lorenzo took to be that river. I felt very much rejoiced, as I hoped to find a house which we could have the privilege of sleeping in; but we were disappointed in our expectation; for when we got over the creek we found there an Indian village. We inquired how far it was to this man's house; they told us by signs it was ten miles, and it was now almost sunset. We started on again, and went perhaps half a mile, when the path became divided into so many little divisions, that we could not tell which to take. Lorenzo went back to an Indian's house, and requested an old Indian to go and pilot us to Nales; the old man hesitated at first, but after understanding that he should be well paid, he took his blanket and wrapping it about his head, he started on before us, and we followed after; by this time it was almost sunset, but we kept on. There was a moon, though it was obscured by a thin cloud, so that it was not of so much use to us as it would otherwise have been. We had not got more than three miles from the Indian's house before it was quite dark. I was very much afraid of our pilot. I strove to lift my heart to God for protection, and felt in some degree supported. Our way lay through a large swamp, intermixed with cane, which made it appear very gloomy; but our pilot was almost equal to a wolf to find his way through this wild unfrequented spot of the earth; he could wind about and keep the path where I would have thought it almost impossible. Having travelled until ten or eleven o'clock, we arrived at the river; but how to get across, that was the next difficulty—we must cross a ferry, and the boat was on the other side. Lorenzo requested the old Indian to go over and fetch it, but he would not move one step until he promised him more money. This was the second or third time he had raised his wages after he started, to keep him on, until we could reach the place that we wished for. However, after he found that he would get more money, he started and went up the river, and found some way across. In a short time he had the boat over, and we went into it with our horses, and the old man set us over. This was perhaps eleven o'clock at night; we came to the house, the family was gone to bed, but the woman got up, and although she was half-Indian, she treated me with more attention than many would have done that had been educated among the more refined inhabitants of the earth!

I felt quite comfortable, and slept sweetly through the remaining part of the night. In the morning we started again, being then thirteen miles from the settlements on the Tombigbee. We passed through some delightful country that day, and about two or three o'clock in the afternoon we reached the first house that was inhabited by white people. It made my heart rejoice to meet again with those that spoke a language which I understood, and above all to find some that loved the Lord.

Lorenzo held several meetings in this neighborhood that were profitable, I trust, to some. We stayed here two nights, and a good part of three days, when we took our leave of them, and departed on our journey through the settlements on the Tombigbee, which extends seventy or eighty miles in length, through a rich and fertile soil. The settlements were flourishing, and the people in some parts hospitable. We arrived at Fort St. Stephen's, situated on the Tombigbee river. It is on an eminence, and makes a handsome appearance, although it is but small. The river is navigable up to this place. It is a beautiful river: the water is as clear as crystal, and the land very fertile, and well situated for cultivation. This will be a delightful country, no doubt, in time.

We got fresh supplies at this place, and made but a few hours' stop before we started on our journey, and crossed the river in a ferry-boat. This was after twelve o'clock. We travelled until late, and came to a small cabin, where we got permission to stay all night, which we did. In the morning we started very early—saw some scattered houses, and at night we got to the Alabama river, where there was a ferry, kept by a man who was a mixture, where we stayed that night. This river is beautiful, almost beyond description. On its pleasant banks stood Fort Mims, that has since been destroyed by the savage Creek Indians, with those that fled to it for protection.

We were now in the bounds of the Creek nation, but without any company. This day we struck the road that had been cut out by the order of the President, from the state of Georgia, to Fort Stoddard. This made it more pleasant travelling, and then we frequently met people removing from the states to the Tombigbee, and other parts of the Mississippi territory.

We travelled betwixt thirty and forty miles that day, and came to a creek, called Murder-creek. It got this name in consequence of a man having been murdered there. This circumstance made it appear very gloomy to me. But we made the necessary preparations for the night, and lay down to rest: although I was so much afraid, I got so weary at times that I could not help sleeping. About twelve o'clock it began to rain so fast that it was like to put out our fire, and we were under the necessity of getting our horses and starting, as we had nothing to screen us from the rain. The road having been newly cut out, the fresh marked trees served for a guide: there was a moon, but it was shut in by clouds.

However, we travelled on ten or twelve miles, and it ceased raining. I was very wet and cold, and felt the need of a fire, more perhaps than I had ever done in my life before.

At last we came in sight of a camp, which would have made my heart glad, but I feared lest it was Indians; yet to my great satisfaction, when we came to it we found an old man and boy, with what little they possessed, going to the country we had left behind, and had encamped in this place, and with their blankets had made a comfortable tent, and had a good fire. This was refreshing to us, as we were much fatigued. We made some coffee, and dried our clothes a little—by this time it was daylight: we then started on our way again. I thought my situation had been as trying as almost could be, but I found that there were others who were worse off than myself.

We came across a family who were moving to the Mississippi. They had a number of small children, and although they had something to cover them like a tent, yet they suffered considerably from the rain the night before; and to add to that, the woman told me they had left an aged father at a man's house by the name of Manack, one or two days before, and that she expected he was dead perhaps by that time. They were as black almost as the natives, and the woman seemed very much disturbed at their situation. I felt pity for her—I thought her burden was really heavier than mine. We kept on, and about the middle of the day we got to the house where the poor man had been left with his wife, son, and daughter. A few hours before we got there, he had closed his eyes in death. They had lain him out, and expected to bury him that evening; but they could not get any thing to make a coffin of, only split stuff to make a kind of box, and so put him in the ground.

I thought this would have been such a distress to me, had it been my case, that it made my heart ache for the old lady. But I found she was of that class of beings that could not be affected with any thing so much as the loss of property; for she began immediately to calculate the *expense* they had been at by this detention; and I do not recollect that I saw her shed one tear on the occasion.

We stayed but a short time, and continued our journey. There we got a supply of bread, such as it was; there we met, also, with three men who were travelling our road, the first company that we had found since we left the Mississippi, being now not more than one-third of the way through the Creek nation. We left this place betwixt one and two o'clock.

I was very glad of some company, for we had been very lonely before. We travelled on without any thing particular occurring for three days, until we arrived at the Chattahoochee river, where we met with some difficulty in getting over, as the boat was gone. This was early in the morning, before sunrise, that we came to the river. There we were detained until ten o'clock, and then had to hire an Indian to take a canoe, and first carry our baggage over, and then swim our horses over. This hindered us until near eleven o'clock before we got ready to start again. We were in hopes of getting to Hawking's, the agent's, that night; but being so long detained at the river, we were obliged to stay at an Indians' camp, our company having stopped before.

I had got a fall from my horse and hurt myself considerably; and I was as much fatigued and worn out by travelling as ever I was in my life. I thought sometimes that I never should stand it, to get through the wilderness, but Providence gave me strength of body beyond what I could have expected. We left the Indians' camp in the morning, and reached Col. Hawking's that night.

This was within about thirty miles of the settlements of Georgia. I felt grateful to the God of all grace for his tender care over us, while in this dreary part of the land, where our ears had been saluted by the hideous yells of the wolf—and we had been surrounded by the savages, more wild than they; and yet we were preserved from all danger, and brought through in safety.

We got to the river that divides the state of Georgia from the Indians' boundaries, about three or four o'clock, and got into the white settlements, which was very satisfactory to me. We got to a friend's house that night about dark, where we were received kindly. This was like a cordial to my heart, as it had been a long time since I had met with a friend.

We stayed that night with them, and the next day we got to a friend's house within twelve or fourteen miles from Milledgeville, the metropolis of Georgia. There Lorenzo had left a small wagon, six weeks or two months before. Here he exchanged the two horses we had for one that would work in carriage, and went on to Milledgeville, where we stayed about a week, and found many kind friends. This was sometime in December.

While we were here the earthquakes began, which alarmed the people very much. It was truly an awful scene, to feel the house shaking under you as sensibly as you could feel the motion of a vessel, when it was moving over the water; and the trees as it were dancing on the hills—all nature seemed in commotion. This was enough to make the stoutest heart tremble! But when the people get so hardened, that mercies nor judgments cannot move them, we may conclude they are in a bad way. This is the case with too many. O that the day would arrive, when the inhabitants of the earth would love and serve the Lord!

We left Milledgeville, and went to a friend's house, where I stayed three or four weeks, while Lorenzo travelled the upper counties, and through the New Purchase—and offered free salvation to crowed congregations. He then returned to where I was, and we started on our journey to Virginia. Lorenzo preached at several places before we got to Louisville, and had a chain of appointments given out which extended to North Carolina. We came to Louisville, intending to stay only for a few days; but there came on such a rain, that it raised the water courses to such a degree, that it was impossible for us to travel for near two weeks—this brought him behind his appointments; but it gave him an opportunity of preaching to the people in Louisville a number of times.

As soon as we could get along we started, and with some difficulty we overtook the appointments—but not without disappointing three or four congregations. We travelled on from Georgia to Carolina in the cold inclement weather, such as we have in January and February; and Lorenzo preached once and twice in the day. The people seemed quite attentive all the way that we came.

I was very anxious to get to Lynchburg, as we had some thoughts of striving to get a small house built there, that we might have a place of re-great in case of necessity—Lorenzo still expecting to travel and preach as long as his strength would admit. But we intended to go on to Connecticut, to his father's, where I expected to have stayed for some time, and then return to Lynchburg; but the Providence of God seemed not to favor the design.

We arrived in Lynchburg about the seventeenth of March, where we calculated to stay but a few days, and then go on to his father's—after making some preparations for building our little house. However, we had not been in Lynchburg but about one week, before I was taken very ill, and confined to my bed, attended by two doctors, Jennings and Owen, who said my affliction was an inflammation of the liver—which confined me for three months to my bed, and I was expected to die. However, after having gone through a course of physic, I got so as to be able to sit up and ride a little; but was very feeble. My sickness had detained Lorenzo from going to the North, as he had intended, and after counting the expense of building, he found that it would not be in his power to accomplish his design in building a house, without involving himself in debt, which he was not willing to do; accordingly he gave it up, and concluded still to continue as we had been, without house or home, and leave the event in the hand of Providence; knowing that we had been provided for all our lives, from a never-failing source—and we felt willing in some degree to trust him still!

We were still at Lynchburg, and had been there for more than three months—and the friends were very kind to me in my sickness.

Lorenzo wished to take me to his father's; but my health was in such a state that it was impossible for me to travel.

There was a man who lived in Buckingham county, about five-and-twenty miles from Lynchburg—we had but a small acquaintance with him: he, coming to Lynchburg, saw Lorenzo, and invited him to come and stay at his house a while. He told him he had no objections, but was thankful to him for his kindness, though he saw no way of conveyance. Mr. John M. Walker, for that was his name, told him he would send his carriage for me the next week, which he did, and we went to his house. This was a kind family. I had not been there but a little more than a week, before I was again confined to my bed, and it was expected that I must die. They gave every attention to me they could have done had I been their own child—may the great Master reward them in this world with every needed blessing, and in the world to come, with a crown of never-fading glory.

My Lorenzo attended me day and night almost from this time, until near Christmas. By this I had got a little better, so as to be taken and wrapped in blankets and put into a close carriage, and carried about half a mile to another dear friend's house, Major William Duval, where I was treated as if I had been a near relation—and provided with every thing necessary to make me comfortable; and they wished me to stay with them all the winter. This was matter of thankfulness to us.

I had got so as to walk about my room a little—and Lorenzo wishing to take a tour to the North, he made the necessary arrangements, and about the twenty-fifth of December he left me and started to Richmond, on his way to the city of Washington, where he stayed for some time, and then on to New York; and so on to his father's in Connecticut.

He expected to return in March, but did not until May. I stayed at brother Duval's, partaking of their hospitality, until some time in March, when brother Walker's family seemed so solicitous that I should go to their house again, and sister Walker coming in her carriage herself, she being very delicate too—I concluded to go. The old gentleman was not at home at the time, or I expect he would not have consented for me to leave his house, until Lorenzo returned.

I feel under great obligations to that dear family that I cannot express. His wife was a lovely woman. May the Lord reward them—for it is not in my power!

I went home with sister Walker. I was at this time much better, but in a few days after I had got to brother Walker's I was again attacked with my old complaint, a pain in my side, very severe. I applied to the remedies that had been made use of, and that was bleeding and blistering, but to little purpose apparently.

I felt very much discouraged; as I thought it more than probable that my time would be but short in this world of wo—and I wished much to see my companion once more in time, but strove to be resigned to the will of the Lord.

My cry was, Lord help me to be willing to suffer all thy goodness sees best to inflict. My pain was at times very severe, and then I would get a little relief. I was taken about the twenty-seventh of March, but three or four days later than it was the spring before, when I was first attacked.

I had received letters from Lorenzo, which informed me that he could not get back before May. My strength was continually declining; and to appearance, I would shortly be an inhabitant of the other world. My mind was variously exercised—it was sometimes cast down, and at other times much comforted. This long and tedious sickness taught me a greater lesson, as it related to the uncertainty of earthly enjoyments, than any thing I had met with before. My desires for temporalities were gone—at least any more than was strictly necessary to make me comfortable—and the Lord that cared for us had provided me with the kindest friends, where I was treated with the greatest attention.

Lorenzo returned in May, as he had wrote me he should. I was at that time unable to get out of my bed without assistance. I had written to him to New York, before I got so bad, that I was threatened with another attack. He had made all the speed that he could, and the day that he got to the place where I was, he had travelled near seventy miles.

I was much rejoiced to see him once more; the God of all grace had granted my request; and returned him in safety to me again. He stayed with me for several weeks, and every means was made use of to restore me to health, that could be—but they all seemed to prove abortive. Dr. Jennings saw me several times after my last attack, and advised the use of mercury, as the only remedy that could be of any service to me. I followed his advice, and was reduced very low, from the disorder and medicine together—so that it was thought by all who saw me that I must die.

I strove to sink into the will of God; knowing whatsoever was best for me would be given—yet I could not divest myself of a desire to get well, and live a little longer: not to enjoy what is commonly called the pleasures of the world, for my prospects were but small at that time—but to live more to the glory of God, and be better prepared to join the blood-washed company above, when I should be called for.

Lorenzo had at this time gone to the lowlands, to fulfil some appointments which had been given out by some of the preachers, which took him about three weeks. I was very ill while he was gone. About the time he returned I began to mend a little, so that I could set up in the bed. The Doctor had advised Lorenzo to carry me to the White Sulpher Springs, as it was the most likely means to restore my health. After a few weeks, I had got so as to be taken and put into a chair and carried as far as Lynchburg, to Doctor Jennings. We had then a chair and a horse of our own—but our horse's back had got injured, so that we were under the necessity of staying in Lynchburg until he should get well, so that we could get on to the Springs.

We were detained for some time before our horse got so as we could use him. I still was very feeble in body—I could not walk one hundred yards without assistance. Our horse had been quite high for near three weeks, and his back had got tolerably well ; so that we were about to make a start, and try to get on to the Springs—but although our horse had brought Lorenzo all the way from New England, and down to the lowlands of Virginia and the Carolinas, and back again to Buckingham, and from there to Lynchburg in the chair, and appeared very gentle ; yet when he put him in the chair to prepare to start for the Springs, he began to act like as if he was frightened, and we were apprehensive he could not be managed by him, considering my weak and helpless state ; and the road through which we must travel was very rough and mountainous, consequently he sold him on the spot, and hired a hack from a Quaker living in that place : he paid four dollars a day for the use of it for ten days, besides bearing all the expenses. We left Lynchburg in the morning, and went the first day to New London, about fifteen miles, and I stood the travel much better than I expected I could. There Lorenzo preached to the people, as he had some appointments sent on before him ; and we stayed all night. The next day we went to Liberty, where we had another appointment—and from there we went to a friend's house, where we were treated kindly—and they called in some of their neighbors, and we had a comfortable little meeting.

The next day to Fincastle, where we stayed all night, and Lorenzo preached twice. We were now within a few miles of the mountains, which were in some places so craggy and steep, that it was with difficulty we could ascend them ; and then we would come into a valley, where the soil would appear as charming and beautiful as the mountains were rugged and barren. We travelled on, and met with nothing particular until we arrived at the Springs, whither we were bound.

The Springs are situated in Greenbriar county, about three miles the other side of the Alleghany mountains, and from Lynchburg upwards of one hundred miles. It is a pleasant place where the man lives who has rented the Springs, and has built a number of cabins, perhaps fifty or sixty. They were placed in a regular form, the yard enclosed, and a beautiful grass-plot, with handsome shade-trees, for the accommodation of those that attend the Springs. They have a large house that stands near the centre, where the boarders dine, &c.

We went there, but the person that had hired the Springs would not take us in! He pretended they were so full that they could not. But they took more after we went there than they had before. But we got in a house perhaps a mile from the Spring. I was better satisfied with this situation than I would have been at the place, for I could have the water brought twice in the day, and there I was in a more retired place. I stayed there near three weeks. Lorenzo was there part of the time, and part of the time he was travelling through the neighborhoods and preaching to the people. He held several meetings at the Springs, by the request of those that were attending there. There were persons from various parts, some for pleasure, and others for the restoration of health. They were people that moved in the higher circles, and were very gay; but they were quite attentive when he spake to them of heavenly things, except one who was a most abandoned character. He thought to frighten him by threatening his life, and abusing him in a scandalous manner. But the enemy was defeated in this, for the gentleman that kept the Springs, and others, soon stopped his mouth, so that he had peace ever after.

There were none just about this place that knew much about religion; but they appeared anxious to hear the glorious sound of the gospel. I began to get my strength in some measure, so that I could walk about considerably well. There was to be a camp-meeting held near Salem, in Botetourt county, which was a distance of seventy or eighty miles, and we were in the mountains, without horse or carriage, and how we should get out we could not tell. But Providence, that had so often opened our way where we could see none, made a way at this time. There was a friend that was a Methodist, who lived at the Sweet Springs, a distance, perhaps, of eighteen miles from the White Sulphur, who had requested Lorenzo to come over there and preach. He told him he would, provided he could send a couple of horses for us to ride. I had by this time got so well that we thought I might be able to ride that distance on horseback.

Accordingly the man sent the horses; and we started and arrived at his house some time in the afternoon. We stayed at the Sweet Springs three or four days, and Lorenzo preached several times. We then, by the assistance of friends, were enabled to get on to Fincastle, which was within twenty miles. We came with the preachers that were going to camp-meeting.

Here we got a chair from a friend to convey us part of the way from this to the place where the meeting was to be held, to another friend's, who let us have his horse and gig to carry us the remaining part of the way. When we got to the camp-ground it was nearly dark; but there we met with some of our old acquaintance, which made my heart to rejoice. The preachers were very friendly. There I met with my dear friend, sister Dunnington, who, perhaps, enjoys as great communion with God as any person I ever saw. She was very kind to me: and I felt it was good to meet with those that truly love and serve the Lord. We stayed at the camp-meeting until the day before it broke up. It was a tolerable good time, and there were a number of souls converted to God. May they continue to walk in the narrow happy road, until they reach the peaceful shores of Canaan.

We left the camp-ground in company with a preacher and his family for Blacksburg, near the Yellow Springs, so called, where I was advised to go and try the water. This was nearly thirty miles from Salem. Here we stayed for two or three weeks, and I made use of the waters, which was, I think, beneficial to me.

We got acquainted with a gentleman from the lowlands of Virginia, who was at the Springs with his wife, on account of her health. These people were possessed of a large property, and had but one child; and they also possessed as great a share of *hospitality* as any I ever met with. They, understanding our situation, gave me an invitation to go home and spend the winter with them, which I thankfully accepted; while Lorenzo took quite a different course to the western country, intending to visit Louisiana before his return. But the Indian war breaking out, flung some obstacles in the way, which were unavoidable. Hence, he sent on a deed of relinquishment to those who had possession of the old mill, which had made such a noise in the world. We had heard that they had got it, or rather built a new one, to do some business; but Lorenzo had never reaped any benefit from any thing that ever he claimed in that country, and I do not expect he ever will.

Here ends the history of his *reported* vast possessions in the Mississippi.

We parted at the Springs. I was to go home with brother Booth, the friend from Virginia, while he pursued his journey to the west. Brother Dunnington, who lived at Salem, happened to be at the Springs at this time, took me in his chair, and carried me to his house, and brother Booth came down the next day. His wife was very unwell, which detained us in the mountains for six or seven weeks.

I stayed with sister Dunnington, until sister Booth was able to travel. We then started for Brunswick, their place of residence, where I was treated with the greatest kindness.

Lorenzo went on to the western states, and from thence to Carolina, and so on to Virginia, to where I was, after an absence of near four months.

He in this tour visited about forty counties, and travelled near two thousand miles. He stayed with me about ten days, and then started on another route through North and South Carolina to Charleston, and visited many places, preaching from one to four times in a day, until he returned, which was about seven weeks. He got back to me on Friday night; preached on Sunday, and on Monday morning we prepared to start for Petersburg.

March 8th, 1814, we bid adieu to my kind friends in Brunswick, where I had found an asylum from the cold winter for near five months, whilst my Lorenzo was ranging through the western and southern states, to call sinners to repentance. The morning that we parted with that dear family will be a memorable one to me: it was like parting with my nearest friends. May the Lord bless them with all such spiritual and temporal mercies as shall prepare them for a seat at the right hand of the Majesty on high.

Brother Booth had furnished us with two horses, a gig, and servant, to go with us to Petersburg; and there we were to take his carriage and continue on to Baltimore. But when we got to Petersburg, the carriage which it was designed we should take from there was taken to pieces for repairing, so that we could not obtain it for our journey, and hence were under the necessity of taking the public stage for Richmond, which was something disagreeable to me. But I strove to put my trust in that hand which had dealt so liberally with me in days that were past by.

The roads were very bad, being so much cut up by the large heavy wagons that were on the road, laden with cotton and other produce for market.

We arrived in Richmond between two and three o'clock, and were received with kindness by brother West and his companion. There we met several preachers, who treated us with friendship, which was very pleasing to me. Oh how sweet it is to meet with those that love and serve the great Master in sincerity and in truth! And if it is so pleasant here, what will it be when we shall meet in that sweet world of rest, where we shall see eye to eye, and be no more subject to erroneous conclusions, as it relates to our brethren! O that I may be enabled to fight my passage through, and to meet with the dear friends of Jesus on the happy banks of everlasting deliverance!

We stayed in Richmond from Wednesday until Monday morning. Lorenzo hired a hack at the rate of five dollars per day to bring us on to Fredericksburg, which cost us near forty dollars; but we came on in safety. I felt my heart often drawn out in prayer to God for protection while we were on the road, that he would attend us on our journey. We were received with kindness also at this place by our old friend, brother Green, and his family, where we stayed for some days.

Lorenzo held several meetings, and then took a seat in the public stage for Alexandria, where we arrived on Sunday, between two and three o'clock. We stopped at a public house, where the people that travel in the stage are accommodated, but did not stay longer than to deposit our baggage, and then to go in search of some friends where we had put up, when in the place some years before, by the name of Slone. We walked down the street for some distance, and as it happened, a gentleman and lady were standing at the door where Lorenzo had formed some acquaintance the preceding winter, and invited us to come in, which we did, and found a pleasant asylum where we could rest from our fatigue of travelling in the stage. O how sweet is it to meet with kind friends after having been confined with those who neither feared God nor regard man!

We stayed at Mr. Warter's two nights, and then by the request of a family of Quakers, by the name of Scholfield, we spent one night with them. It was a very pleasant time to me. They were remarkably kind and friendly. The gentleman in the morning took me in his chair and carried me to the city of Washington, which was about six miles from Alexandria, to another friend's where my Lorenzo had found a kind reception a little more than twelve months before, and who had requested that he would bring me if ever he should travel that way again.

Lorenzo had stayed behind to find some conveyance for our trunks and other baggage. In a short time he found a return hack, which he engaged, and arrived in a short time after me, and was received with affection by the family. They were by name Friends, and they were so by nature.

We stayed with them three nights, and received many marks of friendship from them—for which may the great Master reward them in the day when he cometh to make up his jewels! They had been married for seventeen years, and had no children, except one little adopted daughter, of the lady's brother, which they had taken as their own. They doted on her. She was taken sick the day after I went there, and the second day, at night, they thought she was dying, and the poor little woman was in great anguish of soul on the account. I did not expect the child would live until morning. We had engaged our passage in the stage for that morning at five o'clock, and were up at three. The family had slept very little for two nights; but when we arose in the morning, which was at an early hour, to prepare for our journey, the dear little child was still living, but looked like she had almost finished her course, and would shortly be conveyed to the realms of peace. Brother Friend went with us to the stage-house, where we parted. We came on to Baltimore, where we stayed two nights with brother Hagerty; and Lorenzo preached twice in the town. We then took the steamboat for Philadelphia, where we arrived in about twenty-six or eight hours, and tarried from Tuesday until Friday. There Lorenzo preached two evenings in the African church. We then left Philadelphia, and continued on in the steamboat to Trenton, where we took the stage for New York. We stayed at Princeton one night, and the next evening we arrived at the city of New York, and came to brother Morris D'Camps, from whose house I started when going to the Mississippi—he then lived in Troy—after an absence of about five years and six months from the time we started, and from whom we have received many favors. May that God, who is able and willing to reward those that will be kind, for their benevolence, bless him and all my dear friends, for their kindness to me—and in particular for the last nine years of my life.

SUPPLEMENTARY REFLECTIONS

TO THE

JOURNEY OF LIFE.

I LEFT Lynchburg on the 19th of July, and came to brother Walker's, in Buckingham, where I was taken worse. I stayed there three months, and then went to brother Duval's, where I stayed about five months, and then returned to brother Walker's again, where I continued near two months more—making ten months in all. May the Lord give them the reward that is promised to those that give a cup of cold water to a disciple, in the name of a disciple, for their kindness to unworthy me in this day of adversity.

January 25th. I this morning have been much relieved from melancholy reflections that employed my mind through the last night, as it relates to Lorenzo; as I had not heard from him for several weeks, which gave me much uneasiness, and made me feel my situation, which is something lonely: but what most distressed me was my heart being so prone to distrust the protection of Providence over us, which I had so much reason to rely upon—for his tender care hath been over me from my earliest days until now, and hath brought me through dangers seen and unseen.

> "Through various deaths my soul hath led;
> And turn'd aside the fatal hour,
> And lifted up my sinking head."

O that I may ever feel resigned to the will of God! The day will shortly arrive when we must bid adieu to all sublunary things. May the Lord help me to tear my heart from earth away for Jesus to receive. I long to be dead to all below the sun, and have my affections placed on things above, where sorrow will be turned into joy, where we shall view our Saviour, who hath borne all our sins in his own body on the tree, without a dimming veil between! Lord, enable me to say—

> "Forever here my rest shall be,
> Close to thy bleeding side;
> This all my hope and all my plea,
> For me the Saviour died.
>
> My dying Saviour and my God,
> Fountain for guilt and sin,
> Sprinkle me ever with thy blood,
> And cleanse, and keep me clean."

January 26th. My heart longs to be filled with love and gratitude to God, for his mercy to me: and through his grace strengthening me, I hope to overcome all the evils that may befall me, whether outward or inward. O that I may consider the uncertainty of time—and that I know not the hour when the Son of man may call for me, whether it will be at midnight, or at the cock's crowing—so it stands me in hand to watch and pray, that I may not be surprised when He shall come, but be ready to enter in with the bridegroom to the marriage supper of the Lamb! How sweet rest will be, after the toilsome "journey of life" is over. We shall then be received to those joys that have been purchased at so dear a rate—which cost no less than the precious blood of the Son of God! O what a ransom! That it should be neglected by those who ought to benefit by it—what a pity! O that they may take timely warning, and flee to the outstretched arms of the Saviour, and hide them, until the storms of life be past, that they may be guided safe into the haven of eternal rest.

February 7th, 1813, Sunday. I feel this morning my spirits are very much depressed—I fear that trouble awaits me. O that I may be prepared for whatever may be the will of God concerning me, whether prosperity or adversity. May I ever lay passive at his feet, and feel a disposition to say—Not my will, but thine be done. I am assured that this is a state of trial, wherein we must stand to our arms, or we shall suffer loss —for we are surrounded with enemies on every side, within and without, that are watching to do us mischief. O that I may be on my guard, and watch unto prayer, that the Lord may be fore-front and rere-ward! and although troubles should assail me, and dangers affright, I may be enabled to fly to the arms of Jesus, and find shelter and consolation there! For he hath said, that he will carry the lambs in his bosom, and gently lead those that are with young. O that I may be one of those that can claim this promise and protection from him. I am left as one alone in the earth —but if I can only put my trust in him, I need not fear. Although dangers stand thick through all the ground, yet if the Lord is my shield, I shall not fear what man can do unto me. But I too often sink into a state of despondency, as my situation seems to be very gloomy at present;—not that I am in want of any thing to make me comfortable, as it relates to living—for I am placed in a kind family, for which I desire to be thankful—but my concern for my companion, who hath been gone for near two months, and whom I have not heard of but once, fills my heart with fear, lest something hath befallen him. O that God may preserve him from those that would do him harm—and may I be enabled to give him up into the hands of God; knowing that he will do all things well: and if we meet no more on earth, may we meet in glory, where we shall be reunited never to part again—and receive the crown of glory that is laid up for those that are faithful to the Lord, who bought their pardon on the tree!

February 9th. I am still alive, and enjoy a tolerable degree of health—for which I desire to be thankful: for it is more than I once expected, from the state of my health.

I expected that I should have been an inhabitant of eternity before this—but the Lord hath preserved me for a longer space! O that I may improve the precious moments as they pass, to the glory of God, and for the good of my immortal soul—that when time shall be no more with me, I may be received into glory, where sorrow will be turned into joy; where I may join the blood-washed throng in singing hallelujahs to God and the Lamb for ever!

> "And then my happy soul shall tell,
> My Jesus hath done all things well."

February 15th. I am still alive, and on praying ground. O that I may improve the precious moments as they pass, to the glory of God and the good of my own soul. My heart is too little engaged with God! O that I may never rest until I am filled with love to God and all mankind. May the Lord prepare me for whatever awaits me through this unfriendly world—for I expect that troubles will be my lot, while here, more or less, until I pass over Jordan! God grant that they may end then; and for them may I receive a crown of glory, though unworthy. May God help me to watch and pray without ceasing, that I may be in a state of readiness for whatever may befall me!

> "How happy every child of grace,
> Who knows his sins forgiven!
> This earth, he cries, is not my place,
> I seek my place in heaven.
>
> "A country far from mortal sight,
> Yet, O by faith, I see
> The land of rest, the saint's delight,
> The heaven prepar'd for me."

March 12, 1813. I have reason to bless and praise God, that it is as well with me as it is—that I have some desire still to devote my life and all that I have to the service of that God who hath preserved and brought me to the present moment. O that every power of my soul and body may be, without reserve, devoted to him. He hath been my Preserver and kind Benefactor from my earliest days until the present time! O that my heart may be filled with love and gratitude to Him, for every mercy that I do enjoy. It hath been better than three months since I parted with the friend that I esteem most dear; and I long much to see him—but I must be patient, and strive to give my all to the Lord, and say, not my will, but thine be done.

March 14th. This day has been a day of a good degree of peace and joy to my soul. As I have been so long deprived of meeting with my brethren to praise God! O that I may give my soul and body as a living sacrifice to him day by day—and be prepared to meet my Saviour in the skies, with joy and gladness.

> "Through grace I am determin'd
> To conquer though I die!"

March 21st. I have reason to praise God for his tender mercy to me; that he hath given me a degree of health and strength—and feel a desire to spend the remainder of my days in his service and to his glory. May the Lord bless me with an hungering and thirsting for all the mind that was in Christ, that I may be a comfort to my companion, and a blessing to society, and be prepared for heaven and glory.

> "Come, Lord, from above, these mountains remove,
> O'erturn all that hinders the course of thy love."

I long to be altogether his. The day is fast approaching when it will be of more importance to have an interest at a throne of grace, than to be possessed of all the riches in this lower world! May God help me to realize the worth of time and the length of eternity—and improve my privileges accordingly!

March 21st. I feel to be in some degree thankful to God for the blessings that I do enjoy. May I improve them to the glory of my great Benefactor—and may the Lord reward my kind friends for their friendship to me.

"O that my God would count me meet
To wash his dear disciples' feet."

I feel my heart prone to wander from the God that I desire to love! O that the day may arrive when I shall love my God supremely—above every thing else.

April the 15th, 1813. I am this day out of eternity, but am not well—and know not how long I may be an inhabitant of this world! O that I may be in a state of readiness for death, when it shall come—for whether it be long or short, it will be the same kind of terrors when it comes, if we are not prepared for it. My heart and soul long for full redemption in the blood of Jesus.

"O that my tender soul might fly
The least abhorr'd approach of ill:
Quick as the apple of an eye,
The slightest touch of sin to feel."

I hope the Lord may give me grace to be faithful; that whether my days are many or few, they may all be devoted to him, that when I am called to go I may have a convoy of angels to escort my happy soul to realms of glory. My conflicts are many here, but the hand of the Lord is strong. O that I may be enabled to put my trust in him in every trying hour.

April 21st. I am this day a spared monument of mercy—that I am not cut off as a cumberer of the ground. O that my heart may be filled with real gratitude for the blessings I do enjoy—for kind friends in the day of adversity.

I feel that I need daily suplies from the fountain that was opened in the house of King David for sin and uncleanness; for the enemy thrusts sore at me—and I often fear I shall come short at last. I want the whole armor, and skill to use the weapons, that I may be more than conqueror through the strength of Jesus; that when my sun is setting, I may have a prospect of Canaan's happy land, and view by faith the celestial fruits of paradise, where joys immortal grow—where pain shall be exchanged for pleasure that never shall cease—where we may gaze on the face of our beloved without a dimming veil of mortality between.

April 23d. I have reason to be thankful to God my great Preserver, for the peace that I do feel in my soul this morning. Although my body is afflicted, yet I feel a degree of resignation to the will of God, and hope that I may be prepared for whatever is the will of God concerning me—whether life or death.

"Through grace I am determin'd
To conquer though I die,
And then away to Jesus
On wings of love I'll fly:
And then my happy station
In life's fair tree shall have,
Close by the throne of Jesus,
Shut up with God above."

O that I may consider that my days are as a shadow that passeth away. God grant that I may secure a lot among the blest.

> "My suffering time will soon be o'er,
> Then shall I sigh and weep no more;
> My ransom'd soul shall soar away,
> To sing God's praise in endless day."

The road I have to travel is interspersed with joys and sorrows, and the only way to be happy is to receive the one with gratitude and the other with submission. O that I may have that true resignation to the will of heaven, that may enable me to rejoice evermore, and pray without ceasing, and in every thing to give thanks—thank the Lord for the blessings that I do enjoy, and be patient under sufferings, knowing that it is good for me to be afflicted, that I may know my own weakness the better, and rely only on the strength of him that is able to save all those that put their trust in his clemency and mercy! May the Lord help me to live to his glory while on earth I stay.

May 9th, 1813. I have reason to bless God that it is as well with me as it is! Whether I shall ever enjoy health or not I do not know, and I would not be anxious concerning it: but may I be prepared for whatever is the will of the Lord concerning me, whether life or death, health or sickness, prosperity or adversity. I feel a desire to see my Lorenzo once more in time: but if that is denied me, may I be enabled to say, the will of the Lord be done, and may we meet on Canaan's happy shore, where sorrow will be turned into joy, and all that's earthly in our souls will be done away, and in its place we shall have the nature of angels and saints.

> "O what a happy company—
> Where saints and angels join!"

There will be no more anger nor strife, no more malice nor envyings, evil speaking, nor any thing that shall mar our happiness, or give us pain, but harmony and peace shall for ever abound! May God help us to be faithful to him, and to the spirit of his grace.

> "How tedious and tasteless the hours
> When Jesus no longer I see;
> Sweet prospects, sweet birds, and sweet flow'rs
> Have all lost their sweetness to me.
> The midsummer sun shines but dim—
> The fields strive in vain to look gay;
> But when I am happy in him,
> December's as pleasant as May.

> "His name yields the richest perfume,
> And sweeter than music his voice;
> His presence disperses my gloom,
> And makes all within me rejoice.
> I should, were he always thus nigh,
> Have nothing to wish or to fear—
> No mortal so happy as I,
> My summer would last all the year."

O that I could always be enabled to put my trust in him in every time of trouble, and may the Lord prepare me for death and glory.

> "There on a green and flowery mount
> Our weary souls shall sit;
> And with transporting joy, recount
> The labors of our feet!"

May 10th. I am in a lingering state of health, and whether I shall ever be able to be of any use to myself or others I know not, but I hope that I may be enabled to be resigned to the disposal of Providence, and say, not my will, but thine be done. It is a reality that we are born to die, and after death to come to judgment; and how ought we to live, that we may stand acquitted in that awful day, when Christ in glory shall appear to judge both the quick and the dead! O that I may have "my robes washed and made white in the blood of the Lamb," that I may hear the welcome sentence, Come, ye blessed of my Father, inherit the kingdom prepared for you from the foundation of the world. O happy day, when we shall be delivered from this body of clay, that clogs and weighs down the soul oftentimes, and makes us cry out with the apostle, Who shall deliver me from the body of this death!

How necessary it is for us to watch and pray, that we enter not into temptation, but hold fast the confidence that we have in a blessed Saviour.

"On Jordan's stormy banks I stand,
 And cast a wishful eye,
To Canaan's fair and happy land,
 Where my possessions lie.
O the transporting, happy scene,
 That rises to my sight—
Sweet fields array'd in living green,
 And rivers of delight!

"There generous fruits that never fail,
 On trees immortal grow:
There rocks and hills, and brooks and vales,
 With milk and honey flow
All o'er those wide extended plains,
 Shines one eternal day;
There God the Son forever reigns,
 And scatters night away.

"No chilling winds nor pois'nous breath
 Can reach that healthful shore;
Sickness and sorrow, pain and death,
 Are felt and fear'd no more.
When shall I reach that happy place,
 And be for ever blest?
When shall I see my Father's face,
 And in his bosom rest?

"Fill'd with delight, my raptur'd soul
 Would here no longer stay;
Though Jordan's waves around me roll,
 Fearless I'd launch away:
There on those high and flow'ry plains,
 Our spirits ne'er shall tire;
But in perpetual, joyful strains,
 Redeeming love admire."

It is through the tender mercy of God that I am alive and out of hell! O that I may be rewarded in the spirit of my mind! May all the earthly dispositions of my heart be changed into heavenly, that I may be prepared to bid adieu to this world of sorrow, and find an habitation of peace, where the wicked cease from troubling, and the weary are at rest. May God help me to be faithful the few days that I have to spend on earth. My heart hath been much sunk under a weight of sorrow, when I consider how far from God and heaven and what I would be, I am! O that the cry of my soul may be, Dear Jesus, raise me higher! I long to be holy, as thou art holy. May the Lord help me to rely on his mercy and goodness for all that is to come—and say, without reserve, " The will of the Lord be done."

> " O God, my help in ages past,
> My hope for years to come ;
> My shelter from the stormy blast,
> And my eternal home :"

prepare me for that day, when all the saints shall get home, and sit down on the right hand of God—where we shall be freed from all the toils and troubles of life, and have pleasure without end—where trouble and anguish cannot enter, but all shall be harmony and peace !

> " O what a glorious company,
> When saints and angels meet"—

in robes of white arrayed—when Christ shall wipe all tears from our eyes, and we shall be admitted to sit down with Abraham, Isaac, and Jacob, and all the saints that have gone through much tribulation, and *washed their* robes, and made them white in the blood of the Lamb. May my heart and life be conformed to the gospel, that I may be a comfort to my companion, and a blessing to society.

> " And may my sun in smiles decline,
> And bring a pleasing night."

The men that love the Lord are happy in this world and in the next ! O may that be my happy lot—may the Lord help me to tear every idol from my heart, and may he reign without a rival there. I feel my heart's desire is, to love the Lord with my whole heart.

> " This is a world of trouble and grief, I plainly see ;
> But when in deepest sorrow, O God, I look to Thee !
> Thou deliver'dst Daniel, when in the lion's den—
> And if thou didst protect him, O why not other men !"

Help me to pray without ceasing, and in every thing give thanks ! May my soul's concern and only care be to secure a lot among the blest, that when my days are ended on earth, I may receive an inheritance that can never be taken from me ! May God preserve my companion while absent.

In my days of childhood, the providence of God was over me to preserve me from evil ; although I lost my mother, one of the most invaluable blessings that a child can be deprived of, particularly a female. Yet the Lord was my friend, and brought me up to the years of maturity, with a mind as little tainted with the evil practices that are prevalent among young people as most. My sister was very careful to teach me the way of rectitude in my earliest days, which was of great benefit in my journey through life. And I doubt not, if mothers would begin with their children when they are young, they might mould them into almost any frame they chose. But instead of paying that attention to their morals while their minds are young and susceptible of good impressions, as they ought, they suffer them to mix with those who are wicked to a proverb, thinking there is no danger—they are too young to be injured by any bad example or precept. But they find, when it is too late, that their minds are too easily impressed with evil, and that habits imbibed in childhood are not easily eradicated: and through their neglect, many that might have been shining characters in society, and a blessing to the age they live in, are but a nuisance to mankind, and are rearing up another set to walk in their tracks. Thus the world is contaminated by the mismanagement of mothers! My heart has often been pained to see the dear little innocents run at random, and taught nothing that would be of service to them, either in this world, or in the next! May the Lord open the eyes of those who have the care of children, to see the importance of their charge, and enable them to do their duty, that the rising generation may be more obedient to their parents, more attentive to the duty they owe their God ; then they will be a greater blessing to society, and will be better qualified to fill up that sphere in life which they may be called to, and above all, be prepared for those happy regions, where all will be harmony and peace!

After my marriage, leaving the place where I had lived from my early days, I was placed in quite a different sphere of life. Unacquainted with the variety of manners and dispositions of mankind, I thought all who professed friendship were friends: but I have found myself mistaken in many instances. Some that at one time would appear like as if there was nothing too good that they could do for one, at another time were so cool and distant, that one would be ready to conclude that they could not be the same people! These constant changes have, in some measure, taught me this lesson, that we are all frail mortals, liable to change ; and there is but one source that is permanent. There we may place implicit confidence, and we will not be deceived.

I have abundant cause to be thankful to my great Benefactor, for the continued favors bestowed on me, and for the many kind friends who have administered to my necessities in the time of adversity. May the great Master reward them richly in this world, and in that which is to come, eternal life and glory! It is said to be more blessed to give than to receive ; therefore, those who have it in their power to do good to the needy sons and daughters of affliction, and follow the dictates of charity, will have a double reward. They will feel a sweet peace in their own souls while they are travelling through this unfriendly world ; and when they come to bid adieu to all things below the sun, they will have a glorious prospect of a happy entrance into the blest abode of saints and angels!

"O may my lot be cast with these,
The least of Jesus' witnesses"—

on earth, and at last be joined to that happy company above the skies!

What need there is to watch and pray, and guard against the vain allurements of this world—to steer our course between the rocks on either hand, that we may gain the destined port of eternal repose in the bosom of our once crucified, but now risen and exalted Saviour!

Our hearts are too often fixed on the vain and transient things of time and sense, while the important concerns of eternal happiness or misery are almost, if not quite neglected! We are leaving nothing undone that we can accomplish to lay up treasure on earth, which will perish in the using ; while the immortal part, which will have an existence as long as its Author exists, lieth in ruins! O what madness! This poor body, what is it, but a dying lump of clay, that must in a few revolving days be consigned to the dust from whence it was taken? What will it avail us then, whether we were rich or poor, noble or ignoble? The main point will then be, whether we have spent our time in the service of God, or have devoted it to the pleasures and vanities of the world, to please ourselves instead of obeying the calls of the gospel, and taking up the cross! O that these things may lay with serious weight on our minds, that we may make sure work for eternity, and spend no time unprofitably, but husband it to the best advantage.

The various scenes of life make such an impression on our minds that we are often brought into such perplexities that we hardly know which way to turn. But if we could always live in the enjoyment of that faith, which it is our privilege to possess, we should never be at a loss. I have passed through many trying situations in Europe and America; but the Lord hath been my helper thus far, through all the *vicissitudes* attending the *journey of life!* And I hope one day to outstrip the wind, beyond the bounds of time, where there will be no more uncertainty or disappointment—where peace and harmony shall for ever abound: after all our troubles here, how sweet and consoling rest will be! May the Lord help me to live near to the bleeding side of a crucified Redeemer, willing to take up my cross and follow him wherever he may lead, if it is to go through fire or water. These are trying times—the love of many is waxing cold. How soon we may be called to a fresh trial of our faith, we cannot tell. May we stand firm, knowing that all shall work together for good to those that love God.

How many and various are the difficulties of life, while travelling through this vale of tears, to the place of rest, whither we are all hastening! Were it not for the mixture of pleasure that we find interwoven in those pains, we should often sink under them; but He that rides upon the winds and can command them at a nod, undertakes our cause and makes a way for us when we see none, and cannot tell which way we must go. I am indebted to that great and beneficent hand for all the mercies that I do enjoy. O that my heart may be filled with gratitude to God for these favors.

I arrived in New York with my companion towards the last of March, 1814, where I met with kind friends, particularly brother Munson and his family. They are like as though they were our own dear brothers and sisters: may the Lord reward them in this world and in the next! Here I met with my old friend, sister Lester. She is still the same: may the Lord prosper her on her journey to a glorious eternity! I have found as kind friends of late as I could expect. O that my heart may ever feel grateful to my God for all his mercies to unworthy me! I have felt a greater desire to be all devoted to the Lord, (soul and body, and all that I have and am, for time and eternity,) of late, than I have felt for a long time. I do not expect to find that place, while I am an inhabitant of this lower world, where there is nothing to trouble or afflict either body or mind. May the great Master give me more of the spirit of humility, that it may enable me to be willing to suffer all the righteous will of God; and when called to bid adieu to all below the sun, that I might have a pleasing prospect of a glorious immortality! O how sweet and delightful must be the scene to souls that have been tossed on the ocean of time, and have fought their passage through, and got within a view of the happy land,

> "When all their sorrows will be o'er,
> Their suff'ring and their pain;
> Who meet on that eternal shore
> Shall never part again!"

O may I be prepared to meet those that have gone before, and those that may come after.

May 10th, 1814. We have been in New York for several weeks, and kindly treated by many—may the Lord reward them.

Though many have been my trials and afflictions the last four or five years of my life, yet the Lord hath been my friend—and I feel a desire to devote the remainder of my days to his service. How long I shall be an inhabitant of this world of wo, is uncertain with me; I feel the seeds of death in this mortal frame—and it is my earnest desire to become more and more acquainted with my own heart, that when the summons shall arrive, I may not be alarmed, but rejoice to go and be at rest! O how soon my heart sinks down to earth again! O my Lord, help me to keep my eye upon the prize, and my heart stayed on thee, that this world may have no charms sufficient to draw me from the contemplation of heaven and glory!

> "Was I possessor of the earth,
> And called the stars my own,
> Without thy graces, and thyself,
> I were a wretch undone!
> Let others stretch their arms like seas
> And grasp in all the shore;
> Grant me the visits of thy grace,
> And I desire no more."

May I ever lay at the feet of my glorious Redeemer, who hath bought my pardon on the tree! My soul is pained on the account of those that were once plain, humble followers of the meek and lowly Jesus, but now are so conformed to the world, that they can hardly be distinguished from them! How long will they sleep in security, wandering from God—pursuing a shadow instead of a substance? How vain are all things below the sun! We may have prosperity one day, and the next may prove quite the reverse. How necessary it is to have our hearts detached from the world, and placed on a more durable object!

May 13th, 1814. I am this day under renewed obligations to the great Preserver for the blessings that I enjoy—my life is preserved, and I have kind friends that appear willing to supply all my wants. May God, that is able to give me the inward consolation of the Holy Spirit, enable me to draw water out of the fountain that never will run dry! I long to be more holy in heart and life; and then I shall surely be more happy. O my soul, arise! and shake thyself, and put on thy beautiful garments! and then, I can rejoice in tribulation, knowing that tribulation worketh patience; and what a charming trait it is in the Christian character—that of patience! O that I may learn to possess my soul in patience in this day of trial! The times are gloomy, and we need to be continually at the throne of grace, and cry mightily to God to stand by us; that we may keep the narrow road, and not turn to the right hand or to the left.

Sunday, May 15th, 1814. I thank the Lord that I have once more had the privilege of hearing the sweet sound of the gospel, from these words: "By whom shall Jacob arise, for he is small?" I wish it may sink into the hearts of those that heard it. In the first place, he told what was meant by Jacob or Israel—spiritually the church of Christ; and then went on to tell why it was styled small in those days, as well as at the present day. First, because the professed clergy were not faithful, but were fallen asleep upon their watch-tower; and did not warn the people of their danger as they ought. Secondly, wicked rulers, by their bad example, prevented that good being done as otherwise would be, if they were men that truly loved and feared God. And thirdly, the laity, those that heard the sound of the gospel, did not make that improvement of the precious opportunities which they enjoyed as they ought. Parents set bad examples before their children—this was one great cause why we so seldom saw the young and rising generation turning to God! And fourthly, and lastly, he showed by whom Jacob must arise—it was our duty to pray in faith, but it was God that gave the increase—therefore, we must hope and believe that God would hear our prayers, and convert our children and neighbors, and prosper Zion. If we were united in heart, so as to be like an army with banners, and not let the spirit of division get in among us, and cry out, "I am of Paul, and I am of Apollos, and I of Cephas, and I of Christ"—but all must be of one mind and heart in Christ Jesus the Lord! Then we should see how the church would prosper, and what glorious seasons we should have! But the times are gloomy, and when the cloud will disperse we cannot tell.

May 19th. Lorenzo is quite unwell—trials await us, but may our trust be in the Lord, that he will deliver us from all our troubles at last, and land us safe on the peaceful shores of blest eternity; where all our toils will be over—our suffering and our pain; where we shall join the happy millions that surround the throne of God, and sing hallelujah to God and the Lamb forever and ever!

"Our moments fly apace,
Nor will our minutes stay;
Just like a flood our hasty days
Are sweeping us away."

May our hearts be inspired with love and gratitude to the great Giver of all things, for the mercies we do enjoy—to enable us to improve every moment to the glory of God, and our own good!

May 20th, 1814. We are at Hoboken, a delightful spot of the earth, upon the Jersey side of the river, opposite New York—where, from the window of the room we occupy, we have a grand view of the city, with the majestic steeples of the different churches, reaching their lofty heads almost to the lowering skies—while the beautiful trees that are interspersed among the houses, with the surrounding country, which can also be seen at the same time, conspire to make it a most enchanting prospect. On the other hand, the Jersey side presents to view, decorated with all the charms of spring—green trees and shady groves; while the delightful songsters of the woods tune their harmonious throats in praising their great Creator! These beauties of nature all joined in concert, one would suppose, could not fail to excite gratitude in the hard and obdurate heart of man, the most noble work of our great Creator! But, lamentable to tell, they appear to be less thankful than the birds that fly in open space, or even the reptiles that crawl upon the earth, for they answer the end for which they were made—but man, who was formed in the image of his God, and not only indebted to him for creation, but also for redemption in the blood of Jesus, tramples on his mercies, and despises the offers of his grace; and live more like beasts, than creatures possessed of rationality! O that men would learn to love and serve the Lord!

We are at the house of a kind family, but they do not profess religion. May the Lord make our stay with them a blessing to their souls, and to the neighborhood where they live; for the people in this place, by what I can learn, are quite careless about their souls! O that the Lord may make use of some measures to bring them to a knowledge of the truth—my soul longs to see a revival of religion take place once more.

May 21st. I am still alive, and out of a never-ending eternity: for which may my heart be filled with gratitude to him that sustains and supplies me with every needed blessing; who inclines the hearts of my fellow-mortals to treat me with kindness. O how much I am indebted to my God—and how little is my heart affected with a grateful sense of his goodness! O that he would implant, deep in my soul, love to God and man, with a heart-felt sense of my dependence upon him, for all the favors which I do enjoy.

From Sunday until Monday we were in New York, at brother Munson's the greatest part of the time.—Lorenzo is printing his Journal, with some other tracts; which has detained him in and about this city far longer than he expected to have stayed when we came here—but the way seemed to open for him to print his books, and he thought it best to improve the present opening, and I hope it may prove a blessing to many.

On Wednesday afternoon we came over to Mr. Anderson's again; where we met with the same kind reception which we had experienced some days before. Mrs. Anderson was very sick, but was something better the next day. Lorenzo preached to the people in this place on Wednesday evening, and had a crowded house. May the seed take root in some heart, and bear fruit to perfection! I feel the need of more faith, to be enabled to put my trust in the great Giver of every good and perfect gift—my heart too often wanders from the right source. O that my mind may be stayed on God in every trying hour. I long to be made holy in heart and life; and feel a willingness to bear the cross like a good soldier of Jesus Christ, that when the sun of life shall decline, I may have a pleasing prospect of a happy eternity!

Saturday, May 28th. Through the goodness of God I enjoy better health than I have done for more than two years before. May my heart be filled with love and gratitude to the Great and Beneficent hand that is daily showering down blessings on my unworthy head, and improve my lengthened days, in doing good to myself and others! For why should I be useless in this time of need? But, O! my heart shrinks at the cross!— May the Lord help me to be willing to take it up, and follow Jesus in the way! When we consider the shortness of time, and the length of eternity, we perceive there is no time to lose; but a necessity to improve every moment to the best advantage. May it be impressed on my heart!

May 31st. I desire to have my heart filled with grateful songs of praise, to the God of all grace and mercies, for his favors to me! Through every lane of life, he hath provided me kind friends, in the day of adversity as well as in the day of prosperity. What reason have I to be faithful to my God for all these blessings! May the Lord help me ever to lie at the feet of the Saviour, and learn instruction from his lips! I am still at captain

Anderson's at the beautiful little town of Hoboken, as charming a place as I almost ever saw. O, what a pity there is not (as I know of) one person in this place that enjoys religion; or at least, not many feeling much concern for their souls; and they have no preaching, except by the Baptists, who preach up "particular election" and reprobation, in the strongest terms that I ever heard. I went to hear them on Sunday last, and my heart was truly pained, to hear a man get up and address a number of people, (who were unacquainted with the way of salvation, and for aught I knew, were living in the neglect of their duty altogether,) in this way; that they "could do nothing; they must be taken by an irresistible power, and be brought in." But my heart replied, "Ho, every one that thirsteth, come ye to the waters; and he that hath no money, come buy wine and milk, without money and without price!"—What a pity it is, that men should darken counsel by words without knowledge! For it is expressly said, that all may come that will; and that they shall in no wise be shut out. May God stop the mouths of those that attempt to speak in his name, who are not called and qualified by the Spirit for the work; but bless and prosper those that have taken their lives in their hands, and have gone forth to call sinners to repentance, offering a free salvation to all the fallen race of Adam.

June 1st. What a miracle of mercy it is that I am still spared on this side of eternity, whilst many of my fellow-mortals have been called from the stage of action; their bodies numbered with the pale nations under ground, and their souls taken flight to a world of spirits; whilst I, the most unprofitable, perhaps, of any, am spared, and enjoy a tolerable state of health, so much better than I once expected I ever should! May my heart be made truly sensible of the duty I owe to the great God of heaven and earth; whose name is terrible to all who are in any measure sensible of his majesty and power. And also I desire to know and to do my duty to my fellow-mortals; but I tremble at the cross! O that I may be delivered from "the fear of man, which bringeth a snare!"

"My drowsy powers, why sleep ye so!
Awake, my sluggish soul!
Nothing hath half thy work to do,
Yet nothing is half so dull!

Go to the ants; for one poor grain
See how they toil and strive;
Yet we who have a heaven to obtain,
How negligent we live!

Waken, O Lord, my drowsy sense,
To walk this dangerous road;
That if my soul be hurried hence,"
It may be found in God!

une 2d. I am this day under renewed obligations to that hand which hath supplied all my necessities, from my earliest days, until the present period of time. O that I may lie in the valley of humility, under a sense of the numerous favors bestowed upon me, by the hand of an ever bountiful God, and improve the moments that are allotted me, to the glory of his great name, and the good of my own immortal soul! I feel my heart is too often placed upon things below the sun—may the Lord help me to tear my heart and affections from earth, and place them on things above.

My Lorenzo's mind is exercised and drawn out to visit foreign lands, to call sinners to repentance; and I would not stand in his way above all things, but I feel the need of more grace to acquiesce, in all circumstances, in the will of Providence, which I desire to do more than any thing besides. May the God of all grace enable me to say—"not my will, but thine be done." Lord, may I be made of some use to my fellow-creatures while on earth I stay, that I need not be quite useless, while I am an inhabitant of this lower world! It is now night, and the evening shades prevail. The sun hath set beyond the western sky, and the Lord only knows whether I shall see the return of another day! May he take charge of me this night, and grant that whether I sleep, or whatever I do, I may have a single eye to his glory, and be prepared to meet my "last enemy" in peace! May God reward my kind benefactors with every needed blessing.

Sunday, June 12th. This hath been a day of deep trial to my soul. There having been an appointment made for my Lorenzo to preach in the African church, at six o'clock, and the people appearing anxious to see me, as many of them had not, it was published that I would be there, and perhaps I would subjoin a few words by way of exhortation: this made such an impression on the minds of people, that they came out in such numbers, that they could not get into the house. I took my seat in the altar; and after Lorenzo had given them a discourse from these words, "O earth, earth, earth, hear the word of the Lord," I rose up and spoke a few words; but the cross was so weighty, I did not fully answer my mind. I closed the meeting by striving to lift my heart to God, in prayer, with some degree of liberty. May the Lord deliver me from the fear of man, which bringeth a snare! Why should we be so much under the influence of the enemy, as not to speak for our God in these important times, when wickedness doth so much abound, and the love of many is waxing cold, and others are carrying such burdens! O may the God of all grace stand by and support his people in this day of trial! The storm is gathering fast, and who will be able to stand, while the anger of the Lord is pouring out upon the inhabitants of the earth, for their ingratitude, particularly those of our favored land, America? We have had peace and plenty for many years; but the fulness of bread was the destruction of Sodom! O that it may not be the case with us!

June 13th. May my soul and body be altogether devoted to that God who hath provided for me ever since I have had an existence! I have in some instances been brought into trying circumstances; but there hath always been a way opened for me, so that I have never lacked any thing so much as to say that I was in a suffering condition. For if I had it not, nor wherewith to procure it for myself, yet the Lord that hath the hearts of all men in his hands, would raise up some one to supply my wants. Glory! glory! be to his name for ever and ever, for all his mercies to such an unworthy mortal as me! What is past we know; but what is to come we cannot tell. May we be prepared for whatever lies before us! The cloud seems gathering fast over our land! May the God that rules on high, that all the earth surveys, avert the threatening storms, and deliver us from the power of our enemies. O the charms of America! shall they be destroyed by foreigners? Shall the rich jewel of liberty be plucked from the American crown by tyrants? Forbid it, mighty God! and grant, if we need chastisements, as no doubt we do, as a nation, to let us fall into thy hand, rather than into the hand of man, for thou art merciful! O that the people of this favored land might learn to be wise, in time to save our country from destruction! My soul mourns on account of my fellow-mortals. May they be made sensible of the necessity of making their peace with God, before the evil day shall come, when they shall say, " I have no pleasure in them."

June 14th. Through the favor and goodness of God I am still alive, and am blessed with as good health as I have enjoyed for many months; and trust my face is Zion-ward. For ever praised be the Lord for all his blessings which I do enjoy. O may my soul drink deeper and deeper into that spirit which will enable me to bear the cross with joy; and not shrink from it like a coward, and the crown fall from my head, and others take the prize.

June 18th. Through the tender mercy of the Lord, who is over all and above all, I am still an inhabitant of this lower world, surrounded by dangers and difficulties; liable to stray in bye and forbidden paths: and the way appears so gloomy that I tremble at the prospect. I feel much concerned for the present state of my beloved country. There is so much dissension among the people of this most favored of all lands, that I fear for its consequences. My heart has often been pained, to see the ingratitude which has been prevalent in our peaceful, plentiful, and happy country. Whilst other nations were almost deluged in blood, we have been blessed with peace in our borders; and the glorious gospel has been spread from shore to shore. But these happy days are gone, and for aught I know or can see, it may be long before they will return, unless the Lord should undertake our cause. He can bring low and raise up. He sways kingdoms; and it is through his long-suffering and tender mercy that the world is kept in existence; for it groaneth under the wickedness of its inhabitants! If he were to enter into judgment with us, who could stand before him? And it appears he is about to visit the earth with a curse! It is surely time for those that profess to fear God, to awake and shake themselves from that indolence of spirit, which so prevails in our land, and lay siege to a throne of grace for deliverance; for he is all-sufficient, and can make a way, where it appears to us, short-sighted creatures, impossible for a way to be made. May he undertake our cause, and bring deliverance in whatever channel he thinks best.

Sunday, June 19th. I have been at Capt. John Anderson's, Hoboken, for several weeks, where I have been treated very kindly. Himself and wife are as agreeable a couple as I have met with for a long time, and I believe they wish well to the cause of religion: but they do not enjoy that peace in their own souls as they might. May the God of all grace attend them, and enable them to take up the cross, that they may be prepared for a seat at the right hand of God, at last.

On the twenty-ninth of June, we left New York, after having been there for the space of near three months, for New Haven, in the mail-stage. We travelled through the most delightful country that my eyes ever beheld; the season was so charming! The gardens were in bloom; the fields and meadows clothed in their richest dress; so that the eye might be transported with pleasure at almost every glance. My heart was at the same time contemplating the goodness of God to the once happy land of America; but now, how soon her beauty might be laid in the dust, by the spoiler.

we could not tell, and all her glory brought to nought! But there is a God that rules over all; and I trust he will bring order out of confusion. May the people learn humility and submission, from the present calamity, to the will of the great Ruler of the universe.

We arrived at New Haven about nine o'clock at night; we stopped at the stage-tavern, kept by a man that fears not God nor regards man, if we may judge by the appearance, but we could not get permission to stay there for the night. It being so late we could not find any friends, although there were Methodists in the place; consequently, we were under the necessity of seeking lodgings in another public house: accordingly, we did, and slept there. But in the morning, Lorenzo went out to find the preacher that is stationed at New Haven, and in his way he met with a brother Woolf, and he requested him to breakfast with him, and sent up to the public house for me to come to his house; accordingly I did, but the people where we stayed said that we ought to have eat breakfast with them, as we stayed there the night before; and so charged us one dollar and a half for our lodging, which Lorenzo paid.

The friends in New Haven were very kind, and wished Lorenzo to stay over the Sabbath. This was on Thursday: he was anxious to get to his father's; but by the solicitation of brother Smith, the stationed preacher, and many others, he was prevailed on to stay. He preached on Thursday night and Friday night; and on Sunday he preached four times: the people appeared quite solemn and attentive. The preacher in that place is one of the most affectionate, friendly men, that I ever met with; may the Lord bless him, and make him useful to souls!

On Monday morning I left New Haven, in company with a man and his wife for Branford, in their wagon; while Lorenzo stayed to give them another sermon, as it was the "Fourth of July," and there was an oration to be delivered by the great Mr. T * * * *; accordingly, he spoke something on the present state of our country, to an audience that was attentive. He then left there in a wagon, which belonged to a Quaker, who was going to see his friends in Branford, where he spoke again at night.

The next morning the friend that had brought us to Branford, started with us to North Guilford, to a brother of mine, that I had not seen for near thirty years. We were both very small at that time, but now he had a wife and six children, and I felt much pleased to find that he had been industrious, and appeared to be doing well, as it relates to this world; and I trust he was not altogether indifferent to the things of another. His wife was in a low state of health, but I have no doubt but she enjoys religion. May the God of all grace bless them and their dear children. There I saw my step-mother also, that I had not seen before since I was six years of age: my heart glowed with affection towards her; may her last days be crowned with peace!

My brother took his wagon, and carried us to Durham, on the stage-road, and tarried with us that night; and in the morning bid us farewell, and returned home. A friend living at Durham, lent us a chaise to Middletown; where my Lorenzo held meeting at night. There we met brother Burrows from Hebron, with a wagon, which was to return the next morning, in which we came to his house, where we stayed from Friday until Monday. Lorenzo preached on Friday night, and also on Sunday at the Methodist meeting-house; the people were solemn and attentive. At five o'clock, at another place four or five miles distant, and returned again that night.

This place was about twelve or fourteen miles from his dear father's; and as we had no horse or carriage, and brother Burrows made wagons, he bought a horse and wagon from him; and we started on Monday, about three o'clock in the afternoon, and arrived at his father's just before dark. We were kindly received by his father and the rest of the family. We found the old gentleman in tolerable health; but being a man advanced in years, he was something feeble: we stayed with him from Monday until Saturday. The people of this place are much degenerated from what they once were, when the candle of the Lord shone upon their heads; but now there is scarcely any, that I saw, who appeared to enjoy religion! Our dear old father seemed to be struggling for deliverance in the blood of Jesus; may the great Master appear to his soul, the first among ten thousand, and altogether lovely!

We spent the week, I may say, in a solitary way, in taking our rambles through the lonely walks that my Lorenzo had taken in early days of childhood, before his tender mind was matured; and after he had arrived to the age of fifteen, when his heart was wrought upon by the Spirit of God. Here was the sweet grove, at the foot of a beautiful hill, through which ran a charming rivulet of water, where he used to go to meditate and pray to that God, who was able to save and did deliver his soul, and enabled him to take up his cross, and go forth to call sinners to repentance.

My heart was pained to know and see that some part of the family was not, or appeared not engaged to save their souls.

On Saturday we started for Tolland, and from thence to Square-pond, where Lorenzo preached twice the next day, at the Methodist meeting-house, to an attentive congregation; and at five o'clock at Tolland: the people seemed very solemn. Early on Monday morning we left Tolland, for Hartford, where Lorenzo preached at night, in a Presbyterian meeting-house, to a tolerable congregation. We met with kind treatment from a Doctor Lynds—may the Lord bless him and his! We left Hartford on Tuesday, and went to an aunt of Lorenzo's that night, living about four or five miles from his father's. She appeared very glad to see us; and sent out and called in the neighbors, and Lorenzo gave them a short discourse. The next day Lorenzo was quite unwell, unable to sit up; but towards evening we made ready, and started for his father's, where we arrived in safety. Lorenzo had intended to leave me at his father's, while he took a journey to the east; but circumstances appeared not to favor it, and he concluded to take me with him. Accordingly, we made preparations for our departure, on Saturday morning, July 23d, 1814, after having stayed with his father for ten or twelve days.

I felt truly pained to part with the dear old man: may the Lord bless him, and make his last days abundant in peace! My Lorenzo preached at Vernon at night, and in the morning, to an attentive little company—may the Lord make it like bread cast upon the waters! He preached at Hartford-five-miles, on Sunday, to a crowded congregation.

July 25th. We have this day arrived at Hartford, and my Lorenzo has received his books from New York; and furthermore, we have heard of the arrival of a large force of our enemy's soldiers, landing on our once peaceful happy shore! O that the God that is able to save, would appear for our deliverance! Although, as a nation, we have forfeited all right and title to protection; yet there is nowhere else to fly for deliverance! O that we, as a nation, may be humbled before God, and lift our united cries to the throne of grace for his assistance! May the tumults of the earth be hushed to silence, and people learn war no more! My soul longs to drink deeper into the spirit of love to God and man, that I may be made useful to souls, and a comfort to my wandering companion, that I may be a helpmate indeed.

> "How vain are all things here below,
> How false, and yet how fair!
> Each pleasure has its poison too,
> And every sweet a snare!"

O that the Lord would teach me the emptiness of earthly enjoyments, and help me to rely on him alone for support and comfort! O that my prospects for glory may brighten up, and my soul be struggling for full deliverance from every desire that is not centred in Him that is able to give all things!

I have been reading the exercise of a precious woman, who went with her husband to the East Indies, to help him to preach the gospel to the poor ignorant Hindoos. O that the desire which filled her soul, to spread the good news of glad tidings of the Saviour, may prevail more and more!

We rode three miles from Hartford, the same day that we went there; and Lorenzo preached at night, at East Hartford, to, perhaps, one hundred and fifty or two hundred, (and they were quite attentive,) from these words—"Behold, I stand at the door and knock; if any man hear my voice and open the door, I will come in to him, and sup with him, and he with me." My mind was quite depressed, although I was enabled to close the meeting by prayer. I feel a gloom hanging over my mind, on account of the present state of my country.—O! will the great God deliver our happy land into the hand of the spoiler? O that God would hear and answer prayer; inspire, and then accept the prayer of us poor mortals! My soul longs to be prepared for whatever awaits us on the shores of time. If we live as we ought, we may rely on the providence of God, to protect us from every evil. My Lorenzo is very unwell. O that the Lord may give him grace and strength to do his duty, and call sinners to repentance! May the Lord bless his labors, and make him useful to souls!

I long to get more confidence, to take up my cross, and help him to spread the good news of glad tidings to all people—may God help me!

My desire is, that I may lie at the feet of Jesus, and be willing to love the cross, that I may wear the crown in those happy mansions above the skies. My heart, I find, is too often wandering from my God. O that I may arise and shake myself, and in the strength of Jesus, overcome my enemies, both of a spiritual and a temporal nature! I long to be altogether devoted to my God. Lorenzo expects to preach this evening—may the Lord attend, by the unction of his Holy Spirit.

Lorenzo preached the last night; but I was so unwell that I could not attend: and he is to preach twice to-day—may the Lord stand by him, and make his words sharp and piercing, reaching the hearts of those that hear!

My soul longs to be more alive to God, that I may be made more useful to my fellow-creatures, and help my companion to spread the glorious gospel through this weary land: we are wanderers on earth—we have no abiding home in this world, but are seeking one above—may the God of all grace enable us to keep the prize in view, and deliver us from all our enemies.

My Lorenzo hath spoken once to-day, and is to speak again this evening —may the Lord attend the word with power. Why should we desire to live in this world to be useless? For what would be the benefit if we were to live to the age of Methuselah, and neglect the one thing needful? It would only add to our condemnation! O that these things may be impressed on my heart!

July 28th. Bless the Lord, O my soul, and forget not all his benefits! What reason have I to be thankful to my great Benefactor for mercies to me, a poor wanderer upon the earth, that I am provided with kind friends in this world of wo! May my heart glow with gratitude to my God and my fellow-mortals for the blessings that I enjoy! May the great Master reward those who are willing to administer to the necessities of those that have taken their lives in their hands, and have gone forth to sound the alarm, and call sinners to repentance—to offer them free salvation in the blood of Jesus! My soul longs to see Zion prosper—to hear poor sinners inquiring the way to peace and true happiness. O may the Lord inspire my heart with that living faith, to cry mightily to him who is able to save souls. O, if Christians were more engaged to obtain the height and depth, and length and breadth of the love of God, which is in Christ Jesus our Lord, what a happy time it would be! O my soul, awake! lift up a cry to the God and Father of our Lord Jesus Christ, for full redemption in the blood of Jesus!

Lorenzo preached three times at East Windsor; but the people are like the nether mill-stone, hard and unfeeling: may the Lord soften their hard hearts, and bring them to a sense of their danger! We were at a kind family by the name of Stoten. May the Lord prosper them in the way to glory. My heart hath felt somewhat refreshed since I came to the house of friend Barker's, living in West Windsor. Lorenzo hath been acquainted with the family sixteen years: it does my heart good to meet those who have their faces Zion-ward!

What a sweet meeting it will be when all the tempted followers of Jesus get home!

"There on a green and flow'ry mount
Our weary souls shall sit;
And with transporting joys recount
The labors of our feet."

What a prize! Is it not worth striving for? O may I be more zealous in the way of my duty—more willing to take up the cross!

The news of war is saluting our ears daily. O that God may prepare us for whatever awaits us; and if a scourge is necessary, may it bring us, as a nation, to the feet of Jesus! My heart is pained within me. Lord, prepare me to submit to thy will, with the rest of the poor fallen race of Adam. We have all sinned, and come short of the glory of God, and deserve chastisement. O that we may fall into the hand of God rather than the hand of man—for he is merciful! I feel a desire to submit without murmuring; but our hearts are so refractory, we need the influence of grace, to make us what we ought to be. My Lord, help America!

July 29th. Lorenzo preached last evening to a tolerable company, considering it was a very unpleasant night; and they gave very good attention: may the Lord make it like seed sown on good ground, that it shall bring forth fruit in due time! There seems to be a number in this place that are heaven-born and heaven-bound: may the Lord make them burning and shining lights in the land wherein they live, that they may be like unto the leaven which was hid in three measures of meal, leavening the whole lump; so that the flame may continue to increase until the town shall be filled with the glory of God! My soul longs to see Zion prosper! O God, fill my heart with love to thee and my fellow-sinners. My heart is pained to see so little good done as there is—may God revive his work once more in the land.

> "Through grace I am determin'd
> To conquer though I die;
> And then away to Jesus,
> On wings of love I'll fly!"

I am a stranger and pilgrim on earth, together with my dear companion; but we have the promise of a substantial inheritance, if we are faithful, and continue to the end.

> "The Lord my pasture shall prepare,
> And feed me with a shepherd's care;
> My noonday walks he shall attend,
> And all my midnight hours defend."

O Lord, help me to rely upon thy promises, by faith!

July 31st, 1814. What cause have I to adore that beneficent hand, that hath and doth still provide for such a poor unprofitable creature as I! May my heart be filled with grateful songs of praise to the great Master.

We left Hartford on the morning of the 30th, without knowing whither we went, or where we should find a resting-place for the night; but God provided for us beyond what we could have expected. We met with an old man, and after speaking to him, we found him to be one of those who are striving to walk the narrow happy road. He told us of a family who he thought would be glad to see Lorenzo. Accordingly, we went there, and found it even so: this place is called Barkhamstead. They received us with affection, and every attention possible. Their names were Francis. Lorenzo held two meetings at a barn, within about a mile of this friend's: the people were solemn and attentive. There I met with two of my uncle's daughters very unexpectedly: they lived in the neighborhood. They appeared glad to see me, this being the first time I had ever seen them since I could recollect. I have had as little acquaintance with any of my relation as most people. This circumstance excited a sensation in my heart, that I was almost a stranger to before—I felt such a drawing towards them! O that the Lord would give them to feel the necessity of living up to the requirements of the gospel, that we may meet at last on the happy banks of everlasting deliverance! In the evening we went about five miles further, where Lorenzo preached again. This was the third time he had preached this day: may the Lord strengthen his body and soul, to cry aloud and spare not, to sinners to repent.

Monday morning, August 1st. Lorenzo preaches again this morning at 5 o'clock. O that the Lord would make him more and more useful to nis fellow-mortals. I feel this morning a desire to be more engaged with my God! O that my heart might be filled with all the fulness of the Spirit, that I may be more willing to take up my cross and help my companion to do good! Time is short—we are hastening to eternity! O that our days may be spent in the service of God, helping souls on to the peaceful mansions of rest. We left brother Coe's this morning and went on about seven or eight miles, when our horse was taken sick. We stopped at a public house, and the people seemed willing to help us to administer some relief. I felt my mind quite composed, knowing that he who dealeth out to us, knoweth what is best, and what good may result from it we cannot tell.

The family were desirous Lorenzo should hold a meeting here this evening, and he hath consented. May the Lord stand by him, and enable him to declare the whole counsel of God to those who may come out to hear! May my heart feel more engaged for the salvation of our souls.

August 3d. What cause of gratitude I have to the God of all mercies, that it is as well with me this morning as it is! May my heart be filled with grateful songs of praise for his preservation! We started from the public house, where our horse was sick, on Tuesday morning the 2d day of August. Lorenzo preached the evening before to a small congregation, but quite attentive. I think there were really pious, humble souls; but I left there condemned in my own mind for not taking up my cross: may the Lord forgive, and enable me to be more obedient in future.

We intended to reach Lenox that night, which was about thirty miles, our horse appearing quite well. It was not far from sunrise: the day appeared very gloomy. We travelled until about six o'clock, then we stopped at a tavern and got some refreshments. They made a tolerable heavy charge, which we paid, and Lorenzo gave them two books. He requested the man to let one of them circulate through the neighborhood, hoping it might prove a blessing to some. God grant it for his mercy's sake! We continued on our way through a wood four or five miles, lying nearly on the Farmington river, over a mountain of considerable height. The road was very good, and the prospect delightful to me. The river breaking through the rocks appeared to me very majestic, while the banks were clothed with delightful green. My heart was charmed with the scene. After we got over the mountain, the country seemed more thinly inhabited than any part of Connecticut that I have been in: may the Lord bless the people. We travelled on until between one and two o'clock, and then stopped and gave our horse some food. By this time the clouds began to grow somewhat more gloomy; but we did not think the storm was so near. We started, but had not gone more than a mile and a half before the clouds began to discharge their contents at such a dreadful rate, that we were almost blinded with the rain, and no house so near that we could retreat to. At last we came to a place where there was a house over in a lot, and also a barn. We drove up to the bars, and I got out and ran to the barn; but there seemed no asylum from the impetuous rain. From thence I ran to the house, but no one lived there; so I was compelled to return to the barn, where, by the time Lorenzo had got with his horse and wagon, and drove them into the barn upon the floor, I was wet through and through. I crept upon the mow, and he reached me my trunk. There I changed my clothes; but he was not so well off, for he was under the necessity of keeping his on. We stayed there until the storm was over, and then made the best of our way to Lenox, where we arrived a little before sunset. We got into a friend's house, where we were treated very kind. Lorenzo appeared to have taken some cold; but we have reason to be thankful that it is no worse. We have a trying world to pass through. O that the Lord may enable us to keep the prize in view—that our conflicts may prove blessings to our souls, and we at last come off more than conquerors through him that hath loved us and given himself for us! Lorenzo hath had the privilege of preaching in the courthouse twice, and perhaps he may hold meeting there again this evening: may the Lord that can answer by fire, attend the word with power to the hearts of those that hear! O my soul, look up to him that is able to save, for all the strength that is necessary to enable me to bear with patience whatever may be the will of my heavenly Father to inflict.

My soul longs to enjoy more of the perfect love of God, that I may in all things say, "not my will, but thine be done!"

August 4th. Through the goodness of the Friend of sinners, I am still alive, and better in health than I could expect, considering my exposure for a few days past. May my heart be grateful to him that supplies all my wants. We left Lenox this morning, and have come to Pittsfield. This is a delightful country, but the same gloom appears to hang over the country as it relates to religion. O that the cloud would break, and the work of God revive once more! May my heart glow with love to God and my fellow-sinners. I want to be a true follower of the meek and lowly Jesus—be prepared for life or death, a living witness of his goodness, and when I am called to bid adieu to this world of wo, that I may leave it in peace.

August 5th. How much I am indebted to the rich mercy of a kind Providence, for the many blessings which I do enjoy, the favor of kind friends, while a wanderer on earth! We left Lenox the morning of the 4th, and went to the north part of Pittsfield, to old friend Ward's, where we were received with seeming friendship; but my Lorenzo could not get the people notified as he had expected he might have done, when he thought of going there at night, and concluded to start from there early the next morning; but several people coming in that evening, appeared so anxious that he should preach before he left the place, that he concluded to stay, if they would give notice, which they promised to do, at half past 10 o'clock the following day, and at evening in the centre of the town, it being a day set apart for a fast by the Methodists. Accordingly we repaired at the appointed hour to the meeting-house, where a considerable number of people were collected, and Lorenzo spoke to them on the duty of fasting, from these words, "In those days shall they fast," with a good degree of liberty: the people were very solemn and attentive; may God make it a blessing to some souls. From thence we came to the centre of the town, to a brother Green's, where we were received with great kindness. O that the great Master may reward those who are willing to receive his wandering pilgrims, and make them comfortable with every needed blessing for time and eternity. O that I could always keep the place of Mary, at the feet of Jesus! Lord, give me more of the loving spirit which she possessed, that my soul may enjoy the blessings that are laid up for those that are faithful. My Lorenzo is much afflicted of late with his old complaint—may God give him and me grace to say, The will of the Lord be done.

August 6th. My mind is quite depressed this day, the fluctuating scenes of this life lie too much on my heart. O that my Lord would give me grace to bear them with patience! We are still in Pittsfield; the people are kind, but they have their peculiarities, so inquisitive to know the concerns of others! May the Lord help us to look more carefully into our own hearts, and see that we are right before God! I need more of the spirit of submission to the will of my Master.

August 7th. My poor companion hath been very much afflicted yesterday and the last night with the toothache; in so great a degree, that he could not attend the appointment the last evening, which gave me some pain, as it would be a disappointment to many. I thought if I could have gone and spoken to the people, if I could have spoke any thing to the edification of souls, it would, I thought, have been a great comfort to my mind. My health is but poor; may God strengthen my body: and above all, may my heart be so filled with love to my fellow-sinners, that I may call upon them to close in with the overtures of mercy! I felt such a desire that souls might be benefited, that I could not sleep. O that I may be willing to take up my cross, and if the Lord has any thing for such an unworthy creature as me to do, may I not be so loth to accede to it. I feel many times much distressed on account of my backwardness. O that I may be a cross-bearer indeed. Lorenzo hath gone to speak to those who will assemble to hear the word, in much weakness of body: may that God who is able to bring strength out of weakness, stand by him, and enable him to declare the whole counsel of God. He labors under many weaknesses, but this I trust is his consolation, that when his work is done, he will receive double for all his pain! O that I may willingly take my share with him in this vale of wo, that I may share with him in the reward! May the Lord bless his labors this day. We returned to Pittsfield town in the afternoon, and he preached at 5 o'clock to a crowded congregation. They were really attentive: may the Lord seal conviction on their hearts. This was the third time he had spoken that day; he returned to brother Green's, where we lodged, and seemed much better than he was in the morning: in the evening there was a number who came in, and he spoke to them again, and it was quite a solemn time; my heart was much drawn out in prayer that the Lord would bless them.

We expected to have left the place on Monday morning, but the weather proved so unfavorable that it was impracticable: consequently we stayed until Tuesday; then we left brother Green's and came on to Bennington that night, to a public house, where Lorenzo got permission to hold meeting in a large ball-room. He hired two little boys to go down into the middle of the town to give notice, and others told some, so that there were perhaps more than one hundred that attended; they gave very good attention. God grant they may profit by it. On Tuesday the 9th of August we left Bennington, and came to Cambridge white meeting-house, where we took breakfast. This brought to my recollection former times, when I was a child; the rambles that I have taken among my companions through this delightful spot! Now those that were my companions, are married, and have large families; many have gone to the "silent tomb," whither we are all hastening. May the Lord prepare us for that impor tant day. We than started for my sister's, living near the Batonkill river; where we arrived a little before night. My sister was much rejoiced to see us, and I was not less happy to meet with a sister whom I had not seen but once in more than twenty years. I found her enjoying a good degree of peace and plenty: a kind husband and a sufficiency of this world's goods; and I trust her face is Zion-ward! May God help us to keep on our journey until we meet to part no more!

Sunday, August 14th. Bless the Lord, my soul, for the present mercies that I do enjoy: I have been privileged once more of meeting with a kind sister; my heart warms with affection towards her. She appears to be striving to make her way to Mount Zion. May the Friend of sinners be her guide and support through this vale of tears, and may we meet on the peaceful banks of eternity at last, with those of our friends that have arrived there before us. She is blessed with an affectionate friend and companion; may the Lord make them happy in time and eternity.

Lorenzo is very much afflicted with the old complaint, that has followed him almost all his life. This northern clime disagrees greatly with his health, and I know not what will be the consequence, if he stays long in this part of the world. My sister wishes me to stay with her for some time, but I cannot feel reconciled to let my companion go and leave me behind; and on the whole, I think I had rather go and take my chance with him, until it is the will of our God to part us by his Providence. May the Lord help us to feel resigned to his will in all things, enable us to keep the prize in view, and be faithful to our good God while on earth we stay, and be prepared to shout hallelujahs above, among the blood-washed throng, in the paradise of God!

Monday, 15th. My Lorenzo preached twice yesterday in this place, and some were offended at his doctrine. This shows how prejudiced people are in favor of their own notions. May the Lord help people to discern between truth and error. My heart's desire is to keep the narrow road that leads to joys on high; may the way appear more plain to my understanding, and my heart feel more love to God and man. We know not what is in store for us, nor how many conflicts we may have to pass through. May our days be spent in the service of the great Master, so that whether we have pleasure or pain, we may be enabled to say, the will of the Lord be done! The way of danger we are in, and we need the influence of his grace to speed us on our way. The cloud seems to darken, and what may be the troubles that America may have to encounter we do not know: may that God who is able to deliver nations as well as individuals, undertake our cause, and make it a blessing to the inhabitants of this our once happy land. My soul longs for the prosperity of my country, and that precious souls may be brought to the knowledge of the truth, as it is in Christ Jesus the Lord! O that my heart may feel a greater inward struggle for the welfare of my dear fellow-mortals; and may I keep the crown in view myself!

Tuesday, August 16th. I am still the spared monument of mercy. O that my soul may glow with love and gratitude to my great Benefactor, for all his favors to unworthy me. But my cold heart is too little warmed by all these blessings! O God, give me more of that inward purity of heart, that my life may be like an even-spun thread—my heart and soul engaged in the work, to help my Lorenzo to cry aloud to poor sinners to turn to God, and seek the salvation of their poor souls!

> Come, Lord, from above,
> These mountains remove;
> O'erturn all that hinders the course of thy love."

Wednesday morning, August 17th. We have been one week at my brother-in-law's, and they are very kind; we have taken much satisfaction with my sister and her husband: may their hearts be placed on those riches that are durable and will never fade! I feel my heart too little alive to my God. O that I had more of the power of living faith!

> "The praying spirit breathe,
> The watching pow'r impart;
> From all entanglement beneath,
> Call off my peaceful heart!"

August 19th. We left my dear sister's yesterday, with hearts much affected, not knowing whether we should meet again on mortal shores, but hoping if we meet no more below, we may have a happy meeting in that bright world above, where separation will be dreaded no more!

We travelled about twenty-three miles, and met with a kind family, where we put up for the night. In the morning, by the time the day broke, we started for the Saratoga Springs, where we were aiming, and arrived there by six o'clock. There Lorenzo met a lady from South Carolina, who had treated him with every attention when at the White Sulphur Springs in Virginia, and also at her own house at Charleston. She still appeared much pleased to meet with him here: she invited him to call upon them at their lodgings, at the Columbia Hotel. Accordingly we did, and were treated with great politeness. Lorenzo received an invitation to preach in the afternoon at four o'clock, which he accepted. O may the word come from the heart, and reach the hearts of those that hear; may his labors be blessed to the people in this place! My soul longs to see the work revive, and souls brought to the knowledge of the truth. We are now at the Springs, but which way we shall bend our course when we leave here, I cannot tell. May the Lord direct our steps in that way which will be most for our good and his glory!

I am a wanderer upon the earth: may the Lord help me to be resigned to his will in all things. I feel to shrink from the cross at times; but the desire of my heart is, that I may be a willing follower of the meek and lowly Jesus. My soul's desire and prayer to God is, that the people of America may learn righteousness, and put their trust in that God that is able to save. O! my heart is pained to see so much inattention to the one thing needful, and I also mourn before God for the coldness of my heart! O that I may be stirred up to more diligence in my duty!

Saturday, August 20th. The Springs seem to have a salutary effect upon me. May my soul glow with gratitude to my great and good Benefactor for all his mercies to unworthy me. I am under many obligations to him who supplieth all our necessities; may my soul ever feel sensations of love to my precious Redeemer for these unmerited favors, bestowed on such an unprofitable creature as I! My poor companion is still much afflicted with the asthma, which makes him very feeble in body; but I pray

God to strengthen his soul, and give him wisdom from above to prevail on precious souls to close in with the overtures of mercy! The Lord help us to wait patiently to see the salvation of God!

> "The way of danger we are in,
> Beset by devils, men, and sin!"

But may we view the line drawn by the Friend of sinners, and keep there: so that we may be prepared to pass over Jordan with joy, and everlasting songs of praise to him who conquered death and the grave, and made it possible for the ruined race of Adam to obtain peace and pardon!

Monday, August 22d. Through the tender mercies of a beneficent Providence I am still alive and out of eternity! O may my soul be bowed down at his footstool, feeling gratitude to that hand which hath preserved and provided for me in this unfriendly world! I, of all creatures, have the most reason to be thankful; the Lord hath raised me up friends to supply all my necessities, may the great Master have all the glory. Lorenzo preached at the Springs on Sunday the 20th, to an attentive congregation, though made up of various characters, and some of the first rank; but gentlemen or ladies may be known by their behavior, meet them where you will. At Milling's, (living about six or seven miles from the Springs,) he met a large company, but of quite a different cast: they gave him a quiet hearing! May the Lord turn curiosity into godly sincerity; my soul longs to see Zion prosper! A lady at the Springs had requested us to return in the morning before she should leave there, as she expected to start for the Balston Springs soon after breakfast. Accordingly, we started very soon in the morning, and arrived about six at the Columbian Hotel, where this lady, with one more, had invited us. They appeared very friendly: they were from South Carolina, by the name of Coldon and Harper, the latter made me a present of six dollars: may the Lord reward her as well as others, for their liberality to me!

Thursday, August 25th. I am now at Balston Springs, whither we came on Tuesday, for the benefit of the water. We have met with a kind family, for which I desire to be truly thankful to that gracious Providence who hath opened the hearts of many to show us kindness. May he reward them richly in this world, and in the next bestow on them a crown of glory! Lorenzo hath left me this morning, to fulfil some appointments which have been given out for him: may the great Master attend him with his grace, and bless his labors to precious souls! I should rejoice to see the prosperity of Zion! May the Lord prosper his people, and make them of one heart and of one mind, that they may join together to build up the cause of God, and not stand in the way of sinners! When that happy day will arrive I know not, but whosoever lives to see that period may truly rejoice.

We stayed a few days more in this place. There are but few people here, I am afraid, that truly love and serve the Lord. O that something might take place to bring them to a sense of their danger, and cause them to seek the Lord in good earnest! The way of sin and transgression is hard and dangerous. May the Lord teach me my duty, and enable me to walk in the way of holiness, that my last end my be peace! The prospect before me is something dark and gloomy at times, while I am tossed to and fro upon the boisterous ocean of life, but the Lord hath bee my helper hitherto, and I trust he will save to the end. My soul needs more grace and strength to stem the torrent of difficulties and dangers that I have to encounter, but the arm of the Lord is sufficient! What is before me I know not, but I hope to put my trust in the Lord, who is able to save, and not say my will, but thine be done.

August 27th. My soul is much depressed this morning. I spent the last night at a house where the woman is a Methodist, but the man makes no profession of religion. I felt myself quite embarrassed, as he appeared very unsociable. I have returned to brother Webster's; they are kind, but have a good many in family. My way appears something difficult, but I pray God to help me to sink into his will; and in whatever situation I may be brought in, to learn therewith to be content. O thou Friend of sinners, draw nigh and give me more of the true spirit of Christian love!

I pray my God to give my poor companion strength of body and mind, to be useful to souls, that when his work is finished on earth, he may enter into joys on high. O happy, happy day, when the laborer shall receive his reward! May he be faithful to his God, that he may have a clear sky, and a glorious prospect of that rich inheritance, which is laid up for those that are faithful to their God!

"O may my lot be cast with these,
The least of Jesus' witnesses"

on earth, and at last join the blood-washed throng above!

Sunday, August 28th. This is the day that our all-conquering Saviour burst the bands of death, and led captivity captive; opened the door of mercy to the enslaved sons and daughters of Adam, that they may profit by the rich sacrifice which hath been offered for their redemption. What matter of sorrow it is, that the offers of such unbounded mercy should be neglected by those who are so deeply interested in it, to prepare them for the day of adversity and death; which must assuredly overtake them, whether they will or not—there is no escape. Moments fly on without control, and will shortly bring us to the place appointed for all living. O that it may rest with ponderous weight on the hearts of all concerned in it! And thou, O my soul! look well to thyself, that thou mayest meet thy Judge in peace, when he shall come in the clouds of heaven, attended with his glorious retinue of saints and angels, to sit in judgment on the descendants of the first man and woman, who have *all* had the offers of life and salvation made to them! It will be a joyful day to those who have improved their time, "and washed their robes and made them white in the blood of the Lamb;" but O what horror will seize the guilty soul that squandered away his precious time, and slighted the overtures of mercy—who did despite to the Spirit of grace and the Son, who took upon him the form of a servant, spent many years of toil and pain, and at last gave his life a ransom for our salvation! O what unbounded mercy! O unexampled love! Why are not our souls lost in wonder, love, and praise! May I ever tremble at his word! My departure may be at hand—time is short at the longest. O that I may improve my precious moments as they pass, to the glory of my God, and the good of my own immortal soul!

My Lorenzo is engaged in blowing the gospel trumpet—may the Lord bless and be with him while absent from me, and at last bring us to meet to part no more in that sweet world of love.

August 29th. My companion hath returned this morning. We left the Springs and came on to Greenfield, to Dr. Young's. Lorenzo had an appointment to preach at ten o'clock. The people assembled at the time appointed. Lorenzo was quite feeble in body, but he stood up and gave them a discourse on, " The great day of his wrath is come, and who shall be able to stand ?" with a good degree of liberty. I felt my heart somewhat refreshed under the word, and the people appeared very attentive. I think there are some souls in this place who truly love the great Master— may the Lord prosper them on their journey, and preserve them from the evils that are in the world !

My Lorenzo left it to others to give out a few appointments, which they did, in such a manner, that he would be much pinched for time : consequently, he was under the necessity of getting some person for a pilot, and go on horseback, as that would be a more speedy way of conveyance than his wagon. Accordingly he started, leaving me behind, at the doctor's, until he should return. He had to preach that afternoon, and again at night ; and once or twice, and perhaps three times, the next day. May that God, whom he is striving to serve, strengthen him, soul and body. to cry aloud and spare not, to sinners to repent ! My heart is many times pained on his account. O that I could oftener say, Not my will, but thine be done—that whether our days be many or few, they may all be devoted to God.

August 30th. The Lord is still gracious to unworthy me, in giving me a good degree of strength of body, and a desire in my soul to make my way through this trying world to a peaceful eternity. O that I may have the whole armor to fight the battles of my Master, and through his strength come off victorious !

The days are truly evil, and we need much grace to enable us to keep the narrow way, and not lose our guide ; for we are surrounded by enemies on every hand : some, who profess to love the Lord, are watching for evil, and not for good :—may they be sensible that it was a command of our blessed Saviour, " to love one another" as he hath loved us ! May our hearts overflow with love to God, and our brethren ! My soul longs for more of that spirit, that my heart might melt at human wo. May my soul feel for my dear fellow-sinners, that I may bear them up by faith, to a throne of grace, knowing their souls are in danger while living without God in the world ! My lot is a peculiar one, may God help me to fill the station that hath fallen to me, with true courage and fortitude. My companion is calling sinners to repentance, under many trials and inconveniences: may the Lord stand by him, and give him power and wisdom from above, to give to every one a portion in due season !

Wednesday, August 31st. We have come eight or ten miles this morning, after Lorenzo had preached at sunrise, to a considerable congregation, with a good degree liberty : the people were very serious, and many I trust were true lovers of Jesus. In about two days Lorenzo preached seven times. The last meeting was under the trees by moonlight ; the prospect was delightful ; he addressed the people from these words : " Who is she that looketh forth as the morning, fair as the moon, clear as the sun, and terrible as an army with banners ?" The people were solemn and tender. After this meeting he came to Dr. Young's, where I had been ill two days and one night. May the Lord strengthen his body and soul, that he may cry aloud and spare not, for sinners to repent. The times are truly awful, and alarming; may God send the word home with power to the hearts of the impenitent, that they may take the alarm, and fly to the arms of Jesus for shelter, before troubles shall overtake them.

We have heard a report that the city of Washington is taken by the enemy, and burned, but I hope it is not so: be that as it may, we must strive to sink into the will of the Lord. What though the fire, or plague, or sword, receive commission from the Lord to strike his saints among the rest, their very pains and deaths are blest! O that the Lord would prepare them for every event of his providence! I think I should be willing to go to any part of the world, if the Lord would make duty plain before us; the way seems to be intricate at present, although our way hath been opened in a very wonderful manner since we left Virginia. Bless the Lord, O my soul! and let all within me join to praise his holy name! May he guide us in the way he would have us to go, and teach us our duty, and enable us willingly to bear the cross, that we may wear a crown of glory at last.

If our happy land should be brought into bondage to a foreign foe, the time will be distressing beyond what many imagine. I pray God to deliver us from our enemies, if it is consistent with his will; and if we need a scourge, that we may fall into the hands of God, and not man: my heart is pained on account of my country.

My companion preached on Thursday, 1st of September, three times; first at the Methodist meeting-house in Malta, where we had a sweet and precious time; there were many praying souls present. From thence we came on to a friend's house, where we got some refreshment; we then went to another appointment at a large "steeple house," where he had been requested to preach by some person: but the house was shut when we arrived, and was not opened at all, for what reason I cannot tell, but expect it was through prejudice: but this did not dishearten him, he stood up by the side of the house, and gave them a discourse on "Many are called, but few are chosen." The people were attentive in general, except one or two, who thought their craft in danger; they grumbled a little to themselves, but did not make much disturbance: we had a peaceable waiting before the Lord. From thence we came on to Still Water village, where we had another appointment; there he spoke in the open air, to a tolerable congregation, who gave good attention: there the meeting-house was shut also against him. From thence we came on to the Borough, to a brother Evan's, where we stayed that night, the next day Lorenzo had an appointment at ten o'clock; my prayer to the Lord was that he would stand by him. We were on our way to the city of New York, and what awaited us there I could not tell, the gloomy clouds seemed gathering over our hemisphere; our once happy land is involved in a bloody war, and what will be the end of it, we cannot tell; may the great Master give those that have an interest at the throne of grace, the true spirit of agonizing prayer, to cry mightily to God for deliverance from the thraldom of war!

My Lorenzo is drawn to visit a land far distant from that which gave him birth; may God teach him the way he would have him go! My desire is, that God would direct our steps, and enable us to do our duty; that when the storms of life are over, we may sit down in the paradise of God.

Friday, Sept. 3d. This day Lorenzo hath preached once at the Borough, to an attentive congregation. We found kind friends in this place. From thence we came to Waterford, and stopped at friend King's, where we were received with expressions of kindness. They, with one more, requested Lorenzo to stay over the Sabbath, which he consented to. My soul's desire was, that the Lord would stand by him, and make his stay profitable to souls.

My heart was something gloomy, the prospect was dark, the times precarious; what was before us, I could not tell, and I felt my heart drawn out in prayer to God, that he would help us to walk in the way he would have us to go. My desire is, that I may be prepared for all the troubles and difficulties that I may have to encounter in this world of wo! My dear companion in tribulation is quite feeble in body, which gives me much pain. O that I may learn the lesson of submission: the time is fast approaching when sorrow will be turned into joy to those that are faithful to the God of all grace. O that I may be of that happy number!

Lorenzo is preaching in Waterford still; on Friday and on Saturday night, on Sunday morning at sunrise, and at eight o'clock. The people came out very well, and appeared very solemn, and I trust good was done in the name of the Lord. May the Lord inspire our hearts to cry mightily to him who is able to save, for ourselves and our country. It lies near my heart. O that the people may be interested for its welfare, and lay at the feet of the Master, and humble themselves in the dust, that God may deliver us!

September 6th. We came to Lansingburgh, the appointment having been given out the day before. But Mr. Chichester, a local preacher, who had been a principal man in building the meeting-house in that place, forbid his preaching in it. Consequently the people erected seats by the side of a large brick house, for accommodation beneath its shade, where we had a refreshing time from the presence of the Lord. My heart was grateful that his blessings were not confined to any particular place: for if we fly to the desert, behold he is there—in the city or country—still the throne of grace is accessible to the humble soul! May God ever keep us from pride and vain glory, that we may always keep the intercourse open between our souls and him!

From thence we went to Troy; but the same difficulty existed there, the meeting-house being shut up in this place also. But he repaired to the market-house, where he soon had a large company and spoke to them there. Many appeared quite serious: may conviction fasten on their hearts! We had been in Troy about six years before, and then had more friends than we could visit; but now we were under the necessity of going to a public-house to put up for the night. But, after Lorenzo had done preaching, and we had retired to our lodgings, there was a friend with whom we had no previous acquaintance, who came to the tavern where we were, and requested us to go and sleep at his house, which after some hesitation we accepted, but left our horse where we were.

The different treatment we met with now, from what we had received in years that were past, made a great impression on my mind. Lorenzo had preached in this same place a number of times about six years previous, and was treated with much kindness by the Methodists; but now they were very distant.

We left Troy about eight o'clock on Monday morning, and travelled more than forty miles that day, and stayed at a public house at night. We started early in the morning, and came about seven miles, to a house of entertainment, where we stopped for breakfast. There Lorenzo misse: his pocket-book, containing a considerable sum in bank notes, having left it under his pillow. He took the horse, borrowed a saddle, rode back and found it, which was matter of thankfulness to us. After taking breakfast, we started and came on to Rhinebeck Flats, but made no stop; from thence to the ferry. We had to cross in a sail-boat, and the wind blew quite hard, so that it appeared considerably gloomy to me; but we got over very well. We wished to get to Esopus, or rather Kingston, which was about three miles from the ferry, before we stopped. We came on, and the first thing we saw when the town appeared in view, was a numerous concourse of people assembled together, to see the soldiers take their departure for the city of New York, to defend it, if necessary, from the enemy. This filled my heart with pain and sorrow, when I considered they were liable to fall in the contest, and perhaps leave a wife and children unprotected; and if not a wife and children, they had parents whose hearts were bleeding at the prospect: may God deliver us in his own good time!

We were received by brother and sister Covel with friendship: may the Lord reward them in this world with every temporal blessing necessary, and crown them at last with a crown of glory! It gives me fresh courage when I meet with those who love and serve the Lord, for we find such to be kind and affectionate to all.

The times are truly awful!—may the Lord stand by his followers, and help them to lay at his feet, that they may be prepared for the gathering storm. My God, give me more grace to hang my soul on thee. I know what I have passed through, but what is to come I cannot tell: but if God be for us, who can be against us? O that we may so live, that we may be prepared for the worst.

Since we left our father's, we have travelled several hundred miles, through a delightful country, flowing, as it were, "with milk and honey." Plenty abounds on every hand; nothing is lacking but a grateful sense from whence these mercies flow. May God inspire the hearts of the people with a due sense of their privileges, both of a spiritual and temporal nature, which they enjoy: and may they esteem them as they ought, that they may be saved from destruction!

We stayed two nights and part of three days at friend Covel's; and Lorenzo held two meetings in the town, in the court-house, to a crowded audience. They were as attentive as could be expected, considering what a thoughtless place it was: may God have mercy upon them!

We left friend Covel's on Thursday, September 5th, and travelled on until night, and stopped at a public house. From thence we came on towards Newburg, and about ten o'clock we came to a brother Fowler's, and called; but he not being at home, and the family not choosing to give us an invitation to stop, we kept on to Newburgh. We had been directed to call at a friend's house, by the name of Cowles, but could not find him.

We then continued on our way, intending, the first public house we came to, to stop, and get some refreshment. But in passing a toll-bridge, the old man who attended it knew Lorenzo, and solicited him so earnestly to stop and take breakfast, that he consented. They appeared much pleased, and entertained us as well as we could wish. It was done with such cheerfulness that it made a pleasant repast to us indeed. O that people who have it in their power to do good in the world, would be more liberal, and not let the poor outdo them, and so take their crown!—May God have mercy on the high and lofty ones of the earth, and teach them they are born to die, and perhaps their dust will mingle with the beggar's, and if they are not purified by grace their souls will appear guilty before God! How can they stand in that great day, when the dread alarm shall be sounded—arise, ye dead, and come to judgment! My God make us all sensible of the necessity of being ready to meet our Judge in the air!

From the toll-bridge we came on to a public house, and stopped to feed our horse; and while he was eating, there was a woman, whom we had met in a wagon a little before we had got to this house, who, thinking it was Lorenzo, had returned back to this house, and requested him to stop and preach to the people in this neighborhood. The tavern-keeper also solicited him, saying he would notify the neighbors. Lorenzo then consented to stay, and we went about a mile further, to sleep at a house where they were Methodists. The place where we went to stay was a delightful spot, situated in a valley, between two considerable mountains, covered with shrubs and trees, but not very fertile, which made the contrast more striking. The house was surrounded with meadows and fruit-trees: the scene appeared charming beyond description. This would be a sweet retreat, was suggested to my mind, if we had a few select friends, whose souls were formed for social pleasure, as it relates to spiritual and temporal converse.

But stop, my fancy! stay thy soul on God, who can give peace even on the raging ocean. To him, and him alone would I look for comfort, and not to objects which are so transient. My lot appears to be in a peculiar sphere, and I hope in love and mercy the Master will enable me to fill it with patience and submission.

We left Cornwall on Saturday morning, and proceeded on our way to the city of New York. We made such progress that we got within fifteen or sixteen miles of the city that night, and put up at a public house, where we were much disturbed by some town's people, who, I believe, did it on purpose, on the account of our appearance. O that they may be made sensible of the duty they owe to themselves, their God, and their neighbors.

We started early on Sunday morning, and get to a brother Paradise's, at Bull's Ferry, where we left our horse and wagon. Lorenzo hired a Presbyterian man to keep the horse, and brother Paradise took a small boat and rowed us down to the city. My mind was overspread with gloom, but I strove to put my trust in the Lord. We had a pleasant time on the water. We got down to New York about two o'clock, and went to our old friend brother Munson's, and were received with the same marks of friendship as formerly: may the Lord reward them for their kindness to us. Our situation is as good at present as it has ever been, as it relates to our temporal prospects, but no doubt trials await us still: may the Lord prepare us for whatever may befall us in the way of duty. I have met with another kind family, to whom I am under many obligations for their kindness in days that are past: they still are friends. This is not the case with many. Brother and sister Decamp are true-hearted : may the Lord prosper them on their journey to a peaceful eternity !

The cloud appears to spread over the American hemisphere : may God prepare his children for the shock. What though the fire, or plague, or sword, receive commission from the Lord to strike his saints among the rest, their pains and deaths are blest.

Monday, September 12th. I have this day felt my heart somewhat more composed than I have done for some time.

September 13th. This day we have received more intelligence of the invasion of our once happy land. O that the Lord would prepare us for every event of his providence !

September 14th. I desire to be truly thankful to the Giver of every mercy for the blessings I enjoy this precious morning. I enjoy a tolerable degree of health, and am surrounded with kind friends. O that my soul may be filled with grateful songs of praise to him who so richly provides for me. My situation is as pleasant as it has ever been, perhaps for many years.

"Bless God, my soul, even unto death,
And write a song for every breath."

September 15th. May my heart be made truly sensible of my dependence upon God, who giveth to every one liberally, that seek him with an undivided heart. But I feel this morning as though my heart was too far from that enjoyment which makes happy in this world and in the next. May my heart be revived, and filled with love to God and my fellow-mortals. Religion is low at this time in almost every direction : may our hearts feel interested for the prosperity of the church.

The times are truly alarming, the sound of war is heard in our borders: the alarm is gone forth, "Ye sons of Columbia, to arms, arms." Our sea-boards are likely to be deluged in blood. While our interior is in commotion, our frontiers have been saluted by the warwhoop of the savage ; while tender wives and children have fallen victims to their wanton cruelty. May He that rules on high, that can calm the raging ocean, and bring harmony out of confusion, undertake our cause, and deliver us from the hand of our enemy, and establish peace once more on the earth ! But this may only be the beginning of sorrow to the inhabitants of this terrestrial ball. O that all who have an interest at the throne of grace, would cry mightily to him for strength, to stand in this day of adversity. Lord, prepare us to make our way through all opposition, to the peaceful, happy mansions of unclouded day. O happy, happy land ! when shall we get there ? My God, wash out the stains that sin has made on my immortal soul, that I may have a glorious admittance into those pure regions of everlasting rest ! Trials await me on these mortal shores : may the God of love attend us by his grace, and give us true submission to his will ! May my soul be filled with love and gratitude to that hand which hath provided for me, from my cradle to the present time. How much I owe, yet how little I do as I ought ! O my soul, awake, awake to a sense of duty to the God of all consolation, that thou mayest be filled with all his fulness.

September 16th. Nothing material has taken place in my situation for some days, but a continual clangor of war is saluting our ears, and what will be the final issue, doth not yet appear: may we be prepared for whatever may await us: my soul is truly pained on account of my country. O that God would undertake the cause of America. O that the people may learn humility, and submission to his divine will!

My mind was much depressed this morning, when I arose, but these words came to my mind, "Be still, and know that I am God," with some power; may my heart acquiesce in whatever may be our lot.

We have just heard the joyful tidings, that our dear fellow-citizens of the town of Baltimore are delivered from their troublesome visiters. O that their hearts may be thankful to that hand which was able to save, when appearances were most gloomy! Help us, O thou God of love, to render thee sincere thanks for these mercies; and may America, above all lands, be conformed to the will of him, who hath wrought out such a deliverance for this favored country! May my heart glow with thankfulness to such a good God, and may the remnant of my days be spent in his service.

Sunday, September 18th. This day my soul hath been refreshed under the improvement of brother Daniel Smith; while discoursing on the wickedness of the Jews, the once chosen people of God, in destroying that most worthy servant of God, Stephen—his triumphant death, and ascension to glory. It filled my soul with raptures. I had something of a view of the suffering Christian, bidding adieu to a world of wo, transported by a convoy of angels to his Redeemer's bosom! O what a glorious scene! may that be my happy lot, though unworthy!

September 19th. My heart feels quite gloomy this day. O that these trials might teach me from whence my strength must come! I cannot tell what is before me; may God prepare and help me to hang upon his promises, and lay at the feet of the Redeemer of mankind. I long to be more holy, that my heart may be drawn from earth, and placed on more permanent riches. Through grace I hope one day to out-ride the tempest and storms of life, and reach the fair fields of unclouded day. May God revive his work in the land, and prosper Zion, and fill his church with faithful Christians!

September 21st. Bless the Lord, O my soul, and forget not all his benefits. The days are evil; we have need of more wisdom and humility, to walk the narrow road that leads to joys on high. What a vain, deceitful world we have to travel through! How many snares on every side! May we be as wise as serpents and harmless as doves.

Friday, September 23d. The days are rolling fast away: may I have wisdom and grace, to improve my time to the glory of my Creator and the comfort and satisfaction of my own immortal soul! My heart is often pained to see and feel so little of the life of religion, in almost every direction: may the Lord once more revive his work in the land!

Since I came to the city, my husband and self took a walk to the "Sate Prison," which was a very great satisfaction to me. We gave one shilling for admittance, and had the privilege of going through every apartment in the prison; and to see the neatness and industry that prevail there, was truly charming. This institution is one of the most noble, perhaps, that ever was adopted by any nation: it saves many of those poor unfortunate creatures who have forfeited their life and liberty, from suffering death, and gives them a space for repentance: and furthermore, their labor is very useful to the community. The men were very serious, and appeared downcast; but the women that have been so unfortunate as to get into this place, appear the most hardened creatures I ever saw. This is a striking proof, to what human nature may be reduced. There is a large square in the centre of the prison, where they may range for health, at times. A man may love and serve the Lord in this place, as well as in any other, if he be so minded, and it may be some of these poor mortals will be brought to reflection. The happy day is fast approaching. I trust, when light will shine forth, as the morning, and peace will be established upon the earth.

From the eleventh of September to the seventh of October, Lorenzo spent in New York: then he took his departure for Philadelphia, expecting to return in six or eight weeks; but, when he arrived there, he found his way opened in the city and country, so that he thought best to send for me to come to Philadelphia, where he had concluded to spend the winter. Accordingly I started without delay, in a carriage which was sent for me, and arrived in safety in about three days. I was kindly received by friend Allen and his wife, where I tarried until the return of Lorenzo from the Eastern Shore, whither he had taken a tour two or three weeks previous. When he came back, he wished to find a small room, where we could be retired from the world for a few months; and we were so fortunate as to meet with a friend, (who had plenty of house room, and was willing to accommodate us with a small room, which was made very comfortable by putting up a stove in it,) in a neighborhood of the people called Quakers, where we found it very agreeable. I attended their meetings with much satisfaction: I believe many, very many of those people to be truly spiritual. The friend and his wife, at whose house we stopped, belonged to the meeting, and they both appeared striving to be what they ought. May the Master prosper tham in the way of their duty.

February 27th, 1815. The news of peace salutes our borders, and echoes through the land! It is a truly pleasing sound. May it inspire our hearts with gratitude to that God who hath given us the blessing. O that divine peace may fill every soul, until this favored nation shall become Immanuel's land, and the earth be full of his glory.

May 8th, 1815. We left Philadelphia in the steamboat, for New York, after spending an agreeable winter at Benedict Dorsey's. The weather being very chilly, and my health somewhat impaired by reason of a severe cold I had taken some time previous, this exposure which I passed through, came very near being too much for my feeble constitution. After we arrived at New York I was confined almost two weeks to my bed; but recovering my strength in some measure, we embarked on board a packet for New London, where we had every accommodation necessary; and after a pleasant sail of about thirty hours, we arrived safely and found the people very kind and friendly. But the cold I had taken was so deeply seated on my lungs, it was thought by many it would prove serious in its consequences to me. We arrived here on Saturday. On Sunday, Lorenzo preached four times to crowded congregations, and several times through the week—until he was taken sick: he was attacked very suddenly as he was about to lay down at night, with a pain at his heart, attended with chills. We were then at his brother's. We were all much alarmed. thinking perhaps his dissolution was at hand, yet he appeared composed and serene, with a smile on his countenance, although his pain was beyond description! My soul was poured out to God for his deliverance. After a while he got so much relief that he could be laid down in his bed, but continued very ill for near two weeks; he then had recovered so far as to be able to go on board a boat for Norwich, where we arrived in five or six hours.

We were received with kindness by brother Bentley and his companion. Lorenzo was still very feeble in body, but the people appearing very anxious he should preach, he consented, and at six o'clock that evening the Baptist meeting-house was opened and well filled; he addressed them— his strength holding out beyond what could have been expected. He spoke again on Monday night; it was a solemn assembly, and I hope good was done in the name of the Lord.

Lorenzo hired a wagon and horse to convey us to his father's—which was betwixt twenty and thirty miles. Early on Tuesday morning we started, and arrived there about one o'clock on the 14th of June. We found his dear father, with the rest of the family, in tolerable health.

Lorenzo spent two weeks with us, and then thinking it best to leave me with his father, bid me farewell, and set out on a tour through a part of the states of Rhode Island and Massachusetts, to sound an alarm to the fallen race of Adam in those parts. My heart went with him, in desire that he might be useful to precious souls.

His father's place of residence is very pleasant. I spent my hours as agreeably as the circumstances could admit, seeing I was separated from my companion and had not the opportunity of meeting, there being none within my reach, except the Presbyterian, and that not very convenient. He thought he might be absent three or four months, but returned in five or six weeks unexpectedly to me, and spent a few weeks with us; made preparations to leave me with his father, and start on a long tour which would take him eight or nine months to accomplish. This was something trying to my feelings; but I dare not say do not go, neither do I feel a disposition to prevent him doing his duty.

On the 30th of August, he had got in readiness and bid me adieu— leaving me comfortably provided for as it relates to outward things. The family consisted of his father, sister, and myself. The old gentleman is an affectionate friend and father. We spent our time for the most part quite comfortably; considering the cold inclement season, my health was far better than it had been for years. I frequently received letters from my absent companion, which gave me much satisfaction; this being the only way we could communicate our pleasures or pains to each other. He gave me to understand he expected to return to us in April or May. The last letter I received from him, was dated March 30th, expecting to sail from New Orleans to New York the first of April; and by his writing, it appeared to me, there was a doubt whether he should be brought through in safety—or at least he expected some uncommon difficulty to attend him; which laid me under great anxiety of mind. The season also was so uncommonly blustering, that I, from the first of April until the middle of May, was in a state of mind not to be expressed. This gave my body another shock—for the mind and body are so closely connected, one can not suffer, without the other in some considerable degree feeling affected. I strove hard to apply to Him who is able to save, and at times found some relief: but then, my thoughts would retrace the happy seasons which were past; and the gloomy prospects that now presented to view, made me very wretched. I strove to realize the day, the happy blessed day when we should meet to part no more; but could not so much as I could wish: this gave me greater pain, seeing my heart so attached to earthly objects. Yet under all this, in some measure I was supported: for which may my heart render a tribute of praise to the Giver of all our mercies!

About the 15th of May, I received the pleasing intelligence that Lorenzo had arrived at New York, which removed a heavy burden from my heart, and the 25th he reached his father's. I need not say it was a memorable day to me. May I ever feel true sensations of gratitude for all these favors, and improve them while they are preserved to me! My soul's desire is, to find closer communion with my God; may my soul sink in his will in all things!

After Lorenzo's return, he prepared to steer his course first to Philadelphia, then into the state of New York—from thence to Vermont; and wishing me to go with him, he procured a horse and wagon, and on the 12th of June we left his father's house, it being twelve months lacking two days, since I came there. We went from there to Hebron, where we stayed a few days—met some preachers from the general conference; they were friendly towards Lorenzo. From thence we came on to Durham, where we spent the Sabbath. Lorenzo preached three times. On Monday morning we left there and proceeded on to New Haven—there we met with more preachers and kind friends; here we stayed until Friday. Lorenzo held a number of meetings in the time. From there we came to New York—spent the Sabbath, and he also held three meetings there in the course of the day. I met with old friends, Captain Anderson and his wife, who gave me a pressing invitation to go home with them that evening. Lorenzo was willing, and I accepted the invitation; he was to come over the next morning. Accordingly I went and spent an agreeable evening, and about one o'clock the next day Lorenzo came; but I was quite unwell; the weather having become much warmer, it so debilitated me, that Lorenzo feared lest I could not hold out to travel—and Captain Anderson and his wife wishing me to tarry with them, I concluded to stay. Accordingly, on Tuesday morning, Lorenzo set off on his way to Philadelphia, leaving me behind; he came on that night to Bridgetown, where he preached; and finding such an opening, he spent two or three days in the place. The friends requested him to send for me to come there; accordingly brother Thomas Pitts coming to New York, got brother Washburn to write a few lines to me. I came over from Hoboken and met him at brother Washburn's: the next day we were to go on board the steamboat. I did not expect Lorenzo so soon; but when we came to the ferry-house, and the boat came in, Lorenzo was on board. He intended returning that night or the next day to Bridgetown; consequently I went on, and he returned that night. We have spent some time in this place, and find the people remarkable kind: may they be rewarded for their kindness to us! My soul's desire to God is, that he would reward our kind benefactors, wherever they be.

Visited Woodbridge—had meeting in the meeting-house of the Presbyterians, and returned to Bridgetown and held several other meetings.

July 26th, 1816.

The following letter I received, and think proper to have it subjoined as an Appendix.—L. D.

October 6th, 1816.

DEAR LORENZO,—

Through the tender mercy of a kind providence, I enjoy a better state of health than when you left me, and my mind is in some measure comforted from day to day : I think, also, it is my sincere desire to live a life devoted to God. I view this as uncertain at best. The world is only good in its place, but it will not give peace and comfort to the mind ; but to feel the indwelling spirit of the Saviour is inexpressible peace indeed ; it makes crosses bearable, it gives us the power of resignation to all the will of the Master ; if we are deprived of that we esteem most, we feel to give it up without murmuring at the dispensation. O how sweet such a spirit is! May the Lord give me all that is my privilege, that I may be a comfort to my best friend in this world, and a blessing to myself while a sojourner on these mortal shores.

Our dear father is as well as when you left us, and I, as ever, feel much satisfaction in his company ; we have had peace and harmony in the family since your departure.

I pray God to give all as one, the true spirit of the gospel, and prepare us for a happy exit from this to the world of spirits.

I felt a desire to arise in my soul, that the Master would commission you to preach the everlasting gospel, that your words may be quick and powerful, reaching the sinners' hearts, that their eyes may be opened to see the necessity of peace and pardon on their hearts. May the Lord bless and be with you, make your peace as a gentle running stream from day to day ; and if we meet again in this world, may we find we have made more progress in the divine life than we have ever made before when separated. Through grace, I hope to conquer all my foes.

Remember me to all our friends in Philadelphia, without reserve.

Adieu, my Lorenzo,

PEGGY DOW

QUIETNESS, AS A CANOPY, COVERS MY MIND.

"Great God, thy name be blest,
    Thy goodness be adored;
My soul has been distressed,
    But thou hast peace restored.

"A thankful heart I feel,
    In peace my mind is stayed,
Balsamic ointments heal
    The wounds by sorrow made.

"Though elements contend,
    Though wind and waters rage,
I've an unshaken Friend,
    Who doth my grief assuage.

"Though storms without arise,
    Emblems of those within,
On Christ my soul relies,
    The sacrifice for sin.

"Though inward storms prevail,
    Afflicting to endure,
I've help that cannot fail,
    In Him that's ever sure.

"Though outward war and strife
    Prevail from sea to sea,
I've peace in inward life,
    And that sufficeth me.

"Though clamor rear its head,
    And stalk from shore to shore,
My food is angels' bread,
    What can I covet more?

"Though ill reports abound,
    Suspicions and surmise,
I find, and oft have found,
    In *death* true comfort lies:

"*That* death I mean whereby
    Self-love and will are slain;
For these, the more they die
    The more the *Lamb doth reign.*

"And well assured I am
    True peace is only known
Where He, the harmless Lamb,
    Has made the *heart* his *throne.*

"Then, then may tempests rage,
    Cannon may roar in vain;
The Rock of every age,
    The *Lamb*, the *Lamb* doth *reign.*"

www.ingramcontent.com/pod-product-compliance
Lightning Source LLC
Chambersburg PA
CBHW051158300426
44116CB00006B/363